THE OXFORD HANDBOOK OF

CRIME AND PUBLIC POLICY

THE OXFORD HANDBOOKS IN CRIMINOLOGY AND CRIMINAL JUSTICE

GENERAL EDITOR: MICHAEL TONRY

THE OXFORD HANDBOOKS IN CRIMINOLOGY AND CRIMINAL JUSTICE offer authoritative, comprehensive, and critical overviews of the state of the art of criminology and criminal justice. Each volume focuses on a major area of each discipline, is edited by a distinguished group of specialists, and contains specially commissioned, original essays from leading international scholars in their respective fields. Guided by the general editorship of Michael Tonry, the series will provide an invaluable reference for scholars, students, and policy makers seeking to understand a wide range of research and policies in criminology and criminal justice.

THE OXFORD HANDBOOK OF

CRIME AND PUBLIC POLICY

Edited by

MICHAEL TONRY

Oxford University Press, Inc., publishes works that further
Oxford University's objective of excellence
in research, scholarship, and education.

Oxford New York
Auckland Cape Town Dar es Salaam Hong Kong Karachi
Kuala Lumpur Madrid Melbourne Mexico City Nairobi
New Delhi Shanghai Taipei Toronto

With offices in
Argentina Austria Brazil Chile Czech Republic France Greece
Guatemala Hungary Italy Japan Poland Portugal Singapore
South Korea Switzerland Thailand Turkey Ukraine Vietnam

Published by Oxford University Press, Inc.
198 Madison Avenue, New York, New York 10016
www.oup.com

First issued as an Oxford University Press paperback, 2011

Library of Congress Cataloging-in-Publication Data
Tonry, Michael H.
The Oxford handbook of crime and public policy / Michael Tonry.
p. cm.
ISBN 978-0-19-533617-7 (hardcover) 978-0-19-984465-4 (paperback)
1. Crime. 2. Crime prevention. 3. Criminal justice, Administration of. I. Title
HV6251.T66 2009
364—dc22 2008026686

Printed in the United States of America
on acid-free paper

Preface

This volume aims to provide a reasonably comprehensive overview of current knowledge about crime and public policy responses to it. This may not seem an unusual aim, but it is. Other leading works, including *Crime,* the *Handbook of Crime and Punishment,* and the *Oxford Handbook of Criminology,* mostly deal with the operations of the criminal justice system, the causes of crime and delinquency, theorizing about crime and justice, and crime prevention. Those are fine books and important subjects, but they are not sharply focused on understanding why particular crimes occur and what kinds of public policies might best prevent them or minimize the harm they cause.

The premise of this volume, by contrast, is that policy responses to crime are developed crime-by-crime, and that understanding and formulation of public policy need to take that approach. Police and legislators usually develop policies targeted not on violence in general but on domestic violence or street robbery or gang violence or homicide. Regulators typically develop policies targeted not on white-collar crime but on securities fraud or environmental crime or money laundering or tax evasion. One size seldom fits all.

The chapters in this volume examine a broad range of types of crime. Each explains why crimes happen, how often, whether they are happening more often or less than in earlier times, and what we know about efforts to prevent or contain them. It is impossible to cover the full range of crimes that human beings commit, but we have tried to range far beyond the core common law offenses—homicide, robbery, rape, burglary, aggravated assault, motor vehicle theft, and theft—that the FBI calls index crimes, though six of those are subjects of chapters. Another 18 chapters cover an array of other offenses. Some, such as identity theft, Internet fraud, and money laundering, are modern inventions. Others, such as prostitution, gambling, and drug abuse, are as old as mankind. Still others, including domestic violence, child abuse, and environmental crime, are harmful behaviors that until recently received little attention from policy makers or law enforcement officials. A final group consists of crimes whose salience has increased as the world has become smaller and as markets have become global; these include human smuggling, trafficking in cultural artifacts, and cybercrime.

Chapters have been organized into five categories: violent and sexual crime, property crime, transactional crime, transnational crime, and crimes against morality. The first two are straightforward, and subjects have been distributed among them using conventional criteria. The other categories are leakier and more contestable. The closest synonyms for transactional crime are white-collar crime and organizational crime. The central characteristic of offenses classified as transactional is that understanding them requires that attention be paid to the organizational and other structural contexts in which they occur. The central characteristics of offenses classified as transnational are that they often or always involve behaviors that cross national boundaries and that they are better understood in terms of markets rather than of organizations. Some offenses categorized as crimes against morality could have been placed elsewhere; the common characteristic of the crimes listed under this heading is that they involve behaviors that might or might not be criminalized. Their treatment as crimes in particular places and times is as much a commentary on prevailing morality and norms of personal ethics as on the harms they cause.

Books like this require lots of work by lots of people. Writers worked to tight deadlines, prepared successive drafts to more tight deadlines, and responded gracefully to numerous questions and requests. Better than anyone else the writers know that the book would not exist save for the extraordinary care and professionalism of Adepeju Solarin and Su Smallen in shepherding the chapters to completion and the book into production. I'm grateful to them all.

This book has several goals. One is to provide comprehensive, up-to-date, and authoritative surveys of knowledge about the subjects covered. The chapters do that. Their authors are invariably among the handful of most distinguished active scholars specializing in the subject. A second goal is to provide comprehensive bibliographies of classic and contemporary specialized literatures so that readers new to a subject can quickly identify the important foundation sources and make a running start at turning themselves into experts. A third is to provide accessible, easy-to-read introductions to subjects so that readers can quickly come to grips with each. A fourth is to provide a textbook for courses on criminal justice, crime control policy, and narrower subjects. Those are not small ambitions. Whether they have been achieved, readers will decide for themselves.

Contents

Contributors

Wim Bernasco is Senior Researcher at the Netherlands Institute for the Study of Crime and Law Enforcement.

Harriet Bildsten is a 2009 graduate of the University of Minnesota Law School.

Valerie Braithwaite is Professor of Social Sciences at the Regulatory Institutions Network of Australian National University.

Michael Cherbonneau is a PhD candidate in the Department of Criminology and Criminal Justice at the University of Missouri, St. Louis.

Philip J. Cook is ITT/Sanford Professor of Public Policy at Duke University and Research Associate at the National Bureau of Economic Research.

Heith Copes is Associate Professor of Justice Sciences at the University of Alabama at Birmingham.

John Dombrink is Professor of Criminology at the University of California at Irvine.

Laura Dugan is Associate Professor in the Department of Criminology and Criminal Justice at the University of Maryland.

James Finckenauer is Professor of Criminal Justice at Rutgers University.

Denise A. Hines is Research/Visiting Professor of Psychology at Clark University.

Valerie Jenness is Professor of Sociology in the Department of Criminology, Law and Society at the University of California at Irvine.

Edward R. Kleemans is Senior Researcher at the Research and Documentation Center of the Ministry of Justice, the Netherlands.

Michael Levi is Professor of Criminology in the School of Social Sciences at Cardiff University, Wales.

Jens Ludwig is Professor of Social Service Administration, Law, and Public Policy at the University of Chicago, Nonresident Senior Fellow in Economic

Studies at the Brookings Institution, and Faculty Research Fellow at the National Bureau of Economic Research.

ROBERT J. MACCOUN is Professor of Public Policy, Professor of Law, and Affiliated Professor of Psychology at the University of California at Berkeley.

KATHLEEN MALLEY-MORRISON is Professor of Psychology at Boston University.

KARIN D. MARTIN is a doctoral candidate in public policy at the University of California at Berkeley.

SAMUEL C. MCQUADE III is Professor of Multidisciplinary Studies at the Rochester Institute of Technology.

JODY MILLER is Professor of Criminology and Criminal Justice at the University of Missouri, St. Louis.

PETER REUTER is Professor of Economics in the School of Public Policy and the Department of Criminology at the University of Maryland and Codirector of the Drug Policy Research Center at the RAND Corporation.

RICHARD ROSENFELD is Professor of Criminology and Criminal Justice at University of Missouri, St. Louis.

LISA L. SAMPLE is Assistant Professor at the School of Criminology and Criminal Justice at the University of Nebraska at Omaha.

JENNIFER SCROGGINS is a doctoral candidate in sociology at the University of Tennessee, Knoxville.

NEAL SHOVER is Professor of Sociology at the University of Tennessee, Knoxville.

SALLY S. SIMPSON is Chair of the Department of Criminology and Criminal Justice at the University of Maryland.

A. J. G. TIJHUIS is a partner at Pontius Lawyers in Amsterdam and Research Fellow at the Netherlands Institute for the Study of Crime and Law Enforcement, Free University, Amsterdam.

MICHAEL TONRY is Sonosky Professor of Law and Public Policy at the University of Minnesota Law School and Senior Fellow at the Netherlands Institute for the Study of Crime and Law Enforcement.

Lynne Vieraitis is Assistant Professor of Justice Sciences at the University of Texas at Dallas.

Richard Wright is Curators' Professor in the Department of Criminology and Criminal Justice at the University of Missouri, St. Louis.

Peter Cleary Yeager is Professor of Sociology at Boston University.

THE OXFORD HANDBOOK OF

CRIME AND PUBLIC POLICY

CRIME AND PUBLIC POLICY

MICHAEL TONRY

CRIME, like death and taxes, will always be with us. Stupidity, cupidity psychopathy, greed, intoxication, strong emotion, and impulsiveness are part of the human condition, much as we might wish it were otherwise, and all societies have to deal with their effects.

Not all harmful behaviors are criminal. What is harmful and what is not varies with time and space. Some behaviors, such as killings, rapes, robberies, serious assaults, and taking other people's property, are criminal in almost all places. Some behaviors, such as witchcraft, heresy, adultery, homosexuality, and gambling, are not now crimes in most Western countries, but in earlier times they were. Other behaviors, such as child abuse, domestic violence, drug use, prostitution, and environmental despoliation, were until recently generally not considered the law's business, though now they are. And still other behaviors, including cybercrime, identity theft, human smuggling, hate crimes, and money laundering, became significant crimes only when they recently became technologically possible or were legally proscribed.

Cross-national agreement about what should and should not be considered criminal is narrower than is sometimes recognized. It is conventional to contrast developed Western countries with others, but that is an oversimplification. In many Muslim countries heresy, apostasy, homosexuality, adultery, and failure to observe important cultural conventions remain crimes. In Turkey acts or words showing disrespect for the nation can be criminally prosecuted.[1] Conversely, some behaviors that are criminal in the United States, such as paying fees to middlemen as conditions of winning commercial or government contracts (U.S. law like that of most developed countries considers such payments bribes), are commonplace and sometimes legal in much of the developing world.

However, it is a mistake to assume that even Western countries' notions of what counts as crime are congruent. In much of continental Europe Holocaust denial is a crime, and people are occasionally prosecuted and imprisoned for it; the First Amendment of the U.S. Constitution forbids such laws. In England, Scotland, and some other European countries private possession of handguns and public possession of knives with blades longer than seven inches are crimes; some Americans believe that the Second Amendment to the U.S. Constitution makes criminalization of handgun possession unconstitutional. English law on "antisocial behaviour" allows criminalization of just about any behavior a plaintiff can convince a court is antisocial, and prison sentences up to five years can be imposed for violation of an order to desist. Extreme cases include forbidding an individual "to enter the City of Manchester," forbidding a prostitute to possess condoms, and forbidding an autistic child to stare at people. The law allows for imposition of prison sentences for engaging in prostitution (as a form of antisocial behavior), even though English criminal law long ago decriminalized prostitution, and for begging (as antisocial behavior), even though English criminal law does not authorize prison sentences for begging (Burney 2005).

Prostitution has been legalized in a number of European countries, and drug use and minor trafficking have been decriminalized. Any adult tourist (or other adult) in the Netherlands can legally buy marijuana in coffee shops, and addicts can obtain maintenance doses of other substances from approved medical sources. Italy and Spain likewise tolerate levels and forms of drug distribution that U.S. policy makers deplore. Sweden, by contrast, is as intolerant of drug use as is the United States, but is much less punitive about it. In much of Europe unlawful entry into the country is not a criminal act, though in the United States it is.

Some of the differences described in the preceding few paragraphs are the products of fundamental national differences in judgments about the importance of particular cultural values. Émile Durkheim ([1893] 1933) long ago explained that criminal law is an outgrowth of a society's most fundamental social norms, what he called the conscience collective, and should embody, express, and reinforce them. Dutch tolerance of drugs and prostitution, Austrian intolerance of Holocaust denial, and some Muslim countries' unwillingness to tolerate nontraditional styles of dress are outgrowths of deeply bedded cultural norms, however much outsiders may disagree with them. As cultural norms change, which over time they do, laws change with them, but the transitional periods are typically rocky.

Other differences described in the preceding paragraphs, however, do not so much reflect cultural differences about the desirability of behavior as they do divergent opinions about the most effective ways to deal with it. Dutch drug policies, for example, are predicated on the ideas that less aggregate social harm will result from tolerant than from repressive drug policies, and that treating addicts as unfortunates needing state support will convert them in the eyes of young people from romantic outlaws into pathetic social failures, object lessons of the dismal effects of a hedonistic lifestyle (Leuw 1991; Buruma 2007).

Dutch tolerance of drug use and low-level trafficking is as much a public policy about crime as is American intolerance and prohibitionism. Which is better cannot be answered in any absolute way. Crime and its control raise a motley of instrumental, expressive, emotional, and moral issues about which reasonable people differ. A purely rational approach to drug policy in the United States based on cost-benefit analyses would involve decriminalization of use, regulation of distribution, greatly reduced use of criminal sanctions, and use of greatly reduced criminal sanctions. Such approaches have been beyond reach in recent decades because for some U.S. policy makers and some citizens, drug use is morally wrong and tough drug laws are an expression of that belief. Sometimes prohibition laws are as much defenses of the values of dominant social groups as they are efforts to avoid harms associated with drug or alcohol use.[2] Whether drug policies are effective or just may be less important to their proponents than that such policies make an unambiguous moral statement about the wrongfulness of drug abuse and abusers.

With so many different kinds of crime, so many ways of thinking about them, and so many ways to deal with them, policy making is contested and complicated. This short article provides a bit of background. Section I sets out a typology of policy approaches (criminal law enforcement, prevention, regulation, decriminalization, harm reduction, nonintervention) that operate sometimes as alternatives, sometimes as complements. Section II discusses data on crime rates, patterns, trends, and costs.

Systematic knowledge and analysis concerning most types of crime are remarkably primitive compared with such subjects as the economy, public health, and education (and dentistry, as James K. Stewart, onetime director of the U.S. National Institute of Justice, liked to point out in the 1980s, contrasting his agency's $13 million budget with the National Institute of Dentistry's $165 million; Blumstein and Petersilia 1995). The amount of money devoted to research and evaluation of crime control policy, the size of the specialist research communities, and the quality of government data systems are meager compared with those relating to other policy subjects.

Nonetheless, a few relatively noncontroversial conclusions can be offered about crime and public policy:

- Property crime (theft, burglary, motor vehicle theft) and homicide rates have declined in the United States and in most other developed countries since the early to mid-1990s, but no one has convincingly explained why. It is difficult to conclude that recent tough police practices and sentencing laws explain the American decline; no other country adopted comparable policies, and simultaneous declines occurred in many of them. Less serious violent crimes have almost certainly also been declining, but this is less clear because reduced tolerance of violence means that relatively more crimes are reported to police and to survey researchers than in earlier times. Seemingly higher rates of violence in some countries in recent years probably reflect higher rates of reporting and recording, sometimes more than offsetting, and thereby camouflaging, absolute declines.

- Remarkably little is known about crime rates and trends for many crimes, including cybercrime, identity theft, environmental crime, organizational crime, organized crime, prostitution, human smuggling, child abuse, tax evasion, illegal gambling, and drug trafficking. Anecdotal and journalistic reports suggest that most of these behaviors are becoming more common, but we have no valid and reliable sources of data about them, so it is hard to know what to believe.
- Remarkably little is known about the costs of crime and the cost-effectiveness of alternative crime control approaches. Some American and British academics have attempted to calculate the costs of common law crimes, but their approaches are so ideological and so dependent on calculation of intangible "pain and suffering" costs as not to be believable. For other types of crime, no one has seriously attempted to estimate costs (e.g., human smuggling, domestic violence, child abuse, terrorism, prostitution) or the estimates have a back-of-an-envelope quality and vary by orders of magnitude (e.g., money laundering, drug abuse, organizational crime, environmental crime).
- Countries vary enormously in how they use their criminal justice systems. Some, such as the United States, England, and New Zealand, rely on deterrence and incapacitation to attempt to control crime. Others, notably the Nordic countries, are skeptical about these approaches and rely on punishment's moral educative effects coupled with strong social welfare approaches. Some countries have high imprisonment rates and others have low rates. Some countries send comparatively few people to prison but for long periods; others send comparatively many but for short periods. Some favor short sentences; others oppose short sentences as destructive. Some have experienced five- and sevenfold increases in imprisonment rates in recent decades; some have experienced slight or no increases. Finland and Japan experienced sharp decreases from 1950 to 1990, though Japanese rates have increased since then.
- Every country uses a wide range of criminal justice, regulatory, preventive, and harm-reduction approaches to dealing with crime, and within countries there are typically major differences between crimes. Crime is a legal concept; strictly speaking, a behavior becomes a crime only after a legislature has defined it to be one. In individual cases, acts become crimes only tentatively when a prosecution is initiated and only conclusively when a conviction is entered. In some countries, and for some kinds of crime, policy makers have decided that preventive, regulatory, and harm-reduction approaches are more effective than criminal law enforcement.

I. Aims, Methods, and Functions

Six broad public policy approaches are available for dealing with crime: criminal law enforcement, prevention, harm reduction, regulation, decriminalization, and nonintervention. Sometimes these are alternatives, sometimes complements.

A. Criminal Law Enforcement

Criminal law enforcement is what the criminal justice system does. Police investigate crimes and arrest people. Prosecutors decide whether or not to initiate a prosecution and if so, for what. They negotiate guilty pleas, try cases, and make recommendations to judges about sentences. Judges preside over pretrial proceedings and trials, review and accept (or, rarely, reject) guilty pleas, and impose sentences. Corrections authorities of different sorts run prisons, jails, and probation and parole systems. Governors and the U.S. president have authority to issue pardons and to commute sentences. Legislatures enact and revise laws defining crimes and governing penalties. Sometimes these laws set ranges within which judges may make decisions (e.g., from probation through a prison sentence of ten years); sometimes, as with mandatory minimums and three-strikes-and-you're-out laws, judges ostensibly have very little discretion about the sentences they impose.

In describing roles of officials and agencies, the preceding description gives a false impression of U.S. criminal law enforcement because it implies a mechanistic system. To the contrary, the system is highly discretionary. Police may decide to make an arrest, or not. Prosecutors may charge suspects with serious crimes, less serious crimes, or no crime at all. They may divert obviously guilty suspects into treatment programs. They exercise discretion to make and withdraw charges and to make plea bargains that, constitutionally, is almost unreviewable. Judges sometimes have broad discretion to individualize sentences, and when they legally lack such authority they can cooperate with plea-bargaining lawyers to avoid application of mandatory minimum or three-strikes sentences they consider too severe. Judges do not always exercise discretion to avoid imposition of unjustly severe sentences, however; sometimes they impose them. The system is so riddled with discretion that wide disparities in how cases are handled are inevitable. This can be portrayed as good (officials can take into account ethically meaningful differences between cases) or bad (officials are not good at individualizing and often treat comparable cases starkly differently).

The criminal justice system is premised on legal threats. Criminalization broadcasts the message that certain behavior is forbidden, and sentencing laws threaten what may happen if citizens ignore the criminal law's adjurations. Conventionally it is said that criminal sanctions do their work through deterrence, incapacitation, rehabilitation, and moral education.

The evidence about deterrence is uncertain and contested. The fairest generalizations are that certainty and celerity of punishment are more important than severity and that the jury is out on the question of "marginal deterrence," whether incremental increases in punishment have deterrent effects (Tonry 2008).[3] Some reviews of the evidence conclude that the marginal deterrence hypothesis cannot be confirmed (e.g., von Hirsch et al. 1999; Doob and Webster 2003). Others conclude that a deterrent effect can be confirmed—sometimes, for some crimes, and under some circumstances—but that existing knowledge is so fragmentary that it has no practical relevance to policy (Cook 1980; Nagin 1998*a*).

There is no doubt that some sentences incapacitate some offenders, but there is doubt about the incapacitative efficiency of imprisonment (e.g., Nagin 1998*b*). Some prisoners will not reoffend in any case. Some, such as drug traffickers and gang members, will quickly be replaced; the crime will go on, the criminal will not. Some will age out of crime; "age-crime curves" instruct that crime, especially violence, is a young man's game and that most people age out of criminality at a young age (Farrington 1986). Even most career criminals desist by their thirties. A classic analysis of incapacitation concluded that its policy relevance is questionable (J. Cohen 1983).

The evidence about rehabilitation has been changing rapidly. In the 1970s the conventional view was that few programs could be demonstrated effectively to reduce later offending (e.g., Martinson 1974). Since the early 1990s the consensus view has been that well-managed, well-targeted drug treatment programs can reduce both drug use and offending among drug-using offenders (e.g., Anglin and Hser 1990); that finding is the premise for the modern drug court movement. Similar optimism exists, supported to some extent by research findings, that a wide range of other kinds of focused (e.g., intrafamily sexual abuse) and broad (cognitive-behavioral) treatment programs can reduce later offending (e.g., Gaes et al. 1999).

There is little evidence concerning the criminal law's moral educative effects. The philosopher H. L. A. Hart (1968, p. 6) believed in it; the answer to why acts are criminalized is "to announce to society that these acts are not to be done." The Norwegian criminal law scholar Johannes Andenaes (1974), following Durkheim, believed moral education is the criminal law's most important and powerful effect. Contemporary Scandinavian punishment laws are premised on the view that the criminal law must reinforce basic social norms and, conversely, must take pains not to contravene them (Lappi-Seppälä 2001). It makes apriori sense to me, but we've no empirical evidence that it is true.

B. Prevention

There are three main forms of prevention: situational, developmental, and community. There is no doubt that situational prevention methods—physical measures ranging from bullet-proof glass, CCTV, improved lighting, exact change policies on buses and trams, and myriad other initiatives that make crimes harder to commit—can reduce crime rates, especially for kinds of crime that are often committed impulsively, and without complete displacement to other places (Clarke 2005, 2008).

Similarly, the evidence is overwhelming that a wide range of developmental prevention programs can reduce at-risk children's later likelihood of offending. These programs identify risk and protective factors in children's lives and attempt to weaken the former and strengthen the latter. Cost-benefit analyses show that public investment in developmental prevention is much more cost-effective (three to four times more) than investment in prison sentences (Aos, Miller, and Drake 2006; Farrington and Welsh 2007). Unfortunately, the investment pays off 10 to 15 years later, which is not the reference period that most politicians have in mind when proposing crime control legislation and voting for appropriations to pay for it.

Community prevention takes two main forms. The first is creation of community self-help crime prevention organizations, usually operating under some permutation of the name "neighborhood watch." There is no credible evidence that such organizations, usually organized in low-crime neighborhoods, have any significant effects on crime (Bennett, Holloway, and Farrington 2006). The second is effectively situational crime prevention at community and architectural levels. Community-level initiatives include improving street lighting, altering traffic-flow patterns, and closing off streets; gated communities are an extreme form. Architectural initiatives include building "defensible space" with clear sight lines and plenty of surveillance opportunities that allow residents and others to see what is going on nearby. The evidence on the effectiveness of community prevention approaches is mixed, though some programs appear to be successful (Welsh and Hoshi 2006).

All of these prevention approaches focus on prevention of rather than reaction to crime. Situational and community prevention are premised on making crimes harder to carry out and on the notions that much crime is impulsive and that not all impulses are displaced to other targets. Although the financial choices are less acute than with developmental prevention, the logic is that investment in prevention will pay off more than investments in prosecutions and imprisonment (Welsh and Farrington 2005).

C. Harm Reduction

Jeremy Bentham ([1789] 1948), the inventor of utilitarian analyses of public policy, believed that the greatest good of the greatest number is the best justification of state policies and actions. In carrying out a utilitarian calculation (a "felicific calculus" he called it because felicity, or happiness, is the measure), everyone's interests must be taken into account. If crime prevention might be made more effective by punishing an individual, it should be done only if the suffering (unhappiness) averted for prospective victims was greater than the suffering to be imposed on individual offenders. The state should be parsimonious in the imposition of suffering, he reasoned. The "parsimony principle," the notion that no suffering should be imposed in the name of crime prevention in excess of the minimum necessary to achieve valid public ends, remains influential (Morris 1974).

Harm-reduction strategies are Benthamism revived. Usually associated in the United States with public health professions, harm-reduction strategies aim to achieve policy goals at the lowest aggregate social cost. Dutch drug-control policies are a classic example. Dutch policy makers believe that their approach, combining effective decriminalization of marijuana, medical support and social marginalization of addicts, and law enforcement targeted on large-scale traffickers, manufacturers, and importers, minimizes the social costs of drug use. Dutch and German approaches to prostitution are also based on the goal of harm reduction. Legalizing prostitution but requiring registration of prostitutes and regular medical examinations are seen as ways to protect prostitutes and their customers from health risks and criminal harms associated with unlawful prostitution (Buruma 2007).

American public health officials have long urged a harm-reduction approach to gun injuries and deaths. Current policies focus primarily on increased penalties for criminal use of guns and on preventing felons and mentally ill persons from acquiring guns. The evidence cited above on deterrent effects of incremental changes in penalties offers little reason to believe that mandatory minimum sentences for gun crimes, or mandatory add-ons for crimes in which guns are used, significantly reduce criminal gun use. English and Scottish criminalization of private possession of firearms in the aftermath of the Dunblane school massacre in Scotland in 1996 is based on a harm-reduction rationale. Research on the effects of mandatory arrest policies for misdemeanor domestic violence shows that arrests result in increased violence by minority and unemployed men; a harm-reduction approach would look for other preventive means (Sherman, Schmidt, and Rogan 1992).

The drugs, prostitution, guns, and domestic violence examples are likely to raise hackles in the United States (albeit more for emotional, ideological, and moral than for practical or evidence-based reasons). Many people find harm-reduction proposals much more congenial for business regulatory crimes (e.g., van de Bunt and Huisman 2007). They provide the primary rationale for business and environmental regulatory strategies that focus on negotiation, collaboration, and self-monitoring (e.g., Braithwaite 2002).

Finnish criminal justice policy making explicitly incorporates harm-reduction principles: "The aim of minimalization (not 'elimination') emphasizes the costs and the harmful effects of criminal behavior instead of simply minimizing the number of crimes. By stressing that not only the costs of criminality but also the costs and suffering caused by the control of crime must be taken into account, the formula draws attention to the material and immaterial losses that arise from operation of the system of sanctions" (Lappi-Seppälä 2007, p. 231).

D. Regulation

Regulatory approaches to crime prevention are most often discussed in relation to business crimes, though regulation is much more widely used than that. Approaches to dealing with drugs and prostitution in the Netherlands and some other European countries contain major regulatory elements.

So do American approaches to gun crime. Many states, counties, and cities have laws that limit who can buy guns and under what circumstances. Almost all jurisdictions require waiting periods, all require identity checks, and some require completion of gun safety courses. None of these is especially effective at controlling gun violence (Cook and Ludwig 2001).

Many countries, including the United States, have replaced laws criminalizing many forms of gambling with newer laws and administrative arrangements for regulating gambling and attempting to minimize social costs and harms associated with it. Fifty years ago many states criminalized most forms of gambling, and every city had some form of the "numbers racket." No more. Legalized gambling in the United States began with on-track horse and dog racing. In the past 40 years, however, state lotteries have become nearly ubiquitous, off-track betting parlors have become common, and casinos have proliferated. Vigorous law enforcement coupled with intrusive regulatory regimes have driven organized crime from casino gambling.

Regulatory approaches are better known in connection with organizational crimes, sometimes referred to as white-collar crimes, especially relating to the environment. Administrative law specialists have argued for decades about the best ways to shape organizational compliance with regulatory regimes (e.g., Yeager 1993; Braithwaite 2002; Hawkins 2003). A law enforcement approach emphasizes monitoring of compliance with regulatory standards, backed up by use of civil penalties and criminal prosecutions to punish past and deter future noncompliance. A "responsive" regulatory approach reserves civil and criminal penalties as measures of last resort, preferring negotiated and cooperative approaches (Braithwaite 2002; van de Bunt and Huisman 2007). Proponents of responsive regulation argue that heavier-handed law enforcement approaches are slower and less effective, partly because they are confrontational and condemnatory, which puts people's backs up, and because they invite stonewalling and litigation, which delay identification and implementation of solutions.

Political ideology often predicts whether political leaders favor law enforcement or responsive regulatory approaches. Political conservatives want to avoid shackling business and discouraging entrepreneurship. They typically favor relatively light regulatory regimes and also favor responsive approaches to law-breaking. However, conservatives tend to oppose adoption of regulatory regimes for drugs and prostitution. Political liberals tend to favor tougher law enforcement approaches for dealing with business crime but are typically more receptive than conservatives to proposals for regulatory approaches for dealing with drugs and prostitution.

E. Decriminalization

Decriminalization eliminates crime by definition. Sometimes it happens *de jure*, as when American legislatures repealed laws criminalizing heresy, adultery, and prostitution, or when the U.S. Supreme Court declared laws making flag burning criminal unconstitutional (and as could happen to city ordinances restricting gun ownership now that the Court has decided that the Second Amendment created a constitutional right of private gun ownership). Sometimes it happens *de facto*, as when prosecutors and courts in many U.S. jurisdictions in the 1970s stopped enforcing laws against private possession, use, and sometimes sale of small amounts of marijuana. In many U.S. jurisdictions, adultery, fornication, and homosexuality crimes remained in the statute books long after they ceased being enforced.

If harm reduction in other than business regulatory contexts ever becomes culturally and politically imaginable in the United States, decriminalization coupled with regulation of a wide range of behaviors will become viable. These might include prostitution, drug possession and use, minor drug trafficking, and euthanasia. For the foreseeable future, American moralism and insistence on expressive legislation concerning what are considered immoral behaviors make much decriminalization unlikely.

F. Nonintervention

One policy option that is always available is to do nothing. Edwin Schur (1973) a third of a century ago argued on harm-reduction grounds that the best response to juvenile delinquency often is to do nothing at all. His proposal was based on two empirical realities. The first is that studies of self-reported delinquency show that majorities of male and female adolescents admit to committing criminal acts, but also show that most soon desist from criminality. Delinquency is a common characteristic of adolescence and is in effect an aspect of a developmental stage that is part of growing up. The second is that labeling theory argued and research showed that being processed through the criminal justice system is in various ways criminogenic (children become stigmatized, making future delinquency a self-fulfilling prophecy; first-timers are put into contact with more deviant peers and are socialized by peer influences into further delinquency).

In many cases juvenile justice system intervention thus promised to make children's life chances worse and to increase the likelihood of future delinquency. Putting the two realities together, Schur argued, meant, perversely, that juvenile justice processes make future delinquents of kids who would in the ordinary course otherwise desist from delinquency. Were Schur's book written today, a third reality would be added: black kids are more often brought into contact with the juvenile justice system than are white kids, and at earlier ages (Feld 1999). The perverse effects Schur described disproportionately affect black children.

What I called decriminalization de facto is a form of radical nonintervention. Nonintervention may be the wisest public policy in connection with criminalized behaviors that raise some people's moral hackles: pornography, adultery, fornication, obscenity, homosexuality, drug use, gambling. In many cities in many times police have known where gambling and prostitution took place; for example, during Prohibition, speakeasies were difficult to hide. Those are examples of nonintervention policies. The great danger they pose is that they expose people to blackmail and create circumstances foreseeably conducive to police corruption. They also produce arbitrariness in law enforcement. Formal decriminalization is the safer policy option, but when that is not politically feasible the de facto form is better than none.

II. Rates, Trends, and Costs

Reasonably good evidence is available concerning rates and trends of serious violent and property crimes targeting individual victims. For a few other crimes some observations can be offered with some confidence on the basis of triangulation of longitudinal data from multiple sources. Both the National Family Violence Surveys (Straus and Gelles 1986) and the *National Crime Victimization Survey* (U.S. Department of Justice 2006), for example, show that domestic violence in which women are victims has been declining but that domestic violence involving male victims is not. For most of the crimes discussed in this volume, however, it is difficult to say much with confidence about rates or trends.

The authors in this volume discuss data sources and estimates of rates and trends for particular crimes. For the most part estimates are based on information that has come to the attention of the authorities. Seldom do we know how representative those cases are. Many health and welfare professionals who deal with children, for example, are obliged to report cases of suspected child abuse to state authorities, which in turn report them to federal authorities. Because the categories of professionals required to report have gradually been extended, and because professional reluctance to report may be declining, national data show steadily increasing numbers of abused children. It is not known whether more children are being abused or more incidents of child abuse are being reported.

Knowledge concerning the costs of crime is sparse and not very useful. There is a bit more credible data concerning the cost-effectiveness of alternative law enforcement, regulatory, and prevention strategies.

A. Rates and Trends

A good bit is known from official police crime data and victimization survey findings about rates and trends of the traditional common law offenses (e.g., Tonry and Farrington 2005). The pattern in the United States, which is paralleled by experience in many developed Western countries, is that crime rates began climbing some time in the 1960s, peaked in the early 1990s, and fell rapidly thereafter. The table "Rates per 100,000 Population, Police Data, Selected Crimes and Years, 1970–2006" shows aggregate rates for the seven traditional FBI index offenses (murder, rape, robbery, aggravated assault, burglary, theft, and motor vehicle theft) per 100,000 U.S. population from 1970 to 2006 and rates separately for murder, rape, robbery, burglary, and motor vehicle theft.

Rates per 100,000 population, police data, selected crimes and years, 1970–2006

Category	'70	'75	'80	'85	'90	'95	'98	'00	'05	'06
All index	3,985	5,299	5,950	5,225	5,803	5,275	4,620	4,125	N/A	N/A
Murder	7.9	9.6	10.2	8.0	9.4	8.2	6.3	5.5	5.6	5.7
Rape	18.7	26.3	36.8	36.8	41.1	37.1	34.5	32.0	31.8	30.9
Robbery	172	221	251	209	256	221	166	145	141	149
Burglary	1,085	1,532	1,684	1,292	1,232	987	863	729	727	729
Motor vehicle theft	457	474	502	464	656	560	460	412	417	398

Note: Three- and four-digit numbers rounded.
Source: Sourcebook of Criminal Justice Statistics Online, 31st ed., table 3.106.2006.

Crime rates in every category were much lower in 2006 than their peak levels in the preceding 36 years. U.S. crime rates began rising in the 1960s. They peaked in 1980–81, fell for five years through 1986, rose again for five years through 1990–91, and have fallen continuously since. By 2006 rates for all the crimes shown except rape were 45 to 50 percent below their peaks in 1980 and 1990. With the exception again of rape, rates for all individual offenses were below 1970 levels. Property crime declines have been most pronounced, and, because burglary and motor vehicle theft victims must generally file police reports to collect on property insurance, those rates are probably believable. Homicide rates, because they usually require bodies and because violent deaths can be validated from public health sources, are also generally viewed as reasonably reliable. Rates for robbery, rape, and aggravated assault have fallen least. There has, however, been a steady decline in public tolerance of violence, leading to higher rates of reporting incidents to the police. Apparent declines for these crimes are probably greater than appears because they are offset by higher likelihoods that victims reported incidents to the police.

The table "Household Victimization Rates, in Percentages, Selected Crimes and Years, 1994–2005" shows American household victimization data from 1994 to 2005 for all offenses and separately for rape, robbery, assault, burglary, and motor vehicle theft.[4] Overall, the percentage of American households experiencing the crimes measured by the National Crime Victimization Survey declined from 25 percent in 1994 to 13.9 percent in 2005. Rates for individual offenses fell by half or more.

The pattern of declining crime rates in the United States characterizes most developed countries. The table "International Criminal Victimization Rates, ICVS Data, Various Years 1989–2004" shows results from the International Crime Victimization Survey (ICVS), which has been conducted five times in most developed Western countries, beginning in 1989. A standardized questionnaire is used in all participating countries. The table shows percentages of respondents reporting victimizations by particular crimes. Overall, and separately for auto theft, burglary, robbery, and sexual offenses against women (a broader category

Household victimization rates, in percentages, selected crimes and years, 1994–2005

Category	1994	1995	1996	1997	1998	1999	2000	2002	2003	2004	2005
Any crime	25	23.4	22.4	20.9	19.1	17.7	16.2	14.6	14.7	14.1	13.9
Rape	0.2	0.2	0.1	0.2	0.1	0.2	0.1	0.1	0.1	0.1	0.1
Robbery	1.0	0.9	0.9	0.7	0.6	0.6	0.5	0.4	0.4	0.3	0.4
Assault	6.0	5.4	5.1	4.8	4.4	3.8	3.4	2.8	2.6	2.5	2.4
Burglary	4.6	4.1	4.0	3.7	3.3	2.9	2.7	2.4	2.6	2.5	2.5
Motor vehicle theft	1.7	1.5	1.2	1.2	1.0	0.9	0.8	0.8	0.8	0.8	0.8

Source: Sourcebook of Criminal Justice Statistics Online, 31st ed., table 3.27.2005.

International criminal victimization rates, ICVS data, various years 1989–2004

Crime category	1989	1992	1996	2000	2004
Auto theft	1.2	1.8	1.3	1.0	0.8
Burglary	2.0	2.8	2.0	2.0	1.8
Robbery	1.0	1.3	1.1	1.0	1.0
Sexual offenses against women	2.5	2.5	2.3	2.0	1.7
Overall rate, nine crimes measured all years	17.2	22.4	20.3	18.4	15.7

Source: van Dijk, van Kesteren, and Smit 2007, table A1.

than "rape" alone), rates peaked in 1995 and have fallen continuously since. The authors of the most recent ICVS report observe, "According to ICVS data, the level of common crime in Europe reached a plateau around 1995 and has shown a steady decline over the past ten years. The level of victimization in Europe has now decreased to the level of 1990" (van Dijk, van Kesteren, and Smit 2007, p. 46).

Thus it appears, strongly and credibly, that crime rates for the most common violent and property crimes affecting individuals have been falling for a considerable time in most developed countries. We do not know why.

B. Costs and Cost-Effectiveness

There is little reliable evidence on the costs of crime. Systematic efforts to calculate the costs of common crimes are plagued by errors and conceptual and ideological blind spots. Efforts to calculate the costs of other crimes are plagued by the unavailability of reliable data and a need to make heroic assumptions.

Evidence on cost-effectiveness of alternative policy choices is in better shape, especially in relation to choices between investment in law enforcement and in developmental prevention or rehabilitative programs. That many developmental and treatment programs appear to be sounder public investments than law enforcement approaches is especially striking because the standard ways of making such calculations use data on the cost of crime that greatly exaggerate costs, thereby making benefits harder to cost-justify.

Studies of the costs of crime exaggerate costs of violent crimes enormously. That is because the most commonly used approach, based on work by the economist Mark Cohen (1988; Miller, Cohen, and Wiersema 1996; M. Cohen and Miller 2003), includes victims' pain and suffering as a cost of crime. Cohen developed his estimates from court files on contested cases in which crime victims filed suit for damages and won. This is inappropriate for two reasons.

First, the estimates are exaggerated. They are applied to all crimes falling within generic categories, such as murders, rapes, robberies, and assaults, even though contested civil damages cases are far from being representative of these categories. They are extreme cases, what statisticians call the right-hand tail of the distribution. They are the comparatively rare cases in which the defendant was solvent or insured, in which the prospect of winning was sufficiently high to attract plaintiffs' lawyers willing to work on a contingent fee basis, and in which the crime was so awful or the defendant so unattractive that juries were prepared to award large damages. Pain and suffering costs make up by far the largest share of costs in Cohen's calculations, especially for violent and sexual crimes. In one of Cohen's most widely cited reports, for example, pain and suffering were estimated to constitute $81,400 of the $87,000 total costs of a rape or sexual assault, and $1,910,000 of the $1,940,000 cost of a homicide (net of lost earnings; Miller, Cohen, and Wiersema 1996).

Cohen and others (e.g., Cook and Ludwig 2001) have used additional methods to estimate the costs of crimes. One, taken from environmental economics, is to ask people how much more they would be willing to spend on annual insurance premiums to reduce particular risks by 10 percent. Using the finding that people would be willing to pay an extra $100 to $150 per year to reduce risks of crime, M. Cohen and colleagues (2004) estimate the cost of a rape at $237,000 and the cost of a murder at $9,700,000.

The second problem is that Cohen's estimates are often used by him and others in cost-benefit studies of criminal justice system policies. The difficulty is that cost-benefit analyses take heavy account of victims' "intangible costs" and "lost earnings" but no account of offenders' intangible costs (and little account of their tangible costs such as lost earnings and reduced postprison earnings prospects, and no account of costs incurred by offenders' dependents). In explaining his felicific calculus Bentham made it clear that everyone's happiness and unhappiness should count in deciding whether a practice or policy is justifiable.

I have many times asked economist friends, including Mark Cohen, why offenders' costs are not taken into account, but I have never received a clear answer. Sometimes someone mumbles that offenders' interests are irrelevant because, after all, they are offenders. Omission of the costs of punishment to offenders and their families, including "intangible costs," from cost-benefit calculations of the effectiveness of criminal justice policies, while counting such costs attributed to victims, is the equivalent of putting not a hand but a foot on one side of the scale, and foreordains the apparent cost-effectiveness of many punitive policies.

Cost-effectiveness studies do considerably better. Some of them take offenders' costs into account to some degree. Credible analyses for nearly twenty years have repeatedly shown that many developmental prevention methods and some treatment programs are better public investments than increased use of imprisonment (Welsh, Farrington, and Sherman 2001; Aos, Miller, and Drake 2006).

Many of the contributors to this book discuss cost-of-crime, cost-effectiveness, and cost-benefit analyses and generally suggest that they should be regarded with skepticism. Reuter (1984) long ago showed the tendency of efforts to estimate the costs of crime (in his case, drug abuse) to produce preposterously high numbers, as his title illustrates: "The (Continuing) Vitality of Mythical Numbers."

III. Choosing Policies

Evidenced-based policy for many subjects is in vogue. It implies a rationalistic approach to policy making that takes account of evidence concerning the effectiveness, including cost-effectiveness, of alternative policy options, and takes account of intended and unintended foreseeable effects of policy choices. Efforts to prevent and control crime and minimize its harms and costs are, alas, not fully rational. They implicate economic, political, social, ideological, and moral issues that shape the limits of politically possible policies.

"Wars" on drugs and crime, for example, reflect moral entrepreneurship and political calculation at least as much as dispassionate assessment of how to prevent unwanted behavior and minimize related social costs. Recent policy attention to domestic violence has been motivated both to prevent and respond to harmful behavior and to elevate its visibility in the public mind and in political debate, and through doing so to strengthen the social, economic, and political positions of women.

People concerned single-mindedly about environmental damage or financial chicanery are deeply frustrated when they realize that others are equally or more concerned about the economic and social effects (for business) of vigorous law enforcement. Economic conservatives often see a bit of illegality and corruption as an inevitable and even necessary, if regrettable, effect of unleashing a capitalist economy. Tighter regulation of organizations might yield less unwanted behavior, but it might also yield lower rates of economic growth. Social liberals often see street crime and drug abuse as inevitable but tragic effects of child poverty, disadvantaged lives, and a weak U.S. welfare state, and prefer to try to prevent crime by improving criminogenic social conditions rather than primarily through deterrence, incapacitation, and rehabilitation.

People are not angels, and this side of the Pearly Gates they are never likely to be. People make mistakes, do stupid and cruel things, and commit sins (if you find that concept uncongenial, substitute: behave immorally or in ways that violate fundamental social norms of right conduct). Everyone's happiness and unhappiness should count. Laws and other public policies should be based on best-faith efforts to achieve the greatest public benefit at the least human cost. Finnish policy makers have a distinctive way to say this: crime policy should take all the costs of crime into account, including the costs of law enforcement (by which they mean not only the economic costs of crime and the criminal justice system, but also the economic and intangible costs offenders suffer because of what is done to them; Lappi-Seppälä 2007, p. 231). This is basically a restatement of Bentham's parsimony, the view that no suffering should be imposed on offenders that is not justified by greater suffering from which others are saved. The implication is that policy makers should try as best they can to restrain the influences of emotion and expressive considerations on public policy about crime. Evidence-based policies for dealing with crime, coupled with a sense of human frailty and the transience of life, may be a romantic aspiration, but it is the right aspiration.

NOTES

1. Americans should not feel especially virtuous and tolerant by comparison. Not long ago laws were passed making it a crime to burn the U.S. flag. A Supreme Court decision, *Texas v. Johnson*, 491 U.S. 397 (1989), declared such laws unconstitutional as infringements of the First Amendment's right of free speech.

2. For example, Gusfield's (1963) classic account of prohibition in the nineteenth century (established teetotaling Protestants from England anxious about incoming alcohol-drinking Catholic Irish and German settlers). Musto ([1973] 1987) offers parallel accounts of early twentieth-century criminalization of opiates (associated with Chinese immigrants), cocaine (associated with blacks), and marijuana (associated with Mexicans). This point is often made by contrasting policies concerning alcohol and nicotine, the recreational substances that generate the greatest social costs (in ill health, lost lives, monetary costs) but that are the recreational drugs of the majority population, with policies concerning marijuana and heroin.

3. There is, however, no credible evidence that capital punishment, which can be imposed in the United States only for murder, deters murders better than sentences that can otherwise be imposed (Donohue and Wolfers 2005; Tonry 2008).

4. Victimization rates have generally been declining for a much longer period, beginning not later than 1973, the *National Crime Victimization Survey*'s first year. Major changes in the survey's design were effected in 1993, making the data series discontinuous.

REFERENCES

Andenaes, Johannes. 1974. *Punishment and Deterrence*. Ann Arbor: University of Michigan Press.

Anglin, M. Douglas, and Yih-Ing Hser. 1990. "Treatment of Drug Abuse." In *Drugs and Crime,* edited by Michael Tonry and James Q. Wilson. Vol. 13 of *Crime and Justice: A Review of Research,* edited by Michael Tonry. Chicago: University of Chicago Press.

Aos, Steve, Marna Miller, and Elizabeth Drake. 2006. *Evidence-Based Public Policy Options to Reduce Future Prison Construction, Criminal Justice Costs, and Crime Rates*. Olympia: Washington State Institute on Public Policy.

Bennett, Trevor, Katy Holloway, and David Farrington. 2006. "Does Neighborhood Watch Reduce Crime? A Systematic Review and Meta-Analysis." *Journal of Experimental Criminology* 2(4): 437–58.

Bentham, Jeremy. 1948. *Introduction to the Principles of Morals and Legislation*. Edited by Wilfred Harrison. Oxford: Oxford University Press. (Originally published 1789.)

Blumstein, Alfred, and Joan Petersilia. 1995. "Investing in Criminal Justice Research." In *Crime,* edited by James Q. Wilson and Joan Petersilia. San Francisco: ICS.

Braithwaite, John. 2002. *Restorative Justice and Responsive Regulation*. New York: Oxford University Press.

Burney, Elizabeth. 2005. *Making People Behave—Antisocial Behaviour, Politics, and Policy.* Cullompton, UK: Willan.

Buruma, Ybo. 2007. "Dutch Tolerance: On Drugs, Prostitution, and Euthanasia." In *Crime and Justice in the Netherlands,* edited by Michael Tonry and Catrien Bijleveld. Vol. 35 of *Crime and Justice: A Review of Research,* edited by Michael Tonry. Chicago: University of Chicago Press.

Clarke, R. V. 2005. "Seven Misconceptions of Situational Crime Prevention." In *Handbook of Crime Prevention and Community Safety,* edited by Nick Tilley. Cullompton, UK: Willan.

———. 2008. "Situational Crime Prevention." In *Environmental Criminology and Crime Analysis,* edited by R. Wortley and L. Mazerolle. Cullompton, UK: Willan.

Cohen, Jacqueline. 1983. "Incapacitation as a Strategy for Crime Control: Possibilities and Pitfalls." In *Crime and Justice: A Review of Research,* vol. 5, edited by Michael Tonry and Norval Morris. Chicago: University of Chicago Press.

Cohen, Mark. 1988. "Pain, Suffering, and Jury Awards: A Study of the Cost of Crime to Victims." *Law and Society Review* 22: 537–55.

Cohen, Mark, and Ted R. Miller. 2003. "'Willingness to Award' Nonmonetary Damages and the Implied Value of Life from Jury Awards." *International Review of Law and Economics* 23: 165–81.

Cohen, Mark, Roland T. Rust, Sara Steen, and Simon T. Tidd. 2004. "Willingness-to-Pay for Crime Control Programs." *Criminology* 42: 89–109.

Cook, Philip J. 1980. "Research in Criminal Deterrence: Laying the Groundwork for the Second Decade." In *Crime and Justice: A Review of Research,* vol. 2, edited by Norval Morris and Michael Tonry. Chicago: University of Chicago Press.
Cook, Philip J., and Jens Ludwig. 2001. *Gun Violence: The Real Costs.* New York: Oxford University Press.
Donohue, John J., and Justin Wolfers. 2005. "Uses and Abuses of Empirical Evidence in the Death Penalty Debate." *Stanford Law Review* 58: 791–846.
Doob, Anthony N., and Cheryl Marie Webster. 2003. "Sentence Severity and Crime: Accepting the Null Hypothesis." In *Crime and Justice: A Review of Research,* vol. 30, edited by Michael Tonry. Chicago: University of Chicago Press.
Durkheim, Émile. 1933. *The Division of Labour in Society.* Translated by George Simpson. New York: Free Press. (Originally published 1893.)
Farrington, David P. 1986. "Age and Crime." In *Crime and Justice: A Review of Research,* vol. 7, edited by Michael Tonry and Norval Morris. Chicago: University of Chicago Press.
Farrington, David P., and Brandon Welsh. 2007. *Saving Children from a Life of Crime.* New York: Oxford University Press.
Feld, Barry. 1999. *Bad Kids.* New York: Oxford University Press.
Gaes, Gerald G., Timothy J.Flanagan, Lawrence L. Motiuk, and Lynn Stewart. 1999. "Adult Correctional Treatment." In *Prisons,* edited by Michael Tonry and Joan Petersilia. Vol. 26 of *Crime and Justice: A Review of Research,* edited by Michael Tonry. Chicago: University of Chicago Press.
Gusfield, Joseph R. 1963. *Symbolic Crusade: Status Politics and the American Temperance Movement.* Urbana: University of Illinois Press.
Hart, H. L. A. 1968. *Punishment and Responsibility.* Oxford: Oxford University Press.
Hawkins, Keith. 2003. *Law as Last Resort: Prosecution Decision-Making in a Regulating Agency.* Oxford: Oxford University Press.
Lappi-Seppälä, Tapio. 2001. "Sentencing and Punishment in Finland: The Decline of the Repressive Ideal." In *Sentencing and Sanctions in Western Countries,* edited by Michael Tonry and Richard S. Frase. Oxford: Oxford University Press.
———. 2007. "Penal Policy in Scandinavia." In *Crime, Punishment, and Politics in Comparative Perspective,* edited by Michael Tonry. Vol. 36 of *Crime and Justice: A Review of Research,* edited by Michael Tonry. Chicago: University of Chicago Press.
Leuw, Ed. 1991. "Drugs and Drug Policy in the Netherlands." In *Crime and Justice: A Review of Research,* vol. 14, edited by Michael Tonry. Chicago: University of Chicago Press.
Martinson, Robert. 1974. "What Works? Questions and Answers about Prison Reform." *Public Interest* 35(2): 22–54.
Miller, Ted R., Mark K. Cohen, and Brian Wiersema. 1996. *Victim Costs and Consequences: A New Look.* Washington, DC: U.S. Department of Justice, National Institute of Justice.
Morris, Norval. 1974. *The Future of Imprisonment.* Chicago: University of Chicago Press.
Musto, David. 1987. *The American Disease: Origins of Narcotic Control.* Expanded ed. New York: Oxford University Press. (Originally published 1973.)
Nagin, Daniel S. 1998*a*. "Criminal Deterrence Research at the Outset of the Twenty-First Century." In *Crime and Justice: A Review of Research,* vol. 23, edited by Michael Tonry. Chicago: University of Chicago Press.
———. 1998*b*. "Deterrence and Incapacitation." In *The Handbook of Crime and Punishment,* edited by Michael Tonry. New York: Oxford University Press.

Reuter, Peter. 1984. "The (Continuing) Vitality of Mythical Numbers." *Public Interest* 78 (Spring): 135–47.

Schur, Edwin. 1973. *Radical Nonintervention—Rethinking the Delinquency Problem.* Englewood Cliffs, NJ: Prentice-Hall.

Sherman, Lawrence W., Janelle D. Schmidt, and Dennis P. Rogan. 1992. *Policing Domestic Violence: Experiments and Dilemmas.* New York: Free Press.

Sourcebook of Criminal Justice Statistics Online. 2007. 31st ed. http://www.albany.edu/sourcebook.

Straus, Murray A., and Richard J.Gelles. 1986. "Societal Change and Change in Family Violence from 1975 to 1985 as Revealed by Two National Surveys." *Journal of Marriage and the Family* 48: 465–79.

Tonry, Michael. 2008. "Learning from the Limits of Deterrence Research." In *Crime and Justice: A Review of Research,* vol. 37, edited by Michael Tonry. Chicago: University of Chicago Press.

Tonry, Michael, and David P. Farrington, eds. 2005. *Crime and Punishment in Western Countries, 1980–1999.* Vol. 33 of *Crime and Justice: A Review of Research,* edited by Michael Tonry. Chicago: University of Chicago Press.

U.S. Department of Justice, Bureau of Justice Statistics. 2006. *National Crime Victimization Survey: Criminal Victimization in the United States—2005.* Washington, DC: U.S. Department of Justice.

van de Bunt, Henk, and Wim Huisman. 2007. "Organizational Crime in the Netherlands." In *Crime and Justice in the Netherlands,* edited by Michael Tonry and Catrien Bijleveld. Vol. 35 of *Crime and Justice: A Review of Research,* edited by Michael Tonry. Chicago: University of Chicago Press.

van Dijk, Jan, John van Kesteren, and Paul Smit. 2007. *Criminal Victimisation in International Perspective: Key Findings from the 2004–2005 ICVS and EU ICS.* The Hague: Boom Juridische uitgevers and Research and Documentation Center, Ministry of Justice, the Netherlands.

von Hirsch, Andrew, Anthony E. Bottoms, Elizabeth Burney, and Per-Olof H. Wikström. 1999. *Criminal Deterrence and Sentence Severity: An Analysis of Recent Research.* Oxford: Hart.

Welsh, Brandon C., and David P. Farrington, eds. 2005. *Preventing Crime: What Works for Children, Offenders, Victims, and Places.* New York: Springer.

Welsh, Brandon C., David P. Farrington, and Lawrence Sherman. 2001. *Costs and Benefits of Preventing Crime.* Boulder, CO: Westview.

Welsh, Brandon C., and Akemi Hoshi. 2006. "Communities and Crime Prevention." In *Evidence-Based Crime Prevention,* rev. ed., edited by Lawrence W. Sherman, David P. Farrington, Brandon C. Welsh, and Doris Layton MacKenzie. New York: Routledge.

Yeager, Peter Cleary. 1993. "Industrial Water Pollution." In *Beyond the Law: Crime in Complex Organizations,* edited by Michael Tonry and Albert J. Reiss Jr. Vol. 18 of *Crime and Justice: A Review of Research,* edited by Michael Tonry. Chicago: University of Chicago Press.

PART I

VIOLENT AND SEXUAL CRIME

CHAPTER 1

HOMICIDE AND SERIOUS ASSAULTS

RICHARD ROSENFELD

HOMICIDE and aggravated assault are forms of violent crime. A crime is a violation of criminal law, but what is violence? That turns out to be a difficult question. Should the definition of violence be limited to acts causing physical harm? What about threats of harm? Can mere words or symbols constitute violence? Is defacing religious property or burning a cross on someone's lawn a violent act?

Social scientists do not agree on a single or unified definition of violence. Psychologists generally prefer broad definitions that include behaviors producing emotional harm. The Committee on Family Violence of the National Institute of Mental Health, for example, offers a definition that includes not only acts threatening or inflicting physical harm but those resulting in "restraint of normal activities or freedom, and denial of access to resources" (quoted in Crowell and Burgess 1996, p. 10). By this definition, prisons and poverty could be considered forms of violence.

Criminologists tend to favor narrower definitions of violence focusing on physical harm or threats. Many, but not all, criminologists accept the definition provided by an influential National Research Council study of violence as "behaviors by individuals that intentionally threaten, attempt, or inflict physical harm on others" (Reiss and Roth 1993, p. 2). This definition includes a diverse assortment of behaviors, including homicide, assault, rape, torture, capital punishment, and boxing. But it excludes many acts that are encompassed by other, equally reasonable definitions. How one chooses to define violence prefigures the types of behavior that are counted as violence, the levels of violence observed across place and time, the theories that make sense of violent behavior, and the social response to violence.

Regardless of the definition, not all violence is criminal violence. Violence is made a crime through the *criminalization process*, which entails the selective application of the criminal law to violent acts (Turk 1969). Criminal law, and law itself, are not universal. They have not always existed, and they do not impose uniform standards or sanctions on behavior across societies or in the same society over time. Prior to the emergence of formal law, a creation of the modern, centralized state, behavior was guided and sanctions were imposed by custom rooted in religious, community, and kinship institutions.

It is a criminological truism that acts legally prohibited at one time or place may not be at others (Beirne and Messerschmidt 2000, pp. 10–16). An example is the prohibition of the manufacture, sale, and distribution of alcohol in the United States. But this maxim applies to violent behavior and not just victimless crimes. Until late in the twentieth century in most U.S. states, for example, a man could not be criminally charged with raping his wife; now all states have laws against marital rape (see Brownmiller 1975; Russell 1990). Current controversies over the application of criminal law to violence include the debates over abortion and assisted suicide. Regardless of one's views on these issues, they clearly reveal the *contested* character of the distinction between legal and illegal violence. During his murder trial, Jack Kevorkian, the physician who publicly assisted in the deaths of terminally ill patients, gestured to the prosecutor and told the court, "He calls it a murder, a crime, a killing.... I call it medical science" (quoted in Belluck 1999). Changes in the legal status of specific forms of violence are often brought about by social movements and involve considerable social conflict. The history of the legal regulation of abortion is a good example (Conrad and Schneider, 1992, pp. 10–12). If you are put off by applying the term *violence* to abortion, welcome to the debate.

In this chapter I consider the cultural meanings, empirical patterns, theoretical explanations, and social responses connected with homicide and aggravated assault. I address homicide and aggravated assault trends in the United States over the past several decades; cross-national comparisons of homicide and assault; characteristics of victims, perpetrators, and incidents; relationships between victims and perpetrators; theories of violence; and policies to reduce violent crime.

The main empirical patterns in homicide and serious assault are easily summarized, less easily explained. Rates of homicide and aggravated assault have exhibited substantial volatility in the United States, rising to peak levels by the early 1990s and then falling over the next decade to 30-year lows. Cross-national comparisons reveal strikingly higher rates of homicide, but not assault, in the United States than other developed nations. In all nations where they have been recorded, rates of homicide and serious assault are higher among men and the young than among women and older persons. In the United States the prevalence of homicide and serious assault is greater among African Americans and Hispanics than among non-Hispanic whites. In all groups firearm use greatly increases the risk that a violent encounter will result in the victim's death. Large numbers of victims are acquainted with the perpetrator in homicide and aggravated assault, sometimes intimately. Women are more likely than men to be killed or injured in attacks by an intimate partner. Rates of intimate partner violence have fallen in recent years, but the decrease differs by sex and lethality. Greater reductions in assault victimization have occurred among women than men, and homicide victimization has decreased more among men than women.

Although homicide and serious assault have declined in the United States, the reasons why remain something of a mystery (Rosenfeld 2004; Zimring 2007). Mass imprisonment is one contributor to the crime decline, but its other social consequences are troubling, and even its crime-reduction benefits may dissipate over time. The same sense of political purpose, widespread mobilization, and forceful leadership that ushered in the era of mass imprisonment will be required to bring about needed reforms under the banner of "prisoner reentry," the reintegration of released prisoners into the social and political mainstream. A surprising degree of political support for prisoner reentry exists, but that is likely to last only until violent crime rates begin to rise again.

I began by considering the variable technical definitions and cultural meanings attached to the concept of violence. Explanations of violence, including social science explanations, are subject to the same disciplinary and cultural influences. Lay, legal, and scientific explanations of violence share a fundamental feature: they are based less on the inherent qualities of the behavior than on the social and moral status of the victim and perpetrator. The causal factors emphasized in explanations of the violent behavior of morally suspect persons (e.g., criminals) generally involve individual or social defects, whereas those in explanations of violence carried out by morally upright persons (e.g., soldiers, police officers, executioners, physicians) more often involve considerations of legal or moral obligation. Consider the case of the Stillwater slap.

I. The Stillwater Slap

A Stillwater, Oklahoma, police officer was demoted and charged with assault in 1996 for slapping a teenage boy he caught having sex with his daughter on the couch in his home. He "struck the boy on the nose," according to an Associated Press account. Although he was reinstated in his job and the criminal charges were dropped, the officer pressed for a full exoneration and removal of the incident from his record. "I was acting as a father in my own home," he said at a news conference. He won widespread support for slapping the boy, including from the Oklahoma governor, who was quoted as saying, "I would have slapped him a lot harder" ("Officer Gets Back Job" 1996).

There is nothing exceptional about this story; were it not for the sex, it probably would not have made the news outside of Stillwater. But it raises several relevant questions about the legal status of violent behavior and how such behavior is explained. First, is the Stillwater slap violence? It would seem so, even by the narrow criminological definition given above, although the degree of physical harm in this case was apparently very slight. The police officer's slap qualifies as what criminologists term *simple assault,* which is an assault without a weapon and that does not cause serious physical injury.

Second, is the Stillwater slap a crime? It was, and then it wasn't. The prosecutor believed he had grounds for charging the police officer with an assault, but then dropped the charge after the case attracted widespread public attention. Earlier I characterized crime as a violation of criminal law. Although technically true, the Stillwater case illustrates the fundamentally *contingent* character of the criminalization process. The process depends to some degree on the facts of a case, but the facts are usually open to multiple interpretation.

What are the applicable facts in this case? Granting that violent behavior is at issue, the fact that it did not result in serious injury is clearly germane. What if the officer had slapped the boy hard enough to cause a bruise or abrasion? A bleeding cut requiring stitches? What if he had used a closed fist or struck the boy repeatedly or made contact with a body part more pertinent than the nose to the case at hand? At some point along the continuum of physical harm, the prosecutor would have concluded that he had little choice but to bring the case to court, but reasonable people will disagree about where that point lies.[1]

If the degree of injury is a relevant fact in this case, the social status of the victim and offender also matters. The offender occupied several statuses with powerful and highly pertinent cultural resonance: homeowner, father, adult, police officer. Each is what sociologists call a *redeeming role* that provides moral justification for actions that would elicit social condemnation if carried out by less respectable persons. But although the social status of the participants influences the social response to violence, social status is not inviolable; one note off key can ruin the entire performance. Ask yourself whether the Stillwater prosecutor might have proceeded differently had the father been drunk when he struck the boy or if he had a record of prior assaults.

Status considerations not only influence the criminalization process, they affect the way social scientists explain violent behavior. Because not all fathers would have behaved as the Stillwater police officer did under similar circumstances, it seems reasonable to ask about the characteristics that distinguish him from others. Would it be useful to inquire into the genetic influences that might have predisposed him to behave violently, psychological attributes such as impulsivity or low self-control, or possible brain dysfunction from head injury or early exposure to lead? Such explanations are quite common in contemporary social science research on violent behavior. If they seem odd or irrelevant in this case, that is because we do not ordinarily invoke individual pathology to explain *socially acceptable* behavior, violent or otherwise. We tend to reserve explanations that emphasize individual defects of one kind or another for *problematic* violence or persons, such as adolescents, with few redeeming roles. The acceptable violence of respectable persons usually requires no explanation at all.

If you doubt that social status matters as much as or more than the behavior itself in the explanation of violence, switch the roles of victim and offender in the Stillwater case, leaving everything else the same. Now, instead of the father slapping the boy, the boy slaps the father. Do explanations emphasizing individual defects (e.g., impulsivity, conduct disorder, early exposure to toxins, poor parenting) make more sense when applied to the boy than to the father? I think they would to many social scientists who study violence. And they would not necessarily be incorrect under either scenario. But to the extent that they are invoked selectively to explain *socially disapproved* violence they are not explanations of violent behavior as such, but of behavior that violates commonly held views of the acceptability of violent conduct by persons who lack redeeming roles. In applying such explanations, the social science researcher makes judgments very similar to those of the prosecutor when deciding whether to apply criminal charges to violent behavior, except that prosecutors are usually more self-conscious than researchers about how the moral status of the behavior may affect their judgment.

II. Patterns of Criminal Homicide and Assault

The foregoing discussion implies that how one chooses to define violence and the cultural meanings attached to particular instances of violent behavior will affect how violence is measured, the levels of violence observed across places at any given time, and trends in violence over time. What is true for violent behavior generally is also true for homicide and aggravated assault. Homicide is the willful killing of one human being by another. Some homicides are lawful, such as those committed in warfare or as legal punishment for crime, and some are criminal. Aggravated assault is an attack by one or more persons on another with the purpose of inflicting serious bodily injury, including threats and attempts, or an assault committed with a dangerous weapon—an "aggravating" condition (Federal Bureau of Investigation 2006). As with homicide, the behavior itself does not distinguish a criminal from a noncriminal assault. The sport of boxing is a legally regulated form of assault.

In the United States three sources of data can be used to track levels and trends in criminal homicide and assault: the FBI's Uniform Crime Reports (UCR), the Bureau of Justice Statistics' *National Crime Victimization Survey* (*NCVS*), and the mortality and intentional injury data series from the National Center for Injury

Prevention and Control (NCIPC).[2] The UCR data are based on offenses reported to and recorded by police departments. The *NCVS* data are from representative surveys of the population age 12 and older. The NCIPC data are from hospital and death records. The three data sources complement one another in several ways. For example, the *NCVS* picks up crimes that are not reported to the police, and the UCR and NCIPC count homicides, which are not included in victim surveys (see Lynch and Addington 2007). The NCIPC mortality series includes the nearly 3,000 homicides resulting from the 2001 terrorist attacks, whereas the FBI omitted these victims from its homicide statistics. Finally, the three series categorize rapes and other sexual assaults separately from other assaults (see Sample, chapter 2 in this volume, for a discussion of sexual violence).

A. Recent Trends in the United States

Criminal homicide and aggravated assault rates have exhibited marked fluctuation over the past several decades. Homicide rates between 1960 and 2005 as reported by the UCR are displayed in figure 1.1. These rates were relatively stationary at 4 to 5 homicides per 100,000 population during the 1950s and early 1960s, and then rose substantially over the next several years, peaking at just over 10 per 100,000 in 1980. They cycled between 8 and 10 per 100,000 until the early 1990s, when they began a nearly decade-long drop, what one analyst has called the "Great American Crime Decline" (Zimring 2007). By 2000 U.S. homicide rates had returned to levels not seen since the mid-1960s.

Aggravated assaults are measured in both the UCR and the *NCVS*, using virtually identical definitions. But the two series show very different patterns of change since 1973, the first year of the *NCVS* (see fig. 1.2). Although both UCR and *NCVS* aggravated assault rates have fallen since the mid-1990s, the UCR series rose almost continuously before then, whereas the *NCVS* series decreased from 1973 until the early 1990s, increased for a few years, and then began to fall again.

Some of the early divergence between the two series could be related to the differing age composition of the populations used to create the rates: the UCR rates are based on the total population, and the *NCVS* rates are based on the population age 12 and over. The growth in the UCR series also could reflect a growing willingness by victims to report crimes to the police. In 2005 62 percent of aggravated assault victims told *NCVS* interviewers that they reported the incident to the police (Catalano 2006*a*). Thirty years earlier 56 percent of aggravated assault victims said they reported the crime to the police, but that reporting rate did not change appreciably until the late 1990s. All of the change in reporting to the police occurred well after the *NCVS* and UCR aggravated assault trends began to converge in the 1990s, and therefore cannot explain the divergent trends of the earlier years.[3]

The contrasting trends prior to the 1990s more likely reflect better police recording of crimes with the advent of computerized records and 911 emergency

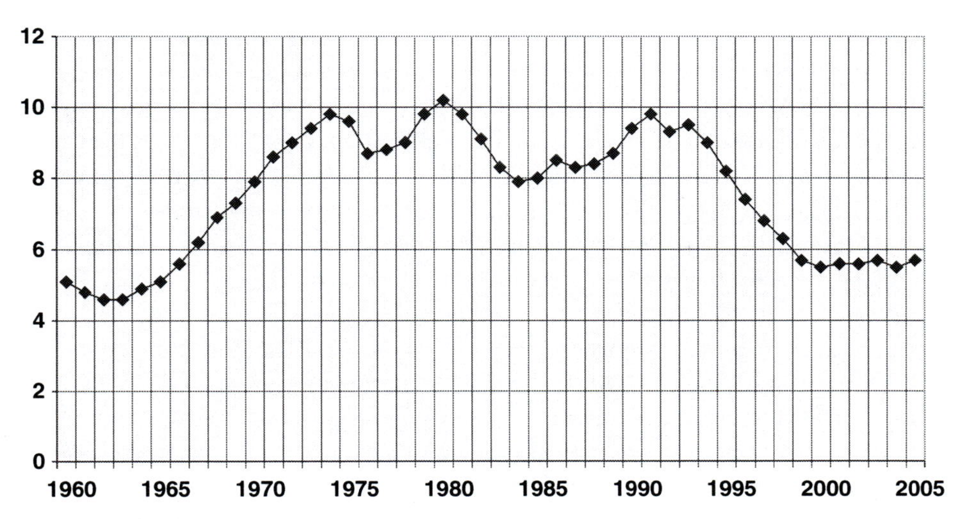

Figure 1.1. Homicides per 100,000 population in the United States, 1960–2005.
Source: Uniform Crime Reports.

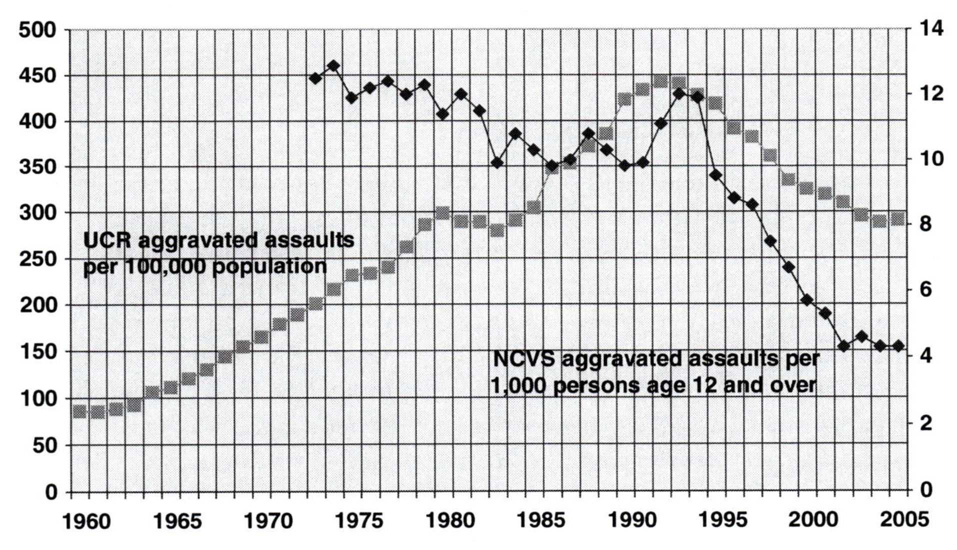

Figure 1.2. UCR and NCVS aggravated assault rates, United States, 1960–2005.
Note: NCVS rates prior to 1993 adjusted to reflect 1992 *NCVS* redesign.
Source: Uniform Crime Reports; *National Crime Victimization Survey.*

call systems and police upgrading of many assaults as aggravated that in the past had been considered less serious crimes. The latter interpretation is supported by evidence showing much stronger correspondence between the UCR and *NCVS* time trends for assaults committed with firearms than those without a firearm. The police are unlikely to record firearm incidents as simple assaults, whereas they have much greater discretion in classifying incidents without firearms. Beginning in the 1970s the women's movement and advocates for criminalizing domestic violence began to press police and prosecutors to treat assaults more seriously, especially those with female victims, and those pressures contributed to the rate increase in aggravated assaults reflected in the UCR data series. Because the *NCVS* is based on standardized screening questions to determine criminal victimization and lacks the police recording filter of the UCR, the *NCVS* aggravated assault series is much less likely to be affected by such changes (see Rosenfeld 2007).

Changes in police recording of assaults provide an excellent illustration of how the cultural meanings of violence are redefined by social movements and affect the definition and measurement of violent crime. Assaults that the police, reflecting commonly held views, once had classified as misdemeanor offenses, or may not have recorded as crimes at all, were upgraded in seriousness with the increasing social status of victims. The rights and prerogatives of crime victims generally have grown during the past thirty years, with victims of domestic violence leading the way. Mandatory and pro-arrest policies have reversed the legal protection once granted to violence occurring in the home. The effects of such policies on the incidence of domestic violence are more difficult to discern (see Sample, chapter 2 in this volume).

B. Cross-National Comparisons

Comparative assessments of changes in homicide or other crime rates over time are important because they can reveal limitations in explanations of crime trends that are restricted to a single nation, as is true of several leading explanations of the recent violent crime decline in the United States (Zimring 2007). Like those in the United States, the homicide rates of many developed nations rose during the 1970s and 1980s and have fallen since then, but there are plenty of exceptions (LaFree and Drass 2002). As an illustration, figure 1.3 displays the homicide rates for Japan, Canada, and the United States between 1960 and 2000.[4] Japan's homicide rate dropped steadily over the 40-year period. By contrast, the Canadian trend mirrors the increases and declines in the United States, as shown by the best-fitting curves superimposed on the two nations' homicide time series. Explanations of recent U.S. crime trends that emphasize the importance of prison expansion and urban crack markets, such as that Blumstein and Rosenfeld (1998) have proposed, leave open the question of why Canada should have experienced many of the same trends without comparable changes in imprisonment or drug markets (Zimring 2007).

Explanations of cross-national differences in homicide also must contend with the substantial difference in homicide *levels* between the United States and other developed nations, regardless of the time period. Even after dropping by 40 percent during the 1990s the U.S. homicide rate greatly exceeds those of other developed nations. Figure 1.4 displays the homicide rates of 14 highly industrialized,

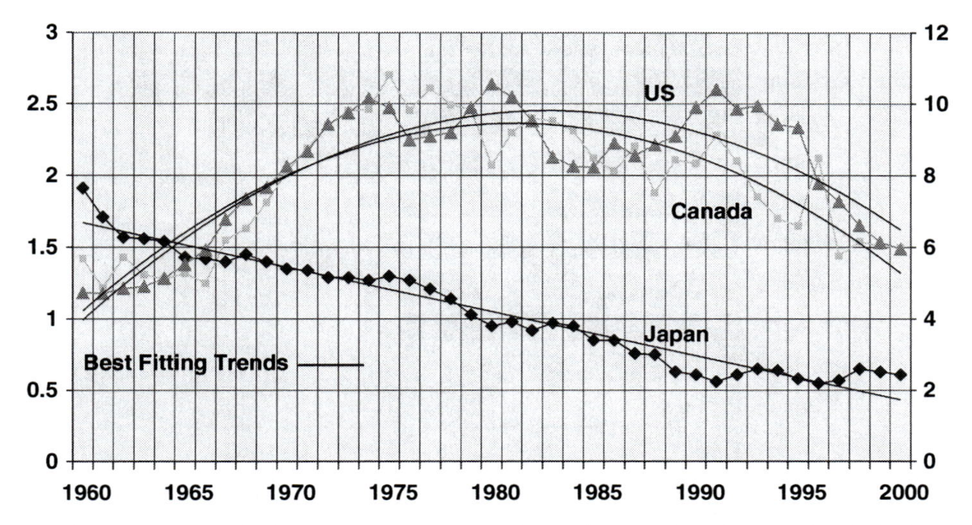

Figure 1.3. Homicides per 100,000 population in Japan, Canada, and the United States, 1960–2000.
Source: World Health Organization, compiled by Gary LaFree.

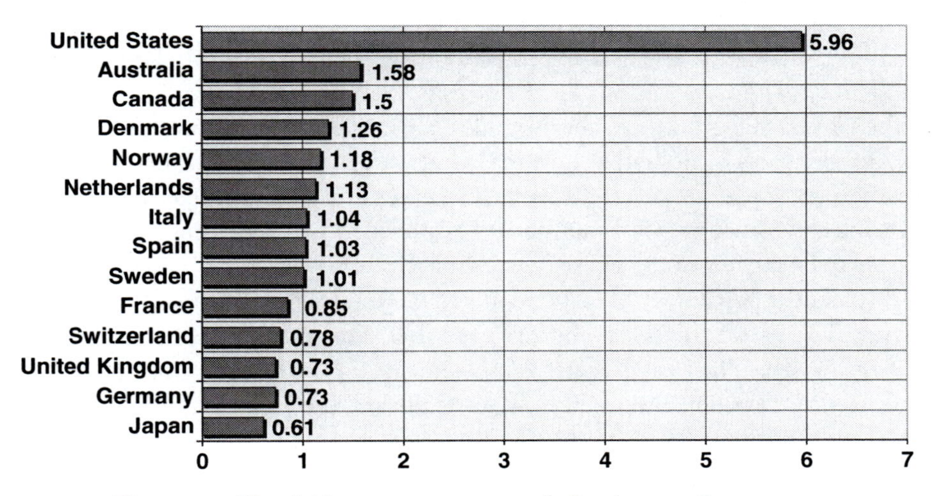

Figure 1.4. Homicides per 100,000 population in 14 nations, 2000.
Source: World Health Organization, compiled by Gary LaFree.

democratic nations in 2000. With 6 homicides per 100,000 population, the United States is the clear outlier in the group. The U.S. homicide rate is three times that of Australia and Canada, its nearest competitors, and over six times the average rate of the remaining 11 nations.

Some analysts attribute the large difference in homicide rates between the United States and other developed nations to the widespread availability of fire-

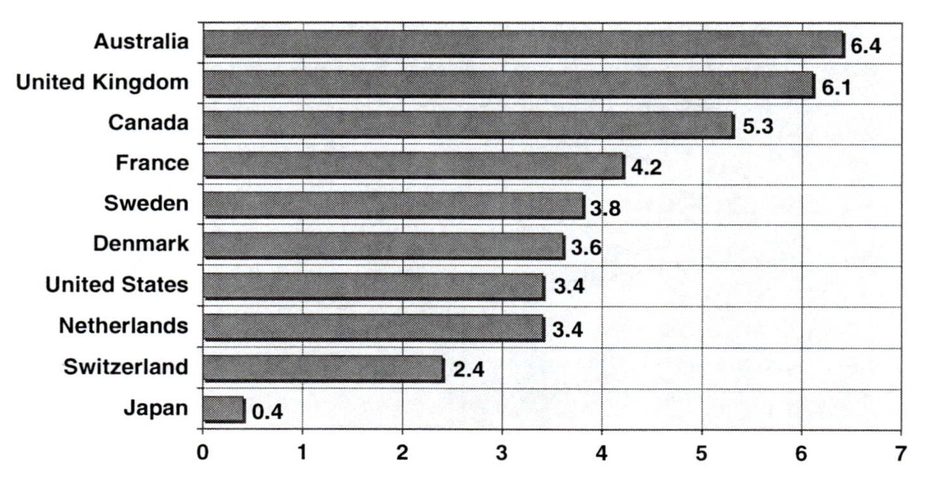

Figure 1.5. Percentage of respondents reporting assault victimization, 1999.
Source: International Crime Victimization Survey.

arms in the United States (Zimring and Hawkins 1997). Others point to the fact that the rate of homicides committed without guns is also greater in the United States than in other developed nations and call attention to a history of racial oppression, economic inequality, and lack of protection from market forces, in addition to the availability of guns, as reasons for the exceptionally high levels of criminal violence in the United States (Currie 1991; Beeghley 2003; Messner and Rosenfeld 2007).

But are rates of nonlethal criminal violence greater in the United States than in other developed nations, or is American exceptionalism limited to homicide, as Zimring and Hawkins (1997) maintain? The prevalence of nonlethal assault does not appear to be greater in the United States than in other developed countries. Figure 1.5 displays the percentage of respondents to the International Crime Victimization Survey (ICVS) in 10 nations who reported that they were victims of one or more assaults in 1999. The United States is far from the top of the list, ranking just below Denmark and Sweden and well below Australia and the United Kingdom.

Caution is in order when interpreting these cross-national comparisons. The ICVS samples are small (1,000 to 2,000 households, compared with about 40,000 households in the U.S.-based *NCVS*), and response rates vary markedly across participating nations. In addition, the ICVS data measure all assaults, not just those with a weapon or that result in serious injury, and simple assaults greatly outnumber aggravated assaults in all nations. Finally, the U.S. assault ranking is largely a product of the crime drop of the 1990s; earlier surveys show the United States closer to the top of the list. Nonetheless, a safe conclusion from the international victimization data is that the United States does not have exceptionally high assault rates. This conclusion favors causal accounts able to explain why the United States dominates international comparisons of homicide but not other forms of criminal violence.

III. Characteristics of Victims and Firearm Use

Nearly everywhere they have been assessed, rates of aggravated assault and homicide are higher among males and the young than among females and older persons. In the United States serious interpersonal violence is also more common among blacks and Hispanics than among non-Hispanic whites. Table 1.1 presents three-year average rates of aggravated assault and homicide in the United States by sex, race, ethnicity (Hispanic and non-Hispanic), and age. The data represent rates

Table 1.1. Characteristics of aggravated assaults and homicide victims age 12 and older and incidents in the United States, 2002–4

	Assaults*	Homicides*	Lethality ratio**
Sex			
Male	563	11.1	50.7
Female	317	2.8	113.2
Race			
White	410	4.1	100
Black	647	26.2	24.7
Ethnicity			
Hispanic***	463	10.1	45.8
Non-Hispanic	437	6.3	69.4
Age			
12–15	670	1.8	372.2
16–19	1,170	10.8	108.3
20–24	977	16	61.1
25–34	533	11.3	47.2
35–49	373	6.5	57.4
50–64	173	3.5	49.4
65+	43	2.3	18.7
Weapon			
Firearm	106	4.8	22.1
Nonfirearm	334	2.1	159
Total	440	6.8	64.7

* Rate per 100,000 population.

** Number of aggravated assaults for every homicide.

*** Hispanics may be of any race.

Source: National Crime Victimization Survey, National Center for Injury Prevention and Control.

of victimization; offending rates exhibit the same demographic patterns, except that offenders tend to be a few years younger than their victims.

Rates of aggravated assault are 78 percent greater among males and 58 percent greater among blacks than among females and whites, respectively. Aggravated assault is somewhat more common among Hispanics than non-Hispanics, but this difference is smaller than the sex and race differences. Age-specific rates of aggravated assault exhibit a distinctive, curvilinear pattern, rising from early to late adolescence and falling steadily thereafter. Persons over the age of 65, with a victimization rate only one-tenth of the average rate of 440 per 100,000, are particularly unlikely to be victims of serious assault. This "age-crime curve" characterizes many common criminal offenses and informs a well-known "general theory" of crime (Gottfredson and Hirschi 1990).

Firearms are used in about one-quarter of aggravated assaults that victims report to the *NCVS* (see Cook and Ludwig, chapter 3 in this volume). Recall that use of a dangerous weapon is one of the aggravating conditions that distinguish aggravated from simple assaults. The other condition is serious bodily injury. It turns out that aggravated assaults involving firearms are much less likely to produce injury than those committed with other weapons or none at all. But if the presence of a firearm reduces the chance of nonfatal injury, it increases the chance that the victim will be killed, thereby converting an aggravated assault into a homicide (Kleck and McElrath 1991).

As shown in table 1.1 the homicide rate for persons 12 and older in the United States is 6.8 per 100,000, meaning that the average American over the age of 11 has a 1 in 14,706 chance of becoming a homicide victim. The sex, race, ethnic, and age patterns in homicide are roughly similar to those in aggravated assault, although the group differences are larger. Males are about four times more likely than females to be the victim of a homicide. The homicide rate among blacks is more than six times that among whites, and the risk of homicide is about 60 percent higher among Hispanics than all others. Like aggravated assaults, homicide rates rise during adolescence but peak a few years later in the early 20s before falling through the remainder of the life course, as shown in figure 1.6. Finally, in contrast to aggravated assault, about two-thirds of homicides are committed with a firearm, so that the firearm homicide rate in the United States is more than twice that of homicides committed without firearms. The United States leads the developed world in both homicides and the proportion of homicides committed with a gun (for comparative data on child and adolescent homicide, see Krug et al. 1998).

The third column in table 1.1 presents the "lethality ratio," or the number of aggravated assault victims for every homicide victim, by characteristics of the victim and whether or not the victim was attacked or threatened by an offender with a firearm. The lethality ratio is a rough approximation of the degree to which death results from the serious violence a group experiences.

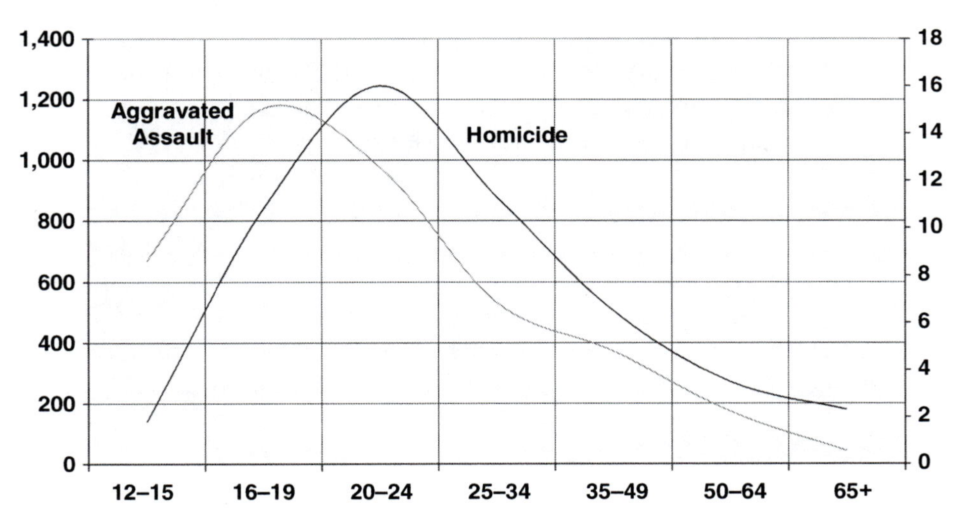

Figure 1.6. Age-specific aggravated assault and homicide victimizations per 100,000 population, United States, 2002–4.
Source: National Crime Victimization Survey; National Center for Injury Prevention and Control.

A full accounting of the lethal outcomes of violent crime would have to include other "precipitating" offenses, such as robbery and rape, in addition to aggravated assault, but the group differences shown in the table would not be altered substantially.

For the population over the age of 11 the average ratio is 65 aggravated assaults for every homicide. Some groups—teenagers, whites, women—have ratios that are much higher than average, meaning that the serious violence they experience is less likely to result in death than is true for groups with lower-than-average ratios, such as blacks and, interestingly, senior citizens. Persons age 65 and over have a lethality ratio of 19 aggravated assaults for each homicide, the lowest ratio shown. It is tempting to attribute this result to the frailty of older persons, which would transform more of their serious assaults into homicides, but their comparatively low homicide rate of 2.3 per 100,000 suggests that is not the full story. Rather, older persons are much less likely to experience interpersonal violence, serious or not, than other age groups. Even their level of simple assault (assaults without a dangerous weapon or serious injury) is far lower than that of younger persons.[5] But when they are attacked they are more likely to be killed.

The group with the largest lethality ratio is near the other end of the age spectrum. Adolescents between 12 and 15 experience 372 aggravated assaults for each homicide. Teenagers, who are said to have replaced fists and knives with guns when they fight, remain far less likely to die in violent encounters than their parents or grandparents.

Finally, attacks involving firearms produce far more deaths per incident than those committed with a knife or club or no weapon. There is no question that firearms are lethal weapons, and many analysts argue that decreases in the availability of firearms would result in fewer homicides (Hemenway 2004). But critics of this view maintain that strict controls on firearm availability would deprive victims of needed protection (Kleck 1997) and even increase violent crime rates if offenders assume their victims are unarmed (Lott 1998). A comprehensive assessment by the National Research Council finds fault with the methods and data used in studies of the "more guns, less crime" hypothesis, regardless of their results (Wellford, Pepper, and Petrie 2004). The relationship between firearms and violence remains a contentious research and public issue in the United States, which is not surprising in a nation with persisting traditions of popular justice and self-protection, high homicide rates, and the largest private arsenal in the world.

IV. Victim-Offender Relationship

Victims of homicide and serious assault are often acquainted with the offender, sometimes intimately. According to the *NCVS,* about 47 percent of aggravated assault victims in 2004 knew their attacker. It is more difficult to determine the proportion of homicide victims who knew their killer, both because the victim is unable to say and because an offender is arrested in only about 60 percent of the homicides committed in the United States (Federal Bureau of Investigation 2006). The FBI's Supplementary Homicide Reports, a detailed compilation of homicide incidents, victims, and known offenders, show that 43 percent of homicide victims in 2004 were acquainted with the offender, 13 percent were strangers, and the victim-offender relationship could not be determined in the remaining 44 percent of cases. Women and younger victims are more likely to know their attackers than are men and older victims. The same patterns emerge in violence among family members and other intimates. About 16 percent of aggravated assault victims and 12 percent of homicide victims in 2004 were attacked by a family member, including spouses or ex-spouses. Intimate partner violence has received widespread attention by researchers, victims' advocates, and policy makers in the United States. It is worth taking a closer look.

Two facts stand out in patterns of intimate partner violence: women are more likely than men to be victims of serious intimate partner violence, and levels of intimate partner violence have declined markedly over time.[6] Both of these patterns are revealed in figures 1.7 and 1.8, which show U.S. trends in nonfatal and fatal intimate partner violence, respectively, by sex of the victim.

Both figures show higher levels of victimization among female than male intimate partners and decreases in victimization over time, but the rate of decline

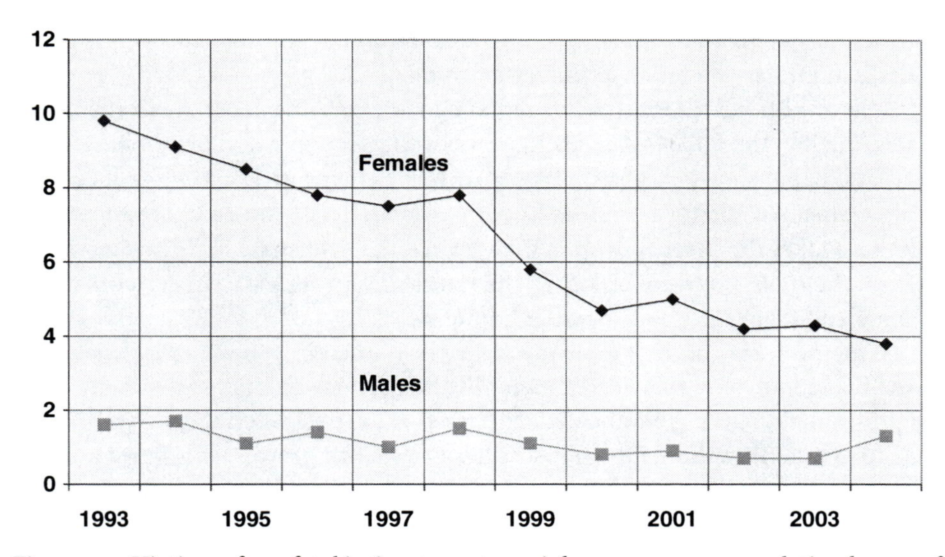

Figure 1.7. Victims of nonfatal intimate partner violence per 1,000 population by sex of victim, United States, 1993–2004.
Source: Catalano 2006*b*.

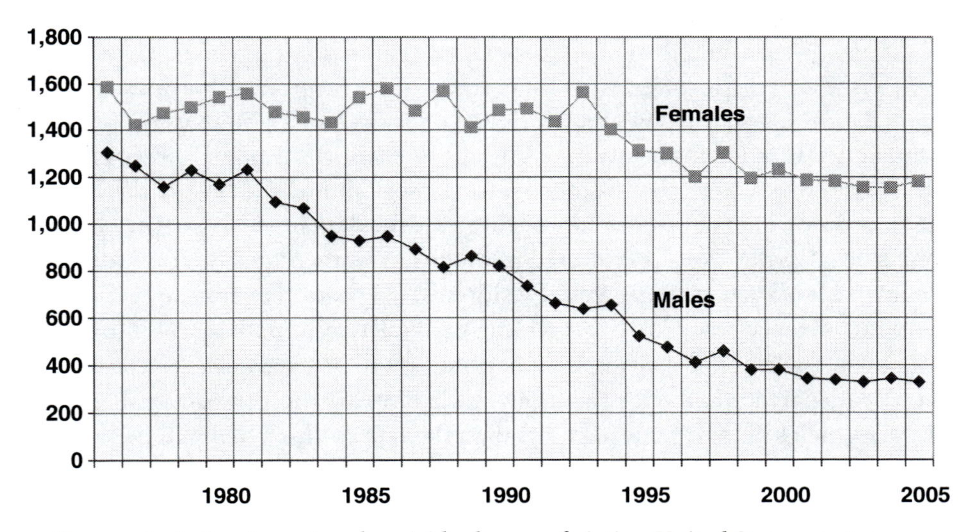

Figure 1.8. Intimate partner homicides by sex of victim, United States, 1976–2005.
Source: Catalano 2006*b*.

differs for men and women by type of victimization. Continuous data from the *NCVS* on nonfatal intimate partner violence are available only since 1993. They show a greater decline in the nonfatal victimization of women than men. By contrast, the drop in male victims of intimate homicide over the past 30 years is steeper than the drop in female victims, which only began in the early 1990s. These contrasting declines are, at first glance, puzzling. What accounts for the sex differences in nonfatal and fatal victimization trends?

The conditions responsible for reducing violent crime generally in the United States during the 1990s—including a booming economy, more police, and a dramatic expansion in imprisonment—might be expected to have reduced violence against women (Levitt 2004; Rosenfeld 2004; Rosenfeld and Fornango 2007). But that makes the sharper drop in male than female intimate homicide victimization all the more puzzling. A key to the puzzle lies in the differing circumstances of male and female intimate partner homicide.

When women kill their male partners, the homicide is much more likely to be "victim-precipitated" than when men kill their female partners (Wolfgang [1958] 1975; Rosenfeld 1997). A homicide is victim-precipitated when the victim initiates the violent conflict that ends in his or her death. The person who starts a fight is not always the one left standing when it ends. When women kill their male partners, they typically do so in response to an attack or threat. The same is not true of men who kill their intimate partners (Rosenfeld 1997). Women are more apt than men to kill as a last resort, when all else fails, to stop the violence directed at them, sometimes over a long period of time. Women, then, should be more willing than men to take advantage of nonviolent alternatives to homicide that effectively reduce their exposure to their partner's violence.

Dugan, Nagin, and Rosenfeld (1999) used that reasoning to explain what otherwise is a very curious result in their study of the impact of hotlines, shelters, legal advocacy, and other domestic violence services and resources on trends in intimate partner killings: intimate killings of men, not women, dropped more rapidly in cities where such resources were more prevalent. It is a fair bet that the domestic violence prevention advocates who demanded more services and greater legal protection for battered and abused women and their children did not intend that their struggle would result in saving batterers' lives. But if we view domestic violence resources as providing nonviolent alternatives to killing a violent partner, it is not surprising in light of the sex difference in the circumstances of intimate partner homicide that they would have a greater impact on the rate at which women kill their male partners than the rate at which men kill their female partners.

In a second study, Dugan, Nagin, and Rosenfeld (2003) found that the homicide reductions associated with domestic violence services and legal reforms were uneven across racial groups and by marital status: the availability of domestic violence resources produced greater reductions among whites and married couples than among blacks and unmarried intimate partners. These results are consistent with evaluations of mandatory and pro-arrest policies for domestic violence, which have found stronger deterrence effects of arrest on subsequent violence for married and employed men than for the unmarried and unemployed (Sherman 1992; see Garner, Fagan, and Maxwell 1995 for a critical review of this research). Domestic violence policy interventions explain only part of the drop in intimate partner homicide; rising divorce rates also contributed to the decline as more women exited relationships with violent or abusive partners (Dugan, Nagin, and Rosenfeld 1999). In fact, an important rationale for liberalizing divorce laws in Europe during the nineteenth and twentieth centuries was to reduce the number of domestic homicides (Gillis 1996). The institution of divorce was the first and arguably remains the most effective program to prevent domestic violence.

V. Theories of Homicide and Assault

Homicide and assault are studied from a variety of theoretical perspectives, and no single theory commands consensus among students of interpersonal violence, even when the focus is limited to criminological perspectives. It is useful to categorize theories of violence according to their level of analysis and whether they apply to all forms of violence, legal as well as criminal, or are restricted to nonnormative or criminal violence. Micro-level theories direct attention to characteristics of individuals or their immediate social context (e.g., family and peer influences) to explain individual differences in violent behavior. Macro-level theories explain the variation in rates of violence across groups, populations, and societies. Both micro- and macro-criminological theories of violence are limited primarily to explaining socially disapproved violence, although two perspectives, R. B. Felson's (2004) interactionist theory and Black's (1976, 1998) theory of social control, encompass normative violence as well.

Though conceptually and analytically distinct, specific micro and macro perspectives share underlying assumptions about the individual and social processes implicated in crime. The three major micro-level perspectives in criminology—social learning theory, social control theory, and strain theory—share behavioral assumptions with three of the major macro-level perspectives on crime: cultural deviance theory, social disorganization theory, and anomie theory, respectively (Messner and Rosenfeld 2007). Social learning theory posits that criminal behavior is learned under the same social conditions that shape learning of all kinds (Sutherland 1947; Akers 1998). Its macro-level counterpart, the cultural deviance perspectives, explain variations in violent crime across groups and communities on the basis of cultural or subcultural values, beliefs, and norms that promote or tolerate violent conduct (Wolfgang and Ferracuti 1967; Anderson 1999).

Social control theory explains criminal behavior as resulting from weakened or absent social bonds that, when strong, discourage crime and delinquency (Hirschi 1969; Kornhauser 1978). Its macro-level analogue, social disorganization theory, specifies the social conditions that weaken social bonds, including economic deprivation, residential instability, and population heterogeneity (Shaw and McKay 1969; Bursik and Grasmick 1993).

Finally, strain theories posit that criminal behavior is a function of failure to attain desired goals, aversive stimuli, and negative emotions (Agnew 2006). At the macro level, anomie theories hold that high levels of crime characterize communities and societies in which cultural goals extol the virtues of economic success for everyone, access to the legitimate means to attain cultural goals are unequally distributed in the population, and the social controls and supports of basic institutions are weakened (Merton 1938; Messner and Rosenfeld 2007; see Baumer and Gustafson 2007 for an excellent overview).

The three pairs of criminological theories make very different assumptions about how criminality is facilitated by personal and social characteristics. Cultural learning theories propose that criminal propensities are generated in interaction with others whose values and beliefs conflict with prevailing legal standards. In sharp contrast, social control theories view criminal behavior as needing no special explanation; what must be explained is not why some people steal or behave violently, but why the rest of us do not. People conform to law, control theorists argue, because not doing so is costly. To the degree nonconformity threatens valued social relationships and investments in rewarding legitimate activities, people will conform. In addition, time and energy devoted to legitimate pursuits limit the time and energy available for criminal activity. Contemporary strain and anomie theories incorporate elements of social learning and control theories but also specify the personal and social processes that weaken social controls and encourage the adoption of deviant or criminal attitudes and beliefs (Messner and Rosenfeld 2007).

None of these perspectives holds a commanding position among criminologists. Researchers tend to mix and match arguments from multiple perspectives, often oblivious to the contrasting assumptions they make about how and why persons violate legal standards (Kornhauser 1978).

In recent years rival theories have emerged that seek to transcend the limitations of established theories or recast them around new insights. Routine activity theory (M. K. Felson 2002) downplays the significance the older perspectives attach to criminal motivations and emphasizes the opportunities to commit crime that emerge when offenders, however motivated, come into contact with victims in situations that facilitate theft or attack (e.g., an unguarded cash register, a lone individual on a darkened or empty street). Self-control theory (Gottfredson and Hirschi 1990) transcends social control theories by locating the source of deviant behavior in early childhood socialization. Poor parenting produces persons incapable of forming deep attachments to others or controlling their impulses and who will commit crimes whenever opportunity permits. Life course theories also emphasize the importance of early childhood in facilitating or retarding delinquent and criminal behavior in adolescence and adulthood but reject self-control theory's deterministic assumption that faulty socialization spells trouble throughout the life course (Laub and Sampson 2003; Sampson and Laub 1993). Age-graded turning points, such as marriage, military service, and a good job, can promote conformity and discourage criminality.

None of these established or emerging criminological perspectives applies specifically to criminal violence; they are intended to explain criminal behavior generally: violent offending, property offending, and public order offending, such as possessing illegal drugs. At the same time the explanatory scope of all of them, unsurprisingly, is restricted to *criminal* violence. That is a significant limitation. None of the criminological theories can explain why some forms of violent conduct are socially condemned while others are not. Implicitly or by design, all take the prevailing legal order as given and therefore are fundamentally culture bound.

Not all theories of violence are so restricted in their application. Black's (1976, 1998) theory of social control views violence as one among several means of conflict management. Whether disputants engage in violent "self-help" rather than avoidance, toleration, mediation, arbitration, or other ways of managing conflict depends on how closely they are related to one another, the degree of economic inequality or cultural difference between them and relevant third parties, and their integration into broader collectivities. Black's theory is intended to explain dispute-related violence of all kinds, at all times, everywhere.

R. B. Felson's (2004) interactionist theory explains both dispute-related and predatory violence. Whereas some persons engage in dispute-related (sometimes termed "moralistic") violence in response to a perceived wrong, predatory violence is committed without real or imagined provocation by the victim. When a parent spanks a child for misbehaving, she is engaging in moralistic violence. When a robber demands his victim's money at gun point, he is engaging in predatory violence. Rejecting the traditional duality of expressive versus instrumental violence, Felson argues that all violence is intended to achieve some goal, whether to exact compliance, achieve justice, or secure a desired social identity. His theory applies to both criminal and noncriminal violence, in any and all societies and historical periods.

To clarify the distinctions among the various criminological perspectives and the points made earlier about how the moral status of victims and offenders influences popular and social science explanations of violent behavior, consider how each of the perspectives would explain the Stillwater slap. Recall that a police officer slapped a boy he found having sex with his daughter, and the local prosecutor initially charged him with assault only to later drop the charges. From the vantage point of Felson's theory, the violence was a form of retribution, punishment for perceived misbehavior. From Black's perspective, the violence was a form of social control and the ambivalent legal response a reflection of the differences in status and social integration separating victim and offender. Both perspectives are able to make sense of the Stillwater slap.

But what about the strain, control, and social learning perspectives? Does it make sense to conceive of the officer's conduct as the product of goal blockage (strain), weakened social bonds (social control), deficient parenting (self-control), or peer influence (social learning)? Perhaps so, if additional information indicated that the officer was drunk, jobless, depressed, or impulsive or had violent friends or a history of angry aggression. Such information would help to recast his violent behavior as *problematic*, and as such a candidate for explanations that locate the sources of violence in personal or social defects. Absent information that threatens the moral status of violence, however, the traditional criminological theories are left speechless.

Many forms of violence are roundly condemned and, in principle, can be explained with reference to the various problems and pathologies highlighted in traditional criminological perspectives. But the commonalities underlying normative and nonnormative violence are obscured by such a restrictive focus on the problematic origins and manifestations of violence. Science craves generality (Black 1995). All else being equal, theories of violence capable of explaining the executioner's behavior, and not merely that of the condemned, are better.

VI. Violence-Reduction Policies and Interventions

Homicide and aggravated assault rates in the United States have declined markedly over the past 15 years. Homicide fell by 43 percent between 1991 and 2005. The UCR aggravated assault rates dropped by 33 percent over the same period. As measured in the *NCVS*, aggravated assault rates fell by 57 percent. Declines of this magnitude in death and serious injury must be counted as good news. But valued effects are not always brought about by equally appealing causes. That is the case with the relationship between recent crime reductions and mass imprisonment in the United States.

Over a quarter of a century ago the United States embarked on an unparalleled program of prison expansion. For most of the twentieth century, U.S. imprisonment rates were on par with those prevailing in Europe and the rest of the developed world. Since the mid-1970s the U.S. imprisonment rate has risen fivefold. No other nation incarcerates its citizens at the levels now customary in the United States.

The rise of mass incarceration resulted from deliberate policy choices and was not the unavoidable outcome of increasing crime rates. One state after another, with strong inducements and pressures from the federal government, instituted mandatory-minimum sentences, sentence enhancements, and truth-in-sentencing provisions to ensure that more convicted felons would be sent to prison and would serve longer sentences (Messner and Rosenfeld 2007, pp. 115–18). Drug offenders were a prime target of the sentencing reforms. Presumably African Americans were not, but changes in drug laws and other get-tough policies, whether intended or not, have disproportionately affected the life chances of African Americans (Tonry 1996; Blumstein and Beck 2005). Fully 10 percent of African American men between the ages of 25 and 29 resided in a state or federal prison in 2002, compared to 2 percent of Hispanic men and 1 percent of white men of the same age (Messner and Rosenfeld 2007, p. 5). It is fair to assume that few policy makers intended or foresaw a quintupling of the prison population as a consequence of the mandatory-minimum sentencing and truth-in-sentencing laws passed over the past 30 years, but once the dramatic escalation in incarceration—and its racially disparate effects—became evident, if policy makers were inclined to limit future imprisonment growth, presumably they would have done so by now (Tonry 1996).[7]

Although debate remains about the size and even the direction of the effect, accumulating research evidence shows that the massive expansion in imprisonment has reduced crime rates in the United States (Marvell and Moody 1994; Levitt 1996, 2002, 2004; Rosenfeld and Fornango 2007; but see DeFina and Arvanites 2002, Tonry 2004). It would be astounding if mass imprisonment at the level used in the United States had no impact on crime rates. But the effects are complex. They are likely to differ by age, with the strongest crime-reduction effects among offenders in their early 30s, who have the longest residual criminal careers, and the weakest effects among juveniles, who are at low risk for incarceration in state and federal prisons. And recent research has shown that the crime-reduction effects of incarceration diminish with increases in the scale of imprisonment (Liedka, Piehl, and Useem 2006).

Mass imprisonment is a stop-gap and costly crime control policy. Most persons released from prison are rearrested for new crimes, and half return to prison within three years (Langan and Levin 2002). The costs of the growing correctional complex are borne primarily by state and local governments, and they have risen at roughly double the rate of state and local outlays for education, health care, and policing over the past 30 years (Hughes 2006). Each additional dollar spent on prisons, jails, and community corrections is money that states and local areas cannot devote to other pressing needs, including improvements in education and early childhood interventions that hold some promise for reducing *criminality* and not just containing crime rates by incapacitating offenders (Greenwood et al. 1998).

Add to the economic costs of mass imprisonment the political and social costs in the form of a growing disenfranchised population of ex-prisoners, further destabilization of the communities hardest hit by the continuous churning of young men moving in and out of prison, the high recidivism rates of ex-prisoners, and the racially disparate impact of prison expansion—and policy alternatives that promise to limit *both* crime rates and prison expansion begin to have growing appeal to policy makers at all levels of government, regardless of political affiliation.[8] A "prisoner reentry" movement has attracted the attention of the Bush administration and state legislatures across the country. Advocates of prisoner reentry point to the limited employment, housing, health, and social services available to persons returning home from prison and the spotty and inconsistent supervision of many ex-prisoners in the community as primary reasons for their high recidivism rates (see Petersilia 2003; Travis 2005). To protect the communities to which they are released and stanch the flow of offenders back to prison, reentry advocates call for sharply lower parole caseloads and enhanced supportive services for ex-prisoners and their families.

It is too early to tell whether current reentry programs reduce recidivism rates, but if they are found to be effective and are widely implemented they could well limit the overall growth in imprisonment, for the simple reason that most persons entering prison in recent years have been there at least once before (Blumstein and Beck 2005). The essential challenge to prisoner reentry programs is finding the right mix of incentives, supports, and controls that will reduce the chances that persons who have already been in and out of prison, and then are reincarcerated, will not return to prison yet again when they are released.

Effective crime-control policy requires more than addressing the needs of released prisoners. The best policy is multifaceted and also should include promising approaches to the prevention and policing of violent crime and in-prison rehabilitation programs of proven effectiveness. There is no shortage of such initiatives (Sherman et al. 1997), but combining them in a coherent policy and providing the resources necessary to bring them to scale pose enormous political challenges.

One is tempted to say the challenge is insurmountable, but recent history indicates it is not. The United States showed the world it is possible to effect startling changes in crime-control policy when the necessary sense of urgency and political will are mobilized. In a nation renowned for its political decentralization and fragmentation, a coherent and self-reinforcing policy of mass imprisonment took hold almost instantaneously across the 50 states with the federal government, no matter which party was in power, leading the way. Limiting the costs of mass imprisonment and instituting effective alternatives are no less possible. The challenge is to mobilize the necessary political resources and instruments before crime rates begin to rise again.

NOTES

1. A year later a Michigan woman faced trial on assault and domestic violence charges for slapping her daughter, twice, for running away and cursing at her. The prosecutor in that case said the charges were justified because the victim sustained a physical injury, although a physician's report found no indication of injury ("Mother May Face" 1997).

2. See "Violent Crime Data Sources" under the references for the data sources used in this chapter.

3. In 1996 55 percent of aggravated assault victims told the *NCVS* they reported the crime to the police. The data for earlier years are from annual paper volumes of the Bureau of Justice Statistics' *Criminal Victimization* publication series (Bureau of Justice Statistics, annual).

4. The cross-national data presented in this section are from the World Health Organization and were kindly provided by Gary LaFree.

5. In 2005 the simple assault rate among persons 65 and older was 1.1 per 1,000, compared with a rate of 13.5 per 1,000 for the total population over the age of 11 (see http://www.ojp.usdoj.gov/bjs/abstract/cvus/age908.htm).

6. The data reported in this section are from a special *NCVS* report by Catalano (2006*b*). As defined in the report, intimate partner violence includes robberies and rapes as well as assaults and homicides, and intimates include same-sex partners.

7. Portions of this section are drawn from Rosenfeld and Messner (2009).

8. For evidence of the political and social costs of mass imprisonment, see Pattillo, Weiman, and Western (2004); Travis and Visher (2005); Manza and Uggen (2006).

REFERENCES

Agnew, Robert. 2006. *Pressured into Crime: An Overview of General Strain Theory*. New York: Oxford University Press.

Akers, Ronald L. 1998. *Social Learning and Social Structure: A General Theory of Crime and Deviance*. Boston: Northeastern University Press.

Anderson, Elijah. 1999. *Code of the Street: Decency, Violence, and the Moral Life of the Inner City*. New York: Norton.

Baumer, Eric P., and Regan Gustafson. 2007. "Social Organization and Instrumental Crime: Assessing the Empirical Validity of Classic and Contemporary Anomie Theories." *Criminology* 45: 617–63.

Beeghley, Leonard. 2003. *Homicide: A Sociological Explanation*. Lanham, MD: Rowman and Littlefield.

Beirne, Piers, and James Messerschmidt. 2000. *Criminology*. Boulder, CO: Westview.

Belluck, Pam. 1999. "Kevorkian Appeals to Emotions of Jurors as They Begin Weighing Murder Charges." *New York Times* (March 26). http://www.nytimes.com.

Black, Donald. 1976. *The Behavior of Law*. New York: Academic Press.

———. 1995. "The Epistemology of Pure Sociology." *Law and Social Inquiry* 20: 829–70.

———. 1998. *The Social Structure of Right and Wrong*. Revised ed. San Diego, CA: Academic Press.

Blumstein, Alfred, and Allen J. Beck. 2005. "Reentry as a Transient State between Liberty and Recommitment." In *Prisoner Reentry and Crime in America*, edited by Jeremy Travis and Christy Visher. New York: Cambridge University Press.

Blumstein, Alfred, and Richard Rosenfeld. 1998. "Explaining Recent Trends in U.S. Homicide Rates." *Journal of Criminal Law and Criminology* 88: 1175–1216.

Brownmiller, Susan. 1975. *Against Our Will: Men, Women, and Rape*. New York: Simon and Schuster.

Bureau of Justice Statistics. Annual. *Criminal Victimization in the United States*. Washington, DC: U.S. Department of Justice.

Bursik, Robert J., Jr., and Harold Grasmick. 1993. *Neighborhoods and Crime: The Dimensions of Effective Community Control*. New York: Lexington Books.

Catalano, Shannan M. 2006*a*. *Criminal Victimization, 2005*. Washington, DC: U.S. Department of Justice.

———. 2006*b*. *Intimate Partner Violence in the United States*. Washington, DC: U.S. Department of Justice. http://www.ojp.usdoj.gov/bjs/intimate/ipv.htm.

Conrad, Peter, and Joseph W. Schneider. 1992. *Deviance and Medicalization: From Badness to Sickness*. Philadelphia: Temple University Press.
Crowell, Nancy A., and Ann W. Burgess, eds. 1996. *Understanding Violence against Women*. Washington, DC: National Academy Press.
Currie, Elliott. 1991. "Crime in the Market Society: From Bad to Worse in the Nineties." *Dissent*, Spring: 254–59.
DeFina, Robert H., and Thomas M. Arvanites. 2002. "The Weak Effect of Imprisonment on Crime: 1971–1992." *Social Science Quarterly* 83: 635–53.
Dugan, Laura, Daniel Nagin, and Richard Rosenfeld. 1999. "Explaining the Decline in Intimate Partner Homicide: The Effects of Changing Domesticity, Women's Status, and Domestic Violence Resources." *Homicide Studies* 3: 187–214.
Dugan, Laura, Daniel Nagin, and Richard Rosenfeld. 2003. "Exposure Reduction or Retaliation? The Effects of Domestic Violence Resources on Intimate Partner Homicide." *Law and Society Review* 37: 169–98.
Federal Bureau of Investigation. 2006. *Crime in the United States 2005*. Washington, DC: U.S. Department of Justice. http://www.fbi.gov/ucr/05cius/.
Felson, Marcus K. 2002. *Crime and Everyday Life*. 3rd ed. Thousand Oaks, CA: Sage.
Felson, Richard B. 2004. "Predatory and Dispute-Related Violence: A Social Interactionist Approach." *Routine Activity and Rational Choice. Advances in Criminological Theory* 5: 103–25.
Garner, Joel, Jeffrey Fagan, and C. Maxwell. 1995. "Published Findings from the Spouse Abuse Replication Project: A Critical Review." *Journal of Quantitative Criminology* 11: 3–28.
Gillis, A. R. 1996. "So Long as They Both Shall Live: Marital Dissolution and the Decline of Domestic Homicide in France, 1852–1909." *American Journal of Sociology* 101: 1273–1305.
Gottfredson, Michael, and Travis Hirschi. 1990. *A General Theory of Crime*. Stanford, CA: Stanford University Press.
Greenwood, Peter W., Karyn Model, C. Peter Rydell, and James Chiesa. 1998. *Diverting Children from a Life of Crime*. Santa Monica, CA: RAND.
Hemenway, David. 2004. *Private Guns and Public Health*. Ann Arbor: University of Michigan Press.
Hirschi, Travis. 1969. *Causes of Delinquency*. Berkeley: University of California Press.
Hughes, Kristen A. 2006. *Justice Expenditure and Employment in the United States, 2003*. Washington, DC: U.S. Department of Justice.
Kleck, Gary. 1997. *Targeting Guns: Firearms and Their Control*. Hawthorne, NY: Aldine de Gruyter.
Kleck, Gary, and Karen McElrath. 1991. "The Effects of Weaponry on Human Violence." *Social Forces* 69: 669–92.
Kornhauser, Ruth R. 1978. *Social Sources of Delinquency: An Appraisal of Analytic Models*. Chicago: University of Chicago Press.
Krug, Etienne G., James A. Mercy, Linda L. Dahlberg, and Kenneth E. Powell. 1998. "Firearm- and Non-Firearm-Related Homicide among Children: An International Comparison." *Homicide Studies* 2: 83–95.
LaFree, Gary, and Kriss A. Drass. 2002. "Counting Crime Booms among Nations: Evidence for Homicide Victimization Rates, 1956 to 1998." *Criminology* 40: 769–99.
Langan, Patrick A., and David J. Levin. 2002. *Recidivism of Prisoners Released in 1994*. Washington, DC: U.S. Department of Justice.

Laub, John H., and Robert J. Sampson. 2003. *Shared Beginnings, Divergent Lives: Delinquent Boys to Age 70*. Cambridge, MA: Harvard University Press.
Levitt, Steven D. 1996. "The Effect of Prison Population Size on Crime Rates: Evidence from Prison Overcrowding Litigation." *Quarterly Journal of Economics* 111: 319–52.
———. 2002. "Deterrence." In *Crime: Public Policies for Crime Control,* edited by J. Q. Wilson and J. Petersilia. Oakland, CA: ICS.
———. 2004. "Understanding Why Crime Fell in the 1990s: Four Factors That Explain the Decline and Six That Do Not." *Journal of Economic Perspectives* 18: 163–90.
Liedka, Raymond V., Anne Morrison Piehl, and Bert Useem. 2006. "The Crime-Control Effect of Incarceration: Does Scale Matter?" *Criminology and Public Policy* 5: 245–76.
Lott, John R., Jr. 1998. *More Guns, Less Crime*. Chicago: University of Chicago Press.
Lynch, James P., and Lynn A. Addington, eds. 2007. *Understanding Crime Statistics*. New York: Cambridge University Press.
Manza, Jeff, and Christopher Uggen. 2006. *Locked Out: Felon Disenfranchisement and American Democracy*. New York: Oxford University Press.
Marvell, Thomas B., and Carlisle E. Moody. 1994. "Prison Population and Crime Reduction." *Journal of Quantitative Criminology* 10: 109–39.
Merton, Robert K. 1938. "Social Structure and Anomie." *American Sociological Review* 3: 672–82.
Messner, Steven F., and Richard Rosenfeld. 2007. *Crime and the American Dream*. 4th ed. Belmont, CA: Wadsworth.
"Mother May Face Year in Jail for Slapping Runaway Daughter." 1997. *St. Louis Post-Dispatch* (October 22): 13A.
"Officer Gets Back Job after Demotion for Slapping Boy in Home." 1996. *St. Louis Post-Dispatch* (September 4): 2A.
Pattillo, Mary, David F. Weiman, and Bruce Western, eds. 2004. *Imprisoning America: The Social Effects of Mass Incarceration*. New York: Russell Sage.
Petersilia, Joan. 2003. *When Prisoners Come Home: Parole and Prisoner Reentry*. New York: Oxford University Press.
Reiss, Albert J., Jr., and Jeffrey A. Roth, eds. 1993. *Understanding and Preventing Violence*. Washington, DC: National Academy Press.
Rosenfeld, Richard. 1997. "Changing Relationships between Men and Women: A Note on the Decline in Intimate Partner Homicide." *Homicide Studies* 1: 72–83.
———. 2004. "The Case of the Unsolved Crime Decline." *Scientific American* 290: 68–77.
———. 2007. "Explaining the Divergence between UCR and NCVS Aggravated Assault Trends." In *Understanding Crime Statistics: Revisiting the Divergence of the NCVS and the UCR,* edited by James P. Lynch and Lynn A. Addington. New York: Cambridge University Press.
Rosenfeld, Richard, and Robert Fornango. 2007. "The Impact of Economic Conditions on Robbery and Property Crime: The Role of Consumer Sentiment." *Criminology* 45: 735–69.
Rosenfeld, Richard, and Steven F. Messner. 2009. "The Normal Crime Rate, the Economy, and Mass Incarceration: An Institutional-Anomie Perspective on Crime-Control Policy." In *Criminology and Public Policy: Putting Theory to Work,* edited by Scott H. Decker and Hugh Barlow. Philadelphia, PA: Temple University Press.
Russell, Diana E. H. 1990. *Rape in Marriage*. Bloomington: Indiana University Press.
Sampson, Robert J., and John H. Laub. 1993. *Crime in the Making: Pathways and Turning Points through Life*. Cambridge, MA: Harvard University Press.

Shaw, Clifford R., and Henry D. McKay. 1969. *Juvenile Delinquency in Urban Areas.* Revised ed. Chicago: University of Chicago Press.

Sherman, Lawrence W. 1992. *Policing Domestic Violence: Experiments and Dilemmas.* New York: Free Press.

Sherman, Lawrence W., Denise Gottfredson, Doris MacKenzie, John Eck, Peter Reuter, and Shawn Bushway. 1997. *Preventing Crime: What Works, What Doesn't. What's Promising.* Report to the U.S. Congress. Washington, DC: U.S. Department of Justice.

Sutherland, Edwin H. 1947. *Criminology.* Philadelphia: Lippincott.

Tonry, Michael. 1996. *Malign Neglect: Race, Crime, and Punishment in America.* New York: Oxford University Press.

———. 2004. *Thinking about Crime: Sense and Sensibility in American Penal Culture.* New York: Oxford University Press.

Travis, Jeremy. 2005. *But They All Come Back: Facing the Challenges of Prisoner Reentry.* Washington, DC: Urban Institute Press.

Travis, Jeremy, and Christy Visher, eds. 2005. *Prisoner Reentry and Crime in America.* New York: Cambridge University Press.

Turk, Austin T. 1969. *Criminality and Legal Order.* Chicago: Rand-McNally.

Wellford, Charles F., John V. Pepper, and Carol V. Petrie, eds. 2004. *Firearms and Violence: A Critical Review.* Washington, DC: National Academies Press.

Wolfgang, Marvin E. 1975. *Patterns in Criminal Homicide.* Montclair, NJ: Patterson Smith. (Originally published 1958).

Wolfgang, Marvin E., and Franco Ferracuti. 1967. *The Subculture of Violence: Towards an Integrated Theory in Criminology.* London: Tavistock.

Zimring, Franklin E. 2007. *The Great American Crime Decline.* New York: Oxford University Press.

Zimring, Franklin E., and Gordon Hawkins. 1997. *Crime Is Not the Problem: Lethal Violence in America.* New York: Oxford University Press.

Violent Crime Data Sources

International Crime Victimization Survey. http://ruljis.leidenuniv.nl/group/jfcr/www/icvs/. Data available from National Archive of Criminal Justice Data, http://www.icpsr.umich.edu/cocoon/ICPSR/SERIES/00175.xml.

National Center for Injury Prevention and Control. Centers for Disease Control and Prevention. Web-based Injury Statistics Query and Reporting System. http://www.cdc.gov/ncipc/wisqars/.

National Crime Victimization Survey. Bureau of Justice Statistics, U.S. Department of Justice. http://www.ojp.usdoj.gov/bjs/.

Supplementary Homicide Reports. Federal Bureau of Investigation, U.S. Department of Justice. Detailed data available from the National Center for Juvenile Justice, http://www.ojjdp.ncjrs.gov/ojstatbb/ezashr/.

Uniform Crime Reports. Federal Bureau of Investigation, U.S. Department of Justice. http://www.fbi.gov/ucr/ucr.htm.

World Health Organization, United Nations. http://www.who.int/en/.

CHAPTER 2

SEXUAL VIOLENCE

LISA L. SAMPLE

Sex crimes have garnered much public attention and concern over the past twenty years, and as a result, sex offenders have been the subject of an unprecedented amount of legislative activity at state and federal levels. Many of the sex offender policies recently enacted are the products of technological advances in the medical, computer, and surveillance fields. For instance, currently all states mandate the drawing of DNA samples from convicted sex offenders so they may be housed in databanks and used by law enforcement agencies to help identify criminal suspects and enact arrests (Stevens 2001). Some states have enacted chemical castration statutes, which promote reductions in victimization through the use of medications that diminish offenders' sex drive. More recently, the federal PROTECT Act of 2003 (PL-108–21, section 604) requires all states to create Internet-based Web sites that contain information about registered sex offenders, and Florida's Lunsford Act (948.30 f.s.) requires global positioning satellite tracking of sex offenders for life once they emerge from prison.

Other sex offender policies enacted since the late 1980s, such as civil commitment and sex offender registration, were simply new versions of old laws repackaged to reflect the public's growing concerns. To date at least twenty-one states have passed civil commitment legislation, which requires the commitment of sex offenders in mental health facilities after their release from prison if they can be diagnosed with a mental disorder that makes future offending likely (Sample 2001). These laws borrowed heavily from the sexual psychopath laws passed by several states in the late 1930s and 1940s (Sutherland 1950). Also, the Jacob Wetterling Crimes against Children and Sexually Violent Offender Registration Act (Title XVII of the Violent Crime Control and Law Enforcement Act of 1994, 42 U.S.C.A. §14071) requires states to create registries of convicted sex offenders. California, however, had enacted a criminal registration statute as early as 1947 (Tewksbury 2002) that offered the same requirement as the Wetterling Act: the registration of offenders' addresses with law enforcement agencies upon criminal convictions.

Still other recent sex offender policies, such as community notification and a national sex offender registry, appear to be natural extensions of preexisting laws. Megan's law was passed in 1996 as an amendment to the Wetterling Act and requires states to provide sex offender registry information to the public so citizens can better protect themselves from convicted offenders. The Pam Lychner Sexual Offender Tracking and Identification Act was also passed in 1996, allowing the FBI to track sex offenders when they move from state to state. In 1998 an act was passed to extend registration requirements to federal military personnel and nonresident students and workers residing in the United States, and this act mandated states to participate in a national sex offender registry (section 115 of the General Provisions of Title I of the Departments of Commerce, Justice, and State, the Judiciary, and Related Agencies Appropriations Act). More recently the Adam Walsh Child Protection and Safety Act of 2005 further enhanced registration requirements for sex offenders and provided additional guidelines for the implementation of the national sex offender registry. In addition, several states over the past decade have enhanced the penalties for various sex crimes, either lengthening the prison sentence to be served or requiring lifetime supervision, and some states now require electronic monitoring of certain types of sex offenders upon their release from prison.

Although many of the sex offender laws to date are either reiterations of or amendments to previous legislation or are the natural outgrowth of technological advances in various fields, a new class of sex offender laws has emerged that appear to be the result of true innovations. Several states and local communities have proposed or enacted laws that prohibit sex offenders from living, frequenting, or loitering in designated public spaces. For instance, in some states sex offenders have been prohibited from living within a certain number of feet (500 to 2,000) from a school, school zone, day care facility, or bus stop (Florida and Iowa offer examples). In other states, sex offenders have been prohibited from frequenting amusement parks, malls, or public parks (Illinois and Texas are examples). Some local communities have proposed prohibiting sex offenders from simply loitering near schools, public parks, and mall parking lots.

The specific sex crimes included under any of these laws vary slightly from community to community and state to state; however, all this legislative activity appears to share a common goal: the protection of the public from sexual victimization. These laws also appear to share common assumptions about sex offenders and offending. In this chapter I review the assumptions underlying sex offender legislation and discuss them in light of what we know about the incidence, prevalence, and causes of sex offending. Assessments of the effectiveness of these laws are also reviewed. I conclude with thoughts on the future of sex offender legislation.

Here are a few things that can reasonably be said about what we know about sex offenders, offenses, and responses to both:

- The majority of sex offenders know their victims, and their crimes generally take place in private residences.
- Recidivism rates for sex offenders are typically lower than that found for other criminal groups.
- Sex offenders with adult victims tend to reoffend with greater frequency than offenders with child victims.
- Sex offenders rarely kill their victims.
- Social incompetencies such as a lack of empathy, a lack of intimacy, exaggerated depression or anger, loneliness, and impulsivity contribute to or facilitate sex offending.
- There have been few evaluations of contemporary sex offender policies to determine their effectiveness at monitoring or controlling sex offenders' behavior or addressing the causes of sex crimes.

I. Assumptions about Sex Offenders and Offending

The sheer amount of sex offender legislation passed since the late 1980s suggests that the public faces a growing threat of sexual victimization. Beyond an inference of a growing sex offender problem, however, the requirements of these laws often imply assumptions about the behavior of sex offenders. Of the three most common assumptions about sex offenders—their inevitable reoffending regardless of their type, their propensity to kill, and their frequent choice of children as victims—the first two are not supported by empirical findings, and research findings are mixed with regard to the third.

Legal scholars and researchers have highlighted what they believe to be assumptions about sex offenders and offending that underpin much of the legislation we have today (Sample and Bray 2003, 2006; Sample 2006; Shajnfeld and Krueger 2006; Levenson et al. 2007). Sample and Bray (2003) suggest that the requirements found in sex offender registration and community notification laws imply an assumption that sex offenders will inevitability reoffend, or at the very least that they reoffend with greater frequency than other types of offenders. Given that registration and notification laws often apply to all sex offenders regardless of the age of their victims or the nature of their crimes, these laws also seem to imply that all sex offenders have an equally high probability of recommitting sex offenses (Sample and Bray 2006). In this way, current sex offender legislation assumes that sex offenders are a homogeneous group who exhibit similar offending patterns irrespective of their type.

Much contemporary legislation, such as the Wetterling Act, Megan's law, and the Lunsford act, are responses to sexually motivated homicides, particularly against children. For example, the enactment of contemporary civil commitment laws can be traced to two trigger offenses (Websdale 1999). In 1988 a work release prisoner with two prior convictions for sexual assault raped and murdered a woman in Seattle (Websdale 1999, p. 92). One year later Earl Shriner drew national media attention for sexually assaulting a 7-year-old Seattle boy, mutilating his genitals, and leaving him for dead. Shriner had been hospitalized for murder in the 1960s and convicted of child molestation in 1977, 1987, and 1988 (Jenkins 1998, p. 191). These crimes precipitated Washington's Community Protection Act, passed in 1990, which became the impetus for many states' civil commitment laws. These laws not only reaffirmed the assumptions that sex offenders will never stop offending, but their passage implied another assumption: that sex offenders often kill their victims. To this end, sex offender laws suggest that sex offending and homicide are almost inevitably intertwined.

Sex offender laws also suggest assumptions about the causes of offenders' behavior. Civil commitment legislation is premised on the notion that sex offenders often possess a mental disorder or defect that drives their behavior. Moreover, chemical castration statutes seem to suggest a biological cause for sex offenders' behavior. Whether assuming a biological or a psychological cause, these laws imply that it is up to the medical community to control the behavior of sex offenders. In light of the assumption that sex offenders will inevitably reoffend, however, lifetime supervision and enhanced prison terms are policies consistent with these causes of behavior.

The last assumption that is readily apparent from contemporary sex offender laws concerns the victims of sex offenders. Residency restrictions and prohibitions from public places such as parks and school zones suggest that children are most often the victims of sexual attacks, or at the very least that children are the population most in need of protection. Given that I know of no laws that prohibit sex offenders from night clubs or other public social places where adult men and women dwell, it seems the victimization of adults is either of less concern to public officials or adults may simply appear less susceptible to sex crimes. Regardless of the reasons for the prohibition of sex offenders from some public places and not others, many current laws seem to suggest that children are frequently the victims of sex crimes. Given the assumptions underlying sex offender laws, it is important to assess the degree to which these assumptions comport to empirical information available about sex offenders and sex crimes.

II. Trends in Sex Offending and Victimization

Although legislative activity surrounding sex offending in recent years may suggest an increased risk of sexual victimization, table 2.1 demonstrates that sex crimes reported to police and incidents of sexual victimization in the United States have

Table 2.1. Trends in incidents of forcible rape and sexual assault

	1996	1998	2000	2002	2005	Percentage change
Forcible rape reported to police*	96,252	93,144	90,178	95,235	93,934	−2.40
Incidents of rape and sexual assault victimization**	291,820	328,130	256,770	247,730	188,960	−35.20

* Rate per 100,000 (Federal Bureau of Investigation, 2006).

** Number of victimization incidents reported (*National Crime Victimization Survey* 1996–2005).

declined over time. There was a slight increase in rapes reported to police from 2000 to 2002, but overall there was a 2.4 percent decline in reports of forcible rape to police from 1996 to 2005 (Federal Bureau of Investigation 2006). Uniform Crime Reports produced by the FBI do not include information on sexual molestations and other less serious sex crimes, so the degree to which their rates increased or declined remains unknown. Despite this caveat, however, even with the slight increase in forcible rapes in the early years of the twentieth century, the number of reported incidents in 2002 remained lower than the number in 1996.

More important, the *National Crime Victimization Survey* data from 1996 to 2005 reveal a 35 percent decline in victimization for rape and sexual assault. There was an increase in incidents of victimization in the late 1990s, but this subsided by 2000, and incidents have continued to decline. Victimization information is available only for persons over 12 years of age, so it remains unknown if the victimization of children under 12 has also declined. Victimization information is necessarily dependent on the way people disclose and interpret sexual activity. It is possible that more sexual victimization occurred than was reported in the National Crime Victimization Survey, as citizens are reticent to disclose their victimization history or simply did not see some unwanted sexual activity as a crime. Nevertheless, this empirically driven information does not support the excessive legislative attention sex offenders have received in the United States in recent years.

The United States is not the only country experiencing declines in sex crimes over time, although cross-national comparisons of the incidence of sex crimes are difficult for several reasons. The definitions of rape, sexual assault, and sex crimes vary across countries, as do reporting and recording practices to and by the police (Tonry and Farrington 2005). These issues are particularly salient when examining official rates of offending. Nevertheless, sources such as the *European Sourcebook of Crime and Criminal Justice Statistics* can provide insight into trends in offending. In 2006 the *Sourcebook* reports that Albania, Georgia, Hungary, Malta, Romania, England and Wales, and Northern Ireland all experienced declines in rape rates between 2000 and 2003 (Aebi et al. 2006). In contrast, police figures report a more than 100 percent increase in rape between 2000 and 2003 in Cyprus and increases between 10 and 100 percent in Croatia, Estonia, France, Germany, Ireland, Italy, and Switzerland. During this same period rates of rape remained relatively stable in Austria, Belgium, Denmark, Finland, Poland, Portugal, and Ukraine. In sum, the declines in sex crimes observed in the United States, as measured through official statistics, have not been witnessed across the globe. What can be definitively stated, however, is that rates of sex offending vary over time from one country to another. Moreover, despite recent declines in the U.S. rate of sex offending, the U.S. rate for sex crimes far exceeds that of other Western countries, such as England, Switzerland, and the Netherlands (Farrington and Jolliffe 2005).

Given the problems inherent in interpreting police statistics on sex crimes, it is essential to examine victimization survey data to get a more accurate picture. Table 2.2 depicts incidence rates of sex crimes against females for several countries from 1989 through 2000. As can be seen, trends in sexual victimization vary. While England and Wales, Finland, and the Netherlands witnessed increases in sexual victimization, Australia, Canada, Belgium, and France experienced declines. As with official statistics, victimization data derived from survey research are not without problems. Respondents may over- or underreport their unwanted sexual experiences depending on personal or cultural willingness to disclose the event. Also, cultural definitions of sexual assault may change over time, thereby making fluctuations in rates more an artifact of changes in the law than changes in the behavior. These facts should be kept in mind when interpreting rates of victimization.

Regardless of the data sources used, it appears that virtually every country experiences some rate of sexual offending and that these rates can vary greatly from one decade to the next. There may be multiple reasons for these fluctuations, such as changes in demographic traits of the population, in the reporting of the behaviors, in the apprehension and punishment of sex offenders, or in drug and alcohol consumption among the population (Farrington and Jolliffe 2005). What cannot be discerned from international statistics for sex crimes, or those from the United States, is the degree to which children are sexually victimized. For this information, we must look to data collected in the United States.

Table 2.2. Victimization incident rates per 100 inhabitants

	1989	1992	2000	Percentage change
Australia	18.9	7.6	7.5	−60
Canada	6.9	7.1	3.8	−45
Belgium	2.3	1.4	2.1	−9
England and Wales	1.2	2.9	6.1	408
Finland	0.5	8.7	8.4	1508
France	1.8	1.7	1.3	−27
Netherlands	5.0	4.1	5.7	14

Source: van Kesteren, Mayhew, and Nieuwbeerta 2000.

Information on those most likely to be the victims of sex crimes is mixed. For instance, Snyder (2000) used National Incident-Based Reporting System (NIBRS) data from 12 states to investigate victims of sex crimes. His findings suggest that children 18 or younger represent over two-thirds of the victimizations of sexual attacks from 1991 through 1996. These children were largely the victims of forcible fondling, forcible sodomy, and sexual assault with an object, whereas adults were more frequently the victims of forcible rape. In contrast, an examination of all persons arrested in Illinois for any offense from 1990 to 1997 reveals that the majority of arrests for sex crimes (63 percent) were for raping an adult 18 years or older, not for crimes against children (Sample and Bray 2006).

Several factors make it difficult to accurately assess trends in sex crimes against children. When reporting arrests or crimes known to the police as sex crimes, most states and countries do not differentiate between sexual crimes against adults and those against children. Data on sexual assaults are represented in the aggregate, irrespective of whether the crime was against someone over or under 18. The U.S. *National Crime Victimization Survey* does not interview anyone under the age of 12, making it impossible to discern the degree to which juveniles 12 and younger experience sexual victimization. What little information we have concerning sex crimes against minors has been gathered at the state level, making it impossible to discern national trends. These deficiencies in data collection make conclusions about trends in offending against children virtually impossible to identify. There is agreement across data sources, however, with regard to the relationship between victims of sex crimes and offenders and where sexual crimes typically occur.

A review of U.S. *National Crime Victimization Survey* data from 1996 to 2005 suggests that the majority of victims of sex crimes knew their attackers (*National Crime Victimization Survey* 2006). Only about one-third of victims were assaulted by a stranger. Snyder's (2000) study of NIBRS data from 12 states reaffirms these results and suggests that only approximately 14 percent of his sample were assaulted by strangers, whereas slightly over 25 percent were assaulted by a family member and the vast majority of victims were attacked by an acquaintance. Given the relationship between offenders and victims, it is not surprising that 70 percent of sexual assaults reported to police occurred in the residence of the victim, the offender, or another individual (Snyder 2000). A greater percentage of sex crimes in 2005 committed by strangers (20.5 percent) and nonstrangers (13 percent) were committed more frequently on a street not near the victim's home or in other areas, such as a private residence (*National Crime Victimization Survey* 2006), than in schools or on public transportation. Approximately 8 percent of sex crimes occurred inside a school or on school property in 2005, regardless of the relationship between the victim and the offender, but this estimate was based on 10 or fewer sample cases.

It thus appears that assumptions regarding children as frequent victims of sexual assault may be valid. Despite impediments in obtaining reliable data on the age of victims, many children do seem to fall victim to sex crimes, but it is not known if children's risk of victimization has increased over the past two decades. What is known is that most victims of sex crimes know their attackers, and fewer sex crimes occur on school property or in public places than occur in private homes. Given the degree to which children are assaulted by family members and other people they know in private residences, it would seem more prudent to remove known sex offenders from the home than forbid their residence in school zones or prohibit them from public places.

III. Sex Offender Recidivism and the Propensity to Kill

The penalties under most contemporary sex offender laws seem to embrace the notion that sex offenders will inevitably reoffend and that those offenses often result in homicide. An examination of empirical research on the recidivism of sex offenders refutes this notion. Recidivism information is reviewed here in terms of general reoffending, sex offenders' general reoffending rates as compared to those for non-sexual offenders, sexual reoffending among sex offenders, and comparisons of general and sexual reoffending across several sex offender types.

Although most scholars have been concerned with the degree to which sex offenders commit another sex crime, some have investigated the degree to which sex offenders recommit any type of crime and how these rates compare to those for other types of non-sexual offenders (Hanson, Scott, and Steffy 1995; Sapsford 1998; Sipe, Jensen, and Everett 1998; Langan and Levin 2001; Sample and Bray 2003). Langan and Levin examined rearrest rates over three years for released prisoners in 15 states (N = 272,111). They found that those convicted of sexual assault (41.4 percent) and rape (46 percent) had comparatively low rearrest rates compared with other offender groups, such as burglars (74 percent), robbers (70.2 percent), and thieves (74.6 percent). In their study of arrested sex offenders in Illinois in 1990, Sample and Bray found relatively low general reoffending rates compared with non-sex offenders. Persons arrested in 1990 for robbery had the highest probability of rearrest (74.9 percent) within five years, followed by arrestees charged with burglary (66 percent), non-sexual assault (58 percent), and larceny (52.9 percent). Persons in the sex offense category had rearrest rates of 21.3 percent, 37.4 percent, and 45.1 percent for any offense within one, three, and five years, respectively. Although almost half of the sex offenders examined in these studies were rearrested for another crime within three to five years after their initial arrest or incarceration, these proportions are low compared with those for other types of criminal offenders. The question that remains, however, is the degree to which any of these rearrests represent a new sex crime.

Several researchers have investigated, both retrospectively and prospectively, sexual reoffending patterns among offenders hospitalized, incarcerated, or under treatment for sex crimes (for reviews, see Furby, Weinrott, and Blackshaw 1989; Becker and Hunter 1992; Hanson and Bussiere 1998). Furby, Weinrott, and Blackshaw reviewed forty-nine published sex offender recidivism studies and found that reported levels of sexual reoffending among treated and untreated sex offenders ranged from 3.8 to 55.6 percent. Those results were consistent with Quinsey's (1984, p. 101) findings and support his conclusion: "The difference in recidivism across these studies is truly remarkable; clearly by selectively contemplating the various studies, one can conclude anything one wants." More recently, Hanson and Bussiere conducted a meta-analysis of sixty-one studies examining sexual reoffending patterns among sex offenders. They found that, on average, the sex offense recidivism rate was 13.4 percent during an average follow-up time of four to five years. Langan and Levin (2001) examined rates of sexual reoffending among released sex offenders from 15 states and found only 2.5 percent of released rapists were rearrested for another rape within three years. Hanson and Bussiere (1998, p. 357) may best summarize this body of literature when they conclude, "The present findings contradict the popular view that sexual offenders inevitably re-offend. Only a minority of the total sample (13.4 percent of 23,393) were known to have committed a new sexual offense."

Despite methodological difficulties, differences in sample size, and variability in follow-up lengths, most studies find some level of general or sexual reoffending among sexual offenders, but generally recidivism rates are much lower for sex offenders than for other offender groups, and sex offense recidivism rates tend to be much lower than sex offender laws imply. Clearly, not all sex offenders inevitably reoffend.

Although these findings may seem to refute assumptions of the compulsiveness of sexual reoffending, it is possible that some types of sex offenders exhibit higher rates of recidivism than others. Scholars have noted variability in the rates of general reoffending for sex offenders with adult, as opposed to child, victims. Most find that rapists, or offenders with adult victims, recidivate at a higher rate than do child molesters (Marques et al. 1994; Quinsey, Rice, and Harris 1995; Quinsey, Khanna, and Malcolm 1998). Marques et al. studied recidivism among treated and untreated child molesters whose victims were 15 or younger and rapists whose victims were 16 or older, using rearrest as their measure for a new offense. A greater proportion of rapists were rearrested for another violent crime (22.7 percent) over a five-year period than were child molesters (7.9 percent). In their meta-analysis of 61 sex offender recidivism studies, Hanson and Bussiere (1998) found that a greater proportion of rapists were rearrested for a new offense (46.2 percent) and for another violent offense (22.1 percent) than were child molesters (36.9 percent for a new offense, 9.9 percent for violent crimes). Sample and Bray (2006) found that persons arrested for child molestation or for the rape of an adult were rearrested more frequently for another crime (51 percent and 49 percent, respectively) than those arrested for pedophilia (sexual assault of a child 12 or younger) or hebophilia (sexual assault of a person 13 to 18 years old), or for possessing or manufacturing child pornography over a five-year period. It appears that sex offenders with adult victims have higher general recidivism rates than those with child victims.

With regard to rearrests for another sexual offense, Sample and Bray (2006) found that those arrested for child pornography (10 percent) and those arrested for an "other" sex crime (such as juvenile pimping or soliciting a juvenile prostitute; 9 percent) were more frequently rearrested for another sex crime than were those arrested for rape, child molestation, pedophilia, or hebophilia within five years. Marques et al. (1994) examined sexual recidivism among sex offenders with child and adult victims and found that a greater proportion of rapists were rearrested for another sex crime (9.1 percent) than were child molesters (4 percent). Despite this information regarding the variability in recidivism rates across sex offender types, these data continue to suggest that sex offenders, irrespective of type, do not reoffend with great frequency.

Differences in sex offenders' recidivism rates have also been found with regard to the relationship they have with their victims, the victims' gender, and the type of sex crime committed. In their review of sex offender recidivism research, Becker and Quinsey (1993, p. 170) found that "extrafamilial child molesters are more likely to recidivate than strictly intrafamilial child molesters." They also found that child molesters with male victims were more likely to repeat their crimes than were molesters with female victims. Hood et al. (2002) found that 26.3 percent of extrafamilial offenders with child victims were reimprisoned for a new sex crime after six years, whereas no intrafamilial offenders with child victims were reimprisoned during that time. Moreover, 9.5 percent of nonstranger offenders with adult victims were reimprisoned after six years for another sex crime, compared with 5.3 percent of stranger offenders with adult victims.

In contrast, some researchers have found little or no significant variability in sex offenders' reoffending rates when offenders are disaggregated by the age of their victims or the sex offense type. Romero and Williams (1983) found that a significantly higher proportion of exhibitionists were rearrested for a new non-sexual offense, but they found no significant differences in the commission of subsequent sex crimes between sex offender subgroups. Over a period of two to five years Hagan and Cho (1996) examined reoffending among 100 adolescent child molesters and youth who raped adults. They found that the difference between the 10 percent of rapists and 8 percent of child molesters who were reconvicted for new sex crimes was not statistically significant. The groups' reconviction rates did not significantly differ for non-sexual offenses.

Research findings are mixed with regard to differences in recidivism rates across subcategories of sex offenders. Nevertheless, there is some evidence to suggest that sex offenders are a homogeneous group, as sex offender laws imply. What this body of literature cannot highlight, however, is the degree to which sex crimes often include or result in homicide.

Several scholars have investigated sexually related homicides or homicides committed by sex offenders, but the vast majority of these examinations have focused either on creating a typology of offenders or explaining the causes of the behavior (Ressler, Burgess, and Douglas 1988; Koesis, Cooksey, and Irwin 2002; Beech, Fisher, and Ward 2005; Johnson 2006; Salfati and Taylor 2006). Only two studies could be found that directly investigated the degree to which sex offenders kill (Francis and Soothill 2000; Sample 2006). Francis and Soothill followed 7,436 convicted sex offenders in England and Wales in 1973 over a 21-year period to determine the degree to which they were reconvicted for a homicide or manslaughter charge. They found that only 2.55 percent (19 of 7,436) were reconvicted for killing another person. Of these 19 people, 11 had committed sex crimes against children (persons 16 or younger) in 1973. They conclude "that those convicted of child-sex offences do go on—on quite rare occasions—to be convicted of homicide, and that there is no difference in rates compared with other sex offenders whose illicit sexual behaviour is targeted on adults" (p. 58).

Sample's (2006) findings from a case study of arrested sex offenders in Illinois from 1990 to 1997 confirm that the percentage of sex offenders who kill their victims is small. When examining simultaneous charges for sex crimes and homicides, she found that only 3 percent of arrests that included a sex offense charge also included a charge for homicide. When data were disaggregated by charges for specific sex crime types, the findings indicated that no homicide charges were enacted in conjunction with arrests for child molestation, child pornography, or hebophilia. One percent of pedophilia charges were accompanied by a homicide charge, and less than 2 percent of arrests for the rape of an adult included charges for murder. More important, Sample found that few sex offenders go on to commit homicides in the future. When sex offenders were compared to other groups of offenders, 8.2 percent of people classified as robbers were rearrested for homicide within five years, which was a greater percentage than for any other group. Only 2.9 percent of arrestees in the sex offense category were rearrested for a homicide within five years, which was smaller than the percentages in the homicide (5.7), burglary (5.4), and larceny (4.2) categories. When the sex offender group was disaggregated by specific sex crime type, a greater proportion of arrestees for child molestation were rearrested for homicide within one year than were other categories of offenders (7.4 percent). However, this percentage is based on 2 of 27 people rearrested for crimes in the homicide category. Few people classified as pedophiles, hebophiles, or rapists were rearrested on a homicide charge.

These findings refute popular and legislative notions about the compulsiveness of sex offenders and the degree to which their behavior turns increasingly toward murder. The studies also suggest that sex offenders are not a homogeneous group of offenders exhibiting similar recidivism patterns. This should be kept in mind when enacting broad-based laws, such as registration, notification, and residency restrictions, that are intended to curb the likelihood of all sex offenders' reoffending equally.

IV. Causes of Sex Offenders' Behavior

Examinations of recidivism rates of sex offenders tell us little about why they reoffend or why they commit an initial sex crime. The research discussed thus far does not examine whether the causes and motivations to commit sex crimes against adults are similar to those for people who offend against children. Several factors can contribute to criminal offenders' behavior, including those of a sociological, psychological, and biological nature. Several theories have been proposed, but the literature suggests that most sex offenders share a fundamental pathway to offending. In general, sex offenders' behavior begins with problems in childhood that affect their attachments to others, social skills development, and personality traits (McClintock 1995; Hudson and Ward 2000; Ward and Sorbello 2003; Howells, Day, and Wright 2004; Knight and Sims-Knight 2004; Alley 2006; Chichester 2006). Weak attachments, particular personality traits, and inadequate social skills result in uninhibited or improper responses to opportunities and situations in which offending may occur (Beech and Ward 2004; Beauregard, Rossmo, and Proulx 2007), thus culminating in sex offending.

Sexual and physical abuse and neglect, are problematic childhood events that can affect attachment, social skills, and personality development (Marshall 1996; Ward and Sorbello 2003; Knight and Sims-Knight 2004). Several factors have been significantly associated with these events and subsequent social incompetencies, including cognitive distortions, a lack of empathy, a lack of intimacy, exaggerated emotions in terms of depression or anger, loneliness, and impulsivity, all of which either contribute to or facilitate antisocial behavior and sex offending (Seidman et al. 1994; Howells, Day, and Wright 2004; Knight and Sims-Knight 2004; Marziano et al. 2006). In addition, early childhood sexual abuse may result in sexual fantasies and operant learning opportunities, which provide techniques and rationalizations that promote sex offending (Siegert and Ward 2003; Beech and Ward 2004; Howells, Day, and Wright 2004). Scholars also suggest that different emotional responses to early childhood abuse may result in different types of sex offending. For instance, anger is related to the rape of adults, whereas depression and loneliness are more closely related to victimizing children (Marshall 1996; Howells, Day, and Wright 2004). Nevertheless, it seems clear that childhood abuse sets in motion a series of emotional, social, and cognitive responses that facilitate sex offending.

Beyond psychological factors, contextual and biological factors have also been examined in relation to sex crimes. Some scholars suggest that sex offending is the product of a rational choice made by offenders based on the routine activities of both offenders and victims and the ways ecological and other contextual factors converge to create opportunities for offending (Beech and Ward 2004; Beauregard, Rossmo, and Proulx 2007). Still other researchers have investigated the roles of brain dysfunction, innate mating rituals, sex hormones, neurotransmitters, and the limbic system in promoting sex crimes (Revitch 1988; Money

1990; Lalumiere, et al. 2005; Fazel et al. 2007). Other features of sex offenders have been noted, although their role in the etiology of the behavior remains unclear. For instance, psychopathy has been found in civilly committed sex offenders, but not to a great degree (Jackson and Richards 2007), and substance abuse is frequently encountered in examinations of sex offenders, but again, the causal order is unclear (Marshall 1996).

Evidence for the degree to which any one theory can explain sex offending is mixed, but scholars have begun to see sex offending as the product of multiple dysfunctions spanning diverse biological, social, and psychological factors. This observation seems to hold regardless of sex offender type, although some factors may be more pronounced in one type of sex offender than another. Given what we know about the factors associated with or influencing sex offending, it is important that we create policies that, to some degree, address these factors in order to prevent future offending. We must then examine how current policies address the known factors of sex crimes.

V. Effectiveness of Sex Offender Laws

Much has been written about contemporary sex offender laws, but to date there have been few empirical evaluations of the laws' effectiveness (Cohen and Jeglic 2007). Some of what we know about sex offender legislation pertains to the public's knowledge and acceptance of the laws (Zevitz and Farkas 2000; Tewksbury 2002, 2005; Levenson 2003; Levenson et al. 2007). Several scholars, for example, have found widespread public knowledge and support for sex offender registration and community notification laws (Philips 1998; Martin and Marinucci 2006; Levenson et al. 2007). Despite public support for these laws, scholars are generally not optimistic about these laws' ability to reduce public fear of victimization or sex offending (Avrahamian 1998; Petrosino and Petrosino 1999; Zevitz and Farkas 2000; Tewksbury 2002).

Registration and notification laws are intended to inform the public as to the whereabouts of convicted sex offenders with the hope of preventing reoffending. Their effectiveness is premised on accurate information, yet empirical and journalistic investigations consistently reveal a significant amount of error in descriptions of sex offenders and their addresses (Tewksbury 2002; Lees and Tewksbury 2006). More important, scholars have not found significant effects of community notification on sex offenders' behavior (Schram and Milloy 1995; Adkins, Huff, and Stageberg 2000; Walker et al. 2005; Levenson 2007; Zevitz 2006). Although notification may not promote significant reductions in recidivism, it appears effective at informing the public. Rather than easing the public's fear of victimization, however, notification meetings may have the opposite effect, increasing public anxiety about sexual crimes (Zevitz and Farkas 2000). To the degree that registration and notification are intended to reduce reoffending and ease public fears, they appear to be falling short. They have, however, succeeded in creating unanticipated consequences for offenders.

Researchers have begun noting the adverse effects, or unintended consequences, that registration and notification have for offenders, their behaviors, and communities (Zevitz 2003; Tewksbury 2005; Mustaine, Tewksbury, and Stengel 2006; Tewksbury and Lees 2006). Sex offenders report harassment, social isolation, stigmatization, and feelings of vulnerability as a result of sex offender laws, all of which may prompt further misbehavior (Tewksbury 2005; Tewksbury and Lees 2006). Zevitz studied feelings of neighborhood residents once a registered sex offender moved into their community and found increased levels of fear and anxiety among citizens, but he suggests these feelings may not translate to long-term destabilization of their community. Moreover, Mustaine, Tewksbury, and Stengel (2006) suggest that registered sex offenders are relegated to living in socially disorganized communities, or communities conducive to criminal offending. Registration and notification may simply move sex offenders to areas of the larger community that more readily facilitate their deviant behavior.

Despite the breadth of research on registration and notification laws, there have been few examinations of civil commitment legislation, which is most likely the result of government regulations on the privacy of mental health information. What little we have learned suggests that these laws generally apply to few sex offenders relative to the convicted population, the financial cost of committing offenders for indefinite periods is quite high, and civilly committed sex offenders are no more likely to recidivate that those not committed (Schram and Milloy 1998; Janus 2000; Fitch and Hammen 2003).

Residency restrictions and prohibitions of sex offenders from public spaces are relatively new legislative efforts and have yet to be thoroughly investigated in terms of their ability to prevent sex crimes. Given what we know about sexual victimization and that crimes are most frequently committed by family members and acquaintances in private residences, it seems unlikely that these laws will have a great effect. Nevertheless some states and scholars have begun to investigate correlations between where sex offenders live and where they offend. Most conclude that recidivism appears to be unrelated to where sex offenders' reside, whether that be near public parks or schools or other places where children dwell (Levenson 2007).

Evaluations of other sex offender policies, such as DNA databanks and chemical castration, are rare to nonexistent. A few observations can be made. First, much more research is needed on sex offender laws before definitive conclusions can be drawn about their potential to enhance public safety. Also, it seems reasonable to suggest that we should assess the effectiveness of existing sex offender laws before passing new ones. Given the evidence to date, it is possible that current policies exacerbate the behaviors they are meant to reduce. To the degree that social isolation, loneliness, anxiety, substance abuse, contextual opportunity, and impulsivity affect people's propensity to commit sex crimes, sex offender registration, community notification, and residency restrictions may increase these conditions and place sex offenders in areas where substance abuse and opportunities for offending proliferate.

VI. Conclusions and Future Directions

Given trends in offending and victimization, rates of recidivism and homicide among offenders, factors known to be associated with sex offending, and findings of evaluations of current sex offender laws, scholars suggest moving toward evidence-based social policies for sex offenders (Lees and Tewksbury 2006; Levenson 2007; Shajnfeld and Krueger 2006). Given the complex nature of the causes of offending, some have suggested that multidisciplinary commissions be established to investigate the effects of sex offender policies on offenders' behavior and their reintegration into the community (Shajnfeld and Krueger 2006). Most scholars embrace the notion of a risk-based classification system for notification, which notifies the public of those predicted to pose the greatest risk to society (Levenson 2007; Sample and Bray 2006; Shajnfeld and Krueger 2006). Community protection policies are more likely to succeed when used in a targeted manner rather than being broadly applied (Levenson 2007). A collaborative risk management approach has been proposed for the supervision of sex offenders in the community that could supersede traditional parole (Levenson 2007). This approach would encourage the evaluation of individuals' risks and needs, reinforce offender strengths, and facilitate social support networks for offenders in order to address many of the emotions and cognitive disorientations associated with sex offending.

Some have called for public education and prevention campaigns (Zevitz and Farkas 2000; Levenson 2007). A few sexually related homicides of children committed by strangers have left the public with the impression that children are at greater risk of victimization from strangers than from acquaintances. Empirical data, however, suggest that this is not true. The myth of the stranger sex offender has affected the techniques by which citizens protect themselves from victimization and may leave them vulnerable to the potential offenders they know. To this end, public safety may be enhanced by better informing the public of trends in sex offending and victimization. After community notification meetings, Zevitz and Farkas noted increased levels of fear among the citizens present, and many left the meetings asking law enforcement officers how to better protect themselves. Few community notification procedures include information on preventive techniques. In light of the potential fear community notification may cause, public awareness policies should be accompanied by prevention campaigns based on empirically driven information about the causes of offending and trends in victimization.

Many of our current sex offender polices are facilitated by technological advances. As technology continues to improve, more sex offender legislation is likely to be enacted. It is also likely that each missing or murdered child will result in new sex offender policies or further enhancements to existing laws. These observations are not meant to dismiss the threat of sex offending, make light of the harm that victims endure, or demean the tragedy of sexually assaulted or murdered children. Nor are they intended to question or demean the desires and intentions of public officials enacting sex offender laws: to protect the public from sexual harm and ease public fear (Sample and Kadleck 2008). Rather, these observations are based on the history of sex offender laws. They offer nothing more than an anticipation of what is to come. Few of us know what the computer, medical, psychiatric, or surveillance fields will invent next, but if history is predictive of future events it seems likely that whatever inventions may come, they will be applied to sex offenders before those in other offending groups. These innovations will also most likely be applied before anticipating all the consequences of their application and will become widespread before evaluation of their effectiveness occurs.

Sex offending is a reprehensible behavior with long-lasting consequences for victims and needs to be managed, controlled, and prevented. This we cannot deny. Sex offenders' crimes invoke great fear from legislators and the public at large, which often prompts public officials into quick legislative action. Before enacting additional policies to control this behavior, however, we need to carefully examine laws currently enacted, thoroughly review the empirical evidence we now possess, more extensively research the causes of the behavior, and thoughtfully synthesize all this information. To the degree that we can enact policies that are empirically driven and address some of the causes of sex offending, rather than simply reaffirming misplaced assumptions about offenders, we may be able to enact laws that enhance public safety and achieve their goals.

REFERENCES

Adkins, G., D. Huff, and P. Stageberg. 2000. *The Iowa Sex Offender Registry.* Des Moines: Iowa Department of Human Rights.

Aebi, Marcelo, Kauko Aromaa, Bruno Aubusson De Cavarley, Gordon Barclay, Beata Gruszczynska, Hanss Von Hofer, Vasilika Hysi, Jorg-Martin Jehle, Martin Killias, Paul Smit. 2006. *European Sourcebook of Crime and Criminal Justice Statistics—2006.* The Hague: Minister of Justice.

Alley, Dawn. 2006. "Attachment Disturbances and Sexual Offending. A Progression from Victim to Offender." In *Sex Crimes and Paraphilia,* edited by Eric W. Hickey. Upper Saddle River, NJ: Pearson Prentice Hall.

Avrahamian, Koresh A. 1998. "A Critical Perspective: Do 'Megan's Laws' Really Shield Children from Sex-Predators?" *Journal of Juvenile Law* 19: 301–17.

Beauregard, Eric, D. Kim Rossmo, and Jean Proulx. 2007. "A Descriptive Model of the Hunting Process of Serial Sex Offenders: A Rational Choice Perspective." *Journal of Family Violence* 22: 449–63.

Becker, Judith V., and John A. Hunter Jr. 1992. "Evaluation of Treatment Outcomes for Adult Perpetrators of Child Sexual Abuse." *Criminal Justice and Behavior* 19(1): 74–92.
Becker, Judith V., and Vernon L. Quinsey. 1993. "Assessing Suspected Child Molesters." *Child Abuse and Neglect* 17: 169–74.
Beech, Anthony, Dawn Fisher, and Tony Ward. 2005. "Sexual Murderers' Implicit Theories." *Journal of Interpersonal Violence* 20(11): 1366–89.
Beech, Anthony, and Tony Ward. 2004. "The Integration of Etiology and Risk in Sexual Offenders: A Theoretical Framework." *Aggression and Violent Behavior* 10(1): 31–63.
Chichester, P. Rich. 2006. *Attachment and Sexual Offending: Understanding and Applying Attachment Theory to the Treatment of Juvenile Sexual Offenders*. London: Wiley.
Cohen, Michelle, and Elizabeth L. Jeglic. 2007. "Sex Offender Legislation in the United States: What Do We know?" *International Journal of Offender Therapy and Comparative Criminology* 51(4): 369–83.
Farrington, David P., and Darrick Jolliffe. 2005. "Cross-National Comparisons of Crime Rates in Four Countries." In *Crime and Punishment in Western Countries, 1980–1999*, edited by Michael Tonry and David P. Farrington. Vol. 33 of *Crime and Justice: A Review of Research*, edited by Michael Tonry. Chicago: University of Chicago Press.
Fazel, Seena, Ian O'Donnell, Tony Hope, Gautam Gulati, and Robin Jacoby. 2007. "Frontal Lobes and Older Sex Offenders: A Preliminary Investigation." *International Journal of Geriatric Psychiatry* 22: 87–89.
Federal Bureau of Investigation. 2006. *Crime in the United States—2005*. Washington, DC: U.S. Government Printing Office.
Fitch, W. Lawrence, and Debra A. Hammen. 2003. "The New Generation of Sex Offender Commitment Laws: Which States Have Them and How Do They Work?" In *Protecting Society from Sexually Dangerous Offenders*, edited by Bruce J. Winick and John Q. LaFond. Washington, DC: American Psychological Association.
Francis, Brian, and Keith Soothill. 2000. "Does Sex Offending Lead to Homicide?" *Journal of Forensic Psychiatry* 11(1) :49–61.
Furby, Lita, Mark R. Weinrott, and Lyn Blackshaw. 1989. "Sexual Offender Recidivism: A Review." *Psychological Bulletin* 105(1): 3–30.
Hagan, Michael P. and Meg E. Cho. 1996. "A Comparison of Treatment Outcomes between Adolescent Rapists and Child Sexual Offenders." *International Journal of Offender and Comparative Criminology* 34(2): 105–13.
Hanson, R. Karl, and Monique T. Bussiere. 1998. "Predicting Relapse: A Meta-Analysis of Sexual Offender Recidivism Studies." *Journal of Consulting and Clinical Psychology* 60(2): 348–62.
Hanson, R. Karl, Heather Scott, and Richard A. Steffy. 1995. "A Comparison of Child Molesters and Nonsexual Criminals: Risk Predictors and Long-Term Recidivism." *Journal of Research in Crime and Delinquency* 32(3): 325–37.
Hood, Roger, Stephen Shute, Martina Feilzer, and Aidan Wilcox. 2002. "Sex Offenders Emerging from Long-Term Imprisonment." *British Journal of Criminology* 42: 371–94.
Howells, Kevin, Andrew Day, and Steven Wright. 2004. "Affect, Emotions, and Sex Offending." *Psychology, Crime and Law* 10(2): 179–95.
Hudson, Stephen, and Tony Ward. 2000. "Interpersonal Competency in Sex Offenders." *Behavior Modification* 24(4): 494–527.
Jackson, Rebecca L., and Henry J. Richards. 2007. "Diagnostic and Risk Profiles among Civilly Committed Sex Offenders in Washington State." *International Journal of Offender Therapy and Comparative Criminology* 51(3): 313–23.

Janus, E. S. 2000. "Sexual Predator Commitment: Lessons for Law and the Behavioral Sciences." *Behavioral Sciences and the Law* 18: 5–21.

Jenkins, Philip. 1998. *Moral Panic: Changing Concepts of the Child Molester in Modern America*. London: Yale University Press.

Johnson, Jeanne. 2006. "Sexual Sadism in Rapists." In *Sex Crimes and Paraphilia*, edited by Eric W. Hickey. New Jersey: Prentice Hall.

Knight, Raymond A., and Judith E. Sims-Knight. 2004. "Testing an Etiological Model for Male Juvenile Sexual Offending against Females." *Journal of Child Sexual Abuse* 13(3/4): 33–55.

Koesis, Richard N., Ray W. Cooksey, and Harvey J. Irwin. 2002. "Psychological Profiling of Sexual Murders: An Empirical Model." *International Journal of Offender Therapy and Comparative Criminology* 46(5): 532–54.

Lalumiere, Martin L., Grant T. Harris, Vernon L. Quinsey, and Marnie E. Rice. 2005. *The Causes of Rape: Understanding Individual Differences in Male Propensity for Sexual Aggression*. Washington, DC: American Psychological Association.

Langan, Patrick A., and David J. Levin. 2001. *Recidivism of Prisoners Released in 1994. Bureau of Justice Statistics*. Washington, DC: U.S. Department of Justice.

Lees, Matthew, and Richard Tewksbury. 2006. "Understanding Policy and Programmatic Issues Regarding Sex Offender Registries." *Corrections Today* 68(1): 54–56.

Levenson, Jill S. 2003. "Policy Interventions Designed to Combat Sexual Violence: Community Notification and Civil Commitment." *Journal of Child Sexual Abuse* 12: 17–52.

———. 2007. "The New Scarlet Letter: Sex Offender Policies in the 21st Century." In *Applying Knowledge to Practice: Challenges in the Treatment and Supervisions of Sexual Abusers*, edited by David Prescott. Oklahoma City: Wood and Barnes.

Levenson, Jill S., Youlanda Brannon, Timothy Fortney, and Juanita Baker. 2007. "Public Perceptions and Community Protection Policies." *Analyses of Social Issues and Public Policy* 7(1): 1–25.

Marques, Janice K., David M. Day, Craig Nelson, and Mary Ann West. 1994. "Effects of Cognitive-Behavioral Treatment on Sex Offender Recidivism: Preliminary Results of a Longitudinal Study." *Criminal Justice and Behavior* 21(1): 28–54.

Marshall, W. L. 1996. "Assessment, Treatment, and Theorizing about Sex Offenders: Developments during the Past Twenty Years and Future Directions." *Criminal Justice and Behavior* 23(1): 163–99.

Martin, M., and C. Marinucci. 2006. "Support behind Tough Sex Offender Initiative." *San Francisco Chronicle* (July 18), pp. B3–4.

Marziano, Vincent, Tony Ward, Anthony Beech, and Philippa Pattison. 2006. "Identification of Five Fundamental Implicit Theories Underlying Cognitive Distortions in Child Abusers: A Preliminary Study." *Psychology, Crime and Law* 12(1): 97–105.

McClintock, T. L. 1995. "Sexual Offending." *International Review of Psychiatry* 7(2): 253–60.

Money, J. 1990. "Forensic Sexology: Paraphilic Serial Rape and Lust Murder." *American Journal of Psychotherapy* 143: 26–36.

Mustaine, Elizabeth Ehrhardt, Richard Tewksbury, and Kenneth M. Stengel. 2006. "Social Disorganization and Residential Locations of Registered Sex Offenders: Is This a Collateral Consequence?" *Deviant Behavior* 27(3): 329–50.

National Crime Victimization Survey: Criminal Victimization in the United States—2005 [and earlier years]. 2006. Washington, DC: U.S. Department of Justice, Bureau of Justice Statistics.

Petrosino, Anthony J., and Carolyn Petrosino. 1999. "The Pubic Safety Potential of Megan's Law in Massachusetts: An Assessment from a Sample of Criminal Sexual Psychopaths." *Crime and Delinquency* 45(1): 140–58.

Phillips, Dretha M. 1998. *Community Notification as Viewed by Washington's Citizens.* Olympia: Washington State Institute for Public Policy.

Quinsey, Vernon L. 1984. "Sexual Aggression: Studies of Offenders against Women." In *Law and Mental Health: International Perspectives,* vol. 1, edited by D. Weisstub. New York: Pergamon.

Quinsey, Vernon L., Arunima Khanna, and P. Bruce Malcolm. 1998. "A Retrospective Evaluation of the Regional Centre Sex Offender Treatment Program." *Journal of Interpersonal Violence* 13(5): 621–44.

Quinsey, Vernon L., Marnie E. Rice, and Grant T. Harris. 1995. "Actuarial Prediction of Sexual Recidivism." *Journal of Interpersonal Violence* 10(1): 85–105.

Ressler, Robert K., Ann W. Burgess, and John E. Douglas. 1988. *Sexual Homicide Patterns and Motives.* Toronto: Lexington Books.

Revitch, E. 1988. "Clinical Reflections on Sexual Aggression." Paper presented at the Conference of the New York Academy of Sciences: Human Sexual Aggression—Current Perspectives. New York, October 24–26.

Romero, J., and L. Williams. 1983. "Group Psychotherapy and Intensive Probation Supervision with Sex Offenders: A Comparative Study." *Federal Probation* 47(4): 36–42.

Salfati, C. Gabrielle, and Paul Taylor. 2006. "Differentiating Sexual Violence: A Comparison of Sexual Homicide and Rape." *Psychology, Crime and Law* 12(2): 107–25.

Sample, Lisa L. 2001. "The Social Construction of the Sex Offender." Ph.D. dissertation, University of Missouri, St. Louis, Department of Criminology and Criminal Justice.

———. 2006. "An Examination of the Degree to Which Sex Offenders Kill." *Criminal Justice Review* 31(3): 230–50.

Sample, Lisa L., and Timothy M. Bray. 2003. "Are Sex Offenders Dangerous?" *Criminology and Public Policy* 3(1): 59–82.

Sample, Lisa L., and Timothy M. Bray. 2006. "Are Sex Offenders Different? An Examination of Re-arrest Patterns." *Criminal Justice Policy Review* 17(1): 83–102.

Sample, Lisa L., and Colleen Kadleck. 2008. "Sex Offender Laws: Legislators' Accounts of the Need for Policy." *Criminal Justice Policy Review* 19(1): 40–62.

Sapsford, R. J. 1998. "Further Research Applications of the 'Parole Prediction Index.'" *International Journal of Criminology and Penology* 6: 247–54.

Schram, Donna D., and Cheryl D. Milloy. 1995. *Community Notification: A Study of Offender Characteristics and Recidivism.* Olympia: Washington State Institute for Public Policy.

Schram, Donna D., and Cheryl D. Milloy. 1998. *A Study of the Characteristics and Recidivism Rates of Sex Offenders Considered for Civil Commitment but for Whom Proceedings Were Declined.* Olympia: Washington State Institute for Public Policy.

Seidman, Bonnie T., W. L. Marshall, Stephen M. Hudson, and Paul J. Robertson. 1994. "An Examination of Intimacy and Loneliness in Sex Offenders." *Journal of Interpersonal Violence* 9(4): 518–34.

Shajnfeld, Adam, and Richard B. Krueger. 2006. "Reforming (Purportedly) Non-punitive Responses to Sexual Offending." *Developments in Mental Health Law* [University of Virginia] 26(1): 31–53.

Siegert, Richard, and Tony Ward. 2003. "Back to the Future? Evolutionary Explanations for Rape." In *Sexual Deviance: Issues and Controversies,* edited by Tony Ward, D. Richard Laws, and Stephen M. Hudson. London: Sage.

Sipe, Ron, Eric L. Jensen, and Ronald S. Everett. 1998. "Adolescent Sexual Offenders Grow Up: Recidivism in Young Adulthood." *Criminal Justice and Behavior* 25(1): 109–24.

Snyder, Howard N. 2000. *Sexual Assault of Young Children as Reported to Law Enforcement: Victim, Incident, and Offender Characteristics.* Washington, DC: U.S. Department of Justice, Office of Justice Programs, Bureau of Justice Statistics.

Stevens, Aaron P. 2001. "Arresting Crime: Expanding the Scope of DNA Databases in America." *Texas Law Review* 79(4): 921–61.

Sutherland, Edwin H. 1950. "The Sexual Psychopath Laws." *Journal of Criminal Law and Criminology* 40(5): 543–54.

Tewksbury, Richard. 2002. "Validity and Utility of the Kentucky Sex Offender Registry." *Federal Probation* 66(1): 24–28.

———. 2005. "Collateral Consequences of Sex Offender Registration." *Journal of Contemporary Criminal Justice* 21(1): 67–81.

Tewksbury, Richard, and Matthew Lees. 2006. "Perceptions of Sex Offender Registration: Collateral Consequences and Community Experiences." *Sociological Spectrum* 26(3): 309–34.

Tonry, Michael, and David P. Farrington. 2005. "Punishment and Crime across Space and Time." In *Crime and Punishment in Western Countries: 1980–1999,* edited by Michael Tonry and David P. Farrington. Vol. 33 of *Crime and Justice: A Review of Research,* edited by Michael Tonry. Chicago: University of Chicago Press.

van Kesteren, John, Pat Mayhew, and Paul Nieuwbeerta. 2000. *Criminal Victimization in Seventeen Industrialised Countries: Key Findings from the 2000 International Crime Victims Survey.* The Hague: Minister of Justice.

Walker, J. T., S. Madden, B. E. Vasquez, A. C. VanHouten, and G. Ervin-McLarty. 2005. "The Influence of Sex Offender Registration and Notification Laws in the United States." http://www.acjc.org.

Ward, Tony, and Laura Sorbello. 2003. "Explaining Child Sexual Abuse: Integration and Elaboration." In *Sexual Deviance: Issues and Controversies,* edited by Tony Ward, D. Richard Laws, and Stephen M. Hudson. London: Sage.

Websdale, Neil. 1999. "Predators: The Social Construction of 'Stranger-Danger' in Washington State as a Form of Patriarchal Ideology." In *Making Trouble: Cultural Constructions of Crime, Deviance, and Control,* edited by Jeff Ferrell and Neil Websdale. New York: Aldine De Gruyter.

Zevitz, Richard G. 2003. "Sex Offender Community Notification and Its Impact on Neighborhood Life." *Crime Prevention and Community Safety: An International Journal* 20(1): 41–61.

———. 2006. "Sex Offender Community Notification: Its Role in Recidivism and Offender Reintegration." *Criminal Justice Studies* 19(2): 193–208.

Zevitz, Richard G., and Mary Ann Farkas. 2000. "Sex Offender Community Notification: Examining the Importance of Neighborhood Meetings." *Behavioral Sciences and the Law* 18(2/3): 393–408.

CHAPTER 3

FIREARM VIOLENCE

PHILIP J. COOK AND JENS LUDWIG

WHEN a criminal assailant uses a gun rather than a knife or other weapon, the chance that the victim will suffer fatal injury is greatly increased, and bystanders are placed at risk. Reducing gun use in violent crime is thus an important public goal, distinct from the goal of reducing the overall rate of violent crime. As a result, firearms transactions, possession, and use are subject to regulation in most of the world.

Compared to other developed nations, the United States is unique with respect to its high rates of both gun ownership and murder (Zimring and Hawkins 1997; Miron 2001; Hemenway 2004; Wellford, Pepper, and Petrie 2005).[1] America has 200 million to 250 million firearms in private circulation and relatively lax federal firearm laws.[2] Certain defined groups, including teenagers and adults who have been convicted of a serious offense or have been institutionalized for mental health problems, are prohibited from owning a gun, but in most states almost anyone else can legally buy and own as many guns and rounds of ammunition as he or she wishes. This permissive approach is the result in part of a powerful national gun lobby and features of the U.S. political system that provide extra political power to rural states where hunting and gun ownership are particularly prevalent. America's lax gun laws stand in contrast to those in many developed nations, including England and Wales, which now basically ban private handgun ownership.

A common distinction is between policies that focus on deterring gun misuse through the threat of extra punishment for using a gun in criminal assault, that is, policies focused on gun use, and policies that seek to preempt gun misuse by focusing on gun access, such as through regulating gun and ammunition design, transactions, possession, and carrying. Both of these approaches, if actually effective in changing the expected punishment or the costs of acquisition and use, have the potential to cause violent people to reduce gun misuse. There are interventions that are intended to work within this framework but are too weak to have much effect on gun violence. We devote particular care to the interpretation of null results, distinguishing between cases where the intervention is weak and cases where gun violence is simply unresponsive to that type of intervention.

Our main conclusions are as follows:

- Private gun ownership may in principle benefit society by deterring certain kinds of criminal behavior, and may also harm society by increasing gun use in criminal assault.
- On balance more guns in circulation seems to increase the overall rate of homicides, with relatively little effect on the volume of crime more generally.
- Many evaluations of firearm regulations have found meager effects on gun misuse, in part because these interventions are relatively weak. For example, the federal Brady Act required background checks for gun purchases at licensed dealers but left unregulated all gun transactions that occur between private parties, the so-called secondary market. Some states and localities have on their own enacted more stringent regulations, but these are difficult to enforce in part because of the ease with which guns can be moved across state lines.
- Despite the limitations of previous gun regulations in the United States, underground gun markets appear to work less efficiently than is commonly thought, particularly in areas where household gun ownership rates are relatively low.
- A variety of enforcement strategies aimed at reducing gun misuse or criminal access to guns seem promising, both in light of the available empirical evidence on gun violence and a general presumption that criminals respond to incentives.

We begin in section I by characterizing the nature and scope of the gun violence problem, including a discussion of the potential benefit from use of guns in self-defense. Section II is devoted to a discussion of access to guns, and section III to a discussion of policies designed to discourage gun misuse directly by making guns a liability to criminals. The final section provides thoughts on further research.

I. Nature and Scope of the Problem

In this section we review some basic facts on the patterns of private gun ownership and violence in the United States and the link between the two. This background helps make sense of the particular constellation of policy approaches that have been adopted in the United States and that are discussed in more detail in the subsequent sections.

A. Statistics on Guns and Violence

Although the United States has 200 million to 250 million firearms in private circulation, enough to arm every American adult, only around one-third of all American households have a gun. The fraction of households keeping a gun has been in long-term decline in part because household composition is changing, becoming smaller and less likely to include an adult male. The upshot is that gun ownership is very concentrated. Most households that own one gun own many. In 1994 three-quarters of all guns were owned by those who owned four or more, amounting to just 10 percent of adults (Cook and Ludwig 1996). Around one-third of America's privately held firearms are handguns, which are more likely than long guns to be kept for defense against crime (Cook and Ludwig 1996) and far more likely than long guns to be used by robbers and other assailants.

The majority of guns in circulation were obtained by their owners directly from a federally licensed firearm dealer. However, the 30 to 40 percent of all gun transfers that do not involve licensed dealers, the so-called secondary market (Cook, Molliconi, and Cole 1995), accounts for most guns used in crime (see Wright and Rossi 1994; Sheley and Wright 1995; Cook and Braga 2001). Despite the prominence of gun shows in current policy debates (Wintemute 2007), the best available evidence suggests that such shows account for only a small share of all secondary market sales (Cook and Ludwig 1996). Another important source of crime guns is theft: over 500,000 guns are stolen each year (Cook and Ludwig 1996; Kleck 1997).

Including homicide, suicide, and accident, 29,569 Americans died by gunfire in 2004, a mortality rate of 10.1 deaths per 100,000 people.[3] This figure is down substantially from 1990 (14.9 per 100,000) but is still higher than what was observed in, say, 1950 (when it was just 7.7).[4] As seen in figure 3.1, the share of all murders, robberies, and aggravated assaults that involve a gun has been on the order of 30 percent during recent years; the figure is more than twice as high for homicide specifically.

Intentional violence is the major exception to the secular decline in injury deaths during the past 50 years (Cook and Ludwig 2000). More Americans die each year by gun suicide than gun homicide (table 3.1). However, more people suffer nonfatal gun injuries from crime than from suicide attempts; the case-fatality rate for gun suicide is much higher than for gunshot wounds from criminal assaults. Several hundred people a year die in gun accidents, a statistic that is heavily influenced by coroners' standards concerning what constitutes an accident as opposed to a homicide or a suicide.

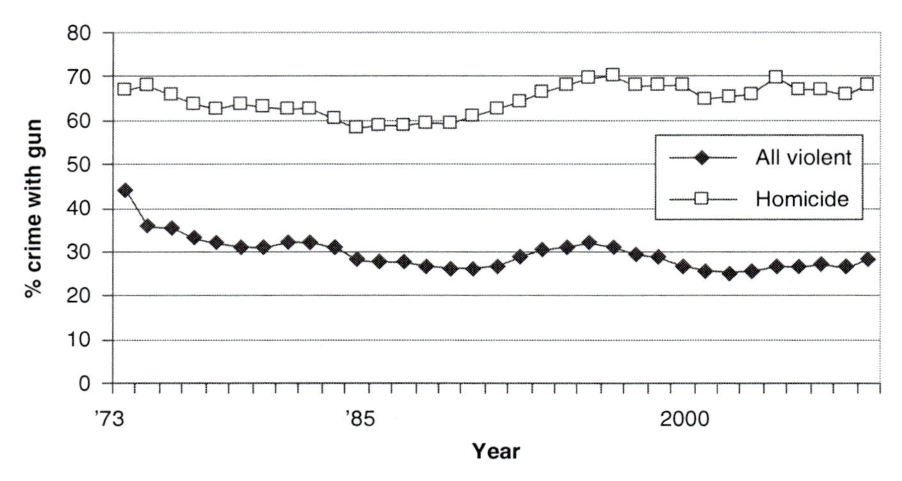

Figure 3.1. Percentage of all violent crimes and percentage of homicides committed with guns, United States, 1973–2005.
Note: "All violent" is the sum of homicides, robberies, and aggravated assaults.
Source: Bureau of Justice Statistics, http://www.ojp.usdoj.gov/bjs/glance/tables/guncrimetab.htm.

Table 3.1. Percentage of all firearm deaths by cause, age, and year

	Unintentional	Suicide	Homicide	Other
All ages				
1991	4	48	47	1
2001	3	57	39	1
Children (<=14)				
1991	28	19	52	1
2001	17	22	59	1
Teens (15–19)				
1991	7	28	63	2
2001	4	33	61	1
Adults (20+)				
1991	3	52	45	1
2001	2	60	37	1

Source: Bureau of Justice Statistics, http://www.ojp.usdoj.gov/bjs/glance/tables/frmdth.htm.

Even though everyone shares in the costs of gun violence, the shooters and victims themselves are not a representative slice of the population. The gun homicide–victimization rate in 2004 for Hispanic men ages 18 to 29 was six times the rate for non-Hispanic white men of the same age; the gun homicide rate for black men 18 to 29 was 100 per 100,000, 23 times the rate for white males in that age group.[5] There appears to be considerable overlap between the populations of potential offenders and victims: the large majority of both groups have prior criminal records (see McGonigal et al. 1993; Kennedy, Piehl, and Braga 1996; Kates and Polsby 2000; Cook, Ludwig and Braga 2005).

The costs of gun violence to society are more evenly distributed across the population than victimization statistics would suggest. The threat of being shot causes private citizens and public institutions to undertake a variety of costly measures to reduce this risk, and all of us must live with the anxiety caused by the lingering chance that we or a loved one could be shot. Quantifying the magnitude of these social costs is difficult. One approach is to use the contingent valuation method. In one such study a nationally representative sample of survey respondents were asked what they would be willing to pay to support a hypothetical public sector intervention that was capable of reducing gun violence by a specified amount; results showed that the social costs of gun violence in the United States were on the order of $100 billion per year in the mid-1990s (Cook and Ludwig 2000). Most ($80 billion) of these costs come from crime-related gun violence. Dividing by the annual number of crime-related gunshot wounds, including homicides, implies a social cost per crime-related gun injury of around $1 million (Ludwig and Cook 2001).[6] Of course, the contingent valuation method is controversial, and the results are sensitive to the details of the procedure. The important point is that the burden is far larger than is suggested by associated medical costs and lost earnings.

B. Instrumentality

Because both guns and homicides are unusually common in the United States compared to other developed nations, it is natural to wonder whether the two phenomena are linked. In the 1950s and 1960s criminologists generally ignored the issue of weapon choice as a determinant of homicide, preferring to focus on more "fundamental" issues. One exception was Marvin Wolfgang (1958), although he argued that the gun itself had little effect on the outcome of a violent encounter—a judgment that he later retracted (Wolfgang 1995).

In two seminal articles, Franklin Zimring (1968, 1972) provided systematic evidence that the weapon type matters independent of motivation. Zimring drew on crime data from Chicago to show that case-fatality rates in gun attacks are a multiple of those in knife attacks, despite the fact that the circumstances are generally quite similar. Zimring (1972) found further confirmation in comparing the case-fatality rates among shootings involving guns of different caliber: victims who were shot with guns that fire larger caliber ammunition were more likely to die than those shot with smaller bullets. For robbery in particular, Cook (1976, 1980) found that although the injury rate was relatively low when the assailant used a gun, the fatality rate was three times as high as for knife robberies. Furthermore, changes in the underlying gun-robbery rate in a large sample of cities were closely associated with changes in the gun-robbery murder rate, suggesting that death can be viewed as a random by-product of robbery (Cook 1987).

C. Self-Defense and Deterrence

The same features of guns that make them valuable to criminals may also make them useful in self-defense. Just how often guns are used in defense against criminal attack has been hotly debated and remains unclear. Estimates from the *National Crime Victimization Survey* (*NCVS*), a large government-sponsored in-person survey that is generally considered the most reliable source of information on predatory crime, suggest that guns are used in defense against criminal predation around 100,000 times per year (Cook, Ludwig, and Hemenway 1997). In contrast are the results of several smaller one-time telephone surveys, which provide a basis for asserting that there are millions of defensive gun uses per year (Kleck and Gertz 1995).

Why do these estimates for the number of defensive gun uses each year differ by more than an order of magnitude? One explanation is that the *NCVS* asks questions about defensive gun use only to those who report a victimization attempt, while the phone surveys ask such questions of every respondent. As a result the scope for false positives will be much greater with the phone surveys compared to the *NCVS* (Cook, Ludwig, and Hemenway 1997; Hemenway, 1997*a*, 1997*b*). Moreover, as the National Research Council (NRC) report notes, "Fundamental problems in defining what is meant by defensive gun use may be a primary impediment to accurate measurement" (Wellford, Pepper, and Petrie 2005, p. 103; see also McDowall, Loftin, and Presser 2000). When respondents who report a defensive gun use are asked to describe the sequence of events, many of the cases turn out to have involved something far less threatening than one might suppose (Hemenway 2004).

Whatever the actual number of defensive gun uses, the mere threat of encountering an armed victim may exert a deterrent effect on the behavior of criminals, a subject we turn to in the next section.

II. Access to Guns

Perhaps the question of primary interest to individual citizens is whether guns make the owners and members of their household more or less safe. Several studies have demonstrated that a gun in the home is far more likely to end up being used to kill a member of the household (including in suicide) than to kill or injure an intruder (Hemenway 2004, ch. 5). But that comparison is not exactly on point: the number of intruders who are shot understates the total number of instances in which an intruder is repelled or scared off. If guns in the home are dangerous to its occupants on balance, then we would predict that people who are victimized in their homes would be more likely to have a gun than nonvictims, other things equal. This prediction has been tested in case control studies that compare gun ownership rates of homicide victims with those of neighbors who share similar sociodemographic characteristics (Kellermann et al. 1993). But it's not clear that these studies have really controlled for other relevant factors. Another problem is that the indicators of gun ownership used in these studies (reports by neighbors or others) may be confounded by the homicide or suicide.

A more subtle concern with case control studies is that they ignore the possibility that individual gun ownership affects other people in the community. These external effects could be salutary if widespread gun ownership deters criminals, or negative if widespread ownership facilitates diversion to criminal use through theft and secondary sales. Hence it is important to assess the effects of overall rates of gun ownership within a community.

A. The Prevalence of Gun Ownership

One way to learn about the effects of community gun prevalence on crime is to compare crime rates across jurisdictions that have different rates of gun ownership. Because there are no administrative data on gun ownership rates, small-area estimates must utilize a proxy. The best generally available proxy for gun prevalence is the fraction of suicides that involve a firearm (FSS), which is highly correlated with survey-based measures of gun ownership rates in cross-sectional data (at both the state and county level) and also tracks movements over time at the regional and state levels (Azrael, Cook, and Miller 2004; Kleck 2004; Cook and Ludwig 2006).

Several studies report a strong positive correlation between the FSS proxy and homicide rates across counties (Cook and Ludwig 2002; Miller, Azrael, and Hemenway 2002).[7] On the other hand, counties with a high prevalence of gun ownership experienced residential burglary rates comparable to or even higher than those with low gun ownership rates, perhaps because guns are attractive loot to burglars (Cook and Ludwig 2003*b*).

In any event, it is difficult to isolate a particular causal mechanism in cross-sectional studies. Gun-rich jurisdictions, such as Mississippi, are systematically different in various ways from jurisdictions with relatively few guns, such as Massachusetts. The usual approach for addressing this "apples and oranges" problem has been to control statistically for the handful of local area characteristics that are available in standard data sources, such as population density, poverty, and the age and racial composition of the population. But these variables never explain very much of the cross-sectional variation in crime rates (Glaeser, Sacerdote, and Scheinkman 1996), suggesting that the list of control variables is inadequate to the task. Also unclear is whether widespread gun ownership is cause or effect of an area's crime problem, since high crime rates may induce residents to buy guns for self-protection. These same concerns are arguably even more severe with cross-sectional comparisons across countries.

Some of the problems with cross-sectional studies can be overcome by using panel data—repeated cross-sections of city, county, or state data measured at multiple points in time—to compare *changes* in gun ownership with *changes* in crime.

Compared with Massachusetts, the state of Mississippi may have much higher homicide rates year after year for reasons that cannot be fully explained by standard sociodemographic or other variables. But by comparing changes across areas we implicitly control for any unmeasured differences across areas that are relatively fixed over time, such as a "southern culture of violence" (see Loftin et al. 1991; Butterfield 1996). The best available panel data evidence suggests that more guns lead to more homicides, which is driven entirely by a relationship between gun prevalence and homicides committed with firearms; there is little association of gun prevalence with non-gun homicides or other types of crimes (Duggan 2001; Cook and Ludwig 2006). We should note that recent empirical estimates are not unanimous on this point: John Lott (2000) comes to the opposite conclusion, although we put more weight on the other studies because of problems with Lott's data and methods (see Cook and Ludwig 2006).

An alternative approach for learning about the effects of gun availability on public health and safety is to examine the effects of policy changes that influence overall gun ownership rates. Although these policy experiments have commanded a great deal of public attention, they are not very informative about the effects of widespread gun availability on violence, primarily because even outright bans on handguns have surprisingly modest effects on gun ownership rates.

One widely cited policy change is Washington, DC's 1976 ban on handgun acquisitions. The available data suggest that homicides and suicides declined by around 25 percent around the time of the District's handgun ban, led by reductions in homicides and suicides with guns (Loftin et al. 1991); this was before the violent tsunami caused by the introduction of crack cocaine. Still controversial is the question of how much of this decline can be attributed to the handgun ban rather than other factors. The nearby city of Baltimore also experienced a decline in gun homicides around the time of DC's gun ban (Britt, Kleck, and Bordua 1996), although unlike DC, Baltimore did not experience a decline in gun suicides (McDowall, Loftin, and Wiersema 1996). Further complicating the interpretation of this evidence is that DC did not seem to experience a decline in overall household gun ownership rates (as proxied by the fraction of suicides committed with guns), either relative to the city's pre-1976 levels or compared to the trend over this period in Baltimore (Cook and Ludwig 2006). In 1982 Chicago followed Washington's lead by essentially banning private ownership of guns, grandfathering only those who had already registered a handgun with the city; as shown in figure 3.2, there was a dip in the percentage of suicides with guns following the ban, but no more so in Cook County (which includes Chicago) than in other counties in Illinois (fig. 3.3).

B. Gun Transactions and Possession

In practice most supply-side regulations in the United States are not intended to have much effect on the overall prevalence of guns, but rather to reduce criminal and

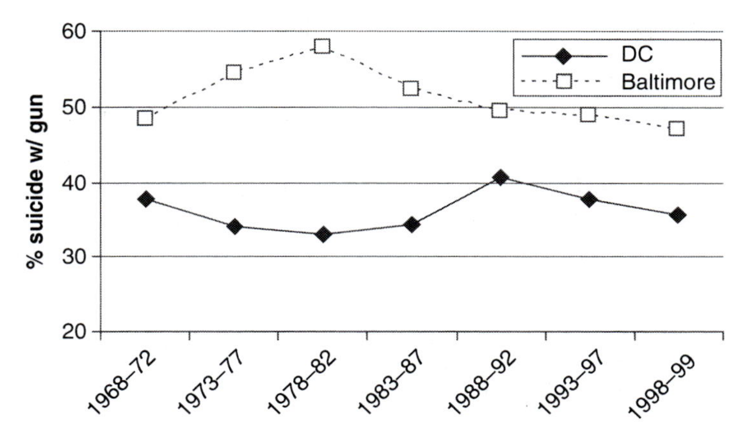

Figure 3.2. Percentage of suicides with guns, Washington, DC, and Baltimore.
Note: Chart presents 5-year averages for percentage of suicides with guns, a proxy for household gun ownership rates (see text).
Source: CDC for Residents Only, http://wonder.cdc.gov/mortsql.html.

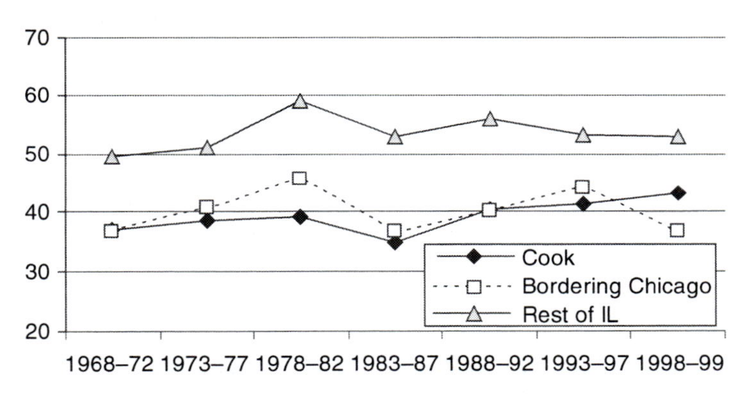

Figure 3.3. Percentage of suicides with guns, Cook County and the rest of Illinois, 1968–99.
Note: Figure represents 5-year averages of percentage of suicides with guns, a proxy for household gun ownership rates (see text). Counties bordering Chicago are DuPage, Lake, McHenry, and Will. Missing data in vital statistics for Illinois counties for 1992. Rates are possibly slightly higher.
Source: CDC Wonder for Residents Only, http://wonder.cdc.gov/mortsql.html.

reckless use of guns by banning possession by certain groups, such as youths and felons. Fortunately an effective program to deny guns to those likely to misuse them does not require a house-to-house search; it would be enough to regulate transactions effectively. The reason is that criminal misuse usually follows rather quickly after gun acquisition. In other words, the millions of current gun possessors will account for little of the violent crime five years from now. A reasonable goal, then, is to increase the effective price of guns to the high-risk segment of the market.

1. *Gun Markets*

To some people, the notion of trying to keep guns away from a small subset of the population with over 200 million guns already in circulation seems hopeless. But targeted regulation in an environment of widespread availability is not always futile, as is suggested by the analogy to minimum drinking age laws (Wagenaar and Toomey 2002). Whether restrictions on gun acquisitions are or could be similarly effective is not clear, although the prospect is somewhat less daunting when we recognize that the stock of guns in the United States probably matters less than the flow. Most guns are in the hands of relatively low-risk people and are likely to remain there (theft notwithstanding) for many years. The large majority of gun crimes are committed by a small group of criminally active people whose criminal careers are typically fairly short in duration. And it is surely relevant to note that most gang members and violent criminals do not own guns (Cook 1991).

Considering that the secondary market is the proximate source for the vast majority of crime guns, one obvious intervention point is the movement of guns from the primary to the secondary markets. The structure of these markets was analyzed in an intensive case study of Chicago (Cook et al. 2007). Professional traffickers seem to play an important role in moving guns across markets, as suggested by ethnographic field interviews in one high-crime part of Chicago. These findings are supported by analysis of Bureau of Alcohol, Tobacco, and Firearms (ATF) investigation files and crime-gun trace data, which links guns confiscated at crime scenes back to the original legal purchaser (see also Cook and Braga 2001). In principle, other traffickers may simply be friends or relatives who engage in one or two straw purchases to provide guns to someone with a disqualifying criminal record. However, these types of straw purchases appear to be rare in Chicago.

Some licensed gun dealers are willing accomplices to gun trafficking or straw purchases or are selling to criminals off the books (Wachtel 1998; Wintemute, Cook, and Wright 2005). One ATF investigation of the relatively small subset of dealers who account for the original retail sale of most crime guns submitted for tracing found that 75 percent were in violation of at least one federal regulation. Most of these were for minor violations, but 20 percent of dealers in this sample were recommended for license revocation (ATF 2000).

If regulation or enforcement could reduce the flow of guns from primary to secondary markets, standard economic analysis suggests that the resulting decline in supply would increase the price of guns in secondary markets. Diverting high-risk buyers from the primary to the secondary market (by, for example, improving background checks or cracking down on rogue dealers) would further increase prices in the latter by increasing demand (Cook and Leitzel 1996).

Enforcement might also help increase the price of guns to high-risk people by targeting retailers in the underground gun market. Cook et al. (2007) found that the underground gun market in Chicago is characterized by high transaction costs. Prices are high relative to the legal primary market, although because quality is often low in this market prices can be low in an absolute sense: the median price paid among one sample of Chicago arrestees was $150, with one-quarter of guns bought for less than $100. Information about buyers and sellers (including the trustworthiness of trading partners) in the underground gun market is scarce, perhaps in part because guns, unlike drugs, are durable goods and so the underground gun market is quite thin, with a relatively small number of transactions. At least in Chicago, many gun transactions are navigated by local brokers who draw on their social networks to match buyers and sellers and advertise their services in part through word of mouth throughout the local underground economy. The costs of doing business for these local brokers and the higher-level suppliers that provide them with guns could presumably be increased through buy-and-bust or sell-and-bust activities by the local police, as well as by offering arrestees incentives to provide information about retailers and sellers in the gun market.

Whether price increases in the underground gun market translate into decreased gun misuse depends on how price-sensitive teens and criminally inclined adults are. Surprisingly little is known on this point, although scattered survey evidence suggests that criminals are not entirely immune to the financial and other costs of getting guns (Wright and Rossi 1994, pp. 128–29; Cook, Molliconi, and Cole 1995). With higher prices we would expect cash-strapped youths to be less inclined to buy a gun and more inclined to sell whatever guns come their way. Further, higher prices would provide an incentive for those who do have a gun to exercise greater caution against theft and confiscation by law enforcement by, for example, leaving the gun at home.

2. *The Brady Act*

One sign of the effectiveness of the 1968 Gun Control Act, which prohibited underage people and those with disqualifying prior criminal records from buying guns, comes from the fact that surveys of prisoners from the 1980s show that only around one-fifth obtained their guns directly from a licensed gun dealer (Wright and Rossi 1994), even though dealers in most states were not required to conduct background checks to verify the buyer's eligibility. The Act's restrictions were strengthened beginning in 1994 by the Brady Handgun Violence Prevention Act, which required gun dealers in states without background check requirements to begin to conduct such checks on prospective buyers. Around 3 percent of potential handgun buyers have been denied handguns following Brady as a result of background checks (Manson and Gilliard 1997), which is to say that hundreds of thousands have been denied since the Brady Act went into effect. Descriptive statistics like these have led many to conclude that the Brady Act has had a substantial effect on crime and suicide.

More direct evidence of the Brady Act's effects on public safety comes from comparing mortality trends in the thirty-two states that were required to abide by Brady's background check and waiting period requirements with the eighteen states (plus the District of Columbia) that already had sufficiently stringent policies in place and as a result were exempt from the Brady provisions. Our analysis,

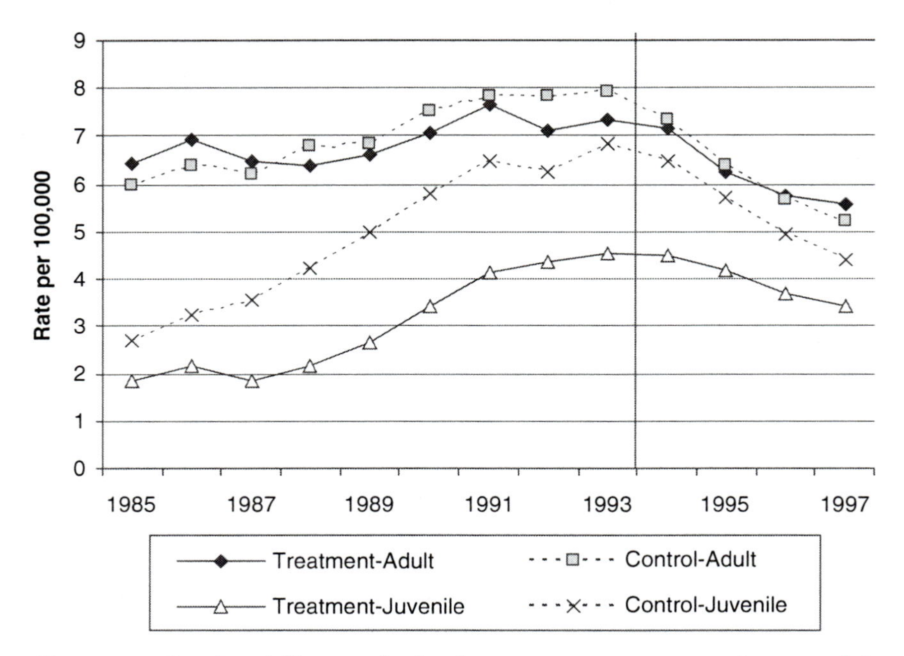

Figure 3.4. Gun homicide rates for Brady treatment versus control states, adults (over 21) and juveniles (under 21), 1985–97.
Source: Ludwig and Cook 2000.

published in the *Journal of the American Medical Association*, exploited this natural experiment using a difference-in-difference analysis. That approach nets out the permanent differences among states in conditions that contribute to homicide and presumes that the "experimental" and "control" states would have followed the same trajectory on average in the absence of the law. That presumption is reasonable both because of our finding that the trajectories were similar *prior* to the law, and because the law in question was exogenous to the individual states; there is no self-selection problem here, as might arise if we were evaluating laws that were changed by act of individual state legislatures (fig. 3.4).[8]

We found no statistically discernible difference in homicide trends between the "Brady" (treatment) and "non-Brady" (control) states among people 21 and older (Ludwig and Cook 2000). Given the standard error of this estimate, it is plausible that there was a true effect on homicide, ranging from an increase of around 8 percent to a reduction of 13 percent. Our focus on *adult* mortality rates is motivated by the different trajectories that juvenile homicides followed in treatment and control states even before the Brady law went into effect. As a result, any differences in juvenile homicide trends following implementation of the Brady Act cannot be confidently attributed to the effects of the law itself. Excluding juvenile victims is not particularly problematic, since most of them were shot by those who would have been too young to be directly affected by the Brady background check requirement (Cook and Laub 1998). Our methodological point is that when evaluating discrete policy interventions, one check on the validity of the control group is whether it follows a trajectory similar to the treatment group *prior* to the intervention.

A distinct concern in evaluating the effects of the Brady Act is that the new law may have reduced gun running from the treatment to the control states, in which case comparing the two groups of states might understate the overall effects of the law. In a nutshell, the concern here is that the control states were in fact affected by the intervention. Some support for this concern comes from ATF trace data in Chicago showing that the fraction of crime guns in the city that could be traced to the Brady treatment states declined dramatically following implementation of the law (Cook and Braga 2001).[9] However, the proportion of homicides in Chicago committed with guns did not change over this period, despite the substantial changes in gun-trafficking patterns (Cook and Ludwig 2003*a*). One explanation of these results is that traffickers can adapt easily to changes in the larger environment. If correct, they suggest that any bias introduced into comparisons of Brady treatment and control states due to changes in across-state gun running is minor.

3. *State Regulations of Gun Acquisition*

Many states have supplemented the minimum requirements of the 1968 Gun Control Act with additional restrictions and regulations for gun transactions. The available evidence on the effects of these state-level regulations in general relies on weak research designs and yields stronger evidence for regulatory impacts on immediate output measures, but not on outcomes that are of more direct policy interest.

For example, a study by Weil and Knox (1996) using ATF firearms trace data found that the fraction of crime guns confiscated in northeastern states that were first purchased in Virginia declined after that state's "one gun a month law" went into effect. While persuasive on its own terms, the net effect of a change in crime-gun source states on the effective price of guns and ultimately on criminal gun use is far from clear. Other studies analyze outcome measures but use weaker designs that leave room for substantial uncertainty about the proper interpretation (Kleck and Patterson 1993; Webster, Vernick, and Hepburn 2001, 2002).

4. *Gun Possession by Violent Misdemeanants*

Perhaps the exception to the generally bleak literature on gun regulation regards initiatives that move the boundary between who is and is not eligible to purchase a firearm. Two recent federal examples include the 1994 ban on gun possession by people under a restraining order for domestic violence, and the 1996 Lautenberg Amendment that extended that ban to anyone convicted of a domestic violence misdemeanor. Encouraging evidence for the effects of these laws comes from study of similar state-level laws.

Elizabeth Richardson Vigdor and James Mercy (2003) found that state laws that prevent those who are subject to a restraining order from owning or purchasing a handgun reduce rates of intimate partner homicides (by about 10 percent); there are no clear effects for prohibitions directed against those with prior misdemeanor convictions for domestic violence. Their use of repeated cross-sections of state-level data enable them to control for at least some of the unmeasured state or period effects that may confound evaluation of these laws. Presumably the difference in the effects of the two laws is due to some combination of the inability of available data systems to identify all those with domestic violence records, the close timing between state and federal laws that keep guns from those convicted of domestic violence misdemeanors, and that there are likely to be more people subject to restraining orders than with prior convictions for domestic violence misdemeanors. The results for the restraining order laws are also more likely to reflect causal policy effects than those for domestic violence misdemeanors. Prohibitions on those with restraining orders are consistently related to intimate partner homicides and unrelated to other crimes that should less clearly be affected by gun regulations; the reverse is true for the domestic violence laws. The data also suggest that states with restraining order prohibitions experience rates of intimate partner homicides quite similar to those observed in other areas before these gun laws go into effect, at least up to one year before passage.[10]

III. Making Guns a Liability to Criminals

Gun control entails regulations on gun commerce and possession; *gun policy* is a broader term that also incorporates laws and programs to reduce misuse directly by making guns a legal liability to those inclined to misuse them. Our discussion begins with penalties for gun use in violent crime, and then considers law enforcement efforts to influence gun carrying.

A. Targeting Gun Use in Crime

There is a growing body of evidence that criminal behavior can be deterred by increases in the likelihood or the severity of punishment (Nagin 1998; Levitt 2001). We generally endorse the presumption that criminals make choices that are generally responsive to the perceived consequences. If guns are hard to get or gun use increases the chance of arrest and severe punishment, then some criminals will substitute other weapons or reduce their participation in violence. That presumption provides qualitative guidance in identifying promising policy approaches.

To date, however, there is no compelling evidence that sentence enhancements deter gun use in crime, perhaps because these laws may not be implemented as intended (see Marvell and Moody 1995), or because any effects might be too modest for available data and evaluation techniques to reliably detect. Most of the studies of sentence enhancements rely on time-series models, some of which find evidence for an effect of such laws on gun involvement in at least some types of crime, but none of these essentially pre-post comparisons is entirely convincing (Loftin and McDowall 1981, 1984; Loftin, Heumann, and McDowall 1983; McDowall, Loftin, and Wiersema 1992).[11] The main problem with these time-series analyses is the possibility of other changes in these jurisdictions over time that can also affect gun involvement in crime. The fact that similar sorts of changes are observed in multiple jurisdictions that enact a policy at different times does not rule out the possibility of confounding factors, since enactment of sentence enhancement laws may be systematically related to local crime trends. For example, if these types of "get tough" laws tend to be enacted in response to increasing rates of gun crime (as seems plausible) and if local crime rates are cyclical (as they tend to be), then subsequent declines in gun crime following sentence enhancements may simply be the result of mean reversion—even if similar patterns are observed in different jurisdictions that enact such laws at different points in time. Even the more sophisticated state-level panel data study by Marvell and Moody (1995) is susceptible to this type of bias to some degree, as we discuss further below in the context of state laws that regulate concealed gun carrying.

Boston's Operation Ceasefire is one of the most widely cited and conceptually appealing gun-oriented enforcement efforts enacted to date (Kennedy, Piehl, and Braga, 1996; Braga et al. 2001). Ceasefire was put into place in June 1996 with the goal of targeting law enforcement resources to both reduce the supply of guns to gangs and increase the costs to gangs of using guns in crime. Of particular interest are the program's activities targeted at gun use, in which gangs were informed by law enforcement that gun use by any member would produce a concentrated crackdown on all the gang's members and activities (including income-generating activities) by law enforcement at all levels of government, a strategy known as "pulling levers." One hope was to help change social norms within the gang about gun crime. Another hope was that a halt in intergang violence would provide a cooling off period that would break the dynamic of violence fueled by "gang beefs" and retaliatory attacks.

Any formal evaluation of Ceasefire as it was implemented in Boston must confront two complications.[12] The first is distinguishing between noise and trend in the city's crime rate during the 1990s. High-frequency (monthly) data suggest that youth homicide counts may have started to decline in Boston in fall 1995, even before Ceasefire went into effect in summer 1996 (Braga et al. 2001, p. 205). When Piehl et al. (2003) search the time series for the "optimal break" in trend starting with the observations for January 1996, the data point to summer 1996 (when Ceasefire was in fact initiated), although there would still seem to be the possibility of a sharp break in trend before their search window.

Short-term fluctuations in the data can be smoothed out in part by looking at annual data over a long-term horizon (fig. 3.5). Homicide rates in Boston, as in

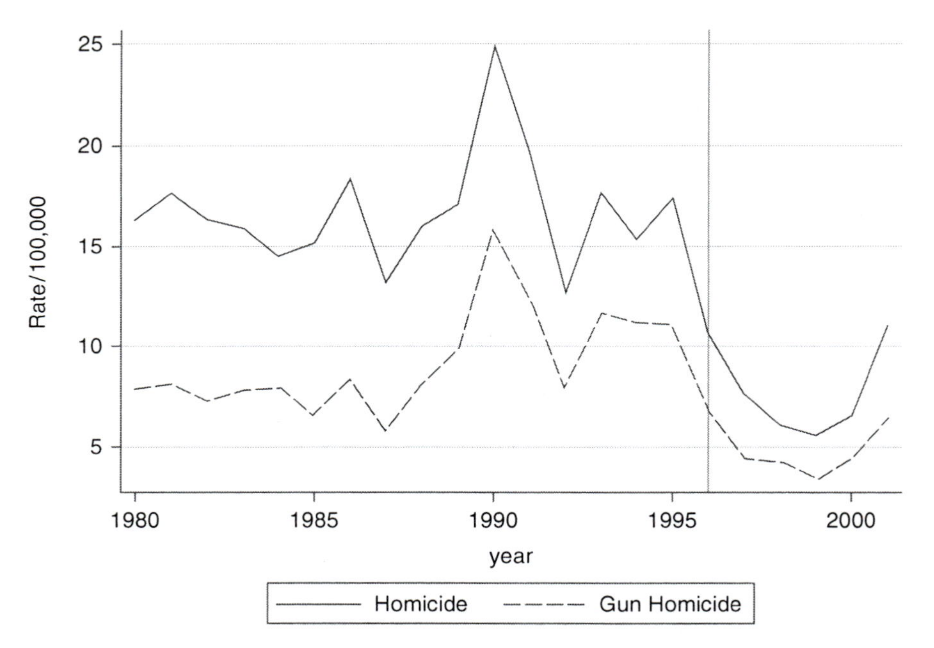

Figure 3.5. Homicide trends in Boston, 1980–2000.
Source: Ludwig 2005.

most of the largest American cities, peaked during the early 1990s and were significantly lower at the end of the decade (Blumstein 2000, p. 38; Eck and Maguire 2000, p. 234; Levitt 2004, p. 168). But one way in which Boston's homicide trend is unusual is that after declining in the early 1990s, rates increased again in 1993–95, despite the trend in "fundamentals" that Levitt argues drove crime rates down everywhere during the 1990s, before resuming their decline.[13] Most studies use this 1993–95 period as the "pretreatment" benchmark period for evaluating Ceasefire. However if the 1993–95 increase represents a temporary deviation from trend, then comparing post-Ceasefire rates to this period may to some extent confound the impact of Ceasefire with that of mean reversion. One way to circumvent this problem is to focus on the long-run trend in homicides in Boston, for example, over the period 1991–2001. Under this approach Boston's decline in homicides was (in proportional terms) about average compared to what was observed in the 25 largest cities in the country (Levitt 2004, p. 168).

Given the limits of quantitative evaluations of Ceasefire, other forms of evidence such as qualitative findings may, in principle, also help shed light on the program's effectiveness. In this case, suggestive support for "pulling levers" comes from ethnographic fieldwork from Chicago's South Side reported in Cook et al. (2007).

Ceasefire's gang-deterrence strategy holds considerable conceptual appeal and enjoys some support from qualitative research, but the limits of the available quantitative evaluations leave us uncertain about the program's actual impacts.

Another source of uncertainty comes from the difficulty of replicating the successful collaboration across agencies that was achieved in Boston, at least as suggested by the Los Angeles experience (Braga 2002; Tita et al. 2003).

B. Gun Carrying

One step back from gun use in crime is illegal carrying, and policies to deter carrying by dangerous people may be an efficient strategy for reducing misuse. As Lawrence Sherman (2000, p. 1193) notes, "To the extent that homicide frequently occurs spontaneously among young men in public places, it is the *carrying* of firearms, rather than their ownership, that is the immediate proximate cause of criminal injury."[14] Others, impressed by the potential value of an armed public in deterring street crime, have successfully advocated for relaxing restrictions on carrying by adults who can pass a criminal record check.

The available empirical evidence in support of policing against illegal gun carrying is currently much stronger than what is available in support of longer prison terms for carrying. The net impact of state laws that make it relatively difficult for normal citizens to get permits to carry guns legally remains unclear. But because just a small share of the population gets concealed-carry permits, even in states with lax permit requirements, and because most of those who get permits have socioeconomic characteristics associated with low risk of either criminal offending or victimization, the net effects of restrictive gun carrying laws are likely to be modest.

1. *Policing against Illegal Guns*

The most straightforward way to keep people from carrying guns illegally is to arrest them when they do so. The widespread belief in the effectiveness of police patrols against illegal gun carrying is motivated in large part by findings from the Kansas City Gun Experiment, in which patrol resources were added in one high-crime neighborhood to search pedestrians and motorists for guns. Lawrence Sherman and his colleagues (Sherman and Rogan 1995; Sherman, Shaw, and Rogan 1995) calculate that gun seizures increased by 65 percent in the target neighborhood during the program, while gun crime declined by 49 percent. In contrast, there was little change over this period in either outcome in a comparison neighborhood several miles away.

Despite the promise of the Kansas City Gun Experiment, it is important to recognize that this program was not an "experiment" in the true sense of the term. There were just two neighborhoods involved, and they experienced different levels and trends in firearm offenses even *before* the policing program was put into place (Sherman, Shaw, and Rogan 1995). As we argued earlier, that difference should make for caution in drawing inferences from differences in crime rates after the program was put into place. Although policy makers in New York City and elsewhere have implemented police patrols against illegal guns, convincing evidence on the effects of this strategy is lacking.

J. Cohen and Ludwig (2003) provide stronger evidence in support of the effects of such patrols by evaluating a model program implemented in Pittsburgh. Their evaluation exploits the fact that gun-oriented patrol was implemented in some parts of the city but not others, and that in the targeted areas the extra patrols were focused on just four evenings each week (Wednesday through Saturday). Their main finding is that during the targeted nights of the week, the target neighborhoods experienced much larger declines in gunshot injuries and citizen reports of shots fired compared to control areas. Evidence that, at least for gunshot injuries, the control neighborhoods provide a reasonable estimate for what *would have* happened in the treatment areas had the program not been enacted comes from the fact that there was little difference in injury trends between treatment and control neighborhoods on days in which the new antigun patrols were *not* scheduled (Sunday through Tuesday). In addition, the treatment and control neighborhoods had similar trends in gunshot injuries *before* the policing program was implemented. However, the neighborhoods did have significantly different experiences with reports of shots fired (the other outcome they examine) even before the program was in effect, so we should be more confident in the results for gunshot injuries than shots fired.

This evaluation supplements existing evidence that police programs targeted against illegal gun carrying may reduce gun violence. Given the substantial costs of gun violence to society these policing programs easily generate benefits to society in excess of their operational costs. Of course, aggressive police patrols may generate other costs, impinging on civil liberties and straining police-community relations. In the Pittsburgh case, at least, the police appear to have been mindful of these concerns and quite restrained.

2. *Enhanced Punishment for Carrying and Possession*

Another approach to deterring illegal gun carrying is to enhance the threatened severity of punishment for those who are caught. In the 1970s this approach was used in Massachusetts, which enacted the Bartley-Fox Amendment mandating a one-year prison sentence for unlicensed gun carrying. The new law prohibited plea bargaining and was widely advertised; it was subsequently evaluated in several careful studies, with somewhat contradictory results (Pierce and Bowers 1981; Wellford, Pepper, and Petrie 2005).

In recent years the most highly touted example of this approach is Richmond, Virginia's, Project Exile, which diverts convicted felons who are arrested for gun possession from state courts into the federal system, where penalties are more severe. Exile now serves as one model for the Bush administration's nationwide Project Safe Neighborhoods initiative. Advocates for Project Exile often point to the 40 percent reduction in gun homicides in Richmond between 1997 and 1998 as evidence (Shannon 1999; "Remarks" 2001). Skeptics point out that homicides actually increased during the last 10 months of 1997 following Exile's launch in February, and that the homicide rate during 1997 as a whole was around 40 percent higher than in 1996. Neither of these simple before-and-after claims is very convincing because without a control group, there remains the obvious question of what Richmond's crime trajectory would have been in the absence of Exile. After all, violent crime rates were declining dramatically across the country during the 1990s (Blumstein and Wallman 2000; Cook and Laub 2002).

The first rigorous evaluation of Project Exile is by Raphael and Ludwig (2003), which offers a negative assessment. They show that Richmond's crime trajectory (even removing 1997 data from the picture) in the late 1990s is not notably better than other cities that had experienced similarly volatile homicide rates since 1980. This null finding is robust to a variety of methodological adjustments, including a check for omitted variables bias that uses juveniles (who are generally exempt from the federal felon-in-possession charges that make up the bulk of Exile prosecutions) as an additional within-city control group. Levitt (2003) notes that expectations of large impacts were probably unrealistic from the start, since Exile engendered only a small objective increase in the threat of punishment. There is also some question whether the program targeted the most dangerous group of offenders (Greenwood 2003).[15]

3. *Relaxing Restrictive Gun-Carrying Laws*

While many big-city police departments devote substantial resources to keeping guns off the street, over the past several decades state governments across the country have made it easier for people to carry guns legally in public. More than 30 states have eliminated their restrictive gun-carrying laws (Dvorak 2002). These legislative changes are not necessarily in conflict with police patrols against illegal gun carrying, because there is not much overlap in the population characteristics of those who apply for permits to carry and those who are targeted in police patrols.

The argument for liberalizing gun-carrying laws is that an increased likelihood of encountering an armed victim would deter criminals, a possibility that receives some support from prisoner surveys: 80 percent in one survey agreed with the statement that "a smart criminal always tries to find out if his potential victim is armed" (Wright and Rossi 1994). But the same data also raise the possibility that an increase in gun carrying could prompt an arms race: two-thirds of prisoners incarcerated for gun offenses reported that the chance of running into an armed victim was very or somewhat important in their own choice to use a gun. Currently criminals use guns in only around 25 percent of robberies and 5 percent of assaults (Rennison 2001). If increased gun carrying among potential victims causes criminals to carry guns more often themselves, or become quicker to use guns to avert armed self-defense, the end result could be that street crime becomes more lethal.

In a provocative series of research papers and books, the economist John Lott (2000, p. 20) has argued that the deterrent effects of eliminating restrictive gun-carrying laws dominate: "Of all the methods studied so far by economists, the carrying of concealed handguns appears to be the most cost-effective method for reducing crime." Lott and fellow economist David Mustard (1997) improved on earlier research by comparing crime changes in states that enact concealed-carry laws with changes in other jurisdictions. Lott has now performed this analysis in a variety of ways, reaching different conclusions about the effect on property crime (Cook, Moore, and Braga 2002), but always finding that ending restrictive gun-carrying laws reduced homicide rates (Lott 2000, pp. 90, 100).

The economist John Donohue (2003) argues that, although Lott's analysis improves on previous research on this topic, in the end Lott's findings cannot support the conclusion that ending restrictive concealed-carry laws reduces crime. Donohue shows that Lott's estimates are sensitive to the correction of several coding errors and to reasonable changes in the model specification. More important, Donohue's reanalysis of the Lott data shows that states that eventually ended restrictive concealed-carry laws had systematically different crime trends from the other states even before these law changes went into effect, violating what we have argued is a minimum necessary condition for deriving unbiased estimates of policy impacts. The violation of this condition implies that the estimated treatment effect may in fact be due to whatever unmeasured factors caused crime trends to diverge before the laws are enacted.

In a response to Donohue, Lott's coauthor, David Mustard (2003), notes that their work tries to address this apparent omitted-variables problem in a number of ways. In our own judgment, as well as that of the NRC panel report, none of these approaches is persuasive.[16] The puzzling pattern of results for robberies and property crimes in this literature is one manifestation of this issue.[17] Another is the finding, by Donohue and the NRC panel's own reanalysis of Lott's data, that right-to-carry laws in the 1980s seemed to reduce crime, whereas those adopted in the 1990s appear to have the opposite effect.[18] Manning (2003) notes in his commentary that few of the estimates reported in this literature may be statistically significant anyway, once one correctly calculates standard errors and the relevant statistical tests.[19]

Whether the net effect of relaxing gun-carrying laws is to increase or reduce the burden of crime, there is good reason to believe that it is not large. One recent study found that in 12 of the 16 permissive concealed-carry states studied, fewer than 2 percent of adults had obtained permits to carry concealed handguns (Hill 1997). The actual change in gun-carrying prevalence will be smaller than the number of permits issued would suggest, because many of those who obtain permits were already carrying guns in public (Robuck-Mangum 1997). Moreover, the change in gun carrying appears to be concentrated in rural and suburban areas, where crime rates are already relatively low, among people who are at relatively low risk of victimization: white, middle-aged, middle-class males (Hill 1997). The available data about permit holders also imply that they are at fairly low risk of misusing guns, consistent with the relatively low arrest rates observed to date for permit holders (Lott 2000). In sum, changes to state laws governing legal gun carrying are likely to induce only modest changes in the incentives facing criminals to go armed themselves or to avoid potentially armed victims.

IV. Implications for Policy and Future Research

There are no feasible policies that would reduce the rate of gun violence in the United States to that of Western Europe. But we believe there are ways to make a substantial dent in the problem. Targeted police patrols against illegal gun carrying, for example, appear more promising than enhanced prison sentences for those who use or carry guns illegally. So we could increase the chances that current government spending in this area reduces gun violence by shifting resources from efforts to impose more lengthy prison terms for illegal gun carrying or use toward directed patrol strategies.

The descriptive and analytical information summarized here opens the door to favorable consideration of a variety of other interventions. For example, we would identify as promising a group deterrence strategy designed to reduce gun misuse by gang members. Formal quantitative evaluation evidence for this approach, as in Boston's Operation Ceasefire, falls short of definitive. But descriptive statistics about the importance of gangs to gun violence in many cities, together with quantitative evidence that many street gangs have important economic interests (Levitt and Venkatesh 2000) and qualitative evidence that gangs regulate gun use by members to protect these economic interests (Cook et al. 2007), suggest to us that this is an approach that is worth pursuing.

Beyond specific interventions, we think it is a useful exercise to consider what an entire portfolio of interventions should look like. For example, if we accept the "rational violence" notion as a guide, then we want to organize a portfolio around making guns a liability to criminals. The goal is to increase the (perceived and actual) likelihood and severity of negative consequences for misusing a gun. If that can be done without much affecting gun access for self-defense by generally law-abiding people, then the expected impact would be beneficial. Included on the list of potentially helpful measures are the following:[20]

- Improve the gun registration system so that guns confiscated by the police can be more reliably traced to their owners
- Increase the use in police investigations of the available technology to analyze the ballistic "fingerprints" on shell casings left at the scene of crimes in order to help investigators match confiscated guns to crimes or to match violent events with each other

- Launch intensive police patrols directed against illicit gun carrying in high-violence neighborhoods
- Offer rewards for information leading to the arrest of people carrying or possessing a gun illegally
- Institute a gun emphasis policy in investigations and prosecutions of violent crimes

Although only one of these interventions has been subjected to a formal impact evaluation (police patrols), all of them receive general support from the evidence on the potential of deterring criminal behavior by increasing the probability of punishment.

Another promising approach is stepped-up enforcement against the underground gun market to reduce access by criminals. Qualitative evidence from Chicago and survey evidence from arrestees in 22 cities suggest that in many cities guns are not readily available to most criminals (Cook et al. 2007). This qualitative evidence also suggests that the underground market is structured in ways that may be vulnerable to regulatory enforcement against scofflaw licensed dealers and buy-and-bust undercover operations against illicit brokers.[21]

Is more research required before policy makers can take any useful steps to reduce gun violence? No. There are lessons to be learned from currently available research. But of course more research is always welcome. One secondary benefit of our conclusion that enforcement activities directed at both access and use seem promising is the possibility for rigorous evaluation. If some law enforcement agencies accept the importance of piloting new enforcement programs before taking them to scale, there would be important scientific opportunities to randomly assign the neighborhoods or townships that receive these pilot programs. In the meantime, prudence requires better use of existing evidence in formulating gun policy.

NOTES

1. Homicides and other deaths are fairly well measured in most developed countries as a result of government collections of death certificate information. What we know about the gun stock in the United States comes from two sources: cumulative counts of annual gun production and imports, which are subject to some uncertainty about the rate at which guns deteriorate (Kleck, 1997), and population surveys, which are subject to some underreporting (Ludwig, Cook, and Smith 1998). Nevertheless the two data sources paint a qualitatively similar picture, and the surveys also tell us something about who owns what.

2. The number of firearms can be estimated through two sources of data: federal tax records on sales and a survey. First, the number of new guns added each year is known from data kept by the federal government on manufactures, imports, and exports.

The annual count of net additions can be cumulated over, say, the past century, with some assumption about the rate of removal through such mechanisms as off-the-books exports, breakage, and police confiscation (Cook 1991; Kleck 1997). The alternative basis for estimating the stock is the one-time National Survey of the Personal Ownership of Firearms (NSPOF), conducted in 1994; this is the only survey that has attempted to determine the number of guns in private hands. (A number of surveys, including the General Social Survey, provide an estimate of the prevalence of gun ownership among individuals and households without attempting to determine the average number of guns per gun owner.) The NSPOF estimate for the number of guns in 1994 was 192 million, a number that is compatible with the "sales accumulation" method, assuming that just 15 percent of the new guns sold since 1899 had been thrown out or destroyed (Cook and Ludwig 1996). Since the survey, the annual rate of net additions to the gun stock has been about 4 million to 5 million per year (ATF 2001, 2002), or 50 million to 60 million by 2006. Given a continued removal rate of just 1 percent, the stock as of 2006 would be around $220 million.

3. http://webappa.cdc.gov/sasweb/ncipc/mortrate.html (accessed February 1, 2006).

4. http://www.cdc.gov/nchs/products/pubs/pubd/vsus/1963/1963.htm (accessed January 17, 2008).

5. http://webappa.cdc.gov/sasweb/ncipc/mortrate.html (accessed February 1, 2006).

6. Note that this estimate is intended to capture the costs of gun misuse and so ignores the benefits to society from widespread gun ownership, in the same way that studies of the social costs of automobile accidents ignore the benefits from driving. The figure comes, in part, from contingent valuation responses about what people say they would pay to reduce crime-related gun violence by 30 percent. One potential concern is that these estimates assume that societal willingness to pay to reduce gun violence is linear with the proportion of gun violence eliminated, which may not be the case. And in practice there remains some uncertainty about the reliability of the contingent valuation measurement technology. In any case, most of the estimated costs of gun violence to the United States appears to come from crime, since suicide seems more like a private concern, and the estimated costs of gun crime by Cook and Ludwig (2000) fits comfortably next to more recent contingent valuation estimates for the social costs of crime more generally (M. A. Cohen et al. 2004).

7. Kleck and Patterson (1993) use a similar proxy with city-level data and find no statistically significant cross-sectional relationship between gun ownership rates and homicide or other crime rates. However, rather than relying on a simple cross-sectional regression-adjusted comparison of crime rates across areas with different rates of gun ownership, they attempt to isolate variation in gun ownership rates that arguably will be unrelated to the unmeasured determinants of local crime rates. Their choice of instrumental variable to explain variation in gun prevalence—per capita rates of hunting licenses and subscriptions to gun magazines—are likely to be biased in the direction of overstating the net deterrent effect of guns on crime (see, for example, the discussion in Cook and Ludwig 2003*b*).

8. The individual state legislatures in the experimental group had chosen to not regulate gun transactions, indicating that they have a different political climate in this respect than the control states. But that difference is part of the permanent cross-sectional difference among states that is netted out by the difference-in-difference procedure. The change in regulations was imposed by the federal law and hence did not reflect a shift in state political climates, which would have confounded our estimates.

9. Cook and Braga (2001) analyzed the age and point of first sale of all guns confiscated in Cook County in 1999. Guns first sold prior to 1994 were much more likely to come from out of state. The change in 1994 is large and abrupt.

10. Wintemute et al. (2001) find encouraging results from an examination of California's law, although the research design employed leaves the estimates susceptible to bias from omitted variables (see Cook and Ludwig 2003*c*).

11. Other studies using the same basic research design have found evidence of some decline in gun use in crime in at least some cities in Arizona (McPheters, Mann, and Schlagenhauf 1984) but not California (Lizotte and Zatz 1986). Kleck (1991) uses a cross-sectional analysis of data from 170 cities and finds no effect on gun use in crime, although the problems with cross-sectional comparisons of this sort are described above.

12. In principle, a third complication with the evaluation of Ceasefire in Boston is the launching in 1992 of the Ten Points Coalition, a collaboration between the Boston Police Department and leading African American clergy in the city. However, the time path of homicides in Boston does not show a decline at this point, although this is admittedly a weak test of the role of this effort (see Berrien, McRoberts, and Winship 2000; Winship 2002; Berrien and Winship 2003).

13. Youth homicides show a similar pattern; see Cook and Ludwig (2004).

14. James Q. Wilson (1994) extends the argument: "Our goal should not be the disarming of law-abiding citizens. It should be to reduce the number of people who carry guns unlawfully, especially in places—on streets, in taverns—where the mere presence of a gun can increase the hazards we all face."

15. Rosenfeld, Fornango, and Baumer (2005) reach a different conclusion about Exile's effects in Richmond. But their analysis considers crime data only back to 1992 and so omits the most important variable explaining why Richmond had an above-average decline in homicide after Exile went into effect: the city's above-average increase in homicides from the mid-1980s to the mid-1990s.

16. For example, the instrumental variables (two-stage least squares) estimates presented by John Lott and David Mustard (1997) yield implausibly large estimates for the effects of right-to-carry laws on crime; see Donohue (2003) as well as Ludwig (1998, 2000). Using nonlinear state-specific trends may yield evidence for right-to-carry laws when separate trends are included for the pre- and postlaw periods, but not when each state's crime trend over the entire sample period as a whole is modeled using a linear and quadratic term (Black and Nagin 1998). Because crime rates follow the same types of cyclical patterns as do many economic indicators and these right-to-carry laws are adopted during periods of increasing crime, isolating their causal effects is quite difficult in practice. That the postlaw crime levels are below the prelaw levels does not rule out the influence of whatever factors drive these crime cycles over time.

17. Mustard (2003) argues that the net effect of right-to-carry laws on a county's or state's robbery rate is ambiguous because not all robberies occur in public places, and right-to-carry laws may cause some criminals to substitute from robbing people in public places to committing such crimes in private areas instead. But the proportion of criminal events that occur in public areas is higher for robbery than for murder, rape, and other violent crimes. Why we should see substitution from public to private areas suppressing the right-to-carry effect on robbery more than for other violent crimes is unclear.

18. Mustard (2003) argues that compared to right-to-carry laws enacted in the 1980s, the laws adopted in the 1990s involved higher fees, more stringent training requirements, and more restrictions on where those with permits can legally carry their firearms.

This argument offers some hypotheses about why the crime-reducing effect of the laws adopted in the 1990s might be muted compared to those enacted in the 1980s, but it cannot explain why Donohue finds that right-to-carry laws adopted in the 1990s seem to increase crime. A similar sort of "treatment heterogeneity" argument is offered by James Q. Wilson in his dissent to the NRC panel report's conclusions about Lott's research (see appendix A in Wellford, Pepper, and Petrie 2005). A more likely explanation in our view for the conflicting results between the laws of the 1980s and 1990s is that both sets of estimates are driven by confounding factors that are not captured by the regression model.

19. The key issue here is that annual observations drawn from counties within the same state may not be statistically independent (for example, if shocks to the state government's budget affect the provision of criminal justice or social services statewide). The NRC panel report is correct that if we are willing to assume that only the unmeasured state shocks have constant effects on crime outcomes over the entire sample period, then they will be absorbed in the county fixed effects included in all of the models that have been employed in this literature (see Wellford, Pepper, and Petrie 2005, p. 138).

20. Most of these measures have been implemented in New York City, among other places. See the report of the Vera Institute of Justice on this subject for a review (Golden and Almo 2004).

21. The importance of scofflaw dealers is suggested by the results of an investigation of large dealers in California, which found widely differing probabilities with respect to the likelihood that a gun sold by a dealer would end up being used in crime (Wintemute, Cook, and Wright 2005)

REFERENCES

Azrael, Deborah, Philip J. Cook, and Matthew Miller. 2004. "State and Local Prevalence of Firearms Ownership: Measurement, Structure, and Trends." *Journal of Quantitative Criminology* 20(1): 43–62.

Berrien, Jenny, Omar McRoberts, and Christian Winship. 2000. "Religion and the Boston Miracle: The Effect of Black Ministry on Youth Violence." In *Who Will Provide?,* edited by Mary Jo Bane, Brent Coffin, and Ronald F. Thiemann. Boulder, CO: Westview.

Berrien, Jenny, and Christian Winship. 2003. "Should We have Faith in the Churches? The Ten-Point Coalition's Effect on Boston's Youth Violence." In *Guns, Crime and Punishment in America,* edited by Bernard E. Harcourt. New York: New York University Press.

Black, David, and Daniel S. Nagin. 1998. "Do 'Right to Carry' Laws Reduce Violent Crime?" *Journal of Legal Studies* 27(1): 209–19.

Blumstein, Alfred. 2000. "Disaggregating the Violence Trend." In *The Crime Drop in America,* edited by Alfred Blumstein and Joel Wallman. New York: Cambridge University Press.

Blumstein, Alfred, and, Joel Wallman. 2000. *The Crime Drop in America*. New York: Cambridge University Press.

Braga, Anthony A. 2002. *Problem-Oriented Policing and Crime Prevention.* Monsey, NY: Criminal Justice Press.

Braga, Anthony A., David M. Kennedy, Elin J. Waring, and Anne M. Piehl. 2001. "Problem-Oriented Policing, Deterrence, and Youth Violence: An Evaluation of Boston's Operation Ceasefire." *Journal of Research in Crime and Delinquency* 38(3): 195–225.

Britt, Chester L., Gary Kleck, and David Bordua. 1996. "A Reassessment of the D.C. Gun Law: Some Cautionary Notes on the Use of Interrupted Time Series Designs for Policy Impact Assessment." *Law and Society Review* 30(2): 361–79.

Bureau of Alcohol, Tobacco, and Firearms. 2000. *ATF Regulatory Actions: Report to the Secretary on Firearms Initiatives.* Washington, DC: U.S. Department of the Treasury.

———. 2001. *Firearms Commerce in the United States.* Washington, DC: U.S. Department of the Treasury.

———. 2002. *Firearms Commerce in the United States.* Washington, DC: U.S. Department of the Treasury.

Butterfield, Fox. 1996. *All God's Children: The Bosket Family and the American Tradition of Violence.* New York: Avon Books.

Cohen, Jacqueline, and Jens Ludwig. 2003. "Policing Gun Crimes." In *Evaluating Gun Policy,* edited by Jens Ludwig and Philip J. Cook. Washington, DC: Brookings Institution Press.

Cohen, Mark A., Roland T. Rust, Sara Steen, and Simon T. Tidd. 2004. "Willingness-to-Pay for Crime Control Programs." *Criminology* 42(1): 89–109.

Cook, Philip J. 1976. "A Strategic Choice Analysis of Robbery." In *Sample Surveys of the Victims of Crimes,* edited by W. Skogan. Cambridge, MA: Ballinger.

———. 1980. "Reducing Injury and Death Rates in Robbery." *Policy Analysis* 6(1): 21–45.

———. 1987. "Robbery Violence." *Journal of Criminal Law and Criminology* 70(2): 357–76.

———. 1991. "The Technology of Personal Violence." In *Crime and Justice: A Review of Research,* vol. 14, edited by Michael Tonry. Chicago: University of Chicago Press.

Cook, Philip J., and Anthony A. Braga. 2001. "Comprehensive Firearms Tracing: Strategic and Investigative Uses of New Data on Firearms Markets." *Arizona Law Review* 43(2): 277–309.

Cook, Philip J., and John H. Laub. 1998. "The Unprecedented Epidemic of Youth Violence." In *Youth Violence,* edited by Michael Tonry and Mark H. Moore. Vol. 24 of *Crime and Justice: A Review of Research,* edited by Michael Tonry. Chicago: University of Chicago Press.

Cook, Philip J., and John J. Laub. 2002. "After the Epidemic: Recent Trends in Youth Violence in the United States." In *Crime and Justice: A Review of Research,* vol. 29, edited by Michael Tonry. Chicago: University of Chicago Press.

Cook, Philip J., and James A. Leitzel. 1996. "Perversity, Futility, Jeopardy: An Economic Analysis of the Attack on Gun Control." *Law and Contemporary Problems* 59(1): 91–118.

Cook, Philip J., and Jens Ludwig. 1996. *Guns in America: Results of a Comprehensive Survey of Gun Ownership and Use.* Washington, DC: Police Foundation.

Cook, Philip J., and Jens Ludwig. 2000. *Gun Violence: The Real Costs.* New York: Oxford University Press.

Cook, Philip J., and Jens Ludwig. 2002. "Litigation as Regulation: The Case of Firearms." In *Regulation through Litigation,* edited by W. Kip Viscusi. Washington, DC: Brookings Institution Press.

Cook, Philip J., and Jens Ludwig. 2003*a*. "The Effects of the Brady Act on Gun Violence." In *Guns, Crime, and Punishment in America,* edited by Bernard E. Harcourt. New York: New York University Press.
Cook, Philip J., and Jens Ludwig. 2003*b*. "Guns and Burglary." In *Evaluating Gun Policy,* edited by Jens Ludwig and Philip J. Cook. Washington, DC: Brookings Institution Press.
Cook, Philip J., and Jens Ludwig. 2003*c*. "Pragmatic Gun Policy." In *Evaluating Gun Policy,* edited by Jens Ludwig and Philip J. Cook. Washington, DC: Brookings Institution Press.
Cook, Philip J., and Jens Ludwig. 2004. "Does Gun Prevalence Affect Teen Gun Carrying After All?" *Criminology* 42(1): 27–54.
Cook, Philip J., and Jens Ludwig. 2006. "The Social Costs of Gun Ownership." *Journal of Public Economics* 90(1–2): 379–91.
Cook, Philip J., Jens Ludwig, and Anthony A. Braga. 2005. "Criminal Records of Homicide Offenders." *Journal of the American Medical Association* 294(5): 598–601.
Cook, Philip J., Jens Ludwig, and David Hemenway. 1997. "The Gun Debate's New Mythical Number: How Many Defensive Gun Uses per Year?" *Journal of Policy Analysis and Management* 16: 463–69.
Cook, Philip J., Jens Ludwig, Sudhir A. Venkatesh, and Anthony A. Braga. 2007. "Underground Gun Markets." *Economic Journal* 117(524): F588–F618.
Cook, Philip J., Stephanie Molliconi, and Thomas B. Cole. 1995. "Regulating Gun Markets." *Journal of Criminal Law and Criminology* 86: 59–92.
Cook, Philip J., Mark H. Moore, and Anthony A. Braga. 2002. "Gun Control." In *Crime: Public Policies for Crime Control,* edited by James Q. Wilson and Joan Petersilia. Oakland, CA: ICS.
Donohue, John J. 2003. "The Impact of Concealed-Carry Laws." In *Evaluating Gun Policy,* edited by Jens Ludwig and Philip J. Cook. Washington, DC: Brookings Institution Press.
Duggan, Mark. 2001. "More Guns, More Crime." *Journal of Political Economy* 109(5): 1086–114.
Dvorak, John A. 2002. "Concealed Weapons Laws Taking Hold." *Kansas City Star* [Knight-Ridder Newspapers], March 1.
Eck, John, and Edward Maguire. 2000. "Have Changes in Policing Reduced Violent Crime? An Assessment of the Evidence." In *The Crime Drop in America,* edited by Alfred Blumstein and Joel Wallman. New York: Cambridge University Press.
Glaeser, Edward L., Bruce Sacerdote, and Jose A. Scheinkman. 1996. "Crime and Social Interactions." *Quarterly Journal of Economics* 111(2): 507–48.
Golden, Megan, and Cari Almo 2004. *Reducing Gun Violence: An Overview of New York City's Strategies.* New York: Vera Institute of Justice.
Greenwood, Peter. 2003. "Comment." In *Evaluating Gun Policy,* edited by Jens Ludwig and Philip J. Cook. Washington, DC: Brookings Institution Press.
Hemenway, David. 1997*a*. "The Myth of Millions of Self-Defense Gun Uses: An Explanation of Extreme Overestimates." *Chance* 10: 6–10.
———. 1997*b*. "Survey Research and Self-Defense Gun Use: An Explanation of Extreme Overestimates." *Journal of Criminal Law and Criminology* 87: 1430–445.
———. 2004. *Private Guns, Public Health.* Ann Arbor: University of Michigan Press.
Hill, Jeffrey M. 1997. "The Impact of Liberalized Concealed Weapon Statutes on Rates of Violent Crime." Unpublished senior thesis, Duke University, Department of Public Policy.

Kates, Don B., Jr., and Daniel D. Polsby. 2000. "The Myth of the 'Virgin Killer': Law-Abiding Persons Who Kill in Fit of Rage." Paper presented at the American Society of Criminology annual meeting, San Francisco, November.

Kellermann, Arthur L., Frederick P. Rivara, Norman B. Rushforth, Joyce G. Banton, Donald T. Reay, Jerry T. Francisco, Ana B. Locci, Janice Prodzinski, Bela B. Hackman, and Grant Somes. 1993. "Gun Ownership as a Risk Factor for Homicide in the Home." *New England Journal of Medicine* 329: 1084–91.

Kennedy, David M., Anne M. Piehl, and Anthony A. Braga. 1996. "Youth Violence in Boston: Gun Markets, Serious Youth Offenders, and a Use-Reduction Strategy." *Law and Contemporary Problems* 59(1): 147–98.

Kleck, Gary. 1991. *Point Blank: Guns and Violence in America*. New York: Aldine de Gruyter.

———. 1997. *Targeting Guns: Firearms and Their Control*. New York: Aldine de Gruyter.

———. 2004. "Measures of Gun Ownership Levels for Macrolevel Crime and Violence Research." *Journal of Research in Crime and Delinquency* 41(1): 3–36.

Kleck, Gary, and Marc Gertz. 1995. "Armed Resistance to Crime: The Prevalence and Nature of Self-Defense with a Gun." *Journal of Criminal Law and Criminology* 86: 150–87.

Kleck, Gary, and Britt E. Patterson. 1993. "The Impact of Gun Control and Gun Ownership Levels on Violence Rates." *Journal of Quantitative Criminology* 9(3): 249–87.

Levitt, Steven D. 2001. "Deterrence." In *Crime: Public Policies for Crime Control,* edited by J. Q. Wilson and J. Petersilia. Oakland, CA: Institute for Contemporary Studies.

———. 2003. "Comment." In *Evaluating Gun Policy,* edited by Jens Ludwig and Philip J. Cook. Washington, DC: Brookings Institution Press.

———. 2004. "Understanding Why Crime Fell in the 1990s: Four Factors That Explain the Decline and Six That Do Not." *Journal of Economic Perspectives* 18(1): 163–90.

Levitt, Steven D., and Sudhir A. Venkatesh. 2000. "An Economic Analysis of a Drug-Selling Gang's Finances." *Quarterly Journal of Economics* 115(3): 755–90.

Lizotte, Alan, and Marjorie Zatz. 1986. "The Use and Abuse of Sentence Enhancement for Firearms Offenses in California." *Law and Contemporary Problems* 49(1): 199–221.

Loftin, Colin, Milton Heumann, and David McDowall. 1983. "Mandatory Sentencing and Firearms Violence." *Law and Society Review* 17(2): 287–318.

Loftin, Colin, and David McDowall. 1981. "'One with a Gun Gets You Two': Mandatory Sentencing and Firearms Violence in Detroit." *Annals of the American Academy of Political and Social Science* 455: 150–67.

Loftin, Colin, and David McDowall. 1984. "The Deterrent Effects of the Florida Felony Firearm Law." *Journal of Criminal Law and Criminology* 75(1): 250–59.

Loftin, Colin, David McDowall, Brian Wiersema, and Talber J. Cottey. 1991. "Effects of Restrictive Licensing of Handguns on Homicide and Suicide in the District of Columbia." *New England Journal of Medicine* 325: 1625–30.

Lott, John R. 2000. *More Guns, Less Crime*. 2nd ed. Chicago: University of Chicago Press.

Lott, John R., and David B. Mustard. 1997. "Crime, Deterrence and Right-to-Carry Concealed Handguns." *Journal of Legal Studies* 16(1): 1–68.

Ludwig, Jens. 1998. "Concealed-Gun-Carrying Laws and Violent Crime: Evidence from State Panel Data." *International Review of Law and Economics* 18: 239–54.

———. 2000. "Gun Self-Defense and Deterrence." In *Crime and Justice: A Review of Research,* vol. 27, edited by Michael Tonry. Chicago: University of Chicago Press.

———. 2005. "Better Gun Enforcement, Less Crime." *Criminology and Public Policy* 4(4): 677–716.

Ludwig, Jens, and Philip J. Cook. 2000. "Homicide and Suicide Rates Associated with Implementation of the Brady Handgun Violence Prevention Act." *Journal of the American Medical Association* 284(5): 585–91.

Ludwig, Jens, and Philip J. Cook. 2001. "The Benefits of Reducing Gun Violence: Evidence from Contingent-Valuation Survey Data." *Journal of Risk and Uncertainty* 22(3): 207–26.

Ludwig, Jens, Philip J. Cook, and Tom W. Smith. 1998. "The Gender Gap in Reporting Household Gun Ownership." *American Journal of Public Health* 88(11): 1715–18.

Manning, Willard. 2003. "Comment." In *Evaluating Gun Policy,* edited by Jens Ludwig and Philip J. Cook. Washington, DC: Brookings Institution Press.

Manson, Donald A., and Darrell K. Gilliard. 1997. *Presale Handgun Checks, 1996: A National Estimate.* NCJ 165704. Washington, DC: U.S. Department of Justice, Bureau of Justice Statistics.

Marvell, Thomas B., and Carlisle E. Moody. 1995. "The Impact of Enhanced Prison Terms for Felonies Committed with Guns." *Criminology* 33(2): 247–81.

McDowall, David, Colin Loftin, and Stanley Presser. 2000. "Measuring Civilian Defensive Firearm Use: A Methodological Experiment." *Journal of Quantitative Criminology* 16(2): 1–19.

McDowall, David, Colin Loftin, and Brian Wiersema. 1992. "A Comparative Study of the Preventive Effects of Mandatory Sentencing Laws for Gun Crimes." *Journal of Criminal Law and Criminology* 83(2): 378–94.

McDowall, David, Colin Loftin, and Brian Wiersema. 1996. "Using Quasi-Experiments to Evaluate Firearms Laws: Comment on Britt et al.'s Reassessment of the D.C. Gun Law." *Law and Society Review* 30(2): 381–91.

McGonigal, Michael D., John Cole, William C. Schwab, Donald R. Kauder, Michael F. Rotondo, and Peter B. Angood. 1993. "Urban Firearm Deaths: A Five-Year Perspective." *Journal of Trauma* 35(4): 532–36.

McPheters, Lee, Robert Mann, and Don Schlagenhauf. 1984. "Economic Response to a Crime Deterrence Program: Mandatory Sentencing for Robbery with a Firearm." *Economic Inquiry* 22(2): 550–70.

Miller, Matthew, Deborah Azrael, and David Hemenway. 2002. "Household Firearm Ownership Levels and Homicide Rates across U.S. Regions and States, 1988–1997." *American Journal of Public Health* 92: 1988–93.

Miron, Jeffrey A. 2001. "Violence, Guns, and Drugs: A Cross-Country Analysis." *Journal of Law and Economics* 44(2): 615–33.

Mustard, David B. 2003. "Comment." In *Evaluating Gun Policy,* edited by Jens Ludwig and Philip J. Cook. Washington, DC: Brookings Institution Press.

Nagin, Daniel S. 1998. "Criminal Deterrence Research at the Outset of the Twenty-first Century." In *Crime and Justice: A Review of Research,* vol. 23, edited by Michael Tonry. Chicago: University of Chicago Press.

Piehl, Anne M., Suzanne J. Cooper, Anthony A. Braga, and David M. Kennedy. 2003. "Testing for Structural Breaks in the Evaluation of Programs." *Review of Economics and Statistics* 85(3): 550–58.

Pierce, Glenn L., and William J. Bowers. 1981. "The Bartley-Fox Gun Law's Short-term Impact on Crime in Boston." *Annals of the American Academy of Political and Social Science* 455: 120–37.

Raphael, Steven, and Jens Ludwig. 2003. "Prison Sentence Enhancements: The Case of Project Exile." In *Evaluating Gun Policy,* edited by Jens Ludwig and Philip J. Cook. Washington, DC: Brookings Institution Press.

"Remarks by the President on Project Safe Neighborhood." 2001. The White House, Office of the Press Secretary, May 14.

Rennison, Callie Marie. 2001. *Criminal Victimization 2000: Changes 1999–2000 with Trends 1993–2000.* NCJ 187007. Washington, DC: Bureau of Justice Statistics.

Robuck-Mangum, Gail. 1997. "Concealed Weapon Permit Holders in North Carolina: A Descriptive Study of Handgun-Carrying Behavior." Unpublished master's thesis, University of North Carolina, School of Public Health.

Rosenfeld, Richard, Robert Fornango, and Eric Baumer. 2005. "Did Ceasefire, Compstat and Exile Reduce Homicide?" *Criminology and Public Policy* 4(3): 419–50.

Shannon, Elaine. 1999. "Have Gun? Will Travel." *Time,* August 16, 154(7).

Sheley, Joseph F., and James D. Wright. 1995. *In the Line of Fire: Youth, Guns, and Violence in Urban America.* New York: Aldine de Gruyter.

Sherman, Lawrence W. 2000. "Gun Carrying and Homicide Prevention." *Journal of the American Medical Association* 283(9): 1193–95.

Sherman, Lawrence W., and James P. Rogan. 1995. "Effects of Gun Seizures on Gun Violence: 'Hot Spots' Patrol in Kansas City." *Justice Quarterly* 12(4): 673–93.

Sherman, Lawrence W., James W. Shaw, and Dennis P. Rogan. 1995. *The Kansas City Gun Experiment.* Washington, DC: National Institute of Justice.

Tita, George K., Jack Riley, Greg Ridgeway, Clifford Grammich, Allan F. Abrahamse, and Peter W. Greenwood. 2003. *Reducing Gun Violence: Results from an Intervention in East Los Angeles.* Santa Monica, CA: RAND.

Vigdor, Elizabeth R., and James A. Mercy. 2003. "Disarming Batterers: The Impact of Domestic Violence Firearm Laws." In *Evaluating Gun Policy,* edited by Jens Ludwig and Philip J. Cook. Washington, DC: Brookings Institution Press.

Wachtel, Julius. 1998. "Sources of Crime Guns in Los Angeles, California." *Policing: An International Journal of Police Strategies and Management* 21(2): 220–39.

Wagenaar, Alexander C., and Traci L. Toomey. 2002. "Effects of Minimum Drinking Age Laws: Review and Analyses of the Literature from 1960 to 2000." *Journal of Studies on Alcohol.* Supp. 14: 206–25.

Webster, Daniel W., Jon S. Vernick, and Lisa M. Hepburn. 2001. "Relationship between Licensing, Registration and Other Gun Sales Laws and the Source State of Crime Guns." *Injury Prevention* 7(3): 184–89.

Webster, Daniel W., Jon S. Vernick, and Lisa M. Hepburn. 2002. "Effects of Maryland's Law Banning 'Saturday Night Special' Handguns on Homicides." *American Journal of Epidemiology* 155(5): 406–12.

Weil, Douglas S., and Rebecca C. Knox. 1996. "Effects of Limiting Handgun Purchases on Interstate Transfer of Firearms." *Journal of the American Medical Association* 275(22): 1759–61.

Wellford, Charles F., John V. Pepper, and Carol V. Petrie. 2005. *Firearms and Violence: A Critical Review.* Washington, DC: National Academies Press.

Wilson, James Q. 1994. "Just Take Their Guns Away: Forget about Gun Control." *New York Times Magazine* (March 20), section 6, pp. 46–47.

Winship, Christopher. 2002. "End of a Miracle? Crime, Faith and Partnership in Boston in the 1990's." Working Paper, Harvard University, Department of Sociology.

Wintemute, Garen J. 2007. "Gun Shows across a Multistate American Gun Market: Observational Evidence on the Effects of Regulatory Policies." *Injury Prevention* 13: 150–55.
Wintemute, Garen J., Philip J. Cook, and Mona Wright. 2005. "Risk Factors among Handgun Retailers for Frequent and Disproportionate Sales of Guns Used in Violent and Firearm-related Crimes." *Injury Prevention* 11: 357–63.
Wintemute, Garen J., Mona Wright, Christiana M. Drake, and James J. Beaumont. 2001. "Subsequent Criminal Activity among Violent Misdemeanants Who Seek to Purchase Handguns." *Journal of the American Medical Association* 265(8): 1019–26.
Wolfgang, Marvin E. 1958. *Patterns of Criminal Homicide*. Philadelphia: University of Pennsylvania Press.
———. 1995. "A Tribute to a View I Have Opposed." *Journal of Criminal Law and Criminology* 86(1): 188–92.
Wright, James D., and Peter H. Rossi. 1994. *Armed and Considered Dangerous: A Survey of Felons and Their Firearms*. Expanded ed. New York: Aldine de Gruyter.
Zimring, Franklin E. 1968. "Is Gun Control Likely to Reduce Violent Killings?" *University of Chicago Law Review* 35: 21–37.
———. 1972. "The Medium Is the Message: Firearm Calibre as a Determinant of Death from Assault." *Journal of Legal Studies* 1: 97–124.
Zimring, Franklin E., and Gordon Hawkins. 1997. *Crime Is Not the Problem: Lethal Violence in America*. New York: Oxford University Press.

CHAPTER 4

ROBBERY

PHILIP J. COOK

ROBBERY is a crime of violence motivated by theft. The spectrum of robbery ranges from schoolyard shakedowns for lunch money to bank holdups with losses reaching into the millions of dollars. Property losses from robbery are, however, usually small or nil. It is the violence that makes robbery such a serious crime.

Robbery is particularly fear-inspiring because it usually involves an unprovoked attack by strangers. In that regard it differs from assault, which typically involves an altercation between acquaintances. The public concern about crime in the streets is to a large extent a concern about robbery, and that concern may have profound effects on the life of the city through its influence on choices about where to live, work, shop, and go out to dinner (Cook and Ludwig 2000). James Q. Wilson and Barbara Boland (1976, p. 183) note, "It is mostly fear of robbery that induces many citizens to stay home at night and to avoid the streets, thereby diminishing the sense of community and increasing the freedom with which crimes may be committed on the streets."

This chapter provides a description of trends and patterns in robbery using police statistics and statistics from crime surveys. The focus is on data for the United States, which has the best established of the national crime surveys. The survey data support a fine-grained analysis of the age, sex, race, and number of robbers and victims involved in an incident, as well as the type of weapon and the outcomes of the confrontation with respect to theft and injury. It is helpful to examine these patterns through the lens of the robbers' instrumental concerns—identifying lucrative targets, preempting resistance, and avoiding arrest—although some violence is simply gratuitous.

Robbery prevention efforts include private protection efforts for prime commercial targets (guards, closed-circuit cameras, reduced cash on hand) and directed police patrols against street robbery. Probably more important has been the evolution toward a cashless economy, reducing the robbers' chances for a quick payoff. Reducing the overall robbery rate is not the only goal; a second public goal is harm reduction. For example, measures to reduce gun use in robbery have the potential to reduce the rate of serious injury and murder.

The chapter consist of four main sections and a conclusion. The first section discusses robbery rate trends in the United States since the 1960s—mainly up through 1981, down since 1991, and fluctuating in between—and relative to rates elsewhere. The second section, based on victimization dates combined for the years 2000 through 2005 (henceforth 2000–5) to provide sufficiently large numbers to support generalizations, examines the demographics of robber perpetration and victimization and robbery outcomes (property loss, injury, and death). The third discusses robbers' strategic choices about whom to rob, how, and with what weapon, and what differences those choices make. The fourth discusses interventions aimed at preventing robberies.

A number of conclusions are offered:

- Although data comparability issues preclude confident assertions, U.S. robbery rates as shown in official data and victims' reports appear comparable to those of other developed countries.
- Official and victim data concur in showing a very substantial decline in robbery rates since the early 1990s.
- Most robbers are male (more than 90 percent in 2000–5), young (74 percent under 30), and black (54 percent).
- Most robberies do not yield high profits for robbers (only 29 percent yielded cash), but nearly half of victims are physically attacked.
- Robberies with guns are less likely to result in victim injuries than are other robberies but are much more likely to result in death.
- A variety of situational and police manpower approaches to robbery reduction have been successful.

I. Data and Trends

The volume, trend, and patterns of crime can be measured by use of two sorts of data: victimization surveys and records of crimes known to the authorities. A careful analysis of data for eight first world nations offers insight into the difficulty in developing reliable measures (Farrington, Langan, and Tonry 2004). As shown in table 4.1, the recorded rates circa 1999 ranged from 0.5 per 1,000 (for Switzerland) up to 1.5 per 1,000 (for both the United States and England and Wales). But the survey estimates were far higher and suggest a different lineup; for example, while the survey rate for the United States was 2.5 times the recorded rate during the 1980s

Table 4.1. Robbery rates, record and survey data

	Time period	Growth, survey data (percentage)	Growth record data (percentage)	Recent recorded rate per 1,000	Ratio: survey to recorded rates
England and Wales	1981–99	95	266	1.5	6.1
Scotland	1981–99	61	22	1.0	3.6
Australia	1983–2000	0	300	1.2	7.9
Canada	1981–98	2	−9	.9	9.7
United States	1981–99	−51	−42	1.5	2.5
Netherlands	1980–99	25	270	1.1	14.8
Sweden	1980–98	N/A	85	.7	9.0
Switzerland	1985–99	41	48	.5	14.2

Source: Cook and Khmilevska 2005, pp. 333, 335.

and 1990s, for the Netherlands the survey rate was nearly 15 times as high as the recorded rate and was a multiple of the U.S. survey rate. Furthermore, in several of these nations the trends in the survey measure look quite different from the trends in the recorded measure.

Of the various national crime surveys, the U.S. *National Crime Victimization Survey* (*NCVS*) is the best established, generating annual estimates since 1973, and also has an important technical advantage over the others. The *NCVS* interviews the same households every six months over seven cycles, encouraging the respondents to use the previous interview as a mental baseline to define the relevant period. That device helps limit an important source of error in survey-respondent reports, namely, the tendency to report important victimization experiences that occurred outside the specified interval (six months or a year), a recall problem known as "telescoping." Other nations do not use this costly procedure and hence may have more telescoping and hence a positive bias to survey results.

The *NCVS* helps uncover the dark figure of crime that goes unreported to the police. In 2005, for example, the *NCVS* estimated 625,000 noncommercial robberies, compared to 417,000 robberies of *all* types tabulated through the Uniform Crime Reports (UCR), which compiles crimes known to the police. Only about 40 percent of noncommercial robberies are reported to the police. The *NCVS* data are also useful in providing the statistical basis for analyzing demographic patterns of violence, both of the victims and of the perpetrators (based on respondents' reports of their impression of the age, race, sex, and number of assailants). They also provide an empirical basis for characterizing process and outcomes of criminal incidents.

Because the interview subjects are households, commercial robberies and other crimes against businesses are not included. According to UCR data, about 42 percent of robberies reported to the police occur in businesses. The true percentage may be lower if businesses are more likely to report victimization than are individuals.

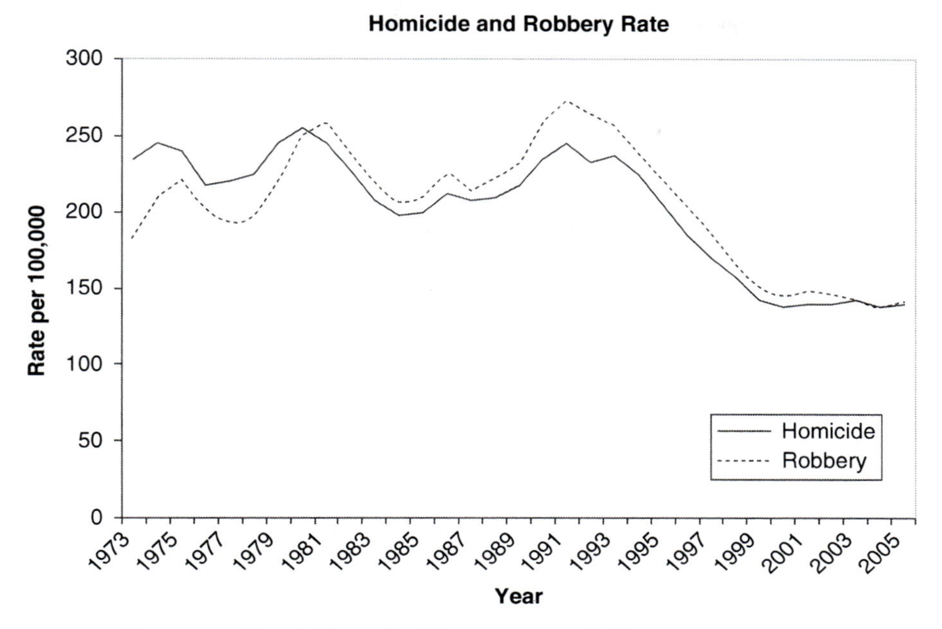

Figure 4.1. Homicide and robbery rates, United States, 1973–2005.
Source: Original computations based on the FBI Uniform Crime Reports and National Archive of Criminal Justice Data (http://www.icpsr.umich.edu).

For the period since 1973, the *NCVS* data indicate that victimization rates for personal robbery were cyclical, with peaks in 1974, 1981, and 1994; since 1994 there has been a sustained drop, from 6.3 per 1,000 to just one-third that level in 2004. UCR robbery rates have roughly the same peaks and valleys as the *NCVS* rates, and they too show a strong downward trend during the 1990s (Blumstein, Cohen, and Rosenfeld 1991). As documented by Alfred Blumstein (2000) and shown in figure 4.1, UCR robbery rates have moved up and down for the past several decades in synch with murder rates, which are the most reliably measured of all crime rates. (Note that the homicide rate has been scaled up by a factor of 25 in this diagram so that it is on a scale similar to the robbery rate.) It appears like a reasonable bet that the UCR robbery trends are reliable.

The extraordinary reduction in robbery and other violent crime during the 1990s remains something of a mystery—no expert *predicted* this decline—but some credit surely goes to increases in the size of police forces and stringent sentencing policies that greatly increased the prison population (Blumstein and Wallman 2000, 2006; Cook and Laub 2002; Levitt 2004; Zimring 2007). The crack epidemic that began in the mid-1980s contributed to the surge and later decline of robbery; by one account, crack users turned to robbery rather than other forms of theft (such as burglary) because it was the quickest method of obtaining cash

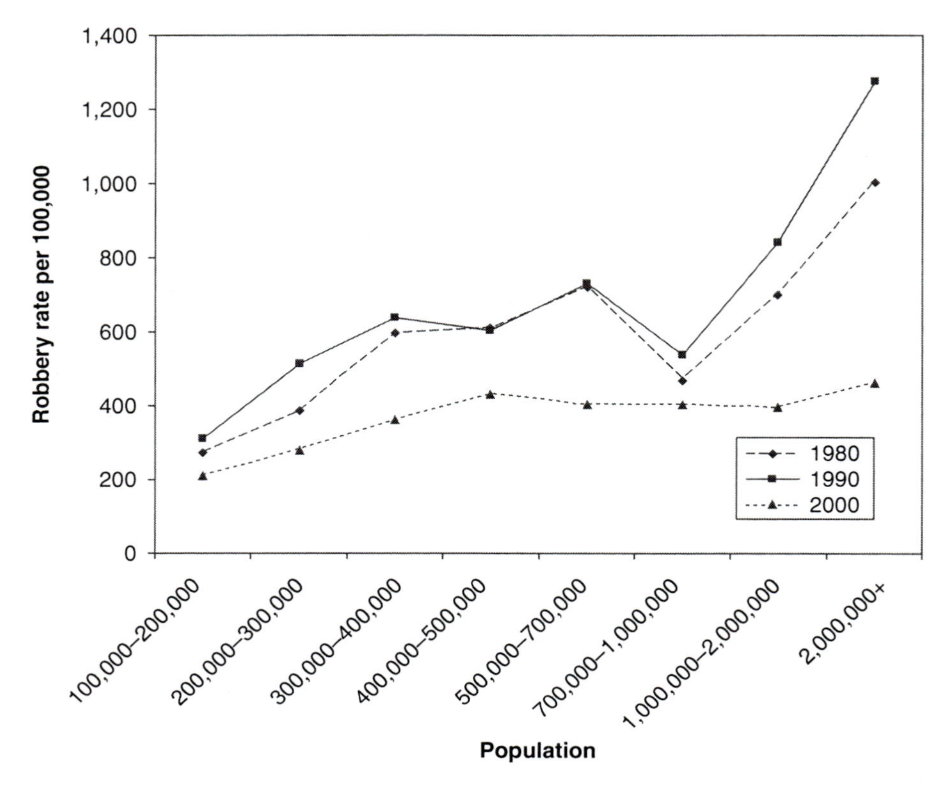

Figure 4.2. Average robbery rate by city size.
Source: Original computations based on the FBI Uniform Crime Reports and National Archive of Criminal Justice Data (http://www.icpsr.umich.edu).

(Baumer et al. 1998). Other plausible (but contested) explanations for the drop in robbery and other violence include the sustained economic expansion of that period, innovations in policing, the delayed effects of the legalization of abortion, and the removal of lead from gasoline.

The 1990s crime drop affected all geographic areas. The greatest percentage of improvements occurred within metropolitan statistical areas, and especially among large cities with populations over 250,000. All the 25 largest cities experienced noteworthy declines in homicide rates from their peak year (mostly in the early 1990s) to 2001, declines that ranged as high as 73 percent for New York and San Diego (Levitt 2004). New York City alone had 17.5 percent of all U.S. robberies in 1990, but just 8.4 percent in 2005. Remarkably, robbery, always the quintessential urban crime, was no longer correlated with city size by 2000. Figure 4.2 shows how the urban pattern of robbery rates changed over three decades.

II. Patterns of Commission, Victimization, and Violence

In what follows, robbery patterns for the United States as a whole are documented by use of data from the *NCVS* on noncommercial robberies. The years 2000–5 are combined to provide an adequate sample of incidents.

A. Demographics

Robberies are often committed by groups of offenders. For the period 2000–5, 18 percent of incidents involved two robbers, and 20 percent involved three or more.[1] Such incidents are classified here according to the victim's or respondent's report of the *oldest* robber's age or race. Groups of robbers almost always consist of demographically similar individuals, with the partial exception of sex: 11 percent of robbery incidents involve at least one female offender, but she teamed up with a man in over one-third of those cases.

In robbery, unlike other types of violent crime, the victim and perpetrator are usually strangers (65 percent of incidents) and are drawn from different demographic distributions. The majority of robbers in the United States are male, young (36 percent under 21, 74 percent under 30), and African American (54 percent), whereas the victims are more representative of the U.S. population. There is some tendency for likes to rob likes with respect to age, race, and sex (Cook 1976), but with notable crossover: a majority of victims of black robbers are white, and most female victims (37 percent of the total) are robbed by males (table 4.2).

Robberies can be classified by location, and for this purpose it is best to get the full spectrum of possibilities, including commercial robberies, which requires UCR data. In 2005, 44 percent of all robberies known to the police were on the street, and 14 percent at a residence. The remaining 42 percent were at convenience

Table 4.2. Race of robbers versus race of victims, 2000–5

	Race of robber (percentage of total)			
Race of victim	White	Black	Other	Total
White	31	29	10	70
Black	1	22	1	24
Other	1	3	2	7
Total	33	54	13	100

Note: Cases with multiple robbers with mixed races are omitted.

Source: Original calculations, *National Crime Victimization Survey*, 1992–2005: Concatenated Incident-Level Files; National Archive of Criminal Justice Data.

stores, gas stations, banks, and other commercial locations. The nationwide drop in the robbery rate during the 1990s was concentrated on street robbery, with relative increases in residential and commercial robbery.

B. Outcomes

When the celebrated bank robber Willie Sutton was asked why he robbed banks, he allegedly replied, "Because that's where the money is." The *NCVS* provides data only on noncommercial robberies, committed by robbers who generally did not follow Willie Sutton's putative guidance. Combining all incident reports for 2000–5 with at least one adult male robber, it turns out that the robbery was unsuccessful in fully 33 percent of the cases, either because the robber was scared off or the victim had nothing to offer. Cash was stolen in only 29 percent of all cases. In the minority of cases that were successful, the median cash stolen was $90. In these and other successful robberies, the loot may include jewelry, clothing, credit cards, household items, and sometimes (in a carjacking) a motor vehicle. But only 25 percent of successful robberies resulted in theft of items worth $250 or more.

The other proximate outcome is injury to the victim. About half of victims report being physically attacked by the robber (rather than just threatened), and one-fifth require medical treatment. Some victims are seriously wounded or killed. In 2005 the FBI classified 921 murders as robbery-related (6 percent of all murders), which suggests as an order of magnitude that 1 in 1,000 robberies resulted in death that year. The true robbery-murder count is probably higher; one detailed study of Chicago robberies found the police department was conservative in using that classification (Zimring and Zuehl 1986).

Because the greatest threat from robbery is the victim's serious injury or murder, it is of considerable interest to know what distinguishes those incidents from the great majority in which the victim comes through unscathed (at least physically). One of my studies compared robbery murders (as documented by the FBI's Supplementary Homicide Reports) to robberies, finding similar distributions with respect to prior relationship (primarily strangers) and demographics (Cook 1987, p. 366). But there was one important difference between robbery and robbery murder: the types of weapons used. About two-thirds of robbery murders are committed with guns, whereas less than one-third of robberies involve guns. Gun robberies are three times more likely to result in the death of the victim than knife robberies, and knife robberies three times more likely than robberies with other weapons (Cook 1987). It has been much debated whether the type of weapon has a separate causal influence on injury (an "instrumentality effect"), as opposed to merely reflecting the offender's intent, yet a variety of evidence favors instrumentality (Zimring 1972; Kleck and McElrath 1991; Wells and Horney 2002). A regression analysis of changes in robbery-murder rates in 43 cities found a close relationship between the robbery rate and the robbery murder rate, as if the latter were simply a probabilistic by-product of the former. Every additional 1,000 gun robberies added four robbery murders to the city's total, while 1,000 non-gun robberies added just one robbery murder (Cook 1987, p. 373).

C. Strategic Choices

Observed outcomes of injury and theft are the result of a series of choices made by the robber and his or her intended victim. The robber (or group of robbers) chooses the victim, the weapon, and the technique, while the victim must decide whether to cooperate or resist. Based on interviews with robbers and other evidence, it is safe to say that robbers' choices reflect a desire to preempt resistance, secure as much loot as possible, and then make a safe getaway, although actual behavior in these fraught encounters is not necessarily rational (Conklin 1972; Wright and Decker 1997; Jacobs 2000). One useful concept is the power of the robber to gain the victim's compliance (Cook 1976). Power depends on the weapon used by the robber; a gun, by creating a lethal threat at a distance, is most powerful, enough for a single robber to control several victims at once. Accomplices also enhance power, as does skill and experience. A solo offender who lacks a gun or accomplices is more likely to select a woman or older person as victim; a majority of gun robberies, on the other hand, are directed against relatively robust commercial targets (Cook 1980).

A multivariate analysis of *NCVS* data for 2000–5 (all robberies committed by an adult male) confirms that the chances of successful theft are greatly enhanced when a gun is used or the robber has accomplices.[2] A gun also enhances the amount of loot in those robberies that are successful, in part because gun robbers are able to choose more lucrative targets (couples, males age 25–54), who might otherwise be in a position to defend themselves. This analysis of the payoff to robbery technique can be used to compute the value of using a gun as opposed to, say, a knife. Other things being equal, the likelihood of successful theft increases by 12.5 percentage points and the average value of loot in successful robberies almost doubles when compared to using a knife (the second best weapon alternative, from the robber's perspective).

Robbers use different methods for gaining compliance, depending in part on the circumstances. The standard technique in gun and knife robberies is to threaten without actually attacking (78 percent and 64 percent of gun and knife noncommercial cases, respectively), which is usually sufficient to gain compliance. The standard technique in unarmed robberies or robberies utilizing sticks and clubs is to attack physically (over 60 percent of cases) and then attempt to take the valuables by force. The chances of injury follow the same pattern, ranging from just 11 percent for gun robberies to 36 percent for robberies with clubs.[3] Of course, when a gun is present and fired, the resulting injury is far more likely to be fatal, and the chances that the victim will be killed are highest for gun robberies (as documented earlier).

Detailed case studies have provided evidence that the violence in robbery is not necessarily instrumental. The offenders may exploit the situation by raping or otherwise tormenting the victim. In some cases of robbery murder it would appear that the killing was purely gratuitous, or even "recreational," stemming from the heat of the moment and the interplay between accomplices (Cook 1980; Zimring and Zuehl 1986). Robbery defendants who injured their victims are more likely than others to be arrested for assault following release from prison than are robbery defendants who did not use violence (Cook and Nagin, 1979; Cook 1987), suggesting a taste for violence.

The strategic choice framework predicts that drug dealers and other actors in the underground economy would be especially attractive targets, both because the loot is likely to include large amounts of cash and drugs and because victims are not likely to inform the police—although they may attempt to retaliate (Jacobs 2000; Topalli, Wright, and Fornango 2002). Crimes of this sort are unlikely to become known unless someone is killed; indeed, it is common to have a drug connection with robbery murder (Zimring and Zuehl 1986). As observed by one group of criminologists studying drug-dealer robbery, "One of criminology's dirty little secrets is that much serious crime... takes place beyond the reach of the criminal law because it is perpetrated against individuals who themselves are involved in lawbreaking" (Topalli, Wright, and Fornango 2002, p. 337).

Victims as well as offenders make decisions that influence the outcome of a robbery. Most important is whether to comply with the robber's demands, and if not, just how to resist. In the *NCVS* sample of noncommercial robberies, about one-third of victims attempted to forcefully resist. Resistance is associated with a reduced chance of successful theft, but an increased chance of injury. Victims of gun robbery are less likely to resist than those confronted with other weapons. A practical question often arises of whether it is prudent to resist a robber, but unfortunately it is not possible to extract a quantitative answer from survey data that lack detailed information on the sequence of events (and hence cannot distinguish between resistance that occurred before or after the injurious attack; Cook 1987). Most victims act on the commonsense rule that it is foolish to resist a robber with a gun, and commercial employers often instruct their clerks that if there is a robbery they should not attempt active resistance.

III. Interventions

The threat of robbery victimization has far-reaching effects on urban life. The effort to avoid this threat may influence choices about where to live, whether and where to go out at night, use of public transportation, and whether to carry a weapon. A reduction in the robbery threat in a city enhances the residents' standard of living and may well contribute to the city's growth and prosperity (Cook and Ludwig 2000). There are a variety of specific measures, both private and public, that hold some promise in this regard, either in reducing the overall robbery rate or reducing the related harms.

The private efforts to reduce robbery are to a large extent applications of situational crime prevention (Clarke 1983, 1995), which attempts to reduce criminal victimization of specific targets by making them less attractive to criminals. The goal is to make it more difficult to complete the crime successfully, reduce the payoff if successful, and increase the risks of arrest and conviction. For especially attractive robbery targets, most notably banks, an array of measures are typically put in place, including guards, surveillance cameras, alarms, and dye packs mixed in with the cash. (Private security against robbery and other crimes is a rapidly growing industry, and there are now as many private guards as there are sworn police officers.) Studies suggest that convenience stores, which are frequent targets of robbery, can reduce the risk by installing bright exterior lighting and keeping at least two clerks on duty at night (Loomis et al. 2002). A variety of common robbery targets, including all-night businesses and public buses, have attempted to discourage robbery by limiting the amount of accessible cash—and advertising that fact.

One of the most controversial private responses to the threat of robbery is keeping a gun handy. The immediate goal for those who keep or carry a gun for self-protection is to enhance one's capacity to resist a robbery, other assault, or criminal intrusion to home or vehicle. But the laws governing gun possession and carrying have taken on great significance in part because of the claim that widespread gun carrying would create a general deterrent to robbery and other assaults that would benefit all. With that in mind, and under pressure from gun rights advocates, most states in the United States have loosened their restrictions on carrying concealed firearms (Vernick and Hepburn 2003), now mandating that all who meet minimum requirements have the right to a concealed-carry permit. These "shall issue" laws have been extensively evaluated, with conflicting results (Lott and Mustard 1997; Black and Nagin 1998; Ludwig 1998; Lott 2000). A careful review of the evidence suggests that the true effects on crime are almost certainly small, and are statistically undetectable given other more powerful forces that influence crime trends (Donohue 2003).

There is less controversy about the public's stake in robbers' choice of weaponry; a gun robbery has a greatly enhanced risk of turning deadly compared with robberies with knives and blunt objects. Gun involvement by young men is closely linked to the prevalence of gun ownership in the community, but there are a variety of regulatory and policing methods that show promise for discouraging gun carrying and criminal use (Cook and Ludwig 2006). One organizing principle for such interventions is to make guns a liability to urban youths and criminals by patrolling against illicit carrying, offering rewards for information on illegal guns, and giving priority to prosecution and sentencing of gun robberies.

More generally, expanding and focusing police resources directed at street crime is a costly but effective method of combating robbery. In England and Wales the Street Crime Initiative provided funding for antirobbery policing in 10 of the 43 police force areas, with large, statistically discernible effects on robbery rates (Machin and Marie 2005). Other studies have also provided support for the conclusion that additional police suppress crime rates (Levitt 2002; McCrary 2002; Levitt and Miles 2007). The effect sizes are large enough to make a strong case for expanded police funding (Donohue and Ludwig 2007).

IV. Conclusions

When people worry about crime in the streets their first concern is robbery. Although the financial losses from robbery are of little consequence overall, the fear of robbery and the actual injuries it causes have a profound effect on the quality of life in certain neighborhoods.

A quick payoff is the allure of robbery for many drug addicts and other criminals. The surest quick payoff is cash, but that is becoming increasingly rare as a means of exchange in the first world nations, except for transactions where preserving anonymity is important. For that reason robbery may focus increasingly on underground markets and as a result become less visible but perhaps more violent. Policies to reduce the scope of the underground market will thus be helpful in the effort to curtail robbery.

NOTES

1. According to *NCVS* data, the solo robbery has become relatively more common over time. For the period under consideration here, 2000–5, 62 percent of robberies were solo, but the percentage prior to 1993 was only about half that number. Specifically, the percentage of robberies with a solo robbery was 48.3 percent in 1979 and 49.9 percent in 1992 and began increasing thereafter (computed from the U.S. Bureau of Justice Statistics, 1996).

2. The logit-regression specification also indicates whether the offender and victim are strangers, the number of victims, race and age of the victim, and whether the robbery occurred during the night. The coefficient estimates for most of these variables are not significantly different from zero. Significantly positive coefficients were estimated for "at home" and "female victim."

3. In a multivariate analysis the likelihood of attack and injury is increased when there are several robbers, the robber is black, and the robbery occurs in a residence.

REFERENCES

Baumer, Eric, Janet L. Lauritsen, Richard Rosenfeld, and Richard Wright. 1998. "The Influence of Crack Cocaine on Robbery, Burglary, and Homicide Rates: A Cross-City, Longitudinal Analysis." *Journal of Research in Crime and Delinquency* 35(3): 316–40.

Black, Dan, and Daniel Nagin. 1998. "Do 'Right to Carry' Laws Reduce Violent Crime?" *Journal of Legal Studies* 27(1): 209–19.

Blumstein, Alfred. 2000. "Disaggregating the Violence Trends." In *The Crime Drop in America*, edited by Alfred Blumstein and Joel Wallman. New York: Cambridge University Press.

Blumstein, Alfred, Jacqueline Cohen, and Richard Rosenfeld. 1991. "Trend and Deviation in Crime Rates: A Comparison of UCR and NCS Data for Burglary and Robbery." *Criminology* 29(2): 237–63.

Blumstein, Alfred, and Joel Wallman. 2000. *The Crime Drop in America*. New York: Cambridge University Press.

Blumstein, Alfred, and Joel Wallman. 2006. "The Crime Drop and Beyond." *Annual Review of Law and Social Science* 2: 125–46.

Clarke, Ronald V. 1983. "Situational Crime Prevention: Its Theoretical Basis and Practical Scope." In *Crime and Justice: An Annual Review of Research*, vol. 4, edited by Michael Tonry and Norval Morris. Chicago: University of Chicago Press.

———. 1995. "Situational Crime Prevention." In *Building a Safer Society: Strategic Approaches to Crime Prevention*, edited by Michael Tonry and David P. Farrington. Chicago: University of Chicago Press.

Conklin, John E. 1972. *Robbery and the Criminal Justice System*. Philadelphia: Lippincott.

Cook, Philip J. 1976. "A Strategic Choice Analysis of Robbery." In *Sample Surveys of the Victims of Crimes*, edited by Wesley Skogan. Cambridge, MA: Ballinger.

———. 1980. "Reducing Injury and Death Rates in Robbery." *Policy Analysis*, Winter: 21–45.

———. 1987. "Robbery Violence." *Journal of Criminal Law and Criminology* 70(2): 357–76.

Cook, Philip J., and Nataliya Khmilevska. 2005. "Cross-National Patterns in Crime Rates." In *Crime and Punishment in Western Countries, 1980–1999*, edited by Michael Tonry and David P. Farrington. Chicago: University of Chicago Press.

Cook, Philip J., and John H. Laub. 2002. "After the Epidemic: Recent Trends in Youth Violence in the United States." In *Crime and Justice: A Review of Research*, vol. 29, edited by Michael Tonry. Chicago: University of Chicago Press.

Cook, Philip J., and Jens Ludwig. 2000. *Gun Violence: The Real Costs*. New York: Oxford University Press.

Cook, Philip J., and Jens Ludwig. 2006. "The Social Costs of Gun Ownership." *Journal of Public Economics* 90(1–2): 379–91.

Cook, Philip J., and Daniel Nagin. 1979. *Does the Weapon Matter? An Evaluation of a Weapons-Emphasis Policy in the Prosecution of Violent Offenders*. Washington, DC: INSLAW.

Donohue, John J. 2003. "The Impact of Concealed-Carry Laws." In *Evaluating Gun Policy*, edited by Jens Ludwig and Philip J. Cook. Washington, DC: Brookings Institution Press.

Donohue, John J., and Jens Ludwig. 2007. *More COPS*. Policy Brief 158. Washington, DC: Brookings Institution.

Farrington, David P., Patrick A. Langan, and Michael Tonry, eds. 2004. *Cross-National Studies in Crime and Justice*. Washington, DC: U.S. Department of Justice, Office of Justice Programs.

Jacobs, Bruce A. 2000. *Robbing Drug Dealers: Violence beyond the Law*. Hawthorne, NY: Aldine de Gruyter.

Kleck, Gary, and Karen McElrath. 1991. "The Effects of Weaponry on Human Violence," *Social Forces* 69: 669–92.

Levitt, Steven D. 2002. "Using Electoral Cycles in Police Hiring to Estimate the Effects of Police on Crime: A Reply." *American Economic Review* 92(4): 1244–50.

———. 2004. "Understanding Why Crime Fell in the 1990s: Four Factors That Explain the Decline and Six That Do Not." *Journal of Economic Perspectives* 18(1): 163–90.

Levitt, Steven D., and Thomas J. Miles. 2007. "The Empirical Study of Criminal Punishment." In *The Handbook of Law and Economics,* vol. 1, edited by A. Mitchell Polinsky and Steven Shavell. New York: North Holland.

Loomis, Dana, Stephen W. Marshall, Susanne H. Wolf, Carol W. Runyan, and John D. Butts. 2002. "Effectiveness of Safety Measures Recommended for Prevention of Workplace Homicide." *Journal of the American Medical Association* 287: 1011–17.

Lott, John. 2000. *More Guns, Less Crime*. 2nd ed. Chicago: University of Chicago Press.

Lott, John R., and David B. Mustard. 1997. "Crime, Deterrence and Right-to-Carry Concealed Handguns." *Journal of Legal Studies* 16(1): 1–68.

Ludwig, Jens. 1998. "Concealed-Gun-Carrying Laws and Violent Crime: Evidence from State Panel Data." *International Review of Law and Economics* 18: 239–54.

Machin, Stephen J., and Oliver Marie. 2005. *Crime and Police Resources: The Street Crime Initiative*. IZA Discussion Paper 1853. Bonn, Germany: Institute for the Study of Labor.

McCrary, Justin, 2002. "Using Electoral Cycles in Police Hiring to Estimate the Effect of Police on Crime: Comment." *American Economic Review* 92(4): 1236–43.

National Archive of Criminal Justice Data. U.S. Department of Justice. http://icpsr.umich.edu/NACJD/.

Topalli, Volkan, Richard Wright, and Robert Fornango. 2002. "Drug Dealers, Robbery and Retaliation." *British Journal of Criminology* 42: 337–51.

U.S. Department of Justice, Bureau of Justice Statistics. [no date]. *Criminal Victimization in the United States, 1996, Statistical Tables*. http://www.ojp.usdoj.gov/bjs/pub/pdf/cvus96.pdf (accessed September 15, 2008).

Vernick, Jon S., and Lisa M. Hepburn. 2003. "State and Federal Gun Laws: Trends for 1970–99." In *Evaluating Gun Policy,* edited by Jens Ludwig and Philip J. Cook. Washington, DC: Brookings Institution Press.

Wells, William, and Julie Horney. 2002. "Weapon Effects and Individual Intent to Do Harm: Influences on the Escalation of Violence." *Criminology* 40(2): 265–96.

Wilson, James Q., and Barbara Boland. 1976. "Crime." In *The Urban Predicament,* edited by William Gorham and Nathan Glazer. Washington, DC: Urban Institute.

Wright, Richard T., and Scott H. Decker. 1997. *Armed Robbers in Action*. Boston: Northeastern University Press.

Zimring, Franklin E. 1972. "The Medium Is the Message: Firearm Calibre as a Determinant of Death from Assault." *Journal of Legal Studies* 1: 97–124.

———. 2007. *The Great American Crime Decline*. New York: Oxford University Press.

Zimring, Franklin E., and James Zuehl. 1986. "Victim Injury and Death in Urban Robbery: A Chicago Study." *Journal of Legal Studies* 15(1): 1–40.

CHAPTER 5

DOMESTIC VIOLENCE

DENISE A. HINES

DOMESTIC violence is commonly conceptualized as a pattern of behaviors involving physical, psychological, and/or sexual abuse between two people currently or previously involved in an intimate relationship. Domestic violence researchers typically define each of these components in their own way and have yet to come to a consensus on the behaviors that constitute each (Malley-Morrison and Hines 2004; Hines and Malley-Morrison 2005). However, the subtype of domestic violence that is usually brought to the attention of authorities is physical assault, and most studies and policies concerning domestic violence concentrate on this type of abuse.

Domestic violence against women is a major social concern, and educational and treatment efforts are widespread in the United States. Feminist advocacy movements of the 1970s brought domestic violence out of the home and into the public eye. It soon became viewed as an issue that researchers, the public, and the criminal justice system had to take more seriously. The first systematic study of domestic violence, *The Violent Home,* was published by Richard J. Gelles in 1974. It addressed such issues as the prevalence and possible causes of domestic violence. This was shortly followed by the first National Family Violence Survey in 1975 (Straus, Gelles, and Steinmetz 1980), a population-based, nationwide study of the extent of family violence in the United States.

Around the same time, grassroots efforts by feminist battered women's advocates led to the opening of the first battered women's shelter, despite widespread public and governmental resistance (Straus 1980). With the spread of shelters, the public stereotype that domestic violence was a problem of the poor, mentally ill, and socially deviant began to fade. Domestic violence became a major social concern not only for researchers and advocates, but for government and the public. Throughout the next two decades, state laws on domestic violence proliferated at a rapid rate that continues to this day. Federal protection occurred in 1994, when the federal Violence Against Women Act was enacted. It provided women with broad protections against violence in their homes and communities. The Act was extended and expanded each time it came up for renewal, in 1998, 2002, and 2005 (Buzawa and Buzawa 2003).

Although there has certainly been much progress in research and policy making surrounding domestic violence, there are still some major problems and contentious issues within the field. Essentially, the field is split into three camps: those who feel that at the heart of all domestic violence is men's need to dominate and control women, those who feel that male dominance does not play a major role in domestic violence and that it is much more complex and often involves women who perpetrate domestic violence, and those who try to resolve this schism. Current policy is based on the first notion; however, much of the empirical research supports the second notion. Thus, what we often find in the field is that our policies do not reflect what we empirically know about domestic violence, and therefore, our policies do not fully or even adequately address the problem. While many of those who experience domestic violence in their lives have certainly benefited from the widespread recognition and acceptance of their problem, there is still much work to be done to adequately address the needs of all people who experience domestic violence.

Our empirical knowledge about domestic violence comes from several major data sources, in addition to the hundreds of studies that have been conducted on a more localized level. The major data sources include the *National Crime Victimization Survey* (*NCVS*) (e.g., Catalano 2006), the National Family Violence Surveys (NFVS) (e.g., Straus and Gelles 1990), and the National Violence Against Women Survey (NVAWS) (e.g., Tjaden and Thoennes 2000). Sponsored by the Bureau of Justice Statistics, the *NCVS* collects victimization data (whether reported to the police or not) twice each year through a standardized interview from a sample of approximately 100,000 individuals living in approximately 50,000 households. The households are rotated every three years, and the *NCVS* has been ongoing since 1972, but was redesigned in the early 1990s to more adequately address domestic violence and sexual assault. Questions related to domestic violence include: "Has anyone attacked or threatened you in any of these ways: (a) with any weapon, for instance, a gun or knife; (b) with anything like a baseball bat, frying pan, scissors, or stick; (c) by something thrown, such as a rock or bottle?" There are also questions about being grabbed, punched, choked or threatened, or raped (or attempted rape), or whether anyone committed any other form of sexual attack or unwanted sexual act against the respondent. If respondents indicate that any of these incidents occurred, they are then asked who the perpetrator was. If the perpetrator was a (ex-)husband or wife or (ex-)boyfriend or girlfriend, the act is considered an instance of domestic violence (Catalano 2007).

The NFVS takes a different approach. These national population-based surveys have been conducted three times: in 1975 (2,143 families), in 1985 (8,145 families), and in 1992 (1,970 families). In contrast to the *NCVS*, these surveys are not crime-based. People are asked to participate in a survey on conflict resolution in families, not on criminal victimization. Thus the survey is framed completely differently. For example, the directions of the survey instrument, the Conflict Tactics Scales (CTS), include these words: "No matter how well a couple gets along, there are times when they disagree, get annoyed with the other person, or just have spats or fights because they're in a bad mood or tired or for some other reason. They also use many different ways of trying to settle their differences. I'm going to read some things that you and your partner might do when you have an argument. I would like you to tell me how many times in the past 12 months you and your partner did each of these things." The CTS addresses behaviors such as talking out the issue, yelling and screaming, slapping, punching, beating up, and using a knife or gun. All items that refer to physical aggression are considered domestic violence items, and they are divided into minor (e.g., slapping, grabbing, pushing) and severe (i.e., those that have a greater likelihood of causing an injury: punching, kicking, beating up) physical aggression (Straus and Gelles 1990).

The NVAWS was a national telephone survey administered between November 1995 and May 1996 to a representative sample of 8,000 women and 8,000 men in the United States. Respondents were asked to participate in a study of crime and personal safety. Multiple, behaviorally specific questions, similar to the items on the CTS, were used to screen respondents for rape, physical assault, and stalking victimization. Respondents who endorsed any of these items were subsequently asked detailed questions about the victimization incident, such as the identity and relationship of the perpetrator, the frequency and duration of the violence, and the extent and nature of injuries they sustained (Tjaden and Thoennes 2000).

Information specific to the field of domestic violence can be found in several scholarly journals that either focus on this issue or have a large percentage of their articles that deal with it, including the *Journal of Family Violence, Violence and Victims*, the *Journal of Interpersonal Violence, Violence Against Women, Aggressive Behavior*, and *Aggression and Violent Behavior*. Overall, some of the major conclusions of forty years of research in this area include the following:

- Exact prevalence rates are difficult to establish. The highest rates come from studies that use the CTS and frame the problem in terms of family conflict. However, these studies are subject to much criticism because they continually find equal rates of violence by men and women.
- Domestic violence against women is still a major social concern, although rates have been steadily declining since the 1970s.
- Domestic violence against men is an unrecognized social problem, and unlike domestic violence against women, there has been no decline in domestic violence against men since the 1970s.

- Major policy changes began to occur in the late 1970s due to feminist advocacy, and laws have continually developed and changed. They are typically based on a feminist model that conceptualizes domestic violence as men's need to control and dominate women, even though empirical research shows that this conceptualization has major flaws.
- Treatment for men who perpetrate domestic violence is also based on a feminist model, and there is no evidence that such treatment works. Nonetheless, these treatment models are typically ordered by courts and mandated to be feminist-based according to state laws. No other treatment options are available for men who are arrested and court-ordered for batterer intervention treatment.
- Batterer intervention programs assume that men are the perpetrators; therefore, treatment for women who perpetrate domestic violence is woefully lacking.

This chapter has five sections. The first discusses data on the prevalence of domestic violence and trends over time. The second discusses five major analytical frameworks that have been employed to understand domestic violence: patriarchy theory, systems theory, alcoholism, personality dysfunction, and ecological models. The third discusses criminal justice system policies: mandatory arrest, no-drop policies, protective orders, and batterer treatment programs. The fourth discusses female batterers and distinctive problems they raise for law enforcement and treatment policies. The last discusses policy implications of current knowledge.

I. Prevalence of Domestic Violence

The *National Crime Victimization Survey,* the National Family Violence Survey, and the National Violence Against Women Survey provide very different estimates of the prevalence of domestic violence. The *NCVS* data show that 3.8 per 1,000 women sustained a physical assault from an intimate partner in 2004. This represents nearly a two-thirds decline from 1993, when 9.8 per 1,000 women sustained domestic violence. By contrast, 1.6 per 1,000 men sustained a physical assault from an intimate partner in 1993, and in 2004, 1.3 per 1,000 men did (Catalano 2006). Data from the *NCVS* represent only those incidents of domestic violence that were deemed criminal by the survey respondent. Thus, the *NCVS* provides the lowest rates of domestic violence of all major studies because most people do not consider violence perpetrated against them by family members to be criminal, particularly if it is by a woman (Straus 2004). The NFVS frames the study of domestic violence around issues of family conflict, and these surveys show much higher rates: 11.6 percent of men used some type of violence against their female partners, most of which was minor (e.g., slapping, shoving, pushing), and 3.4 percent used severe

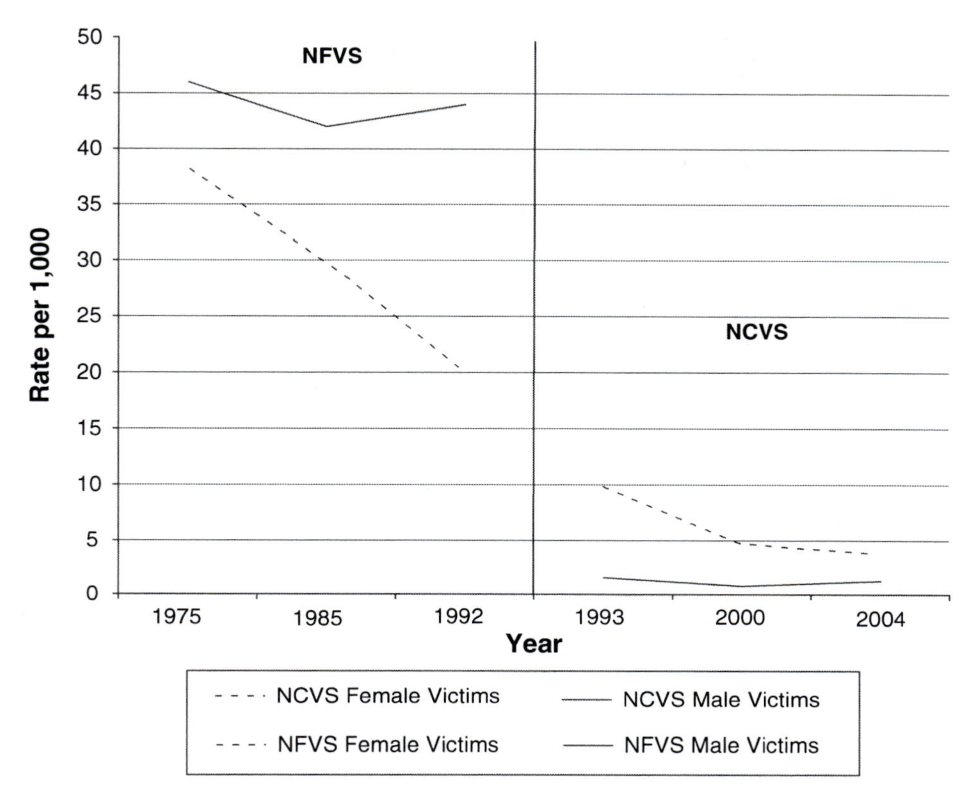

Figure 5.1. Trends in domestic violence, 1975–2004.

Note: The *NFVS* was conducted three times (1975, 1985, 1992). The results presented are for severe violence victimization only. In 1993 the *NCVS* changed its methodology for surveying domestic violence; therefore, results prior to 1993 are not comparable to the current *NCVS*.

violence, which was defined as violence that had a high likelihood of causing an injury (e.g., beating up, punching, using a knife or gun). In addition, 12.4 percent of women used some type of violence against their male partners, and 4.8 percent used severe violence (Straus and Gelles 1986).

Despite differing methodologies, the three NFVS were similar to the *NCVS* in that they also showed declines in rates of physical assault against female partners but consistent rates of physical assaults against male partners. The NFVS showed that between 1975 and 1985, there was a 27 percent decrease in the rate of severe violence perpetrated by male partners, culminating in a projected national incidence of 1.8 million female victims of severe violence in 1985. By contrast, there was no decline in rates of severe violence perpetrated by female partners: The projected national prevalence of severe violence sustained by male partners at both time periods was 2.6 million (Straus and Gelles 1986).

Figure 5.1 displays the domestic violence prevalence data over time for both the *NCVS* and the NFVS. The NFVS was conducted three times, and only the severe violence victimization data are shown. For the *NCVS*, only data from 1993 on are displayed because the survey questions regarding domestic violence were revised beginning with the 1993 survey to better assess domestic violence. Although both surveys show declines in domestic violence for female victims, there is little evidence of decline in domestic violence for male victims. Moreover, the rates for the *NCVS* are substantially lower than those for the NFVS. These differences are due to the different contexts in which the surveys are presented (i.e., crime surveys versus family conflict surveys).

A final source of information on domestic violence rates comes from the NVAWS. According to the 1995–96 NVAWS, 1.8 percent of women and 0.8 percent of men were victims of physical assaults from a current or former intimate partner within the prior 12 months (Tjaden and Thoennes 2000). These NVAWS rates are approximately five to six times as great as the *NCVS*, but are one-sixth to one-fifteenth the rate of the NFVS. The reason for the intermediate rates is that the NVAWS used a methodology that was similar to that used for the *NCVS* (e.g., respondents were told they were being interviewed about personal safety issues and their perception of male violence) but used a measure of domestic violence that was based on the NFVS (i.e., Conflict Tactics Scales).

The prevalence rates reported in all of these national studies show that despite the apparent decline in rates of physical assault against female partners, domestic violence continues to be a major social problem. Moreover, the steady rates of domestic violence against male partners over the past 30 years show that this is a social problem we have done little to address.

II. Contextual and Causal Mechanisms: Major Theoretical Perspectives

Several major theoretical perspectives guide research on domestic violence. Some individual-level predictors that have found considerable empirical support are family-of-origin violence, alcohol abuse, and personality dysfunction. Researchers have also been concerned with how societal structures, neighborhood conditions, socioeconomic status, stressful situations, and family dynamics contribute to domestic violence. Theories that address these variables are reviewed next, although this discussion is not exhaustive of all theoretical perspectives.

A. Patriarchy Theory

Patriarchy theory dominates policy making on domestic violence (Dutton and Corvo 2006). The cause of domestic violence, patriarchal theorists hold, is the gendered structure of society. Men have economic, political, social, and occupational power over women, and this power structure is reflected in intimate heterosexual relationships. Men use violence strategically to maintain their dominant status over women and have been socialized to believe that violence against women to maintain dominance is justified (e.g., Dobash and Dobash 1979). Thus all domestic violence is a result of men operating within a global patriarchal system that denies equal rights to women and legitimizes violence against women (Hammer 2003).

There is limited empirical support for this theoretical perspective. In a meta-analysis of studies investigating domestic violence against women and the male partner's patriarchal ideology (Sugarman and Frankel 1996), the only component of patriarchal ideology that consistently predicted wife assault was the perpetrator's attitude toward violence, which is not necessarily a component of patriarchal ideology. A more recent meta-analysis found that traditional sex role ideology and domestic violence against women were only moderately associated (Stith et al. 2004). Moreover, there is abundant evidence that contradicts patriarchy theory, including the consistent findings that women physically assault their partners at rates comparable to men (Archer 2000), that the majority of women's use of domestic violence is not self-defensive (Hines and Malley-Morrison 2001), that the overwhelming majority of men do not think that physically assaulting their female partner is acceptable (Simon et al. 2001), and that the rates of domestic violence in gay and lesbian couples are at least as high as in heterosexual couples (Hines and Malley-Morrison 2005).

B. Systems Theory

Systems theorists argue that domestic violence takes place within a dyadic system and that the system works in such a way as to maintain those dysfunctional interactional styles. Interactions within couples are bidirectional, and both members interact in ways that promote domestic violence. Thus domestic violence is not simply one member of the couple abusing the other, but is a function of the stresses of everyday life in which conflicts arise, negative interactions escalate, and violence is sometimes a response (e.g., (Giles-Sims 1983). Systems theory is supported by empirical findings that many domestic violence situations are bidirectional (e.g., Stets and Straus 1990) and that there is assortative mating for antisocial behaviors (e.g., Capaldi, Kim, and Shortt 2004; Moffitt et al. 2001; Serbin et al. 2004).

Systems conceptual frameworks have been valuable in highlighting the complexity of domestic violence and have led to the development of effective therapeutic techniques for domestic violence that address both members of the couple (Holtzworth-Munroe et al. 1995; O'Leary, Heyman, and Neidig 1999; Stith, Rosen, and McCollum 2003). However, they have consistently been challenged by patriarchal theorists as frameworks that blame the victim (i.e., the female partner) and put her in danger (Bograd 1984). Thus, therapeutic techniques based on systems frameworks are precluded under most states' laws.

C. Alcohol Abuse

Abuse of alcohol is a consistent predictor of domestic violence. This link has primarily been demonstrated among clinical samples of male batterers (e.g., Fals-Stewart 2003), but has also been shown in community samples of men (e.g., Leonard 1993) and men and women in convenience (e.g., Hines and Straus 2007) and population-based (e.g., Caetano, Schafer, and Cunradi 2001) samples. The model that currently receives the most empirical support to explain this association is a mediational model, in which certain dispositions of the drinker may influence the association between alcohol abuse and domestic violence perpetration. Specifically, people with elevated levels of antisocial personality traits display an increased likelihood of perpetrating domestic violence while drinking (e.g., Fals-Stewart, Leonard, and Birchler 2005; Hines and Straus 2007; Murphy et al. 2001).

The influence of alcohol abuse on domestic violence is particularly striking when one considers treatment studies of male alcoholics who are also batterers. When male alcoholics stop using alcohol through the administration of empirically based alcohol treatment programs, their rates of domestic violence perpetration decrease significantly and mirror those of population-based samples (O'Farrell et al. 2003). This finding demonstrates the importance of screening for and treating alcoholism in male batterers. In fact, alcoholism treatment has a stronger effect on reducing recidivism rates for battering than do treatment programs specifically designed to treat battering.

D. Personality Dysfunction

There is also empirical support for the prediction of domestic violence perpetration by personality dysfunction. Dutton et al. (1994) found that several personality dysfunctions—borderline personality, antisocial personality, aggressive-sadistic personality, and passive-aggressive personality—are related to domestic violence perpetration by men. They theorize that this association is due to long-standing attachment disorders that have their roots in paternal rejection, exposure to abuse in childhood, and a "failure of protective attachment." These men seem to have developed a "fearful-angry" attachment style, which causes them to lash out violently toward their female partners during confrontations and perceived separations.

Holtzworth-Munroe and Stuart (1994) have also found that personality dysfunction predicts some male battering and theorized that there were three types of male batterers. Violence by *family-only batterers* results from a combination of stress and low-level risk factors, such as childhood exposure to marital violence and poor relationship skills. On occasion, during escalating conflicts, these men may engage in aggression that typically does not escalate. *Borderline-dysphoric batterers* come from a background involving parental abuse and rejection, which leads them to have difficulty forming stable and trusting attachments to an intimate partner. Instead, they are highly dependent on, yet fearful of losing, their female partner. Consistent with this attachment style and their borderline personality traits, these batterers are jealous, lack adequate relationship skills, and have hostile attitudes toward women. *Generally violent-antisocial batterers* resemble other antisocial, aggressive men. They have experienced high levels of family-of-origin violence and associate with deviant peers. They are impulsive, lack interpersonal skills, have hostile attitudes toward women, and view violence as acceptable. Their domestic violence is part of their general engagement in antisocial behavior, and their female partners are readily accessible victims, but not their only victims.

Findings of personality dysfunction among male batterers suggest that treatment modalities addressing these underlying issues would lead to improvements in violent behavior. Moreover, the Holtzworth-Munroe and Stuart (1994) typology points to different prevention and intervention programs depending on the type of batterer. If we ignore the existence of different types of batterers, we will not be effective in ameliorating domestic violence because our treatment programs will be based on the notion that all batterers are alike.

E. Ecological Models

Increasingly, domestic violence researchers embrace an ecological model (e.g., Gelles 1998; Hines and Malley-Morrison 2005; Dutton 1985). This perspective developed because of the recognition that no one theory can explain all domestic violence, and therefore it is necessary to view domestic violence within a set of nested levels of influences. The *microsystem* consists of the individual's immediate setting (e.g., the home). The *mesosystem* consists of relations among the settings in which the individual is involved (e.g., between home and work). The *exosystem* includes the larger neighborhood, the mass media, and state agencies. Finally, the *macrosystem* consists of broad cultural factors (Bronfenbrenner 1979). Belsky (1993) and Hines and Malley-Morrison (2005) argue that it is also important to consider biological characteristics that exist even before birth and that individuals bring to every interaction.

An ecological perspective conveys the notion that to understand how someone may commit domestic violence, we need to understand the genetic endowments of the individual, the microsystem in which he or she grew up, the microsystem in which he or she is currently embedded, characteristics of the neighborhood within which he or she functions (including the availability of social services and the criminal justice system), and the larger society that either condones or condemns domestic violence (Hines and Malley-Morrison 2005). Inherent in an ecological perspective is the notion that to properly prevent and intervene in domestic violence, the treatment modality must match the level of the ecological model.

III. Law Enforcement Policies

The primacy of the criminal justice system in domestic violence cases has to do with the way it is structured: The police provide a free service 24 hours a day, seven days a week, and their responsibilities include serving and protecting the public. They are the obvious source for help for people in the midst of a domestic dispute. The police are highly visible authority figures and usually provide a quick response to allegations of assault (Buzawa and Buzawa 2003). In the 1970s the criminal justice system began undergoing a major overhaul in how it addressed issues of domestic violence. These changes resulted from criticisms by the feminist community about how the police typically handled domestic violence calls, which were relegated to the bottom of the call list and addressed only after other, "more important" calls had been dealt with (Ford 1983; Martin 1979; Berk and Loseke 1980–81). Because most crimes against women happened in the home, the perception that the police essentially ignored domestic violence was viewed by feminists as a sign that the criminal justice system was sexist (Buzawa and Buzawa 2003).

Because feminist advocates were the major proponents of change within the criminal justice system, current criminal justice policies and procedures are rooted in feminist theory and exemplified in the Duluth Model, which stresses that male battering is a calculated choice by men to exert their power and control over women (Pence and Paymar 1983). Although there is evidence that the criminal justice system is currently more sensitive to cases of domestic violence than in earlier times (Buzawa and Buzawa 2003), there are serious problems in how domestic violence cases are handled. I discuss four major interventions—mandatory arrest, no-drop policies, protective orders, and batterer intervention programs—for cases of domestic violence, when and why they were instituted, and the evidence concerning their efficacy.

A. Mandatory Arrest

The policy of mandatory arrest (or pro-arrest) quickly became widespread following the release of the initial results of the Minneapolis Domestic Violence Experiment (Sherman and Berk 1984). Over the course of a year and a half, 51 patrol officers in two Minneapolis precincts were randomly assigned to respond to cases of domestic violence in one of three ways: separate the parties, advise the couple of alternatives, or arrest the offender. Of the 330 domestic violence cases included in the study, recidivism rates were lowest in the arrest group. Ten percent of the arrested offenders reoffended, compared with 24 percent of the separation group and 19 percent of the alternatives group.

Based on these initial results, Sherman and Berk (1984) argued that arrest had by far the best deterrent effect of all alternatives, and political activists subsequently lobbied for mandatory or preferred arrest policies. The number of police jurisdictions that changed their policies to pro-arrest policies tripled within one year, and more than one-third of police departments changed their policies in response to this study and ensuing media coverage (Cohn and Sherman 1987).

Various researchers subsequently pointed out the flaws of the Minnesota Domestic Violence Experiment. The most pressing problem was that it was a preliminary study that took place in only two precincts in Minneapolis, and the results were not necessarily generalizable across the country, or even everywhere in Minneapolis. A second problem was that officers had advance knowledge of the response they were supposed to make and therefore could reclassify a domestic violence case if they did not wish to make the assigned response. This reclassification happened an unknown number of times, and it is not known what would have happened to the results if officers had strictly followed the study protocol. A third problem was that officers sometimes gave a "treatment" that they were not supposed to; this happened in 17 percent of cases, all of which were dropped from the study and not analyzed. These dropped cases may have differed substantially from the cases that were analyzed; after all, they led officers to deviate from the mandates of the study. A final problem was that only 49 percent of the victims agreed to be interviewed to establish recidivism rates (Binder and Meeker 1988; Lempert 1989). This is particularly significant given that later analyses showed that the deterrent effect of arrest was found only when using victim data (Gartin 1991). It is likely that victims who were not revictimized composed the majority of victims who participated in the follow-up interview; they could be located more easily, would have had less ambivalence coming in to be interviewed about their domestic violence problems, or were happy with the police response.

These caveats were ignored. Advocates for battered women pushed for legislation that mandated arrest, and much of that legislation continues to be enforced today.

However, because of the methodological problems and widespread policy effects of this study, the U.S. National Institute of Justice funded five replications (Buzawa and Buzawa 2003). These five studies found that arrest had only a short-term overall effect on recidivism rates and that this effect was no longer apparent one year following the initial arrest. Moreover, arrest worked only for those offenders who had something to lose—for example, their marriage, job, or home—as a result of being arrested. Arrest had no impact on offenders who were unemployed, were not married, did not own a home, or had been arrested previously (Dunford, Huizinga, and Elliott 1989; Sherman et al. 1992; Hirschel et al. 1991; Berk et al. 1992; Pate and Hamilton 1992). Thus the deterrence effects of arrest worked only against those who had a low likelihood of reoffending anyway but did little to deter the most dangerous, chronic offenders.

One particularly disconcerting finding from the Milwaukee replication showed that domestic violence recidivism *increased* for arrested black men but decreased for arrested white men (Sherman et al. 1992). Using these data, Mills (2003) concluded that arresting all male domestic violence offenders would prevent 2,504 acts of domestic violence against white women but cause 5,409 black women to sustain additional acts of domestic violence.

Nonetheless, proponents of mandatory arrest still argue that it is a necessary policy. Their argument centers around four issues. First, because these women are basically trapped in their relationships they may not be able to express their preference for arrest when the police arrive. Second, they may not understand the danger they are in. Third, arrest allows the victim to consider her options, such as going to a shelter or filing for a protective order. Fourth, arrest puts the responsibility for punishment where it belongs, on the state, and prevents the victim from resorting to vigilante justice (Stark 1996).

Others argue that relieving victims of their decision-making power by mandating arrest is ultimately patronizing to battered women (e.g., Buzawa and Buzawa 2003; Mills 2003). Often victims simply want the violence to stop or fear the consequences that may accompany arrest, such as retaliation by their batterer or loss of his income. In addition, victims might be deterred from calling the police in the future or obtaining medical help for injuries if they fear that their abuser might be arrested. Thus true victim empowerment would be achieved by giving victims some control over the outcome of police intervention, as occurs in nondomestic assault situations. Of course, there are situations in which arrest is indicated; however, it is only one of several alternatives that should be considered.

Implicit in many of the arguments for mandatory arrest is the notion that all battering incidents are the same. However, not all batterers are the same, not all battering incidents are the same, and not all victims are the same. Thus having one overarching policy that is supposed to be based on what victims really want ignores the complexity of the situation. Some victims merely want the police to stop the abuser and take him or her away to cool off; some want their abuser arrested. Some fear, probably rightfully, that if their abuser is arrested, he or she will exact revenge. It is important to consider these individual issues in these battering incidents.

B. No-Drop Policies

Mandatory arrest policies were instituted at a time when the nation was expanding its "war on drugs" and prosecutors were pressured to increase the prosecution of drug crimes. Thus mandatory arrest policies for domestic violence had some consequences that initially were unanticipated but probably should have been. Because police officers now had to arrest domestic violence offenders, more and more cases were referred to the prosecutor, without concomitant increases in budgets or manpower to handle such cases. The already overstrained systems were on the verge of breaking because of these additional domestic violence cases (Balos and Trotsky 1988; Cahn 1992).

One study in Milwaukee showed that backloads of cases, time to disposition, and pretrial crime increased after mandatory arrest policies were instituted, whereas convictions and victim satisfaction with how prosecutors handled cases decreased (Davis, Smith, and Nickles 1998). Without adequate resources, prosecutors' offices often were unable to handle effectively the increase in domestic violence caseloads, and the typical response was to reduce charges dramatically. This practice was criticized because it subverted what mandatory arrest laws were trying to accomplish (Davis and Smith 1995). However, prosecutors saw their actions as reasonable, especially given the noncooperation of many victims. In 60 to 80 percent of domestic violence cases, victims ultimately repudiate the case because they want to drop the charges; often they refuse to appear in court as a witness (e.g., Ford 1983; Rebovich 1996).

Because domestic violence cases were getting dismissed by the prosecutors' offices or dropped by victims, states began to enact "no-drop" policies, which effectively limited the discretion of victims and prosecutors. Under no-drop policies, prosecutors cannot drop cases unless there are documented failures to find evidence that a crime occurred. In addition, if the victim wants to prosecute the prosecutor must follow the victim's wishes. For victims, these policies imposed restrictions that limited their ability to drop charges, and in some jurisdictions, if a victim refuses to testify in court he or she can be subpoenaed and held in contempt of court (Buzawa and Buzawa 2003).

Although these no-drop policies sound strict, prosecutors nonetheless find them to be flexible. Many jurisdictions screen out cases prior to instituting the no-drop policy, and fewer than 20 percent of jurisdictions reported that these policies had any severe effects on how they handled cases (Rebovich 1996).

Studies of sites that instituted no-drop policies have shown some positive impact. For example, in Washington, DC, the prosecution rates of domestic violence cases began to approximate those of nondomestic misdemeanor cases, and some cities seem to have experienced a decrease in recidivism rates (Epstein 1999). However, limited resources for prosecutors' offices to handle such cases, in addition to continued victim noncooperation, still pose problems for the effective institution of such policies (Buzawa and Buzawa 2003; Wills 1997). Another documented problem is the issue of victim "disempowerment." Studies have shown that women who were forced to prosecute, even though they felt that it would be dangerous, were more likely to be revictimized than those who were not forced to prosecute (Buzawa et al. 1999).

C. Protective Orders

Changes to protective orders are a major innovation in the criminal justice system's handling of domestic violence cases. Prior to the 1970s women typically had to be divorcing their husband if they hoped to get a restraining order (Chaudhuri and Daly 1992), and judges used restraining orders sparingly. The situation has changed drastically, however; restraining orders are now much easier to get and are probably the instruments most used to combat domestic violence. Battered women's advocates were largely behind this movement to make restraining orders easier to obtain in an effort to circumvent the perceived reluctance of police, prosecutors, and judges to deal with domestic violence. Moreover, under the federal Violence Against Women Act, protection orders must be fully enforced nationwide, no matter what the original jurisdiction; they must be accessible and affordable; and penalties were established for individuals who cross state lines to continue abusive behavior (Buzawa and Buzawa 2003).

Although thousands of women and many men apply for protective orders every year, only about half of female applicants receive them, primarily because they do not follow through with the process (Malecha et al. 2003). One difference between women who complete the process and those who do not is that women who drop the process are more likely currently to be in a relationship and living with their batterer three months after their initial application for the order. These are the women most likely to continue being abused (Malecha et al. 2003).

The use of protective orders has several advantages. First, they are flexible in the provisions that can be imposed, and judges have discretion to impose provisions they feel are necessary for each individual case. Second, because they are designed to operate prospectively they can prevent future violence, particularly in relationships where violence is in the early stages. Third, they provide police with tangible means to arrest an offender: violations of protective orders are subject to warrantless arrests in most states, and, in some, repeated violations are considered a felony. Fourth, the police may be motivated to take action in domestic violence cases involving restraining orders, even if only because they cannot then be accused of not following procedures that ultimately led to victim injury. With a restraining order in hand, police know that they can and must arrest. Fifth, obtaining a restraining order may empower the victim, who now has control over the home, possessions, and children, and the ability to call the authorities if the offender violates the restraining order. Sixth, protective orders cost less than other means of dealing with domestic violence. For the victim, they may prevent future abuse without the necessity of going through a lengthy trial or having the batterer incarcerated and thus unable to make child support payments. For the offender, a protective order does not jeopardize employment. For the courts, it takes less time and money to prevent future crime than to arrest and prosecute a crime that has already occurred. Seventh, relief from violence is quicker; in contrast to the prosecution process, which may take weeks or months, restraining orders can be obtained immediately, and the preliminary hearing can be scheduled within a day or two after the complaint is filed. Finally, violation of a protective order can be useful for the prosecutor in convicting an offender, especially if other physical evidence and victim cooperation are not forthcoming (Buzawa and Buzawa 2003).

Nonetheless, protective orders have several disadvantages. Some judges are reluctant to issue them because protective orders can impinge on the defendant's constitutional rights without due process of law. This is especially so with ex parte protective orders because the defendant is not present to defend himself or herself. A second problem is that restraining orders must be initiated and pursued by the victim, which in some states requires filing fees and may involve contact with unsupportive court personnel. When, in addition, batterers threaten the victim with retaliation, obtaining a restraining order is a large obstacle for the victim (Buzawa and Buzawa 2003).

Several studies show that restraining orders give victims a sense of empowerment, but that this empowerment may be illusory because restraining orders do not seem to protect victims from repeat abuse (e.g., Klein 1996; Grau, Fagan, and Wexler 1985; Harrell, Smith, and Newmark 1993; Harrell and Smith 1996; Keilitz, Hannaford, and Efkemann 1997; Mears et al. 2001). These studies also show that men who are served with restraining orders tend to be the most seriously violent offenders and have criminal histories. These are also the men who most likely violate a restraining order. Thus restraining orders, like mandatory arrest policies, do not seem to work well for the most serious offenders.

D. Batterer Intervention Programs

One of the main diversionary programs mandated by judges for male batterers is completion of a batterer intervention program. These have several goals, including helping the batterer take responsibility for his behavior, changing the batterer's attitudes toward violence, eliminating violent behavior toward his partner, and protecting the victim. Most states have developed a number of mandates for these programs, the most controversial of which include (a) provision of group intervention and avoidance of both individual and couples' interventions, and (b) inclusion of issues of power and control in program content (Hamby 1998). These provisions are controversial because there is little evidence that group intervention is better than individual or couples' therapy, and there is very little evidence that using power and control issues as the focus of program content is an effective way to reach the goals of such programs. In fact, current evidence suggests that these programs do not work (e.g., Davis, Taylor, and Maxwell 1998; Feder and Forde 2000).

State-mandated program models are organized around the feminist notion that battering is a social problem stemming from the patriarchal organization of society. The male batterer is seen as intentionally committing violence to maintain a patriarchal structure in which he is superior and the woman is inferior within the relationship (Hamby 1998). Most programs that focus on power and control issues use the Duluth Model, developed in Duluth, Minnesota, by a small group of battered women's activists (Pence and Paymar 1983). The model is based on Pence and Paymar's experience with four male batterers and five female victims who completed the Duluth program. The model assumes that the sole cause for all battering is the batterers' need to control and dominate their partners. This issue of power and control is seen as an exclusively male phenomenon, and all female violence is viewed as self-defensive. Changing this dynamic is the key to changing batterers' behavior. The facilitator of the program is encouraged to use slavery as an analogy for how male batterers maintain control over their female partners, and all other risk factors for domestic violence (e.g., alcohol abuse, personality disorders, anger control issues, impulsivity, communication skills deficits, couple interaction styles, stress) are viewed as excuses. Program developers consider any psychological diagnosis of the male batterer to involve a rationalization for his behavior and thus inaccurate (Pence and Paymar 1983).

Studies of the effectiveness of Duluth-type batterer intervention programs show that they do not work. There are no differences in recidivism rates or attitudes toward women and domestic violence between male batterers who attend these programs and those who do not (e.g., Davis, Taylor, and Maxwell 1998; Feder and Forde 2000). Moreover, attrition rates of men who attend an initial batterer intervention program session have been shown to be between 40 and 60 percent, even when attendance is mandated as a condition of probation and failure to attend can result in incarceration (Buttell and Carney 2002).

Dutton and Corvo (2006) argue that by taking an adversarial and judgmental stance against batterers (and by disbelieving or dismissing batterers' often valid claims of alcoholism, mental illness, and mutuality of abuse), Duluth treatment providers preclude any opportunity to form a therapeutic bond with the batterers, which is the strongest predictor of successful treatment outcome. Thus it is not surprising that Duluth Model treatment does not work and leads to high attrition rates.

Programs that focus on psychological issues, anger problems, communication problems, impulse control issues, and couple interaction problems are often shunned by domestic violence advocates and prohibited by state laws. However, there is evidence that such intervention programs work for male batterers and their female partners. For example, couples' therapy that addresses underlying negative interactions that precede violence has shown positive results (O'Leary, Heyman, and Neidig 1999; Stith, Rosen, and McCollum 2003). Treatments based on psychological and family systems models have also been shown to be more effective than the Duluth Model (e.g., Babcock, Green, and Robie 2004). Even programs that focus on the treatment of alcoholism (without addressing issues of battering) have shown substantially greater reductions in domestic violence among alcoholic batterers than do Duluth Model programs (e.g., O'Farrell et al. 2003).

Despite such evidence, batterer intervention programs that focus on power and control are still mandated by state laws as programs of choice for batterers, whereas programs that are effective are shunned or, worse, specifically prohibited. For example, Georgia law prohibits any batterer intervention program that links "causes of violence to past experiences," includes "communication enhancement or anger management," addresses addiction, or has a systems theory focus (State of Georgia 2002). The rationale for such state prohibitions is that the Duluth Model guarantees a victim's safety. However, it makes no sense to assume that a program that does not work is better at protecting victims' safety than are programs that do work (Dutton and Corvo 2006).

IV. Female Perpetrators

The ideology that guides criminal justice policies and procedures for domestic violence has made the issue of female perpetrators a thorny one. According to the Duluth Model, female perpetrators do not and cannot exist because domestic violence is an issue of power and control of which only men are capable. Therefore, when women have been arrested for domestic violence the police have been faulted for instituting a "backlash" against mandated policies (Mills 2003), and if women are prosecuted there is no place for them to receive treatment because current batterer intervention programs assume they do not exist. This is significant because about 15 percent of people arrested for domestic violence are women (Mills 2003).

Despite the Duluth Model's insistence that female perpetrators do not exist, there is much evidence that they do and that most of their violence is not self-defensive. There is also an abundance of evidence that women can be the sole perpetrators of domestic violence and that much domestic violence is mutual (Hines and Malley-Morrison 2001), that the strongest predictor of one partner's violence is the other partner's violence, and that there is assortative mating for violent behavior (Capaldi, Kim, and Shortt 2004; Moffitt et al. 2001; Serbin et al. 2004). Thus there is an apparent discrepancy between research and policy on female perpetrators of domestic violence.

Some researchers have tried to resolve this discrepancy by arguing that women tend to engage in low-level violence that is often mutual with their partner, but that severe violence and control that can be labeled "intimate terrorism" is the domain of male batterers (e.g., Johnson 1995). However, several recent comprehensive population-based studies have cast serious doubt on this argument. These studies show that at least a substantial minority of all "intimate terrorists" are women (Ehrensaft, Moffitt, and Caspi 2004; Laroche 2005), who strike just as much fear in their male partner as male intimate terrorists do in their female partner (Laroche 2005). Moreover, there is evidence that a strong predictor of women's use of violence is a history of antisocial behavior from adolescence on (e.g., Ehrensaft, Cohen, and Johnson 2006; Moffitt et al. 2001; Capaldi, Kim, and Shortt 2004).

Why aren't arrest rates reflected in the research findings? The principal reason seems to be that the Duluth-type ideology has permeated police departments, with the result that men are disproportionately arrested for domestic violence, even when their violence is equivalent to that of women (Brown 2004). Another factor seems to be the institution of "primary aggressor" policies. These policies grew out of the mandatory arrest movement, when it was found that mandatory arrest resulted in an increased likelihood of dual arrest, principally because officers did not know who was at fault for the violence. Given that most violence is mutual, the officers were probably correct in arresting both partners, but "primary aggressor" policies were instituted to provide police with guidelines in determining which party was at fault. Backers of these policies wanted to reduce the number of women arrested for domestic violence; they felt that battered women were being arrested for defending themselves (Goldberg 1999, Nov. 23).

To learn how to identify the primary aggressor, officers typically undergo training that encourages them to consider these factors: relative age, height, and weight of the parties; criminal history of the parties; whether one of the parties is on probation for domestic violence; evidence of fear in one of the parties; whether injuries appear offensive or defensive; the relative seriousness of injuries; whether either party has a motive to lie; the relative strength and skill of the parties; whether one of the parties used alcohol or drugs; who called 911; who in the relationship poses the most danger; whether one party is more at risk for future harm; the demeanor of each party; whether there exists a protective order against one of the parties; and how detailed each parties' statement is (Strack n.d.). Many of these criteria would apply to the male party, regardless of whether he is the primary aggressor. In addition, guidelines sometimes encourage police to ask, "Have you ever called a battered women's hot line?" and "Has he hit you before?" (Goldberg 1999, Nov. 23). The mind-set behind such questions is that women are victims and men are perpetrators.

In addition, men face several internal and external barriers to seeking help from the criminal justice system. For example, men are not likely to seek help for issues that society deems non-normative or for which society deems they should be able to handle themselves (Addis and Mihalik 2003). Even when men who sustain domestic violence do overcome these internal barriers and call the police, they may experience significant external barriers. For example, some report that they, not their violent female partner, are arrested, prosecuted, and sentenced for being a batterer. Sometimes a male victim is required to enter a batterer intervention program, even if there is no evidence that he hit his female partner but substantial evidence that he had been injured by her (Hines, Brown, and Dunning 2007). Moreover, policies in some jurisdictions discourage the arrest of women as domestic violence offenders. For example, in Boulder, Colorado, male victims were three times as likely to be arrested during a dual arrest as were female victims (Jones and Belknap 1999). In Massachusetts, when the man was the victim an arrest was five times less likely than when a woman was a victim in a similar situation. In addition, sometimes officers made no arrest or arrested the man (Buzawa and Hotaling 2000).

V. Policy Implications

Current policies do not work well, principally because they are built on the faulty notion that *all* domestic violence is perpetrated by men who instrumentally and consciously choose to exhibit violently their power and control over their female partner. There are certainly plenty of domestic violence cases in which this happens; however, these cases are a small minority. Thus a one-size-fits-all policy for how we should deal with domestic violence is doomed to fail. Not all battering relationships and motives are the same, and if our policies do not recognize this, then the policies designed to help those involved in domestic violence may make the problem worse for some, as has been shown already with arrest policies (Sherman et al. 1992).

Policy makers in the criminal justice system need to pay attention to what research shows is driving domestic violence and what works in domestic violence prevention and intervention. In no other field is there such a schism between evidence and practice. As Dutton and Corvo (2006, p. 478) write:

> Against a national movement toward evidence-based practice and best-practice criteria for assessing program continuance, interventions with perpetrators of domestic violence remain immune to those evaluative criteria. The stranglehold on theory and policy development that the Duluth Model exerts confounds efforts to improve treatment. There is no rational reason for domestic violence to be viewed outside of the broad theoretical and professional frameworks used to analyze and respond to most contemporary behavioral and psychological problems.... No other area of established social welfare, criminal justice, public health, or behavioral intervention has such weak evidence in support of mandated practice.

Current laws and policies often make it impossible to deliver interventions or prevention models not consistent with the Duluth ideology. Even though current interventions are not effective, state policies prohibit the execution of effective practices. We need to change these policies so that we can move away from this unicausal model of domestic violence to one that considers the complex dynamics of the relationships in which domestic violence exists, the complex psychology of those who are violent, and the complex social systems in which domestic violence is embedded. Policy makers should embrace the multilevel ecological model and tailor their policies to the level that they are targeting for intervention or prevention.

It is also time to move away from the notion that there are distinct perpetrators and victims in domestic violence and accept that women can and do use aggression in their intimate relationships. Police are often forced to identify *the* victim and *the* perpetrator; however, the best designed studies show that, in at least half of domestic violence cases, both parties are violent. Thus it is time to realize that the roles of victim and perpetrator may be constantly shifting and that even in the context of a single argument these roles can shift.

The proponents of the Duluth Model that underlies all current policies should be congratulated for their initial movement to bring domestic violence into public awareness. However, it is time that they abandon their faulty ideology and stronghold on domestic violence policies and let effective prevention and intervention programs be put in place.

REFERENCES

Addis, Michael E., and James R. Mihalik. 2003. "Men, Masculinity, and the Contexts of Help Seeking." *American Psychologist* 58(1): 5–14.

Archer, John. 2000. "Sex Differences in Aggression between Heterosexual Couples: A Meta-Analytic Review." *Psychological Bulletin* 126(5): 651–80.

Babcock, Julia C., Charles E. Green, and Chet Robie. 2004. "Does Batterers' Treatment Work? A Meta-Analytic Review of Domestic Violence Treatment Outcome Research." *Clinical Psychology Review* 23(8): 1023–53.

Balos, Beverly, and Katie Trotsky. 1988. "Enforcement of the Domestic Abuse Act in Minnesota: A Preliminary Study." *Law and Inequality* 6(2/3): 83–125.

Belsky, Jay. 1993. "Etiology of Child Maltreatment: A Developmental-Ecological Approach." *Psychological Bulletin* 114(3): 413–34.

Berk, Richard A., Alec Campbell, Ruth Klap, and Bruce Western. 1992. "Bayesian Analysis of the Colorado Springs Spouse Abuse Experiment." *Criminal Law and Criminology* 83(1): 170–200.

Berk, Sarah F., and Donileen R. Loseke. 1980–81. "'Handling' Family Violence: Situational Determinants of Police Arrests in Domestic Disturbances." *Law and Society Review* 15: 317–46.

Binder, Arnold, and James Meeker. 1988. "Experiments as Reforms." *Journal of Criminal Justice* 16: 347–58.

Bograd, Michele. 1984. "Family Systems Approaches to Wife Battering." *American Journal of Orthopsychiatry* 54: 558–68.

Bronfenbrenner, Urie. 1979. *The Ecology of Human Development: Experiments by Nature and Design*. Cambridge, MA: Harvard University Press.

Brown, Grant A. 2004. "Gender as a Factor in the Response of the Law-Enforcement System to Violence against Partners." *Sexuality and Culture* 8(3–4): 1–139.

Buttell, Fred P., and Michelle M. Carney. 2002. "Psychological and Demographic Predictors of Attrition among Batterers Court Ordered into Treatment." *Social Work Research* 26(1): 31–42.

Buzawa, Eve S., and Carl G. Buzawa. 2003. *Domestic Violence: The Criminal Justice Response*. Thousand Oaks, CA: Sage.

Buzawa, Eve S., and Gerald Hotaling. 2000. *The Police Response to Domestic Violence Calls for Assistance in Three Massachusetts Towns*. Final report. Washington, DC: National Institute of Justice.

Buzawa, Eve S., Gerald Hotaling, Andrew Klein, and James Byrne. 1999. *Response to Domestic Violence in a Pro-Active Court Setting*. Final report. Washington, DC: National Institute of Justice.

Caetano, Raul, John Schafer, and Carol B. Cunradi. 2001. "Alcohol-related Intimate Partner Violence among White, Black, and Hispanic Couples in the United States." *Alcohol Research and Health* 25: 58–65.

Cahn, Naomi 1992. "Prosecuting Domestic Violence Crimes." In *Domestic Violence: The Changing Criminal Justice Response,* edited by Eve Schlesinger Buzawa and Carl G. Buzawa. Westwood, CT: Auburn House.

Capaldi, Deborah M., Hyoun K. Kim, and Joann W. Shortt. 2004. "Women's Involvement in Aggression in Young Adult Romantic Relationships." In *Aggression,*

Antisocial Behavior, and Violence among Girls, edited by Martha Putallaz and Karen L. Bierman. New York: Guilford.
Catalano, Shannan. 2006. "Intimate Partner Violence in the United States." http://www.ojp.usdoj.gov/bjs/intimate/ipv.htm.
———. 2007. "Intimate Partner Violence in the United States." http://www.ojp.usdoj.gov/bjs/intimate/ipv.htm.
Chaudhuri, Molly, and Kathleen Daly. 1992. "Do Restraining Orders Help? Battered Women's Experiences with Male Violence and Legal Process." In *Domestic Violence: The Changing Criminal Justice Response,* edited by Eve Schlesinger Buzawa and Carl G. Buzawa. Westwood, CT: Auburn House.
Cohn, Ellen G., and Lawrence W. Sherman. 1987. *Police Policy on Domestic Violence 1986: A National Survey.* Washington, DC: Crime Control Institute.
Davis, Robert C., and Barbara Smith. 1995. "Domestic Violence Reforms: Empty Promises of Fulfilled Expectations." *Crime and Delinquency* 41(4): 541–52.
Davis, Robert C., Barbara Smith, and Laura Nickles. 1998. "Prosecuting Domestic Violence Cases with Reluctant Victims: Assessing Two Novel Approaches in Milwaukee." In *Legal Interventions in Family Violence: Research Findings and Policy Implications.* Washington, DC: National Institute of Justice, American Bar Association.
Davis, Robert C., Bruce G. Taylor, and Christopher D. Maxwell. 1998. "Does Batterer Treatment Reduce Violence? A Randomized Experiment in Brooklyn." *Justice Quarterly* 18: 171–201.
Dobash, Rebecca E., and Russell P. Dobash. 1979. *Violence against Wives: A Case against the Patriarchy.* New York: Free Press.
Dunford, F. W., David Huizinga, and Delbert Elliott. 1989. *The Omaha Domestic Violence Police Experiment: Final Report to the National Institute of Justice and the City of Omaha.* Boulder, CO: Institute of Behavioral Science.
Dutton, Donald G. 1985. "An Ecologically Nested Theory of Male Violence towards Intimates." *International Journal of Women's Studies* 8(4): 404–13.
Dutton, Donald G., and Kenneth Corvo. 2006. "Transforming a Flawed Policy: A Call to Revive Psychology and Science in Domestic Violence Research and Practice." *Aggression and Violent Behavior* 11: 457–83.
Dutton, Donald G., Keith Saunders, Andrew J. Starzomski, and Kim Bartholomew. 1994. "Intimacy Anger and Insecure Attachment as Precursors of Abuse in Intimate Relationships." *Journal of Applied Social Psychology* 24(15): 1367–86.
Ehrensaft, Miriam K., Patricia Cohen, and Jeffrey G. Johnson. 2006. "Development of Personality Disorder Symptoms and the Risk of Partner Violence." *Journal of Abnormal Psychology* 115(3): 474–83.
Ehrensaft, Miriam K., Terrie E. Moffitt, and Avshalom Caspi. 2004. "Clinically Abusive Relationships in an Unselected Birth Cohort: Men's and Women's Participation and Developmental Antecedents." *Journal of Abnormal Psychology* 113(2): 258–71.
Epstein, Deborah. 1999. "Effective Intervention in Domestic Violence Cases: Rethinking the Roles of Prosecutors, Judges, and the Court System." *Yale Journal of Law and Feminism* 11(1): 3–50.
Fals-Stewart, William. 2003. "The Occurrence of Partner Physical Aggression on Days of Alcohol Consumption: A Longitudinal Diary Study." *Journal of Consulting and Clinical Psychology* 71(1): 41–52.

Fals-Stewart, William, Kenneth E. Leonard, and Gary R. Birchler. 2005. "The Occurrence of Male-to-Female Intimate Partner Violence on Days of Men's Drinking: The Moderating Effects of Antisocial Personality Disorder." *Journal of Consulting and Clinical Psychology* 73(2): 239–48.

Feder, Lynette, and David R. Forde. 2000. *A Test of the Efficacy of Court-Mandated Counseling for Domestic Violence Offenders: The Broward Experiment*. Washington, DC: National Institute of Justice.

Ford, David A. 1983. "Wife Battery and Criminal Justice: A Study of Victim Decision-making." *Family Relations* 32(4): 463–75.

Gartin, Patrick. 1991. *The Individual Effects of Arrest in Domestic Violence Cases: A Reanalysis of the Minneapolis Domestic Violence Experiment*. Final report. Washington, DC: National Institute of Justice.

Gelles, Richard J. 1974. *The Violent Home: A Study of Physical Aggression between Husbands and Wives*. Beverly Hills, CA: Sage.

———. 1998. "Family Violence." In *The Handbook of Crime and Punishment*, edited by Michael Tonry. New York: Oxford University Press.

Giles-Sims, Jean. 1983. *Wife Battering: A Systems Theory Approach*. New York: Guilford.

Goldberg, Carey. 1999. "Spouse Abuse Crackdown, Surprisingly, Nets Many Women." *New York Times* (November 23). p. A16.

Grau, Janice, Jeffrey Fagan, and Sandra Wexler. 1985. "Restraining Orders for Battered Women: Issues of Access and Efficacy." In *Criminal Justice Politics and Women: The Aftermath of Legally Mandated Change*, edited by Claudine Schweber and Clarice Feinman. New York: Haworth.

Hamby, Sherry L. 1998. "Partner Violence: Prevention and Intervention." In *Partner Violence: A Comprehensive Review of 20 Years of Research*, edited by Jana L. Jasinski and Linda M. William. Thousand Oaks, CA: Sage.

Hammer, Rhonda. 2003. "Militarism and Family Terrorism: A Critical Feminist Perspective." *Review of Education, Pedagogy, and Cultural Studies* 25: 231–56.

Harrell, Adele, and Barbara Smith. 1996. "Effects of Restraining Orders on Domestic Violence Victims." In *Do Arrests and Restraining Orders Work?*, edited by Eve Schlesinger Buzawa and Carl G. Buzawa. Thousand Oaks, CA: Sage.

Harrell, Adele, Barbara Smith, and Lisa Newmark. 1993. *Court Processing and the Effects of Restraining Orders for Domestic Violence Victims*. Washington, DC: Urban Institute.

Hines, Denise A., Jan Brown, and Edward Dunning. 2007. "Characteristics of Callers to the Domestic Abuse Helpline for Men." *Journal of Family Violence* 22(2): 63–72.

Hines, Denise A., and Kathie Malley-Morrison. 2001. "Psychological Effects of Partner Abuse against Men: A Neglected Research Area." *Psychology of Men and Masculinity* 2: 75–85.

Hines, Denise A., and Kathie Malley-Morrison. 2005. *Family Violence in the United States: Defining, Understanding, and Combating Abuse*. Thousand Oaks, CA: Sage.

Hines, Denise A., and Murray A. Straus. 2007. "Binge Drinking and Violence against Dating Partners: The Mediating Effect of Antisocial Traits and Behaviors in a Multinational Perspective." *Aggressive Behavior* 33(5): 441–57.

Hirschel, David J., Ira W. Hutchison, Charles W. Dean, Joseph J. Kelley, and Carolyn E. Pesackis. 1991. *Charlotte Spouse Assault Replication Project: Final report*. Washington, DC: U. S. Department of Justice.

Holtzworth-Munroe, Amy, Howard Markman, K. Daniel O'Leary, Peter Neidig, Doug Leber, Richard E. Heyman, Dena Hulbert, and Natalie Smutzler. 1995.

"The Need for Marital Violence Prevention Efforts: A Behavioral-Cognitive Secondary Prevention Program for Engaged and Newly Married Couples." *Applied and Preventive Psychology* 4(2): 77–88.

Holtzworth-Munroe, Amy, and Gregory L. Stuart. 1994. "Typologies of Male Batterers: Three Subtypes and the Differences among Them." *Psychological Bulletin* 116: 476–97.

Johnson, Michael P. 1995. "Patriarchal Terrorism and Common Couple Violence: Two Forms of Violence against Women." *Journal of Marriage and the Family* 57(2): 283–94.

Jones, Dana A., and Joanne Belknap. 1999. "Police Responses to Battering in a Progressive Pro-Arrest Jurisdiction." *Justice Quarterly* 15: 249–73.

Keilitz, Susan L., Paula L. Hannaford, and Hillery S. Efkemann. 1997. *Civil Protection Orders: The Benefits and Limitations for Victims of Domestic Violence. Executive Summary.* Washington, DC: Department of Justice.

Klein, Andrew. 1996. "Re-abuse in a Population of Court-Restrained Male Batterers: Why Restraining Orders Don't Work." In *Do Arrests and Restraining Orders Work?,* edited by Eve Schlesinger Buzawa and Carl G. Buzawa. Thousand Oaks, CA: Sage.

Laroche, Denis. 2005. *Aspects of the Context and Consequences of Domestic Violence: Situational Couple Violence and Intimate Terrorism in Canada in 1999.* Quebec: Institut de la statistique du Quebec.

Lempert, Richard. 1989. "Humility Is a Virtue: On the Publicization of Policy Relevant Research." *Law and Society Review* 23(1): 145–61.

Leonard, Kenneth E. 1993. "Drinking Patterns and Intoxication in Marital Violence: Review, Critique, and Future Directions for Research." In *U.S. Department of Health and Human Services. Research Monograph 24: Alcohol and Interpersonal Violence: Fostering Multidisciplinary Perspectives,* edited by S. E. Martin. Rockville, MD: National Institutes of Health.

Malecha, Anne, Judith McFarlane, Julia Gist, Kathy Watson, Elizabeth Batten, Iva Hall, and Sheila Smith. 2003. "Applying for and Dropping a Protection Order: A Study with 150 Women." *Criminal Justice Policy Review* 14: 486–504.

Malley-Morrison, Kathleen, and Denise A. Hines. 2004. *Family Violence in a Cultural Perspective: Defining, Understanding, and Combating Abuse.* Thousand Oaks, CA: Sage.

Martin, Del. 1979. "What Keeps a Woman Captive in a Violent Relationship? The Social Context of Battering." In *Battered Women,* edited by Donna M. Moore. Beverly Hills, CA: Sage.

Mears, Daniel P., Matthew J. Carlson, George W. Holden, and Susan D. Harris. 2001. "Reducing Domestic Violence Revictimization: The Effects of Individual and Contextual Factors and Type of Legal Intervention." *Journal of Interpersonal Violence* 16: 1260–83.

Mills, Linda G. 2003. *Insult to Injury: Rethinking Our Response to Intimate Abuse.* Princeton, NJ: Princeton University Press.

Moffitt, Terrie E., Avshalom Caspi, M. Rutter, and Phil A. Silva. 2001. *Sex Differences in Antisocial Behaviour: Conduct Disorder, Delinquency and Violence in the Dunedin Longitudinal Study.* Cambridge: Cambridge University Press.

Murphy, C. M., T. J. O'Farrell, William Fals-Stewart, and M. Feehan. 2001. "Correlates of Intimate Partner Violence among Male Alcoholic Patients." *Journal of Consulting and Clinical Psychology* 69: 528–40.

O'Farrell, T. J., William Fals-Stewart, M. Murphy, and C. M. Murphy. 2003. "Partner Violence before and after Individually Based Alcoholism Treatment for Male Alcoholic Patients." *Journal of Consulting and Clinical Psychology* 71: 92–102.

O'Leary, K. D., R. E. Heyman, and P. H. Neidig. 1999. "Treatment of Wife Abuse: A Comparison of Gender-Specific and Couple Approaches." *Behavior Assessment* 30: 475–505.

Pate, A., and E. Hamilton. 1992. "Formal and Informal Deterrents to Domestic Violence: The Dade County Spouse Assault Experiment." *American Sociological Review* 57: 691–97.

Pence, Ellen, and Michael Paymar. 1983. *Education Groups for Men Who Batter: The Duluth Model*. New York: Springer.

Rebovich, Donald J. 1996. "Prosecution Response to Domestic Violence: Results of a Survey of Large Jurisdictions." In *Do Arrests and Restraining Orders Work?*, edited by Eve Schlesinger Buzawa and Carl G. Buzawa. Thousand Oaks, CA: Sage.

Serbin, Lisa A., Dale M. Stack, Natacha De Genna, Naomi Grunzeweig, Caroline E. Temcheff, Alex E. Schwartzmann, and Jane Ledinham. 2004. "When Aggressive Girls Become Mothers." In *Aggression, Antisocial Behavior, and Violence among Girls*, edited by Martha Putallaz and Karen L. Bierman. New York: Guilford.

Sherman, Lawrence, and Richard Berk. 1984. "The Specific Deterrent Effects of Arrest for Domestic Assault." *American Sociological Review* 49: 261–72.

Sherman, Lawrence W., Joel D. Schmidt, Dennis P. Rogan, Douglas A. Smith, Patrick R. Gartin, Ellen G. Cohn, J. Collins, and Anthony R. Bacich. 1992. "The Variable Effects of Arrest on Criminal Careers: The Milwaukee Domestic Violence Experiment." *Journal of Criminal Law and Criminology* 83: 137–69.

Simon, T. R., M. Anderson, M. P. Thompson, A. E. Crosby, G. Shelley, and J. J. Sacks. 2001. "Attitudinal Acceptance of Intimate Partner Violence among U.S. Adults." *Violence and Victims* 16: 115–26.

Stark, Evan. 1996. "Mandatory Arrest of Batterers: A Reply to Its Critics." In *Do Arrests and Restraining Orders Work?*, edited by Eve Schlesinger Buzawa and Carl G. Buzawa. Thousand Oaks, CA: Sage.

State of Georgia. 2002. *Family Violence Intervention Provider Statute*. Atlanta: State of Georgia.

Stets, Jan E., and Murray A. Straus. 1990. "Gender Differences in Reporting Marital Violence and Its Medical and Psychological Consequences." In *Physical Violence in American Families: Risk Factors and Adaptation to Violence in 8,145 Families*, edited by Murray A. Straus and Richard J. Gelles. New Brunswick, NJ: Transaction.

Stith, Sandra M., Karen H. Rosen, and Eric E. McCollum. 2003. "Effectiveness of Couples Treatment for Spouse Abuse." *Journal of Marriage and Family Therapy* 29: 407–26.

Stith, Sandra M., Douglas B. Smith, Carrie E. Penn, D. B. Ward, and D. Tritt. 2004. "Intimate Partner Physical Abuse Perpetration and Victimization Risk Factors: A Meta-Analysis Review." *Aggression and Violent Behavior* 10(1): 65–98.

Strack, Gael B. n.d. "She Hit Me, Too: Identifying the Primary Aggressor. A Prosecutor's Perspective." http://www.peaceathomeshelter.org/domestic violence/readings/aggressor/She_hit_me.pdf.

Straus, Murray A. 1980. "Wife-Beating: How Common and Why?" In *The Social Causes of Husband-Wife Violence*, edited by Murray A. Straus and Gerald T. Hotaling. Minneapolis, MN: University of Minnesota Press.

———. 2004. "Women's Violence toward Men Is a Serious Social Problem." In *Current Controversies on Family Violence*, edited by Donileen R. Loseke, Richard J. Gelles, and Mary M. Cavanaugh. Thousand Oaks, CA: Sage.

Straus, Murray A., and Richard J. Gelles. 1986. "Societal Change and Change in Family Violence from 1975 to 1985 as Revealed by Two National Surveys." *Journal of Marriage and the Family* 48: 465–79.

Straus, Murray A., and Richard J. Gelles, eds. 1990. *Physical Violence in American Families.* New Brunswick, NJ: Transaction.
Straus, Murray A., Richard J. Gelles, and Suzanne Steinmetz. 1980. *Behind Closed Doors: Violence in the American Family.* Garden City, NY: Anchor.
Sugarman, David B., and Susan L. Frankel. 1996. "Patriarchal Ideology and Wife Assault: A Meta-analytic Review." *Journal of Family Violence* 11: 13–40.
Tjaden, Patricia, and Nancy Thoennes. 2000. *Extent, Nature, and Consequences of Intimate Partner Violence: Findings from the National Violence against Women Survey.* http://www.ojp.usdoj.gov/nih/victdocs.htm#2000.
Wills, Donna. 1997. "Domestic Violence: The Case for Aggressive Prosecution." *UCLA Women's Law Journal* 7: 173–99.

CHAPTER 6

CHILD ABUSE

KATHLEEN MALLEY-MORRISON
AND DENISE A. HINES

PUBLIC policies regarding child abuse have expanded and undergone several changes in direction since the publication in 1962 of Henry Kempe and his colleagues' groundbreaking article on the battered child syndrome. In 1962 the U.S. Children's Bureau required physicians to report cases of child abuse to social service agencies. Within five years all states had passed child abuse reporting laws for physicians, with provisions designed to protect them from civil or criminal liability (Zellman and Fair 2002). By the 1970s sexual abuse, emotional maltreatment, and neglect had been added to the Children's Bureau's definition of child abuse. By 1986 nearly every state had added nurses, social workers, other mental health professionals, teachers, and school staff to the list of mandated reporters (Zellman and Fair 2002).

Early laws, for example, the Child Abuse Prevention and Treatment Act of 1974 (CAPTA; P.L. 93–247), gave states the power to remove children from their homes if they were deemed to be in danger (Myers 2002; Zellman and Fair 2002). Most typically such children were placed into foster care, a form of intervention that often proved inimical to the child's well-being (Jonson-Reid and Barth 2000*b*). The 1980 Adoption Assistance and Child Welfare Act required states to make every reasonable effort to prevent the removal of children from their families and to reunite them quickly with families if removal seemed initially necessary. More recent laws, for example, the 1997 Adoption and Safe Families Act (42 U.S. Code § 671(a)(15)(A); Myers 2002), are designed to facilitate the quick adoption of abused children into safe, stable homes when efforts to keep the family together fail (Malley-Morrison and Hines 2004). Despite such legislative efforts, child abuse rates continue to be high.

In addition to mandating a broadening array of child abuse reporters and providing resources to states for child abuse prevention and intervention activities, CAPTA required the secretary of the U.S. Department of Health, Education, and Welfare to undertake longitudinal research on the incidence of child abuse and neglect and to identify trends in child maltreatment. This led to four National Incidence Studies (NIS), conducted in 1979–80, 1986–87, 1993–95, and 2005–08. As amended in 1988, CAPTA also directed the secretary of the U.S. Department of Health and Human Services (DHHS) to establish a national data collection and analysis program on state child abuse and neglect reporting information; this led to the establishment of the National Child Abuse and Neglect Data System (NCANDS), which publishes annual summaries of child abuse reports.

In this chapter we summarize current knowledge concerning child abuse in the United States. A number of findings stand out:

- The National Family Violence Surveys (NFVS) provide the highest estimates of child physical maltreatment because many parents admitted to behaviors, such as beating, that were never reported to any child protection agency.
- Rates of child abuse appear to be particularly high if corporal punishment is included in the definition of child abuse.
- The next highest estimates come from the NIS survey data on the number of cases identified as abusive by mandated reporters but not necessarily reported to authorities.
- The lowest rates come from the NCANDS data on number of child maltreatment reports.
- The actual number of substantiated cases is even lower than the reported cases identified by NCANDS and clearly underestimate the actual number of child maltreatment cases.
- Girls are at higher risk of sexual abuse than boys, but boys appear to be at higher risk for severe physical abuse and serious injury, particularly at younger ages. Mothers appear to administer more punishment and to be identified more often for neglect, whereas fathers and father figures are more likely to be identified as sexual abusers.
- A comparison of rates across the three major approaches provides useful information for estimating the percentage of child abuse cases that are actually receiving services in relation to the number of cases parents acknowledge, which is itself likely to be an underestimate of the amount of child abuse that is occurring.
- Risk factors that predict child abuse and neglect include individual, family, and neighborhood characteristics; effective interventions must address factors at multiple levels.
- Physical abuse during childhood is associated with reduced life chances, including greater risk of delinquency and of becoming a child abuser later in life.

- Gaps or holes exist in current knowledge about patterns of abuse victimization and about the effects of policy interventions. Improving policy will depend on the availability of new and better knowledge.
- A new National Family Violence Survey, in which the CTS-PC is administered to families using the same approach as the first survey (personal interviews), and again summarizing self-report rates for both corporal punishment and more severe forms of physical assault, is essential for better estimates of child abuse rates than are possible through the other methodologies.
- Efforts to deal with child abuse will be improved if child protection and criminal justice agencies learn to work together more closely and more effectively.

In section I of this chapter we discuss the major approaches to assessing the incidence and prevalence of child abuse, including the NFVS, NIS, and NCANDS surveys, estimates of abuse rates provided by the different data sources, apparent changes in prevalence rates over time, and possible explanations of these changes. We also consider ethnic differences in rates of child abuse and data relating to ethnic differences. Section II provides an overview of competing definitions of child abuse and the major theories of why child abuse occurs. In section III we describe the criminal justice system's response to the problem, and in section IV we consider implications of research for public policy.

I. Incidence and Prevalence

Determining child abuse *incidence rates* (the frequency with which acts occur within a specific population during a specified period) and *prevalence rates* (the percentage of the population experiencing those acts within a particular period) is difficult because of sampling and methodological differences across surveys and because of differences in operational definitions of abuse and reporting biases (for example, tendencies to over- or underreport cases based on extraneous characteristics such as ethnicity). Government agencies and independent investigators have collected three major types of data: self-reports of aggressive behavior from nationally representative samples of parents; tallies of reported cases from child protective service (CPS) agencies; and self-reports of numbers of identified cases from mandated reporters who may or may not have reported those cases to CPS. Because these different approaches yield different estimates, we describe each one briefly.

A. Major Types of Assessments

Funded by the National Institute of Mental Health and the University of New Hampshire, Murray A. Straus, the director of the Family Research Laboratory at the University of New Hampshire, and his colleagues conducted the first study of rates of family violence in a nationally representative sample of American families, the 1975 National Family Violence Survey (Straus, Gelles, and Steinmetz 1980). Researchers conducted face-to-face interviews with parents in two-parent families. Using the Conflict Tactics Scales (CTS; Straus 1979) they elicited self-reports concerning the frequency with which parents used corporal punishment (for example, grabbing, shoving, hitting, spanking the child) or more extreme violence (for example, kicking, biting, beating up, burning the child). Ten years later, in the second NFVS (Straus and Gelles 1986; Straus 1990), the CTS were administered over the phone by Harris pollsters to another nationally representative sample. The second study indicated some decline in child abuse rates, although this may have been related to the different method used to collect the data. In a third study (1995) of a nationally representative sample, initiated and sponsored by the Gallup Organization, parents from two-parent and one-parent homes completed a revised and improved form of the CTS (which included sexual abuse and neglect items) over the phone (Straus et al. 1998). Because of differences in sample characteristics and changes in the CTS, it is difficult to draw inferences concerning changes in rates over time.

In contrast to CTS self-report studies of aggression against children in representative community samples, the three completed National Incidence Studies of Child Abuse and Neglect (NIS-1, NIS-2, and NIS-3; Sedlak and Broadhurst 1996) and NIS-4, which was scheduled for completion in February 2008, focused on "caught cases" of child abuse by soliciting information from community professionals mandated to report child abuse cases (professionals from schools, hospitals, law enforcement agencies, and welfare offices) and CPS agencies. This methodology permits researchers to compare the cases reported by the professionals with the reports received by CPS from professionals and from nonprofessionals such as neighbors, family members, and friends. All four NIS studies were conducted by Westat, an employee-owned contract research organization, under contracts with the Administration for Children and Families of the U.S. Department of Health and Human Services.

Finally, annual reports from state CPS agencies to the NCANDS summarize such statistics as the number of children and families receiving preventive services, the number of reports and investigations of child abuse and neglect, the number of child fatalities, and the major "dispositions" (i.e., substantiated, "reason to suspect," and "unsubstantiated") of child maltreatment reports. NCANDS data are collected and funded by the Children's Bureau, Administration on Children, Youth and Families, Administration for Children and Families, DHHS. Because NCANDS data include only officially reported cases they are generally assumed to be only the tip of the child abuse iceberg. By contrast, the NIS data provide a more complete estimate of the number of child abuse cases actually seen (but not necessarily reported) by professionals, although critics are concerned that not all professionals will honestly indicate the number of cases they have seen but not reported.

Finally, the CTS studies have been criticized for their reliance on parent reports, restrictions on participation eligibility (for example, two-parent homes only in the first study), and for asking about parental behaviors in the context of conflict. However, Straus et al. (1998) have provided strong evidence for the reliability and validity of the modified CTS, and despite the limitations their data consistently provide the highest estimates of child abuse of all the major surveys.

B. Reported Rates

What have we learned from these different data sources about the incidence and prevalence of child maltreatment in the United States? Table 6.1 presents a summary of the disparate results obtained from the three major sources. According to a 1995 CTS telephone study conducted by the Gallup Organization (Straus et al. 1998), corporal punishment of children was reported at a rate of 614 per 1,000 children, and severe physical assault of a child at a rate of 49 per 1,000. Straus et al. noted that the rates of physical assault reported by parents on the CTS in 1995 were more than 10 times higher than the rate of 4 per 1,000 for cases reported to child protective services in 1994 (U.S. DHHS 1998, pp. 2–5), and five times higher than the rate of 9.1 per 1,000 found in NIS-3 (Sedlak and Broadhurst 1996). These differences are due in part to the differences in methodology. The lowest rates (from NCANDS) represent only reported cases. The highest rates (from CTS) are gathered through self-report surveys in which participants are told they are taking a survey on how family members handle conflicts. The NIS-3 rates fall in between. These numbers represent the cases that come to the attention of mandated reporters, who do not always report suspected cases and do not always know that some of the children they see are physically assaulted by their parents.

According to the NIS, child maltreatment reports have been increasing nationally since at least the time of the first study. Analysis of NIS-3 responses revealed that in 1993 an estimated 1,553,800 children in the United States were identified as having experienced harm from abuse or neglect. This NIS-3 total reflects a 67 percent increase since the NIS-2 (1986) estimate of 931,000 maltreated children and a

Table 6.1. **Rates of child maltreatment based on three different surveys: 1995 CTS study performed by Gallup, NIS-3 of 1993–94, and the 1994 NCANDS report**

Data source	Rate per 1,000 children
1995 CTS study: corporal punishment	614
1995 CTS study: severe assault	49
NIS-3: physical abuse	9.1
1994 NCANDS report: physical abuse	4.0

Sources: Sedlak and Broadhurst 1996; U.S. Department of Health and Human Services 1998; Straus et al. 1998.

149 percent increase since the NIS-1 (1980) estimate of 625,100 maltreated children (Sedlak and Broadhurst 1996). Physical abuse nearly doubled, and sexual abuse, emotional abuse, physical neglect, and emotional neglect all more than doubled between NIS-2 and NIS-3 (Sedlak and Broadhurst 1996).

Table 6.2 displays the number of children reported maltreated in NIS-2 and NIS-3, disaggregated by type of abuse and according to the two standards that NIS uses: the harm standard, which is defined as "an act or omission resulting in demonstrable harm" (Sedlak and Broadhurst 1996, p. 5), and the endangerment standard, which "allows children who were not yet harmed by maltreatment to be counted in the abused and neglected estimates if a non-CPS sentinel considered them to be endangered by maltreatment or if their maltreatment was substantiated or indicated in a CPS investigation" (Sedlak and Broadhurst, 1996, p. 6). Rates increased according to both standards and for all types of abuse between NIS-2 and NIS-3.

The 2005 NCANDS report corroborates a continued increase in child abuse investigations since 2001. For example, while the rate of investigations was 43.2 children per 1,000 in 2001 (which is approximately 3,136,000 children), the rate in federal fiscal year 2005 was 48.3 per 1,000 (an estimated 3,598,000 children; U.S. DHHS 2005). Of these cases, as in prior years, the majority were for neglect (62.8 percent); 16.6 percent of the cases were physical abuse, 9.3 percent were emotional abuse, and 7.1 percent were sexual abuse. Although child maltreatment reports and investigations have increased overall, analysis of NCANDS data from 1995 to 2004 revealed a 37 percent decline in substantiated child sexual abuse cases (U.S. DHHS, 1999, 2004; see fig. 6.1). It is unclear whether this decline is due to successful intervention and prevention programs or simply a decline in the number of cases being reported and investigated (Finklehor and Jones 2004).

In addition, figure 6.1, based on NCANDS data, shows that rates of child physical abuse and neglect also declined over the 10-year period from 1995 to 2004. Physical

Table 6.2. Trends in child maltreatment according to NIS-2 and NIS-3 by type of abuse

	Child physical abuse	Child sexual abuse	Neglect	Emotional/ psychological abuse
Harm standard				
NIS-2 (1986–87)	269,700	119,200	474,800	
NIS-3 (1993–94)	381,700	217,700	879,000	
Endangerment standard				
NIS-2 (1986–87)	311,500	133,600	710,700	188,100
NIS-3 (1993–94)	614,100	300,200	1,920,200	532,200

Note: Numbers represent the projected number of child victims.
Source: Sedlak and Broadhurst 1996.

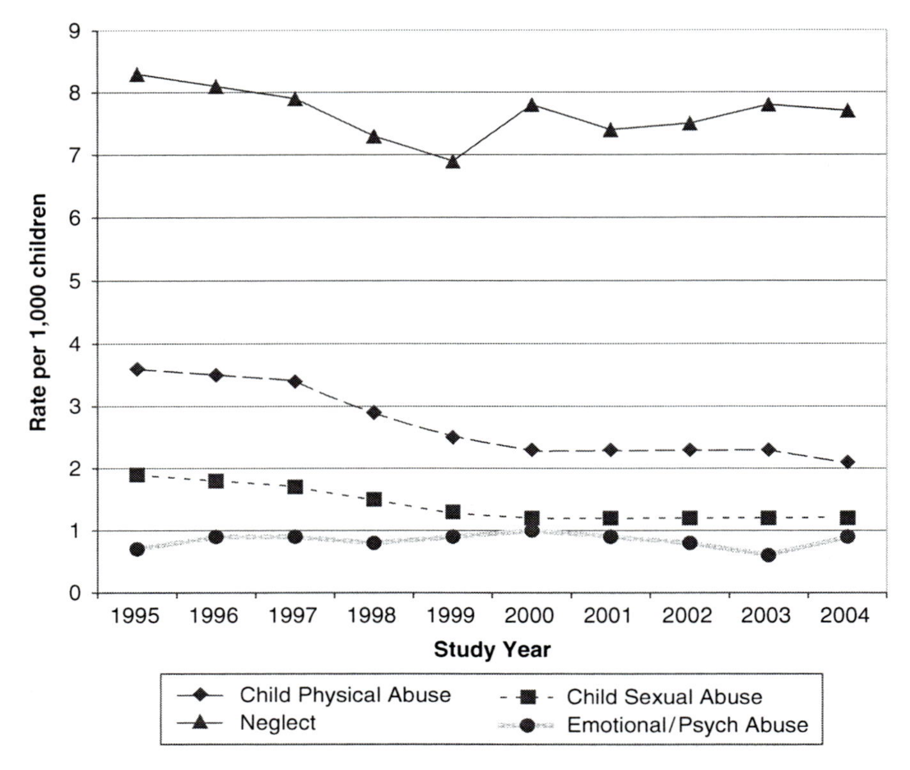

Figure 6.1. Trends in child abuse, 1995–2004, NCANDS Reports.
Source: U.S. Department of Health and Human Services 1998, 1999, 2004.

abuse rates declined 42 percent and neglect rates declined 7 percent. Emotional or psychological abuse rates remained steady, however (U.S. DHHS 1999, 2004). The NFVS surveys of 1975, 1985, and 1995 show a similar trend in that self-reported rates of child physical abuse declined over that 20-year period (fig. 6.2).

C. Gender

Findings concerning the role of gender in child abuse vary somewhat depending on which methodology was used and the type of abuse under consideration. Based on responses to the original CTS, the 1985 National Family Violence Resurvey (Wauchope and Straus 1990) revealed no differences in parents' self-reported *incidence* of physical punishment or physical abuse as a function of their sex or the sex of the target child; however, an analysis of self-reported *chronicity* rates (i.e., frequency of physically assaulting a child who has been physically assaulted at least once) revealed that both mothers and fathers physically punished sons more often than daughters and that fathers punished both sons and daughters significantly

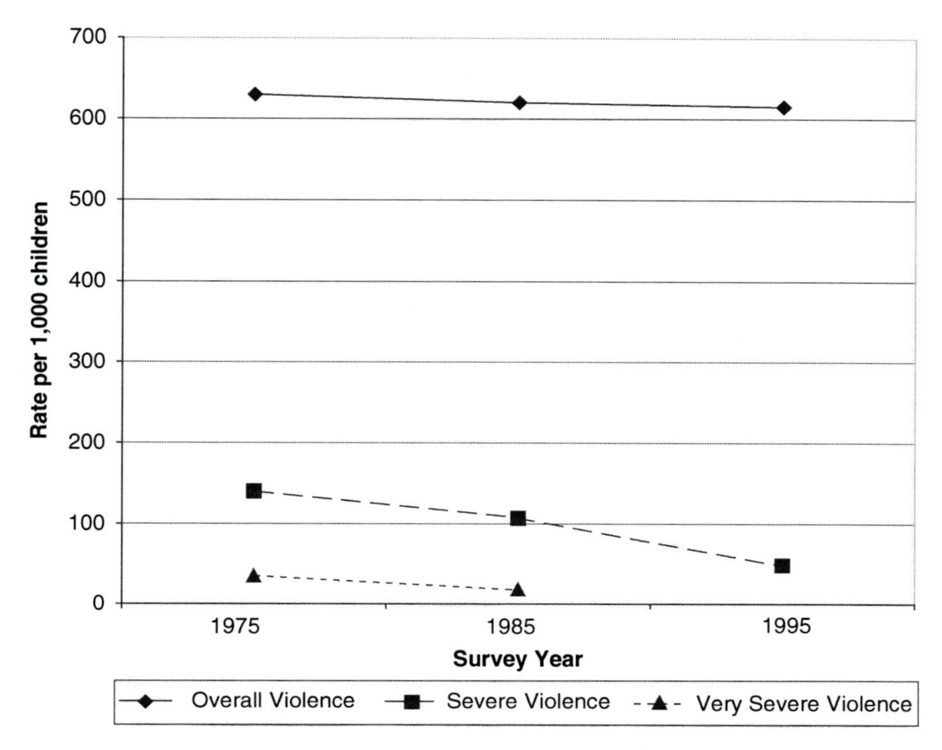

Figure 6.2. Trends in child abuse, 1975–95, National Family Violence Surveys.
Source: Straus and Gelles 1986; Straus et al. 1998.

more often than mothers did. Research with the revised CTS revealed a different pattern. Mothers physically punished more than fathers, significantly so in regard to young children, and reported physically assaulting their children twice as much as fathers did.

Recent data (2005) from the NCANDS, which are generally consistent with NCANDS findings from earlier years, show that a little more than half of the victims of child maltreatment were girls, although infant boys had the highest fatality rates. When children were abused by just one parent, the abuser was more than twice as likely to be their mother (40.4 percent) than their father (18.3 percent), although 17.3 percent of child victims were abused by both parents.

NIS-3 data indicated that girls were sexually abused three times more often than boys, and boys were at higher risk for emotional neglect and serious injury than girls. In regard to the sex of the perpetrator, mothers and mother figures were reported for neglect at a substantially higher rate (87 percent compared to 43 percent) than fathers and father figures, whereas physical and sexual abuse rates were reported at substantially higher rates for men than for women: 89 percent of identified sexual abusers were men.

D. Race and Ethnicity

Attending to issues of race and ethnicity in regard to child maltreatment is important because of concerns about the overrepresentation of ethnic minorities in the child welfare and juvenile justice systems. Obtaining accurate estimates of child abuse incidence and prevalence becomes challenging when investigators try to determine racial and ethnic differences in rates, partly because different investigators have "operationalized" (i.e., measured) race and ethnicity in different ways. For example, in some of the NFVS analyses for corporal punishment and physical abuse (e.g., Straus and Donnelly 2001), race and ethnicity were coded as either non-Hispanic white or minority (with all ethnic minority group members lumped together). By contrast, Sedlak and Broadhurst (1996), in their analyses of NIS data, compared whites (including non-Hispanic whites) with nonwhites. In another analysis of NIS data, Hampton and Newberger (1985) compared reports on Caucasian Americans, blacks, and Hispanics and "others." The NCANDS reports provide frequencies of child maltreatment reports separately for whites, African Americans, Hispanics, American Indian/Alaska Natives, and Asian/Pacific Islanders.

Underlining much of the attention to incidence and prevalence rates of child abuse within different ethnic communities is widespread concern about disproportionality (overrepresentation) and disparities based on race and ethnicity. As explained by Ryan et al. (2007, p. 1036), "Overrepresentation refers to a situation in which a greater proportion of a specific group is present at a specific stage within the service system. For example, 35 percent of the children in foster care are African American, yet African American children represent only 15 percent of the child population (U.S. Department of Health and Human Services 2005). Disparity refers to a situation in which the probability of receiving a specific outcome is contingent upon one's group status."

At the heart of the debate over racial bias in the reporting of child abuse cases are the discrepancies among the findings of different studies, particularly the NIS. In one study (Straus et al. 1998), in which the revised form of the CTS was administered to a nationally representative sample of 1,000 parents of children under 18, there were no significant differences between European Americans and African Americans in amounts of corporal punishment reported, but the African American rate of 148 severe assaults per 1,000 was significantly higher than the European American rate of 34 per 1,000. The NCANDS report on investigated cases in 2005 revealed that African American children, American Indian or Alaska Native children, and Pacific Islander children were overrepresented in the investigated cases, with rates of 19.5, 16.5, and 16.1 per 1,000 children of the same race or ethnicity, respectively. White children and Hispanic children had rates of approximately 10.8 and 10.7 per 1,000 children of the same race or ethnicity, respectively, and Asian children had the lowest rate: 2.5 per 1,000 children of the same race or ethnicity. Although there were no significant differences between blacks and whites in numbers of cases of child maltreatment identified (but not necessarily reported), a recent analysis of NIS data (Baird, Ereth, and Wagner 1999) revealed substantial differences in types of maltreatment reported by race, with African Americans having a higher rate of neglect reported and whites having a higher rate of abuse reported.

Despite the apparent discrepancies between NCANDS and NIS data, there has long been recognition that ethnic minority children are overrepresented in the child welfare system. Many investigators point to high levels of poverty and stress in many minority communities and attribute the disproportionate identification of child maltreatment cases in those communities to such factors. For example, in their analysis of poverty and microsystem stress characterizing the NIS neglect cases, Baird, Ereth, and Wagner (1999) pointed out that many more African Americans than whites had annual incomes under $15,000 (30.4 percent vs. 11.6 percent), single female caretakers (52 percent vs. 18 percent), and three or more children in the home (14 percent vs. 9 percent), all of which are risk factors for neglect. Other investigators (e.g., Hill 2004) attribute the overrepresentation of black children in the child welfare system to institutional racism. Hill presents evidence indicating that processes occur at each successive stage of CPS operations that screen in black children and screen out white children. For example, Hill (2004) reported that in regard to placement in foster homes, an analysis of the National Study of Protective, Preventive, and Reunification Services data revealed that black children were twice as likely as white children to be placed in foster care (56 percent vs. 28 percent) but that white families were almost twice as likely as black families to receive services with their children at home (72 percent vs. 44 percent).

II. Definitions and Theories

Definitions of child abuse vary in their inclusiveness (for example, whether corporal punishment should be considered abusive) and differ within and across research, social service, and legal domains. Moreover, theories of child abuse differ in the perspectives they offer on abusers (Are they overstressed, or were they taught inappropriate forms of parenting?) and appropriate types of intervention (for example, provide services to the parents or prosecute them). Differences in the definitions and theories informing research and practice influence the likelihood that children and families will receive interventions from the legal, medical, or social service professions.

A. Definitions

Since the enactment of CAPTA, millions of children have been reported to the child welfare system for child abuse or neglect, yet there continues to be considerable debate as to how child abuse should be defined. The federal Child Abuse Prevention and Treatment Act, as amended by the Keeping Children and Families Safe Act of 2003, indicates that child abuse and neglect involve, at a minimum, "any recent act or failure to act on the part of a parent or caretaker which results in death, serious physical or emotional harm, sexual abuse or exploitation; or an act or failure to act which presents an imminent risk of serious harm." Within those general standards each state has its own definitions and criteria, and there are discrepancies between definitions of maltreatment used in the CPS system and those used in the NIS (Runyan et al. 2005). Moreover, the use of CPS definitions may be influenced by local agency and policy issues (for example, reluctance of community-based agencies to report cases of neglect to the police; Runyan et al. 2005).

In regard to the CAPTA definition, major debates center on the criteria for harm and on the appropriateness of defining maltreatment (which we use to include both abuse and neglect) in terms of outcomes and potential outcomes, which can be difficult to assess, rather than in terms of specific behaviors (for example, hitting). In regard to harm, there has been considerable research indicating that corporal punishment (spanking, slapping) can have harmful long-term consequences for children (e.g., Mulvaney and Mebert 2007; Douglas and Straus 2008), yet in the United States corporal punishment is not only legal but generally not considered abusive.

Similarly, there is substantial evidence (e.g., Vissing et al. 1991) of long-term negative effects of psychological aggression against children (for example, belittling), yet the child welfare and criminal justice systems appear ill-equipped to address this form of maltreatment. Although the majority of children who enter the child welfare system do so because of accusations of neglect, the construct of neglect has consistently been neglected by child maltreatment experts (Dubowitz et al. 2005; Dubowitz 2007; McSherry 2007).

Finally, given the strong links between indices of poverty and child maltreatment, there are important issues concerning who should be considered responsible for the maltreatment: the parents who are unable to escape poverty because of racism, discrimination, and lack of education, or the social forces and "structural" or "systemic" forms of violence that contribute to and maintain inequity (e.g., Gil 1989; Pilisuk 1998; Gelles 1999). Dubowitz (2007, p. 605) asks, "Should not poverty be construed as a form of societal neglect, especially in countries with substantial resources?"

B. Theories

Numerous theories have been developed to account for the existence of child abuse and neglect. Tzeng, Jackson, and Karlson (1991) identified 46 different theories of child maltreatment, and their list is not inclusive. The majority (25) focus on physical child abuse; 15 address some aspect of sexual abuse; and there are three theories each for child psychological maltreatment and child neglect.

Building on Belsky's (1993) developmental-ecological approach to the etiology of physical child abuse and neglect, Hines and Malley-Morrison (2005) presented an ecological framework in which family violence theories are classified on the basis of the level of the causal mechanisms identified: individual developmental factors (for example, behavioral genetics, psychopathology, attachment deficits, and social learning theories); microsystem and family factors (for example, systems and stress theories); exosystem and neighborhood factors (for example, ecological and sociocultural theories); and macrosystem, cultural, and historical factors (for example, feminist theories). Hines and Malley-Morrison summarize evidence indicating that risk factors at each of these levels contribute to child abuse and neglect. They conclude that child maltreatment cannot be explained solely by factors at any one level and that greater attention to the contexts of child maltreatment is important if the problems are to be addressed adequately.

Although not as extensively researched as individual-level contributors to child maltreatment, there is evidence that context plays an important role in the etiology of child maltreatment. For example, evidence concerning the contribution of neighborhood characteristics to child maltreatment continues to accrue. In a review of 25 years of studies examining neighborhood characteristics in relation to child maltreatment, Freisthler, Merritt, and LaScala (2006, p. 263) found "a stable ecological relationship among neighborhood impoverishment, housing stress, and rates of child maltreatment, as well as some evidence that unemployment, child care burden, and alcohol availability may contribute to child abuse and neglect." Also working within an ecological perspective, Zielinski and Bradshaw (2006) considered how child maltreatment outcomes may be influenced by the contexts (families, peer groups, schools, and communities) in which children develop. Their review indicated that contextual factors not only influence the incidence of maltreatment but can also moderate its developmental effects. One of the advantages of an ecological approach, as noted by Dubowitz (2007), is that recognizing multiple and interacting contributors to child maltreatment may help in avoiding the tendency inherent in some theories (and by some agencies) to blame the victim, who in some cases is as much the parental victim of abusive social forces as the child victim of the parent's frustrations and misapprehensions.

Among the most important theories that can be usefully integrated within an ecological framework, particularly in regard to child abuse in families of color, are social learning theories, stress theories, and neighborhood risk theories, each of which we consider briefly.

1. *Social Learning Theory*

Social learning theory is at the core of a number of explanations of the intergenerational transmission of violence. According to this theory, much of human behavior, including aggressive behavior, is learned through both operant conditioning (rewards and punishments) and modeling one's own behavior on behaviors observed in important role models. Studies addressing this theory have found at least partial support for the hypothesis that individuals abused in childhood will be at risk for later abusing others, including their own children (Jackson et al. 1999; Gershoff 2002). However, it is clear that not all children who are abused by their parents become abusers themselves (Kaufman and Zigler 1987).

2. *Stress Theories*

Stress theories have focused on every level of human ecological systems: the microsystem (family), exosystem (neighborhood), and macrosystem (broader culture). For example, exosystem stress theories focus on contextual factors *external* to the individual and the family (for example, poverty, unemployment), whereas microsystem-level stress theories place greater emphasis on stresses *inherent* in the family as a social structure (for example, overcrowding, too many children, children with disabilities). However, despite considerable empirical support for a relationship between stress and child abuse, violence is only one of many possible responses to stress.

For example, in a study of 1,146 families with a child age 3 to 17 in the home, Straus (1980) found a positive association between the number of stressors experienced in a year and rates of child abuse. However, he also found that growing up in a violent family with low marital satisfaction and social isolation played a role in the stress–child abuse relationship. He concluded that stress can lead to child abuse among people who learned to use violence during childhood and believe that hitting other family members is justified. However, without those conditions, the relationship between stress and child abuse was minimal.

3. *High-Risk Neighborhoods*

Garbarino and Sherman (1980) argued that to understand child maltreatment we must focus not just on high-risk families but also on high-risk neighborhoods (that is, neighborhoods with elevated rates of child maltreatment). Based on extensive interviews in communities matched on socioeconomic status and race but differing in rates of child maltreatment reports, Garbarino and Sherman found that in neighborhoods with elevated levels of child abuse, isolated families competed for scarce resources rather than assisting each other. In Chicago, neighborhoods with high rates of child abuse were characterized by social disorganization (for example, criminal activity) and lack of access to social services and support networks (Garbarino and Kostelny 1992).

Consistent with neighborhood risk theories, a recent review of 25 studies on the influence of neighborhoods on child maltreatment provided strong evidence that child maltreatment cases are concentrated in disadvantaged areas and that many socioeconomic characteristics of neighborhoods are correlated with frequency of child maltreatment reports to child protective service agencies (Coulton et al. 2007). To understand the processes that link child maltreatment reports to neighborhood characteristics, Coulton et al. argued that it is essential to make distinctions among three pathways that may account for the relationship: behavioral influences (for example, availability of social support, which may in turn be related to levels of neighborhood crime); definition, recognition, and reporting (which may be influenced by relationships between neighborhoods and social service agencies); and characteristics of neighborhoods that are independent of characteristics of the families within those neighborhoods.

In sum, research addressing major theories of child maltreatment confirms the influence of risk factors at all levels of the ecological system. Risk factors include characteristics of individuals (for example, substance abuse, a history of abuse, belief in the efficacy of punitive child-rearing methods); characteristics of homes (for example, poverty, overcrowding); and characteristics of neighborhoods (for example, high crime levels, socially isolating circumstances). Some individuals who abuse their children would not do so if they were living and working in safer and more congenial environments. If we are to address the problem of child abuse adequately, it will be necessary to combat not only individual risk factors but also attributes of environments that increase the risk of child abuse. Although the criminal justice system is geared primarily to action at the individual level (for example, arrest and prosecution), it can also contribute to solutions at the neighborhood level (for example, through crime reduction), although its role in regard to the neighborhood is likely to benefit from expanded and more successful collaborations with social service and other agencies seeking nonpunitive solutions to child maltreatment. There is reason to be concerned about the observation of Meyers (2006, cited in Dubowitz 2007, p. 605) that "a long social work tradition of helping families in need has largely been replaced with much monitoring/policing."

III. The Criminal Justice System's Response

CAPTA provided for the expenditure of millions of federal dollars to support state child protection agencies and required all states to conform their child abuse reporting laws to the federal standards, create policies and procedures for reporting and investigating alleged child abuse, offer treatment services to identified families, and remove children from homes when they are deemed to be in danger (Myers 2002; Zellman and Fair 2002). This legislation, in essence, mandated cooperation regarding child abuse prevention and intervention between the criminal justice and the social service systems—an often uneasy alliance due to different philosophies and approaches. Research findings and changing social philosophies have led to shifts over time in relative emphases on the two approaches and evidence concerning their effectiveness in helping children and families.

A. Child Abuse Reporting Laws

The 1980 Adoption Assistance and Child Welfare Act required all states to conform their child abuse reporting laws to the federal standards, create policies and procedures for reporting and investigating alleged child abuse, offer treatment services to identified families, and remove children from the home if they were deemed to be in danger (Myers 2002; Zellman and Fair 2002). Subsequent legislation included a 1997 amendment to the Adoption and Safe Families Act specifying that "in making reasonable efforts, the child's health and safety shall be of paramount concern" (42 U.S. Code § 671(a)(15)(A); Myers 2002). This act represented a shift from emphasizing family reunification for children placed in out-of-home care to expediting permanent placements for those children in order to make it easier to remove them from home environments deemed to be dangerous. CAPTA, as amended by the Keeping Children and Families Safe Act of 2003, includes amended versions of the Adoption Opportunities program and Abandoned Infants Assistance Act. The 2003 CAPTA amendments include provisions for improving systems of technology designed to track child maltreatment reports from intake through final disposition and allow interstate and intrastate information exchange; improving the skills, qualifications, and availability of service providers; and supporting and improving interagency collaboration between the child protection system and the juvenile justice system.

B. Child Protection and the Criminal Justice System

The response to domestic violence cases often begins within the criminal justice system with a request for the police to intervene in a domestic dispute. For child maltreatment, the first level of response generally comes from the social service system. Child maltreatment has generally been regarded as a child welfare rather than a criminal justice matter. Federal regulations require state child protective service agencies, which are generally housed in state departments of social services, to receive incoming calls regarding potential child abuse cases, investigate these cases, decide on a disposition based on the available evidence, and take appropriate action. When child protective workers determine that child abuse has taken place or that the child is at risk, they generally bring the case to juvenile or family courts, which act on civil rather than criminal law principles.

Nevertheless, an increasing number of child maltreatment cases involve the police and are being investigated and adjudicated in the criminal justice system (Finkelhor and Ormrod 2001). Analyses of 1997 data from the FBI's National Incident-Based Reporting System (NIBRS) revealed that 19 percent of violent crimes against juveniles (ages 0–17) reported to the police and 4 percent of violent crimes against persons of any age were incidents of child abuse (Finkelhor and Ormrod

2001). Nearly three-quarters of these cases were physical assaults, with most of the rest being sexual. Although neglect and psychological aggression are included in federal and state definitions of child abuse, they are not, as already noted, generally reported to law enforcement agencies, and therefore are not included in the NIBRS statistics, even though they are probably the most frequent forms of child maltreatment.

Child-maltreating parents are often arrested and adjudicated within the criminal court system, not for maltreating their children but for other reasons, such as drug abuse. In a study of randomly selected protective custody cases brought before the family court in Clark County, Nevada, during a one-year period, parental methamphetamine use, homelessness, lack of resources, and outstanding warrants unrelated to the child's safety were factors contributing to arrest and incarceration of the parents and out-of-home placements for the children (Pelton 2008). Perhaps illustrative of the absence of an ecological perspective in the child welfare and criminal justice systems, the parents often were offered counseling for their substance abuse and other issues but rarely were offered concrete assistance, such as help with housing.

The most severe cases of child physical assault and child sexual abuse (including noncoercive Internet-related sex crimes) are most likely to be adjudicated in criminal courts, where a major concern is the validity of testimony by children. One approach to this problem has been the development of children's advocacy centers. Their primary purposes are to increase the number of successful criminal prosecutions of child sexual abuse cases and to conduct child-friendlier criminal investigations (Faller and Palusci 2007). The growth of these centers reflects an increasing emphasis on prosecution of child sexual abusers, but Faller and Palusci debate the extent to which successful prosecutions should be considered the gold standard for outcomes of child sexual abuse cases. They note that there is considerable research indicating that testifying in criminal court can have a detrimental impact on child well-being, especially when there are long delays between discovery of sexual abuse and court testimony, or when the prospect of prison rather than rehabilitation may increase the defense's focus on discrediting the child, interviewers, investigators or supportive care providers. Because unsubstantiated cases do not receive child protection services, if the criminal standard of proof is not met the children may be at even greater risk than before.

Although evaluation studies are rare and the long-term outcomes of criminal prosecutions of sexually abusive family members are unknown, one study of children evaluated at a child abuse assessment center revealed that significantly more of their cases were filed rather than no-actioned, significantly more overall counts were charged in the filed cases, more counts were charged against alleged perpetrators who were biological fathers and stepfathers, and more defendants pled or were found guilty compared with cases involving children not seen at the center (Faller and Palusci 2007).

C. From Child Maltreatment to Child Welfare and into the Criminal Justice System

One unfortunate connection between child protective services and the criminal justice system is the prosecution of former victims of child abuse and neglect for criminal behavior that is likely to be in large part an outcome of their victimization. Several studies have shown that victims of child maltreatment are at enhanced risk for delinquency. A prospective longitudinal study of 574 children from three cities in two states, followed from age 5 to age 21, revealed that individuals who had been physically abused in the first five years of life were less likely to graduate from high school, more likely to have been fired in the past year, more likely to have become a teen parent, and at greater risk for being arrested as juveniles for violent, nonviolent, and status offenses (Lansford et al. 2007). Physical abuse in the first five years of life was more strongly related to negative outcomes for African American than for European American adolescents and for young adults for both nonviolent and violent offenses documented in juvenile court records, self-reported arrests, and court evidence of arrest (Lansford et al. 2007).

The negative and potentially criminogenic effects of early maltreatment may be particularly pronounced in individuals taken into the child welfare system. One study (Ryan and Testa 2005) indicated that delinquency rates are approximately 47 percent higher in youth who have had at least one substantiated report of maltreatment. Another study, of 159,549 school-age children reported for abuse and neglect in 10 California counties, revealed a rate of 8 per 1,000 children who were later incarcerated in the juvenile corrections system (Jonson-Reid and Barth 2000*b*). Children who entered their first placement between the ages of 12 and 15, children with multiple placements, and children whose placements following child welfare involvement were supervised by probation were at greater risk of incarceration for a serious or violent offense during adolescence (Jonson-Reid and Barth 2000*a*). Another study indicated that significantly more members of a sample of women who had been incarcerated for sexual abuse were themselves survivors of childhood sexual abuse than were women incarcerated for other crimes, and significantly more of the sexually abusive women suffered from symptoms of borderline personality disorder (Christopher, Lutz-Zois, and Reinhardt 2007)—further evidence of childhood victimization being followed by later and systemic victimization.

Involvement in the child welfare system also appears to contribute to overrepresentation of African American youth in the juvenile justice system (Ryan et al. 2007). Among all new arrests in Los Angeles from 2002 to 2005, for example, 7 percent were former child welfare cases; however, 14 percent of the new arrests of African Americans came from the child welfare system. African American and Hispanic youth were both less likely than white and Asian youth to have their cases dismissed and more likely to enter the correctional system.

IV. Implications for Public Policy

We believe it is time for a new National Family Violence Survey, in which the modified CTS is administered to families face-to-face rather than through telephone interviews and results are summarized using self-report rates for both corporal punishment and more severe forms of physical assault. Moreover, although research using the modified CTS and aimed at identifying predictors and outcomes of child abuse is important, more research concerning the outcomes of various forms of intervention and prevention programs is even more crucial. To what extent are our interventions hurting rather than helping children? To what extent does the nature of the interventions vary in regard to child ethnicity? Do variations in type of intervention influence outcomes independent of ethnicity? The research community has barely scratched the surface of such questions. Continued collection of NCANDS and NIS data is also useful, but those data best tell us how identification and reporting of child abuse changes across time and the characteristics of children and families being identified and reported, but do not provide reliable data on levels of child abuse occurring in homes.

Related to our recommendation for a new National Family Violence Survey are several others. First, the United States should ratify the United Nations Convention on the Rights of the Child and thereby end its ignominy as the only country besides Somalia to have failed to do so. Second, the United States should follow in the footsteps of the European Union and identify corporal punishment of children as a violation of their human rights. Third, the United States should not treat corporal punishment, psychological aggression, and neglect as criminal offenses but should invest more in social service solutions to problems and to evaluation and reporting of the results of those efforts. Fourth, the U.S. government should expand its support of research on the effects of racism and poverty, with particular emphasis on whether and how they contribute to the entry of children into the child protection and juvenile justice systems.

There is a role for the criminal justice system in the community response to severe cases of child physical and sexual abuse, particularly so long as national, state, and local governments are unwilling to invest sufficiently in intervention programs to stop the cycle of violence and combat factors (for example, drug abuse, poverty-related stresses) that contribute to child maltreatment. At the same time, it is important to attend to findings suggesting that higher welfare benefits and lower unemployment rates may serve as protective factors for children (Berger 2004).

CAPTA emphasizes the importance of interagency collaboration in the management of child maltreatment cases. Saunders (2003) frets about the "Balkanization" (division into small, hostile, competing groups) of the professions that address issues of child maltreatment, interpret problems in different ways, and recommend different solutions. In his view, unless there is significant sharing, cooperation, and colleagueship among professionals from different fields, children exposed to violence will continue to suffer. Professionals in different fields need to have some modesty concerning when their approaches are most useful and when they are not. It may well be, for example, that efforts to address and avoid the harmful effects of corporal punishment, psychological aggression, and neglect are not best housed in the criminal justice system.

Although our own bias is for collaborations among criminal justice, social service, and other community programs to *prevent* child maltreatment both directly and through combating its causes, collaboration after maltreatment remains essential. A case study in one community regarding child sexual abuse revealed that collaboration between CPS and law enforcement personnel can increase the number of confessions in child sexual abusers, even in the absence of testimony by victims (Faller and Henry 2000).

Some efforts at preventive collaboration between the criminal justice system and other services hold promise. For example, preliminary findings from a five-site evaluation of the Safe Kids/Safe Streets program (developed by the U.S. Department of Justice to help communities reduce child maltreatment and its negative outcomes through collaborations among criminal justice, social service, and local community agencies and representatives) suggested considerable progress toward the program's goals (Cronin et al. 2006). Local stakeholders reported progress in such areas as providing multiagency responses to child victims affected by domestic violence, educating the community about child abuse and neglect, improving services for children and families at risk of falling through the cracks, and decreasing community tolerance for child maltreatment. Research on family treatment drug courts (FTDC), which are designed to improve outcomes for substance-abusing families involved in the child welfare system, shows that, compared with a non-FTDC sample, FTDC parents entered substance abuse treatment more quickly and stayed in treatment longer. They were also more likely to be reunified with their children (Green et al. 2007). In our view, such innovations, operating in a multilevel prevention and intervention approach, provide good models for criminal justice collaborations with other agencies to address the child maltreatment problem.

REFERENCES

Baird, Christopher, Janice Ereth, and Dennis Wagner. 1999. *Research-Based Risk Assessment: Adding Equity to CPS Decision Making. The National Incidence Studies.* Madison, WI: Children's Research Center.

Belsky, Jay. 1993. "Etiology of Child Maltreatment: A Developmental-Ecological Approach." *Psychological Bulletin* 114: 413–34.

Berger, Lawrence Marc. 2004. "Income, Family Structure, and Child Maltreatment Risk." *Children and Youth Services Review* 26: 725–48.

Child Abuse Prevention and Treatment Act (CAPTA) of 1974. P.L. 93–247. http://www.acf.hhs.gov/programs/cb/laws_policies/cblaws/capta/index.htm

Christopher, Kelly, Catherine J. Lutz-Zois, and Amanda R. Reinhardt. 2007. "Female Sexual-Offenders: Personality Pathology as a Mediator of the Relationship between Childhood Sexual Abuse History and Sexual Abuse Perpetration against Others." *Child Abuse and Neglect* 31: 871–83.

Coulton, Claudia J., David S. Crampton, Molly Irwin, James C. Spilsbury, and Jill E. Korbin. 2007. "How Neighborhoods Influence Child Maltreatment: A Review of the Literature and Alternative Pathways." *Child Abuse and Neglect* 31: 1117–42.

Cronin, Roberta, Francis Gragg, Dana Schultz, and Karla Eisen. 2006. "Lessons Learned from Safe Kids/Safe Streets." *Juvenile Justice Bulletin*. http://www.ncjrs.gov/pdffiles1/ojjdp/213682.pdf (accessed March 15, 2008).

Douglas, Emily M., and Murray A. Straus. 2008. "Discipline by Parents and Child Psychopathology." In *International Handbook of Psychopathology and the Law,* edited by Alan Felthouse and Henning Sass. Hoboken, NJ: Wiley, 303–18.

Dubowitz, Howard. 2007. "Understanding and Addressing the 'Neglect of Neglect': Digging into the Molehill." *Child Abuse and Neglect* 31: 603–6.

Dubowitz, Howard, Steven C. Pitts, Alan J. Litrownik, Christine E. Cox, Desmond K. Runyan, and Maureen M. Black. 2005. "Defining Child Neglect Based on Child Protective Services Data." *Child Abuse and Neglect* 29(5): 493–511.

Faller, Kathleen C., and James Henry. 2000. "Child Sexual Abuse: A Case Study in Community Collaboration." *Child Abuse and Neglect* 24: 1215–25.

Faller, Kathleen C., and Vincent J. Palusci. 2007. "Children's Advocacy Centers: Do They Lead to Positive Case Outcomes?" *Child Abuse and Neglect* 31: 1021–29.

Finkelhor, David, and Lisa M. Jones. 2004. *Explanations for the Decline in Child Sexual Abuse Cases.* Washington, DC: Department of Justice, Office of Justice Programs, Office of Juvenile Justice and Delinquency Prevention.

Finkelhor, David, and Richard Ormrod. 2001. "Child Abuse Reported to the Police." Washington, DC: Department of Justice, Office of Justice Programs, Office of Juvenile Justice and Delinquency Prevention.

Freisthler, Bridget, Darcey H. Merritt, and Elizabeth A. LaScala. 2006. "Understanding the Ecology of Child Maltreatment: A Review of the Literature and Directions for Future Research." *Child Maltreatment* 11: 263–80.

Garbarino, James, and Kathleen Kostelny. 1992. "Child Maltreatment as a Community Problem." *Child Abuse and Neglect* 16: 455–64.

Garbarino, James, and Deborah Sherman. 1980. "High-Risk Neighborhoods and High-Risk Families: The Human Ecology of Child Maltreatment." *Child Development* 51: 188–98.

Gelles, Richard James. 1999. "Policy Issues in Child Neglect." In *Neglected Children: Research, Practice, and Policy,* edited by Howard Dubowitz. Thousand Oaks, CA: Sage.

Gershoff, Elizabeth Thompson. 2002. "Corporal Punishment by Parents and Associated Child Behaviors and Experiences: A Meta-Analytic and Theoretical Review." *Psychological Bulletin* 128: 539–79.

Gil, David G. 1989. "Exposing or Concealing the Roots of Violence." Review of *Intimate Violence,* by Richard J. Gelles and Murray A. Straus. *Contemporary Sociology* 18: 236–38.

Green, Beth L., Carrie Furrer, Sonia Worcel, Scott Burrus, and Michael W. Finigan. 2007. "How Effective Are Family Treatment Drug Courts? Outcomes from a Four-Site National Study." *Child Maltreatment* 12: 43–50.

Hampton, Robert L., and Eli H. Newberger. 1985. "Child Abuse Incidence and Reporting by Hospitals: Significance of Severity, Class, and Race." *American Journal of Public Health* 75: 56–60.

Hill, Robert B. 2004. "Institutional Racism in Child Welfare." *Race and Society* 7: 17–33.

Hines, Denise A., and Kathleen Malley-Morrison. 2005. *Family Violence in the United States: Defining, Understanding, and Combating Abuse.* Thousand Oaks, CA: Sage.

Jackson, Shelly, Ross A. Thompson, Elaine H. Christiansen, Rebecca A. Colman, Jennifer Wyatt, Chad W. Buckendahl, Brian L. Wilcox, and Reece Peterson. 1999. "Predicting Abuse-Prone Parental Attitudes and Discipline Practices in a Nationally Representative Sample." *Child Abuse and Neglect* 23: 15–29.

Jonson-Reid, Melissa, and Richard P. Barth. 2000*a*. "From Maltreatment Report to Juvenile Incarceration: The Role of Child Welfare Services." *Child Abuse and Neglect* 24(4): 505–20.

Jonson-Reid, Melissa, and Richard P. Barth. 2000*b*. "From Placement to Prison: The Path to Adolescent Incarceration from Child Welfare Supervised Foster or Group Care." *Children and Youth Services Review* 22(7): 493–516.

Kaufman, Joan, and Edward Zigler. 1987. "Do Abused Children Become Abusive Parents?" *American Journal of Orthopsychiatry* 57: 186–92.

Keeping Children and Families Safe Act of 2003, Public Law 108–36. http://www.acf.hhs.gov/programs/cb/laws_policies/policy/im/2003/im0304a.pdf.

Kempe, C. Henry, Frederic N. Silverman, Brandt F. Steele, William Droegemuller, and Henry K. Silver. 1962. "The Battered Child Syndrome." *Journal of the American Medical Association* 181: 17–24.

Lansford, Jennifer E., Shari Miller-Johnson, Lisa J. Berlin, Kenneth A. Dodge, John E. Bates, and Gregory S. Pettit. 2007. "Early Physical Abuse and Later Violent Delinquency: A Prospective Longitudinal Study." *Child Maltreatment* 12: 233–45.

Malley-Morrison, Kathleen, and Denise A. Hines. 2004. *Family Violence in a Cultural Perspective.* Thousand Oaks, CA: Sage.

McSherry, Dominic. 2007. "Understanding and Addressing the Neglect of Neglect: Why Are We Making a Mole-Hill out of a Mountain?" *Child Abuse and Neglect* 31: 607–14.

Mulvaney, Matthew K., and Carolyn J. Mebert. 2007. "Parental Corporal Punishment Predicts Behavior Problems in Early Childhood." *Journal of Family Psychology* 21: 389–97.

Myers, John E. B. 2002. "The Legal System and Child Protection." In *The APSAC Handbook on Child Maltreatment,* 2nd ed., edited by John E.B. Myers, Lucy Berliner, John Briere, C. Terry Hendrix, Carole Jenny, and Theresa A. Reid. Thousand Oaks, CA: Sage.

Pelton, Leroy H. (2008). "An Examination of the Reasons for Child Removal in Clark County, Nevada." *Children and Youth Services Review* 30: 787–99.

Pilisuk, Marc. 1998. "The Hidden Structure of Contemporary Violence." *Peace and Conflict: Journal of Peace Psychology* 4: 197–216.

Runyan, Desmond, Christine Cox, Howard Dubowitz, Rae Newton, Mukund Upadhyaya, Jonathan B. Kotch, Rebecca Leeb, Mark Everson, and Elizabeth Knight. 2005. "Describing Maltreatment: Do Child Protective Service Reports and Research Definitions Agree?" *Child Abuse and Neglect* 29: 461–77.

Ryan, Joseph P., Denise Herz, Pedro M. Hernandez, and Jane M. Marshall. 2007. "Maltreatment and Delinquency: Investigating Child Welfare Bias in Juvenile Justice Processing." *Children and Youth Services Review* 29: 1035–50.

Ryan, Joseph P., and Mark F. Testa. 2005. "Child Maltreatment and Juvenile Delinquency: Investigating the Role of Placement and Placement Instability." *Children and Youth Services Review* 27: 227–49.

Saunders, Benjamin E. 2003. "Understanding Children Exposed to Violence: Toward an Integration of Overlapping Fields." *Journal of Interpersonal Violence* 18: 356–76.

Sedlak, Andrea J., and Diane D. Broadhurst. 1996. *Executive Summary of the Third National Incidence Study of Child Abuse and Neglect.* http://www.childwelfare.gov/pubs/statsinfo/nis3.cfm.

Straus, Murray A. 1979. "Measuring Intrafamily Conflict and Violence: The Conflict Tactics (CT) Scales." *Journal of Marriage and the Family* 41: 465–99.

———. "Stress and Physical Child Abuse." *Child Abuse and Neglect* 4: 75–88.

———. "The Conflict Tactic Scale and Its Critics: An Evaluation and New Data on Validity and Reliability." In *Physical Violence in American Families: Risk Factors and Adaptations to Violence in 8,145 Families* edited by Murray A. Straus and Richard J. Gelles. New Brunswick, NJ: Transaction.

Straus, Murray A., and Denise Donnelly. 2001. *Beating the Devil Out of Them: Corporal Punishment and Its Effects on Children.* Boston: Lexington Books.

Straus, Murray A., and Richard J. Gelles. 1986. "Societal Change and Change in Family Violence from 1975 to 1985 as Revealed by Two National Surveys." *Journal of Marriage and the Family* 48: 465–79.

Straus, Murray A., Richard J. Gelles, and Suzanne Steinmetz. 1980. *Behind Closed Doors: Violence in the American Family.* Garden City, NY: Anchor Books.

Straus, Murray A., Sherry L. Hamby, David Finkelhor, David W. Moore, and Desmond Runyan. 1998. "Identification of Child Maltreatment with the Parent-Child Conflict Tactics Scales: Development and Psychometric Data for a National Sample of American Parents." *Child Abuse and Neglect* 22: 249–70.

Tzeng, Oliver, Jay Jackson, and Henry C. Karlson, eds. 1991. *Theories of Child Abuse and Neglect: Differential Perspectives, Summaries, and Evaluation.* New York: Praeger.

U.S. Department of Health and Human Services, Administration on Children, Youth, and Families. 2005. *Child Maltreatment 2005.* http://www.acf.hhs.gov/programs/cb/pubs/cm05/index.htm.

U.S. Department of Health and Human Services, National Center on Child Abuse and Neglect. 1998. *Child Maltreatment 1996: Reports from the States to the National Child Abuse and Neglect Data System.* Washington, DC: U.S. Government Printing Office.

U.S. Department of Health and Human Services, National Center on Child Abuse and Neglect. 1999. *Child Maltreatment 1999: Reports from the States to the National Child Abuse and Neglect Data System.* Washington, DC: U.S. Government Printing Office.

U.S. Department of Health and Human Services, National Center on Child Abuse and Neglect. 2004. *Child Maltreatment 2004: Reports from the States to the National Child Abuse and Neglect Data System.* Washington, DC: U.S. Government Printing Office.

Vissing, Yvonne M., Murray A. Straus, Richard J. Gelles, and John W. Harrop. 1991. "Verbal Aggression by Parents and Psychosocial Problems of Children." *Child Abuse and Neglect* 15: 223–38.

Wauchope, B. A., and Murray A. Straus. 1990. "Physical Punishment and Physical Abuse of American Children: Incidence Rates by Age, Gender, and Occupational Class." In *Physical Violence in American Families: Risk Factors and Adaptations to Violence in 8,145 Families,* edited by Murray A. Straus and Richard J. Gelles. New Brunswick, NJ: Transaction.

Zellman, Gail L., and C. Christine Fair. 2002. "Preventing and Reporting Abuse." In *The APSAC Handbook on Child Maltreatment,* 2nd ed., edited by John E. B. Myers, Lucy Berliner, John N. Briere, C. Terry Hendrix, Carole Jenny, and Theresa A. Reid. Thousand Oaks, CA: Sage.

Zielinski, David S., and Catherine P. Bradshaw. 2006. "Ecological Influences on the Sequelae of Child Maltreatment: A Review of the Literature." *Child Maltreatment* 11: 49–62.

PART II

PROPERTY CRIME

CHAPTER 7

BURGLARY

WIM BERNASCO

BURGLARY is very common. Most people will be a victim of burglary at least once in their lifetime. Although commonly listed as a property offense, most victims agree that the illegal entry into their home causes more emotional turmoil and more enduring stress than the monetary loss and inconveniences they suffer. Burglary is one of the most extensively studied offenses, and it is an illusion that a single scholar could ever read all that has been written about it. A comprehensive essay on burglary appeared in the fourteenth volume of *Crime and Justice* (Shover 1991). I took that as the starting point for this chapter, focusing mostly on research that has appeared since. Several conclusions can be drawn:

- Burglary is the actual or attempted illegal entry into a dwelling with the intent to steal. Definitions vary between jurisdictions (and surveys) with respect to details, for example whether the actual entry requires force or destruction and what precisely constitutes a dwelling.
- Our knowledge about burglary is derived from victimization surveys, from the police and other criminal law organizations, and from offenders. Victimization surveys are preferred when the aim is to assess incidence and prevalence.
- Burglary is a common crime that occurs in industrialized countries with a decreasing annual rate of currently roughly 4 burglaries per 100 households. Burglary is most common in Anglo-Saxon countries. Victims report 40 percent of attempted burglaries and 80 percent of completed burglaries to the police, depending on the size of the loss involved.
- Burglars tend to burglarize in disadvantaged urban neighborhoods with poor social control. They prefer dwellings that are unoccupied and easily accessible and unobservable from the street, and they prefer items that

are CRAVED (concealable, removable, available, valuable, enjoyable, and disposable), the ideal being cash. Victimization risk is most strongly related to the amount of time a dwelling is left unoccupied. Victims quite often know the offenders.

- The majority of the people who commit burglaries are young males who burglarize to sustain an expensive lifestyle, often including drug use. Juvenile burglars are more likely to co-offend than adult burglars. Specialization in burglary is uncommon, as most burglars also commit other offenses, including violent ones.
- Burglaries are subject to time cycles that correspond to the times that dwellings are unoccupied. Although precisely for the reason of variation itself (absence of the occupants), the exact time of burglary is often unknown, and the daily time cycle shows most variation. Burglaries do not seem to vary a lot over the days of the week, but there is some seasonality in burglary data. In the United States most burglaries are committed during the summer, in Europe during the winter.
- Many burglaries are repeat burglaries of the same address. Often the second burglary involves the same offender as the first, and the second tends to take place within a few weeks or months after the first. The elevated victimization risk after burglary extends to dwellings in the immediate environment of the burglarized dwelling, which may indicate that a blocked repeat burglary elsewhere is displaced to nearby victims.
- Most conventional preventive measures against burglary are target-hardening devices that strengthen the physical barriers against unlawful entry to the property and measures that draw attention to illegal entries. There is some evidence that target-hardening devices are effective in reducing burglary. Preventing repeat victimization of recent burglary victims has been particularly successful.
- Large parts of Shover's (1991) essay remain valid in 2008, in particular the characteristics of offenders, victims, and offending. Three notable changes are that burglary rates have dropped considerably worldwide, that more sources of information on burglary have become available worldwide, and that repeat burglary victimization has been introduced as a useful concept for prevention, especially in the United Kingdom. Future work could address the offender-victim nexus, as well as burglary detection by contemporary technologies such as CCTV and DNA. More ethnographic work along lines initiated by Wright and Decker (1994) would be welcomed.

This chapter comprises nine sections. Section I kicks off by addressing how burglary is defined in various countries and jurisdictions, in criminal law as well as in victimization survey questions. Section II discusses victims, offenders, and the police as sources of information. In section III data are presented on the current prevalence of burglary in the United States, England and Wales, and other countries. Long-term burglary trends are addressed, as is the decision of victims whether or not to report a burglary to the police. Section IV discusses burglary "targets": the areas where offenders commit burglaries, the types of houses they enter, from whom they steal, and what they steal. Section V reviews what we know about the people who commit burglaries. Burglars are described in terms of their demographic attributes, motivations for burglary, co-offending patterns, and level of planning involved in the commission of a burglary. The burglary daily time cycle and its relation to target choice are described in section VI. Section VII is dedicated to the issue of repeated burglaries against the same or nearby addresses, a phenomenon that has received considerable attention during the past decades. Section VIII discusses evidence on the effectiveness of situational burglary prevention measures. Section IX concludes by discussing whether and how our understanding of burglary has increased since Shover's (1991) essay and by enumerating future research priorities.

I. What Is Burglary?

When someone enters an inhabited dwelling without permission and with the intent to steal, many people would agree that the person is committing a burglary; if a lock is broken to get inside and if valuable items are taken away, virtually everyone will agree. However, definitions of burglary differ between jurisdictions and over time (Mawby 2001, p. 4).

In the United States the Uniform Crime Reporting (UCR) program defines burglary as the unlawful entry of a structure used as a permanent dwelling to commit a felony or theft. To classify an offense as a burglary, it is not required that force be used to gain entry. The UCR program has three subclassifications for burglary: forcible entry, unlawful entry where no force is used, and attempted forcible entry. In many jurisdictions, including England and Wales, burglary also includes "distraction burglary," where falsehood, trick, or distraction is used on an occupant to gain access to the property in order to steal (Thornton et al. 2003). Various gradations of burglary can be distinguished depending on whether the offender was armed, whether there were co-offenders, whether the burglary took place at nighttime, and whether the property was occupied when entered. In Australia legislation introduced in 1999 replaced break-and-enter offenses with a range of so-called criminal trespass offenses, making it possible to distinguish larceny and criminal damage from illegal entry in various gradations of seriousness (South Australian Department of Justice 2007).

For statistical purposes, an important distinction is whether failed burglary attempts are included in the definition, as it has been suggested that there are nearly as many attempted burglaries as completed burglaries (Budd 1999). For example, when an offender is disturbed upon entering by an alarm system or by the occupants and flees, this is viewed as a burglary attempt (i.e., "attempted forcible entry" in the UCR classification).

Definitions of burglary differ with respect to the nature of the property entered; some countries exclude theft from a secondary residence or from an attic or basement in multidwelling buildings, and some countries include theft from a car (Aebi et al. 2006). A particularly important distinction is whether to include illegal entry and theft from structures not used as a dwelling, such as schools, offices, and shops. These are sometimes called commercial or nonresidential burglaries, as opposed to domestic or residential burglaries. This chapter deals with residential or domestic burglary only.

Because we increasingly rely on accounts of victims rather than on police records for understanding the nature and extent of burglary, the legal definition of burglary may be less important than how burglary is defined in survey questionnaires and interviews. In the International Crime Victimization Survey (ICVS), the definitions of burglary and attempted burglary are reflected in what questions respondents are asked (van Dijk, van Kesteren, and Smit 2008: appendix 8, Q60 and Q65), for example:

> Over the past five years, did anyone actually get into your home/residence without permission, and steal or try to steal something? I am not including here thefts from garages, sheds or lock-ups.
>
> Apart from this, over the past five years, do you have any evidence that someone tried to get into your home/residence unsuccessfully? For example, damage to locks, doors or windows or scratches around the lock?

In the British Crime Survey, burglaries include all break-ins and attempts, regardless of intent, to all inhabited dwellings (any house or flat or any outhouse or garage linked to the dwelling via a connecting door; Nicholas, Kershaw, and Walker 2007, p. 75). The questions refer to a period of 12 months preceding the interview. Affirmative answers to these questions are indicative of burglary or attempted burglary:

> During the last 12 months...has anyone GOT INTO this house/flat without permission and STOLEN or TRIED TO STEAL anything?
>
> [Apart from anything you have already mentioned], in that time did anyone GET INTO your house/flat without permission and CAUSE DAMAGE?
>
> [Apart from anything you have already mentioned], in that time have you had any evidence that someone has TRIED to get in without permission to STEAL or to CAUSE DAMAGE?

Questions in the U.S. *National Crime Victimization Survey* (*NCVS*), a rotating panel survey, refer to the six months that precede the interview (U.S. Dept. of

Justice 2007*a*): "In the last 6 months, has anyone broken in or ATTEMPTED to break into your home by forcing a door or window, pushing past someone, jimmying a lock, cutting a screen, or entering through an open door or window?" Based on the answers to subsequent follow-up questions, and in line with the UCR classification, the *NCVS* distinguishes between completed burglaries (either "forcible entry" or "unlawful entry without force") and "attempted forcible entries."

II. Sources of Knowledge on Burglary

What we know about residential burglary comes either from the police and other agencies in the criminal justice system, from victim accounts, or from offender accounts. In the United States, the Uniform Crime Reports (UCR) are the major source of information at the federal level collected by law enforcement agencies. These are compiled from reports transmitted to the Federal Bureau of Investigation. In the United Kingdom, the Recorded Crime Statistics are based on crimes notified to the Home Office by police forces. Other countries collect and publish similar statistics on crime recorded to the police and other law enforcement agencies. The European Sourcebook of Crime and Criminal Justice compiles and harmonizes crime and justice data, including burglary statistics, from about 40 European countries (Aebi et al. 2006).

Before the advent of population surveys to measure criminal victimization, burglary data recorded by the police and other criminal justice agencies were the only data available to measure the size of the burglary problem. In the 1970s the criminal victimization survey was discovered as a way to measure the "dark figure" of crime not reported to or not recorded by the police and other law enforcement agencies. In the United States the *National Crime Victimization Survey* started in 1972 and was designed to serve as a benchmark for UCR statistics (Rand and Rennison 2002, p. 48). The *NCVS* is an ongoing panel survey designed to be nationally representative of households and persons age 12 and over in the United States, collected by the Census Bureau under the direction of the Bureau of Justice Statistics (Lauritsen 2005). Each year about 134,000 persons in 77,200 households are interviewed. A special methodological feature of the *NCVS* is that it employs a rotating panel design: households remain in the sample for, at most, seven interviews, a feature that affords longitudinal data, albeit over a relatively short period. Another distinctive feature is the use of the first interview as a "bounding interview" to minimize the telescoping effect, that is, the tendency of respondents to report that incidents are more recent than they actually are.

The British Crime Survey (BCS) started in 1982; subsequent sweeps were in 1984, 1988, 1992, 1994, 1996, 1998, 2000, before it moved to an annual cycle in 2001. The BCS asks adults in private households about their experience of victimization in the previous 12 months.

In terms of geographical coverage, the International Crime Victimization Survey (ICVS) is the most comprehensive of the surveys. The ICVS was started in 1987 as an initiative of a group of European criminologists to produce estimates of victimization that can be used for international comparison. There have been five main sweeps of the ICVS (1989, 1992, 1996, 2000, 2004–5). It is the only standardized victimization survey that includes respondents from a large number of countries. In the most recent sweep 38 countries were represented, of which 30 were sampled nationwide.

Offender accounts are the last source of information used to gain knowledge on burglary. Because the detection rate of burglary is universally low, offender accounts are not useful for estimating the size of the burglary problem. Rather, offender accounts help us understand why offenders burglarize and how they do it. Except for youth population surveys, such as the National Youth Survey (Elliott, Huizinga, and Ageton 1985) and the National Longitudinal Study of Adolescent Health in the United States (Harris et al. 2003), most studies have used accounts of detained offenders (Bennett and Wright 1984; Ashton et al. 1998; Rengert and Wasilchick 2000; Palmer, Holmes, and Hollin 2002) and active offenders "out on the street" (Cromwell, Olson, and Avary 1991; Wright and Decker 1994). Nee (2003) reviews the various ways offender accounts have been used for understanding the cognitive and social processes that play a role in the commission of burglaries.

III. Incidence, Prevalence, Trends, and Reporting to the Police

Because not all burglary victims report to the police, victimization surveys are generally seen as the best available source for estimating the size of the domestic burglary problem in quantitative terms. Three related measures have been used to determine burglary victimization quantitatively (Trickett et al. 1992; Tseloni et al. 2002). *Prevalence* is the number of burglary victims as a percentage of the population; *incidence* (or the burglary rate) is the number of burglaries per person or household; and *concentration* is the number of burglaries per victim. For example, if 10 households in a population of 100 have been burglarized, of which 5 have been burglarized twice, the prevalence is 10, the incidence is 15, and the concentration is 1.5. This distinction is potentially important because a substantial number of burglaries have been shown to be repeat burglaries of the same address within a relatively short span of time.

Burglary is a prevalent crime worldwide. For the industrialized countries that took part in the 2004–5 ICVS, annually there were on overage 4.4 completed or attempted burglaries per 100 households (see fig. 7.1). With the exception of Mexico (8.8 burglaries per 100 households), the burglary rate tends to be highest

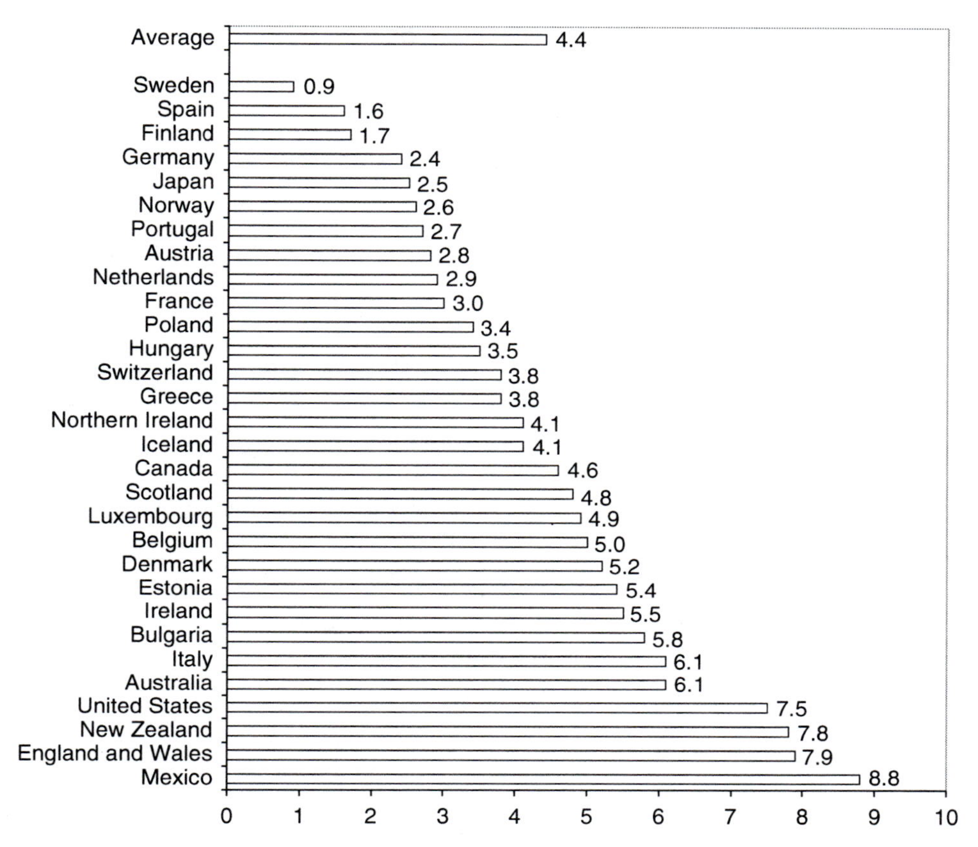

Figure 7.1. Burglary incidence (attempted and/or completed), ICVS 2004–5.
Source: van Dijk, van Kesteren, and Smit 2008.

in Anglo-Saxon countries, in particular England and Wales (7.9 percent). New Zealand (7.8), the United States (7.5), and Australia (6.1). Countries with a low burglary rate are Japan, Spain, and the northern European countries of Sweden, Finland, Norway, and Germany.

A. The Burglary Drop around the World

In most countries for which data are available, the ICVS shows that the incidence and prevalence of burglary have been decreasing since the early 1990s (van Dijk, van Kesteren, and Smit 2008, pp. 66–68). The ICVS findings on the long-term trend in burglary rates are supported by data from individual countries, such as the *NCVS* in the United States and the BCS in England and Wales, which may be more reliable because they are updated annually and survey a large within-country sample.

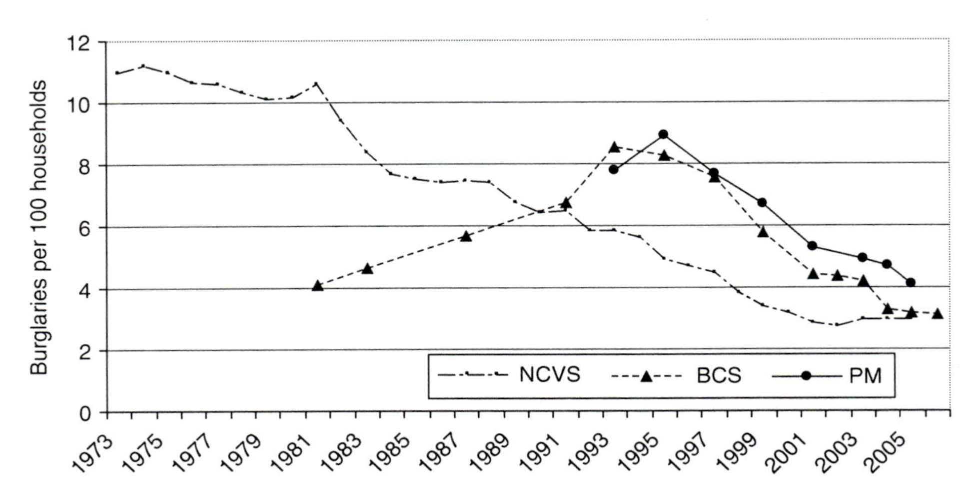

Figure 7.2. Burglary rate trends in the United States (*NCVS*), England and Wales (BCS), and the Netherlands (PM), 1973–2005.
Source: National Crime Victimization Survey (U.S. Dept. of Justice 2005); British Crime Survey (Nicholas, Kershaw, and Walker 2007, and previous main reports on subsequent sweeps of the British Crime Survey; see http://www.homeoffice.gov.uk/rds/bcs1.html for a full list); Netherlands Police Monitor (Intomart Gfk. 2005).

As shown in figure 7.2, according to *NCVS*-based estimates, the burglary rate (incidence) in the United States has been decreasing steadily, from 11 burglaries per 100 households in 1973 to fewer than 3 in 2005. In England and Wales the long-term trend since 1981 is not linear. From 1982 onward the burglary rate steadily increased until it reached a peak in the early 1990s. Thereafter, however, from 1995 to 2005, the number of burglaries dropped by 59 percent (Nicholas, Kershaw, and Walker 2007, p. 74). In the Netherlands the rate has been decreasing since 1993. In sum, there is substantial evidence for a general decline in the burglary rate in the industrialized world. It has been suggested that this continuing decrease is the consequence of the increased use of antiburglary devices and measures, such as alarm systems, locks and bolts, and improved lighting (van Dijk, van Kesteren, and Smit 2008). The evidence for this claim is reviewed in the section on prevention.

B. Reporting to the Police

Not all crime victims report to the police. The seriousness of an offense, in terms of durable physical injury or monetary loss or other harm, is the best predictor of whether a victim reports to the police (Goudriaan 2006). In the case of burglary, as is shown in table 7.1, victims of burglary attempts are less likely to report to the police than are victims of completed burglaries; victims

Table 7.1. Percentages of burglaries reported to the police in 2005, by offense and household characteristics

Variable	% reported
Total (average)	56.30
Burglary subcategory	
Forcible entry	74.70
Unlawful entry/without force	46.90
Attempted forcible entry	51.70
Value of loss	
$10–$49	37.70
$50–$99	27.40
$100–$249	38.70
$250–$499	48.10
$500–$999	63.10
$1,000+	85.90
Sex of head of household	
Male	54.90
Female	57.60
Property ownership	
Owned	58.40
Rented	53.20
Household annual income	
Less than $7,500	54.40
$7,500–$14,999	55.90
$15,000–$24,999	49.60
$25,000–$34,999	55.80
$35,000–$49,999	61.00
$50,000–$74,999	65.30
$75,000 or more	63.90

Source: U.S. Department of Justice 2006, tables 93a, 98, 99, 100.

of completed burglaries are more likely to report if force was used to gain entry; and victims with (larger) monetary losses are more likely to report than those who lost nothing or little. Further, female-headed households report slightly more often than male-headed households; home owners report slightly more often than renters; but higher income groups do not systematically report more or less often than lower income households. These relationships also hold within the subcategories of forcible entry, illegal entry without force, and attempted forcible entry.

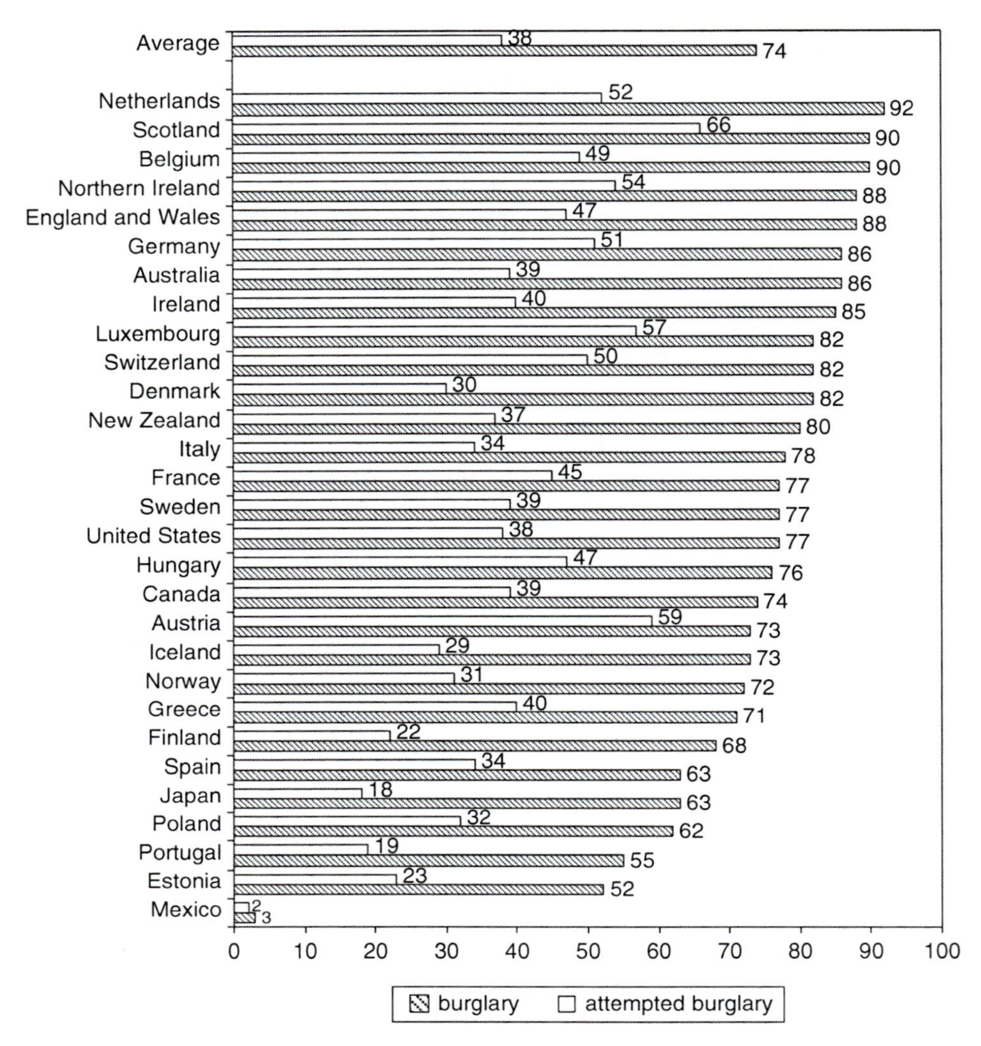

Figure 7.3. Percentage of reported burglaries (completed and attempted), ICVS 2004–5.
Source: van Dijk, van Kesteren, and Smit 2008.

When victims are asked in retrospect about their motivations to report or not report crimes to the police, the reasons they give vary from perceived moral obligations ("crimes should be reported") to cost-benefit considerations ("to recover property," "to collect insurance"), but the answers are likely to be justifications after the fact (Goudriaan 2006, pp. 11–12).

Burglary reporting rates vary across countries. As figure 7.3 shows, no less than 90 percent of completed burglaries are reported in the Netherlands, Belgium, and Scotland. The difference between the reporting rates of completed and attempted burglaries is remarkably constant: in most countries covered, completed burglaries are reported about twice as often as attempted burglaries. The reporting rate in Mexico is much lower than elsewhere, a phenomenon that had been observed for many participating developing countries in prior ICVS sweeps (van Dijk, van Kesteren, and Smit 2008, p. 114).

IV. Targets

Burglaries do not take place randomly. There is a pattern in the areas where offenders commit burglaries, which particular houses they target, what they steal, and from whom they steal. All of these (i.e., areas, houses, items, and victims) have been referred to as "burglary targets," but in individual cases it may not always be clear what precisely the target of a burglary is.

The burglary target selection process has been described as a spatially structured hierarchical process (Brantingham and Brantingham 1978; Cornish and Clarke 1986), in which the offender first selects a geographic area that fits his or her purposes and subsequently targets a specific street segment and a specific property in the chosen area. Once the burglar is inside the property, the items to be stolen become the actual targets. Alternatively, in some cases burglary is a relational offense, for example, when a former husband burglarizes the home of his ex-wife for retaliation, so that the victims rather than their possessions are the real targets. In any case, it is useful to review which characteristics of areas and which characteristics of individual houses are associated with burglary risk and what items tend to be stolen.

A. Areas

Leaving aside the global variation in burglary rates (see van Wilsem 2003; van Dijk, van Kesteren, and Smit 2008), it has generally been found that urbanized areas have higher burglary rates than rural areas, and that in urbanized areas inner-city neighborhoods suffer more from burglary than do suburban neighborhoods (Sampson and Groves 1989). Empirical research further consistently demonstrates that burglary rates (and crime rates generally) are elevated in deprived areas, ethnically mixed areas, and areas with high residential turnover, all measured at various levels of geographical aggregation.

The relationships between burglary risk and deprivation, ethnic heterogeneity, and residential turnover have been found to be indirect for two very different reasons. The first is that all three are associated with a lack of social control among residents (Bursik and Grasmick 1993; Sampson, Raudenbush, and Earls 1997). When social control (which is also captured in the slightly more complex concepts of social organization and social efficacy) is lacking, residents are less likely to take notice of incivilities or offenses taking place in their environment, and if they do, are less likely to intervene personally or call the police to stop it. Thus, where social control is lacking burglars run lower risks of apprehension and residents run higher risks of victimization.

The second reason is that most offenders themselves live in deprived, ethnically mixed, and unstable areas and usually offend within their own awareness spaces (Forrester, Chatterton, and Pease 1988; Wiles and Costello 2000). Thus these measures are largely synonymous to being nearby and exposed to concentrations of motivated offenders (Bernasco and Luykx 2003). This may explain the paradox that although offenders themselves claim that they select prosperous targets (Wright and Logie 1988), the empirical evidence on actual targets is that burglary is concentrated in deprived areas.

Studies of crime surveys have shown that characteristics related to individuals and area deprivation interact with the more visibly affluent households (e.g., detached and semidetached properties as opposed to terraced properties and flats) in the most deprived areas having the highest risks of burglary victimization (Trickett, Osborn, and Ellingworth 1995; Bowers, Johnson, and Pease 2005). Apparently offenders' preferences for prosperous targets are local preferences: they prefer the most prosperous targets within the (deprived) area they are familiar with.

B. Premises

Following the work of urban planners (Jacobs 1961; Newman 1973), other studies have focused on the role of the physical design of residential environments and burglary risk. A number of physical characteristics of residential units have been associated with burglary risk. Some of these apply to the location of the house in the urban landscape or street network or to the design of its immediate environment. Others apply to the structure of the unit itself. Proximity to major thoroughfares increases the risk, and being located in a dead-end street or cul-de-sac decreases it (Budd 1999; Hakim, Rengert, and Shachmurove 2001), possibly because the former are more and the latter are less likely to become part of many offenders' awareness spaces, although the findings are also compatible with a preference on the part of burglars for houses that allow for multiple exit routes. With respect to the units themselves, it has been shown that properties at the corner of a street block have larger burglary risks than properties in the middle of the block, and that the burglary risk is elevated in detached and semidetached houses (as compared to terraced properties and flats), especially if they border playgrounds, woods, or other nonresidential area or if parts of the house are not visible from the street.

Three general property selection criteria have been identified (Cromwell, Olson, and Avary 1991): surveillability, occupancy, and accessibility. Surveillability indicates whether properties can be overseen by other people, obviously a risk factor for the offender. Surveillability is indicated by distance from the street, the absence of trees or hedges that block sightlines, and the absence of lighting. Occupancy is whether there are people at home; this is also a risk factor. Occupancy is indicated by the presence of noise or light in the house, a car on the driveway, toys in the garden, or the absence of unopened mail. Accessibility indicates how easy it is to break into the property. Open doors and windows are a case in point, although they might also signal occupancy. The presence of a dog and target-hardening devices such as window locks and alarm systems restrict accessibility. The evidence for their effectiveness is mixed, however, as discussed below.

C. Victims

The lifestyles of potential victims play a major role in their victimization risk. Because to commit their offense burglars mostly depend on the times that residents are away from home, a major predictor of burglary victimization is the proportion of time a property is unoccupied, a variable that is directly related to the frequency with which residents go out in the evening and go shopping, and indirectly to the composition of the households (single-person households and single-parent families have higher risks) and age (younger households have higher risks; Tseloni et al. 2004). Renters (as opposed to home owners) and unemployed residents also have elevated burglary risks, but the reason is unlikely to be related directly to the proportion of time their houses are unoccupied.

Although the issue is not reported extensively in the literature, some results suggest that burglary is not always a crime directed against anonymous victims. In the 1998 British Crime Survey it was found that in 41 percent of the burglaries victims were able to say something about the offenders. The offender was a complete stranger to the victims in only 49 percent of these cases (Budd 1999); in other cases the offender was casually known (17 percent) or even well known (34 percent). While Budd rightly remarks that the 41 percent of cases in which the victim was able to say something about the offender is probably not representative for all burglaries, it emphasizes that burglary offenders and victims quite often know each other. In some cases, for example those in which a former spouse burglarizes his or her partner's home, it may essentially be the victim who is the burglary target.

D. Items

If the victim is not the target of a burglary, the item to be stolen is the ultimate focus of acquisitive crime (Hearnden and Magill 2004; Wellsmith and Burrell 2005). What do burglars steal? Police records and victim surveys show that the most frequently stolen items are cash, jewelry, and portable electronic gear such as cell phones, cameras, audio and video equipment, computers, game consoles, and TVs. Most of these items would fit the CRAVED model (Clarke 1999) of "hot products," that is, products that have attractive features for thieves in general and burglars in particular. Cash is the ultimate CRAVED item.

V. Offenders

Burglary is a covert crime. Victims are seldom confronted with the offenders and may not know who the offenders are. Our knowledge is hampered by the fact that the detection (clearance) rates of burglary tends to be low: 12.6 percent in the United States in 2006, and generally below 10 percent in cities with a population above 500,000, much like those of other covert crimes (Federal Bureau of Investigation 2007, table 45). As a consequence, our knowledge of offenders is based on interviews with those who have been arrested (Taylor and Nee 1988; Rengert and Wasilchick 2000; Palmer, Holmes, and Hollin 2002; Hearnden and Magill 2004) or sometimes on observations of and interviews with active burglars in their natural settings (Cromwell, Olson, and Avary 1991; Wright and Decker 1994).

When asked about motives or precipitating factors in the decision to commit a burglary, most offenders mention financial need (Wright and Decker 1994). Often offenders are driven by the wish to continue a lifestyle they cannot afford without offending. In particular, the continued use of expensive drugs appears to motivate burglars (Mawby 2001, pp. 66–67). The influence of others further seems to trigger the involvement in burglaries (Bennett and Wright 1984, p. 33), and some mention boredom and a need for thrills. Burglaries tend to be committed by young males. Of the burglars arrested in the United States, 86 percent are male and half of them are younger than 22 (Federal Bureau of Investigation 2007, tables 39 and 40).

Among juvenile offenders burglary tends to be a joint activity. The major reason for this appears to be social rather than practical, as the group setting induces potential offenders for various reasons to join a risky endeavor they would not get involved in on their own (Shover and Honaker 1992; Hochstetler 2001). For practical reasons, such as the possibility of carrying stolen items and the usefulness of having one offender act as a lookout, one would expect co-offending to be common in burglary. Offender accounts, however, suggest that adult offenders are solitary burglars most of the time (Mawby 2001, pp. 69–71), although one might question whether these accounts are always valid, as interviewed burglars tend to be very reluctant to talk about their (nonarrested) accomplices.

Unlike popular images of the persistent burglar, burglary specialization is uncommon. Most offenders are highly versatile, and this appears to be true for burglars as well. There is no evidence that burglars will use violence only when they are unexpectedly confronted with victims or bystanders. Many offenders who commit burglaries also commit violent offenses.

Some authors have proposed a typology of burglars. Maguire and Bennett (1982) distinguish "high-level burglars," "middle-level burglars," and "low-level burglars," a typology that is confirmed by the offense styles described by Bennett and Wright (1984, pp. 43–49), who distinguish between "planners," "searchers," and "opportunists," respectively. Although their typology is basically a typology of offenses rather than of offenders, Bennett and Wright find that most offenders can be characterized by a single offense style. Opportunistic offenses occur when a burglary opportunity presents itself and is immediately, without further planning, acted upon. The decision to burglarize, the selection of the target, and the burglary itself take place with little or no time gaps in between. In the searching offense, there is a time gap between the decision to commit a burglary and the selection of a target, but not between the target selection and the act of burglary; in other words, the searcher explicitly searches for a target and attacks when it is found. A planned burglary involves time gaps both between the decision to burglarize and the target selection and between the target selection and the actual burglary; thus there is forethought and preparation before each phase. As these findings are based on accounts of arrested offenders, and because it is possible that offense styles are related to the likelihood of apprehension, it is virtually impossible to estimate how these styles are distributed in the population.

VI. Temporal Distribution

Like all human behavior, the commission of a burglary is subject to temporal cycles, and its frequency may depend to some extent on the time of the day, the day of the week, and the season of the year. Because burglars tend to avoid confrontations with residents and prefer unoccupied targets, the exact timing of a burglary is often unknown; it is typically discovered when the residents find their place burglarized on returning home. The timing of burglaries is specified in police records using a time window that reflects when residents left their home and when they returned (Ratcliffe 2002). According to the *NCVS* (U.S. Dept. of Justice 2006, table 59), in 28 percent of the burglaries in the United States in 2005, the victims or the police had no idea what time of day the burglary was committed, although daytime burglaries (between 6 a.m. and 6 p.m.) were slightly more common (53 percent) than nighttime burglaries (47 percent) in those cases whose timing was known. In England and Wales 61 percent of burglaries occur between 6 a.m. and 6 p.m. (Budd 1999, p. 19). But the patterns display much larger variations (e.g., Andresen and Jenion 2004), with the least likely burglary hours being those that most residents spend at home.

As about 30 percent of burglaries occur during the weekend, from 6 p.m. on Friday evening to 6 a.m. on Monday morning (Budd 1999, p. 19), there is little evidence for a weekly time cycle in burglaries.

Like most types of crime, burglary appears to fluctuate systematically over the seasons of the year. In the United States burglary rates peak during the summer months and are below average in winter. This is shown in figure 7.4, which plots

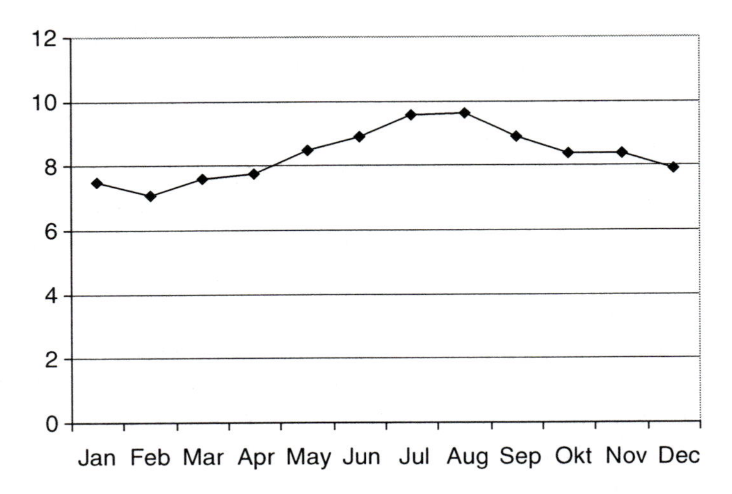

Figure 7.4. Seasonality of U.S. burglaries, 1992–2005.
Source: NCVS 1992–2005 concatenated incident files (U.S. Department of Justice 2005).

the months in which completed and attempted burglary incidents took place and which was prepared for this chapter using the *NCVS* concatenated incident files from 1992 to 2005 (U.S. Dept. of Justice 2007b). Interestingly, the pattern is reversed in England and Wales, which are also in the northern hemisphere but where burglaries peak in the winter, especially December and January (Farrell and Pease 1994; Hird and Ruparel 2007).

As to the explanation of temporal cycles, in the classic study that launched routine activity theory (Cohen and Felson 1979) the authors linked crime rate trends to changing social patterns, in particular a dispersion of activities away from homes. Clearly, some, if not all, of the temporal variation in the timing of burglaries is induced by the time use of potential victims or guardians: burglaries usually take place when residents or housekeepers are away from home and sometimes when they are asleep. In addition, offenders themselves have routine activities, such as school or work, that may give rise to burglary opportunities during certain times of the day.

Another part of the (daily and seasonal) temporal variation is induced by burglars' preference to offend under the cover of darkness in order to minimize their risk of being seen and recognized and arrested. As a preference for darkness is not always compatible with a preference for unoccupied homes, burglars' preference for darkness may depend on attributes of the potential targets. For example, it was found that in daylight burglars select targets in up-market low-density residential areas where residents are employed, whereas in darkness they preferred to target dwellings in deprived high-density areas (Coupe and Blake 2006).

VII. Repeat Victimization and Risk Communication

It has become widely recognized that crime is concentrated among relatively few victims, who are victimized repeatedly (Hindelang, Gottfredson, and Garafalo 1978). Repeat burglary victimization occurs when a property is burglarized more than once within a specified period (e.g., a year). Many studies have demonstrated that previous burglary victimization is associated with an elevated risk of future burglary victimization (e.g., Johnson, Bowers, and Hirschfield 1997; Budd 1999). Repeat burglaries tend to occur swiftly (Polvi et al. 1990, 1991). Thus, the risk of revictimization is greatest immediately after the event. After a short period the risk declines rapidly until it reaches its original level. Often, revictimization takes place within days or weeks. For example, in Tallahassee, Florida, it was found that 25 percent of the repeats took place within a week and 51 percent within one month (Robinson 1998). While the data, methodologies, and outcomes differ somewhat across studies, a characteristic exponential decay in the time course of repeat burglary victimization has been confirmed in many studies (Spelman 1995; Johnson, Bowers, and Hirschfield 1997; Ratcliffe and McCullagh 1998; Townsley, Homel, and Chaseling 2000).

There are two explanations for these findings (Tseloni and Pease 2003). The first is that burglary victimization simply *flags* properties with lasting attributes that attract offenders. According to this explanation, both the initial burglary and the repeated burglary reflect the elevated risk associated with stable attributes of the target. The second mechanism is that the initial victimization *boosts* the likelihood of a repeat. Under this mechanism, the initial burglary alters something about the property or the victim that increases the risk of revictimization.

It has been argued that the temporal pattern of repeat burglaries in particular often suggests the involvement of the same offender or offender group in both offenses (Polvi et al. 1991). Indeed, the boost explanation is compatible with the possibility that a repeat offense against the same premise involves the same offender who committed the initial offense and who returns to collect items not stolen during the initial burglary or that have been replaced since then. On the other hand, in the wake of a burglary one should expect victims to be extremely vigilant and maybe to install burglary prevention devices, which should logically decrease the risk of repeat victimization. The typical time course of repeat burglary has been viewed as supporting the boost explanation of repeat victimization. In particular, it has been viewed as tentative evidence that in a typical repeat burglary, the perpetrators are the same people who were involved in the initial event. Although the exponential decay in the time course itself is not sufficient evidence for this claim, as it may also indicate unobserved risk heterogeneity (Townsley, Homel, and Chaseling 2000; Morgan 2001; Sagovsky and Johnson 2007), there is also evidence from interviews and offender accounts that returning to a previously targeted property is a common burglar strategy, especially among prolific offenders (Ericsson 1995; Ashton et al. 1998; Palmer, Holmes, and Hollin 2002).

It has recently been shown that the elevated victimization risk after burglary applies not only to the victimized property, but that it generalizes to the immediate environment of that property. In other words, burglary victimization appears to be contagious. In the wake of a burglary properties near the victim's property run heightened burglary risks as well. The phenomenon was first established in Beenleigh, a police division near Brisbane in southeastern Queensland, Australia (Townsley, Homel, and Chaseling 2003), and Liverpool, England (Johnson and Bowers 2004; Bowers and Johnson 2005), and its ubiquity has recently been demonstrated in no fewer than 10 regions around the world (Johnson et al. 2007). Because of modus operandi similarity in near repeats, it has been argued that involvement of the same offenders is also likely in these cases (Bowers and Johnson 2004; Bernasco 2008). Near repeats could be displaced repeats, for example if an offender returns to a previously burglarized property but finds it well secured and subsequently targets an alternative nearby property.

VIII. Prevention

What preventive measures have been taken to reduce burglary, and what do we know about their effectiveness? Burglary prevention is not typically concerned with changing the attitudes of offenders, partly because efforts to change the delinquent attitudes and behavior of burglars cannot be very specific, as offenders are quite versatile. Another reason is that the burglary detection rate is so low that only a small minority is ever arrested and eligible for rehabilitation (Coupe and Griffiths 1996). Increases in the burglary detection rate may decrease the number of burglaries, as increased detection will translate into burglary's being perceived as a much more risky crime for offenders than before. Thus, although improving burglary detection cannot prevent the burglary that has been detected, it may deter the same and other offenders from committing future burglaries. In this respect, new developments in DNA profiling are promising, as DNA is most helpful in crimes that are the most difficult to detect. Although DNA samples currently make a relatively small contribution to all detections, they make a powerful contribution to those cases in which they are available (U.K. Home Office 2005).

Most conventional preventive measures against burglary can be categorized as situational crime prevention, that is, measures directed to change the immediate situation in which a burglary could potentially occur. Situational measures against burglary can be taken at various levels. First, target-hardening measures can be taken at the level of the individual property. Data on target-hardening measures of individual properties in the ICVS demonstrate that the penetration of burglar alarms and special door locks is higher in Anglo-American countries (England and Wales, Australia, United States, Canada, Scotland, Northern Ireland) than in Europe and Japan, and that it is higher in England and Wales than anywhere else (van Dijk, van Kesteren, and Smit 2008, pp. 135–39). Typically, at country level the dissemination of target-hardening devices is more or less proportional to the burglary rate. For example, England and Wales and Australia have the highest burglary rates and the highest levels of installed target-hardening devices. The most likely explanation of this finding is that citizens respond to high burglary rates by trying to defend themselves against burglaries.

According to findings from the British Crime Survey, a considerable number of British householders have installed devices that strengthen the physical barriers against unlawful entry to their property, such as double locks or deadlocks (76 percent), window locks (80 percent), and security chains on doors (32 percent). Further, many have taken measures that draw attention to illegal entries, such as outdoor (40 percent) or indoor (24 percent) sensor or timer lights and burglar alarm systems (29 percent). These home security measures might appear to be a key defense against burglary victimization. Households with no home security measures were almost 10 times more likely to have been burgled as households where there were simple security measures such as deadlocks on doors and window locks. Alarm systems only weakly differentiate between victimized and nonvictimized households. That simple security measures such as locks help to keep burglars out is also suggested by the fact that victimized households that experienced an attempted burglary were more likely to have double locks or deadlocks than those where entry was gained (Nicholas, Kershaw, and Walker 2007, p. 76). This is not the case with respect to alarm systems: an equal percentage of victims of completed burglaries and victims of attempted burglaries has an alarm system. If alarms are not effective this might be due to the frequency of false alarm activations. LeBeau and Vincent (1997) found that 98 percent of alarm activations in Charlotte, North Carolina, were false alarms.

The simple negative correlations between target-hardening measures and burglary risk may be spurious and may indicate that low-risk households (e.g., home owners, high-income groups) invest more in burglary prevention than do high-risk households, for reasons not directly related to the actual or perceived burglary risk (e.g., because the rich can better afford antiburglary devices or because home owners can expect longer term benefits).

Some target-hardening measures apply to larger entities than individual premises. Alley-gating, for example, is a measure that prevents unauthorized entry from the rear of properties of a block of houses; it is a target-hardening measure that has been shown to be successful (for an overview, see Armitage and Smithson 2007).

There is probably no government in the world that has invested as much in reducing burglary as England and Wales, starting with the Safer Cities project in

1988 and more specifically with the Reducing Burglary Initiative that started in 1999. As most of these initiatives are being constantly evaluated (many of them applying quasi-experimental designs with control groups and pre-intervention and postintervention measurements), this has also generated a host of information on the effectiveness of various prevention methods.

A comprehensive evaluation of nearly 300 antiburglary schemes in England and Wales (Ekblom, Law, and Sutton 1996, p. 41) found that a combination of target-hardening and community-oriented action (such as fostering Neighborhood Watch, property marking, raising burglary awareness among residents) worked best, but that target hardening could also work alone. This is in line with other research on target-hardening interventions, which has concluded that whole-area target hardening can reduce local burglary rates in the short term if continuous publicity is heard or viewed by prospective offenders (Tilley and Webb 1994, p. 26).

Independently of the prevention tactic chosen, publicity appears to increase the effects of prevention schemes (Bowers and Johnson 2003). Apparently this works because it informs and deters potential offenders from burgling in the area, although publicity may also sensitize potential victims and increase their vigilance. When publicity precedes the implementation it often reduces burglary in the period before the actual intervention (this may actually undermine the proper evaluation of the effect of the intervention itself, however). It may also reduce crime in a larger geographic area than where the intervention is implemented, and it may prolong the benefits of the intervention.

At a very general level, the largest burglary reductions are to be obtained by focusing on the areas or on the victims with the highest burglary risks. This may be the main reason for the success of schemes that have been inspired by the concept of repeat victimization. The prevention of repeat burglary victimization by varying means has received a great deal of success and attention in England, where the Kirkholt project and the Huddersfield project (Anderson, Chenery, and Pease 1995; Chenery, Holt, and Pease 1997) resulted in substantial burglary reductions through multitactic interventions. The success may not have been caused by any specific method of intervention, but by addressing a very high risk population who was recently victimized and thus sensitive to and aware of the emotional and material consequences.

IX. Conclusion

Although there has been a lot of continuity in the literature since Shover's (1991) review, some important developments may be highlighted. The first is the worldwide drop in burglary. The debate on the causes of the drop is ongoing, but the drop itself cannot be mistaken.

The second development concerns the nature and comprehensiveness of information on burglary. In 1991 the *National Crime Victimization Survey* had been under way in the United States for nearly 20 years; the British Crime Survey had just started in 1982 and did not yet follow an annual cycle; and the International Crime Victimization Survey gained momentum only during the 1990s. Similar developments can be observed with respect to police-reported burglary. In the United States the Uniform Crime Reports have been reported for decades, yet many other countries have lagged behind. The European Sourcebook is an example of a new initiative to collect and standardize information from various countries and to stimulate international comparison. It is also noteworthy that just after publication of Shover's essay some innovative studies were taken up to study offender accounts of burglary. In addition to the more conventional strategy of interviewing convicted burglars in prison (Rengert and Wasilchick 2000), some researchers studied target selection processes by taking arrested burglars back to places they had burglarized and having them reflect on the choices they made (Cromwell, Olson, and Avary 1991); others went as far as to interview active burglars out on the streets (Wright and Decker 1994).

A third development to be highlighted since Shover's essay is that much more is known about the large percentage of burglaries that are repeat victimizations. The success of the repeat burglary prevention programs in the United Kingdom has shown that repeats can be prevented, thereby reducing overall burglary rates substantially. An emerging line of research generalizes repeat victimization by showing that risk of revictimization can be communicated to nearby dwellings.

By way of a tentative agenda for research in the next decade, a few issues deserve to be studied in greater detail. One issue is the offender-victim nexus. It has been demonstrated repeatedly that offenders are disproportionately likely to be crime victims themselves, (Lauritsen and Laub 2007); another question is whether offenders and victims in the same incident are strangers to each other. Although the issue has not been studied extensively, a finding from the 1998 British Crime Survey (Budd 1999) indicates that quite often victims have an idea of who the offenders are. Ethnographic research shows that offenders quite often know who their victims are, as they tend to select them from a pool of acquaintances (Wright and Decker 1994; Hearnden and Magill 2004).

A second issue is the effectiveness of situational crime prevention measures. Although it has been argued that surveys demonstrate strong negative correlations between target-hardening and burglary risk, and although trend analyses show that increasing levels of burglary prevention devices are aligned with decreasing burglary rates, the evidence has not always been compelling, and the findings stand in strong contrast to the accounts of offenders, who generally emphasize that target-hardening measures play a minor role in the selection of dwellings.

The detection of burglary should be a third research priority. Worldwide the detection rate of burglary is low and a concern to the police. Possibilities for burglary detection offered by contemporary detection methods and tools (such as DNA matching, CCTV surveillance) have not yet been systematically investigated. The low burglary detection rate should also concern investigators who base their findings on police data or on accounts of arrested burglars. If fewer than 10 percent of the burglaries are detected, is there any guarantee that those arrested are representative of the total burglar population? DNA databases may help to solve this puzzle, not by increasing the detection rate but by providing evidence of the behavioral patterns (geographic, temporal, modus operandi) of those offenders who have never been arrested but whose DNA stains have been left at multiple burglary scenes. If the behavioral patterns of these burglars resemble those of arrested offenders, it would increase confidence in present findings based on arrested offenders only.

With respect to research methodologies, priority should be given to ethnographic research along lines set out by Richard Wright and his colleagues. They have shown not only that field research among offenders "in the wild" can provide important data and insights, but also that investments in such research can be translated into academic achievements and recognition.

REFERENCES

Aebi, Marcelo Fernando, Kauko Aromaa, Bruno Aubusson de Cavarlay, Gordon Barclay, Beata Gruszczyñska, Hanns Von Hofer, Vasilika Hysi, Jörg-Martin Jehle, Martin Killias, Paul Smit, and Cynthia Tavares. 2006. *European Sourcebook of Crime and Criminal Justice Statistics—2006, Third edition, Reeks Onderzoek en beleid, nr. 241.* The Hague: Boom Juridische uitgevers.

Anderson, David, Sylvia Chenery, and Ken Pease. 1995. *Biting Back: Tackling Repeat Burglary and Car Crime.* London: Home Office Police Department.

Andresen, Martin A., and Greg W. Jenion. 2004. "The Unspecified Temporal Criminal Event: What Is Unknown Is Known with Aoristic Analysis and Multinomial Logistic Regression." *Western Criminology Review* 5: 1–11.

Armitage, Rachel, and Hannah Smithson. 2007. "Alley-gating: A Review of Evidence, Policy and Legislation." *Internet Journal of Criminology.* http://www.internetjournalofcriminology.com (accessed September 15, 2008).

Ashton, Julie, Imogen Brown, Barbara Senior, and Ken Pease. 1998. "Repeat Victimisation: Offender Accounts." *International Journal of Risk, Security and Crime Prevention* 3: 269–79.

Bennett, Trevor, and Richard Wright. 1984. *Burglars on Burglary: Prevention and the Offender.* Aldershot, UK: Gower.

Bernasco, Wim. 2008. "Them Again? Same Offender Involvement in Repeat and Near Repeat Burglaries." *European Journal of Criminology* 5: 411–31.

Bernasco, Wim, and Floor Luykx. 2003. "Effects of Attractiveness, Opportunity and Accessibility to Burglars on Residential Burglary Rates of Urban Neighborhoods." *Criminology* 41: 981–1001.

Bowers, Kate J., and Shane D. Johnson. 2003. *The Role of Publicity in Crime Prevention: Findings from the Reducing Burglary Initiative*. London: Home Office Research, Development and Statistics Directorate.

Bowers, Kate J., and Shane D. Johnson. 2004. "Who Commits Near Repeats? A Test of the Boost Explanation." *Western Criminology Review* 5(3): 12–24.

Bowers, Kate J., and Shane D. Johnson. 2005. "Domestic Burglary Repeats and Space-Time Clusters: The Dimensions of Risk." *European Journal of Criminology* 2: 67–92.

Bowers, Kate J., Shane D. Johnson, and Ken Pease. 2005. "Victimisation and Re-victimisation Risk, Housing Type and Area: A Study of Interactions." *Crime Prevention and Community Safety: An International Journal* 7: 7–17.

Brantingham, Paul J., and Patricia L. Brantingham. 1978. "A Theoretical Model of Crime Site Selection." In *Crime, Law and Sanctions: Theoretical Perspectives,* edited by M. D. Krohn and R. L. Akers. Beverly Hills: Sage.

Budd, Tracey. 1999. *Burglary of Domestic Dwellings: Findings from the British Crime Survey*. London: Home Office.

Bursik, Robert J., Jr., and Harold G. Grasmick. 1993. *Neighborhoods and Crime: The Dimensions of Effective Community Control*. New York: Lexington Books.

Chenery, Sylvia, John Holt, and Ken Pease. 1997. *Biting Back II: Reducing Repeat Victimisation in Huddersfield*. London: Police Research Group, Home Office.

Clarke, Ronald V. 1999. *Hot Products: Understanding, Anticipating and Reducing Demand for Stolen Goods*. Police Research Series, Paper 112. London: Home Office.

Cohen, Lawrence E., and Marcus Felson. 1979. "Social Change and Crime Rate Trends: A Routine Activity Approach." *American Sociological Review* 44: 588–608.

Cornish, Derek B., and Ronald V. Clarke. 1986. Introduction. In *The Reasoning Criminal: Rational Choice Perspectives on Offending,* edited by D. B. Cornish and R. V. Clarke. New York: Springer-Verlag.

Coupe, Timothy, and Laurence Blake. 2006. "Daylight and Darkness Targeting Strategies and the Risks of Being Seen at Residential Burglaries." *Criminology* 44: 431–64.

Coupe, Timothy, and Max Griffiths. 1996. *Solving Residential Burglary*. London: Home Office, Police Research Group.

Cromwell, Paul F., James N. Olson, and D'Aun Wester Avary. 1991. *Breaking and Entering: An Ethnographic Analysis of Burglary*. London: Sage.

Ekblom, Paul, Ho Law, and Mike Sutton. 1996. *Safer Cities and Domestic Burglary*. London: Research and Statistics Directorate, Home Office.

Elliott, Delbert S., David Huizinga, and Suzanne S. Ageton. 1985. *Explaining Delinquency and Drug Use*. Beverly Hills: Sage.

Ericsson, Ulrica. 1995. "Straight from the Horse's Mouth." *Forensic Update* 43: 23–25.

Farrell, Graham, and Ken Pease. 1994. "Crime Seasonality: Domestic Disputes and Residential Burglary in Merseyside 1988–90." *British Journal of Criminology* 34(4): 487–98.

Federal Bureau of Investigation. 2007. *Crime in the United States 2006*. Washington, DC: U.S. Department of Justice. http://www.fbi.gov/ucr/cius2006/index.html.

Forrester, David, Mike Chatterton, and Ken Pease. 1988. *The Kirkholt Burglary Prevention Project, Rochdale*. Crime Prevention Unit Paper #13. London: Home Office.

Goudriaan, Heike. 2006. *Reporting Crime: Effects of Social Context on the Decision of Victims to Notify the Police*. Veenendaal, Netherlands: Universal Press.

Hakim, Simon, George F. Rengert, and Yochanan Shachmurove. 2001. "Target Search of Burglars: A Revised Economic Model." *Papers in Regional Science* 80: 121–37.

Harris, Kathleen Mullan, Francesca Florey, Joyce Tabor, Peter S. Bearman, Jo Jones, and J. Richard Udry. 2003. *The National Longitudinal Study of Adolescent Health: Research Design*. http://www.cpc.unc.edu/projects/addhealth/design.

Hearnden, Ian, and Christine Magill. 2004. *Decision-making by House Burglars: Offenders' Perspectives*. London: Home Office.

Hindelang, Michael, Michael R. Gottfredson, and James Garafalo. 1978. *Victims of Personal Crime: An Empirical Foundation for a Theory of Personal Victimization*. Cambridge, MA: Ballinger.

Hird, Celia, and Chandni Ruparel. 2007. *Seasonality in Recorded Crime: Preliminary Findings*. London: Home Office.

Hochstetler, Andy. 2001. "Opportunities and Decisions: Interactional Dynamics in Robbery and Burglary Groups." *Criminology* 39: 737–63.

Intomart Gfk. 2005. *Politiemonitor Bevolking 2005: Tabellenrapport* [Police Population Monitor: Report of Tables]. Hilversum, the Netherlands: Intomart Gfk.

Jacobs, Jane. 1961. *The Death and Life of Great American Cities*. New York: Random House.

Johnson, Shane D., Wim Bernasco, Kate Bowers, Henk Elffers, Jerry Ratcliffe, George Rengert, and Michael Townsley. 2007. "Space-Time Patterns of Risk: A Cross National Assessment of Residential Burglary Victimization." *Journal of Quantitative Criminology* 23: 201–19.

Johnson, Shane D., and Kate J. Bowers. 2004. "The Burglary as Clue to the Future: The Beginnings of Prospective Hot-Spotting." *European Journal of Criminology* 1: 237–55.

Johnson, Shane D., Kate J. Bowers, and Alex. Hirschfield. 1997. "New Insights into the Spatial and Temporal Distribution of Repeat Victimization." *British Journal of Criminology* 37: 224–41.

Lauritsen, Janet L. 2005. "Social and Scientific Influences on the Measurement of Criminal Victimization." *Journal of Quantitative Criminology* 21(3): 245–66.

Lauritsen, Janet L., and John H. Laub. 2007. "Understanding the Link between Victimization and Offending: New Reflections on an Old Idea." In *Surveying Crime in the 21st Century: Crime Prevention Studies,* vol. 22, edited by M. Hough and M. Maxfield. Monsey, NY: Criminal Justice Press.

LeBeau, James L., and Karen L. Vincent. 1997. "Mapping It Out: Repeat-Address Burglar Alarms and Burglaries." In *Crime Mapping and Crime Prevention,* edited by D. Weisburd and T. McEwen. Monsey, NY: Criminal Justice Press.

Maguire, Mike, and Trevor Bennett. 1982. *Burglary in a Dwelling: The Offense, the Offender and the Victim*. London: Heinemann.

Mawby, Rob I. 2001. *Burglary*. In *Crime and Society (Series),* edited by H. Croall. Cullompton, UK: Willan.

Morgan, Frank. 2001. "Repeat Burglary in a Perth Suburb: Indicator of Short-term or Long-term Risk?" In *Repeat Victimization,* edited by G. Farrell and K. Pease. Monsey, NY: Criminal Justice Press.

Nee, Claire. 2003. "Burglary Research at the End of the Millennium: An Example of Grounded Theory?" *Security Journal* 16: 37–44.

Newman, Oscar. 1973. *Defensible Space: Crime Prevention through Urban Design*. New York: Macmillan.

Nicholas, Sian, Chris Kershaw, and Alison Walker, eds. 2007. *Crime in England and Wales 2006/07*. London: Home Office.

Palmer, Emma J., Angela Holmes, and Clive R. Hollin. 2002. "Investigating Burglars' Decisions: Factors Influencing Target Choice, Method of Entry, Reasons for

Offending, Repeat Victimisation of a Property and Victim Awareness." *Security Journal* 15: 7–18.

Polvi, Natalie, Terah Looman, Charlie Humphries, and Ken Pease. 1990. "Repeat Break and Enter Victimisation: Time Course and Crime Prevention Opportunity." *Journal of Police Science and Administration* 17: 8–11.

Polvi, Natalie, Terah Looman, Charlie Humphries, and Ken Pease. 1991. "The Time-Course of Repeat Burglary Victimisation." *British Journal of Criminology* 31: 411–14.

Rand, Michael R., and Callie Marie Rennison. 2002. "True Crime Stories? Accounting for Differences in Our National Crime Indicators." *Chance* 15(1): 47–51.

Ratcliffe, Jerry H. 2002. "Aoristic Signatures and the Spatio-Temporal Analysis of High Volume Crime Patterns." *Journal of Quantitative Criminology* 18: 23–43.

Ratcliffe, Jerry H., and Michael J. McCullagh. 1998. "Identifying Repeat Victimization with GIS." *British Journal of Criminology* 38: 651–62.

Rengert, George F., and John Wasilchick. 2000. *Suburban Burglary: A Tale of Two Suburbs*. Springfield, IL: Charles C. Thomas.

Robinson, Matthew B. 1998. "Burglary Revictimization: The Time Period of Heightened Risk." *British Journal of Criminology* 38: 78–87.

Sagovsky, A., and Shane D. Johnson. 2007. "When Does Repeat Victimisation Occur?" *Australian and New Zealand Journal of Criminology* 40: 1–26.

Sampson, Robert J., and Byron W. Groves. 1989. "Community Structure and Crime: Testing Social Disorganization Theory." *American Journal of Sociology* 94: 773–802.

Sampson, Robert J., Stephen W. Raudenbush, and Felton Earls. 1997. "Neighborhoods and Violent Crime: A Multilevel Study of Collective Efficacy." *Science* 277: 918–24.

Shover, Neal. 1991. "Burglary." In *Crime and Justice: A Review of Research*, vol. 14, edited by Michael Tonry. Chicago: University of Chicago Press.

Shover, Neal, and David Honaker. 1992. "The Socially Bounded Decision Making of Persistent Property Offenders." *Howard Journal* 31: 276–93.

South Australian Department of Justice. 2007. *Crime and Justice in South Australia, 2006*. Adelaide: South Australian Department of Justice, Office of Crime Statistics and Research.

Spelman, William. 1995. "Once Bitten, Then What? Cross-Sectional and Time Course Explanations of Repeat Victimization." *British Journal of Criminology, Delinquency and Deviant Social Behaviour* 35: 366–83.

Taylor, Max, and Claire Nee. 1988. "The Role of Cues in Simulated Residential Burglary: A Preliminary Investigation." *British Journal of Criminology* 28: 396–401.

Thornton, Amanda, Chris Hatton, Caroline Malone, Tamsin Fryer, David Walker, Joanne Cunningham, and Nazia Durrani. 2003. *Distraction Burglary amongst Older Adults and Ethnic Minority Communities*. London: Home Office, Research, Development and Statistics Directorate.

Tilley, Nick, and Janice Webb. 1994. *Burglary Reduction: Findings from Safer Cities Schemes*. London: Home Office.

Townsley, M., R. Homel, and J. Chaseling. 2000. "Repeat Burglary Victimisation: Spatial and Temporal Patterns." *Australian and New Zealand Journal of Criminology* 33(1): 37–63.

Townsley, Michael, Ross Homel, and Janet Chaseling. 2003. "Infectious Burglaries: A Test of the Near Repeat Hypothesis." *British Journal of Criminology* 43: 615–33.

Trickett, Alan, Denise R. Osborn, and Dan Ellingworth. 1995. "Property Crime Victimisation: The Roles of Individual and Area Influence." *International Review of Victimology* 3: 273–95.

Trickett, Alan, Denise R. Osborn, Julie Seymour, and Ken Pease. 1992. "What Is Different about High Crime Areas?" *British Journal of Criminology* 32: 81–89.

Tseloni, Andromachi, Denise R. Osborn, Alan Trickett, and Ken Pease. 2002. "Modelling Property Crime Using the British Crime Survey: What Have We Learnt?" *British Journal of Criminology* 42: 109–28.

Tseloni, Andromachi, and Ken Pease. 2003. "Repeat Personal Victimization: 'Boosts' or 'Flags'?" *British Journal of Criminology* 43: 196–212.

Tseloni, Andromachi, Karin Wittebrood, Graham Farrell, and Ken Pease. 2004. "Burglary Victimization in England and Wales, the United States and the Netherlands." *British Journal of Criminology* 44: 66–91.

U.K. Home Office. 2005. *DNA Expansion Programme 2000–2005: Reporting Achievement.* London: Home Office, Forensic Science and Pathology Unit.

U.S. Dept. of Justice, Bureau of Justice Statistics. 2006. *Criminal Victimization in the United States, 2005. Statistical Tables.* Washington, DC: U.S. Department of Justice, Office of Justice Programs, Bureau of Justice Statistics. http://www.ojp.usdoj.gov/bjs/pubalp2.htm#cvus.

———. 2007*a*. *Crime and Victims Statistics.* Washington, DC: U.S. Department of Justice, Bureau of Justice Statistics, August 8. http://www.ojp.gov/bjs/cvict.htm.

———. 2007*b*. *National Crime Victimization Survey, 1992–2005: Concatenated Incident-Level Files* [computer file]. U.S. Dept. of Commerce, Bureau of the Census. ICPSR04699-v1. Ann Arbor, MI: Inter-university Consortium for Political and Social Research.

van Dijk, Jan J. M., John N. van Kesteren, and Paul Smit. 2008. *Criminal Victimisation in International Perspective: Key Findings from the 2004–2005 ICVS and EU ICS.* The Hague: Boom Legal Publishers.

van Wilsem, Johan. 2003. *Crime and Context: The Impact of Individual, Neighborhood, City and Country Characteristics on Victimization.* Amsterdam: Thela Thesis.

Wellsmith, Melanie, and Amy Burrell. 2005. "The Influence of Purchase Price and Ownership Levels on Theft Targets: The Example of Domestic Burglary." *British Journal of Criminology* 45: 741–64.

Wiles, Paul, and Andrew Costello. 2000. *The "Road to Nowhere": The Evidence for Traveling Criminals.* London: Home Office, Research, Development and Statistics Directorate.

Wright, Richard, and Scott Decker. 1994. *Burglars on the Job: Streetlife and Residential Break-Ins.* Boston: Northeastern University Press.

Wright, Richard, and Robert H. Logie. 1988. "How Young House Burglars Choose Targets." *Howard Journal* 27: 92–104.

CHAPTER 8

AUTO THEFT

MICHAEL CHERBONNEAU
AND RICHARD WRIGHT

IN a comprehensive review of the literature on motor vehicle theft, Ronald Clarke and Patricia Harris (1992*a*) identified a profound lack of academic research.[1] Since then, many studies of auto theft have been published, exploring the offense in detail and at varying units of analysis. The majority of those studies, however, have been conducted in non-U.S. jurisdictions such as Australia, Canada, and the United Kingdom. For example, more than half of the contributions to the recent edited collection *Understanding and Preventing Car Theft* (Maxfield and Clarke 2004) address auto theft patterns and prevention in countries other than the United States.

In retrospect, it is surprising that the 1992 Clarke and Harris article did not stimulate substantial U.S.-based research on auto theft. Motor vehicle theft rates in the United States reached historically high levels at about this time, accompanied by rising public concern about car crime. In response, the U.S. Congress passed the Anti–Car Theft Act of 1992, the fourth installment of federal legislation targeting motor vehicle theft, beginning with the Dyer Act in 1919. The 1992 Act focused on automobile title fraud and made it a federal crime to own, operate, maintain, or control a chop shop (National Highway Traffic Safety Administration 1998). Armed vehicle theft, or "carjacking," was added to the bill prior to its signing, after several atypical but well-publicized carjackings focused national attention on such crimes. Under the Anti–Car Theft Act of 1992 carjacking became a federal offense punishable by sentences ranging from 15 years to life, depending on the severity of injury suffered by the victim(s).

The paucity of auto theft research in the United States is more perplexing still when you consider the symbolic and cultural importance of cars to Americans

(Copes 2003), the way asphalt has changed our urban centers and shaped our suburbs over the past several decades (Davies 1975; St. Clair 1986), and how urban sprawl has increased the interpersonal divide between social classes (Porter 1999). The car not only ushered in so-called urban sprawl and efficient "access to the rapidly expanding middle-class suburbs, but was a status item in its own right tied to notions of gender, status, and individual freedom" (McShane 1994, p. 227). The importance of self-sufficient transportation in twenty-first century America transcends age, gender, and socioeconomic status (Ornati 1969; Paaswell and Recker 1978). The United States exhibits much higher rates of automobile ownership than many other industrialized countries (van Dijk and Mayhew 1992), and a car is the first or second most expensive item that most Americans own (McCaghy, Giordano, and Henson 1977). Vast sums of money are spent in the United States each year insuring vehicles against theft (Insurance Information Institute 2007).

In the 15 years between 1895 and 1910 the number of automobiles in the United States rose from four to almost half a million (Hall 1952). Twenty years later there were approximately 27 million motor vehicles registered in the country (Federal Highway Administration [FHA] 1997). As with any new product of value, the proliferation of publicly and privately owned motor vehicles, which now exceed 247 million nationwide (FHA 2006), created new opportunities for various sorts of lawbreaking. Some would-be criminals viewed the automobile as a "crime facilitator" (Clarke 1995), that is, as a new way to commit the same old crimes (see, e.g., Goddard 1932). Others saw it as a crime target in its own right, with the proliferation of car ownership opening up new lines of criminal enterprise, namely vehicle-related theft (Wilkins 1964; Laycock 2004).

This chapter reviews what we currently know about automobile theft. Section I defines the crime and outlines its prevalence. In section II we examine the social and economic consequences of auto theft. Section III deals with patterns of auto theft in the United States and elsewhere. In section IV we discuss forms of motor vehicle theft, including various types of offenders and offender motivations. Section V discusses victim and offender characteristics, correlates of victimization risk, and types of vehicles stolen. Section VI discusses motor vehicle theft offenders. The final section examines the ways auto theft is controlled, concluding with a discussion of policy-relevant issues and directions for future research.

Some of the important findings that emerge include the following:

- Motor vehicle theft is an important property crime. One million stolen motor vehicles are reported to police each year for a total property loss exceeding $7 billion. Although technically a form of larceny, auto theft is treated as a separate offense in crime statistics due to the magnitude and seriousness of the offense and to the social and economic costs it engenders.
- Motor vehicles have the highest recovery rate of all stolen property. Roughly 6 in 10 vehicles stolen in 2006 were recovered.

- Auto theft in the United States has declined overall by 37 percent over the past 15 years, but has increased by 33 percent in western states since 1999. Vehicle theft is not evenly distributed throughout the United States. It is concentrated in urban rather than rural areas and generally is higher in states and cities near international and coastal boarders.
- Cross-national comparisons indicate that auto theft rates in the United States are substantially lower than in most other industrialized countries, though the offense is declining in many of these nations too.
- Many auto theft typologies have been constructed as a way to organize the varied motivations for auto stealing. Most such schemes are too rigid to capture the fluid quality of offenders' motives.
- Auto theft victims and offenders are much like those found in other sorts of serious crime, tending to be young and poor and to live in urban rather than rural areas.
- The majority of auto thefts occur near the victim's residence during the nighttime hours. Automobiles are stolen at a much higher rate than trucks, buses and other types of vehicles. Additional factors that contribute to a vehicle's theft risk include differing levels of security, its attractiveness to certain types of thieves, its age, and local crime patterns.
- Auto thieves are unlikely to be identified and arrested by law enforcement agencies; only a small fraction of thieves arrested each year are actually prosecuted; most prosecutions do not result in a felony conviction; and fewer than half of felony convictions for auto theft involve a prison sentence. All this suggests that the criminal justice system is unlikely to deter auto theft through sanction threats alone.
- Opportunity-reduction techniques that manipulate the perceived effort required to commit an auto theft, the perceived risk of detection, and the perceived rewards of the offense have been shown to be effective in preventing motor vehicle thefts in certain situations.

I. Definitions and Prevalence

Motor vehicle theft is a form of larceny that involves the unlawful taking or attempted taking of a motor vehicle. This definition does not include situations in which a person has *lawful* access to a motor vehicle for temporary use or when prior authority can be assumed, such as in the case of chauffeurs, rental car agreements, and family situations (Federal Bureau of Investigation [FBI] 2004). According to the Uniform Crime Reports (UCR), a "motor vehicle is self-propelled and runs on land surface and not on rails" (FBI 2005, p. 505) and includes automobiles, vans, trucks, buses, motorcycles, motor scooters, snowmobiles, and all-terrain vehicles

(FBI 2004). Thefts that involve water craft, construction equipment, airplanes, and farming equipment are counted as larcenies and thus are not counted as motor vehicle thefts (FBI 2004). Although technically a form of larceny, auto theft has been counted separately by the UCR since 1933 (the *National Crime Victimization Survey* has done likewise since 1973) owing to the volume and seriousness of the offense and to the monetary loss it engenders (see especially FBI 1958).

Over 1.2 million vehicles, one of every 200 registered nationwide, were reported stolen to police in 2005, for an estimated total property loss of $7.6 billion, or an average per theft loss of $6,173 (FBI 2006; FHA 2006). The sheer number of vehicles reported stolen accounts for a nontrivial fraction of the property crime index in any given year—12 percent in 2006 (FBI 2007). This figure does not include related offenses such as theft of motor vehicle accessories and theft from motor vehicles, which together account for the highest proportion of reported larcenies each year—36 percent in 2006 (FBI 2007). Such offenses are given consideration here because researchers often explore all three in tandem under the term "car/ vehicle crime" (e.g., Webb and Laycock 1992; Sallybanks and Brown 1999) and because these minor forms of theft often mutate into the more serious crime of auto theft (Copes and Cherbonneau 2006).

II. Associated Costs and Vehicle Recovery Rates

When assessing the costs of auto theft, researchers typically distinguish between the economic costs and social costs incurred by victims, criminal justice agencies, and the larger society (Clarke and Harris 1992*a;* Field 1993; Curtin et al. 2005). Auto theft exacts a heavy economic toll. The estimated $7.6 billion lost to auto theft in 2005 outpaced the costs associated with all other individual property crimes and accounted for the largest proportion (46 percent) of the estimated $16.5 billion (excluding arson) in total property crime losses (FBI 2006). Such estimates, however, are somewhat misleading because they do not take into account vehicle recovery rates. It is well known that motor vehicles are more likely than other types of stolen property to be recovered. In 2006 alone 59 percent of *locally stolen motor vehicles* in the United States were later recovered, meaning that somewhere in the region of $4.1 billion of the $6.9 billion loss attributed to such thefts was eventually recouped (FBI 2007). Undoubtedly vehicle recovery operations lessen the economic impact of auto theft, but recovered vehicles often are damaged, thus diminishing their worth (Decker and Bynum 2003).

Beyond direct economic losses related to the value of the vehicle itself, victims often face a litany of indirect costs. These can include money spent on rental vehicles, insurance deductibles, automobile impound or retrieval costs, new license plate and registration fees, opportunity and inconvenience costs related to the unavailability of a vehicle, and loss of time from work or earnings (Clarke and Harris 1992*a;* Field 1993; Curtin et al. 2005). Estimating the cost associated with most items on this list is difficult because systematic data are lacking or nonexistent; however, victimization surveys report that auto theft victims are more likely to miss work than any other type of crime victim, whether violent or property (Bureau of Justice Statistics 2006).

Of course, there also are criminal justice system costs associated with the apprehension, prosecution, and punishment of car thieves (see e.g., Field 1993; Curtin et al. 2005). And because "the patrol officer is in the most opportune position to look for and come in contact with stolen vehicles" (Brickell and Cole 1976, p. 46), auto theft and vehicle recovery operations can consume precious police manpower, resources, and time (Anderson 1987). One study of the traffic activities of patrol officers in six British police constabularies found that more man-hours were allocated to vehicle-related theft than to all other crime incidents (Ogilvie-Smith, Downey, and Ransom 1994). Traffic policing costs emanating from vehicle crime in these constabularies outpaced those of all other offenses. Extrapolating these costs to all police forces in England and Wales indicates that an estimated £8.6 million is expended annually on car crime there (Ogilvie-Smith, Downey, and Ransom 1994).

In the aggregate, the threat of auto theft creates far-reaching costs borne by all car owners. Simon Field (1993) refers to such expenses as "precautionary costs," which include money spent on aftermarket antitheft devices, increased prices for new vehicles with built-in security enhancements, and higher insurance premiums. The Consumer Electronics Association reports that purchases of electronic antitheft devices totaled $227 million in 2001 (cited in Curtin et al. 2005). Perhaps most salient to vehicle owners is the cost of insurance, especially for metropolitan area residents who pay higher premiums for their greater risk of theft. In 2006 insurers paid out over $2 billion to victims of vehicle theft, which equates to an average of $23 in theft losses per insured passenger vehicle (Highway Loss Data Institute 2007*b*). Field (1993) estimated the cost of theft-related insurance premiums in 1985 to be double the average theft losses for all insured vehicles.

III. Trends and Distribution

Drawing on data from the UCR, the U.S. Federal Highway Administration, the most recent International Crime Victimization Survey (ICVS), and official crime and vehicle registration information from other countries, in this section we address auto theft trends in the United States, the distribution of auto theft across various units of aggregation, and comparative rates of auto theft cross-nationally.

A. Trends in the United States

Vehicle theft rose gradually from 1933 through 1960, reflecting the proliferation of motor vehicles in the United States, which increased threefold during this time (FHA 1997).[2] Upon closer inspection, however, vehicle theft remained relatively stable throughout the Great Depression, when the demand for motor vehicles was modest. Substantial rises occurred only after the Second World War, which ushered in a demand for motor vehicles among Americans. The rise in auto theft was the result of offender adaptations to changing opportunity structures, namely, increased vehicle ownership (Gould 1969; Mansfield, Gould, and Namenwirth 1974).

As indicated by figure 8.1, the rate of vehicle theft per 100,000 persons increased steadily between 1960 and 1971, flattened out until 1983, and then exhibited a dramatic eight-year, 53 percent increase that peaked in 1991 at a rate of 659 motor vehicle thefts per 100,000 persons. Since reaching this high point, auto theft has dropped by 37 percent over the past 15 years, standing at 417 thefts per 100,000 persons in 2005. With the exception of the eight-year increase that began in 1983, variation in the rate of motor vehicle theft from 1960 onward tracks the fluctuation found in other forms of serious property theft, such as burglary and robbery (Clarke and Harris 1992*a*).

Instead of calculating auto theft rates to reflect prevalence in the general population, many contend that such rates should be based on the number of *registered vehicles* in a jurisdiction, not the number of inhabitants (Wilkins 1964). Measuring auto theft in this way allows researchers to account for "vehicle availability" (Mayhew 1990), which is a "necessary condition" (L. E. Cohen and Felson 1979) in the opportunity structure of this crime (Sparks 1980). The upper trend-line in figure 8.1 shows the rate of auto theft in the United States per 100,000 registered vehicles. The most obvious difference is that the opportunity-standardized rate is much higher at every data point in the series. For example, in 1991, the year motor vehicle theft peaked, the rate of auto theft per 100,000 inhabitants was 659, while the rate per 100,000 vehicles was 864, a 31 percent difference. Although substantially higher, rates based on vehicle availability waxed and waned over time, tracking the trend-line determined by the population-based rate; thus the two correlate strongly ($r = .77$, $n = 46$ observations). In recent years the difference between the two rates has been narrowing owing to declining registered vehicles relative to population growth in the 1990s.

B. Distribution within the United States

Auto theft rates vary by geographic region, state, and city size. Figure 8.2 plots variation in regional motor vehicle theft rates per 100,000 registered vehicles from 1960 through 2005. At present, auto theft rates are substantially higher in western states (807 per 100,000 vehicles) than in other regions: 1.8 times greater than in the South (457), 2.1 times more than in the Midwest (388), and 3.6 times higher

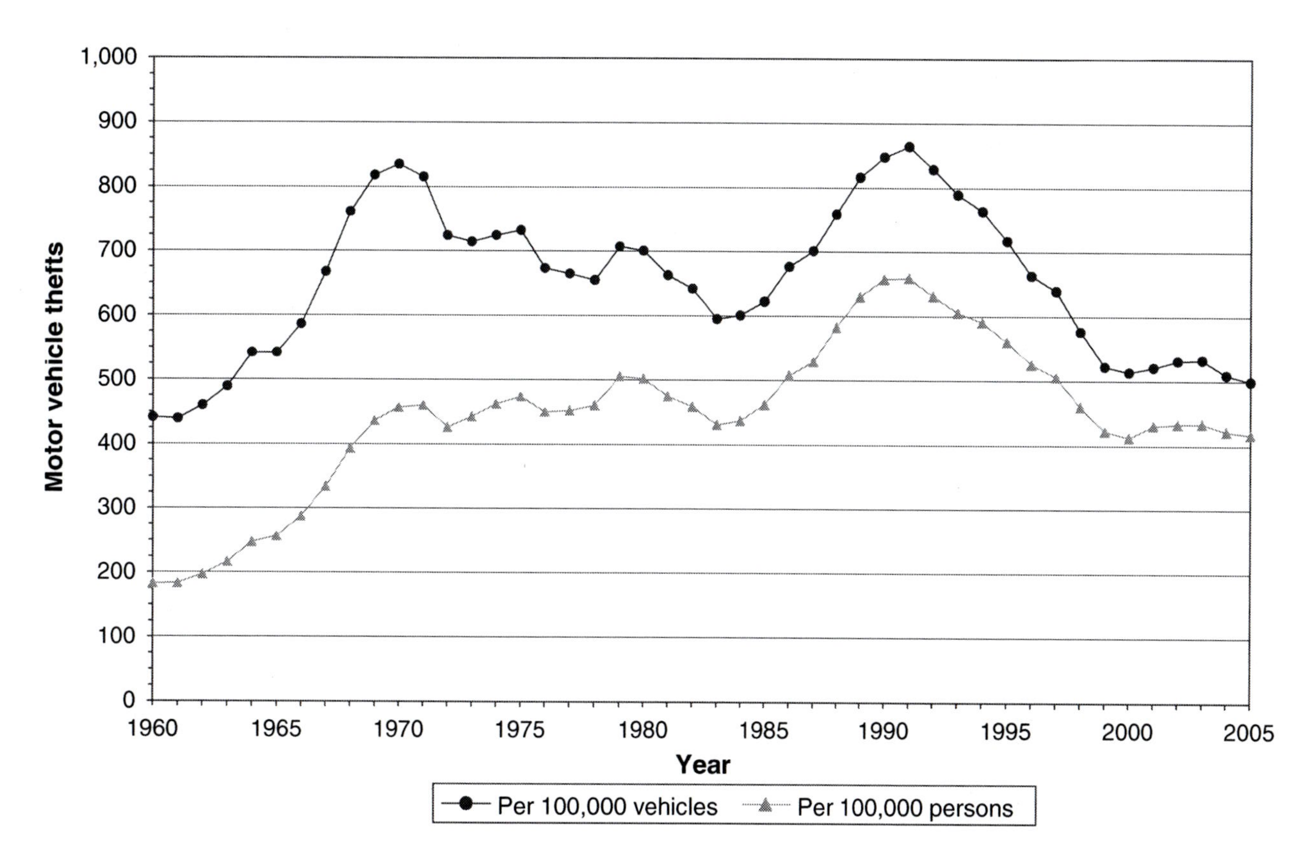

Figure 8.1. Motor vehicle theft in the United States per 100,000 vehicles registered and per 100,000 population, 1960–2005.
Source: Uniform Crime Reports; Highway Statistics.

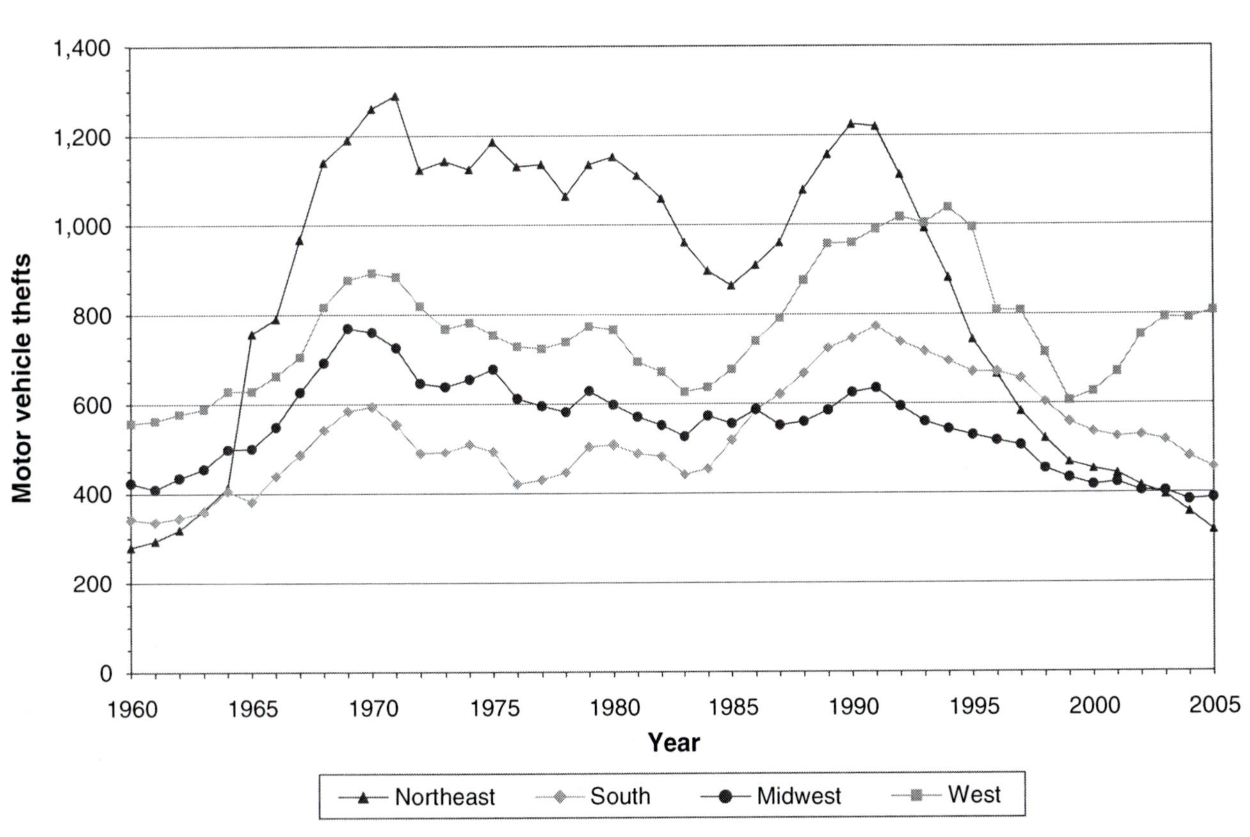

Figure 8.2. Motor vehicle theft in the United States per 100,000 vehicles registered by region of country, 1960–2005.
Source: Uniform Crime Reports; Highway Statistics.

than in the Northeast (316). Exploring regional disaggregation over time indicates that, for the most part, regional variability in auto theft rates mirrors national trends from 1960 to the early 1990s. Specifically, auto theft rates increased rapidly in the late 1960s and early 1970s, leveled off until the mid-1980s, and then began to climb once again into the early 1990s. Rates of auto theft in the Northeast, South, and Midwest then declined dramatically throughout the 1990s, but decreased only gradually thereafter. Rates of auto theft in the West, however, reached a high point much later than in other regions, with 1,035 thefts per 100,000 vehicles in 1994. As with the other regions, rates of auto theft in western states fell dramatically during the rest of the 1990s; yet unlike other regions, auto theft in western states has increased 33 percent since 1999.

The volume and rate of auto theft differs across states. Table 8.1 ranks states by auto thefts per 100,000 vehicles registered in 2005 (FBI 2006; FHA 2006). The highest rates of auto theft were reported by police agencies in the District of Columbia, Nevada, Colorado, Arizona, and Hawaii. Not surprisingly, 7 of the top 10 states were located in the West. The same table also shows corresponding rankings per 100,000 residents, which reveals results very similar to those based on vehicle registrations, with a few exceptions: Colorado was ranked eighth rather than third, Washington moved up from sixth to fourth, and Michigan dropped out of the top 10 to 11th. Although state-wide differences exist in terms of the volume of auto theft, the correspondence between registered vehicle and population rankings indicates that other factors account for the variation. One such factor is proximity to U.S. borders, which facilitates vehicle export and trafficking operations (Clarke and Harris 1992*a;* Field, Clarke, and Harris 1992; Highway Loss Data Institute 2007*a*). For example, four of the top 10 states are adjacent to the U.S.-Mexico or U.S.-Canadian borders, and six are coastal states. Another factor is the varying degree of urbanicity across jurisdictions. South Dakota had the lowest auto theft rate in 2005 (93 per 100,000 vehicles), followed by New Hampshire (108), Wyoming (109), Maine (121), and Vermont (121), all of which are fairly rural states (not presented in table 8.1).

Clearly, auto theft is mostly a "big city problem." In 2006, for instance, 94 percent of auto thefts occurred in metropolitan statistical areas (MSAs), resulting in a rate three times greater than in nonmetropolitan counties (448 and 133 per 100,000 inhabitants, respectively; FBI 2007). The urban-rural gap is unique to auto theft compared to other property crimes; however, it has been narrowing over the years (cf. Clarke and Harris 1992*a*). The 10 MSAs with the highest auto theft rates per 100,000 population in 2006 are all located in the West: Las Vegas (1,355), Phoenix (1,024), Seattle (1,010), Tucson (999), Stockton, California (935), Visalia, California (930), San Francisco (924), Yakima, Washington (924), Modesto, California (910), and Sacramento (900; FBI 2007).

Rates of auto theft also vary greatly by city size. In 2006, for example, the auto theft rate in cities with a population of 250,000 or greater was 827 per 100,000 inhabitants, whereas it was 304 in cities with under 100,000 residents, 254 in towns with under 50,000 residents, and 202 in areas with less than 10,000 in population (FBI 2007).

Table 8.1. Motor vehicle theft in U.S. states ranked by thefts per 100,000 vehicles registered, 2005

Registered vehicle rank (per 100,000 vehicles)	State	Region	Population rank (per 100,000 residents)	Reported theft rank (in thousands)
1 (3,237)	District of Columbia	South	1 (1,402)	35 (7.7)
2 (1,924)	Nevada	West	2 (1,115)	15 (26.9)
3 (1,356)	Colorado	West	8 (560)	16 (26.1)
4 (1,349)	Arizona	West	3 (924)	4 (54.9)
5 (940)	Hawaii	West	5 (716)	31 (9.1)
6 (854)	Washington	West	4 (784)	5 (49.3)
7 (777)	California	West	6 (713)	1 (257.5)
8 (775)	Maryland	South	7 (608)	11 (34.1)
9 (649)	Oregon	West	9 (529)	20 (19.3)
10 (567)	Michigan	Midwest	11 (476)	6 (48.2)

Source: Federal Bureau of Investigation 2006; Federal Highway Administration 2006.

Among U.S. cities with populations greater than 250,000, the 10 cities with the highest motor vehicle theft rates per 100,000 residents in 2006 were Oakland (2,645), Detroit (2,592), Saint Louis (2,492), Newark (1,815), Phoenix (1,586), Sacramento (1,558), Las Vegas (1,496), Cleveland (1,443), Milwaukee (1,418), and Seattle (1,396; FBI 2007). At the bivariate level, auto theft rates generally are higher in cities and census tracts with high levels of ethnic diversity, population turnover, unemployment, single-parent families with children, and low median income (Miethe and Meier 1994).

Two explanations can be offered for the lower levels of auto theft in rural jurisdictions. First, rates of vehicle ownership are much higher in rural than in urban areas owing to low population density, lack of public transportation, and the dispersion of important places of interest such as shopping centers, gas stations, schools, entertainment areas, and commercial and economic centers. The practicality of managing a vast activity space encourages vehicle ownership among rural residents, whereby legitimate access to vehicles decreases motivations for auto theft and is indicative of Biles's (1977) "deprivation hypothesis." Second, rural communities often are characterized by dense social networks. This makes it difficult for would-be thieves to steal a motor vehicle without being noticed by police or community members. Indeed, this appeared to be the case for a group of "small-town" thieves in British Columbia whose auto theft involvement was moderated by a perceived lack of anonymity in their home communities (Fleming, Brantingham, and Brantingham 1994).

C. International Patterns of Auto Theft

Auto theft rates in the United States pale in comparison to those in most other industrialized nations. Data from the 2000 ICVS (van Kesteren, Mayhew, and

Nieuwbeerta 2000) reveal that among 17 industrialized countries, the United States shared 12th place with three other countries; only one-half percent of U.S. car owners interviewed for that survey reported one or more auto theft victimizations. Figure 8.3 displays in rank order the percentage of car owners in 17 industrialized countries who reported one or more auto thefts in 1999 (adapted from van Kesteren, Mayhew, and Nieuwbeerta 2000, p. 25).

Across the 17 countries the average number of car owners victimized once or more in 1999 was 1.2 percent. Eight countries were above average: England and Wales (2.6), Australia (2.1), France (1.9), Poland (1.7), Canada (1.6), Sweden (1.6), Northern Ireland (1.5), and Denmark (1.4).[3] Because very few respondents reported repeat victimizations (van Kesteren, Mayhew, and Nieuwbeerta 2000) measures of prevalence correspond closely to rates of incidence. In this sense, percentages can also be viewed as reflecting the rate of auto theft per 100 car owners.

In line with official U.S. auto theft statistics, victimization survey data indicate that auto theft is declining in many other industrialized countries too (see especially van Kesteren, Mayhew, and Nieuwbeerta 2000, appendix A, table 3 pp. 182–83). Figure 8.4 provides a closer look at falling auto theft rates in select non-U.S. countries with above-average victimization levels. Trends in officially reported auto theft per 100,000 registered vehicles for Australia, Canada, England and Wales, plus the United States are illustrated.[4] Auto theft in Australia, England and Wales, and the United States has declined since reaching a high point in the early 1990s, with Canada following a few years later (for additional cross-national comparisons and trends using both victimization and official data, see Farrington, Langan, and Tonry 2004).

IV. Types of Auto Theft

Perhaps more than any other crime, auto theft is characterized by a wide variety of goals. Indeed, auto theft researchers caution that "it is misleading to view auto theft as a uniform offense" (Maxfield 2004, p. 5), "if only because of the multitude of reasons why cars are stolen" (McCaghy, Giordano, and Henson 1977, p. 377). In response, they have constructed auto theft typologies to reflect the varied nature of the offense, its offenders, and their motives, and to guide thinking about preventive measures with greater specificity.

One of the first classification schemes was developed by Jerome Hall (1952), who viewed the motivations for auto theft as dichotomous, with amateur joyriders on one side and professional auto thieves on the other. Hall argued that the majority of auto thefts reported each year were the work of amateurs, primarily young males interested in joyriding. "Youth with its desire to ride in an automobile," Hall contended, "is the constant and most important single factor in large-scale

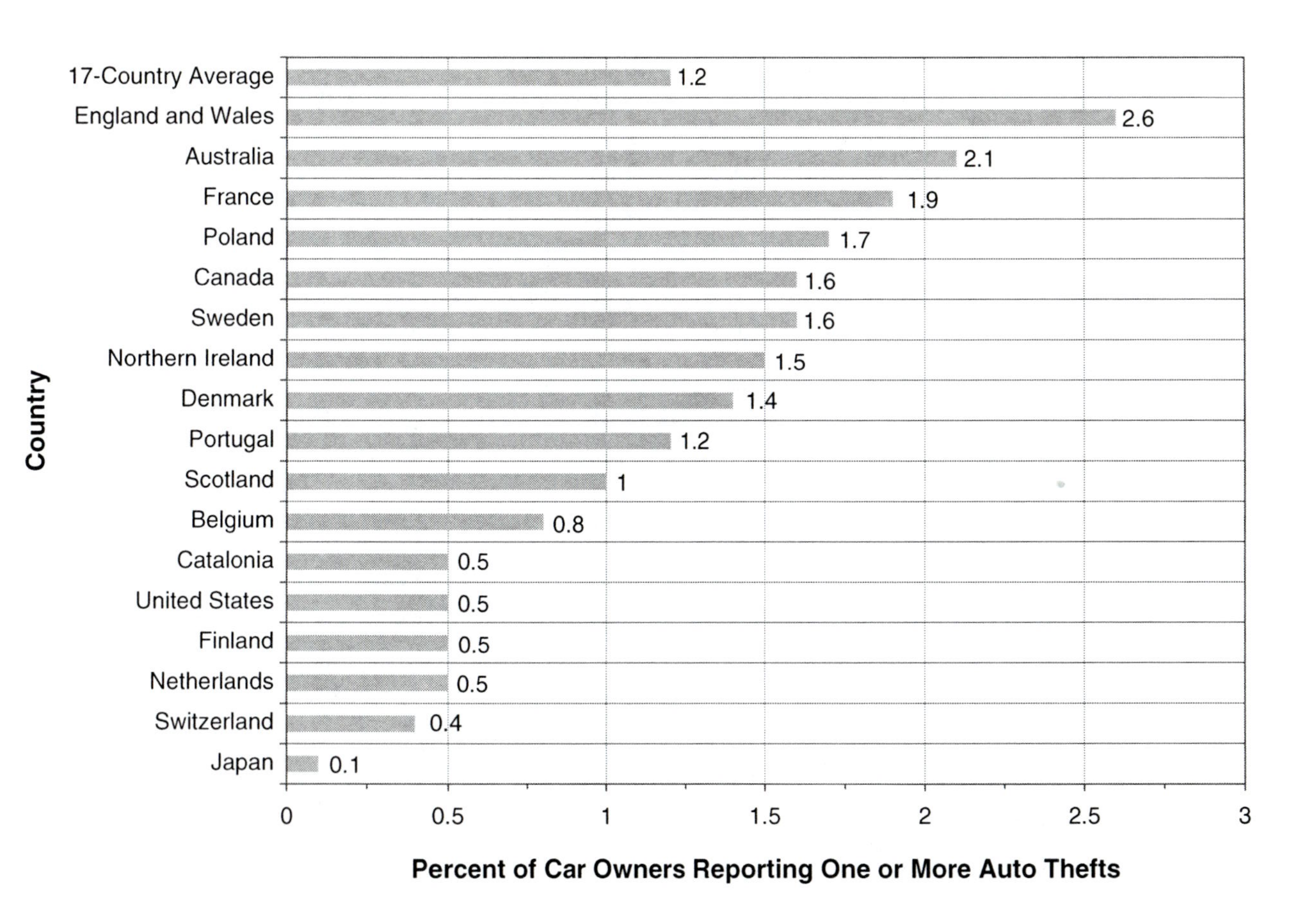

Figure 8.3. Percentage of motor vehicle theft victims in 17 countries, 1999.
Source: van Kesteren, Mayhew, and Nieuwbeerta 2000; International Crime Victimization Survey.

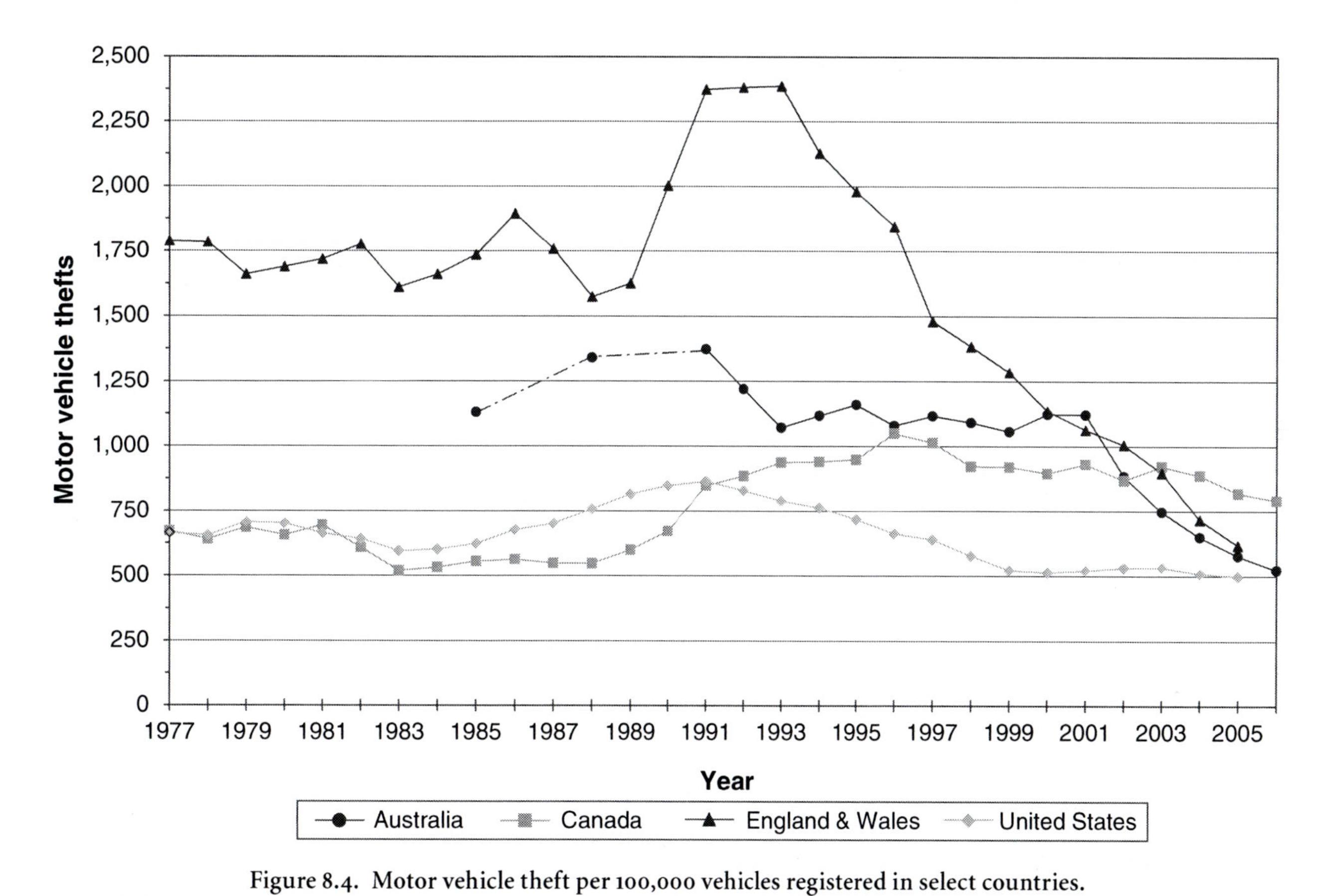

Figure 8.4. Motor vehicle theft per 100,000 vehicles registered in select countries.

Source: Recorded Crime—Victims, Australia; Motor Vehicle Census, Australia; Uniform Crime Reporting Survey (Canada); Road Motor Vehicles, Registrations (Canada); Recorded Crime Statistics (United Kingdom); Transport Statistics Great Britain; Uniform Crime Reports (United States); Highway Statistics (United States).

automobile theft" (p. 249). Joyriding amateurs steal for thrills and to show off. Their misdeeds need not be protracted to garner such expressive rewards, as vehicles typically are appropriated for only a short period and hastily abandoned. Hall posited that at its core, joyriding "expresses the attitudes of the young, especially those who feel deprived of a common pleasure" (p. 256). Skill-wise, amateurs are mechanically inept compared to their professional counterparts. Some amateurs have usable knowledge of the basic techniques of auto theft, but many more rely on found opportunities and criminogenic situations facilitated by careless car owners (see e.g., Herzog 2002; Copes and Cherbonneau 2006).

Professionals, on the other hand, have mastery over more varied and sophisticated skill sets which allow them to create opportunities. By Hall's account, professionals are a much rarer breed than amateurs and therefore are responsible for a smaller proportion of auto thefts each year. Professional thieves are motivated by tangible gains rather than excitement, their modus operandi exudes organization and planning rather than haphazard spontaneity, and they are connected to criminal receivers and to the more general market in stolen property. Tow trucks, keys obtained through repair shop connections, inventive frauds, and parts stripping (for individual resale or to be fitted on refurbished vehicles) are more than just the methods that professionals use; as Hall saw it, they are what best discriminates between amateur and professional thieves.

A more nuanced understanding of auto thieves' motivations began to emerge on the heels of the classic study of motor vehicle theft by McCaghy, Giordano, and Henson (1977). Drawing on police records of 103 auto thefts resulting in arrest in Toledo, Ohio, during an eight-month period from 1975 to 1976, McCaghy, Giordano, and Henson identified five distinct motivations for auto theft. The first and most common was joyriding. Defined as the recreational short-term use of a stolen car, joyriding is not motivated by economic or transportation needs, but by a desire for excitement, to prove one's manhood, or to gain status. In short, "the car is not stolen for what it does, but for what it means" (p. 378).

The second motivational category involved short-term transportation, with the car stolen for a brief period with the sole purpose of specific transportation, and not for a thrill. Usually the short-term car thief succumbs to situational pressures in which immediate transportation is seen as necessary.

Long-term transportation is a third reason for stealing a vehicle. The primary goal in this type of auto theft is to keep the car indefinitely. This category is unusual in that recovered vehicles often are found to be in better shape than when they were stolen. The offenders also are different from the other types of car thieves, tending to be older and to live farther from where the vehicle was stolen.

The fourth motivational category for auto theft involved stealing cars for profit. This category includes individuals who steal vehicles to sell parts or whole, as well as professional organizations that operate chop shops, in which automobiles are broken into parts for sale. The goal is purely economic. Theft of the vehicle is based on the automobile as a saleable commodity, not as a symbol or a form of transportation.

The final motivation involved stealing a vehicle for use in another crime. This was found to be the rarest type of auto theft, prompting McCaghy, Giordano, and Henson (1977) to conclude that in the grand scheme of things, vehicles stolen to facilitate the commission of another crime matter little. In more recent times, however, a growing awareness of vehicle theft insurance fraud calls that conclusion into question.

The McCaghy, Giordano, and Henson (1977) typology is widely credited with identifying the common types of auto theft that exist in the United States and elsewhere (Challinger 1987). Since publication of that typology, however, other auto theft researchers have attempted to elaborate or refine it in various ways. For example, Herzog (2002) collapsed the short- and long-term transportation motives into a single category of self-transportation and amended the typology to include auto theft for equipment supplement, insurance fraud, dismantling of car parts, assignment of a new identity, and for transfer across national borders. Challinger (1987) took a different tack: he reformulated the five-part McCaghy et al. typology into three main motivational types—recreational, transport, and money-making—to allow for a more targeted approach to the prevention of various sorts of auto theft. Clarke and Harris (1992*a*) also proposed a three-part typology of motor vehicle theft consisting of theft for temporary use, namely, joyriding and short-term transportation; professional theft in which thieves intend to deprive the owner permanently of the vehicle for purposes of extended use, parts chopping, resale, or export; and thefts from vehicles, such as car batteries, radios, and personal possessions inside the vehicle.

Copes (2001) took a slightly different approach, dividing the reasons auto thieves gave for their crimes into four broad motivational categories: recreational, economic instrumental, noneconomic utilitarian, and retribution. Recreational motives included cruising around and thrill seeking. Economic instrumental motives involved thefts for "exchange value," meaning resale of the entire vehicle or its individual parts, and its polar opposite, "use value," which included thefts for permanent personal retention or to strip parts for use on thieves' own cars. The noneconomic utilitarian category included thefts for short-term transportation, commission of another crime, and motives related to offenders' desire to learn how to drive. The final category of motives involved retribution directed at a particular individual and carried out as a form of social control to rectify a perceived wrong.

V. Victims and Victimization Risk

The *National Crime Victimization Survey* (*NCVS*) indicates that certain car owners are more vulnerable than others to auto theft. The characteristics of those who experienced an auto theft in 2005 are presented in table 8.2 (Bureau of Justice Statistics

Table 8.2. Motor vehicle theft victimization by victim and household characteristics, 2005

Characteristic	Rate per 1,000 households
Age category	
12–19 years old	14.4
20–34 years old	12.5
35–49 years old	9.8
50–64 years old	7.0
65 and older	2.8
Race	
White	7.6
Black	12.7
Other	9.9
Hispanic origin	
Hispanic	19.0
Non-Hispanic	7.1
Annual household income	
Less than $7,500	9.4
$7,500–$14,999	9.8
$15,000–$24,999	12.4
$25,000–$34,999	9.9
$35,000–$49,999	6.6
$50,000–$74,999	7.2
$75,000 or more	7.1
Home ownership	
Rented	13.3
Owned	6.1
Household size	
One	5.0
Two–three	8.5
Four–five	11.5
Six or more	15.3
Housing unit	
Single	7.0
Two	12.3
Three	20.7
Four	14.5
Five–nine	9.4
Ten or more	11.4
Number of years at residence	
Less than 6 months	17.1

(*continued*)

Table 8.2. (continued)

Characteristic	Rate per 1,000 households
6 months to 1 year	16.7
1 year	10.3
2 years	12.2
3 years	9.3
4 years	4.8
5 years or more	6.7
Location of residence	
Urban	12.7
Suburban	7.7
Rural	4.6

Source: Bureau of Justice Statistics 2006.

2006). In terms of age, race, and ethnicity, those most susceptible to auto theft are young (between the ages of 20 and 34) rather than old, African American rather than white or another race, and nearly three times more likely to be Hispanic than non-Hispanic. There is usually a direct inverse relationship between income and victimization risk for major forms of crime. Auto theft, however, is somewhat different. Households with incomes between $15,000 and under $25,000 are most vulnerable to auto theft and 1.3 times more likely to experience an auto theft than households with an income under $7,500. This is likely due to opportunity in terms of vehicle ownership. Put bluntly, you cannot be an auto theft victim if you do not own a car. Additional household characteristics associated with higher auto theft victimization risk include renters rather than home owners, household sizes of four or more occupants, multi-unit dwellings, and having lived less than one year in your current residence. Consistent with UCR data on the urban-rural divide, urban households are nearly three times more likely than rural ones to experience an auto theft.

A. Timing and Theft Locations in Victimization Risk

Some of the more robust auto theft patterns concern the nexus between time and place of occurrence. Beginning with theft location, victimization risks are highest in and around the immediate vicinity of the victim's household—67 percent of incidents in 2005 (Bureau of Justice Statistics 2006). Thirty-five percent of auto thefts occurred near residences (e.g., private driveway, carport), and another 16 percent occurred on the street outside the victim's home (Bureau of Justice Statistics 2006). For thefts that occurred away from the home, the majority were in public parking lots or garages (31 percent), while a noteworthy 9 percent involved targets parked on public streets. Similar patterns have been documented by victimization surveys conducted in other countries. In a survey of 500 auto theft victims in British Columbia, for instance, 63 percent reported vehicles stolen from their residence

(Fleming, Brantingham, and Brantingham 1994). Likewise, British Crime Survey data for 2000 revealed that 64 percent of auto theft incidents occurred close to victims' homes (36 percent were committed on the street outside residences and 26 percent in semiprivate driveways); thefts in public car parks comprised 17 percent of thefts, and 5 percent occurred in car parks near to where victims worked (Kinshott 2001).

Turning to the dimension of time, the vast majority of auto thefts (nearly 68 percent) occur during the evening and nighttime hours between 6:00 p.m. and 6:00 a.m., with a substantially greater number of thefts occurring in the second half of this interval (Bureau of Justice Statistics 2006). This is supported by research in Philadelphia's city center, which found that 65 percent of such thefts occurred at night (Rengert 1997).

The intersection of time and place in auto theft can be tied to the routines of vehicle owners and motivated offenders as well as to target availability and levels of guardianship (Clarke and Mayhew 1994; Rengert 1997; Hollinger and Dabney 1999). This is explored more fully in British Crime Survey data, which reveal that 75 percent of near-home thefts (street or driveway) took place at night between 6:00 p.m. and 6:00 a.m. (Kinshott 2001). Auto thefts in public car parks were four times more likely to occur in the morning and afternoon hours, and those in work car parks were nearly eight times more likely to occur during these hours than in the same locations during the evening and nighttime. Research based on interviews with offenders supports these patterns. Of the 100 auto thieves interviewed by Light, Nee, and Ingham (1993), 40 percent operated after dark; 52 percent claimed to operate at any time. Eighty percent of those who targeted vehicles outside homes did so only after dark, whereas 69 percent of those favoring car parks operated at any time of the day.

B. Types of Stolen Vehicles

In terms of the most common type of vehicle stolen, cars constitute nearly 75 percent of reported thefts each year, while trucks and buses comprise 18 percent; other types of vehicles account for the remaining 9 percent (FBI 2007). This distribution is not uniform across the nation and is sensitive to local patterns. For example, Burns (2000) attributes the higher rate of truck theft in the South and West relative to the proportion of trucks registered to cultural imperatives favoring such vehicles in these locales. Moreover, the degree to which a particular vehicle is targeted depends on its attractiveness to certain types of offenders. This is especially evident in the work of Clarke and Harris (1992*b*), who found a strong relationship between the motives of auto thieves and the vehicles they choose. Other factors that account for differences in the types of vehicles stolen include differing levels of security, vehicle age, vehicle's location in relation to international borders, and the proportion of that type of vehicle on the road (Sallybanks and Brown 1999; Clarke and Brown 2003; Plouffe and Sampson 2004).

VI. Car Thieves

We now turn our attention to the offenders responsible for the patterns described above. We draw from official data on offenders and on previous offender-based research to examine thieves' social and demographic characteristics, patterns of involvement, and career progression and the social context in which the skill sets and techniques of auto theft are acquired and honed.

A. Demographic Profile

The demographic profile of the typical thief is difficult to determine with great confidence because the parameters of the total population of auto thieves are unknown. Official arrest records, however, can offer some guidance. Nationally, motor vehicle theft arrestees are disproportionately male, young, and members of a racial minority group. Among persons arrested for auto theft in 2006, 82 percent were male, 25 percent were under age 18 (57 percent were under age 25), and 37 percent were nonwhite (FBI 2007). Prison samples almost certainly overrepresent males and members of racial minorities. Thus it is not surprising that of those serving a sentence for auto theft in adult state prisons in 2003, an estimated 95 percent were male and 60 percent were nonwhite (Harrison and Beck 2006). Offender profiles for any type of crime generated through the use of official records are open to suspicion, but two interrelated factors make this especially problematic for auto theft. Vehicle theft has an exceptionally high reporting rate—92 percent of completed thefts were reported to police in 2005 (Bureau of Justice Statistics 2006)—yet it typically has one of the lowest clearance rates: only 13 percent were cleared by an arrest or other means in the same year (FBI 2006). Thus the actual makeup of the total population of auto thieves cannot be determined with great precision because the vast majority of them go undetected each year (Biles 1977).

B. Social and Economic Background

Research in Australia, North America, and the United Kingdom indicates that many young thieves come from economically distressed and working-class inner-city areas characterized by high unemployment, low median income, and a general lack of leisure facilities and economic opportunities for young people (Sullivan 1989; Dawes 2002; Stephen and Squires 2003).[5] In terms of the family unit, auto thieves often experience transitory living arrangements or frequent family moves and come from single-parent homes; family involvement in car crime, such as by a sibling or cousin, is not uncommon (Light, Nee, and Ingham 1993; Fleming, Brantingham, and Brantingham 1994; Dawes 2002; O'Connor and Kelly 2006). Car thieves appear to invest little energy in academic achievement or school-supported activities, and their aspirations for gainful employment frequently are low, aimless, or uncertain (Spencer 1992; Fleming 1999; Dawes 2002). When asked about career ambitions, the modal response includes mention of some sort of car-related career (Light, Nee, and Ingham 1993; Stephen and Squires 2003).

C. Age and Motives for Involvement

Auto theft involvement typically begins at an early age (see, e.g., Cooper 1989; Spencer 1992; Fleming, Brantingham, and Brantingham 1994). In a sample of 100 auto thieves in England and Wales, nearly 8 out of 10 first participated in auto theft between the ages of 13 and 16, with 47 percent stealing their first vehicle between the ages of 14 and 15 (Light, Nee, and Ingham 1993). Somewhat similarly, Briggs (1991) reported that 82 percent of his sample committed their first auto theft between the ages of 13 and 15. The pursuit of excitement, alleviation of boredom, and peer influences are the main reasons given by auto thieves for taking up the crime (Spencer 1992; Light, Nee, and Ingham 1993; Dawes 2002; Stephen and Squires 2003).

For many marginalized youths, a stolen car can provide a degree of escape, if only temporarily, from their social and economic dislocation (Dawes 2002). Stealing cars enables them to offset the boredom that infuses their day-to-day lives (Stephen and Squires 2003). And few activities, legal or illegal, can trump the elation and sense of freedom derived from auto theft (Campbell 1993; Copes 2003). Indeed, the "excitement of theft and the status gained among peers must not be discounted as powerful sources of reinforcement of joyriding" (Clarke and Harris 1992*a*, p. 22).

Beyond a search for excitement and to alleviate boredom, some car thieves desire to gain prestige and establish a reputation among their peers (Sullivan 1989). Marginalized youth have little in the way of economic opportunities, stable families, or educational aspirations, but what they lack in these important spheres of life can be assuaged by the status conferred through the social context of the peer group for their competence in car crime (Campbell 1993; Dawes 2002, p. 203).

D. Social Context of Auto Theft

For novices, car theft is almost invariably a group activity; very few offenders begin by stealing cars on their own (Spencer 1992; Light, Nee, and Ingham 1993; Stephen and Squires 2003). This is hardly surprising given that entering cars and defeating ignitions requires technical know-how and a degree of mechanical proficiency that transcends common sense. As already alluded to, auto theft involvement is facilitated through interaction with neighborhood peers, usually older and more experienced males or, as Spencer (1992) describes them, "local heroes" whom neighborhood youngsters look up to. Novices learn from these "technical advisors" (Fleming, Brantingham, and Brantingham 1994) the skills needed to steal and drive cars through a role best described as an "apprenticeship" (Spencer 1992; Light, Nee, and Ingham 1993). Status within the group is stratified by skill (cf. Stephen and Squires 2003). Initially, novices typically are relegated to the role of lookout and passenger. This learning period may not last long; in many cases peers move quickly from apprentices to co-offenders (Light, Nee, and Ingham 1993; Fleming 1999).[6]

This suggests that there is a car crime culture operating within certain neighborhoods in which the skills and techniques of auto theft are transmitted from seasoned offenders to neophytes. Indeed, there is compelling indirect evidence for this in the crime prevention literature. In 1971 Great Britain passed legislation that required *only* new cars manufactured in or imported into England and Wales to be fitted with a steering column lock, while older cars were left unchanged. Although the new locks resulted in a substantial decline in thefts of newer vehicles, it was to the detriment of older, unsecured vehicles, for which thefts rose correspondingly (Webb 1994). Thus the sizable pool of unprotected vehicles relative to protected ones essentially offset the preventive gains achieved by the new locks (Webb and Laycock 1992). By comparison, West Germany made steering column locks compulsory on all cars (and motorcycles), both old and new, in 1961. The result was an immediate 20 percent reduction in motor vehicle thefts (Webb 1994). After controlling for the growth in registered vehicles, the introduction of steering column locks had a lasting impact on auto theft in West Germany spanning nearly three decades (Webb and Laycock 1992; Webb 1994). Clarke (1997) attributes the decline to a disruption of car crime culture in West Germany. Because it took substantial time to figure out how to defeat the new locks, many thieves, both young and old, became discouraged with auto theft. As a result, the car crime culture was undermined and never rebounded to previous levels because "participation in vehicle crime [was] no longer an offending 'norm' for young men" (Brown 2004, p. 116).

VII. Criminal Justice Response

The ability of criminal justice agencies to control auto theft hinges on sustained efforts to detect, arrest, prosecute, and punish offenders. It is widely held that objective threats communicated by the criminal justice system, coupled with individuals' subjective interpretation of those threats, are important in the production of law-abiding behavior. Thus the risk of punishment must be perceived as certain and associated sanctions severe if already punished thieves are to be dissuaded from offending in the future and individuals not so punished are to be discouraged from contemplating and carrying out an illegal act. Alas, the objective arrest certainty for auto theft, crudely measured by the ratio of police arrests to reported thefts, is dramatically low—one out of every nine in 2006 (FBI 2007). Along with burglary, auto theft has shared the long-standing distinction of being one of the least likely Index offenses to be cleared by arrest. This is compounded by a negligible likelihood of sanction delivery. Motor vehicle theft constituted less than 2 percent of adult felony convictions processed in state courts in 2004 and, at about 16 percent, auto theft arrests were less likely to lead to a conviction than other major crimes. Put differently, state courts attained approximately 16 felony convictions for every 100 auto theft arrests in 2004 (Durose 2007).

Despite the low probability of arrest and conviction for auto theft, a sentence of incarceration was given in 86 percent of felony convictions (41 percent prison and 45 percent jail), while only 10 percent resulted in probation (Durose 2007). In 2004 the median sentence for those receiving a prison or jail sentence for auto theft was 12 months, and recently released prisoners served an estimated 60 percent of their original sentence or 17 months on average (Durose 2007).

Taken together, these objective indicators of the punishment properties for auto theft correspond closely to offenders' subjective perceptions. Offender decision-making research indicates that many auto thieves show remarkable indifference to the risk of detection and arrest and to the legal ramifications if apprehended. In terms of getting caught, very few offenders (22 percent) in the Light, Nee, and Ingham (1993) sample believed that continued offending would lead to their capture. Most discounted arrest potentials by relegating such thoughts to the back of their minds, attempted to reduce such risks on a situational basis (see also Fleming 1999), and displayed confidence in their "skills for evasion" (Jacobs 1996) should they ever come under police scrutiny (see also Cherbonneau and Copes 2006). Relatedly, thieves in Fleming's sample were confident about their chances of avoiding punishment at every stage of the offense. Their poise in this regard even extended into the realm of police chases and court proceedings following apprehension. In general, they too exhibited a carefree attitude when asked about the potential legal consequences of auto theft, which most calculated to be negligible. Most interesting, however, was a view among younger thieves that their status as juveniles insulated them from the most serious repercussions.

Even after arrest and punishment auto thieves remain an especially incorrigible bunch. Among prisoners released in 1994 auto thieves had the highest three-year recidivism rate (79 percent), and auto theft was the most serious offense they were likely to be rearrested for (Langan and Levin 2002). In a 2002 study of felony defendants in the 75 largest urban counties in the United States auto thieves were more likely than others to be on probation or parole at the time of their arrest, and 70 percent had one or more previous felony arrests (T. Cohen and Reaves 2006).

Simply put, the criminal justice system is incapable of deterring many would-be auto thieves, and persistent thieves are keenly aware of this. Offenders are unlikely to be detected; a small fraction of the 12 percent arrested each year will be prosecuted; most of these prosecutions will not result in a felony conviction, and fewer than half of felony convictions will involve a prison sentence. And it is unlikely that this trend will be reversed anytime soon. Local, state, and federal law enforcement and prosecution agencies give precedence to more serious (albeit less prevalent) violent and personal crimes than they do to auto theft (Lee and Rikoski 1984).

A. Auto Theft Prevention and Policy

Despite the criminal justice system's inability to respond effectively to auto theft, the fact remains that the offense has been declining for the past 15 years. Whether this is part and parcel of nationwide declines experienced for all major forms of crime remains unclear, though that must be part of the story. What is abundantly clear, however, is that programs based on situational measures have been shown to produce meaningful reductions in auto theft, at least over the short term. Situational prevention encompasses a broad range of proactive initiatives meant to address specific forms of lawbreaking or problem behaviors. The aim of such initiatives is not to decrease criminal motivation per se, but rather to lessen criminal opportunities by increasing the perceived effort involved, enhancing the perceived risk of detection, or reducing the perceived rewards of the targeted crime (Clarke 1995, 1997).

Opportunity-reducing techniques that serve to increase the perceived risks of auto theft include enhanced informal and formal surveillance. Examples of informal surveillance include security cameras placed in parking lots and active surveillance by employed security guards, which have been shown to correspond with lower levels of theft in protected areas (Webb, Brown, and Bennett 1992; Hollinger and Dabney 1999; Sampson 2004). Measures of formal surveillance include vehicle tracking devices such as LoJack and OnStar that are becoming more commonplace on vehicles. An even newer technology is license plate recognition systems. Recognition systems are either fixed or mobile and automatically cross-check the license plates of parked and moving vehicles with a national criminal database of wanted vehicles (e.g., stolen, wanted felon, "be on the lookout," Amber Alert). Some of these systems employ global positioning coordinates for each plate scanned so that officers can return to it, such as in the case of abandoned vehicles. Such devices capitalize on the fact that many arrests are made through police stops; evaluations in the United Kingdom have shown them to aid in the apprehension of auto thieves and in the recovery of abandoned vehicles (Henderson et al. 2004). Although these technologies are more widespread among police forces in the United Kingdom, U.S. cities, including Chicago, Miami, and Salt Lake City, recently have adopted them specifically for use against auto theft. Research with auto thieves indicates that while driving they feel particularly vulnerable to formal detection and are hypersensitive to immediate risks (Cherbonneau and Copes 2006). Thus further development of such technologies is likely to be fruitful in deterring auto thieves and undermining some of the incentives the offense has to offer.

The primary preventive approach to reducing the rewards of auto theft involves car part marking initiatives, the most common of which is the vehicle identification number, or VIN, a unique 17-digit serial number assigned to each vehicle. The Motor Vehicle Theft Law Enforcement Act of 1984 required manufacturers to stamp the VIN on 14 different vehicle components, including the engine, transmission, hood, doors, fenders, and bumpers (National Highway Traffic Safety

Administration 1998). Although part marking serves many purposes, the primary preventive goal is to make it difficult to conceal the true identity of a vehicle, a process Tremblay, Talon, and Hurley (2001) refer to as "body switching," and thereby reduce the number of vehicles stolen and dismantled in chop shops (Linden and Chaturvedi 2005).

By far the most common opportunity-reduction techniques used to combat auto theft involve various forms of target hardening, which aim to make it harder for would-be thieves to commit such crimes. Vehicles are now more difficult to steal than ever before as people have begun to take proactive measures to protect their vehicles by purchasing alarms, clubs, and other security devices. At the same time, the convenience of keyless entry systems, which now come standard on many vehicle lines, means that a greater number of unattended vehicles are being properly secured by owners. In addition, automobile manufacturers have begun designing more theft-resistant vehicles, often in response to legislation requiring them to do so.

The most recent development in target-hardening initiatives by manufacturers is the electronic immobilizer. In 1995 the European Union mandated that all cars manufactured after October 1998 be fitted with electronic immobilizers (Levesley et al. 2004). This antitheft device uses a computer chip on the key to prevent would-be thieves from bypassing a vehicle's ignition. Police reports from Great Britain show that there was a decline in the rate of auto thefts for cars manufactured after 1998 (Levesley et al. 2004). Australia and, more recently, Canada have passed similar legislation. Although such mandates are absent in the United States, immobilizers are becoming more commonplace on luxury and midrange vehicles. As Clarke (1983, p. 246) points out, however, the problem with many antitheft programs is that "within easy reach of every house with a burglar alarm, or car with an antitheft device, are many others without such protection." Indeed, the introduction of compulsory immobilization in Australia and the United Kingdom reduced auto theft, yet partial displacement toward older, unprotected vehicles was evident in both countries (Brown and Thomas 2003; Kriven and Ziersch 2007). Additionally, some auto thieves have responded to increased vehicle ignition hardening by searching locked and unlocked cars for hidden keys or burglarizing dwellings to obtain keys (Levesley et al. 2004; Copes and Cherbonneau 2006; Donkin and Wellsmith 2006). And some "professional thieves" apparently already know how to defeat immobilizers; an increasing number of vehicles fitted with such devices are being stolen and not recovered (see Brown 2004, p. 101). History suggests that it is only a matter of time before such knowledge becomes diffused throughout the criminal subculture.

The one sure thing that can be concluded about the prevention of auto theft is that would-be thieves will likely adapt to any new target-hardening initiative, so the best we can hope for is to stay one or two steps ahead of them. Viewed in relation to crimes such as burglary, robbery, homicide, and assault, auto theft is a recent phenomenon. Automobiles have been with us for only a little over a century, and, in the face of climate change and escalating fossil fuel prices, they may not be around for much longer, at least not in their current form. Certainly cars—and all forms of transportation, whether private or public—are destined to undergo substantial change in the years ahead. It will be interesting to see how this change alters the face of auto theft.

B. Future Research

For all that has been learned about auto theft, a number of important questions about the offense remain to be answered. For example, the value of motivational typologies has yet to be demonstrated convincingly. Copes (2003) warns us that it is common for auto thieves to report that the motivations underpinning any given auto theft may mutate as the offense progresses, say, from joyriding to use in another crime to parts stripping. As he puts it, "Typologies imply exclusivity and stability, they are based on the idea that offenders in one group are qualitatively different from the offenders in the other group.... [But] motivational categories are not mutually exclusive.... The fluid nature of offenders' motivations suggests that typologies may obscure the nature of auto theft more then they illuminate it" (p. 327).

Auto theft is unlike other types of crime in that it is much less spatially and temporally bound as offenders drive from place to place, often keeping vehicles for substantial periods of time. This has strong implications for deterrence and prevention policies that may be more or less germane as any given offense evolves. Although offenders clearly are indifferent to protracted and remote threats of punishment, recent research suggests that they may be hypersensitive to risks of immediate detection. This is important because at no other time in the course of an auto theft do concerns about detection risk seem to be more prominent than when actually driving the stolen vehicle (Cherbonneau and Copes 2006). More research into the dynamic relationship between auto theft and deterrence is badly needed.

Most of what is known about car thieves and how they operate has been derived through self-report and offender-based research. Unfortunately most such studies have relied almost exclusively on samples contacted through criminal justice channels; precious few have been based on offenders located through other means (e.g., Parker 1974; Sullivan 1989). Findings derived from samples of known thieves are difficult to generalize to populations of free-ranging offenders because by definition they exclude those who have escaped detection and almost certainly underrepresent persons with middle-class backgrounds. Additionally, the bulk of the existing literature on auto theft focuses on joyriding and thereby disproportionately represents young males. Although some researchers have endeavored to include older, more experienced thieves (e.g., Copes 2003; O'Connor and Kelly 2006), at present there is not a single study devoted solely to the study of such offenders. Nor has there been much theorizing about the dynamics of their auto theft participation. With age and experience offenders hone their skills, and, around the time they reach adulthood, many are in a position to use their knowledge and connections to engage in auto theft for financial gain, even though only a fraction appear to do so on a regular basis (Light, Nee, and Ingham 1993; Spencer 1992). How and why this is so remains poorly understood.

NOTES

1. Hereafter, the terms *auto theft, car theft,* and *vehicle theft* are used interchangeably with *motor vehicle theft.*

2. Even though most experts view UCR rates up until 1958 with caution (owing in part to lower agency coverage and imprecise population estimates), as far as the reliability of auto theft counting during this period is concerned, the high rate of police notification for the offense (FBI 1958) may offer some exception to this rule.

3. For important limitations of ICVS data, see Rosenfeld (this volume).

4. Several issues regarding the cross-national statistics presented in figure 8.4 deserve special mention. The Australian series has some missing data issues. Prior to 1991 reliable vehicle registration data for Australia is available only for the years 1985 and 1988. This gap in consecutive-year data is indicated by the broken line at the start of the series. In addition, registration data are not available for the years 1992, 1994, and 2000. Crime data are also missing for 1988 and 1992; in both cases the midpoint was used. Despite these limitations, we are confident in the overall patterns that emerge from the series, especially because previous Australian research based on registration or population data has reported similar patterns (K. Higgins 1997).

There are two concerns with the Canadian series. First, the Canadian UCR survey includes theft of farm and construction equipment in its definition of motor vehicle theft; however, Gannon (2001) views the impact of these counting differences as "minor." Second, in 1999 changes were made to the annual Survey of Road and Motor Vehicle Registrations, rendering comparability with prior years problematic (Wallace 2003). In a separate analysis we found no significant differences associated with the 1999 changes.

Finally, recent changes in recording and reporting practices of crime data in England and Wales have created important comparability issues. Starting in April 1998 crime is reported on a fiscal year rather than calendar year basis, and the introduction of the National Crime Recording Standard in 2002 increased the number of annually recorded auto thefts by approximately 9 percent (Simmons, Legg, and Hosking 2003). Auto theft counts from 2002 onward are not adjusted to account for this increase.

5. Auto thieves' socioeconomic standing has been the focus of substantial debate (e.g., McCaghy, Giordano, and Henson 1977; P. Higgins and Albrecht 1982). The earliest profiles were based on samples of known delinquents in large U.S. cities and found auto theft to be an activity of greater salience among the socially advantaged, that is, white middle-class youth from privileged, usually suburban, homes (Wattenberg and Balistrieri 1952; Schepses 1961). This view of adolescent auto theft became known as the "favored-group" thesis (Wattenberg and Balistrieri 1952). Commentators argued that middle-class youth develop "car-consciousness" at an earlier age compared to less privileged youth, owing to their frequent exposure to cars and driving abilities within the family unit (Schepses 1961).

6. It may be worthwhile to note the findings from an empirical exploration of auto thieves' participation and career progression. Examining the criminal histories of juveniles prosecuted for various offenses in Coventry, England, Slobodian and Browne (1997) found support for a three-stage car crime career, whereby offenders were more likely to be arrested for being a passenger in a stolen vehicle before they were arrested for stealing property from a vehicle or the vehicle itself. Additionally, they were more likely to be arrested for stealing property from a vehicle before being arrested for actually committing an auto theft.

REFERENCES

Anderson, Rex. 1987. "The Practical Impact of Car Theft on the N.S.W. Police." In *Car Theft: Putting on the Breaks, Proceedings of Seminar on Car Theft, May 21*. Sydney: National Roads and Motorists' Association and the Australian Institute of Criminology.

Biles, David. 1977. "Car Stealing in Australia." In *Delinquency in Australia: A Critical Appraisal*, edited by Paul R. Wilson. St. Lucia, Australia: University of Queensland Press.

Brickell, David, and Lee Cole. 1976. *Vehicle Theft Investigation*. Santa Cruz, CA: Davis.

Briggs, Jeffrey. 1991. "A Profile of the Juvenile Joyrider and a Consideration of the Efficacy of Motor Vehicle Projects as a Diversionary Strategy." Master's thesis. University of Durham, Department of Sociology and Social Policy.

Brown, Rick. 2004. "The Effectiveness of Electronic Immobilization: Changing Patterns of Temporary and Permanent Vehicle Theft." In *Understanding and Preventing Car Theft, Crime Prevention Studies*, vol. 17, edited by Michael G. Maxfield and Ronald V. Clarke. Monsey, NY: Criminal Justice Press.

Brown, Rick, and Nerys Thomas. 2003. "Aging Vehicles: Evidence of the Effectiveness of New Car Security from the Home Office Car Theft Index." *Security Journal* 16: 45–53.

Bureau of Justice Statistics. 2006. *Criminal Victimization in the United States, 2005—Statistical Tables*. Washington, DC: Bureau of Justice Statistics.

Burns, Ronald. 2000. "Culture as a Determinant of Crime: An Alternative Perspective." *Environment and Behavior* 32: 347–60.

Campbell, Beatrix. 1993. *Goliath: Britain's Dangerous Places*. London: Methuen.

Challinger, Dennis. 1987. "Car Security Hardware—How Good Is It?" In *Car Theft: Putting on the Breaks, Proceedings of Seminar on Car Theft, May 21*. Sydney: National Roads and Motorists' Association and the Australian Institute of Criminology.

Cherbonneau, Michael, and Heith Copes. 2006. "'Drive It Like You Stole It': Auto Theft and the Illusion of Normalcy." *British Journal of Criminology* 46: 193–211.

Clarke, Ronald V. 1983. "Situational Crime Prevention: Its Theoretical Basis and Practical Scope." In *Crime and Justice: A Review of Research*, vol. 4, edited by Michael Tonry and Norval Morris. Chicago: University of Chicago Press.

———. 1995. "Situational Crime Prevention." In *Building a Safer Society*, edited by Michael Tonry and David P. Farrington. Vol. 19 of *Crime and Justice: A Review of Research*, edited by Michael Tonry. Chicago: University of Chicago Press.

———. 1997. Introduction. In *Situational Crime Prevention: Successful Case Studies,* 2nd ed., edited by Ronald V. Clarke. Guilderland, NY: Harrow and Heston.

Clarke, Ronald V., and Rick Brown. 2003. "International Trafficking in Stolen Vehicles." In *Crime and Justice: A Review of Research,* vol. 30, edited by Michael Tonry. Chicago: University of Chicago Press.

Clarke, Ronald V., and Patricia M. Harris. 1992*a*. "Auto Theft and Its Prevention." In *Crime and Justice: A Review of Research,* vol. 16, edited by Michael Tonry. Chicago: University of Chicago Press.

Clarke, Ronald V., and Patricia M. Harris. 1992*b*. "A Rational Choice Perspective on the Targets of Automobile Theft." *Criminal Behaviour and Mental Health* 2: 25–42.

Clarke, Ronald V., and Pat Mayhew. 1994. "Parking Patterns and Car Theft Risks: Policy-Relevant Findings from the British Crime Survey." In *Crime Prevention Studies,* vol. 3, edited by Ronald V. Clarke. Monsey, NY: Criminal Justice Press.

Cohen, Lawrence E., and Marcus Felson. 1979. "Social Change and Crime Rate Trends: A Routine Activities Approach." *American Sociological Review* 44: 588–608.

Cohen, Thomas, and Brian Reaves. 2006. *Felony Defendants in Large Urban Counties, 2002*. Washington, DC: U.S. Department of Justice.

Cooper, Barrymore. 1989. *The Management and Prevention of Juvenile Crime Problems.* Crime Prevention Unit Paper 20. London: Home Office.

Copes, Heith. 2001. "Finding a Ride: Decision-Making among Auto Thieves." PhD dissertation, University of Tennessee, Department of Sociology.

———. 2003. "Streetlife and the Rewards of Auto Theft." *Deviant Behavior* 24: 309–32.

Copes, Heith, and Michael Cherbonneau. 2006. "The Key to Auto Theft: Emerging Methods of Auto Theft from the Offenders' Perspective." *British Journal of Criminology* 46: 917–34.

Curtin, Patrick, David Thomas, Daniel Felker, and Eric Weingart. 2005. "Assessing Trends and Best Practices of Motor Vehicle Theft Prevention Programs, Final Report." Washington, DC: U.S. Department of Justice.

Davies, Richard O. 1975. *The Age of Asphalt: The Automobile, the Freeway, and the Condition of Metropolitan America*. New York: J. B. Lippincott.

Dawes, Glenn. 2002. "Figure Eights, Spin Outs and Power Slides: Aboriginal and Torres Strait Islander Youth and the Culture of Joyriding." *Journal of Youth Studies* 5: 195–208.

Decker, Scott, and Tim Bynum. 2003. "Auto Theft Problem-Solving." In *Police Department Information Systems Technology Enhancement Project (ISTEP): Phase II Case Studies.* Washington, DC: U.S. Department of Justice, Office of Community Oriented Policing Services.

Donkin, Susan, and Melanie Wellsmith. 2006. "Cars Stolen in Burglaries: The Sandwell Experience." *Security Journal* 19: 22–32.

Durose, Matthew. 2007. *State Court Sentencing of Convicted Felons, 2004—Statistical Tables.* Washington, DC: U.S. Department of Justice.

Farrington, David, Patrick Langan, and Michael Tonry. 2004. *Cross-National Studies in Crime and Justice*. Washington, DC: U.S. Department of Justice.

Federal Bureau of Investigation. 1958. *Uniform Crime Reports: Special Issue, 1958.* Washington, DC: U.S. Department of Justice.

———. 2004. *Uniform Crime Reporting Handbook*. Washington, DC: U.S. Department of Justice.

———. 2005. *Uniform Crime Report: Crime in the United States, 2004*. Washington, DC: U.S. Department of Justice.

———. 2006. *Uniform Crime Report: Crime in the United States, 2005*. Washington, DC: U.S. Department of Justice.

———. 2007. *Uniform Crime Report: Crime in the United States, 2006*. Washington, DC: U.S. Department of Justice.

Federal Highway Administration. 1997. *Highway Statistics, Summary to 1995*. Washington, DC: U.S. Department of Transportation.

———. 2006. *Highway Statistics, 2005*. Washington, DC: U.S. Department of Transportation.

Field, Simon. 1993. "Crime Prevention and the Costs of Auto Theft: An Economic Analysis." In *Crime Prevention Studies,* vol. 1, edited by Ronald V. Clarke. Monsey, NY: Criminal Justice Press.

Field, Simon, Ronald V. Clarke, and Patricia Harris. 1992. "The Mexican Vehicle Market and Auto Theft in Border Areas of the United States." *Security Journal* 2: 205–10.

Fleming, Zachary. 1999. "The Thrill of It All: Youthful Offenders and Auto Theft." In *In Their Own Words: Criminals on Crime,* 2nd ed., edited by Paul Cromwell. Los Angeles: Roxbury.

Fleming, Zachary, Patricia Brantingham, and Paul Brantingham. 1994. "Exploring Auto Theft in British Columbia." In *Crime Prevention Studies,* vol. 3, edited by Ronald V. Clarke. Monsey, NY: Criminal Justice Press.

Gannon, Maire. 2001. "Crime Comparisons between Canada and the United States." *Juristat* 21, no. 11. Ottawa: Canadian Centre for Justice Statistics.

Goddard, Calvin. 1932. "The Motor Car and Crime." *Journal of Criminal Law and Criminology* 22: 650–51.

Gould, Leroy. 1969. "The Changing Structure of Property Crime in an Affluent Society." *Social Forces* 48: 50–59.

Hall, Jerome. 1952. *Theft, Law and Society.* Indianapolis: Bobbs-Merrill.

Harrison, Paige, and Allen Beck. 2006. *Prisoners in 2005*. Washington, DC: U.S. Department of Justice.

Henderson, Charlie, Panikos Papagapiou, Adrian Gains, and Jim Knox. 2004. *Driving Crime Down: Denying Criminals the Use of the Road*. London: Home Office, Police Standards Unit.

Herzog, Sergio. 2002. "Empirical Analysis of Motor Vehicle Theft in Israel, 1990–97." *British Journal of Criminology* 42: 709–28.

Higgins, Karl. 1997. *Exploring Motor Vehicle Theft in Australia*. Trends and Issues in Crime and Criminal Justice No. 67. Canberra: Australian Institute of Criminology.

Higgins, Paul, and Gary Albrecht. 1982. "Cars and Kids: A Self-Report Study of Juvenile Auto Theft and Traffic Violations." *Sociology and Social Research* 66: 29–41.

Highway Loss Data Institute. 2007*a*. *Theft Losses: By Metropolitan Areas of the United States*. Arlington, VA: Insurance Institute for Highway Safety.

———. 2007*b*. *Theft Losses: Historical Trends in Losses of New Passenger Vehicles, 1985–2006*. Arlington, VA: Insurance Institute for Highway Safety.

Hollinger, Richard, and Dean Dabney. 1999. "Motor Vehicle Theft at the Shopping Centre: An Application of the Routine Activities Approach." *Security Journal* 12: 63–78.

Insurance Information Institute. 2007. *Insurance Fact Book, 2007.* New York: Insurance Information Institute.

Jacobs, Bruce. 1996. "Crack Dealers' Apprehension Avoidance Techniques: A Case of Restrictive Deterrence." *Justice Quarterly* 13: 359–81.

Kinshott, Graham. 2001. *Vehicle Related Thefts: Practice Messages from the British Crime Survey*. London: Home Office.

Kriven, Sophie, and Emma Ziersch. 2007. "New Car Security and Shifting Vehicle Theft Patterns in Australia." *Security Journal* 20: 111–22.

Langan, Patrick, and David Levin. 2002. *Recidivism of Prisoners Released in 1994*. Washington, DC: U.S. Department of Justice.

Laycock, Gloria. 2004. "The U.K. Car Theft Index: An Example of Government Leverage." In *Understanding and Preventing Car Theft, Crime Prevention Studies*, vol. 17, edited by Michael G. Maxfield and Ronald V. Clarke. Monsey, NY: Criminal Justice Press.

Lee, Beverly, and Giannina Rikoski. 1984. *Vehicle Theft Prevention Strategies*. Washington, DC: U.S. Department of Justice, National Institute of Justice.

Levesley, Tom, Greg Braun, Michael Wilkinson, and Cymone Powell. 2004. *Emerging Methods of Car Theft: Theft of Keys*. Home Office Findings No. 239. London: Home Office.

Light, Roy, Claire Nee, and Helen Ingham. 1993. *Car Theft: The Offender's Perspective*. Home Office Research Study No. 130. London: Home Office.

Linden, Rick, and Renuka Chaturvedi. 2005. "The Need for Comprehensive Crime Prevention Planning: The Case of Motor Vehicle Theft." *Canadian Journal of Criminology and Criminal Justice* 47: 251–70.

Mansfield, Roger, Leroy Gould, and J. Zvi Namenwirth. 1974. "A Socioeconomic Model for the Prediction of Societal Rates of Property Theft." *Social Forces* 52: 462–72.

Maxfield, Michael G. 2004. Introduction. In *Understanding and Preventing Car Theft, Crime Prevention Studies*, vol. 17, edited by Michael G. Maxfield and Ronald V. Clarke. Monsey, NY: Criminal Justice Press.

Maxfield, Michael G., and Ronald V. Clarke. 2004. *Understanding and Preventing Car Theft, Crime Prevention Studies*, vol. 17. Monsey, NY: Criminal Justice Press.

Mayhew, Patricia. 1990. "Opportunity and Vehicle Crime." In *Police and Theory in Criminal Justice: Contributions in Honour of Leslie T. Wilkins*, edited by Don M. Gottfredson and Ronald V. Clarke. Brookfield, VT: Avebury.

McCaghy, Charles H., Peggy C. Giordano, and Trudy Knicely Henson. 1977. "Auto Theft: Offender and Offense Characteristics." *Criminology* 15: 367–85.

McShane, Clay. 1994. *Down the Asphalt Path: The Automobile and the American City*. New York: Columbia University Press.

Miethe, Terance, and Robert Meier. 1994. *Crime and Its Social Context: Toward an Integrated Theory of Offenders, Victims, and Situations*. Albany: State University of New York Press.

National Crime Victimization Survey. Bureau of Justice Statistics, U.S. Department of Justice. http://www.ojp.usdoj.gov/bjs/.

National Highway Traffic Safety Administration. 1998. *Auto Theft and Recovery: Effects of the Anti Car Theft Act of 1992 and the Motor Vehicle Theft Law Enforcement Act of 1984—Report to the Congress*. Washington, DC: U.S. Department of Transportation.

O'Connor, Christopher, and Katharine Kelly. 2006. "Auto Theft and Youth Culture: A Nexus of Masculinities, Femininities and Car Culture." *Journal of Youth Studies* 9: 247–67.

Ogilvie-Smith, Adam, Alan Downey, and Elizabeth Ransom. 1994. *Traffic Policing: Activity and Organisation*. Police Research Series Paper No. 12. London: Home Office.

Ornati, Oscar. 1969. *Transportation Needs of the Poor: A Case Study of New York City*. New York: Praeger.

Paaswell, Robert, and Wilfred Recker. 1978. *Problems of the Carless*. New York: Praeger.

Parker, Howard. 1974. *View from the Boys: A Sociology of Down-Town Adolescents*. Newton Abbot, UK: David and Charles.

Plouffe, Nanci, and Rana Sampson. 2004. "Auto Theft and Theft from Autos in Parking Lots in Chula Vista, CA: Crime Analysis for Local and Regional Action." In *Understanding and Preventing Car Theft, Crime Prevention Studies*, vol. 17, edited by Michael G. Maxfield and Ronald V. Clarke. Monsey, NY: Criminal Justice Press.

Porter, Richard. 1999. *Economics at the Wheel: The Cost of Cars and Drivers*. New York: Academic Press.

Rengert, George. 1997. "Auto Theft in Central Philadelphia." In *Policing for Prevention: Reducing Crime, Public Intoxication and Injury. Crime Prevention Studies*, vol. 7, edited by Ross Homel. Monsey, NY: Criminal Justice Press.

Sallybanks, Joanna, and Rick Brown. 1999. *Vehicle Crime Reduction: Turning the Corner*. Police Research Series Paper 119. London: Home Office.

Sampson, Rana. 2004. *Theft of and from Autos in Parking Facilities in Chula Vista, California. A Final Report to the U.S. Department of Justice, Office of Community Oriented Policing Services*. Washington, DC: U.S. Department of Justice.

Schepses, Erwin. 1961. "Boys Who Steal Cars." *Federal Probation* 25: 56–62.

Simmons, Jon, Clarissa Legg, and Rachel Hosking. 2003. *National Crime Recording Standards (NCRS): An Analysis of the Impact of Crime in England and Wales 2002/2003. Part One: The National Picture*. London: Home Office.

Slobodian, Paul, and Kevin Browne. 1997. "Car Crime as a Developmental Career: An Analysis of Young Offenders in Coventry." *Psychology, Crime and Law* 3: 275–86.

Sparks, Richard. 1980. "Criminal Opportunities and Crime Rates." In *Indicators of Crime and Justice: Quantitative Studies*, edited by Stephen E. Fienberg and Albert J. Reiss Jr. Washington, DC: U.S. Department of Justice.

Spencer, Eileen. 1992. *Car Crime and Young People on a Sunderland Housing Estate*. Crime Prevention Unit Series Paper No. 40. London: Home Office.

St. Clair, David. 1986. *The Motorization of American Cities*. New York: Praeger.

Stephen, Dawn, and Peter Squires. 2003. "'Adults Don't Realize How Sheltered They Are': A Contribution to the Debate on Youth Transitions from Some Voices on the Margins." *Journal of Youth Studies* 6: 145–64.

Sullivan, Mercer. 1989. *Getting Paid: Youth Crime and Work in the Inner City*. New York: Cornell University Press.

Tremblay, Pierre, Bernard Talon, and Doug Hurley. 2001. "Body Switching and Related Adaptations in the Resale of Stolen Vehicles: Script Elaborations and Aggregate Crime Learning Curves." *British Journal of Criminology* 41: 561–79.

van Dijk, Jan, and Patricia Mayhew. 1992. *Criminal Victimisation in the Industrialised World: Key Findings of the 1989 and 1992 International Crime Surveys*. The Hague: Netherlands Ministry of Justice, Department of Crime Prevention.

van Kesteren, John, Pat Mayhew, and Paul Nieuwbeerta. 2000. *Criminal Victimisation in Seventeen Industrialized Countries: Key Findings from the 2000 International Crime Victimization Survey*. The Hague: Netherlands Ministry of Justice, Research and Documentation Centre.

Wallace, Marnie. 2003. "Motor Vehicle Theft in Canada—2001." *Juristat* 23, no. 1. Ottawa: Canadian Centre for Justice Statistics.

Wattenberg, William, and James Balistrieri. 1952. "Automobile Theft: A 'Favored-Group' Delinquency." *American Journal of Sociology* 57: 575–79.
Webb, Barry. 1994. "Steering Column Locks and Motor Vehicle Theft: Evaluations from Three Countries." In *Crime Prevention Studies*, vol. 2, edited by Ronald V. Clarke. Monsey, NY: Criminal Justice Press.
Webb, Barry, Ben Brown, and Katherine Bennett. 1992. *Preventing Car Crime in Car Parks*. Crime Prevention Unit Series Paper No. 34. London: Home Office.
Webb, Barry, and Gloria Laycock. 1992. *Tackling Car Crime: The Nature and Extent of the Problem*. Crime Prevention Unit Paper No. 32. London: Home Office.
Wilkins, Leslie. 1964. *Social Deviance: Policy, Actions, and Research*. London: Tavistock.

Figure Data Sources

Highway Statistics. Federal Highway Administration, U.S. Department of Transportation. http://www.fhwa.dot.gov/policy/ohpi/hss/hsspubs.htm.
International Crime Victimization Survey. Dutch Ministry of Justice, Research and Documentation Centre. http://www.unicri.it/wwd/analysis/icvs/pdf_files/key2000i/.
Motor Vehicle Census, Australia. Australian Bureau of Statistics. http://www.abs.gov.au/.
Recorded Crime—Victims, Australia (previously: Recorded Crime, Australia; National Crime Statistics). National Crime Statistics Unit, Australian Bureau of Statistics. http://www.abs.gov.au/.
Recorded Crime Statistics. Research Development Statistics, Home Office. http://www.homeoffice.gov.uk/rds/recordedcrime1.html.
Road Motor Vehicles, Registrations. Transportation Division, Statistics Canada. http://www.statcan.ca/start.html.
Transport Statistics Great Britain. Department for Transport, National Statistics. http://www.dft.gov.uk/pgr/statistics/datatablespublications/vehicles/.
Uniform Crime Reports. Federal Bureau of Investigation, U.S. Department of Justice. http://www.fbi.gov/ucr/ucr.htm. Data extracted from the Bureau of Justice Statistics. http://bjsdata.ojp.usdoj.gov/dataonline/.
Uniform Crime Reporting Survey. Canadian Centre for Justice Statistics, Statistics Canada. CANadian Socio-economic Information Management (CANSIM) system, Table 252–0013. http://cansim2.statcan.ca/cgi-win/cnsmcgi.exe?CANSIMFile=CII/CII_1_E.HTM&&RootDir=CII/.

CHAPTER 9

FINANCIAL CRIMES

MICHAEL LEVI

Financial crimes is an imprecise term, and it is not self-evident what it includes and excludes. Conventional usage among American, British, and international regulators and policing bodies suggests that financial crimes include fraud, market abuse (e.g., insider trading), money laundering, and other forms of illicit corporate conduct for profit. The 2007 *Financial Crimes Report to the Public* (Federal Bureau of Investigation [FBI] 2008*a*), and its predecessor (FBI 2007, p. 4) has separate sections on corporate, securities and commodities, health care, mortgage, insurance, and mass marketing frauds; identity theft; and asset forfeiture and money laundering. Financial crimes are dynamic, in the sense that, to an even greater extent than other crimes for gain, the prevalence, incidence, and techniques of particular forms of crime evolve over time in a process of adaptation between the skills and organization of offenders *anywhere in the world* and the informal and formal controls of victims and the criminal justice system (Levi 2007*a*, 2008*a*, 2008*b*). We may witness this dynamism in the discussion of financial institution failures (FIF) by the FBI:

> Since the 1992 peak of the savings and loan crisis, the FBI has been able to refocus its investigative efforts from failed financial institution cases to other high-priority FIF matters. At the close of FY 2005, the total number of pending FIF investigations for the FBI was 5,041. Of this total, 62 failure cases, or less than 1 percent, involved criminal activity related to a failed financial institution.... Convictions related to major case investigations have remained constant since FY 1995, surpassing total convictions for major cases during the 1992 peak.
>
> During the late 1980s and early 1990s, approximately 60 percent of the fraud reported by financial institutions related to bank insider abuse. Since then, external fraud schemes have replaced bank insider abuse as the dominant FIF

> problem confronting financial institutions. The pervasiveness of check fraud and counterfeit negotiable instrument schemes, technological advances, as well as the availability of personal information through information networks, has fueled the growth in external fraud. (Federal Bureau of Investigation, 2007, p. 1)

Since then, the "credit crunch" and—in its wake—the rise in revealed mortgage frauds and other financial services misconduct has given the FBI's mission (and that of the long-term activist district attorney for Manhattan, Robert Morgenthau) a sharper focus in the public eye. At the end of 2007, FBI field offices were dealing with 529 corporate fraud cases (Federal Bureau of Investigation, 2008*b*). They later engaged in U.S.-wide arrests for mortgage frauds under Operation "Malicious Mortgage." Of course, this tells us only about frauds against financial institutions, not about those involving the manipulation of accounts by top executives in major corporations—such as Enron, Parmalat, Tyco, and WorldCom—which were not primarily financial institutions, though they used major corporate secrecy devices and banking facilities that facilitated frauds and their frauds dominated media headlines for a while when they happened.

The use of the term *fraud* or *financial crimes* (and its popular continental European equivalent, *economic crimes*) takes some of the social status controversy out of the term *white-collar crime,* where there is often a problem of determining the point when someone ceases to be "blue-collar" (Shapiro 1990). However, in the process, these terms may submerge important differences in the opportunities available to "trusted criminals" (Friedrichs 2006) and in the way we treat people and companies that overall are deemed to be "socially useful," unlike "organized criminals" and others (e.g., social security fraudsters) deemed "socially unproductive." Fraud in essence is the obtaining of goods and/or money by deception. But what are its boundaries as "crimes"? Are firms that engage in price fixing "criminals"? U.S. and (but only since 2002) U.K. legislators would answer yes, but most world legislators would say that price fixing is at most an administrative offense, even though, as some American companies such as Microsoft as well as cement and pharmaceutical businesses have discovered, the European Commission can raid their headquarters and fine their businesses hundreds of millions of euros for violations, theoretically up to 10 percent of global turnover (see Connor 2006; Harding 2007).

Given the difficulties of determining the boundaries of financial crime, what do we know about the social distribution of offending? In the United States systematic socioeconomic or organizational status data are available only from research studies rather than from official offender statistics, especially prior to the National Incident–Based Reporting System (Barnett 2000). Weisburd, Wheeler, and Waring (1991) entitled their book *Crimes of the Middle Classes,* though many U.S. federal fraud offenders were blue rather than white collar, and arguably not middle class, and a recent study comparing British and German cases (Karstedt and Farrall 2006) stresses the everyday nature of offenders and offending. As far as we know and as seems plausible, there are many more check and payment card fraudsters than there are embezzling accountants and senior executives, so by personnel volume, financial crimes are not typically elite offending.[1] In essence, deception is socially widespread and—perhaps even more than theft in practice—can readily be committed by the more against the less powerful as well as by the poor and by professional criminals against those with many assets to lose, making it broader than white-collar crime. A typology based on the interests that are affected is set out in box 9.1 (see also Levi and Pithouse forthcoming).

This chapter begins by examining the evidence on the extent and costs of financial crimes. I then present an analysis of how financial crimes are organized at a general level before discussing subtypes of fraud, based on their techniques and victim sectors. I conclude with an examination of the major regulatory and criminal justice policy options. Some key observations are the following:

- Financial crimes include a broad variety of deceptions against a spectrum of poor and wealthy individuals and businesses.
- Although their costs are sometimes amplified by entrepreneurs seeking to get more public and policing attention, they are greater than those conventionally seen as constituting "the crime problem."
- We should understand the organization of fraud (and other crimes) in terms of how would-be offenders confront problems of gaining finance, gaining access to crime opportunities, and retaining their freedom and crime proceeds.
- Though many of the major frauds are committed by corporate insiders, globalization has enabled easier targeting of victims from overseas and the concealment of offenders and their crime proceeds from civil and criminal process.
- Regulatory policies tend to focus on financial services rather than "real" industry, though after the Enron case rules were introduced to force more

Box 9.1. Types of economic crime

1. Crimes that harm government or taxpayer interests
2. Crimes that harm *all* corporate as well as social interests—systemic risk frauds that undermine public confidence in the system as a whole; domestic and motor insurance frauds; maritime insurance frauds; payment card and other credit frauds; pyramid selling of money schemes; high-yield investment frauds and "boiler room" scams
3. Crimes that harm social and some corporate interests but benefit other "mainly legitimate" ones—some cartels, transnational corruption (by companies with business interests in the country paying the bribe)
4. Crimes that harm corporate interests but benefit mostly illegitimate ones—several forms of intellectual property violation—sometimes called "piracy" or "theft"—especially those using higher quality digital media

responsibility on senior directors. Given the long gestation of many frauds, it is too early to tell whether these have been effective.
- The more aggressive and proactive policing and sentencing of fraud in the United States compared with the United Kingdom and other jurisdictions generate faster and more efficient sanctions for frauds, but whether this acts as a deterrent is unknown, especially given the ability to organize frauds from outside the United States.

I. The Extent and Costs of Financial Crimes

There are two dimensions of harm: economic damage (perhaps best seen in terms of the effects on individual and corporate victims' abilities to restore themselves to their precrime economic welfare level) and psychological and health damage (including disruption of expectations about future security and welfare). What is the level of harm, including but not restricted to direct economic costs, of these different categories? The answer is harder and the evidence far patchier than we might have hoped, and it differs significantly between countries (as do crime rates generally). Although there have been some modest attempts to develop measures of estimating the prevalence and incidence of some white-collar offenses (Rebovich and Layne 2000; Bussman and Werle 2006; Kane and Wall 2006; Karstedt and Farrall 2006), the financial cost and other impacts of deception offenses have been more items of rhetoric than of serious empirical investigation. In the few criminological texts that address such matters, historic (and uncritically evaluated) data that show the heavy costs of white-collar crimes are juxtaposed with the much lower costs of street crimes for which most people are imprisoned (see, e.g., Reiman 2007). Unfortunately more sophisticated reviews of the costs of crime (e.g., Cohen 2005; Dubourg, Hamed, and Thorns 2005) that examine the collateral costs (health and psychological) have focused hitherto on conventional household and street crimes, and neither frauds nor other forms of corporate crime get more than a passing mention.[2]

If we include the costs of criminal justice in the costs of crime, as is conventional in such studies, then it is plain that our politicized decisions about what to do about them have a significant impact on costs. (For example, in the United States, though less so in continental Europe, courts imprison drug sellers and violent criminals for a long time and seldom jail all but the most egregious white-collar ones for long.)[3] In white-collar crimes, especially in the United Kingdom but also in the United States (data for most countries being unavailable), relatively modest resources overall are expended in investigation, prosecution, and imprisonment, despite the fact that high-profile cases individually may be extremely expensive to investigate and to prosecute. Logically one might add to criminal justice costs the costs of business regulation, though some might then question whether these should properly be called "costs of corporate or white-collar crime" rather than the costs of harm reduction or business compliance.

Following a systematic review of existing studies commissioned by the British Home Office, excluding income tax fraud (which is difficult to estimate) and intellectual property crimes (which are seldom considered fraud),[4] the direct costs of fraud were found to total a conservatively estimated minimum of £12.9 ($26) billion, fairly equally distributed between private and public sectors (Levi et al. 2007; Levi and Burrows 2008). Comprehensively collated or critically assessed cost information is not available for fraud in the United States (see ACFE 2006; Friedrichs 2006; Rosoff, Pontell, and Tillman 2006). The FBI (2007) states that at the end of fiscal year 2006, 490 corporate fraud cases were under investigation, 19 of which involved losses to public investors of over $1 billion. However, though there are possible overlaps of data, information is available on the following categories of activity:

1. Consumer fraud. In 2005, the second Federal Trade Commission survey (involving telephone interviews with 3,888 adults) found that an estimated 13.5 percent of U.S. adults—30.2 million consumers—were victims of one or more of the consumer scams covered in the previous year; there were an estimated 48.7 million incidents of these frauds. In the much larger survey on identity "theft" conducted by the Bureau of Justice Statistics, Baum (2007) found that about 1.6 million households experienced theft from existing accounts other than a credit card (such as a banking account), and 1.1 million households discovered misuse of personal information (such as a social security number). Ten percent of the households with incomes of $75,000 or higher experienced identity theft, about twice the percentage of households earning less than $50,000. Across all types of identity theft, the average amount lost per household was $1,620. On the basis of an annual panel survey of 5,000 people, Javelin Research (2008) reports that a much larger total of 8.1 million Americans were victimized by identity fraud, costing a total of $45 billion (which works out to be the much larger sum of $5,555 per person). It is difficult to adjudicate between these competing estimates of harm, incidence, and prevalence. (See also Copes and Vieraitis, this volume.)
2. Commodities and securities frauds. The FBI (2007) estimates this category to be $40 billion, though no underlying methodology or references for this estimate are given.
3. Mortgage frauds. Suspicious activity reports on mortgage frauds totaled $1.4 billion in 2006, though even if investigated fully, by no means all of these suspicions will turn out to be evidentially founded.
4. Insurance fraud. The Coalition against Insurance Fraud estimated (on what basis is unknown) this category of fraud to be $80 billion.

Many estimates of fraud and money laundering are based on very limited evidence, derive from institutional profile raising, and take on a life of their own as "facts by repetition," seldom critiqued either by media always hungry for sensational headlines (Levi 2006) or by pressure groups (and some academics) happy to swallow "evidence" of the enormous cost of white-collar crimes. On the other hand, if we rely on cases brought to conviction, the data may be absurdly low in both harm and case complexity, the most subtle cases being hardest to prove beyond a reasonable doubt (see Levi and Reuter, this volume).[5]

Many of the larger frauds coming to light in, say, 2008 will have been committed some years before. A foreseeable illustration is lies told by brokers to lenders about the income of mortgage applicants to meet loan criteria (sometimes with the active or passive collusion of all three parties, plus valuers); so long as people can keep up the payments, these frauds will remain hidden (and anyway may not be treated as crimes). Some brokers and even lenders may also have lied to applicants for mortgages and other forms of credit about the risks involved in order to generate the trading volumes needed to hit their productivity targets and to get bonuses that are often much larger than their salaries.[6] Another example is the "rogue trading" in sophisticated financial instruments committed by Nick Leeson at Barings in 1995 (http://www.nickleeson.com) and Jérôme Kerviel at Société Générale in 2007–8. In both cases it was alleged by the primary suspected offenders that more senior managers turned a blind eye to the risk taking either because they were incompetent (Barings) or because they stood to gain if the risks paid off (Barings and Société Générale). The popular explanation for this is greed, but because greed is the engine that drives business performance in capitalism this is not a helpful discriminator between those who both see and take fraud opportunities and those who do not.[7]

The boundary between fraud, organized crime, and money laundering can be hard to discern. Properly analyzed, money laundering is a subcategory of both, being proceeds of crimes that are saved and perhaps reinvested with their criminal origins concealed (see van Duyne and Levi 2005; Levi and Reuter 2006, this volume). Thus in calculating the costs of crime it would be a mistake simply to add the amounts laundered to the amounts defrauded, since a significant proportion of the laundering is of the proceeds of fraud, and that would be double-counting.

II. Understanding the Organization of Financial Crimes

As in other areas of crime, patterns of financial crimes follow the general levels of opportunities available as well as motivations to offend and existing crime networks and organizations (where needed to commit fraud). In terms of what sort of people commit what sorts of offenses, it is difficult not to be seduced by the assumption that the *Godfather*- or *Sopranos*-type hierarchical, deeply embedded cultural and family mode of organization is the natural evolution of all serious crime. The general public, criminals, and the police are all subjected to (and sometimes entranced by) these images of power and "threat to society." However, though fraud and other white-collar crimes may be committed as part of a transnational "serious crime community" (Block and Weaver 2004) that often can outwit the forces of criminal or civil justice control anywhere in the world,[8] they are also capable of functioning unconnected to "organized crime," at least as the latter term is commonly conceptualized by police investigators and politicians. (Though there may be nothing in the least disorganized about how financial criminals go about committing their crimes: a serious problem with that terminology.)

To understand financial crimes, it is helpful to place them in the context of a process map of crime for gain (see box 9.2; Levi 2007*a*).

These steps are not necessarily sequential; for example, we may see a financial crime opportunity only when we meet professionals able to facilitate it, or we may already have in place all the steps. Criminal finance, some or all criminal personnel, and the "tools of crime" may come from or go to another country, constituting "transnational" crimes; if they remain within one country they constitute "national" crimes. (In the United States, Australia, Germany, and other countries with separate federal and state jurisdictions, there may be other enforcement bodies involved, though the United States has federalized most frauds via the application of interstate or federal insurance criteria.) In the case of fraud, offenders may start with differential access to local, national, or international resources, but the exploitation of interstate and international regulatory and criminal justice asymmetries—for example, different levels of enforcement in the states or countries in which the fraudsters operate—represents a positive advantage for fraud compared with most other crimes.

Box 9.2. The process of crime for gain

- See a situation as a "financial crime opportunity."
- Obtain finance.
- Find people willing and able to offend (if necessary for the crimes contemplated and/or if already part of a "criminal organization").
- Obtain any tools and data needed to offend.
- Neutralize immediate enforcement and operational risks.
- Carry out offenses in domestic and/or overseas locations with or without physical presence in jurisdiction(s).
- Launder or hide *safely* unspent funds (at home and/or overseas).
- Decide which jurisdiction offers the optimal balance between (a) social and physical comfort and (b) asset forfeiture and criminal justice sanctions.

We can see from box 9.2 one important difference between frauds and most traditional crimes that have victims: at the time when the offense is committed (which, in contrast with other property offenses, may happen over years), the fraudster can be but does not normally need to be in the same place or even on the same continent as the victims or their property. However, few frauds *need* to be executed on an international basis, and some fraudsters (like gangsters) have their domestic geographic comfort zones. Fraudsters, like other organized criminals, may be part of ethnic or national diasporas operating globally, of whom Nigerians are the most prominent in fraud, followed by Russians and other Eastern Europeans in computer-related crimes.[9] It is quicker for a credit card fraudster or telemarketer to fly or drive from New York to Toronto than to do so from New York to Miami or Los Angeles, and that can be important when the rate of fraud on a stolen or counterfeited card is time-critical. However, in many other cases, fraud is not time-critical, so choice of offender or victim location is determined by other factors (such as the large number of relatively wealthy but still anxious elderly people in Florida). Fraudsters—and, for that matter, any other criminals including terrorists—crossing international borders to and from the United States with large quantities of cash or monetary instruments (e.g., checks) run the risks of forfeiture and conviction for nondeclaration of funds but may benefit from there being greater turf wars and legal cooperation difficulties in international than in merely local or national cases. In the larger cases, professional intermediaries and bank accounts are necessary components in presenting a plausible front and in obtaining and laundering the funds; in others, funds may be wired via money service bureaus to foreign or sometimes domestic locations.

III. Some Types of Fraud

It would occupy too much space in a work of this kind to exhaustively examine all the subtypes of financial crimes (see Rosoff, Pontell, and Tillman 2006 for an extended discussion). However, it may illuminate the subject to examine a set of frauds, clustered around a victimcentric typology, crudely broken down into fraud against business, against individuals, and against government. In economic terms there may be some overlapping impacts; for example, if people are frightened by identity fraud, they may transact less online (though off-line shopping may have collateral noneconomic benefits in the form of interacting with others locally and increasing their happiness and the community's "capable guardianship"). In addition, it is worth noting that the combination of globalization, digitization, and the Internet has created vast opportunities for the counterfeiting of legitimate products, which have the advantage (for the offenders) of being transportable and saleable in a more open way than is the case with wholly illicit commodities (e.g., narcotics) or smuggling or trafficking of prohibited immigrants.[10] Thus an alternative model of thinking about financial crimes might involve clustering them as the skill sets, contacts, start-up capital, and running costs that they require.

A. Frauds against Business

1. *Accounting Manipulation*

Accounts can be manipulated by junior clerical staff taking advantage of poor controls in circumstances that often attract media headlines. But the most damaging frauds are mostly perpetrated by elites, often acting out of a sense of entitlement and with a feeling of impunity (Friedrichs 2006; Shover and Hochstetler 2006), which has been likened to the culture of masculinity more commonly attributed to violent offending (Levi 1994). One question that sometimes arises is why, if opportunities to offend are so ubiquitous, all corporations and individual elites do not offend. The ultraskeptical answer is that they may all do, but (deliberately or otherwise) our intelligence gathering is not sufficiently good to detect many. The less skeptical answer is that rotten apples and rotten barrels arise to commit fraud against consumers, against the tax authorities, and against the corporation itself. In the case of rotten barrels, cultural pressures of conformity are strong and penalties for nonparticipation are high. Insufficient monitoring is done to stop dictatorial senior executives from surrounding themselves with the corrupt or merely quiescent and overriding controls (Tillman and Indergaard 2005, 2007*a*, 2007*b*). Thus Tillman and Indergaard (2007*a*, p. 2) ask, "How were senior executives at so many firms able to engage in financial statement fraud despite the presence of numerous control agents—boards of directors, internal and external auditors—whose function is to prevent those very abuses?. . . . One way of getting at this question is to ask *who* was involved in these frauds."

According to Black (2005), accounting fraud is an optimal strategy for many white-collar crimes because it simultaneously produces record (albeit fictitious) profits and prevents (or, perhaps more accurately, delays) the recognition of real losses. The fact that top-tier audit firms sometimes do not notice or do not blow the whistle on the false profits provides some cover to the CEO against fraud prosecutions and is thus preferable to simple embezzlement of funds. To take an illustration, at Enron senior staff (and most of the potential whistle-blowers) were bought off with shares in offshore special purpose entities, abusing accounting rules to artificially boost their profits without apparently counting as corporate costs (which few of us can do at home!). In the contemporary era, many rewards are paid via stock options granted to executives, and the start date at which such stock is notionally booked can make a great difference to profits; hence the temptation (often indulged) to book options at times that do not obviously correspond to initial contract or other key periods. Such insider profits (e.g., shares bought or sold via nominees with advance knowledge of likely price movements) may never be visible to outsiders.[11]

One of the main themes that emerged from the data examined by Tillman and Indergaard (2007*a*) was the extent to which networks of organizations and individuals were involved in multiple instances of financial statement fraud. Though they do not use the term, they might plausibly be termed recidivist offenders. For the firms in their sample accused of fraud, the average number of defendants or respondents was 7.2, suggesting (unless there was a selection bias in prosecutions) the need or desire to corrupt multiple players in order to achieve a substantial financial hit. Another important finding was that among all organizational defendants and respondents named in class action law suits or in actions taken by the Securities and Exchange Commission, over half were companies other than the firm whose profits had to be restated (i.e., changed downward); many of these were accounting firms and banks.[12] It was too crude to state that auditors colluded (or did not collude) with senior managers at restating firms. What seemed important was the extent to which external auditors resisted efforts by senior managers to engage in fraudulent financial reporting, and whether that resistance was consistent or inconsistent.

At the lower level, accounting records may simply be fabricated. An example in terms of cyber-assisted fraud is as follows (Serious Fraud Office Annual Report 2004–5): Robert Damon-Aspen was sentenced to prison for two and a half years after pleading guilty to 81 offenses of deception and nine offenses of forgery. Through his business, CFT Group Insurance Services, based in Canary Wharf, London, he advertised on the Internet as an insurance intermediary. His advertising focused on small IT companies that needed professional indemnity insurance cover. Applicants completed online application forms. Around 5,000 applicants paid about £1.3 million in premiums. However, the defendant did not place any insurance contracts; instead, he simply forged insurance certificates. Administrative errors in his dealings with clients prompted some of them to contact Lloyds of London, which then notified the regulator, the Financial Services Authority. The case was referred to the Serious Fraud Office.

2. *Insider Abuse of Trust*

Insider trading involves the use of as yet undisclosed price-sensitive information obtained in one's privileged professional capacity to make personal profit or avoid loss. Depending on legislative drafting, families, friends, and professional associates are all covered, but both elites and their personal assistants may commit these offenses; only those not in the know are excluded from opportunity. Although such conduct may generally be seen as corrupt, there is no obvious loser. Other insider financial crimes are closer to theft: they simply involve using corporate or personal accounts as if they were one's own, a possibility that arises from the separation of control between principal and agent. Prior to his dismissal, Lord Conrad Black simply negotiated lucrative personal deals not to compete with the newspapers his companies sold to others (violating his fiduciary responsibilities) and charged to corporate expenses extravagant personal parties and more (Bower 2007). Other scandals include frauds by the former chief executive of Tyco, jailed in 2005. These are readily committed by persons in authority, especially if they have surrounded themselves with greedy, overpaid subordinates dependent on them.

Such insider frauds are also possible—though usually for less money—for trusted junior personnel, who may defraud the firm or individuals working within it. In one sensational British case in 1998, socially ambitious Joyti de Laury worked as a personal assistant to a Goldman Sachs partner, Scott Mead, who made up to $20 million annually in salary and bonuses in his peak earning years. He received a request in 2001 to make a donation to his former university (Harvard) and asked de Laury to get his account statements from an account he held in New York. When she kept failing to produce the statements, he ordered them himself and noticed discrepancies that included one transfer of over £2 million to someone who turned out to be de Laury's mother. De Laury had started by stealing over £1 million from a previous Goldman employee and, by the time she began on Mead's account, had developed an organized system to use forged and genuine signatures sent by fax to "authorize" transfers for her employers. Her busy employers often asked her to undertake similar, legitimate activities for them and gave her full access to their account details. She (and her husband and mother, who were also convicted) spent the money on flashy cars, Cartier jewelry, a powerboat, and property in Cyprus and England.[13]

3. *Bankruptcy and Other Credit Frauds*

A popular enduring theme is fraudsters who do not obtain money directly but rather obtain goods on credit for which they do not pay; instead, they give false identities and disappear altogether, or they give false explanations for nonpayment and false valuations of assets, sometimes in league with dishonest company liquidators. In some cases, professional fraudsters or gangsters set up new businesses, building up credit with the intention of fraud, but in other cases, they find businesspeople in trouble and either persuade them or threaten them to turn their businesses into fraudulent ones. In still other cases, a business continues to order goods for which there is no reasonable chance of payment, hoping against objective evidence that "something will turn up" (Levi 2008*b*). In bad economic conditions, such as a credit crunch (which affects businesses as well as private individuals), firms may simply manufacture invoices which they sell at a discount in order to obtain funds. The Internet has enabled "phishing" and "pharming" of corporate identities, enabling simulation of legitimate businesses to order goods on credit or obtain financial intelligence from the public: a corporate form of identity fraud. In a variant, the company may make up artificial sales of, say, computers, using credit card details taken from elsewhere and defraud the card companies by getting reimbursed for the card receipts before the cardholders get their statements and realize they have been defrauded. In such cases, the credit card firms are the losers, though the individual cardholders may also be distressed.

Some individuals and groups commit credit and loan frauds on an international basis. Banks may lose hundreds of millions of dollars in "letter of credit" frauds on the basis of false documentation pretending to have underlying assets. They may also lose money to overvalued homes, due to conspiracies between mortgage brokers, lawyers, and appraisers to inflate prices, which lenders discover when the purchasers—real or with a fake identity—walk away without paying their mortgages. At a lower level, people may rent cars using false documents and then make the cars "disappear," sometimes driving them across borders to be sold. Until everyone adopts PINs with chip cards to replace magnetic stripes (as in Europe), people in key positions (hotel receptionists, car rental agents, store clerks) may copy card details electronically and send them to their confederates overseas, who may create good counterfeit cards or encode the magnetic stripe data onto unembossed "white plastic" for use when no one looks at the actual card.

4. *Insurance Frauds*

There are many ways in which insurance companies can be defrauded, from large-scale commercial frauds (ship scuttling and arson for profit) to the more common inflation of losses from genuine burglaries and auto theft. Arson can be a technique of concealment for bankruptcy fraudsters who have sold their goods, and maritime fraudsters may offload their genuine cargo elsewhere before their ship is sunk in waters that are hard to excavate. More ambiguously, health care professionals may defraud insurers (as well as Medicare and Medicaid) for consultations or operations that are not performed or are unnecessary. One area that has provoked increasing concern is staged accidents involving networks of offenders, often within the same ethnic or national group (for mutual trust reasons), and sometimes in collusion with auto repair firms, doctors, or specialist claims lawyers, who claim multiply for damage to vehicles and hard-to-falsify injuries such as whiplash or back pain. They may rotate the personnel involved in different roles or take advantage of the absence of data-sharing or sophisticated analysis among corporate victims.

B. Frauds against Individuals

1. *Consumer Scams*

There are a variety of types of consumer fraud. Some lure via e-mail, sent for almost zero cost in telecoms or labor. Others persuade by telephone or letter.[14] Shover, Coffey, and Sanders (2004) explain how U.S. criminal telemarketing works. Sales agents call potential customers, make the initial pitch, and weed out the worst prospects. They do not call individuals randomly but work instead from "lead lists" (also known as "mooch lists"). Lead lists are purchased from other telemarketing fraudsters or from any of dozens of businesses that compile and sell information on consumer behavior and expressed preferences, implicit in which is risk appetite. Individuals whose names appear on lead lists typically are distinguished by assets and previously demonstrated interest in promotions of one kind or another. On the phone, fraudulent sales agents—like many legitimate ones—work from written scripts that lay out successful sales approaches and responses to whatever reception they meet. Promising contacts are turned over to "closers," who are more experienced and better paid sales agents. "Reloaders" are the most effective closers.

Much like account executives in legitimate businesses, fraudulent agents maintain contact with individuals who have previously sent money to their company. Examples of commonly employed schemes include prize and sweepstakes deals, magazine sales, credit card sales, work-at-home schemes, advance-fee loan offers, credit card loss protection programs, buyers' clubs, and travel and vacation offers. As Shover, Coffey, and Sanders (2004, pp. 65–66) put it, "To the unsuspecting, the day-to-day activities of a fraudulent telemarketing operation may be indistinguishable from those of a legitimate business."

2. *Fraudulent Investment Schemes*

There are many types of investment fraud, including the following:

- The simple "419" frauds (named after the relevant section of the Nigerian Penal Code) that many of us receive regularly by mail or e-mail, offering the opportunity to share the unclaimed billion-dollar wealth of whichever African kleptocrat has most recently been in the news, if only we will give them our bank details ($25 billion or $12.5 billion is the normal sum to be transferred)
- "Boiler room" scams, in which high-pressure telemarketers persuade us that we have a chance of getting the inside track of "sure thing" investments, and sometimes then sell "sucker lists" to other fraudsters who offer us a chance of recouping our initial losses
- High-yield investment frauds, often with the alleged complicity of lawyers, in which implausibly high rates of return are offered by apparently prestigious firms
- Far more ambiguous schemes in which the victims may never realize that they have been swindled but instead think that their investments have legitimately failed or have made less money than hoped

In some of these schemes the victims are innocent dupes, but in others, such as some 419 schemes, victims may be viewed as attempted conspirators in transnational frauds and corruption, or hypothetically may even be charged criminally as such. Some citizens have a higher risk appetite than others, and this may not correlate obviously with particular demographics. In their analysis of a Ponzi scheme,[15] Trahan, Marquart, and Mullings (2005) noted that the majority of victims reported investing with no particular financial purpose other than to "get ahead."

C. Frauds against the Public Sector

The patterns of fraud against the government (i.e., taxpayers and recipients of government services) vary by the kinds of activities that are in public ownership.[16] By European standards, the United States has a very high proportion of activities in private ownership, though the United Kingdom has been catching up, and its social security welfare provisions are low. Thus in the United Kingdom and other European countries with a socialized health care system there are relatively few opportunities to defraud medical insurers, whereas in the United States there have been widespread frauds against both medical insurance firms (and consequently those who pay premiums) and the government via Medicare and Medicaid.

Taxation levels are more difficult to compare transnationally, as are corruption opportunities. However, immense contract opportunities are created in routine relationships between "good old boys"—which may not involve direct exchanges of money and gifts that are easier to detect and prove than longer term "understandings"—and by episodic events such as 9/11, Hurricane Katrina, and Iraq reconstruction, especially when there is a rush to get things done, and through single-tenderer contracts awarded to firms such as Halliburton or their affiliates and subsidiaries. More generally, the opportunities for concealment offered by offshore and sometimes domestic (e.g., Delaware, Montana) corporate arrangements are legion for those willing to take modest risks. Successive reports by the General Accounting Office and by inspectors general provide vivid testimony. Some offenders are involved with organized crime groups, some with professional fraudsters unconnected to organized crime. Others are intermittent offenders, working with or without other knowing conspirators.

In Europe carousel frauds are facilitated by European internal market rules (House of Lords 2007). Carousel fraud in its simplest form is known as "missing trader fraud." A fraudster sets up a company, imports items such as mobile phones from another European country free of value-added tax (VAT), sells the goods with VAT added, and then disappears without handing the VAT to Revenue and Customs. However, some fraudsters continually reexport and reimport the goods in a "carousel" system, reclaiming millions of pounds of VAT at the point of export each time because goods are zero-rated for VAT when they cross an EU border.

Contra trading involves setting up two overlapping carousels spinning between various EU countries and countries outside the EU. One will often involve services such as software or licenses and the other goods such as mobile phones. Some of the trades will be legitimate, and a gang will often make a small VAT payment in one country to disguise a much bigger reclaim in another. In some cases, no physical goods move at all: there are merely paper transactions, sometimes aided by corrupt Customs officers.

In Canada criminals take advantage of the tax-exempt status of businesses based on Native American reservations. Known as "flipping," a common method involves the sale and resale of cars, trucks, and heavy building equipment such as bulldozers, and the fraudulent claiming of a goods and services tax (GST) rebate on each transaction. Typically, a vehicle will be sold and resold several times, in and out of a reservation, with the result that it is treated as an export. A 6 percent rebate is claimed on each transaction, and some criminals have been accused of making millions of Canadian dollars. In one case in Ontario, fraudsters were jailed for up to four years after defrauding the Canadian government of $20 million in a fraud in which cars appeared to be sold and resold several times a day in different parts of the country. None of the vehicles actually changed hands.

IV. Policy Responses to Financial Crimes

The control of financial crimes is as large a topic as the control of property crimes, so one cannot hope to do justice here to the immense complexity of the subject matter. Disregarding money laundering per se, frauds and intellectual property violations involve a range of victim-offender relationships and techniques. In keeping with the victimcentric typology, one might think of individual, business, and governmental responses, which can be interwoven and only some of which involve the criminal justice process. We might also think of the resources and skill sets needed for different forms of financial crime and examine how, if at all, these cluster and may be dealt with to minimize harm.

Paradoxically, one of the things that we can learn from the way that we traditionally control white-collar crimes is that less punitive and criminal justice–dependent and more social forms of crime control are possible, that is, by individual and collective efforts at prevention or loss mitigation and by self-regulation and formal regulation (e.g., financial services), supplemented by formal criminal justice controls. One difficult policy question is where market failure occurs (i.e., when self-regulation is bound to be inadequate) and when that failure is sufficiently serious to require major interventions (though there is no scope for zero-tolerance models). In the light of the seismic crashes of the financial services industry in 2008, it is certain that market failure has arisen from reckless lending, even if that is not defined as fraud.

The growth of multilateral information exchange and mutual legal assistance agreements have boosted variable national efforts against financial crimes. However, it is extremely unlikely that the policing panopticon will ever extend to encompass all types of fraud. For despite the growth in public concern about their direct and indirect (via pension funds) investments in the stock markets and about identity theft and other crime risks associated with the cyberworld, the iconography of fear of crime is more difficult to develop and sustain for white-collar than for organized crime and terrorism. Though banks often report frauds under money-laundering regulations, police in many jurisdictions make comparatively little use of these reports as an investigative trigger or to locate proceeds (Fleming 2005; Levi and Reuter, this volume).

Politician lawmakers and resource grantors both respond to and help create social constructions of harm. In keeping with the more general moral entrepreneurship of U.S. "law and order" politics, the U.S. media, politicians, and law enforcement officials are paradoxically more likely than their U.K. counterparts to discuss white-collar crimes, both for crimes against business (e.g., credit card fraud) and crimes against investors (especially senior citizens) by businesses both prestigious and run by racketeers. Although interest in white-collar crimes is commonly associated with left-of-center politics, efficient markets and popular capitalism depend on some level of trust that it is in the interests of capitalism to sustain. Elaborate mechanisms try to ensure that gatekeepers, such as accountants, bankers, credit rating agents, lawyers, and stock analysts, do not let management defraud significant sums, and the U.S.A. Patriot Act of 2001 requires some gatekeepers to report suspicions to the authorities. However, as revealed by Enron and other huge corporate scandals exposed (but not begun) in the twenty-first century, those mechanisms have fault lines that are wider than San Andreas: excessive closeness of "independent professionals" to their clients, the bonus focus of individual partners within professional firms and within business, and the normality of offshore special purpose entities, other nontransparent forms of business structure that reduce tax and other liabilities but conceal self-dealing, and other frauds in international money-laundering schemes.

Some large aggregate frauds against government treasuries, such as evasion of excise duty on smuggled alcohol and tobacco, are viewed as serious organized crime threats in high-tax countries (SOCA 2006), but even those that are not organized (in that special sense) generate huge losses. Throughout the Western world the increased proportion and longevity of senior citizens and the privatization of pensions and savings have created new classes of victims whose magnitude constitutes a political as well as a financial risk that calls for a response. In addition, the Internet has intensified the risk of transnational fraud by making available—more temptingly than by mail or random phone call—lures that then can be followed up by old tech methods such as the telephone. These telemarketing frauds tend to be carried out by criminals more middle class than traditional (Shover, Coffey, and Hobbs 2003) and who have better verbal skills to prey on the rising number of people with spare disposable wealth on the lookout for (apparently) better-than-average returns on investment. This, in turn, has tempted American mafiosi to ally themselves with Russian-origin and with non-Mafia Americans who have the skills and the front companies to exploit penny stock and other fraud opportunities (Block and Weaver 2004; Diih 2005). However, those fraudsters who are not associated with the usual suspects kept under surveillance or with infiltration remain able to force the police to deal with them reactively; especially when overseas, they may end up in the "too difficult" category for hard-pressed or ill-motivated police to pursue.

The FBI (2007, p. 4) states, "Based upon field office crime surveys, current trends in the White Collar Crime arena, and directives established by the President, the Attorney General, and the Criminal Investigative Division, the following national priorities for the White Collar Crime Program have been established: Public Corruption, Corporate Fraud/Securities Fraud, Health Care Fraud, Financial Institution Fraud, Insurance Fraud, and Money Laundering." When they fall below $1 million in aggregate scale,[17] consumer scams tend to be dealt with, if at all, by the Federal Trade Commission and a plethora of state and local police and regulators rather than by the FBI. (There are parallels in the United Kingdom, except that, usually, the alternative to a case being dealt with by a police Fraud Squad or Economic Crime Unit is no police intervention at all.)

Financial crimes are not the only offenses that present difficulties for policing, but in the hierarchy of transnational threats they are ranked lower than terrorism and organized crimes (though there is some overlap). If Canadian "boiler room" stock fraudsters or telemarketers operating from Spain rip off British or American victims and place the funds in an honest (to depositors) but noncooperative offshore finance center, who will have sufficient motivation to spend vast sums of money unraveling the case with an uncertain outcome? U.S. agencies typically have more money to spend than their counterparts around the world, especially in the Third World, but parochial interests predominate everywhere.

Another policy response, as in organized crime, is to stimulate fear and risk of detection by covert operations and by conspirator betrayal. This includes FBI sting operations and the policy that generates lenient treatment for the first person or company to volunteer information about a cartel prior to government investigations of it. Such inquiries require considerable skills and freedom from political interference, and can go disastrously wrong (Greising and Morse 1991; Eichenwald 2001). Connor (2006) notes that the United States is almost always the first to investigate and sanction international cartels, and its investigations are about seven times faster than those of the EU, the second most powerful antitrust busters.

For corporate misconduct committed by top management, greater corporate governance is one approach. In the United States the Sarbanes-Oxley Act of 2002 established a new quasi-public agency, the Public Company Accounting Oversight Board, to oversee, regulate, inspect, and discipline accounting firms in their roles as auditors of public companies. The Act also covers issues such as auditor independence, corporate governance, internal control assessment, whistle-blowing, and enhanced financial disclosure. Quite apart from the need to do something, the aim is to reduce the risk of reoccurrence of major corporate scandals such as Enron and WorldCom. However, endemic conflicts of interest and the right of CEOs to choose their own auditors (who may also receive generous fees for corporate consultancies) lead many to question the benefits compared with compliance costs. The French Société Générale case of 2007–8 indicates the importance of internal audit and follow-up of allegedly unauthorized trading, at least for cases that do not involve the complicity of top management.

As for criminal and administrative penalties, the absence of systematic reoffending data and general offending data makes it difficult to be clear about what works and for which types of financial crimes (Braithwaite 2002, 2005; Korsell 2004). Besides, as with policing, it is difficult to know what the purposes of sanctions are; quite apart from deterrence or crime reduction, penalties can combine retributive or demonstrative effects to show that the act is serious, with penal populism motivated by the desire for reelection. Hence, in part, the popularity of asset forfeiture as a way of showing the public and potential offenders that the fruits of crime will be returned to the public and identifiable victims.

Levi (2007*b*) examined the sentencing of fraud in the United Kingdom and the United States. Since that research U.S. guidelines have recommended increased sentences for some frauds.[18] The most recent available sentencing data are recorded in table 9.1. By contrast, in 2004 only a quarter of offenders sentenced for fraud and forgery offences in England and Wales Crown Courts were imprisoned, and the average jail term was 9.2 months (though this includes many cases that in the United States would be state or local cases). The 109 persons convicted in U.K. Serious Fraud Office cases between 2000 and 2005—the top of the seriousness range—received an average of 31.7 months imprisonment; half of them received three years or less. Comparable U.S. fraud sentences tend to be higher than sentences in Australasia, Canada, and Europe (but they are higher for other offences also). Looking at Serious Fraud Office cases in a victim-focused way, for frauds against business creditors the average was 27.4 months; investment frauds against business investors was 37.7 months; investment frauds on individuals was 40.4 months; market abuse was 12 months (though in one of the two cases all four defendants received suspended prison sentences, showing how distorted averages can be); procurement fraud or corruption was 19.9 months; and frauds on government was 36.8 months (but only three cases). In 17 cases (about a third) at least one defendant was disqualified from company directorship—a sentence not available in the United States—for an average of over seven years. This reflects not just legal powers but also a belief that this is an appropriate financial punishment (reducing future earnings) and will be effective as incapacitation. The latter is an open

Table 9.1. U.S. federal financial crimes sentences, October 2006–7

Offense	Number sentenced (% imprisoned)	Mean sentence (months)	Median sentence (months)
Fraud	6,906 (71.3)	19.0	10.0
Embezzlement	424 (48.3)	8.7	4.0
Forgery/counterfeiting	1,066 (70.7)	14.7	10.0
Tax	588 (61.9)	14.8	10.0
Money laundering	812 (83.7)	34.9	24.0
Antitrust	15 (73.3)	15.9	5.0

Source: Sentencing Commission, http://www.ussc.gov/sc_cases/Quarter_Report_4th_07.pdf.

question: it certainly would affect those who need to play an upfront role as a director, but the extent of shadow directorships among those subject to disqualification is unknown and very difficult to discover even in principle.[19]

As for antitrust offenses, Connor (2006) notes that median U.S. government fines average less than 10 percent of businesses affected, but rise to about 35 percent in the case of multicontinent conspiracies. Civil settlements in jurisdictions where they are permitted are typically 6 to 12 percent of sales. Canadian and U.S. fines and settlements imposed higher penalties than other jurisdictions; fines on cartels that operated in Europe averaged a bit more than half of their estimated overcharges; those prosecuted only in North America paid civil and criminal sanctions of roughly the same as their damages; and global cartels prosecuted in both jurisdictions typically paid less than single damages. It seems plausible that a more aggressive approach would deter corporations more than the present system does, but the individuals making the price-fixing decisions are unlikely to be in post when their illegalities are discovered, and to the extent that frauds are committed to stop firms from sliding into liquidation, increased fines would reduce competition and lead to unemployment.

If offenders perceive that they will have both a low chance of conviction and a light sentence for complex, multijurisdiction frauds obtaining vast sums of money compared with other types of crime for gain, then unless this shift is an intentional policy objective (as a choice between evils), this is cause for reflection on the justice gap in fraud, though as Braithwaite (2002) is keen to stress at a general level, superficial fairness may not be the appropriate objective. The relativities between fraud and other sentences are salient, especially (in the deterrence mode) to those choosing between different crime types within their capacities, but also to justice between different sets of both offenders and victims. The systematic information about offender and potential offender expectations of sanctions for fraud is not yet available to make any clear evidence-based decisions about deterrent penalties. Nor, following the corporate death of the accounting firm Arthur Andersen for shredding Enron files (though the conviction was reversed by the U.S. Supreme Court on appeal), do we have any clear idea of whether deferred prosecutions, currently fashionable in the United States, carry a credible threat that will produce either special or general deterrence. Major accounting firms and banks know that the market disruption that would follow their conviction makes corporate prosecution unlikely, even though U.S. corporate criminal liability rules make conviction easier than in other jurisdictions. The capacity to boost shame in contemporary societies is limited not just by the often tolerant reactions of business and political elites, but also by the ability of the sociopathic to enjoy themselves in isolation from the censurers. Actual prevention is limited by the ability—despite individual and corporate customer identification requirements in regulations against money laundering around the world—to anonymize oneself in many commercial settings, though this does not mean that attempts to reduce the harms from financial crimes have not been successful. Successes will remain tentative, especially without a sustained set of preventive efforts backed by administrative and criminal justice sanctions that must be conducted on a more than purely national basis.

In conclusion, levels of regulation tend to lurch from one extreme to another, as both prosecutions and tighter prevention follow scandals. Since the Wall Street crash of 1929 and the Great Depression of the 1930s, the United States has adopted tougher approaches than the United Kingdom to regulating capitalism, and when it has not, major problems have arisen, as in the Savings and Loans scandals of the 1980s and the dot.com bubble and other corporate scandals of the late 1990s, early 2000s, and the Wall Street collapses of 2008. Globalization has created special challenges for international cooperation to pursue both offenders and their proceeds, supported by political pressure for "functional equivalence" in legislation and for investigative resources to deal with transnational financial crimes. The extent to which both restorative and retributive justice, as well as preventive regulation, will be reconfigured in the light of the economic and moral panics of 2008 (Levi 2009) remain to be seen.

NOTES

1. Are price-fixing corporate executives short-run hedonists with poor self-control?

2. These estimates of the broader impact of street and household crimes are themselves not uncontroversial, since there is much scope for disagreement on the criteria by which we should estimate collateral damage. Some other studies have tackled the costs of organized crime, which involves the still more difficult task of combining often victimless crimes with particular modes of crime delivery, that is, setting a threshold for the label "organized" (Dubourg and Prichard, forthcoming).

3. There are national variations, but corporations and professional firms whose liquidation would generate collateral damage tend to receive "restorative justice," often outside the criminal justice process, or (in the United States) "deferred prosecutions," whereas the poor and the organized criminals who commit fraud are dealt with unambiguously as real criminals. Of course, if elites are not prosecuted, they cannot be imprisoned!

4. People buying counterfeit products almost invariably know that they are fake because of the price and context, though sometimes stores sell counterfeit products as genuine.

5. Note also that just because a high harm calculation comes from a source that has an interest in inflating a problem does not mean that the source is wrong.

6. This might then be termed "corporate crime," though it is arguable that it is for the personal benefit of bonus "earners" rather than truly for the benefit of the corporation.

7. Seeing situations as opportunities for fraud is not an automatic process. Such cognitive issues, as well as the more usual ones of socialization and rationalizations, are properly a part of explaining financial crimes (Levi 2008*b*). There is no space here for an extended discussion of fraud motivation; for good reviews, see Shover and Hochstetler (2006) and Friedrichs (2006). Though this is culturally variable between and within countries and over time, we tend to define greed as the search for superprofits, often obtained in a too upfront way that may produce a negative political reaction.

8. Or, especially in less transparent, mostly developing, countries where economic power is centralized, the corruption may be committed by leading government figures themselves.

9. Of course, Nigerians have variable family, regional, and religious affiliations and should not be seen as a homogeneous group. Canadians also are prominent in boiler room and telemarketing frauds.

10. For a general discussion of these transnational illicit phenomena, see Naim (2005).

11. For good journalistic accounts of Wall Street scandals, see Eichenwald (2005*a*, 2005*b*).

12. Though the latter may owe something to their having deep pockets to sue and to the U.S. civil racketeering punitive damages provisions, which are not found in other jurisdictions.

13. For an intriguingly sympathetic radical feminist interview with her, see *The Guardian*, September 17, 2005.

14. For a British guide, see http://www.oft.gov.uk/oft_at_work/consumer_initiatives/scams/. Reflecting a more active consumer rights political culture, U.S. guides include http://postalinspectors.uspis.gov/; http://www.peoples-law.org/consumer/scams/consumer_scams.htm; http://www.consumer.gov/; http://www.sec.gov/investor/pubs/cyberfraud.htm.

15. Ponzi is a generic term for schemes in which the organizers rob Peter to pay Paul, building up confidence while the racket expands.

16. Though other frauds against the private sector may result in fewer taxes being paid, and therefore are indirectly frauds against the government or us, its citizens.

17. There is an important question (as in serial killings and rapes) of the extent to which frauds that are in fact connected are identified by victims or authorities as part of aggregate behavior by the suspects. This linkage depends on resources and competence.

18. See Sentencing Council (2007) for a subsequent British discussion of sentencing guidelines in fraud. For detailed U.S. sentencing issues, see Sentencing Commission (2007, 2008), though the guidelines are no longer as mandatorily prescriptive as they were.

19. If the companies to which they are shadow directors get into visible trouble, there may be a reasonable chance that their involvement will be uncovered (if there are financial traces or if anyone "grasses"); however, we may overestimate the extent to which director disqualification and even de-authorization from financial services—a regulatory sanction that is available in the United States as well as the United Kingdom—actually incapacitate.

REFERENCES

ACFE. 2006. *2006 ACFE Report to the Nation: On Occupational Fraud and Abuse*. Austin, TX: AFCE. http://www.acfe.com/documents/2006-rttn.pdf.

Barnett, Cynthia. 2000. *The Measurement of White-Collar Crime Using Uniform Crime Reporting (UCR) Data*. Washington, DC: U.S. Department of Justice.

Baum, Katrina. 2007. *Identity Theft 2005*. Washington, DC: Bureau of Justice Statistics. http://www.ojp.usdoj.gov/bjs/pub/pdf/ito5.pdf.

Black, William K. 2005. *The Best Way to Rob a Bank Is to Own One*. Austin: University of Texas Press.

Block, Alan, and Constance Weaver. 2004. *All Is Clouded by Desire*. New York: Praeger.

Bower, Tom. 2007. *Conrad and Lady Black: Dancing on the Edge*. London: Harper Perennial.

Braithwaite, John. 2002. *Responsive Regulation*. Oxford: Oxford University Press.

———. 2005. *Markets in Vice, Markets in Virtue*. Oxford: Oxford University Press.

Bussman, Kai D., and Markus M. Werle. 2006. "Addressing Crime in Companies: First Findings from a Global Survey of Economic Crime." *British Journal of Criminology* 46: 1128–44.

Cohen, Mark. 2005. *The Costs of Crime and Justice*. London: Routledge.

Connor, John. 2006. "Effectiveness of Antitrust Sanctions on Modern International Cartels." *Journal of Industry, Competition and Trade* 6(3): 195–223.

Diih, Sorle. 2005. "The Infiltration of New York's Financial Market by Organised Crime: Pressures and Controls." PhD thesis, Cardiff University.

Dubourg, Richard, Joe Hamed, and Jamie Thorns. 2005. *The Economic and Social Costs of Crime against Individuals and Households 2003/04*. Home Office Online Report 30/05. www.homeoffice.gov.uk/rds/pdfs05/rdsolr3005.pdf.

Dubourg, Richard, and Stephen Prichard, eds. Forthcoming. *The Impact of Organised Crime in the U.K.: Revenues and Economic and Social Costs*. London: Home Office.

Eichenwald, Kurt. 2001. *The Informant*. New York: Broadway Books.

———. 2005*a*. *Conspiracy of Fools: A True Story*. New York: Broadway Books.

———. 2005*b*. *Serpent on the Rock*. New York: Broadway Books.

Federal Bureau of Investigation. 2007. *Financial Crimes Report to the Public, Fiscal Year 2006*. Washington, DC: FBI. http://www.fbi.gov/publications/financial/fcs_report2006/publicrpt06.pdf

———. 2008*a*. *Financial Crimes Report to the Public, Fiscal Year 2007*. Washington, DC: FBI. http://www.fbi.gov/publications/financial/fcs_report2007/financial_crime_2007.htm.

———. 2008*b*. *2007 Mortgage Fraud Report*. Washington, DC: FBI. http://www.fbi.gov/publications/fraud/mortgage_fraud07.htm.

Fleming, Matthew. 2005. *U.K. Law Enforcement Agency Use and Management of Suspicious Activity Reports: Towards Determining the Value of the Regime*. London: University College London.

Friedrichs, David. 2006. *Trusted Criminals*. 3rd ed. Belmont, CA: Wadsworth.

Greising, David, and Larry Morse. 1991. *Brokers, Bagmen, and Moles: Fraud and Corruption in the Chicago Futures Markets*. New York: Wiley.

Harding, Chris. 2007. *Criminal Enterprise: Individuals, Organisations and Criminal Responsibility*. Cullompton, UK: Willan.

House of Lords. 2007. *Stopping the Carousel: Missing Trader Fraud in the EU*. European Union Committee, 20th Report of Session 2006–7. http://www.publications.parliament.uk/pa/ld200607/ldselect/ldeucom/101/101.pdf.

Javelin Research. 2008. *2008 Identity Fraud Survey Report: Consumer Version*. http://www.idsafety.net/803.R_2008%20Identity%20Fraud%20Survey%20Report_Consumer%20Version.pdf.

Kane, John, and April Wall. 2006. *The National Public Household Survey 2005*. Glen Allen, VA: National Center for White-Collar Crime.

Karstedt, Suzanne, and Stephen Farrall. 2006. "The Moral Economy of Everyday Crime: Markets, Consumers and Citizens." *British Journal of Criminology* 46: 1011–36.

Korsell, Lars. 2004. "Four Decades of Policies and Practices in Sweden against White-Collar Crime." Paper presented at the Helsinki Seminar "Regulating Corporate Crime: Developments across Europe." http://www.bra.se/extra/measurepoint/?module_instance=4&&name=0409142164.pdf&&url=/dynamaster/file_archive/050120/37c7bc6b4bf534ad5894d7356142df71/0409142164.pdf.

Levi, Michael. 1994. "Masculinities and White-collar Crime." In *Just Boys Doing Business,* edited by Tim Newburn and Betsy Stanko. London: Routledge.

———. 2006. "The Media Construction of Financial White-Collar Crimes." *Markets, Risk and Crime,* Special Issue of *British Journal of Criminology* 46: 1037–57.

———. 2007*a*. "Organised Crime and Terrorism." In *The Oxford Handbook of Criminology,* edited by Mike Maguire, Rod Morgan, and Robert Reiner. 4th ed. Oxford: Oxford University Press.

———. 2007*b*. *Sentencing Frauds: A Review.* Research paper commissioned by the Attorney General's Fraud Review. http://www.cardiff.ac.uk/socsi/resources/Levi_GFR_Sentencing_Fraud.pdf.

———. 2008*a*. "'Organised Fraud' and Organising Frauds: Unpacking Research on Networks and Organisation." *Criminology and Criminal Justice* 8(4): 389–420.

———. 2008*b*. *The Phantom Capitalists: The Organisation and Control of Long-Firm Fraud.* 2nd ed. Aldershot, UK: Ashgate.

———. 2009. "Suite Revenge? The Shaping of Folk Devils and Moral Panics about White-Collar Crimes." *Moral Panics 36 Years On,* Special Issue of *British Journal of Criminology* 49: 1.

Levi, Michael, and John Burrows. 2008. "Measuring the Impact of Fraud in the U.K.: A Conceptual and Empirical Journey." *British Journal of Criminology* 48(3): 293–318.

Levi, Michael, John Burrows, Matthew Fleming, and Matt Hopkins, with the assistance of Kent Matthews. 2007. *The Nature, Extent and Economic Impact of Fraud in the U.K.* London: Association of Chief Police Officers. http://www.acpo.police.uk/asp/policies/Data/Fraud%20in%20the%20U.K.pdf.

Levi, Michael, and Andrew Pithouse. Forthcoming. *White-Collar Crime and Its Victims.* Oxford, UK: Clarendon.

Levi, Michael, and Peter Reuter. 2006. "Money Laundering." In *Crime and Justice: A Review of Research,* vol. 34, edited by Michael Tonry. Chicago: University of Chicago Press.

Naim, Moses. 2005. *Illicit.* New York: Doubleday.

Operation "Malicious Mortgage." http://www.youtube.com/watch?v=9fMlGGABcHs and http://www.fbi.gov/pressrel/pressrel08/mortgagefraud061908.htm.

Rebovich, Don, and Jenny Layne. 2000. *The 1999 National Public Survey on White-Collar Crime Completed.* Morgantown, WV: National White-Collar Crime Center.

Reiman, Jeffrey. 2007. *The Rich Get Richer and the Poor Get Prison.* 8th ed. New York: Allyn and Bacon.

Rosoff, Stephen M., Henry N. Pontell, and Robert Tillman. 2006. *Profit without Honor: White-Collar Crime and the Looting of America.* 4th ed. Upper Saddle River, NJ: Prentice Hall. (Originally published 2004.)

Sentencing Commission. 2007. *Federal Sentencing Guidelines Manual.* http://www.ussc.gov/2007guid/TABCON07.html.

———. 2008. *Supplement to the 2007 Guidelines Manual*. http://www.ussc.gov/2007guid/20080303_Supplement_to_2007_Guidelines.pdf.
Sentencing Council. 2007. *Consultation Paper on Sentencing for Fraud Offences*. http://www.sentencing-guidelines.gov.uk/docs/Fraud%20Consultation%20Paper%20-%20version%20for%20printing%202007-08-07.DB.pdf.
Serious Fraud Office. 2005. *Annual Report 2004–5*. http://www.sfo.gov.uk/publications/annual_2005.asp.
Shapiro, S. 1990. "Collaring the Crime, Not the Criminal: Liberating the Concept of White-Collar Crime." *American Sociological Review* 55: 346–64.
Shover, Neal, Glenn S. Coffey, and Dick Hobbs. 2003. "Crime on the Line: Telemarketing and the Changing Nature of Professional Crime." *British Journal of Criminology* 43(July): 489–505.
Shover, Neal, Glenn S. Coffey, and Clinton R. Sanders. 2004. "Dialing for Dollars: Opportunities, Justifications, and Telemarketing Fraud." *Qualitative Sociology* 27(1): 59–75.
Shover, Neal, and Andrew Hochstetler. 2006. *Choosing White-Collar Crime*. Cambridge: Cambridge University Press.
SOCA. 2006. *U.K. Assessment of the Threat of Serious Organised Crime 2006/7*. London: Serious and Organised Crime Agency. http://www.soca.gov.uk/assessPublications/downloads/threat_assess_unclass_250706.pdf.
Tillman, Robert, and Michael Indergaard. 2005. *Pump and Dump: The Rancid Rules of the New Economy*. New Brunswick, NJ: Rutgers University Press.
Tillman, Robert, and Michael Indergaard. 2007*a*. *Control Overrides in Financial Statement Fraud*. Report for the Institute of Fraud Prevention. http://www.theifp.org/research%20grants/tillman%20final%20report_revised_mac-orginal-EDITED.pdf.
Tillman, Robert, and Michael Indergaard. 2007*b*. "Corporate Corruption in the New Economy." In *International Handbook of White-Collar and Corporate Crime*, edited by Henry Pontell and Gilbert Geis. New York: Springer.
Trahan, Adam, James W. Marquart, and Janet Mullings. 2005. "Fraud and the American Dream: Toward an Understanding of Fraud Victimization." *Deviant Behavior* 26(6): 601–20.
van Duyne, Petrus, and Michael Levi. 2005. *Drugs and Money*. New York: Routledge.
Weisburd, David, Stanton Wheeler, and Elin Waring. 1991. *Crimes of the Middle Classes: White Collar Offenders in the Federal Courts*. New Haven, CT: Yale University Press.

CHAPTER 10

IDENTITY THEFT

HEITH COPES AND LYNNE VIERAITIS

In the past ten years identity theft has captured the public's attention as "the fastest growing crime in America" (Cole and Pontell 2006, p. 125). Consumers are bombarded on a seemingly daily basis with stories detailing the latest data breach, the newest scams used by identity thieves, the dangers faced in doing routine transactions, and the latest products and services advertised to decrease the likelihood of victimization. Perhaps driven by this widespread attention by the media, identity theft has also captured the attention of lawmakers. In 1998 Congress passed the Identity Theft Assumption and Deterrence Act (18 USC 1028), making identity theft a federal offense and charging the Federal Trade Commission (FTC) with collecting complaints from consumers. State lawmakers have passed similar bills criminalizing the act of identity theft. Attention from lawmakers reached unprecedented levels at the end of 2007 as more than 200 bills focusing on the issue were pending at the state level (Aite Group 2007).

Identity theft is a complex crime and, as the following cases indicate, can take a variety of forms. It includes credit card and bank fraud, government benefits fraud, mortgage fraud, and a variety of other categories of fraud. Because it is often difficult to encompass identity theft within a single description, illustrative cases help shed light on the range of behaviors committed by identity thieves. In 2003 an identity thief placed holds on several victims' mail, picked up the mail at the post office, and used personally identifying information in the stolen mail to create counterfeit checks in the victims' names. The checks were then used to purchase items from various merchants. In 2007 a former Social Security Administration employee was charged with illegally disclosing personal information she took from a government computer that was then used by others to commit identity theft. Her accomplice supplied her with a name and date of birth, and in turn the employee obtained other identifying information, such as the person's social security number or mother's maiden name. This information was used to make approximately $2.5 million worth of unauthorized charges to credit card accounts. In 2007 a man was sentenced to five years in federal prison for committing identity theft by taking over credit card accounts belonging to others and opening new accounts. He used people's personally identifying information to order credit cards, including the information of his father, who had died the previous year.

While the media and lawmakers have focused much attention on identity theft in the past several years, academic research on the crime is limited. However, considering the available data collected by various agencies and organizations as well as existing research studies, we can conclude the following:

- Although there is no set definition of identity theft, most agree that it includes the misuse of another individual's personal information to commit fraud.
- Available data suggest that approximately seven to eight million people are victims of identity theft each year.
- Persons between the ages of 18 and 55 with incomes greater than $75,000 are at greatest risk of victimization, and older persons, especially those over the age of 75, are at least risk.
- Identity thieves come from a variety of backgrounds, criminal histories, and lifestyles.
- Offenders use a variety of methods to acquire information, including buying information from other street offenders or employees of various businesses and agencies and stealing from mailboxes.
- Offenders use a variety of methods to convert information to cash or goods, including using the information to acquire or produce additional identity-related documents such as driver's licenses and state identification cards, making checks, ordering new credit cards, and applying for various loans.
- Although more research needs to be done, the following recommendations concerning preventions are based on what we know so far: increase the effort and risks of acquiring information and converting information into cash or goods; remove excuses for acquiring information and converting information to cash and goods; and advertise the potential legal consequences of identity theft.

This chapter provides an overview of what is known about identity theft. Section I elaborates on the ambiguity and difficulties in defining the crime. In section II we describe patterns and incidences of identity theft and identify the primary sources of data that have illuminated the extent and costs of this crime. Sections III and IV discuss what is known about those who are victimized by the crime and those who engage in it. In section V we offer two theoretical explanations for why offenders choose to commit identity theft. Section VI offers a description of the most common techniques to locate information and convert it into cash or goods. In section VII we discuss policy ideas, including existing legislation directed toward identity theft prevention, and the policy implications of current knowledge about identity theft. The final section presents an agenda for future research.

I. Defining Identity Theft

Despite the widespread attention given to identity theft, there is no general consensus regarding what behaviors and activities constitute the crime. Recent research has drawn attention to the problem with defining identity theft (see Newman and McNally 2005; Bureau of Justice Statistics [BJS] 2006; Cole and Pontell 2006). In its report on identity theft, the Bureau of Justice Statistics (p. 2) explains that "there is no one universally accepted definition of identity theft as the term describes a variety of illegal acts involving theft or misuse of personal information." The term *identity theft* has been used to describe a variety of offenses, including checking account fraud, counterfeiting, forgery, auto theft using false documentation, trafficking in human beings, and terrorism. Although no definitive definition of identity theft exists, basic patterns have emerged among policy makers and researchers trying to establish one. At the heart of these definitions is the idea that identity theft is "the misuse of another individual's personal information to commit fraud" (President's Identity Theft Task Force 2007, p. 2).

In 1998 identity theft became a federal crime when Congress passed the Identity Theft and Assumption Deterrence Act (ITADA). According to ITADA, it is unlawful if a person "knowingly transfers or uses, without lawful authority, a means of identification of another person with the intent to commit, or to aid or abet, any unlawful activity that constitutes a violation of Federal law, or that constitutes a felony under any applicable State or local law." Although the federal statute supplied the first legal definition of identity theft, it provided little help to researchers (Newman and McNally 2005). The Identity Theft Act of 1998, therefore, was an attempt to address the growing problem of repeat victimizations.

The difficulty in precisely defining identity theft is challenging for researchers. For example, the *National Crime Victimization Survey* (*NCVS*) includes three behaviors in its definition of identity theft: (1) unauthorized use or attempted use of existing credit cards, (2) unauthorized use or attempted use of other existing accounts such as checking accounts, and (3) misuse of personal information to obtain new accounts or loans or to commit other crimes (BJS 2006). The *NCVS*'s inclusion of the unauthorized use or attempted use of existing credit cards, that is, credit card fraud, is an illustration of the definitional problem for researchers. If an offender steals a credit card, makes a purchase, and then discards the card, has the victim's identity been stolen? Does the use of a *financial account identifier* or *identifying data* constitute identity theft? An offender can use a credit card number (financial account identifier) to make unauthorized purchases or use a social security number (identifying data) to open a new credit card account and make purchases. In their study Copes and Vieraitis (2007) employed the definition of identity theft specified by the federal statute but included only offenders who had used identifying data to commit their crimes. Allison, Schuck, and Lersch (2005) used a similar definition of identity theft (use of or transfer of another's personal information) and treated credit card fraud and check fraud as separate offenses. The definitional problem also makes it difficult to gauge the extent and pattern of identity theft with data collected by public and private agencies. In sum, there is no consistent definition or use of the term *identity theft* across agencies or organizations that collect data.

II. Patterns of Identity Theft

Reliable information on the extent and cost of identity theft is difficult to ascertain with currently available data. Data sources include government agencies, nonprofit organizations, popular trade and media sources, and credit reporting agencies (Newman 2004). These sources provide varying estimates of the extent of identity theft and its costs to businesses and citizens. The discrepancies are likely due to the varying definitions of identity theft and methodologies used by data collectors. The paucity of data and the seriousness and perceived widespread incidence of identity theft prompted the BJS (2007*a*) to add questions to the *NCVS* in July 2004 to provide annual estimates of identity theft victimization.

The Identity Theft Data Clearinghouse is the most comprehensive database in the United States on the topic. It was implemented by the Federal Trade Commission (FTC) in 1999 to collect consumer complaints related to identity theft. Using information from victims who report via phone or the Website the database includes information about the victim, contact information for the local police department that took the victim's report, type of offense, and the companies involved. According to the FTC, law enforcement can gain access to the database to find victims of identity theft, including their experiences, and other information about identity thieves to assist in their investigations (http://www.ftc.gov/idtheft).

The Internet Crime Complaint Center, an alliance between the National White Collar Crime Center and the Federal Bureau of Investigation, receives complaints related to Internet crime, including identity theft. The Center accepts online Internet crime complaints from persons who believe they were defrauded or from a third party to the complainant. The data include information on the victim and offender by state, demographic characteristics, monetary losses, and law enforcement contact (http://www.ic3.gov).

A variety of nonprofit and for-profit research groups have also gathered data on identity theft through Internet, mail, and telephone surveys and interviews. They include the California Public Interest Research Group (CALPIRG; http://www.calpirg.org), Javelin Strategy and Research (http://www.javelinstrategy.com/research), Gartner, Inc. (http://www.gartner.com), Harris Interactive (http://www.harrisinteractive.com/news/), and the Identity Theft Resource Center (ITRC; http://www.idtheftcenter.org/). The data collected by these groups are based on information from victims of identity theft, with the exception of CALPIRG, which also conducted a study of police officers. Although not as long running and extensive as the FTC's data collection program, the ITRC has conducted annual victimization surveys since 2003. The surveys are limited to "confirmed" victims of identity theft who have worked with the ITRC.

A. Extent of Identity Theft

Numerous sources support the claim that identity theft has risen considerably over the past decade. Reports of identity theft increased from nearly 86,212 to 214,905 in three years, nearly a 250 percent increase (FTC 2004). According to the Gartner Survey and the Privacy and American Business (2003) survey, the incidence of identity theft almost doubled from 2001 to 2002. The Social Security Administration's Fraud Hotline received approximately 65,000 reports of social security number misuse in 2001, a more than fivefold increase from about 11,000 in 1998 (U.S. General Accounting Office 2002). It should be noted, however, that the FTC cautions that this dramatic increase in identity theft may be attributed in part to victims' greater willingness to report their victimization. Recent data from the FTC indicate that identity theft reports have been relatively stable over the past three years. There were approximately 247,000 reports filed in 2004 and again in 2006 (FTC 2007). Identity theft is the most prevalent form of fraud committed in the United States, constituting 36 percent (246,035) of the 674,354 complaints filed in the year 2006 (FTC 2007).

In 2007 the FTC released a report on estimates of the incidence and costs of identity theft. According to the report, approximately eight million people experienced identity theft in 2005, and total losses were nearly $16 billion (Synovate 2007). Estimates from the *NCVS* vary from the FTC report. These differences may be due to differences in methodologies. According to the *NCVS*, in 2005, 6.4 million households, representing 5.5 percent of the households in the United States, reported that at least one member of the household had been the victim of identity theft during the previous six months. The estimated financial loss reported by victimized households was about $3.2 billion (BJS 2006).

The FTC (2007) data also show regional variation: Arizona (147.8 per 100,000 residents), District of Columbia (131.5), Nevada (120.0), California (113.5), and Texas (110.6) had the highest identity theft victimization rates; the lowest rates were reported in West Virginia (39.3), Iowa (34.9), South Dakota (30.2), North Dakota

(29.7), and Vermont (28.5). The three metropolitan areas in the United States with the highest rates of identity theft complaints are Phoenix (178.3 per 100,000), Las Vegas (158.5), and Riverside, California (145.7). According to the *NCVS* data, households in the West were approximately 1.5 times more likely than those in the Northeast, Midwest, or South to experience identity theft, and rural households (4 percent) were less likely than urban (6 percent) or suburban (6 percent) households to have a member experience identity theft (BJS 2007*a*).

B. Clearance Rates

Clearance rates for identity theft are very low. Offenders are seldom detected and rarely apprehended. Allison, Schuck, and Lersch (2005) reported an average clearance rate of 11 percent over a three-year period. Similarly, law enforcement officials interviewed by Owens (2004) and Gayer (2003) estimated that only 10 and 11 percent, respectively, of identity theft cases received by their departments were solved. According to the U.S. General Accounting Office (2002), several obstacles make the investigation of identity theft cases and the likelihood of arrests difficult: identity theft cases can be highly complex, or the offender may have committed the theft in a jurisdiction different from where the victim resides, making it difficult to secure an arrest warrant. Limited departmental resources may be directed toward the investigation of violent and drug-related offenses rather than identity thefts. Allison, Schuck, and Lersch's study supported these claims and also noted that law enforcement found it difficult to obtain cooperation from affected financial institutions.

III. Victims

According to Anderson's (2006) analysis of the FTC's 2003 data, consumers ages 25 to 54, those with higher levels of income, particularly those with incomes greater than $75,000, households headed by women with three or more children, and consumers residing in the Pacific states are at the greatest risk. Older persons, particularly those age 75 and older, and persons in the mountain states are at the lowest risk. Educational attainment and marital status had no effect on risk of victimization (Anderson 2006). Similarly, Kresse, Watland, and Lucki's (2007) study of identity thefts reported to the Chicago Police Department from 2000 to 2006 found that over 65 percent of victims were between the ages of 20 and 44 and that young people (under age 20) and older persons (over 65) were underrepresented. The *NCVS* (BJS 2007*b*) reported that households headed by persons ages 18 to 24 were most likely to experience identity theft, and households headed by persons ages 65 and older were least likely. Households in the highest income bracket, those earning $75,000 or more, were also most likely to be victimized.

It is difficult to get a clear assessment of the costs incurred by victims of identity theft. In the more common forms of identity theft, it is typically credit card companies or merchants that lose money. In most cases, the victim whose information was misused is not legally responsible for the costs of the fraudulent transaction. However, victims may incur expenses from time spent resolving problems created by the theft. To deal with the crime they may have to close existing accounts and open new ones, dispute charges with merchants, and monitor their credit reports, all of which take time.

A CALPIRG survey found that the average amount of time spent by victims to regain financial health was 175 hours, and on average extended over two years. According to the Identity Theft Resource Center's 2003 survey, the average time spent by victims clearing their financial records is close to 600 hours. Moreover, victims of identity theft experience a great deal of emotional distress, including feelings of anger, helplessness, and mistrust, disturbed sleeping patterns, and lack of security (Davis and Stevenson 2004). Much of this distress stems from the hundreds of hours and large sums of money spent trying to resolve the problems caused by the theft of their identity (LoPucki 2001).

A number of organizations and agencies have attempted to assess the financial costs of identity theft to consumers and businesses, but here again the estimates vary across the available data. The FTC Identity Theft Clearinghouse estimates the total financial cost of identity theft at over $50 billion a year, with the average loss to businesses being $4,800 per incident and an average of $500 of out-of-pocket expenses to the victim whose identity was misused (Synovate 2003). Estimates from the most recent report are considerably lower, but the FTC cautions that changes may be attributed to changes in methodology between the 2003 and 2006 surveys. In the 2006 survey the average amount obtained by the offender was $1,882 and the average victim loss was $371 (Synovate 2007). The most recent data from the *NCVS* (BJS 2007*b*) showed that the estimated loss for all types of identity theft reported by victimized households averaged $1,620 per household. However, households that experienced misuse of personal information reported an average loss of $4,850, while theft of existing credit card accounts resulted in the lowest average losses ($980). These figures represent losses that may or may not have been covered by a financial institution, such as a credit card company.

A. Special Victims

Anyone can become a victim of identity theft, including newborns and the deceased. These groups are unique in that the people whose information is used illegally are not likely to incur any out-of-pocket expenses. Instead, their information is used by thieves to defraud others, usually businesses, or to hide from law enforcement. Historically, deceased victims have been thought to be the targets of choice for identity thieves (Newman and McNally 2005). According to CIFAS, a U.K. fraud prevention service, the fastest growing victim group is the deceased. They indicate that this type of identity theft has grown from 5,000 cases in 2001 to over 20,000 by 2004 (cited in Newman and McNally 2005). Identity thieves obtain information about deceased individuals in various ways. It is common for them to watch obituaries, steal death certificates, and even get information from Websites that offer Social Security Death Index files. Additionally, some thieves may be family members who take advantage of the situation. In a survey by Pontell, Brown, and Tosouni (2008), they found very few cases of deceased victims. They argue that this may be because the family is unaware of the victimization. If they are aware, it may have little effect on their lives as the cost of this type of identity theft is incurred by businesses and by family who must sort out the matter.

Child identity theft occurs when an offender uses a child's identifying information for personal gain. Using data from the Consumer Sentinel Network, Newman and McNally (2005) report that in 2004 there were 9,370 victims who were under the age of 18 (4 percent of all cases reported). The Identity Theft Resource Center estimates that they receive reports on approximately 104 to 156 child victims a year. Similarly, Kresse, Watland, and Lucki (2007) reported that only 3.5 percent of victims were under the age of 20.

The perpetrator of child identity theft is typically a family member who has easy access to personal information. According to Pontell, Brown, and Tosouni (2008), over three-quarters of those who stole the identities of victims under the age of 18 were the victim's parents. Similarly, the ITRC 2006 survey data indicated that in child identity theft cases, 69 percent of the offenders were one or both parents or a stepparent. In 54 percent of these cases the crime began when the victim was under 5 years of age (ITRC 2007). However, strangers also target children because of the lengthy amount of time between the theft of the information and the discovery of the offense. Evidence suggests that child identity theft is relatively rare, but when it does occur it takes a considerable amount of time to discover. Typically, the cost to the child whose identity was stolen does not take place until the child applies for a driver's license, enrolls in college, or applies for a loan or credit.

B. Victim-Offender Relationship

The relationship between victims and offenders in identity theft is difficult to assess with currently available data. Available data suggest that the majority of victims do not know their offenders. The FTC reports that 84 percent of victims were either unaware of the identity of the thief or did not personally know the thief, 6 percent of victims said a family member or relative was the person responsible for misusing their personal information, 8 percent reported that the thief was a friend, neighbor, or in-home employee, and 2 percent reported that the thief was a coworker (Synovate 2007). Although the figures are lower than those reported by the FTC study, Allison, Schuck, and Lersch (2005), Gordon et al. (2007), and the ITRC (2007) also report that the majority of victim-offender relationships, approximately 60 percent, involved individuals who did not know each other. In contrast, in Kresse, Watland, and Lucki's (2007) study of identity thefts reported to the Chicago Police Department, in over 60 percent of the cases where the means or method of theft was known (282 of 1,322), the victim's identity was stolen by a friend, relative, or person otherwise known to the victim. According to a victim survey administered by the Javelin Strategy and Research group (2005), for those cases where the perpetrator was known, 32 percent were committed by a family member or relative; 18 percent were committed by a friend, neighbor, or in-home employee; and 24 percent were committed by strangers outside of the workplace.

IV. Offenders

The paucity of research on identity theft coupled with the low clearance rate makes it difficult to have a clear idea of what those who engage in this offense are like. To gain an understanding of the type of individual who commits identity theft Gordon et al. (2007) examined closed U.S. Secret Service cases with an identity theft component from 2000 to 2006. They found that most offenders (42.5 percent) were between the ages of 25 and 34 when the case was opened; 33 percent fell within the 35 to 49 age group. Using data from a large metropolitan police department in Florida, Allison, Schuck, and Lersch (2005) found that offenders ranged in age from 28 to 49, with a mean age of 32.

Both studies found similar patterns regarding race. Gordon et al. (2007) found that the majority of the offenders were black (54 percent), with white offenders accounting for 38 percent and fewer than 5 percent of offenders being Hispanic. Allison, Schuck, and Lersch (2005) found that the distribution of offenders was 69 percent black, 27 percent white, and less than 1 percent Hispanic or Asian. The two studies differed in terms of the sex of offenders. Gordon et al. found that nearly 66 percent of the offenders were male; Allison. Schuck, and Lersch found that 63 percent of offenders were female.

Gordon et al. (2007) also examined the place of birth of the offenders. They found that nearly one-quarter of offenders were foreign-born. The countries most represented, in rank order, were Mexico, Nigeria, the United Kingdom, Cuba, and Israel.

In their qualitative study of identity thieves, Copes and Vieraitis (2007, 2008) asked convicted federal offenders to describe their past and current family situations. Most offenders were currently or had been married in their lifetimes: 25 percent of the offenders were married, 31 percent were separated or divorced, 32 percent had never been married, and 5 percent were widowed. Approximately 75 percent had children. The majority had at least some college.

Prior arrest patterns indicated that a large proportion had engaged in various types of offenses, including drug, property, and violent crimes (Copes and Vieraitis 2007, 2008). Yet the majority claimed that they committed only identity thefts or comparable frauds (e.g., check fraud). In total, 63 percent of the offenders reported prior arrests; most were arrested for financial fraud or identity theft (44 percent), but drug use or sales (19 percent) and property crimes (22 percent) were also relatively common. This is consistent with the study by Gordon et al. (2007), who found that a majority of defendants had no prior arrests, but those who did tended to commit fraud and theft-related offenses.

Copes and Vieraitis (2007) also questioned identity thieves about their prior drug use. Approximately 58 percent had tried drugs in their lifetime, mostly marijuana, cocaine in various forms, and methamphetamine. Only 37 percent reported having been addicted. Of those who said that they were using drugs while committing identity theft, only 24 percent reported that the drug use contributed to their offense. Gordon et al. (2007) discovered that nearly 10 percent of the defendants whose cases they studied had previous arrests for drug-related offenses.

The common perception is that identity theft is a white-collar crime, so most would expect those who commit the bulk of these crimes to resemble typical white-collar offenders. They are just as likely, however, to exhibit the characteristics of street offenders as of more privileged offenders. Identity theft appears to attract offenders from a wide range of family backgrounds, criminal histories, and lifestyles.

V. Explaining Identity Theft

The bulk of academic research has focused on describing how identity thieves get sensitive information, how they convert this information into valued goods, the extent and scope of the problem, and the characteristics of victims. Little has been done to construct a theory to explain these patterns. This section summarizes two explanations as to why identity theft is an attractive choice for some.

A. Lifestyle and Criminal Choice

To understand why people choose to commit crime, it is important to examine the worlds in which they spend much of their lives (Shover 1996). To do this it is necessary to situate their decisions within the principal lifestyle that frames their choices. Numerous studies of street-level property offenders and fraudsters find that their primary motivation is the need for money (Shover 1996; Shover, Coffey, and Sanders 2004), and this seems to be true of identity thieves. Overwhelmingly, the identity thieves interviewed by Copes and Vieraitis (2008) claimed that the sole reason they became involved in these crimes was for the financial rewards. Indeed, identity theft can be richly rewarding. Estimates of the amount of money gained from individual identity thefts evidences these claims (BJS 2006; Gordon et al. 2007).

How do they spend the money gained through their illegal enterprises? Offender motivations are best understood in the context of their lifestyles. They hail from a variety of backgrounds, but it is possible to group them into two categories: those embedded in streetlife and striving to lead a "life as party" and those trying to maintain a comfortable middle-class life. Thus the proceeds of their crimes are used to fund their chosen lifestyles. For those living a "life as party" (Shover and Honaker 1992; Jacobs and Wright 1999), proceeds are more likely to be spent maintaining lifestyles filled with drug use and fast living rather than putting money aside for long-term plans. Money is used to get high, live fast, and spend quickly. These offenders have much in common with persistent street thieves who indulge in streetlife.

However, not all indulged in such a lifestyle. Some show restraint in their spending; many use their stolen money to support what would generally be considered a conventional life or to drift between the two lifestyles. These offenders make efforts to conceal their misdeeds from their friends and family and to present a law-abiding front to outsiders. They use the proceeds of identity theft to finance comfortable middle-class lives, including paying rent or a mortgage, buying expensive vehicles, and splurging on the latest technological gadgets. Their lifestyles are also in line with the telemarketers interviewed by Shover, Coffey, and Sanders (2004). This is not to say that they do not indulge in the trappings of drugs and partying, as many do. Nevertheless, these offenders put forth an image of middle-class respectability.

B. Neutralizing Identity Theft

Although the financial benefits of their crimes are important, offenders must be able to make sense of their actions and maintain a positive self-image even when violating the law. While acknowledging that they needed money to support their lifestyles, identity thieves will not engage in just any crime. They choose identity theft because they can more easily justify their actions (Sykes and Matza 1957; Maruna and Copes 2005). It is by use of verbal techniques that internal controls that normally serve to check deviant motivations and decisions are "rendered inoperative, and the individual is freed to engage in [deviance] without serious damage to his self-image" (Sykes and Matza 1957, p. 667). These verbalizations are more than simply rhetorical attempts to relieve cognitive dissonance or to save face in front of questioning others; they are instrumental in the persistence of crime. While these justifications for wrongdoing may not have been the spark that set their actions in motion, the use of these rhetorical devices facilitates the continued commission of crime.

According to Copes, Vieraitis, and Jochum (2007), the most common way identity thieves justify their crimes is by denying that they caused any "real harm" to "actual individuals." It is not uncommon for identity thieves to argue that stealing identities is only a minor hassle to victims and that no real harm is caused because the victim can repair any credit damage with a few calls and, consequently, not suffer any direct financial loss. This indicates that these criminals draw on incorrect yet common stereotypes regarding the harmlessness of white-collar crimes in order to neutralize their deviant behaviors. Thus a direct connection between the social realities of white-collar and common crime does not exist in the social worlds of these offenders, and this is an important element in the justification of their crimes.

When identity thieves do acknowledge victims, they describe them as large, "faceless" organizations that deserve victimization. Identity thieves argue that the only people who lose from their crimes are banks, corporations, and other victims who are thought not to deserve sympathy. When portraying victims as faceless or "plastic," distancing oneself cognitively from the crime becomes remarkably easy.

Individuals who work within an organization to carry out their crimes sometimes rely on the diffusion of responsibility to excuse themselves. Although large amounts of money are eventually appropriated, many of the self-proclaimed low-level organizational members claim that they play only a minimal role in the crime; thus, by comparison, they should not be judged like others. Additionally, these individuals point to the small amount of money they make as evidence that they "really didn't do anything."

Many identity thieves also seek to make sense of and justify their crimes by pointing out that their actions are done with the noble intention of helping people. They set aside their better judgment because they think their loyalties to friends and family are more important at that time. These offenders argue that their crimes were done to help friends in need or to support their families.

VI. Techniques

Identity thieves use a variety of methods to acquire a victim's personal information and convert that information into cash or goods. Data from victimization surveys and interviews with offenders are used to describe the techniques identity thieves commonly employ to commit their crimes.

A. Acquiring Identities

A key component to the successful commission of identity theft is obtaining people's personal information. It is relatively easy for offenders to do so. Personal information is obtained from wallets, purses, homes, cars, offices, and businesses or institutions that maintain customer, employee, patient, or student records (Newman 2004). Social security numbers, which provide instant access to a person's personal information, are widely used for identification and account numbers by insurance companies, universities, cable television companies, military identification, and banks. The thief may steal a wallet or purse, work at a job that affords access to credit records or purchase the information from someone who does (e.g., employees who have access to credit reporting databases, commonly available in auto dealerships, realtors' offices, banks, and other businesses that approve loans), or find victims by stealing mail, sorting through the trash, or searching the Internet (Lease and Burke 2000; LoPucki 2001; Davis and Stevenson 2004; Newman 2004).

Based on victim surveys, most offenders commit identity theft by obtaining a person's credit card information, which they use to forge a credit card in the victim's name and make purchases (Privacy and American Business 2003). According to the Privacy and American Business survey, 34 percent of victims reported that their information was obtained this way. In addition, 12 percent reported that someone stole or obtained a paper or computer record with their personal information on it; 11 percent said someone stole their wallet or purse; 10 percent said someone opened charge accounts in stores in their name; 7 percent said someone opened a bank account in their name or forged checks; 7 percent said someone got to their mail or mailbox; 5 percent said they lost their wallet or purse; 4 percent said someone obtained the information from a public record; and 3 percent said someone created a false identity to get government benefits or payments (Privacy and American Business 2003).

According to the FTC data, of those who knew how their information was obtained (43 percent), 16 percent said it was stolen by someone they personally knew; 7 percent said it was stolen during a purchase or financial transaction; 5 percent reported their information was obtained from a stolen wallet or purse; 5 percent cited theft from a company that maintained their information; and 2 percent reported theft from the mail (Synovate 2007). In organized rings a person is planted as an employee in a mortgage lender's office, doctor's office, or human resources department to more easily access information. Similarly, these groups will bribe insiders such as employees of banks, car dealerships, government, and hospitals to get the identifying information. Others have obtained credit card numbers by soliciting information using bogus e-mails (phishing) or simply by watching someone type in a calling card number or credit card number (Davis and Stevenson 2004).

Interviews with offenders indicate that they use a variety of methods to procure information and then convert this information into cash or goods. According to Copes and Vieraitis (2008), most identity thieves did not specialize in a single method but preferred to use a variety of strategies. Although some offenders acquired identities from their place of employment, mainly mortgage companies, the most common method of obtaining a victim's information was to buy it. Offenders bought identities from employees of various businesses and state agencies who had access to personal information such as name, address, date of birth, and social security number. Information was purchased from employees of banks, credit agencies, a state law enforcement agency, mortgage companies, state departments of motor vehicles, hospitals, doctors' offices, universities, car dealerships, and furniture stores. Offenders also purchased information from persons they knew socially or with whom they were acquainted on the streets. In some cases, the identity thieves bought information from other offenders, who obtained it from burglaries, thefts from motor vehicles, prostitution, and pickpocketing.

B. Converting Information

After they obtain a victim's information, offenders often convert that information into cash or goods. Offenders may use the information to acquire or produce additional identity-related documents, such as drivers' licenses or state identification cards. They may use these new documents to conceal illegal activities and avoid arrest or to conduct a variety of financial transactions. Offenders apply for credit cards in the victims' names (including major credit cards and department store credit cards), open new bank accounts and deposit counterfeit checks, withdraw money from existing bank accounts, apply for loans, open utility or phone accounts, and apply for public assistance programs.

According to the FTC (2007), the most common type of identity theft was credit card fraud, followed by "other" identity theft, phone or utilities fraud, bank fraud, employment-related fraud, government documents or benefits fraud, and loan fraud.[1] Although not directly comparable due to differences in methodology, units of analysis, and definition of identity theft, data from the *NCVS* indicate that of the 6.4 million households reporting that at least one member of the household had been the victim of identity theft, the most common type was unauthorized use of existing credit cards (BJS 2007*a*).

According to Copes and Vieraitis's (2008) study of offenders, the most common strategy for converting stolen identities into cash was by applying for credit cards. Most of the offenders used the information to order new credit cards, but in a few cases the information was used to get the credit card agency to issue a duplicate card on an existing account. They used credit cards to buy merchandise for their own personal use, to resell the merchandise to friends or acquaintances, or to return the merchandise for cash. Offenders also used the checks that are routinely sent to credit card holders to deposit in the victim's account and then withdraw cash or to open new accounts. Offenders also applied for store credit cards such as from department stores and home improvement stores. Other common strategies for converting information into cash or goods included producing counterfeit checks that they cashed at grocery stores or used to purchase merchandise or pay bills, opening new bank accounts to deposit checks or to withdraw money from an existing account, and applying for and receiving loans.

VII. Policy

Policy makers at federal and state levels have generally addressed the problem of identity theft by enacting legislation to define the crime, establish penalties for offenders, and improve protection to consumers and victims. We provide an overview of this legislation and then turn our attention to the policy implications of our current knowledge of identity theft. Because there are a number of well-publicized efforts to educate consumers on how to reduce their chance of victimization (e.g., shredding documents with personally identifying information, limiting the use of social security numbers) we focus our discussion on situational crime prevention techniques targeted at offenders. These techniques include increasing the effort an offender must use to acquire and convert information, increasing the risks of getting caught, removing excuses that may be used to justify their crime, and changing offenders' perceptions of punishment.

A. Identity Theft Legislation

A wide range of federal laws covers identity theft, including laws pertaining to social security fraud, welfare fraud, computer fraud, wire fraud, and financial institution fraud. This review focuses on specific laws designed and enacted to criminalize the act of identity theft. The first federal law enacted to prevent identity theft was the 1998 Identity Theft Assumption and Deterrence Act (18 USC 1028). This Act made identity theft a separate crime against the person whose identity was stolen, broadened the scope of the offense to include the misuse of information and documents, and provided punishment of up to 15 years of imprisonment and a maximum fine of $250,000. Under U.S. Sentencing Commission guidelines a sentence of 10 to 16 months' incarceration can be imposed even if there is no monetary loss and the perpetrator has no prior criminal convictions (U.S. General Accounting Office 2002). Violations of this crime are subject to investigation by federal law enforcement agencies, including the U.S. Secret Service, the FBI, the U.S. Postal Inspection Service, and the Social Security Administration's Office of the Inspector General.

In 2004 the Identity Theft Penalty Enhancement Act (ITPEA; H.R. Doc. 1731, 108th Congr. 2 [July 2004]) established a new federal crime: aggravated identity theft, defined as the knowing and unlawful transfer, possession, or use of a means of identification of another person during and in relation to any of more than 100 felony offenses, including mail, bank, and wire fraud, immigration and passport fraud, and any unlawful use of a social security number. The law mandates a minimum of two years in prison consecutive to the sentence for the underlying felony. In addition, if the offense is committed during and in relation to one of the more than 40 federal terrorism-related felonies, the penalty is a minimum mandatory five years in prison consecutive to the sentence for the underlying felony.

In an effort to protect consumers against identity theft and assist those who have been victimized, Congress passed the Fair and Accurate Credit Transactions Act (FACTA; H.R. Doc. 2622, 108th Congr. 1 [Dec. 2003]) in 2003. The Act grants consumers the right to one credit report free of charge every year; requires merchants to leave all but the last five digits of a credit card number off store receipts; requires a national system of fraud detection to increase the likelihood that thieves will be caught; requires a nationwide system of fraud alerts to be placed on credit files; requires regulators to create a list of red flag indicators of identity theft drawn from patterns and practices of identity thieves; and requires lenders and credit agencies to take action before a victim knows a crime has occurred. In addition, FACTA created a National Fraud Alert system.

To stop credit grantors from opening new accounts, FACTA also allows consumers to place three types of fraud alerts on their credit files. Individuals who suspect they are, or are about to become, the victim of identity theft can place an "initial alert" in their file. Individuals who have been victims of identity theft and have filed a report with a law enforcement agency can then request an "extended alert." After an extended alert is activated, it will stay in place for seven years, and the victim may order two free credit reports within 12 months. For the next five years, credit agencies must exclude the consumer's name from lists used to make prescreened credit or insurance offers. Finally, military officials are able to place an "active duty alert" when they are on active duty or assigned to service away from their usual duty station.

States have also passed laws in efforts to protect consumers and victims of identity theft. To date, all but two states have laws designed specifically to counter identity theft. In 2006 states continued to strengthen laws to protect consumers by increasing penalties and expanding law enforcement's role in investigating cases. Laws were also enacted to assist victims of identity theft, including prohibiting discrimination against an identity theft victim, allowing the records related to the theft to be expunged, and creating programs to help victims in clearing their name and financial records (see http://www.ncsl.org for each state's laws). Thirty-nine states and the District of Columbia have enacted laws that allow consumers to freeze their credit files. In addition, as of November 1, 2007, the three major credit bureaus (Equifax, Experian, and TransUnion) offer the security freeze to consumers living in the 11 states that have not adopted security freeze laws and to all consumers in the four states that limit the option to victims of identity theft (http://www.consumersunion.org/campaigns/learn_more/003484indiv.html).

The effectiveness of legislation pertaining to identity theft has not yet been determined. These laws have provided law enforcement with the tools to fight identity thieves, but whether thieves have desisted because of these laws is unclear. If identity thieves are like other fraudsters, and indicators suggest that they are, then they will adapt to law enforcement strategies aimed at stopping them. Thus, as Holtfreter and Holtfreter (2006) suggest, ITADA, FACTA, and ITPEA will likely be amended to adjust to changing technology and adaptations of thieves.

B. Situational Crime Prevention

In contrast to the broad-brush programs typical of crime-prevention initiatives just a few years ago, the past two decades have seen increasing acceptance of the need for better focused efforts. Referred to broadly as "situational crime prevention," this approach emphasizes measures directed at highly specific forms of crime that involve the management, design, or manipulation of the immediate environment in as systematic and permanent a way as possible to reduce the opportunities for crime and increase its risks as perceived by a wide range of offenders (Clarke 1983). Grounded in rational choice theory, the logic of situational crime prevention suggests that the level of criminal activity can be reduced by manipulating features of given social situations so as to cause potential offenders to believe that excessive effort would be required to secure criminal gains, which likely would be small in any case, or that the risks are too high. A variety of techniques have been identified for reducing criminal opportunities by causing change in one or more of these conditions (Clarke 1997).

1. *Increase Effort and Risk*

According to Copes and Vieraitis (2007), the situations where identity thieves are most exposed to law enforcement are getting the appropriate information and entering banks or stores to cash in on the crime. Controlling access to places such as dumpsters and mailboxes and monitoring how documents are disposed of (e.g., shredding documents with identifying information) would restrict the number of areas from which offenders get their information (see Newman and McNally 2005 for a review). Media campaigns warning individuals to engage in such target-hardening actions are widespread; however, such programs and any other measures for controlling access to information will be ineffective if information is compromised by individuals who have legitimate access to these data.

Organizations whose employees have access to personal information must therefore take steps to reduce the likelihood that identity thieves can acquire this information from employees. Such strategies may include limiting the number of employees with access to the information, conducting careful background checks of employees, establishing additional oversight and independent checking mechanisms, maintaining a positive work environment, and alerting employees to the serious consequences of identity theft for both victims and perpetrators.

Most crime reduction strategies focus on preventing the acquisition of information by encouraging individuals and businesses to protect their information, but this is not the only strategy. Banks could make simple changes in procedures that would increase the effort and risk of identity theft. For instance, they could require passwords to withdraw money from accounts or cash checks, even when customers engage in these transactions in person. This strategy would clearly not deter thieves who have inside partners or who gain access to the bank's computer system, but these types of identity theft are rare.

Stores should require identification when customers pay by check or credit card. Although many identity thieves produce fake identification, not all have the capability of doing so effectively. For this strategy to be effective, it is necessary for all stores to be consistent in checking identification. With experience and inside knowledge, identity thieves learn which stores check identification and what dollar amounts require proof of identification or manager approval. If some stores do not follow these policies, target displacement is likely to occur (Clarke 1983). The problem with many antitheft programs is that, "within easy reach of every house with a burglar alarm, or car with an antitheft device, are many others without such protection" (Clarke 1983, p. 246). Thus, it is necessary that all stores require proof of identification or there will be too many suitable targets within easy reach of offenders and the deterrent effect of the program will be undercut.

2. *Remove Excuses*

Situational crime prevention programs have been developed based on the neutralization theoretic premise. The theory is that by learning the linguistic devices that offenders use to make their crimes palatable, program designers can attack these belief systems. By "neutralizing the neutralizations," such programs would deny offenders the opportunity to define their actions as noncriminal, and thus they would refrain from criminal behavior (Clarke 1997; Clarke and Homel 1997; Copes and Williams 2007). True to the roots of situational crime prevention, removing excuses in this way does not entail making long-term changes in the disposition of the offender, as do cognitive-based programs in correctional settings. Instead, situational crime prevention theorists argue that programs geared toward removing excuses should still focus on highly specific forms of crime and should be presented at the time criminal decisions are being made. The idea is to "stimulate feelings of conscience at the point of contemplating the commission of a specific kind of offense" (Clarke 1997, p. 24).

These principles can be applied to identity theft. For this approach to work, it is necessary to present the antineutralization message at the immediate situation of the crime. Although this may prove difficult for identity theft, there are ways it can be accomplished successfully. A large proportion of the identity thefts described by participants in Copes and Vieraitis's (2007) study required thieves to go into banks to cash checks or withdraw funds. It is here that messages could be placed reminding offenders that their actions harm individuals. The goal is to make potential offenders recognize the harm they are doing in those locations where they carry out their crimes. Publicity campaigns similar to those used to deter movie piracy and cable theft could be implemented for identity theft. The best locations for these campaigns are banks, retail stores, and any other location where thieves must go to convert stolen identities into cash or merchandise.

Identity thieves also obtain information from people who have legitimate access to this information; dishonest employees play a large role in the prevalence of identity theft. The "remove excuses" campaigns would also serve to educate employees who might be tempted to misuse their position to illegally sell sensitive information to others (Pelfrey 1984; Lim 2002).

3. *Change Perceptions*

Identity thieves in Copes and Vieraitis's (2008) study repeatedly made reference to their expectations of lenient punishment if they were apprehended. With the promise of large rewards with relatively little effort and perceptions of inconsequential punishments, it is easy to understand why they chose to commit identity theft. But the actual punishments these offenders received typically exceeded their expectations. Instead of being given probation or a year of incarceration, they were given sentences ranging from 12 to 360 months.

The underestimates of potential sentences likely contributed to their habituation to identity theft. It is therefore likely that educating potential thieves about the true consequences of being convicted, at least at the federal level, could persuade them to desist. It is always a difficult task to educate target populations about the costs of crime, but it is possible. Following principles of situational crime prevention, these deterrent messages can also be delivered at the scene of the crime. Just as messages informing offenders of the real harm they cause can be presented at the locations of the crimes, so too can these deterrent messages.

Decades of deterrence research have shown that perceived punishments have a greater deterrent effect than actual punishments, so it is necessary to change the perceptions of punishment held by identity thieves. Campaigns designed to create the impression that law enforcement agencies consider identity theft to be a serious crime and that cases will be prosecuted to their fullest extent may go a long way in changing offender perceptions about this offense. If successful, these informational campaigns would likely reduce identity theft. Although there is disagreement about the effectiveness of publicity campaigns, "publicity campaigns may represent a powerful yet cost-effective tool in crime prevention" if planned properly (Johnson and Bowers 2003, p. 497).

VIII. Conclusion

Identity theft is a widespread problem affecting approximately eight million people each year. A common scenario involves an offender who obtains or buys a victim's personally identifying information from an acquaintance or employee of an agency with access to such information. The offender then uses the information to acquire or produce additional identity-related documents, such as drivers' licenses and state identification cards, make checks, order new credit cards, and cash checks. The victim is likely between the ages of 18 and 55 with an income greater than $75,000 and does not know the offender.

Like most offenders, identity thieves are motivated by a need for money. For some identity thieves the need for money is fueled by a desire to maintain a partying lifestyle characterized by drug use and fast living. Others use the proceeds of their crimes to support a conventional life, including paying rent or a mortgage and utilities or buying the latest technological gadgets. Although the desire for money is a common motivation among street-level and white-collar offenders, the selection of identity theft as their crime of choice may be attributed to the ease with which they can justify their actions. Many identity thieves are able to justify their crimes by denying that they caused any real harm to actual individuals.

Most official attempts to control identity theft have been in the form of legislation. As discussed in section VII, federal and state lawmakers have approached the problem by passing legislation defining identity theft as a crime, delineating penalties for offenders, and increasing protection to consumers and victims of identity theft. In addition to legislative action, numerous nonprofit agencies, organizations, and private companies have launched campaigns to educate consumers on how to protect their personally identifying information. Although limited, the currently available data suggest that certain situational crime prevention techniques may be useful in decreasing the incidence of identity theft. These techniques include increasing the effort and risks, removing excuses, and advertising consequences.

To understand the crime of identity theft and thus increase the likelihood that policy makers and law enforcement are effective in reducing this crime, more research needs to be done. First, a number of laws have been passed to provide help to consumers and victims of identity theft and to assist law enforcement. However, the effectiveness of these laws has not yet been assessed. Although much of this legislation is relatively new, future research should evaluate the degree to which legislation is an effective strategy in reducing identity theft. Second, there is very little research on identity thieves themselves. To date, only three published studies examine offenders (Allison, Schuck, and Lersch 2005; Copes and Vieraitis 2007; Gordon et al. 2007), and of those only Copes and Vieraitis interviewed identity thieves. Researchers should consider further developing this line of inquiry by expanding the sample of identity thieves to include active offenders and offenders convicted at federal, state, and local levels.

NOTE

1. "Other identity theft" includes the following subtypes: uncertain, miscellaneous, Internet or e-mail, evading the law, medical, apartment or house rental, insurance, property rental fraud, securities and other investments, child support, bankruptcy, and magazine subscriptions. Bank fraud includes fraud involving checking and savings accounts and electronic fund transfers.

REFERENCES

Aite Group. 2007. "Looking Ahead: An Analysis of Pending State Legislation and Financial Institutions." http://www.aitegroup.com/reports.php.

Allison, Stuart, Amie Schuck, and Kim M. Lersch. 2005. "Exploring the Crime of Identity Theft: Prevalence, Clearance Rates, and Victim/Offender Characteristics." *Journal of Criminal Justice* 33: 19–29.

Anderson, Keith B. 2006. "Who Are the Victims of Identity Theft? The Effect of Demographics." *Journal of Public Policy and Marketing* 25: 160–71.

Bureau of Justice Statistics. 2006. *Identity Theft, 2004*. Washington, DC: U.S. Government Printing Office.

———. 2007*a*. *Identity Theft, 2005*. Washington, DC: U.S. Government Printing Office.

———. 2007*b*. "National Crime Victimization Survey: Crime and the Nation's Households, 2005." *Data Brief*. Publication no. NCJ217198. Washington, DC: U.S. Government Printing Office.

Clarke, Ronald V. 1983. "Situational Crime Prevention: Its Theoretical Basis and Practical Scope." In *Crime and Justice: An Annual Review of Research*, vol. 4, edited by Michael Tonry and Norval Morris. Chicago: University of Chicago Press.

——. 1997. *Situational Crime Prevention: Successful Case Studies*. Guilderland, NY: Harrow and Heston.

Clarke, Ronald V., and Ross Homel. 1997. "A Revised Classification of Situational Crime Prevention Techniques." In *Crime Prevention at a Crossroads*, edited by Steven P. Lab. Cincinnati, OH: Anderson.

Cole, Simon A., and Henry N. Pontell. 2006. "'Don't Be Low Hanging Fruit': Identity Theft as Moral Panic." In *Surveillance and Security*, edited by Torin Monahan. London: Routledge.

Copes, Heith, and Lynne Vieraitis. 2007. "Identity Theft: Assessing Offenders' Strategies and Perceptions of Risk." Technical Report for the National Institute of Justice, NCJ 219122, NIJ Grant No. 2005-IJ-CX-0012. http://www.ncjrs.gov/pdffiles1/nij/grants/219122.pdf.

Copes, Heith, and Lynne Vieraitis. 2008. "Stealing Identities: The Risks, Rewards and Strategies of Identity Theft." In *Crime Prevention Studies: Identity Theft and Opportunity*, edited by Graeme Newman and Megan McNally. New York: Criminal Justice Press.

Copes, Heith, Lynne Vieraitis, and Jennifer M. Jochum. 2007. "Bridging the Gap between Research and Practice: How Neutralization Theory Can Inform Reid Interrogations of Identity Thieves." *Journal of Criminal Justice Education* 18: 444–59.

Copes, Heith, and Patrick Williams. 2007. "Techniques of Affirmation: Deviant Behavior, Moral Commitment, and Resistant Subcultural Identity." *Deviant Behavior* 28: 247–72.

Davis, Kristin, and Alison Stevenson. 2004. "They've Got Your Numbers." *Kiplinger's Personal Finance* 58 (January): 72–77.

Federal Trade Commission. 2004. "National and State Trends in Fraud and Identity Theft." January–December 2003. http://www.ftc.gov/.

———. 2007. "National and State Trends in Fraud and Identity Theft." January–December 2006. http://www.ftc.gov/.

Gayer, Jennette. 2003. "Policing Privacy: Law Enforcement's Response to Identity Theft." Los Angeles: CALPIRG. http://www.calpirg.org/report.

Gordon, Gary R., Donald Rebovich, Kyung-Seok Choo, and Judith B. Gordon. 2007. "Identity Fraud Trends and Patterns: Building a Data-Based Foundation for Proactive Enforcement." Center for Identity Management and Information Protection. http://www.utica.edu/academic/institutes/cimip/publications/index.cfm.

Holtfreter, Robert E., and Kristy Holtfreter. 2006. "Gauging the Effectiveness of U.S. Identity Theft Legislation." *Journal of Financial Crime* 13: 56–64.

Identity Theft Resource Center. 2003. "Identity Theft: The Aftermath 2003." http://www.idtheftcenter.org/index.html.

——— 2007. "Identity Theft: The Aftermath 2006." http://www.idtheftcenter.org/index.html.

Jacobs, Bruce, and Richard Wright. 1999. "Stick-Up, Street Culture, and Offender Motivation." *Criminology* 37: 149–73.

Javelin Strategy and Research. 2005. *2005 Identity Fraud Survey Report*. Pleasanton, CA: Javelin Strategy and Research Group.

Johnson, Shane D., and Kate J. Bowers. 2003. "Opportunity Is in the Eye of the Beholder: The Role of Publicity in Crime Prevention." *Criminology and Public Policy* 2: 497–524.

Kresse, William, Kathleen Watland, and John Lucki. 2007. "Identity Theft: Findings and Public Policy Recommendations." Final report to the Institute for Fraud Prevention. http://info.ethicspoint.com/files/web_seminars/2008/Red_Flag/Identity_Theft_Xavier_Study.pdf.

Lease, Matthew L., and Tod W. Burke. 2000. "Identity Theft: A Fast-Growing Crime." *FBI Law Enforcement Bulletin* 69: 8–13.

Lim, Vivien K. G. 2002. "The IT Way of Loafing on the Job: Cyberloafing, Neutralizing and Organizational Justice." *Journal of Organizational Behavior* 23: 675–94.

LoPucki, Lynn M. 2001. "Human Identification Theory and the Identity Theft Problem." *Texas Law Review* 80: 89–135.

Maruna, Shadd, and Heith Copes. 2005. "What Have We Learned from Fifty Years of Neutralization Research?" *Crime and Justice: A Review of Research*, vol. 32, edited by Michael Tonry. Chicago: University of Chicago Press.

Newman, Graeme R. 2004. *Identity Theft: Problem-Oriented Guides for Police*. Problem-Specific Guide Series No. 25. Washington, DC: U.S. Department of Justice, Office of Community Oriented Policing Services. http://www.cops.usdoj. gov.

Newman, Graeme R., and Megan McNally. 2005. *Identity Theft Literature Review*. Washington, DC: U.S. Department of Justice, National Institute of Justice.

Owens, Megan. 2004. "Policing Privacy: Michigan Law Enforcement Officers on the Challenges of Tracking Identity Theft." Ann Arbor: Public Interest Research Group in Michigan. http://pirgim.org/reports/policingprivacy04.pdf.

Pelfrey, William V. 1984. "Keep Honest Employees Honest." *Security Management* 6: 22–24.

Pontell, Henry N., Gregory C. Brown, and Anastasia Tosouni. 2008. "Stolen Identities: A Victim Survey." In *Crime Prevention Studies: Identity Theft and Opportunity*, edited by Graeme Newman and Megan McNally. New York: Criminal Justice Press.

President's Identity Theft Task Force. 2007. "Combating Identity Theft: A Strategic Plan." http://www.idtheft.gov/reports/StrategicPlan.pdf.

Privacy and American Business. 2003. "Identity Theft: New Survey and Trend Report." http://www.bbbonline.org/idtheft/IDTheftSrvyAug03.pdf.

Shover, Neal. 1996. *Great Pretenders: Pursuits and Careers of Persistent Thieves*. Boulder, CO: Westview.

Shover, Neal, Glenn Coffey, and Clinton Sanders. 2004. "Dialing for Dollars: Opportunities, Justifications and Telemarketing Fraud." *Qualitative Sociology* 27: 59–75.
Shover, Neal, and David Honaker. 1992. "The Socially Bounded Decision Making of Persistent Property Offenders." *Howard Journal of Criminal Justice* 31: 276–93.
Sykes, Gresham, and David Matza. 1957. "Techniques of Neutralization: A Theory of Delinquency." *American Sociological Review* 22: 664–70.
Synovate. 2003. "Federal Trade Commission—Identity Theft Survey Report." http://www.ftc.gov/os/2003/09/synovatereport.pdf.
———. 2007. "Federal Trade Commission—2006 Identity Theft Survey Report." http://www.ftc.gov/os/2007/11/SynovateFinalReportIDTheft2006.pdf.
U.S. General Accounting Office. 2002. *Identity Theft: Prevalence and Cost Appear to Be Growing*. Report to Congressional Requesters GAO-02-363. http://www.gao.gov/new.items/d02363.pdf.

PART III

TRANSACTIONAL CRIME

CHAPTER 11

ORGANIZATIONAL CRIME

NEAL SHOVER AND
JENNIFER SCROGGINS

HISTORICALLY, the study of criminology and criminal justice has focused almost entirely on crimes committed by individuals. The corpus of published criminological theory and empirical work, therefore, is replete with efforts to account for why some individuals are more prone to criminal participation than others and why the severity of criminal punishment varies across individuals and categories of offenders. Increasingly, however, organizations and the dynamics by which they facilitate or in other ways increase the odds of criminal choice have come under scrutiny by scholars, policy makers, and crime-control managers. Reasons for this development are few and easily understood; they begin with the fact that when individuals commit criminal acts they do so not in their private lives but while at work, in their employment roles. In the industrialized and postindustrialized world, overwhelmingly these are situated in organizations. In universities, in charitable organizations, in military units, in religious organizations, and in business firms individuals labor on behalf of their employers. In doing so, they sometimes commit crime. The appellation *organizational crime* is applied to violations of criminal statutes committed in the context or in pursuit of the goals of legitimate organizations, organizational subunits, or work groups.

Much has been learned about organizational crime and efforts to control it:

- Both aggregate rates of organizational crime and rates of criminal participation by organizations vary substantially. Theory and research point to a number of risk and protective factors that contribute to

this variation. They include the state of the economy and economic trends; the intensity of organizational competition over resources and markets; the prevalence of socially acceptable rhetorical explanations for noncompliance; and the credibility of oversight.
- Oversight of potential organizational criminals is more intense and effective when well organized and supported by sustained political movements.
- Criminal prosecution, the most severe response to organizational crime, is rare. Occasional citizen movements and officially designated crackdowns against organizational crime generally are short-lived and almost certainly lacking in long-term effectiveness.
- Concern for the economic health of a nation, region or industry is a major constraint on oversight by decision makers at all levels of the oversight process.
- With the intensification of global economic competition a significant shift in regulatory paradigms has occurred; deterrence-based approaches generally have given way to programs of responsive regulation that emphasize educative, flexible, and cooperative strategies.
- The record of research on organizational crime shows the need for increased attention to international organizational crime, enhanced understanding of the contexts and meanings of organizational crime, comparative studies of regulatory oversight styles, and better statistical information.

In this chapter we review and assess theory and research on organizational crime. Section I notes the behavioral distinctiveness of acts subsumed under this rubric; in section II we describe sources of data and methods used in studies of organizational crime. Section III documents variation in the distribution of organizational crime and how rational choice theory can be applied to the challenge of explaining it. In section IV we describe what is known about organizational criminal careers. Section V reports what has been learned about state and private responses to organizational crime. In section VI we examine the effects of economic globalization on competition, oversight, and organizational crime. Section VII presents a research agenda for further attention and investigation.

I. Definitional Matters

Many crimes committed by individuals while at work are committed exclusively or primarily for personal benefit or in pursuit of largely individual objectives (Clinard and Quinney 1973). Public officials who accept clandestinely delivered gratuities from citizens in return for favorable action on their requests exemplify crime committed in the occupational role for personal award.

A conceptual distinction generally is drawn between *occupational* and *organizational* crimes (Friedrichs 2007). The former includes crimes committed by organizationally unattached individuals in their occupational role and, as in the example, crimes committed for exclusively personal goals or benefit by employees, managers, or owners of legitimate organizations. Many times occupational crimes victimize the offender's employer.

Organizational crime, by contrast, is distinguished by the subsidiary importance of anticipated individual reward in favor of organizational benefit. When corporate officials knowingly report false information to state regulatory officials on the firm's disposal of hazardous materials generated in the production process, they do so in the interest of their employer. This does not deny that participants may benefit personally in some way from organizational criminal participation; they may gain recognition, for example, as team players or be rewarded with economic bonuses or other career-enhancing payoffs denied to peers. To talk of organizational crime, however, is neither to reify collectivities nor endow them with volitional properties (Cressey 1995). Organizations act through individuals and groups. The fact that organizations at law are treated as persons for some purposes does not change this fact.

A. Organizational and Organized Crime

The rationale for distinguishing organizational crime from other types of crime is based on the belief that organizational properties and dynamics can be causally autonomous and significant constraints on its genesis, its development, and responses to it. Characteristic features of organizations, from authority differentials and an emphasis on loyalty to task specialization and the situational importance of secrecy, can affect the strength and effectiveness of normative constraints. By itself, hierarchy, which essentially provides that some will control the work activities of others, may increase the odds of criminal conduct (Tittle 1995, 2004; N. L. Piquero and Piquero 2006). Organizational arrangements can obscure decision-making participation and dynamics and thereby increase the difficulties of oversight (Simpson 2002). Additionally, they can diffuse responsibility for misconduct, and this may facilitate individual willingness to participate. The potential importance of organizational conditions in causing crime is most obvious when there are long-standing patterns of criminal violation in organizations. In these circumstances the pathologies of individuals fail as explanation, and the causes must be sought instead in organizational life. This is the case in police departments, for example, where corruption and abuse are pervasive and long-standing.

Criminogenesis need not be confined to the internal world of organizations; the nature of the organizational environment also affects the odds of crime. This is exemplified by industries where there is evidence of significant criminality over many years or where there are recurring cycles of crime (Reuter 1993). The fluid milk industry, for example, has a history of antitrust activities that surfaces periodically in exposés and criminal convictions. In one of the most common abuses, milk producers reap criminal profit by collectively fixing prices charged to local school districts for milk served in federally supported school lunch programs (Shover and Hochstetler 2006). Those searching for the sources of price fixing in the fluid milk industry would be foolish to limit their focus to the inner world of individual firms; no less, if not more, worthy of attention is how the critical environments and structure of the industry affect the proportion of firms in which individuals and groups choose to commit organizational crime.

The category of organizational crime excludes crime committed in the context and in pursuit of goals of organizations in which crime is the principal means of livelihood and collective success. The crimes of international drug smugglers and other syndicated criminals, for example, are organized, but they are not organizational crime. Empirically, the distinction between organizational crime and organized or syndicated crime can become blurred, as when legitimate businesses are converted gradually into criminal ones, or when they serve as nothing more than a respectable-appearing shell for activities that are largely, if not exclusively, criminal (Passas and Nelken 1993; Baker and Faulkner 2003). In structure and management, for example, criminal telemarketing firms can be indistinguishable from legitimate firms in the direct marketing industry (Shover, Coffey, and Sanders 2004). The sometimes ambiguous empirical distinction between organizational crime and organized crime is seen also in the conduct of some small-business owners who, faced with declining profits and gloomy prospects, commit crimes of the kind more characteristic of experienced confidence men; using the appearance of stable and profitable enterprises, for example, they purchase inventory before closing the business and reneging on their bills (Levi 2007, 2008). Legitimate organizations also may establish and maintain mutually beneficial relationships with criminal organizations (Ruggiero 1996).

B. Corporate and State-Corporate Crime

Although organizational properties and dynamics conducive to crime presumably operate in like fashion across all organizations, this has not deterred investigators from distinguishing for analytic attention specific types of organizational crime. *Corporate crime* is crime committed by officers, managers, or employees of profit-seeking organizations or firms in pursuit of employer objectives (Yeager 2007). It ranks as the most important example of a type of organizational crime given autonomous analytic status by many investigators (Geis 2006). The chief rationale for distinguishing this and other subtypes of organizational crime is the belief that some organizations are unusually criminogenic or that causal conditions are more characteristic of them and their environments. The emphasis in for-profit organizations, for example, on unalloyed economic calculation coupled with possibly distinctive structural and cultural features may make them unusually criminogenic

(Pearce 2001). Among the first to assert this belief, at the dawn of the twentieth century, Ross (1907, p. 109) indicted them as entities that "transmit the greed of investors, but not their conscience." Other rationales for isolating and examining corporate crime include the pervasiveness and power of large corporations and the corporate form, the high cost of corporate crime to victims and the larger community, and the somewhat distinctive and difficult control challenges it presents.

Others contend that there is no compelling reason to single out for special criminological attention any particular organizational form because of belief that much can be learned about organizational crime by examining it in a variety of settings. Whether they are philanthropic, voluntary, profit-seeking, or state sector organizations, moreover, may be unimportant; corporations *are* organizations. Whatever distinguishes them from one another, the fact that they are organizations may contribute substantially to the commission of crime in their confines. There may be benefit, for example, in studies of illegal conduct by law enforcement officials for understanding crime by business executives. This in no way denies that large corporations, which are among the most powerful institutions and political actors in the modern world, may be unusually criminogenic settings. Whether and under what circumstances this is true are issues that remain unsettled empirically.

Corporate crime is not the only type of organizational crime singled out for closer examination by some investigators (Michalowski and Kramer 2006). *State-corporate crime* is crime "that occur[s] when one or more institutions of political governance pursue a goal in direct cooperation with one or more institutions of economic production and distribution" (Kramer, Michalowski, and Kauzlarich 2002, p. 263). Commonplace in occurrence, it is seen where state agencies are willfully or negligently lax in oversight. Some see the explosion of the *Challenger* space shuttle as evidence of criminal negligence by the National Aeronautics and Space Administration (Kramer, Michalowski, and Kauzlarich 2002). State-corporate crime is also found in the behavior of corrupt public officials who troll for and receive gratuities from corporate interests in exchange for access and favors. It can also take the form of complicity in crime committed by profit-seeking organizations. Michalowski and Kramer (2006) suggest that the National Highway Traffic Safety Administration was complicit in deaths resulting from Ford Explorer rollovers that occurred in the early to mid-1990s because it did not actively push Ford to comply with a recall of tires that were a major contributor to fatalities caused by loss of driver control.

Regardless of whether individual investigators choose to single out and empirically examine either corporate crime or state-corporate crime, studies in these areas highlight the great importance of the state in understanding organizational crime and reactions to it. Directly and indirectly, it is a leading supplier of criminal opportunity. More important, the stance adopted by the state toward criminal conduct and regulation of markets sends a powerful message to organizational decision makers (V. Braithwaite and Braithwaite 2006). What is obvious from our conceptual overview of organizational and related forms of crime is that anyone wanting unambiguous and widely agreed upon definitional distinctions will not find them in the area of white-collar and organizational crime.

C. Illegalities and Unethical Conduct

Illegalities and unethical conduct are types of organizational rule breaking that do not rise to the level of crime (Baucus and Dworkin 1991). The former consist primarily of violations of administrative or regulatory rules of the kind ubiquitous in modern states. They are regarded as civil violations and typically are met with warnings or minor civil fines. Investigations of illegalities continue to receive attention from investigators, but any increase that may have occurred in recent years is nothing like the rapid expansion of interest in *unethical conduct* in organizations. University business schools, law schools, and the public pronouncements of corporate managers are settings for theory and research on ethical violations in organizations. The explosion of interest in corporate governance in recent years has been focused almost entirely on unethical conduct by corporate insiders that victimizes the employer or its shareholders. Academics and corporate managers, who disproportionately shape discourse on corporate governance, are remarkably silent on the matter of corporate crime and the potential overarching importance of obedience to the law (Shover and Hochstetler 2002). Organizations in which there are high levels of illegalities and unethical conduct, however, likely are places also where crime is more common; diverse forms of rule breaking, from the unethical to the criminal, probably have their origins in similar organizational conditions. These are relationships deserving of much greater attention.

II. Data Sources

There are three major categories of data on organizational crime: victimization surveys; self-report studies; and reports issued by criminal investigative agencies, regulatory agencies, and the courts. Few of these data sources categorize and report information specifically on organizational crimes. Most reporting categories instead are based on and reflect statutory crime definitions. Fraud and antitrust offenses are prime examples. This helps explain why some of the most revealing and useful research on organizational crime examines antitrust offenses (Simpson 1986, 1987; Jamieson 1994; Szockyj and Geis 2002). It also means that investigators interested in organizational crime must construct a picture inferentially, however tentative, of the problem and key aspects of it. Many, if not most, investigators are more interested in corporate crime specifically than organizational crime in general, but usually they treat the two as coextensive. Studies of corporate crime make up by far the largest part of what is known about organizational crime. There is substantially less work on crime in not-for-profit organizations.

Official data on organizational crime and criminals pales in quality, comprehensiveness, and ease of use beside the systematically collected and issued, bountiful, and readily available data on street crime. In the United States the Bureau of Justice Statistics annually issues a torrent of descriptive research on robbers, burglars, drug offenders, and other street criminals; it publishes next to nothing on organizational crime or corporate crime. Citizens and investigators interested in these offenses are not routinely presented with a "crime clock" of the kind that opens the Uniform Crime Reports. Federal and state regulatory agencies do a better job; the bulk of their reports detail the number and types of regulatory violations recorded in the preceding year. Increasingly, these reports on illegalities are available on the Internet and therefore readily accessible to citizens, organizations, and investigators (e.g., U.S. Environmental Protection Agency 2007). Despite the potential value of regulatory enforcement data, they fall far short of what is needed to arbitrate satisfactorily theoretical claims about organizational crime.

Organizational crime is not a priority for public agencies and departments that fund research on crime and offenders. They focus instead on narrower categories of crime and illegalities that reflect their legislative charge. This is one reason it can require painstaking work to collect useful statistical data on organizational crime, and compiling time-series data over more than a few decades is both challenging and labor intensive. In addition it is impossible to know whether the results provide a representative picture of any larger population of theoretical or policy significance (Geis and Salinger 1998; Szockyj and Geis 2002). The net result of shortcomings in data is inability to measure with comprehensiveness or confidence the volume and distribution of organizational crime. Put simply, the principal dependent variable in organizational crime research is undeterminable.

Arguably there is more information available on organizations as victims of crime than on organizations as offenders, albeit victimization data are concentrated in areas of economic crime. Data on a larger range of organizational crimes is scarce; remarkably little is known, for example, about victims of industrial espionage. There is no doubt, however, that victimization of profit-seeking organizations is not uncommon, although the proportion of crimes that are committed by other organizations is undeterminable in most victimization studies (Bussmann and Werle 2006; Association of Certified Fraud Examiners 2007).

Past research on organizational crime includes a high proportion of case studies. Journalists and academics alike have provided detailed descriptions and postmortem analyses of some of the most arrogant, destructive, and costly organizational crimes. The crimes of Enron Corporation, for example, were the subject of several detailed print media reports, insider accounts, and cinematic productions in the years following its collapse. Industries in which notable crimes or long-term or cyclical patterns of criminality occur have been examined as well (Jesilow, Pontell, and Geis 1993). What is often obscured by attention to newsworthy organizational crimes are the mundane organizations and crimes that more typically draw attention from regulators, police, and prosecutors (Karstedt and Farrall 2006, 2007). Case studies are useful, however, for the insight they provide on organizational and interpersonal dynamics that can result in crime. Some shed light also on the dynamics of denial and coverup. In the same way that life history narratives can yield enhanced understanding and important hypotheses about individual crime, case studies, despite their shortcomings, are useful for what they can teach investigators about organizational crime.

III. Explaining Variation in Organizational Crime

Rates of white-collar crime vary temporally, spatially, and across organizations. Although we lack data needed to demonstrate this with precision, no one doubts what the outcome would be if adequate data were available. The sources of variation in organizational crime are matters of considerable theoretical agreement and a gradually expanding corpus of research. Rational choice theory or approaches that are logically compatible with it predominate. As an organizing paradigm rational choice theory accommodates logically and integrates in a straightforward fashion a range of other theoretical approaches (Needleman and Needleman 1979; Finney and Lesieur 1982; Hirschi 1986; N. L. Piquero, Exum, and Simpson 2005). In the United States and other nations it has been used extensively to understand street criminals and their pursuits and to develop crime-control strategies. The success enjoyed by rational choice theory as a rationale for revolutionary changes in the way street crime is responded to suggests that it may hold promise also for enhancing understanding of organizational crime and potential responses to it.

In the logic of rational choice theory, crime results from a decision-making process in which actors balance diverse utilities with their respective potential risks and rewards. The latter are diverse, but where organizational personnel are concerned they include anything from increased organizational profit or market share to increased personal income, whereas the former includes loss of reputation or income and formal penalties imposed by the state. This in no way denies that contextually remote conditions may contribute to crime occurrence but assumes instead that they are important primarily because of their effects on situationally specific decision making. Discretion resides with the individual, who chooses whether or not to transgress. With its focus on decision making, rational choice theory provides a way of understanding how the world beyond organizations and also their internal conditions and dynamics shape the odds of crime (Paternoster and Simpson 1993; Shover and Bryant 1993; Cohen and Simpson 1997; Shover and Hochstetler 2006).

A. Aggregate Level

When applied to the problem of explaining aggregate-level variation in crime, rational choice theory highlights two principal causes: the volume of criminal opportunities and the size of the pool of tempted individuals and predisposed organizations prepared to exploit them. *Lure* and the absence of credible oversight are the twin components of criminal opportunity. Lure is arrangements or situations that turn heads. Like tinsel to a child, it draws attention. Lure is a purse left unattended where there is heavy pedestrian traffic, cost-plus contracts between government and business firms, officers and representatives of Fortune 500 corporations doing business with officials of fledgling nations eager for investment and economic development. Lure need not be economic, however. It is also access to dependent and vulnerable populations, whether these be children, prisoners, the sick, the aged, or economically marginal workers.

Changes in the forms and supply of lure have been pronounced in the half-century since World War II (Shover and Hochstetler 2007). These changes have occurred not only in the United States but in other nations as well. The onset and developmental pace of the expansion of state largesse, the financial services revolution, new technologies for information sharing and financial transactions, and the globalization of economic markets and relationships vary from one nation to another, but these changes have affected the supply of lure around the globe (Friedman 2006). The growth of the state's public welfare programs, for example, expanded payments to and subsidies for citizens across the income spectrum. The vast majority of state largesse, however, goes not to individuals but to organizations; in 2002 alone, U.S. corporations received $125 billion in government subsidies (Citizens for Tax Justice 2003). Criminal exploitation of subsidies and other programs that make funds available to businesses may require "not much more than the ability to read, write, and fill out forms, along with some minimum level of presentation of a respectable self" (Weisburd et al., 1991, pp. 182–83).

Recognition of lure makes the tempted and criminally predisposed sensitive to whether or not their actions are being monitored and how oversight might be defeated. Lure by itself is not criminal opportunity, but in the absence of credible oversight it is. Organizational criminal opportunities are objectively given situations or conditions encountered by organizational personnel that offer attractive potential for furthering organizational objectives by criminal means. Opportunity is in the eye of the beholder, but there is an objective and commonsense aspect to many criminal opportunities. This is why a high proportion of adults see and recognize it in similar circumstances. It is the reason we are cautioned and recognize wisdom in the admonition not to leave our automobile keys in the ignition switch or leave attractively wrapped gifts in plain sight while away from our cars. Understandably, opportunities for organizational crime cluster in the workplace. In geographic areas, at times, or in industries where there are abundant opportunities for organizational crime we expect correspondingly high rates of it. Where there is a paucity of opportunities the rate of organizational crime contracts.

The size of the pool of predisposed organizations in which individuals are at increased odds of crime commission is a function of economic trends and the level of uncertainty in critical organizational markets; competition over resources and markets; cultures of noncompliance that gain acceptance and legitimacy in specific areas, industries, or historical eras; and prevailing beliefs about the credibility of oversight. Fluctuation in the business cycle has been linked repeatedly to changes in the size of the pool of white-collar offenders (Staw and Szwajkowski 1975; Clinard and Yeager 1980; Simpson 1986, 1987; Baucus 1994). Economic downturns depress both income and prospects for the future, which increases fear and competition. As larger numbers of citizens and organizations are pushed closer to insolvency, desperation escalates, which can cause respectable organizational employees to consider behavioral options they normally would find unacceptable. This may be true particularly for entrepreneurs and small businesses operating near the margin of insolvency.

Fluctuations of the business cycle are important also because they complicate and make more uncertain predictions of market trends. To acquire financing, personnel, raw materials, and other resources needed for production, organizations must participate in a variety of markets. Conditions in any combination of these markets may range from financially depressed or unsettled to strong and predictable. When the former is the case market uncertainty increases. For officers and managers of business firms, this complicates planning, further escalates anxiety, and pushes an increasing proportion toward desperation and crime.

Organizations of all kinds compete with other organizations. They compete not only over the prices charged for their products but also in credit and labor markets. In a competitive world progress is assessed by comparison with peers, and inevitably there are winners and losers. Desire to be the former is fueled in part by fear of becoming the latter. Competition need not be economic, however. Establishing or maintaining respect by peers for exceptional achievement is a priority for many, but humans compete for attention from superiors, for plum assignments, and for possible career advancement. Competition presumably operates also in the realm of nongovernmental organizations. Charitable organizations, for example, must compete annually for funds and other resources to meet their operating budgets and philanthropic objectives. The pervasive insecurity generated in competitive environments provides powerful motivational pushes toward misconduct (Schweitzer, Ordonez, and Douma 2004). By elevating and rewarding success above all else they provide both characteristic understanding of and justifications for misconduct (Coleman 1987). In such environments normative restraints are transformed into challenges to be circumvented or used to advantage.

Whenever and wherever a culture of noncompliance gains acceptance and strength it increases the supply of potential offenders by providing perspectives and justifications that conflict with ethical maxims (Barnett 1986; Reichman 1993; Jamieson 1994; Punch 2000; Simpson and Piquero 2002). Cultures of noncompliance are important because they make available to individuals and groups interactionally permissible rhetorical constructions of illicit conduct. These *techniques of neutralization* or *accounts* excuse, justify, or in other ways facilitate crime by blunting the moral force of the law and neutralizing the guilt of criminal participation (Sykes and Matza 1957; Scott and Lyman 1968; Maruna and Copes 2004). Techniques of neutralization need not be determinants of decision making in all organizations, however. *Techniques of restraint* are linguistic constructions of prospective behaviors that dampen the proportion of firms where crime occurs by shaping preferences, perceived options, and the odds of criminal choice. Techniques of restraint are publicly spoken admonitions such as "Virtue is its own reward," "Honesty is the best policy," and "Protection of the environment is part of our job." The proportionate mix of techniques of neutralization and techniques of restraint is the key determinant of the dominant culture of industries, regions, time periods, and individual organizations (J. Braithwaite 1989).

Prevailing beliefs about the credibility of oversight occupy a prominent place in rational choice theory as partial explanation for variation in the aggregate rate of crime. Just as uncertainty rooted in economic conditions, market fluctuations, and cultural support for criminal actions increase the supply of predisposed offenders, weak or inconsistent oversight does the same. This is because the level of commitment to and resources invested in rule enforcement by the state shapes collectively held notions about the legitimacy and credibility of oversight. Oversight by the state and other organizations can take the form of direct observation or impersonal monitoring via periodic audits, television cameras, or computer programs. It can also include policies and programs supported by professional associations and trade groups. When it is widely believed that oversight is unwarranted and too costly, when the odds of detection and sanctioning for criminal conduct are thought to be minimal, or when penalties threatened by the law or others are dismissed as inconsequential, the pool of individuals and organizations predisposed to offend grows.

B. Organization Level

There is little doubt that the incidence of crime and illegalities varies across organizations. Kagan and Scholz (1984, p. 71) put the matter well, noting that even when "there are [business] firms in the same industry in the same city, with ostensibly equal opportunities for gain and equal detection, some violate regulations frequently and some do not." The variable structure, culture, and dynamics of organizations are major reasons (Hogan, Patterson, and Coleman 2002; Vaughan, 2007). Four aspects of their internal worlds are significant for their potential effects on the odds of crime by executives, managers, or employees of legitimate organizations: performance pressure, doubt about the credibility of oversight, organizational cultures that excuse or permit commission of infraction, and signaling behavior by executives and managers that obedience to the law is not an organizational priority. These as well as other organizational conditions present individuals with different understandings and beliefs about the likely consequences of their decisions. By constraining the calculus of decision making in organizational contexts, variation in these conditions can cause decision makers to believe alternatively that one runs grave risks in choosing crime or that the risks are improbable.

No cause of variation in organizational compliance is asserted with as much confidence as belief that pressure and strain produced by the need to meet acceptable levels of performance increases the probability of crime. When the organizational employer is not doing well and pressure is on to do better, it can embolden decision makers or make them desperate and cause them to make reckless, if calculated, choices. In market-based economies the need for firms to maintain profitability is of paramount importance; declining income and falling profits are a source of pressure for improved performance (Coleman 1987). For-profit nursing homes, for example, are significantly more likely than nonprofit ones to break the law and deliver substandard care (Jenkins and Braithwaite 1993). Apparently top-down pressure to meet the bottom line creates incentive to cut corners in patient treatment, to leave necessary maintenance unfinished, and to look the other way in the face of potentially hazardous working conditions. For employees, the source of performance pressure is a combination of organizational and personal determination to succeed.

Largely because of their effects on organizational performance, the dynamics of economic markets and relationships are among the strongest constraints on criminal choice. The relationship between economic conditions, performance pressure, and the supply of potential organizational criminals may be curvilinear, however; severe economic upturns and downturns alike may increase the number of individuals and organizations weighing criminal options. Crime is stimulated during boom times by a widespread belief that everyone is getting rich. When everyone seems to be doing well, belief that it is foolish to hold back and not engage in the games of the moment finds broad appeal. Many come to believe that to pass up any opportunity is to miss the boat. Those who choose crime may be emboldened by an assumption that a rising economic tide hides their activities and increases their chances of criminal success. Strong and sustained economic growth can also create both a sense of entitlement to the fruits of a thriving economy and belief that now is the time to strike.

Performance pressure is not a condition that occurs only in profit-seeking organizations. All organizations must acquire resources sufficient in quality and price to remain viable if not enhance their level of success. University faculty and researchers, for example, are not immune from performance pressure, and scientific misconduct, some of it criminal, is the result. Faced with pressures to produce new knowledge, publish, and gain promotion and tenure, scientists may tread carelessly or injudiciously along the boundary demarcating the unacceptable (Petersdorf 1989). The rapid corporatization of universities in recent decades presumably has increased the prevalence of crime and scientific misconduct by administrators and faculty alike.

Nearly as important as performance pressure as a source of crime in organizations are organizational cultures that cause decision makers to emphasize the importance of goal achievement, with less emphasis paid to how this is accomplished (Schneider, 1990; Ashkanasy, Wilderom, and Peterson 2000; Cooper, Cartwright, and Earley 2001; Vaughan, 2007). The culture of an organization can make social outcasts of those who behave criminally or welcome them as close colleagues and suitable candidates for increased administrative responsibilities. More than two decades of research is the basis of striking agreement on culture as a "social force that controls patterns of organizational behavior by shaping members' cognitions and perceptions of meanings and realities" (Ott 1989, p. 69). Variation in organizational culture has been linked to an array of variables, including financial performance, adaptability, and goal effectiveness.

Organizational culture has been defined and conceptualized in a variety of ways, but an approach employed by many sees it as the normative beliefs and shared expectations in an organization or organizational unit (Cooke and Szumal 1993). It is well established that some organizational arrangements and cultures are more conducive to compliance than others (Baucus and Near 1991). Just as the dominant culture of industries, regions, or time periods is determined by the proportionate mix of techniques of neutralization and techniques of restraint, the same is true of organizational cultures. An imbalance in the approved use of either constrains the odds of criminal conduct; where techniques of neutralization dominate the odds of crime increase, and where techniques of restraint dominate the odds are reduced.

Another cause of organizational variation in crime commission is the stance on criminal conduct communicated by executives and managers. Differentials of authority are inherent in work organizations; superiors and subordinates are unavoidable aspects of their structure and dynamics. Policies and decisions by executives and managers are meant to influence subordinates' actions in ways that contribute to organizational success. Evidence is clear that in doing so they function as moral exemplars for peers and subordinates (Brown, Trevino, and Harrison 2005; Trevino, Weaver, and Reynolds 2006). Investigators surveyed 1,227 readers of the *Harvard Business Review* about business ethics and inquired especially about factors respondents believe influence executives to make unethical decisions. Analysis suggested that "behavior of one's superiors is the primary guidepost" (Brenner and Molander 1977, p. 66). Research into factors that inhibit impermissible conduct by industrial sales personnel revealed that "one of the consistent and early points that came up was the example set for the company by the behavior of top management" (Sonnenfeld and Lawrence 1978, p. 152).

Similar findings are reported by Clinard (1983) based on interviews with 64 retired middle management executives who formerly were employed by Fortune 500 corporations. This *signaling behavior* by executives, managers, and team leaders communicates to all the degree to which lawful behavior is valued and expected (Hambrick and Mason 1984). When they signal to colleagues and employees that misconduct will not be tolerated, the message is not lost (J. Braithwaite 1985). When they fail to insist on obedience to the law, it signals that compliance is not a priority. The result can be a steady if imperceptible growth of laxness and even indifference about ethics and compliance. If superiors treat standards of ethical conduct in cavalier fashion, subordinates will be quick to realize that the risks of misconduct for them are reduced as well. In these circumstances the proportion of managers and employees who are criminally predisposed or tempted grows (Gobert and Punch 2007).

IV. Organizational Criminal Careers

The ascendance of rational choice theory in the closing decades of the twentieth century as an explanation for criminal participation was matched by renewed interest in *criminal careers*. This concept now figures prominently in criminological research, in textbook analyses of crime, and in public policy debates over what should be done about it. The principal reason is obvious: some offenders have only a brief fling with crime, whereas others commit it repeatedly and may endure repeated convictions and imprisonment. Dubbed "career criminals," these persistent offenders have captured the attention of elite academics and political leaders alike (A. R. Piquero, Farrington, and Blumstein 2003). Research on criminal careers and career criminals has focused most intensely on street offenders and shows indisputably that the great majority eventually desist from their earlier patterns.

As with individual offenders, some organizational criminals may cross the line into crime only once, whereas others cross it repeatedly and endure repeated criminal convictions. Some have lengthy records of transgression; others have exemplary records of compliance with laws and regulations. Sutherland ([1949] 1983) tabulated the adverse decisions of courts and administrative commissions against 70 of the largest U.S. manufacturing, mining, and mercantile corporations over their entire life span. There were 980 adverse decisions total, although only 16 percent (158) were criminal convictions. Sixty percent of the 70 firms had been convicted in criminal courts and had an average of four convictions each. Clinard and Yeager (1980) later analyzed administrative, civil, and criminal actions initiated or completed during 1975 and 1976 by 25 federal agencies against 582 of the largest publicly owned corporations in the United States. Like Sutherland, they employed a broad definition of crime that included not only criminal acts but also administrative violations and adverse civil decisions. Of the 582 firms, 60.1 percent were targets of at least one federal action during the two-year period, and they averaged 4.4 actions each. Of the 477 manufacturing firms in the sample, 38 accounted for 52 percent of all violations, or an average of 23.5 violations each. Simply put, these studies suggest that a minority of business firms are career criminals in the sense that decisions by their executives and managers are frequently at odds with the criminal law.

Although the careers of street criminals have received close and sustained attention, the dimensions and dynamics of organizational criminal careers have been all but ignored, and remarkably little is known about them. Geis and Salinger (1998, p. 95) note, "It is a bit surprising that no research of which we are aware has spanned the life history of one or, better yet, a number of organizations and the relationship between aspects of its or their existence and troubles with the law.... [A] richness of information... could be gleaned from the life story of individual companies that have gone through cycles of fiscal prosperity and famine." There is little doubt that there is substantial variation in the length and intensity of organizational criminal careers. Presumably there are typical patterns of onset, continuity, and desistance when it occurs. Greater awareness of the dimensions and qualities of organizational criminal careers would be important for policy makers interested in crafting more effective oversight of lure.

V. Responses to Organizational Crime

Three primary means to constrain and sanction organizational crime and misconduct are available. Regulatory agencies have a variety of rule-making, monitoring, and sanctioning tools available to them. Criminal prosecutions and sanctions are often available. Other private actors—customers, victims, and informants—can be given motives to uncover and take action against crime and other misconduct.

A. Regulatory Agencies

An array of regulatory agencies at all levels of government make up the first line of oversight of potential organizational criminals. Historically, they are charged with promulgating and enforcing rules for the fair and safe conduct of organizational business in specified areas of activities. To accomplish their legislative charge, agencies employ technical staff to provide expertise, attorneys to draft regulations and pursue penalties in cases of serious or long-standing violations, and inspectors to monitor compliance by organizations. Agencies have considerable discretion deciding how to exercise oversight and respond to violations, but referrals for criminal prosecution are rare (Hawkins 2003). They tend to be sensitive to industry concerns and problems, which finds expression in the content of their regulations and also in their light-handed approach to enforcement (Yeager 1993). In some Western nations the traditional approach to regulation has been supplanted by new programs that rely less on enforcement and penalties and more on assisting organizations to comply with regulatory requirements. The effectiveness of the newer approaches has yet to be subjected to extensive empirical testing (May 2003; Nielsen 2006; V. Braithwaite 2007).

B. Investigation and Prosecution

In the United States several federal investigative agencies have responsibility for organizational crimes, but the Federal Bureau of Investigation is prominent among them. During 2006 it investigated 490 corporate fraud cases, resulting in 171 indictments and 124 convictions of corporate criminals (U.S. Department of Justice 2006). The U.S. Environmental Protection Agency's Criminal Enforcement Program investigates the most significant and egregious violators of environmental laws that pose a significant threat to human health and the environment. Organizations can be targets of criminal investigation and stand as defendants in cases where culpable individuals cannot be identified or where the likely costs of prosecuting successfully those who are culpable is considered prohibitive.

The technical challenges of detecting, investigating, and prosecuting organizational crime are substantial. Many crimes go unreported, either because victims are unaware when they fall prey or because they prefer not to make public their misfortune. Officials who are made aware of organizational crimes may lack the expertise needed to investigate them adequately. Routinely task forces comprised of personnel from multiple agencies are required. Identifying culpable individuals and establishing criminal intent can be difficult. These are chief among the reasons prosecutors frequently opt for civil prosecution and the lower standard of proof required to sustain a successful outcome. They are also among the reasons why primary responsibility for oversight rests with regulatory agencies and the regulatory process.

There is considerable regional and temporal variation in referrals for organizational criminal prosecutions. The former has received little attention from investigators, but in the United States referrals for prosecution of white-collar crime increased noticeably in the period 1987–96. The proportion of referrals made up of organizational crimes is unknown. Stimulated in part by events of September 11, 2001, and the subsequent adjustment of federal law enforcement priorities, referrals for prosecution of white-collar crimes have returned to below the 1987 level (Shover and Hochstetler 2006). The years of increased referrals for prosecution saw only a modest increase in prosecuted cases. Whatever the reasons, official campaigns against white-collar and organizational criminals are uncommon, rarely result in significant escalation of sanctions, are applied to few organizations, and generally are not sustained for long (Schlegel, Eitle, and Gunkel 2001; Shover and Hochstetler 2006).

When they screen cases of reported white-collar and organizational crime, prosecutors pay attention particularly to the number of victims, the extent of harm, and whether there is evidence of multiple offenses. They carefully weigh local economic conditions and interests and sometimes elect not to pursue aggressively crimes committed by businesses for fear of harming employment and the local economy (Benson and Cullen 1998; N. L. Piquero and Davis 2004). Likewise, concern for possible economic repercussions occurs on a grander scale in crimes where massive financial losses caused by organizational crime potentially could destabilize important financial institutions or national economies (Levi 1987; Leeson and Whitley 1996). At every level and stage of the oversight process, its potential economic impacts affect the way options are weighed. The same occurs in other English-speaking nations where judges are permitted broad discretion in sentencing (Law Reform Commission, Australia 2001; Department of Justice, Canada 2002).

The most powerful weapon in the arsenal of prosecutors in the United States is the Racketeer Influenced and Corrupt Organization statute (RICO). Enacted by Congress in 1970, RICO was aimed at organized crime groups, but it has been used also against legitimate businesses. Use of RICO has been controversial, with supporters and opponents equally aroused. Opposition has caused tighter restrictions on its use; from a high of 972 cases brought in 1991, case filings under RICO have declined. In RICO cases the stakes are high for defendants, which can make for complex and vigorous defenses. The resources required if the state is to prevail can be extremely costly.

C. Courts and Sentencing

When organizations are sentenced for committing crimes, the range of options available to prosecutors and judges differs somewhat from what is available when individuals are sentenced; incarceration, for example, is not an option, since organizations cannot be confined. In other ways, however, the range of options expands and allows for sentences that either cannot be imposed on individuals or would be illegal or unethical (Cohen 1989). Other sentencing possibilities available for individuals lack a cognate option when organizations are defendants, but functionally equivalent ones can be employed; organizations cannot be put to death as individuals are, but their license to do business can be revoked, and for all intents and purposes the effect of this may in some ways be comparable to death. Organizations can be compelled to change their internal structure in ways that would not be applicable when sentencing individuals; the latter cannot be ordered to develop a conscience, but organizations can be compelled to establish internal compliance units. The federal guidelines used when sentencing convicted organizations or officers permit sentencing judges to weigh as an aggravating factor the absence of an effective compliance and ethics program (U.S. Sentencing Commission 2007).

In 1991 the U.S. Sentencing Commission (n.d.) promulgated guidelines for sentencing convicted organizational defendants. The guidelines establish fine ranges meant to deter and punish criminal conduct, require full restitution to compensate victims for any harm and disgorging of illegal gains, regulate probationary sentences, and implement forfeiture and other potential statutory penalties (Murphy 2002; Levi 2006). The organizational guidelines apply to all felonies and serious misdemeanors committed by organizational defendants, but their fine provisions are applicable primarily to offenses for which pecuniary loss or harm can be quantified more easily (e.g., fraud, theft, and tax violations). In 1995 111 organizations were sentenced in U.S. district courts, and fine provisions were applicable to 83 of the defendants (U.S. Sentencing Commission 1995). Between 2002 and 2007 there were 1,236 corporate fraud convictions in U.S. district courts (U.S. Department of Justice, 2002, 2005, 2006, 2007).

Published tallies of organizational offenses are limited primarily to financial offenses and fraud, and they generally do not report on other types of crime. Environmental crime is a notable example. In the years 1995–2006 the number of organizational defendants sentenced annually in the United States fluctuated from a low of 45 (2006) to a high of 304 in 2000 (Shover and Hochstetler 2006; U.S. Sentencing Commission, 1995–2007). Given the extremely large number of organizations, these numbers seem minuscule and inconsequential.

As compared with what is known about the characteristics of individual white-collar offenders, the picture of *organizational* defendants is much less clear. Data on 601 organizations sentenced in U.S. district courts in 1988 and 1989 show that fewer than 1 percent of sentenced firms were nonprofit organizations (U.S. Sentencing Commission n.d.). Closely held companies represented 90.7 percent of sentenced firms, and 8.2 percent were publicly traded firms. Fraud and antitrust offenses accounted for 57.2 percent of all offenses, and environmental offenses constituted 9.3 percent. Convicted organizational criminals disproportionately are small and midsize business firms. Apart from the question of whether this reflects higher levels of crime in smaller firms, studies in both the United States and other nations suggests that they are more likely than larger businesses to be singled out for investigation and prosecution (Grabosky and Braithwaite 1986). As compared with the risks and costs of targeting the large and powerful, settlements or convictions are attained most economically by concentrating efforts on firms less likely to mount vigorous or sustained resistance. For organizations convicted and sentenced for crimes in 1988 and 1989, "the typical case [was] a fraud that [involved] a loss of approximately $30,000" (U.S. Sentencing Commission n.d., p. 3). These are hardly crimes of the same sort or magnitude as those committed by Enron and other corporate criminals in the past decade, but they almost certainly are more typical of the larger population of organizational crimes; a substantial if undeterminable proportion are unremarkable, if not mundane.

D. Private Actions: Victims and Informants

As with victims of white-collar crime generally, citizens and organizations victimized by organizational crime may be unaware of their victimization. Because many of these crimes have the look and feel of routine transactions, they may not stand out in victims' experience. In marked contrast to armed robbery, for example, billing customers for services that were not provided can get lost and remain hidden from victims in lengthy and complex financial statements. Understandably, those unaware of being victimized are in no position to respond to victimization.

Both individuals and organizations aware that they have been harmed by what they believe are criminal actions can pursue civil remedies to recover losses and press for punitive damages. It is impossible to determine from official data on civil litigation how many victims of organizational crime take civil action against organizations on the basis of alleged criminal conduct. *Class-action* lawsuits usually are filed by a large number of parties, all of whom believe they have been harmed by a common offender. Class-action suits make it possible for parties who otherwise could not afford litigation to pool their resources, form a class, and pursue redress. They originate in all areas of commercial life, including building and construction products, stocks and securities, drug and medical products, and motor vehicle products. In many class-action suits the cost of litigation exceeds the eventual settlement or court award.

Whistle-blowers are citizens who divulge to enforcement agencies or personnel suspicion or knowledge of wrongdoing in an organization. Some whistle-blowers are officers or employees who report actions by their employer, but others are outsiders who learn about or observe suspicious conduct and report it. Internal informants and whistle-blowers are one of the most important sources of discovery of crimes that victimize organizations (Association of Certified Fraud Examiners 2007; Government Accountability Project 2007). A global survey of more than 5,500 corporations found that law enforcement detected only 4 percent of crimes in which responding firms were victims of economic offenses perpetrated against them (PriceWaterhouseCoopers 2006). Of the remaining cases in which companies were victimized, 60 percent learned from informants and 36 percent learned by accident (Bussmann and Werle 2006). The number of firms that were victimized not by individuals but by organizations is not reported.

In the United States the Whistleblower Protection Act of 1989 as amended provides that whistle-blowers can receive a portion of any settlement or recoveries in cases where they provide key information. This is meant to spur insiders with knowledge of wrongdoing to come forward and report to authorities. During 2006 the federal government recovered $3.1 billion in funds from whistle-blower suits, and of this sum whistle-blowers were entitled to $190 million. The majority of recovered funds came from cases originating in the health care sector (U.S. Department of Justice 2006). Like the federal government, nearly all of the states have enacted legislation providing employment protection and monetary rewards for whistle-blowers.

Whistle-blowers have been targets of retaliatory and discriminatory actions by many organizations whose suspicious or illicit actions were reported to outside authorities (Glazer and Glazer 1989). Retaliation is most likely and most severe when the reported conduct is systematic and significant, particularly if it is part of an organization's profit accumulation process (Rothschild and Meithe 1999). Organizational officials typically combat the allegations of whistle-blowers by questioning their motives and character and painting them as renegades (Nichols 1991). Given the often unwelcome notoriety and the financial costs of legal representation to resist retaliatory actions, the experience of whistle-blowing can be extremely disruptive of life, work, and career (Hastings 2007; National Whistleblower Center 2007). The toll on physical and emotional health can be devastating. Some organizations do not sit by when subjected to public criticism or rebuke; some use their resources not only to bully but to retaliate against private citizens and civic groups. SLAPP (strategic litigation against public participation) gets its name from the fact that plaintiffs generally are experienced users of the court, whereas defendants more likely are private citizens or groups that have resisted the plaintiffs' efforts or in other ways cast them in an unfavorable public light (Canan and Pring 1988; Pring and Canan 1996).

In the United States persons who allege that they are victims of retaliation for being identified as whistle-blowers can file complaints in which they must show that they engaged in protected activity, the employer knew about that activity during the course of their employment, the employer subjected them to adverse employment action, and the protected activity contributed to it (U.S. Department of Labor 2007). Most states offer general whistle-blower protection to public employees who disclose mismanagement, waste, or abuse of authority, but fewer than half offer the same protection to private sector workers (U.S. Office of Special Counsel 2007). Federal sentencing guidelines include provisions to enhance protection of whistle-blowers (Solow 2003). The targets of retaliatory actions by organizations usually prevail, but the financial and emotional costs of resisting SLAPP litigation and retaliation for whistle-blowing can be staggering.

Nearly two decades of experience with policies encouraging whistle-blowers and promoting other private actions as mechanisms for enhancing organizational obedience to the law leaves questions of organizational impact and efficacy unanswered. Additionally, more is known about the fate of those who inform than of the organizational consequences of their actions.

VI. Economic Globalization

Globalization designates the increasing number and complexity of political and economic relationships that cross national borders. Economic indicators demonstrate clearly that globalization is on the march (Brahmbhatt 1998; Baca, Garbe, and Weiss 2000; Cavaglia, Brightman, and Aked 2000; Brooks and Del Negro 2002; Forbes and Chinn 2003). Old barriers of time and distance have been obliterated as technology enables the conduct of complex commercial transactions almost instantaneously over enormous geographic distances (Lippens 2001). As the links between national economies strengthen and expand, and "because capital is at once mobile and in short supply, the desire to attract foreign capital makes it difficult to control a nation's capital" (Guehenno 1995, p. 10). Globalization of production and markets is a powerful constraint on oversight, and it has set off a vigorous debate over how nations should respond (J. Braithwaite and Drahos 2000).

A. Competition, Lure, and Oversight

One of the most important reasons for this debate is another by-product of globalization: increased governmental and business competition for resources and markets. Growing global competition means that what once was commonplace but largely confined to the competitive dynamics of national economies now is produced on a grander scale. The difficulties of controlling corporations were enormous in a world of national economies and corporate actors, but efforts to impose credible oversight on their activities cause firms to locate elsewhere or to threaten relocation. Concern that jobs are in danger contributes to public reluctance to regulate industries and firms close to home. Corporate executives are astutely aware of pressures on governments caused by global competition. They demand lure and weak oversight in return for favorable siting decisions and permit requirements. This dynamic is played out across the globe as they negotiate with political leaders for low taxes, low-cost government services, free infrastructure, and limited restrictions on their autonomy. In return they promise jobs.

Industries and companies in one nation do not take lightly competitive recruitment by representatives of other nations with promises of largesse and pro-business environments unavailable to them. Nor are they willing to accept easily that because home offices are located within their borders, their operations should be regulated and taxed more stringently than companies that keep parts of the company abroad. As pressure to loosen regulatory requirements and oversight intensifies, the challenge of maintaining levels of oversight comparable to what some nations once exercised domestically becomes greater (Guehenno 1995).

In contemporary cross-border exchanges, the variety, scale, and complexity of transactions also are significant barriers to credible oversight. The technical and administrative capacity for effective oversight is within reach of few, if any, nations (Cho 2007). The signatories to international trade agreements typically pledge to adopt and enforce in their home countries elementary regulations for environmental protection, worker rights, and product safety, but police and prosecutors generally lack the budget, expertise, and other resources to pursue cases that arise. It seems clear that as oversight becomes more distant geographically and less certain in application, its efficacy suffers. This dynamic becomes more common in a world where state control increasingly is "bypassed by global flows of capital, goods, services, technology, communication and information" (Castells 2004, p. 303).

B. Regulation as Compliance Assistance

In the closing decades of the twentieth century, as economic globalization began increasing rapidly, Western nations witnessed a revolutionary change in the dominant approach to regulatory oversight. Traditionally regulatory agencies promulgated regulations for their areas of responsibility, maintained an enforcement staff to monitor organizational compliance, imposed small civil fines on organizations found to be in violation, and occasionally referred cases of egregious and serious offenses for possible criminal prosecution. The underlying justification for this approach is grounded in notions of deterrence. Dubbed "command-and-control regulation" by critics, by the beginning of the 1980s it came under increasing attack and eventually was displaced (V. Braithwaite 2007).

In its place enforced self-regulation and "responsive regulation" de-emphasize direct state oversight of production processes with insistence on organizational self-monitoring of compliance and creation of internal oversight mechanisms to ensure it (J. Braithwaite 1983, 2002, 2005; Ayres and Braithwaite 1992; New York Stock Exchange 2007). At the same time, efforts are made to involve other parties in the regulatory process; professional organizations, business groups, and community organizations are seen as playing roles in efforts to minimize noncompliance by organizations. The growth of the new regulatory style means that the state has shifted the bulk of its regulatory efforts to programs to educate the regulated about what is required of them and to assist them in developing and operating internal compliance programs. Increased competition caused by rapid globalization of economic production and markets is a major factor contributing to the rapid diffusion of responsive regulation. The effectiveness of the new approach may vary depending on industry characteristics, the nature of organizational variation, and official resolve (Stretesky 2006; Job, Stout, and Smith 2007).

C. Trends in Organizational Crime

The absence of systematic and comprehensive data on organizational crime means that little can be said confidently about even short-term trends. When rational choice theory is used as an organizing framework for examining organizational crime, however, there are good reasons to believe we are witnessing a tide of it: lure has increased, oversight has not kept pace, and competition is stoked to new intensity by economic recession and globalization of production and markets. Deterrence research suggests that the certainty of threatened punishment has a modest deterrent effect, but the severity of threatened punishment has little, if any (von Hirsch et al. 1999; Simpson 2002). The severity of penalties imposed on some organizational criminals increased noticeably in the decade before the new millennium, but what is significant about this development is the small number of organizational defendants during the same time period; the certainty of punishment for organizational criminals was and remains strikingly low. The small number of organizations prosecuted for and convicted of crime by U.S. courts casts severe doubt on the deterrent effect of current levels of punishment. The combined effects of this and the movement to programs of cooperative regulation likewise give reason for doubt.

VII. Research Agenda

Development and elaboration of theoretical interpretations of organizational crime have far outpaced empirical description and testing. The need for more and for more methodologically diverse investigations of organizational crime is apparent to anyone who examines the corpus of research in this area of white-collar crime. Key theoretical explanations and constructs have received remarkably little empirical scrutiny. The influence of organizational culture is a prime example (Shover and Hochstetler 2002). Investigators are unanimous in agreement that culture is linked to the odds of criminal offending and to aggregate offending rates. As Vaughan (1996, p. 406) notes, "Consistently, scholars have assigned great importance to [an organization's culture] as a cause of organizational... misconduct." This high level of consensus, however, is supported by an extremely thin record of well-designed research into the matter. Much of the support for the culture-crime relationship, however, is based on post hoc interpretation of anomalous research findings (Barnett 1986; Baucus and Near 1991; Simpson and Koper 1992). Consequently, what was true two decades ago remains true today: there are no studies "that develop systematic and independent measures of both business [compliance] and corporate or industry cultures" (Yeager 1986, p. 100). The culture-crime nexus merits much greater attention from investigators.

Despite the relatively large body of knowledge detailing the careers of street criminals, there is much to be learned about the dimensions and dynamics of organizational criminal careers. That some organizations are repeat offenders there is no doubt, but reasons for recidivism are poorly understood. Additional research that examines patterns of organizational offending may provide insight into conditions that increase the likelihood of continued offending and also information that may be instrumental in understanding why and how some organizations desist from a long-term pattern of crime. This information could be extremely important for policy responses to organizational crime.

The impact on organizational crime of the shift to regimes of cooperative regulation is unclear, but it appears they require as backup effective state oversight and official willingness to employ criminal penalties in cases of serious willful or negligent noncompliance (Russell and Gilbert 2002). Despite the wholesale shift to programs of cooperative regulation, no one advocates sole reliance on organizational self-regulation. Data collected from 999 Australian business firms shows that "on the whole, the implementation of... compliance systems is partial, symbolic and half-hearted." Notably, the investigators add that "enforcement action... improves the level of implementation" (Parker and Nielsen 2005, p. 441). There is much to be learned about the most efficacious mix of cooperative practices and tough enforcement for cases of willful and repeated offenses.

Finally, globalization of production and markets is a powerful constraint on oversight. Across the globe determination by states to confront organizational crime has flagged substantially as businesses argue that state oversight is unnecessary and costly, puts them at competitive disadvantage, and harms local economies. Increased competition caused by rapid globalization of economic production and markets has set off a vigorous debate over how nations should respond (J. Braithwaite and Drahos 2000). States have moved significantly in the direction of cooperative regulation. The effectiveness of these regimes and conditions that erode or complement it are pressing areas for empirical investigation (V. Braithwaite 2007).

The greatest challenge facing investigators of organizational crime is the absence of anything approaching systematic and comprehensive data on its occurrence and responses to it. Investigators must develop and test theoretical explanations with available information that falls short of what would be needed to complete critical studies of the frequency and scope of organizational offending and the social costs related to it. Improvements in this state of affairs have been very slow in coming, although some kinds of data are being made available and can be accessed easily via the Internet (e.g., Association of Certified Fraud Examiners 2007). Victimization surveys have become more commonplace, although the crimes they inquire about are rarely serious offenses and victim losses generally are not large. It is unlikely that significant improvements in organizational crime data will occur in the short term, which almost certainly means that the gap between theory and research into organizational crime will remain wide and a major impediment to improved explanation, prediction, and control.

REFERENCES

Ashkanasy, Neal M., Celeste Wilderom, and Mark F. Peterson, eds. 2000. *Handbook of Organizational Culture and Climate*. Thousand Oaks, CA: Sage.

Association of Certified Fraud Examiners. 2007. *2006 Report to the Nation on Occupational Fraud and Abuse*. Austin, TX: Association of Certified Fraud Examiners. http://www.acfe.com/documents/2006-rttn.pdf.

Ayres, Ian, and John Braithwaite. 1992. *Responsive Regulation*. Cambridge: Cambridge University Press.

Baca, Sean P., Brian L. Garbe, and Richard A. Weiss. 2000. "The Rise of Sector Effects in Major Equity Markets." *Financial Analysts Journal*, September: 35–40.

Baker, Wayne E., and Robert R. Faulkner. 2003. "Diffusion of Fraud: Intermediate Economic Crime and Investor Dynamics." *Criminology* 41: 1601–34.

Barnett, Harold C. 1986. "Industry Culture and Industry Economy: Correlates of Tax Noncompliance in Sweden." *Criminology* 34: 553–74.
Baucus, Melissa S. 1994. "Pressure, Opportunity and Predisposition: A Multivariate Model of Corporate Illegality." *Journal of Management* 20: 699–721.
Baucus, Melissa S., and T. M. Dworkin. 1991. "What Is Corporate Crime? It Is Not Illegal Corporate Behavior." *Law and Policy* 13: 231–44.
Baucus, Melissa S., and Janet P. Near. 1991. "Can Illegal Corporate Behavior Be Predicted? An Event History Analysis." *Academy of Management Journal* 34: 9–36.
Benson, Michael L, and Francis T. Cullen. 1998. *Combating Corporate Crime: Local Prosecutors at Work.* Boston: Northeastern University Press.
Brahmbhatt, Milan. 1998. "Measuring Global Integration: A Review of the Literature and Recent Evidence." Unpublished World Bank paper. http://www1.worldbank.org/economicpolicy/globalization/documents/measuring.pdf.
Braithwaite, John. 1983. "Enforced Self-Regulation: A New Strategy for Corporate Crime Control." *Michigan Law Review* 80: 1466–507.
———. 1985. *To Punish or Persuade.* Albany: State University of New York Press.
———. 1989. "Criminological Theory and Organizational Crime." *Justice Quarterly* 6: 333–58.
———. 2002. *Restorative Justice and Responsive Regulation.* Oxford: Oxford University Press.
———. 2005. *Markets in Vice, Markets in Virtue.* Oxford: Oxford University Press.
Braithwaite, John, and Peter Drahos. 2000. *Global Business Regulation.* Cambridge: Cambridge University Press.
Braithwaite, Valerie. 2007. "Responsive Regulation and Taxation: Introduction." *Law and Policy* 29: 3–10.
Braithwaite, Valerie, and John Braithwaite. 2006. "Democratic Sentiment and Cyclical Markets in Vice." *British Journal of Criminology* 46: 1110–27.
Brenner, Steven N., and Earl A. Molander. 1977. "Is the Ethics of Business Changing?" *Harvard Business Review* 55: 57–71.
Brooks, Robin J., and Marco Del Negro. 2002. "Firm-Level Evidence on Global Integration." Paper presented at International Monetary Fund Global Linkages Conference, Washington, DC, April.
Brown, Michael, Linda K. Trevino, and D. Harrison. 2005. "Ethical Leadership: A Social Learning Perspective for Construct Development." *Organizational Behavior and Human Decision Processes* 97: 117–34.
Bussmann, Kai-D., and Markus M. Werle. 2006. "Addressing Crime in Companies: First Findings from a Global Survey of Economic Crime." *British Journal of Criminology* 46: 1128–44.
Canan, Penelope, and George W. Pring. 1988. "Strategic Lawsuits against Public Participation." *Social Problems* 35: 506–19.
Castells, Manuel. 2004. *The Power of Identity.* 2nd ed. Malden, MA: Blackwell.
Cavaglia, Stefano, Christopher Brightman, and Michael Aked. 2000. "The Increasing Importance of Industry Factors." *Financial Analyst Journal,* September: 41–54.
Cho, David. 2007. "Energy Traders Avoid Scrutiny as Commodities Market Grows, Oversight Is Slight." *Washington Post.* (October 27), p. A01. http://www.washingtonpost.com/wp-dyn/content/article/2007/10/20/AR2007102001203.html?hpid%3Dtopnews&sub=AR
Citizens for Tax Justice. 2003. "Surge in Corporate Welfare Drives Corporate Tax Payments Down to Near Record Low." *Corporate Tax Justice Analysis,* April 17.

Clinard, Marshall B. 1983. *Corporate Ethics and Crime: The Role of Middle Management.* Beverly Hills, CA: Sage.

Clinard, Marshall B., and Richard Quinney. 1973. *Criminal Behavior Systems: A Typology.* 2nd ed. New York: Holt, Rinehart and Winston.

Clinard, Marshall B., and Peter C. Yeager. 1980. *Corporate Crime.* New York: Free Press.

Cohen, Mark A. 1989. "Corporate Crime and Punishment: A Study of Social Harm and Sentencing Practices in the Federal Courts, 1984–1987." *American Criminal Law Review* 26: 605–62.

Cohen, Mark A., and Sally S. Simpson. 1997. "The Origins of Corporate Criminality: Rational Individual and Organizational Actors." In *Debating Corporate Crime,* edited by William S. Lofquist, Mark A. Cohen, and G. A. Rabe. Cincinnati: Anderson.

Coleman, James William. 1987. "Toward an Integrated Theory of White-Collar Crime." *American Journal of Sociology* 93: 406–39.

Cooke, Robert A., and Szumal, Janet L. 1993. "Measuring Normative Beliefs and Shared Behavioral Expectations in Organizations." *Psychological Reports* 72: 1299–330.

Cooper, Cary L., Sue Cartwright, and P. Christopher Earley, eds. 2001. *The International Handbook of Organizational Culture and Climate.* West Sussex, England: Wiley.

Cressey, Donald R. 1995. "Poverty of Theory in Corporate Crime Research." In *White-Collar Crime: Classic and Contemporary Views,* edited by Gilbert Geis, Robert F. Meier, and Lawrence M. Salinger. New York: Free Press.

Department of Justice, Canada. 2002. *Government Response to the Fifteenth Report of the Committee on Justice and Human Rights: Corporate Liability.* http://www.canada-justice.ca/en/dept/pub/ccl_rpm/index.html.

Finney, H. C., and Henry R. Lesieur. 1982. "A Contingency Theory of Organizational Crime." In *Research in the Sociology of Organizations: A Research Annual,* vol. 1, edited by Samuel B. Bacharach. Greenwich, CT: JAI.

Forbes, Kristin J., and Menzie D. Chinn. 2003. "A Decomposition of Global Linkages in Financial Markets Over Time." National Bureau of Economic Research, Working Paper No. w9555. Cambridge, MA. http://www.nber.org/papers/w9555.pdf.

Friedman, Thomas L. 2006. *The World Is Flat: A Brief History of the Twenty-First Century.* New York: Farrar, Straus and Giroux.

Friedrichs, David O. 2007. *Trusted Criminals: White-Collar Crime in Contemporary Society.* 3rd ed. Belmont, CA: Wadsworth.

Geis, Gilbert. 2006. *White-Collar and Corporate Crime.* Upper Saddle River, NJ: Prentice-Hall.

Geis, Gilbert, and Lawrence S. Salinger. 1998. "Antitrust and Organizational Deviance." In *The Sociology of Organizations: Deviance in and of Organizations,* vol. 14, edited by Peter A. Bamberger and William J. Sonnenstuhl. Stamford, CT: JAI.

Glazer, Myron P., and Penina M. Glazer. 1989. *The Whistleblowers: Exposing Corruption in Government and Industry.* New York: Basic Books.

Gobert, James, and Maurice Punch. 2007. "Because They Can: Motivations and Intent of White-Collar Criminals." In *International Handbook of White-Collar and Corporate Crime,* edited by Henry Pontell and Gilbert Geis. New York: Springer.

Government Accountability Project. 2007. http://www.whistleblower.org/template/index.cfm.

Grabosky, Peter, and John Braithwaite. 1986. *Of Manners Gentle: Enforcement Strategies of Australian Business Regulatory Agencies.* Melbourne: Oxford University Press.

Guehenno, Jean-Marie. 1995. *The End of the Nation-State*. Trans. Victoria Elliott. Minneapolis: University of Minnesota Press.

Hambrick, Donald C., and Phyllis A. Mason. 1984. "Upper Echelons: The Organization as a Reflection of Its Top Managers." *Academy of Management Review* 9: 193–206.

Hastings, Deborah. 2007. "Whistleblowers on Fraud Facing Penalties." *Forbes.com*. http://www.forbes.com/feeds/ap/2007/08/24/ap4052736.html.

Hawkins, Keith. 2003. *Law as Last Resort: Prosecution Decision-Making in a Regulating Agency*. New York: Oxford University Press.

Hirschi, Travis. 1986. "On the Compatibility of Rational Choice and Social Control Theories of Crime." In *The Reasoning Criminal*, edited by Derek B. Cornish and Ronald V. Clarke. New York: Springer.

Hogan, Andrew J., Ronald Patterson, and James William Coleman. 2002. "Is Research Misconduct Contagious? Evidence from the Swazey, Louis and Anderson Survey." Presented at the Research Conference on Research Integrity, Potomac, MD, November.

Jamieson, Katherine M. 1994. *The Organization of Corporate Crime: Dynamics of Antitrust Violation*. Thousand Oaks, CA: Sage.

Jenkins, Anne, and John Braithwaite. 1993. "Profits, Pressure and Corporate Lawbreaking." *Crime, Law and Social Change* 20: 221–32.

Jesilow, Paul, Henry N. Pontell, and Gilbert Geis. 1993. *Prescription for Profit: How Doctors Defraud Medicaid*. Berkeley: University of California Press.

Job, Jenny, Andrew Stout, and Rachael Smith. 2007. "Culture Change in Three Taxation Administrations: From Command-and-Control to Responsive Regulation." *Law and Policy* 29: 84–101.

Kagan, Robert A., and John T. Scholz. 1984. "The Criminology of the Corporation and Regulatory Enforcement Strategies." In *Enforcing Regulation*, edited by Keith Hawkins and John M. Thomas. Boston: Kluwer-Nijhoff.

Karstedt, Susanne, and Stephen Farrall. 2006. "The Moral Economy of Everyday Crime: Markets, Consumers and Citizens." *British Journal of Criminology* 46: 1011–36.

Karstedt, Susanne, and Stephen Farrall. 2007. *Law-Abiding Majority? The Everyday Crimes of the Middle Classes*. London: Kings College, Centre for Crime and Justice Studies.

Kramer, Ronald C., Raymond J. Michalowski, and David Kauzlarich. 2002. "The Origins and Development of the Concept and Theory of State-Corporate Crime." *Crime and Delinquency* 48: 263–82.

Law Reform Commission, Australia. 2001. *Sentencing: Corporate Offenders*. http://www.lawlink.nsw.gov.au/lrc.nsf/pages/ip20chp03.

Leeson, Nick, with Edward Whitley. 1996. *Rogue Trader*. Boston: Little, Brown.

Levi, Michael. 1987. *Regulating Fraud: White-Collar Crime and the Criminal Process*. London: Tavistock.

———. 2006. *Sentencing Frauds: A Review*. Cardiff, UK: School of Social Sciences, University of Cardiff.

———. 2007. "Reflections on Changes and Continuities in the Organization and Control of Bankruptcy Fraud: Introduction and Postscript to the Second Edition of the *Phantom Capitalists*." Cardiff, UK: University of Cardiff.

———. 2008. *Phantom Capitalists: The Organisation and Control of Long-Firm Fraud*. Rev. ed. Aldershot, UK: Ashgate.

Lippens, Ronnie. 2001. "Rethinking Organizational Crime and Organizational Criminology." *Crime, Law and Social Change* 35: 319–31.

Maruna, Shadd, and J. Heith Copes. 2004. "Excuses, Excuses: What Have We Learned from Five Decades of Neutralization Research?" In *Crime and Justice: A Review of Research,* vol. 32, edited by Michael Tonry. Chicago: University of Chicago Press.

May, Peter J. 2003. "Performance-Based Regulation and Regulatory Regimes: The Saga of Leaky Buildings." *Law and Policy* 4: 381–401.

Michalowski, Raymond J., and Ronald C. Kramer. 2006. *State-Corporate Crime: Wrongdoing at the Intersection of Business and Government.* Camden, NJ: Rutgers University Press.

Murphy, Diana E. 2002. "The Federal Sentencing Guidelines for Organizations: A Decade of Promoting Compliance and Ethics." *Iowa Law Review* 87: 697–719.

National Whistleblower Center. 2007. http://www.whistleblowers.org/.

Needleman, Martin L., and Carolyn Needleman. 1979. "Organizational Crime: Two Models of Criminogenesis." *Sociological Quarterly* 20: 517–28.

New York Stock Exchange. 2007. *Disciplinary Actions.* http://www.nyse.com/DiscAxn/discAxnIndex.html.

Nichols, Lawrence T. 1991. "Whistleblower or Renegade: Definitional Contests in an Official Inquiry." *Symbolic Interaction* 14: 395–414.

Nielsen, Vibeke Lehmann. 2006. "Are Regulators Responsive?" *Law and Policy* 28: 396–416.

Ott, J. Steven. 1989. *The Organizational Culture Perspective.* Pacific Grove, CA: Brooks/Cole.

Parker, Christine E., and Vibeke Lehmann Nielsen. 2005. "Do Businesses Take Compliance Systems Seriously? An Empirical Study of the Implementation of Trade Practices Compliance Systems in Australia." *Melbourne University Law Review* 30: 441–94.

Passas, Nikos, and David Nelken. 1993. "The Thin Line between Legitimate and Criminal Enterprises: Subsidy Frauds in the European Community." *Crime, Law and Social Change* 19: 223–43.

Paternoster, Raymond, and Sally Simpson. 1993. "A Rational Choice Theory of Corporate Crime." In *Routine Activity and Rational Choice,* edited by Ronald V. Clarke and Marcus Felson. New Brunswick, NJ: Transaction.

Pearce, Frank. 2001. "Crime and Capitalist Business Corporations." In *Crimes of Privilege: Readings in White-Collar Crime,* edited by Neal Shover and John Paul Wright. New York: Oxford University Press.

Petersdorf, R. G. 1989. "A Matter of Integrity." *Academic Medicine* 64: 119–23.

Piquero, Alex R., David P. Farrington, and Alfred Blumstein. 2003. "The Criminal Career Paradigm: Background and Recent Developments." In *Crime and Justice: An Annual Review of Research,* vol. 30, edited by Michael Tonry. Chicago: University of Chicago Press.

Piquero, Nicole Leeper, and Jason L. Davis. 2004. "Extralegal Factors and the Sentencing of Organizational Defendants: An Examination of the Federal Sentencing Guidelines." *Journal of Criminal Justice* 32: 643–54.

Piquero, Nicole Leeper, M. Lyn Exum, and Sally S. Simpson. 2005. "Integrating the Desire-for-Control and Rational Choice in a Corporate Crime Context." *Justice Quarterly* 22: 252–80.

Piquero, Nicole Leeper, and Alex R. Piquero. 2006. "Control Balance and Exploitative Corporate Crime." *Criminology* 44: 397–429.

PriceWaterhouseCoopers. 2006. *Global Economic Crime Survey 2005.* New York, NY: PwC.

Pring, George W., and Penelope Canan. 1996. *SLAPPS: Getting Sued for Speaking Out.* Philadelphia: Temple University Press.

Punch, Maurice. 2000. "Suite Violence: Why Managers Murder and Corporations Kill." *Crime, Law and Social Change* 33: 243–80.

Reichman, Nancy. 1993. "Insider Trading." In *Beyond the Law: Crime in Complex Organizations,* edited by Michael Tonry and Albert J. Reiss Jr. Vol. 18 of *Crime and Justice: A Review of Research,* edited by Michael Tonry. Chicago: University of Chicago Press.

Reuter, Peter. 1993. "The Cartage Industry in New York." In *Beyond the Law: Crime in Complex Organizations,* edited by Michael Tonry and Albert J. Reiss Jr. Vol. 18 of *Crime and Justice: A Review of Research,* edited by Michael Tonry. Chicago: University of Chicago Press.

Ross, Edward Alsworth. 1907. *Sin and Society.* Boston: Houghton Mifflin.

Rothschild, Joyce, and Terance D. Miethe. 1999. "Whistle-blower Disclosures and Management Retaliation: The Battle to Control Information about Organization Corruption." *Work and Organizations* 26: 107–28.

Ruggiero, Vincenzo. 1996. *Organized and Corporate Crime in Europe: Offers That Can't Be Refused.* London: Dartmouth.

Russell, Steve, and Michael J. Gilbert. 2002. "Social Control of Transnational Corporations in the Age of Marketocracy." *International Journal of the Sociology of Law* 30: 33–50.

Schlegel, Kip, David Eitle, and Steven Gunkel. 2001. "Are White-Collar Crimes Overcriminalized? Some Evidence on the Use of Criminal Sanctions against Securities Violators." *Western State University Law Review* 28: 117–40.

Schneider, Benjamin, ed. 1990. *Organizational Climate and Culture.* San Francisco: Jossey-Bass.

Schweitzer, Maurice E., Lisa Ordonez, and Bambi Douma. 2004. "Goal Setting as a Motivator of Unethical Behavior." *Academy of Management Journal* 47: 422–32.

Scott, Marvin B., and Stanford Lyman. 1968. "Accounts." *American Sociological Review* 33: 46–62.

Shover, Neal, and Kevin M. Bryant. 1993. "Theoretical Explanations of Corporate Crime." In *Understanding Corporate Criminality,* edited by Michael B. Blankenship. New York: Garland.

Shover, Neal, Glenn S. Coffey, and Clinton R. Sanders. 2004. "Dialing for Dollars: Opportunities, Justifications, and Telemarketing Fraud." *Qualitative Sociology* 27: 59–75.

Shover, Neal, and Andy Hochstetler. 2002. "Cultural Explanation and Organizational Crime." *Crime, Law and Social Change* 37: 1–18.

Shover, Neal, and Andy Hochstetler. 2006. *Choosing White-Collar Crime.* New York: Cambridge University Press.

Shover, Neal, and Andy Hochstetler. 2007. "Sources and Control of Financial Crime." Paper presented at the International Symposium on Financial Crime in the Context of Globalization, Renmin University of China, School of Law, Beijing, August 27.

Simpson, Sally S. 1986. "The Decomposition of Antitrust: Testing a Multi-level, Longitudinal Model of Profit-Squeeze." *American Sociological Review* 51: 859–75.

———. 1987. "Cycles of Illegality: Antitrust Violations in Corporate America." *Social Forces* 65: 943–63.

———. 2002. *Corporate Crime, Law and Social Control*. New York: Cambridge University Press.

Simpson, Sally S., and Christopher S. Koper. 1992. "Deterring Corporate Crime." *Criminology* 30: 347–75.

Simpson, Sally S., and Nicole Leeper Piquero. 2002. "Low Self-control, Organizational Theory and Corporate Crime." *Law and Society Review* 36: 509–48.

Solow, Steven P. 2003. "Environmental Crime Update: What Is the State of Federal Environmental Crime Enforcement?" Paper presented at the 32nd annual American Bar Association, Section on Environment, Energy and Resources, Conference on Environmental Law, Keystone, CO, March.

Sonnenfeld, Jeffrey, and Paul R. Lawrence. 1978. "Why Do Companies Succumb to Price Fixing?" *Harvard Business Review* 56: 145–57.

Staw, Barry M., and Eugene Szwajkowski. 1975. "The Scarcity Munificence Component of Organizational Environments and the Commission of Illegal Acts." *Administrative Science Quarterly* 20: 345–54.

Stretesky, Paul B. 2006. "Corporate Self Policing and the Environment." *Criminology* 44: 671–708.

Sutherland, Edwin H. 1983. *White-Collar Crime: The Uncut Version*. With an introduction by Gilbert Geis and Colin Goff. New Haven, CT: Yale University Press. (Originally published 1949.)

Sykes, Gresham, and David Matza. 1957. "Techniques of Neutralization: A Theory of Delinquency." *American Sociological Review* 22: 667–70.

Szockyj, Elizabeth, and Gilbert Geis. 2002. "Insider Trading: Patterns and Analysis." *Journal of Criminal Justice* 30: 273–86.

Tittle, Charles R. 1995. *Control Balance: Toward a General Theory of Deviance*. Boulder, CO: Westview.

———. 2004. "Refining Control Balance Theory." *Theoretical Criminology* 8: 395–428.

Trevino, Linda K., Gary R. Weaver, and Scott J. Reynolds. 2006. "Behavioral Ethics in Organizations: A Review." *Journal of Management* 32: 951–90.

U.S. Department of Justice. 2002. *Justice Department Recovers over $1 Billion in FY 2002: False Claims Act Recoveries Exceed $10 Billion Since 1986*. http://www.usdoj.gov/opa/pr/2002/December/02_civ_720.htm.

———. 2005. *Justice Department Recovers $1.4 Billion in Fraud and False Claims in Fiscal Year 2005: More Than $15 Billion Since 1986*. http://www.usdoj.gov/opa/pr/2005/November/05_civ_595.html.

———. 2006. *Financial Crimes Report to the Public, Fiscal Year 2006*. http://www.fbi.gov/publications/financial/fcs_report2006/financial_crime_2006.htm#CorporateFraud.

———. 2007. *Fact Sheet: President's Corporate Fraud Task Force Marks Five Years of Ensuring Corporate Integrity*. http://www.usdoj.gov/opa/pr/2007/July/07_odag_507.html.

U.S. Department of Labor, Office of Investigative Assistance. 2007. *The Whistleblower Program*. http://www.osha.gov/dep/oia/whistleblower/index.html.

U.S. Environmental Protection Agency. 2007. *Compliance and Enforcement: Annual Results—FY 2006*. http://epa.gov/compliance/data/results/annual/fy2006.html.

U.S. Office of Special Counsel. 2007. *Whistleblower Disclosures*. http://www.osc.gov/wbdisc.htm.

U.S. Sentencing Commission. 1995. *Organizational Sentencing Practices*. http://www.ussc.gov/corp/1995org.PDF.

———. 1995–2007. *Sourcebook of Federal Sentencing Statistics*. http://www.ussc.gov/ANNRPT/2006/SBTOC06.htm.
———. 2007. *Organizational Guidelines*. http://www.ussc.gov/orgguide.htm.
———. n.d. *The Federal Sentencing Guidelines for Organizational Crimes: Questions and Answers*. Washington, DC: U.S. Sentencing Commission. http://www.ussc.gov/training/corpq&&a.pdf.
Vaughan, Diane. 1996. *The Challenger Launch Decision: Risky Technology, Culture, and Deviance at NASA*. Chicago: University of Chicago Press.
———. 2007. "Beyond Macro- and Micro-Levels of Analysis: Organizations and the Cultural Fix." In *International Handbook of White-Collar and Corporate Crime*, edited by Henry N. Pontell and Gilbert Geis. New York: Springer.
von Hirsch, Andrew, Anthony E. Bottoms, Elizabeth Burney, and P.-O. Wikstrom. 1999. *Criminal Deterrence and Sentence Severity: An Analysis of Recent Research*. Portland, OR: Hart.
Weisburd, David, Stanton Wheeler, Elin Waring, and Nancy Bode. 1991. *Crimes of the Middle Classes*. New Haven, CT: Yale University Press.
Yeager, Peter Cleary. 1986. "Analyzing Corporate Offenses: Progress and Prospects." In *Research in Corporate Social Performance and Policy*, vol. 8, edited by James E. Post. Greenwich, CT: JAI.
———. 1993. "Industrial Water Pollution." In *Beyond the Law: Crime in Complex Organizations*, edited by Michael Tonry and Albert J. Reiss Jr. Vol. 18 of *Crime and Justice: A Review of Research*, edited by Michael Tonry. Chicago: University of Chicago Press.
———. 2007. "Understanding Corporate Lawbreaking: From Profit Seeking to Law Finding." In *International Handbook of White-Collar and Corporate Crime*, edited by Henry N. Pontell and Gilbert Geis. New York: Springer.

CHAPTER 12

ORGANIZED CRIME

JAMES FINCKENAUER

It seems that everyone has a view of what organized crime is. They know something about the "mob" and "gangsters," which they mostly associate with the "mafia." They also know something about what the government, that is, the FBI, is doing about it. How do they know this? Most people's knowledge of organized crime is vicarious rather than direct, and it comes from the popular media, especially movies and television. The best examples are *The Godfather* films and the enormously successful TV series *The Sopranos.* And it is not only the general public who are so informed, but also public officials and law enforcement authorities. This means that the popular culture images of organized crime have a surprisingly large influence on organized crime control policy (see Smith 1975; Finckenauer 2007). A mafia stereotype has been promulgated by the media. This stereotype, which equates nearly all organized crime with the mafia, has had and continues to have serious implications for our ability to appreciate the threat of organized crime and to combat it.

The overreliance on media portrayals should not be taken to mean that there has not been serious scholarly work on organized crime. An eclectic mix of excellent book-length sources include works by Cressey ([1969] 2008), Albini (1971), Ianni (1972), Chambliss (1988), Anderson (1979), Reuter (1983), Gambetta (1993), Stille (1995), Finckenauer and Waring (1998), Jacobs (1999), Naylor (2002), Godson (2003), and Raab (2006). The journal *Trends in Organized Crime* regularly publishes current studies and reports on both domestic and transnational organized crime, and the National Criminal Justice Reference Service (http://www.ncjrs.gov) of the U.S. Department of Justice catalogues a host of reports on these subjects.

Anticipating the discussion that follows, my principal conclusions and observations are these:

- With respect to organized crime control policy, there is a need for constant vigilance to avoid the moral hazards and unacceptable costs presented by controversial and sensitive investigative and prosecutorial methods.
- There is very little hard empirical evidence of success of the various means for combating organized crime.
- There are strong arguments that a control policy that continues to focus exclusively on individual criminals and criminal organizations will not make a serious dent in the organized crime problem.
- Much greater collaboration between researchers, practitioners, and policy makers is needed to better understand organized crime and to improve the effectiveness of methods to combat it.
- Much more attention must be devoted to prevention-oriented approaches to organized crime.

My aim is to examine current U.S. organized crime control policy and its attendant practices in light of some recent criticisms that have been leveled against it. This first requires establishing the context for the policy: What is it about the nature and character of criminal organizations and organized crime that might (as some argue) require special, even extraordinary means for combating them? Second, given this extraordinary nature of various organized crime control practices, what are the risks and costs associated with their use? Specifically, are there moral hazard costs, that is, ethical or moral issues or issues of legitimacy raised by the use of certain methods? Third is the question of efficacy: Just how effective are the various tools in the U.S. policy tool kit for combating organized crime? Fourth, I turn to the most fundamental question for policy makers: Do the ends justify the means? Policies and practices that might be quite effective may nevertheless be deemed unacceptable because they are not considered the right thing to do. Here, "right" can mean legal and constitutional as well as moral and ethical. Are the risks and moral hazards inherent in particular organized crime control strategies and tactics justifiable when weighed against their demonstrated effectiveness?

I. What Is *Organized* Crime?

The "crime" part of organized crime is not what gives it its particular character. Murder, robbery, theft, assault, and even threats and conspiracies to commit same are, after all, part of the repertoire of individual criminals as well as of unorganized and disorganized collections of criminals. Certain crimes by their nature can be committed only by groups of people possessing some level of organization; various types of transnational crime involving the trafficking of drugs or guns or people across national borders are examples. These crimes require planning and groups of people to carry them out. The groups do not necessarily have to be recognized or traditional organized crime per se, but the crimes themselves have to be organized in some sense.

These latter crimes that are organized differ from organized crime in that they typically entail the opportunistic coming together of a group of criminals to exploit a specific criminal opportunity. Depending on the nature of the crime, the offenders must have the necessary expertise or skills required to carry it out. Truck hijackings, for example, require the ability to drive; money laundering demands some knowledge of accounting and banking; human smuggling and trafficking require knowledge of immigration laws and documentation. Once the criminal opportunity has been exploited, the offenders operating in this fashion tend then to go their own ways. They, or at least some of them, may come together again to commit another crime, but they don't usually stay together.

A key difference, therefore, between this particular form of crime and true organized crime is that those engaged in the latter have continuity over time and over crimes. This distinction has important implications. Most frequently used investigative methods assume this kind of continuity. When offenders compose a kind of amorphous, free-floating network, it is measurably more difficult to target them.

Given these distinctions, what is it about criminal organizations and the crimes they commit that warrant special attention? One answer is their capacity for harm. The crimes of all criminals are harmful, but the crimes of criminal organizations are especially so. If we think of criminal harms as being of four types—economic, physical, psychological, and societal (see Maltz 1990)—then we can consider whether certain configurations of criminals have greater capacity for causing these harms. By configurations, I mean organization.

Let me propose first that groups of criminals have greater harm capacity than individual criminals.[1] Second, among criminal groups those that possess more of certain characteristics have greater harm capacity than those that possess less. In particular, criminal organizations that are larger, that are more criminally sophisticated (use planning, knowledge, and skill in committing their crimes), whose structure is characterized by a division of labor and stability, whose members clearly identify themselves as members of a particular organization, and that have the authority of reputation (have the ability to intimidate) have greater capacity for committing economic, physical, psychological, and societal harm than do criminal organizations that have less of each of these characteristics.

It is what we might think of as "high-end" criminal organizations that present the greatest challenge for policy makers. What criminal organizations generally fit this classification? The Italian mafia, La Cosa Nostra, and the Chinese Triads qualify. So do certain outlaw motorcycle gangs, such as the Hells Angels. Criminal organizations such as these use corruption as an insurance policy to protect themselves from law enforcement. In so doing they undermine the credibility and integrity of the political and judicial processes. They often seek to gain monopoly control over particular criminal enterprises so as to maximize profits and eliminate competition. Above all, they use violence and the threat of violence to intimidate victims and witnesses and generally to facilitate their criminal activities.

Another characteristic of organized crime that creates particular problems in combating it is that criminal organizations generally deal in illegal or regulated goods and services. Drugs, prostitution, and gambling are examples; so too are cigarettes, alcohol, firearms, stolen cars, and babies for adoption, and services such as illegal waste disposal. The law says these things are illegal or restricted in some fashion. Enough people, however, continue to want them that meeting the demand is a profitable—often enormously profitable—business. The purchasers of the illicit goods and services—people who often regard themselves as honest, upright citizens—are in reality the enablers of much of organized crime.

This particular aspect of organized crime activity feeds hypocrisy and corruption and fuels ongoing debates about legalization, decriminalization, and deregulation. The prime historical example is the U.S. experience with Prohibition in the 1920s.

II. Prevalence, Trends, and Costs

If one looks to any of the usual sources of data and information on crime, such as FBI Uniform Crime Reports, to get information about organized crime, nothing will be found. There are no listings of arrests, prosecutions, and convictions for organized crime. There are no prevalence or trend data. This is because organized crime, like white-collar crime, is not a specific legal category. It is a composite of other crimes. This absence of specification, when combined with organized crime's clandestine character, makes it very difficult (impossible?) to get a precise handle on its costs and scale. For instance, La Cosa Nostra monopoly control of the waste carting business in New York City through the 1990s clearly increased the costs of waste disposal for every business and residential building in the city. But by exactly how much is incalculable. The same is true of La Cosa Nostra domination of the Teamsters Union, which meant that the cost of every item that traveled by truck had a cost add-on passed on to consumers.

Any attempt to get a sense of just how much organized crime there is, whether it is increasing or decreasing, and what its costs are to society must rely on a mosaic of estimates derived from what are believed to be relevant dimensions of organized crime. What follows is one such mosaic.

An international business research organization, FIA International Research, Ltd., issued a report in 2001 on so-called cargo crime (dealing in contraband goods and products), which is believed to be largely controlled by organized crime groups. According to the report, cargo crime accounted for estimated direct merchandise losses worldwide of as much as $50 billion a year. The losses in the United States alone were estimated to be $25 billion. Contraband tobacco, the report said, is a major profit area for international organized crime. The report estimates that the global market for smuggled cigarettes costs $16 billion a year in lost tax revenues, and that one-tenth of those losses, or an estimated $1.75 billion, was incurred in the United States. With respect to the counterfeiting of goods, the estimate was that American manufacturers are losing $200 billion a year because of fake versions of their products. Although we know that not all of these losses are due to organized crime, we do not know just what proportion is.

In a later report to the U.S. Congress by the Congressional Research Service (Wagley 2006), the counterfeit loss figure was raised to between $200 and $250 billion per year in lost sales. The trade in counterfeit goods has grown eight times faster than legitimate trade since the early 1990s, according to Interpol (2007). Interpol further reports that New York City, for example, annually loses about $500 million in state sales tax revenue due to the sale of counterfeit goods. Again, however, how much of this is specifically attributable to organized crime is unknown.

The CRS report also offered a number of other observations bearing on the costs and scale of organized crime (Wagley 2006). For instance, it is estimated that every year illegal drugs kill about 17,000 Americans. In addition to the human toll, illicit drugs are estimated to result in about $160 billion in social and economic costs (lost productivity, health care, etc.) and $67 billion in direct costs (law enforcement, treatment, rehabilitation, etc.) in the United States annually. The illicit drug trade is valued at between $500 and $900 billion worldwide. The lion's share (admittedly an ambiguous amount!) of these figures is attributable to organized crime. The same is true of international car theft, where Interpol (2007) estimates that the illicit trafficking of vehicles is a form of organized crime that generates huge profits, estimated at $19 billion per year.

The CRS congressional report also dealt with human trafficking for sexual exploitation or forced labor, citing an FBI estimate that human trafficking generates about $9.5 billion annually for its perpetrators (some of whom are suspected of organized crime involvement) (Wagley 2006). The report estimated that 600,000 to 800,000 people are trafficked across international borders annually. When combined with domestic trafficking, the total was believed to be between two and four million. With respect to money laundering, a crime very much associated with organized crime, the CRS estimated that it is valued at 2 to 5 percent of world GDP, which is currently about $50 trillion.

The Internet is another area where organized crime has a growing presence (Williams 2002). According to Williams, there are a number of disturbing trends: use of the Internet for major fraud and theft activities by organized crime groups; infiltration of Wall Street by U.S. and Russian criminal organizations employing stock manipulations known as "pump and dump" schemes; Internet-related stock frauds amounting to $10 billion a year in losses for investors; use of the Internet for money laundering; and cybercrimes linked to organized crime originating in jurisdictions having few or lax laws regulating such activities.

It is a safe assumption that a significant proportion of all the crimes outlined above are attributable to organized crime. Why can we assume this? Because the complexity of organization and sophistication necessary to carry them out, the political connections required, and the ability to intimidate and monopolize that is reflected in the commission of these crimes are all hallmarks of true organized crime groups. This is troubling. Even more troubling are the indications that crime is increasing in all of these areas.

III. The Challenge for Policy

Determining that a crime has been committed and who has committed it requires information. Information about crimes and criminals usually comes to the police in one of several ways. Officers may observe a crime in progress (quite rare); a crime is reported to police (the usual way); or police gain information through surveillance and intelligence collection (the usual way when organized crime is involved).

Criminal organizations are very adept at keeping information about themselves and their criminal activities from coming to the authorities. Although the lowest level members may be exposed to police detection and citizen crime reporting, the higher-ups are not. They are insulated and protected by hierarchical or pyramid-like structures. Sometimes criminal activities are arranged in cell-like structures in which the cells are isolated, and people in one cell do not know who is in another cell and what they may be doing. If and when there is exposure, or the possibility of exposure, violence or threats of violence or corruption is used to eliminate it.

The challenge for law enforcement is finding out who is doing what, to prosecute those responsible, and to eliminate the criminal enterprise: "How do we cripple national and international organized crime syndicates that strangle free enterprise and raise the level of violence, fraud, and corruption in our cities? By using every capability and tool we've got: undercover operations; surveillance; confidential sources; intelligence analysis and sharing; forensic accounting; multi-agency investigations; and the power of racketeering statutes that help us take down entire enterprises. We also work closely with our international partners—in some cases, swapping personnel—to build cases and disrupt syndicates with global ties" (Federal Bureau of Investigation 2007). The core element of U.S. organized crime policy is the seeking of information about the who, what, and how of criminal enterprises. The majority of the approaches pursued have this objective. Before examining such practices as wiretapping, the use of informants, immunity, and witness protection, and their justification and efficacy, let us turn to the criticisms mentioned at the outset.

IV. Critical Perspectives on U.S. Organized Crime Policy

There is no shortage of opinions about U.S. policy with respect to combating organized crime. Some are positive, some negative, and some are mixed. A few Canadian and European experts have been particularly critical of what they regard as the overemphasis on get-tough, law-and-order, and mostly supply-side approaches entailed in U.S. efforts. The few examples that follow are intended to be illustrative of the negative criticism. It will be noted that these examples share a common theme.

Woodiwiss and Bewley-Taylor (2005) strongly argue that U.S. organized crime policy wrongly emphasizes coercive and law enforcement measures and utterly fails to address the root causes of organized crime. Instead of seeking to reduce opportunities for harmful activity, the U.S. concern, they say, focuses on arresting and punishing harmful people. Although many important criminal convictions have been gained, "they have not significantly affected the extent of organized crime activity" (p. 24). Moreover, according to these authors, this approach has infected the international policy arena:

> The current international response to transnational organized crime is inadequate, misdirected and in many ways counter-productive. This is largely because the international community has accepted an understanding of organized crime that closely resembles the limited and "blame-shifting" approach of the United States to the problem. The international community, represented most prominently by the United Nations (UN), therefore seeks to control transnational organized crime using methods pioneered in the United States.... The "dumbing down" of public and professional understanding of organized crime in the United States... [and] the impact of [the] nation's moral crusade against such activities as gambling and drugs... [led to] most Americans [thinking] the problem was synonymous with a foreign crime group usually known as the Mafia. (p. 5)

Instead, they suggest, "the key to understanding organized crime is opportunity." It is the chance to make large illegal profits with minimal risks that encourages organized crime. The focus of organized crime control policy, according to this thinking, should be on eliminating or minimizing criminal opportunities and not on simply catching bad guys.

In a similar vein, Paoli and Fijnaut (2006) criticized what they call the "one-sidedness" and the "predominantly repressive bias" of recently developed organized crime control policy in Europe. They too suggest that a preventive approach to organized crime has been largely neglected. Although they did not attribute this to the undue influence of the United States, the implication seems clear.

Marcus Felson (2006) referred to what he called "the dramatic fallacy" that distorts the image of organized crime in the United States. He argued that misplaced attention on the most dramatic crimes and criminal organizations creates an intellectual distraction. The derivative policy that focuses on "big fish" then lets many smaller fish swim free: "The most common prescription for controlling organized crime is to cut off the head—to find and arrest the most important offenders. I would argue that it makes more sense to *cut off the feet*, that is, to remove or impair the settings where cooperative crime meets the public or where small-time criminals meet one another. The point is that organized crime is most vulnerable in its most public settings. Moreover, those settings are most subject to situational interference with minimal arrests" (p. 12).

Felson (2006) proposed that the way to combat organized crime is to focus on the acts and not the criminal groups. Forget the bosses, he says, and instead monitor and thwart the opportunities for small-time crime. This is similar to Woodiwiss and Bewley-Taylor's (2005) idea of focusing on harmful acts as opposed to harmful people. And it echoes Paoli and Fijnaut's (2006) view that more attention be devoted to the prevention of organized crime.

In sum, these critics more or less strongly suggest that U.S. organized crime control policy is misdirected, that it neglects preventive approaches, and that it has been less than effective. A number of other authorities agree with these criticisms, particularly with respect to effectiveness—and most specifically with the general absence of definitive information concerning effectiveness. Other scholars, for example Braithwaite (2000) and Jacobs (2007), give credit to a shift in U.S. policy that has moved toward a regulatory strategy, denying licenses to mob-controlled businesses, and monitoring the cleansing of mob-controlled unions. These steps are very much in line with what critics like Woodiwiss et al. have been calling for.

Before I discuss the critical effectiveness question, it may be useful to summarize what some of the principal operatives and advocates of existing policy have to say.

V. From the Front Lines

Bruce Ohr is the chief of the Organized Crime and Racketeering Section in the Criminal Division of the U.S. Department of Justice. He has more direct, day-to-day responsibility for organized crime policy than any other U.S. official. Speaking before a Japanese forum in 2000, Ohr described in some detail what he called "effective methods" to combat organized crime.

William J. Nardini is an assistant U.S. attorney responsible for carrying out this policy. His assessment of the legal tools used to investigate and prosecute organized crime in the United States is contained in a recent paper, "The Prosecutor's Toolbox" (Nardini 2006).

Ohr (2000, p. 47) stressed that the fight against organized crime and transnational organized crime would continue to "rely first and foremost on the investigative techniques and prosecutive tools developed in our long struggles against the American Mafia." Ironically, this is just what critics such as those cited above say is wrong with U.S. policy. Before I comment on that disagreement, a look at the techniques and tools being extolled by Ohr and others responsible for U.S. organized crime policy is called for.

A. Electronic Surveillance

According to Ohr (2000, p. 47), electronic surveillance (wiretaps and eavesdropping) "represents the single most important law enforcement weapon against organized crime." The tapping of phones, the monitoring of phone numbers through pen register systems, and the installation of listening devices illustrate the critical importance of information, and in particular insider information, discussed earlier. An argument for the use of electronic surveillance is that those in the upper reaches of criminal organizations may be exposed only through their own words, discussing crimes and conspiring to commit new crimes. Nardini (2006, p. 531) writes, "Not only can electronic surveillance give investigators a window into the operations of the group, but it also provides some of the most compelling evidence at an eventual trial." Juries in criminal trials are greatly influenced by hearing defendants describing their own criminal activities. Their words are almost as good as a confession, and this is therefore a very powerful prosecutorial tool. It is not, however, one that is risk-free.

In line with the criticisms discussed earlier, electronic surveillance focuses on what are believed to be harmful individuals as opposed to focusing on harmful acts. The investigators and prosecutors target persons they have probable cause to believe have engaged in or are currently engaging in criminal activity. These are usually targets in the upper echelons of an organization, the bosses or big fish. They are not the low-level players suggested for attention by Felson (2006); they are not likely to be targeted for electronic surveillance because doing so is not feasible in terms of costs and benefits, and it would be difficult to satisfy a judge (from whom permission must be received) that no other less-intrusive investigative methods are possible with such low-level suspects.

Even more important, electronic surveillance techniques constitute an invasion of privacy. Personal and private conversations are listened to and recorded by government agents. Although there is monitoring and there are restrictions on its use, mistakes and abuses nevertheless occur. Thus investigators, prosecutors, and judges are supposed to weigh the potential costs and benefits carefully in requesting and approving permits for surveillance. These very same issues are, of course, raised in the current war on terrorism. In both instances, the privacy of harmful or potentially harmful people is invaded by electronic means. This technique represents a classic illustration of the dilemma of whether the ends justify the means.

B. Undercover Operations

Another way to penetrate a criminal organization is through the use of undercover agents. Ohr (2000) suggested that this approach is second only to electronic surveillance in its value for investigating organized crime. It too is a way of seeking inside information that might lead to arrest and prosecution, and it too targets what are regarded as harmful individuals and groups. The risks include the possibility of entrapment. Undercover investigators, in their zeal to uncover crimes and in their desire to portray themselves as true members of the organization, may cross the line that prohibits fomenting or instigating criminal behavior. Crossing that sometimes ambiguous line will severely jeopardize the prosecutor's ability to use the fruits of the investigation.

A second risk with undercover investigations concerns the safety of the agents involved. These agents have to live three lives—as government agent, as pseudo-mobster, and as whoever they are in their personal life—a balance that is difficult to maintain. The story of FBI agent Joe Pistone (1987) as told in the book and movie (1997) *Donnie Brasco* is an excellent illustration of the risks and hazards involved.

C. Informants

Just as government agents are used to get inside a criminal organization to gain information, other private or nongovernmental persons may be used for this purpose. Who best knows what a criminal organization might be up to, how they are doing whatever they are doing, and who is doing it? Somebody on the inside or who can get inside and be privy to this information. Consequently, investigators and prosecutors hire paid informants or they use various tools for what Nardini (2006, p. 533) described as "incentivizing cooperation among criminals."

Bruce Ohr (2000, p. 49) described the use of informants as follows: "Confidential informants are typically motivated to provide information to the authorities in exchange for money or lenient treatment regarding charges pending against them or likely to be brought against them. In many cases confidential informants are themselves engaged in criminal activities which enables them to provide valuable direct evidence of criminal activities by their criminal associates. Confidential informants frequently provide the information that enables law enforcement officials to obtain judicial warrants authorizing electronic surveillance."

The focus is again on bad guys and their organization. Weighing against the potential benefits of the information that might be gained are considerable risks. Informants are usually criminals (often serious criminals) whose continuing crimes might be ignored or seemingly condoned in exchange for the information they pass on to police. But who is to say that some crimes are more or less harmful than other crimes? Certainly to their victims the crimes of informants are not less harmful. In addition to their criminality, informants may provide false information to implicate their enemies or drive out their competition. These are, after all, not particularly trustworthy people.

One of the most egregious examples of the abuse of the informant system, and of how this sort of "getting into bed with the devil" can have severe consequences, was the FBI's mishandling of the Boston gangster James "Whitey" Bulger and his gang during the 1990s (see *United States v. Connolly*, 341F.3d 16 [1st Cir. 2003]; Lehr and O'Neill 2001). Agents corrupted by their supposed informant Bulger permitted a virtual crime spree to take place in the Boston area. The FBI special agent handling Bulger was convicted of racketeering, obstructing justice, and making false statements to federal investigators. It was determined that the agent had been co-opted by the very criminal group he was supposedly investigating. Though certainly not a proud moment in FBI history, this case has the potential benefit of raising a red flag with respect to the hazards involved in the practice of using informants.

Cognizant of its dangers, Bruce Ohr (2000, p. 50) nevertheless concluded as follows with respect to informant policy: "On balance...experience teaches us that as a general rule, the benefits from the use of informants greatly outweigh the risks. But, we must be ever vigilant of the risks."

D. Immunity

Sticking with the goal of seeking inside information and of sometimes having to rely on shady characters to get it, a technique that shares certain elements with the use of informants is that of offering immunity from prosecution in return for testimony. The Fifth Amendment to the U.S. Constitution gives every individual the right to refuse to testify against himself or herself. Among the persons who may, and do, avail themselves of this right are members or suspected members of organized crime groups. "The immunity system allows the government to force an individual to testify in return for a promise that the testimony may not be used against the witness in any subsequent criminal case.... [A court order granting 'use' immunity is sought] when, in the judgment of the government, the testimony or other information is necessary to the public interest and the individual has asserted or is likely to assert his or her privilege against self-incrimination" (Ohr 2000, pp. 53–54).

As with the other methods described, the practice of granting immunity can be and has been abused. *Use immunity* is a circumscribed grant of immunity. *Transactional immunity* is much broader; used by the federal government until 1970, it immunized persons against prosecution for any transaction related to their testimony or other provision of evidence. Under the transactional form there was risk of criminals receiving in effect an "immunity bath." Criminals would abuse the system by offering up mere crumbs of information or false testimony in return for large grants of blanket immunity.

Sometimes individuals refuse to testify even after being granted immunity and ordered to testify. In such cases, prosecutors or investigative bodies may then move to have them held in contempt for this refusal. In the 1970s, for example, the New Jersey State Commission of Investigation held several suspected mobsters in prison for lengthy periods because of their refusal to testify after being granted immunity. These individuals had neither been charged nor convicted of a crime but were nevertheless imprisoned. Here, the end—the value and importance of an individual's testimony—must be justified against the means: overriding an individual's constitutional protection against self-incrimination and forcing him or her to testify.

E. Witness Protection Programs

Threatening individuals and their families is one way organized crime protects itself against prosecution. Both insiders (the vast majority of protected witnesses have criminal records) and outsiders who have direct knowledge of criminal activity that would be critical to a successful prosecution can be intimidated and prevented from testifying or otherwise disclosing what they know to the authorities. Witness protection was devised as a way of overcoming their understandable reluctance.

The U.S. Department of Justice created the Federal Witness Security Program in 1970. Since then, roughly 7,000 witnesses and 10,000 family members have been admitted into the program. The average costs are $75,000 per witness and $125,000 per family—a not insubstantial sum. Ohr (2000, p. 55) concluded that the program has been worth the price: "Since its inception... over 10,000 defendants have been convicted through the testimony of witnesses in the Program.... Overall, the Witness Security Program has proven to be extremely beneficial and effective in the prosecution against organized crime groups."

In their independent assessment Fyfe and Sheptycki (2006, p. 322) are much less laudatory: "The government's policy of witness protection appeared to place harm to the public from organized crime above harm to the public from protecting witnesses." These authors describe, for example, the "unintended victims of witness relocation," for example, individuals and organizations unable to recover debts from witnesses and dependents; nonrelocated parents denied access to their children taken into the program; and the receiving communities where witnesses are moved, keeping in mind that most relocated witnesses are criminals. They also describe an understaffed and undertrained U.S. Marshals Service that has led to breaches in security. Fyfe and Sheptycki conclude that "witness protection programs clearly deal with the symptoms rather than the causes of intimidation. They are concerned with 'risk minimization' not the reasons behind witness intimidation" (p. 333).

F. Forfeiture

The principal goal of criminal organizations is to make money. To the extent that they seek power and political influence, it is toward the ultimate end of facilitating the making of more money. It is this characteristic that primarily distinguishes criminal organizations (organized crime) from terrorist organizations. Given this, taking the profit out of crime through forfeiture laws has become a major tactic used in combating organized crime.

Forfeiture provisions permit judges to order convicted defendants to forfeit all profits or proceeds derived from criminal activity. In addition to any cash and financial instruments such as stocks and bonds, these proceeds can include homes, cars, boats, airplanes, jewelry, and clothes. There are both criminal and civil forfeiture laws; the latter are the most far-reaching in their scope in that property used in the facilitation of crime, even though not a direct fruit of the crime, can also be seized.

The forfeiture of items such as homes and cars affects not only defendants themselves, but also their family. Thus the consequences can be quite significant. There is a risk that innocent victims will be punished through these seizures. For example, when union pension funds were seized by the U.S. government after union leaders were convicted of operating a racketeering enterprise, innocent union members suffered the loss of their pensions. Ironically, this was a double victimization for them. In the first instance, their pension funds were being exploited by mobsters, and in the second they were taken by the government.

Ohr's (2000, p. 56) assessment was that "criminal and civil forfeiture laws are powerful weapons in the prosecutor's arsenal to take the profit out of crime." As an element of criminal sentencing, forfeiture can be viewed in terms of its achievement of certain sentencing goals, and in this instance, deterrence and retribution seem the most applicable. Whether those are actually being achieved through present practice is unsubstantiated.

G. The Racketeer Influenced and Corrupt Organizations Act

I have saved until last discussion of what is generally agreed to be the most powerful weapon in the law enforcement arsenal against organized crime: the Racketeer Influenced and Corrupt Organizations Act (RICO) that was part of the Organized Crime Control Act of 1970. The power of RICO rests in its giving prosecutors the ability to get at the bosses of organized crime groups through linking them to a criminal enterprise that is shown to be engaging in a pattern of racketeering activity, and in the severe penalties that include life imprisonment and heavy fines and forfeitures. Prosecutors do not have to establish that higher-ups are directly involved in crime, and the punishments available can be used as incentives (i.e., threats) to get little fish to give up bigger fish.

RICO incorporated a host of state and federal felonies as possible predicate offenses. If any member of a criminal enterprise has been convicted of any of these crimes within the past 10 years, then all the members of the enterprise can be charged under RICO. As Nardini (2006, p. 536) described it, "[RICO links] together a number of crimes committed by various subsets of participants, so long as they all relate to the activities of a *single overarching criminal enterprise....* The government must prove the existence of the enterprise, and that any given defendant participated in a 'pattern of racketeering activity' comprising at least two qualifying offenses." These two offenses, one the predicate and one a current offense, must have been committed within a 10-year period.

Ohr (2000) said RICO recognized that organized crime is made up of many crimes, and that all are linked through a single chain of command to the same enterprise. "In essence," he said, "RICO made it a crime to be in the business of being a criminal" (p. 50). He concluded with this very strong assessment: "It is evident that the control of organized crime in the United States would be inconceivable without RICO" (p. 51).

So what are its downsides? And how effective has RICO been? The answer to the first question is that there are many risks and costs. Based on interviews with 23 judges, prosecutors, and defense attorneys, Urbina and Kreitzer (2004) reported a number of negative consequences. For example, 14 defense attorneys indicated that given that big fish and little fish are mixed together, it is difficult to separate them, and the reasonable doubt standard may get stretched to cover "peripheral players." At least one prosecutor agreed that RICO has a net-widening effect to include persons who would not normally be charged. Some judges expressed concern that the law is too broad and vague, that due process is devalued, and that civil liberties are diminished when people are charged on the basis of limited or questionable evidence.

Other critics and court challenges to RICO have argued that although RICO is a powerful tool, it has on occasion been applied injudiciously and indiscriminately. Prosecutors are accused of wielding RICO against groups for which it was never intended and of threatening such groups with labeling as "mafia" organizations.

Do the ends justify the means with RICO? We saw what Ohr (2000) had to say. In the Urbina and Kreitzer (2004) study, 15 respondents indicated that RICO's benefits do not outweigh its costs, and seven said they did. Of course, we should bear in mind that 14 members of the sample were defense attorneys! One of the prosecutors spoke volumes on the ends-means issue with this observation: "The ends justify the means in RICO. Some small people may have to go down to get the larger people" (quoted in Urbina and Kreitzer 2004, p. 310).

VI. The Efficacy of Organized Crime Control Policy

Unfortunately in the case of RICO, as with all of the other methods described, there are no hard empirical data on which to base informed judgments about its effectiveness. What we have is mostly anecdotal information of the case-specific variety on which subjective judgments are formed. Most analysts would agree that what is sorely lacking in the organized crime policy area—as in so many others—is rigorous and independent evaluation of the effectiveness of any of the major anticrime measures. This complicates and compromises our ability to address the kinds of questions about means and ends that I posed earlier.

Among the very few efforts to find and assess the efficacy of organized crime control measures I describe, two recent ones show more about the rudimentary state of policy analysis with regard to organized crime policy than about the effectiveness of any policies and practices. One attempt to collect this sort of information is described in what is called an "evidence-based critique" paper (Levi and Maguire 2004). Levi and Maguire concluded that despite all the laws aimed at combating organized crime passed during the 1990s, "there have been no major research studies in any key areas that conform to the normal canons of evaluation" (p. 407).

Reflecting criticisms of the predominant tunnel-vision approach to organized crime that relies almost exclusively on law enforcement, their premise is that there must be two core elements in any organized crime control policy: a focus on harmful acts to prevent or reduce particular forms of serious crime and a focus on harmful actors to reduce the growth and development of organized crime groups. Echoing the Felson (2006) criticism discussed earlier, Levi and Maguire (2004) challenge the assumption of most organized crime fighters that disrupting organized crime groups and arresting their leaders will reduce crime. This assumption, they say, is not self-evident. "Action against dominant groups may lead to greater levels of violence... as competitors seek to take advantage of an opportunity which formerly was regulated by an internal criminal market" (p. 401). A reduction in the number of organized crime groups may result in a consolidation of criminal power among the remaining groups. This would have no effect on reducing the overall crime rate, and the opposite may occur. This is consistent with the view that reactive picking off of individual targets, in the prevailing focus on harmful actors, fails to do anything about the structures and conditions that facilitate criminal enterprises and the rise of criminal organizations.

Levi and Maguire (2004) analyzed survey and case study data mainly from European countries collected in 2000, seeking examples of successful and unsuccessful efforts against organized crime. They found almost no evaluative data in any of the responses. "It is not surprising that this research study found little evidence of use of any particularly detailed and systematic analysis in initiatives against organized crime. The examples of 'good practice' obtained were predominantly law enforcement operations. Most comprised what may be described as primarily 'repressive' police operations relying on standard intelligence gathering methods such as the use of informants, surveillance and/or financial investigation" (p. 457). It is safe to say that a similar undertaking in the United States would produce similar results.

Unlike some of the critics cited earlier, however, Levi and Maguire (2004) are less skeptical about the value of law enforcement measures (used together with other approaches) in combating organized crime. They suggest, for example, that there may be certain retributive effects from this approach and that the growth of criminal organizations may be inhibited. With respect to ends and means, however, goals such as retribution and deterrence have always defied precise measurement. What constitutes appropriate and just retributive criminal policies, and whether these are indeed being achieved, are subjective judgments, governed by a variety of political and societal conditions. Deterrence is also impossible to measure. How many youth would have joined criminal organizations, how many criminal organizations came into or went out of existence or grew or diminished because of particular policies and practices? We do not know, nor can we know in any reliable way. Perhaps the one saving grace here is that organized crime control policy is no different in this respect from any other crime control policy.

The second analysis is from an as yet unpublished paper by Allan Castle (2007) of the Royal Canadian Mounted Police. He assessed recent data and other materials provided by a variety of law enforcement agencies in the United States and elsewhere. Castle's conclusions are in line with much of what critics of organized crime control policy have said and largely concur with those of Levi and Maguire (2004). Castle agrees that the policy focus is on agents (the harmful actors) rather than outcomes (the harmful acts). The focus is on "legislative tools designed to identify and incapacitate those agents, and towards measurements of success in terms of tangible impacts on those agents themselves. Lost is a sense of urgency to demonstrate *why* we continue to focus resources on this hard-to define criminal population, let alone how we are doing in that area. To go after the group presumes that the group contributes to one or more social ills and that removing that group will have a demonstrable and proportionate benefit to society. The rub is in the latter statement and in ignoring that we have confused the means with the ends" (Castle 2007, p. 14).

What are needed for evaluative purposes, Castle (2007) argues, are street-level indicators of crime (perhaps à la Felson) and other outcome variables, instead of measures of effects on organized crime groups. Law enforcement has come to believe that outcomes in terms of the criminal justice process (arrests, prosecutions, convictions) equal factual damage to the target criminal organizations. But, says Castle, they have not taken any steps to operationalize and measure outcomes in a persuasive manner (pp. 8–9). "When policing seeks to disrupt and incapacitate criminal organizations and their membership, this is not the end product we desire but merely a strategic choice on the way to our goal.... [Law enforcement presumes] that tackling criminal organizations will have measurable impacts in terms of thefts, health care usage, assaults, homicides, cases of corruption, and other direct consequences of organized crime.... We do not, however, provide much evidence of this linkage" (pp. 29–30).

There is a remarkable convergence of views around several fundamental points here. First, the focus of organized crime control policy has been disproportionately weighted toward the law enforcement side. Other approaches that might be lumped together under the rubric of prevention have largely been neglected. One exception to the approach of arresting, prosecuting, and convicting is the creation of trusteeships and monitoring mechanisms to run certain Teamsters Union locals and oversee the trash carting business and the Fulton Fish Market in New York City (see Jacobs 2007).

Second, the prevailing law enforcement approach has largely been concentrated on trying to disrupt criminal groups by arresting and prosecuting their members under the implicit assumption that if you put enough of these bad guys away organized crime will decline. Unfortunately, hard evidence to test that critical assumption is pretty much nonexistent, which leaves the elusive retributive and deterrence goals.

As both the Levi and Maguire (2004) and the Castle (2007) analyses make clear, most of what we know about law enforcement practices is limited to anecdotal information or, at best, process evaluation information. There are no good outcome or impact data that would allow comparisons over time or across different initiatives or across jurisdictions. And there are no data that would allow valid causal explanations to be made. This does not mean that organized crime policy is not working. But it does mean that we do not know what might or might not be working and why. We do not know why certain actions fail, but we also do not know why our successes succeed. Thus, in the end, we do not really know whether the ends justify the means.

VII. Conclusions

Organized crime control policy, like most crime control policy, is driven more by politics and ideology than by any empirical evidence of success. I suspect that this state of affairs is even more characteristic of organized crime policy, because the target of the policy is so ill-defined, poorly understood, and poorly measured. As a result, normative judgments about ends and means become even more important.

These normative judgments are heavily shaped by media depictions of organized crime—mainly by movies and television, and to a lesser degree by books, magazines, newspapers, and other popular media. This is how the public and public officials, including the law enforcement community, are informed about organized crime. It is thus critically important that criminologists and policy analysts become more active in this area and that they inform policy makers of the findings and the policy implications of their research.

Recent scholarship of researchers such as Varese (2001), Chin (2003), Paoli (2003, 2004), Morselli (2005), and Zhang (2007) demonstrates that this can be and is being done. Their work is much better grounded empirically and theoretically than what has too often passed for scholarship on organized crime. The latter has been heavily weighted toward the descriptive, toward journalistic accounts, and toward sensationalism. Just as it is not easy to combat, so organized crime is not easy to study. It can be very difficult and even dangerous under certain circumstances. This in part explains the overreliance on questionable secondary sources by researchers. The new breed show us that the phrase "solid empirical work on organized crime issues" is not an oxymoron.

So what ought to be on the near horizon of the organized crime research agenda?

- Assess the character of criminal organizations on the dimensions of size, criminal sophistication, division of labor, stability, self-identity, and authority of reputation, juxtaposed against their capacity for economic, physical, psychological, and societal harm. Can criminal organizations be validly classified on the basis of their harm capacity?
- Evaluate policy interventions using more rigorous assessment methods. For example, Jacobs, Cunningham, and Friday (2004, pp. 452–53) argue that the "ongoing experiment" in reforming corrupt labor unions using civil RICO and court-appointed trustees is of vital importance to policy makers and that we must "determine what has worked and what hasn't in order to perfect this strategy."
- Explore cross-national comparative research and evaluation possibilities. For instance, as of this writing the state of South Australia is proposing to pass legislation that would enable the police to get control orders proscribing association or membership in outlaw motorcycle gangs (so-called "bikie" gangs). Such a law would pose clear means-and-ends controversies, and whether it will work to reduce or even eliminate the crimes of these gangs is still an empirical question. Researchers should have a look at it.
- Investigate the effects of the change in the nature of U.S. organized crime from a form dominated by La Cosa Nostra and other traditional groups to a form in which street gangs, especially "super gangs" such as the Latin Kings, the 18th Street Gang, and the Mara Salvatrucha, are now holding sway. How has this affected organized crime control policy, and how will it affect policy in the future?

These are just a few of the areas where organized crime research and control policy could be productively combined. And such combination is very much needed. With regard to the need for greater attention to organized crime prevention, I recommend looking to recent efforts undertaken in Sicily and Hong Kong. What is clear in those examples is that citizen involvement and the building of a strong civil society are essential to any prevention efforts. As the former mayor of Palermo (Orlando 2001) emphasized, the civil sector (schools, media, churches, civic associations) must work hand-in-hand with law enforcement if any society is effectively to fight the scourge of organized crime.

NOTE

1. Serial killers would, of course, be one exception to this proposition.

REFERENCES

Albini, Joseph L. 1971. *The American Mafia: Genesis of a Legend*. New York: Appleton-Century-Crofts.

Anderson, Annalise G. 1979. *The Business of Organized Crime*. Stanford, CA: Stanford University Press.

Braithwaite, John. 2000. "The New Regulatory State and the Transformation of Criminology." *British Journal of Criminology* 40(2): 222–38.

Castle, Allan. 2007. "Measuring the Impact of Law Enforcement on Organized Crime." Paper presented at the 2007 annual meeting of the Criminal Intelligence Service of Canada Executive Committee, Ottawa.

Chambliss, William J. 1988. *On the Take: From Petty Crooks to Presidents*. 2nd ed. Bloomington: Indiana University Press.

Chin, Ko-lin. 2003. *Heijin: Organized Crime, Business, and Politics in Taiwan*. Armonk, NY: M. E. Sharpe.

Cressey, Donald R. 2008. *Theft of the Nation: The Structure and Operations of Organized Crime in America*. New Brunswick, NJ: Transaction Publishers. (Originally published 1969.)

Federal Bureau of Investigation. 2007. "Organized Crime." http://www.fbi.gov/hq/cid/orgcrime/ocshome.htm.

Felson, Marcus. 2006. *The Ecosystem for Organized Crime*. No. 26. HEUNI Papers. Helsinki, Finland: European Institute for Crime Prevention and Control.

FIA International Research, Ltd. 2001. "Contraband, Organized Crime and the Threat to the Transportation and Supply Chain Function." Report. Washington, DC: FIA International Research, Ltd.

Finckenauer, James O. 2007. *The Mafia and Organized Crime*. Oxford, UK: Oneworld Publications.

Finckenauer, James O., and Elin J. Waring. 1998. *Russian Mafia in America: Immigration, Culture, and Crime*. Boston: Northeastern University Press.

Fyfe, Nicholas, and James Sheptycki. 2006. "International Trends in the Facilitation of Witness Co-operation in Organized Crime Cases." *European Journal of Criminology* 3(3): 319–55.

Gambetta, D. 1993. *The Sicilian Mafia: The Business of Private Protection*. Cambridge, MA: Harvard University Press.
Godson, Roy, ed. 2003. *Menace to Society: Political-Criminal Collaboration around the World*. New Brunswick, NJ: Transaction.
Ianni, Francis A. J. 1972. *A Family Business: Kinship and Social Control in Organized Crime*. Ithaca, NY: Russell Sage Foundation.
Interpol. 2007. "The Impact and Scale of Counterfeiting." http://www.interpol.int/Public/News/2004/Factsheet51PR21.asp.
Jacobs, James B. 1999. *Gotham Unbound*. New York: New York University Press.
———. 2007. *Mobsters, Unions, and Feds: The Mafia and the American Labor Movement*. New York: New York University Press.
Jacobs, James B., Eileen M. Cunningham, and Kimberly Friday. 2004. "The RICO Trusteeships after Twenty Years: A Progress Report." *Labor Lawyer* 419: 419–80.
Lehr, Dick, and Gerard O'Neill. 2001. *Black Mass: The True Story of an Unholy Alliance between the FBI and the Irish Mob*. New York: Perennial.
Levi, Michael, and Mike Maguire. 2004. "Reducing and Preventing Organised Crime: An Evidence-Based Critique." *Crime, Law and Social Change* 41: 397–469.
Maltz, Michael. 1990. *Measuring the Effectiveness of Organized Crime Control Efforts*. Huntsville, TX: OICJ Publications.
Morselli, Carlo. 2005. *Contacts, Opportunities, and Criminal Enterprise*. Toronto: University of Toronto Press.
Nardini, William J. 2006. "The Prosecutor's Toolbox: Investigating and Prosecuting Organized Crime in the United States." *Journal of International Criminal Justice* 4: 528–38.
Naylor, R. T. 2002. *Wages of Crime: Black Markets, Illegal Finance, and the Underworld Economy*. Ithaca, NY: Cornell University Press.
Ohr, Bruce G. 2000. "Effective Methods to Combat Transnational Organized Crime in Criminal Justice Processes." Annual report for 2000 and Resource Material Series No. 59. Tokyo, Japan: UNAFEI.
Orlando, Leoluca. 2001. *Fighting the Mafia and Renewing Sicilian Culture*. San Francisco: Encounter Books.
Paoli, Letizia. 2003. *Mafia Brotherhoods: Organized Crime, Italian Style*. New York: Oxford University Press.
———. 2004. "Italian Organised Crime: Mafia Associations and Criminal Enterprises." *Global Crime* 6(February): 1.
Paoli, Letizia, and Cyrille Fijnaut. 2006. "Organised Crime and Its Control Policies." *European Journal of Crime, Criminal Law and Criminal Justice* 14(3): 307–27.
Pistone, Joseph. 1987. *Donnie Brasco: My Undercover Life in the Mafia*. New York: New American Library.
Raab, Selwyn. 2006. *Five Families: The Rise, Decline, and Resurgence of America's Most Powerful Mafia Empires*. New York: St. Martin's.
Reuter, Peter. 1983. *Disorganized Crime: The Economics of the Visible Hand*. Boston: MIT Press.
Smith, Dwight C. 1975. *The Mafia Mystique*. New York: Basic Books.
Stille, Alexander. 1995. *Excellent Cadavers: The Mafia and the Death of the First Italian Republic*. New York: Pantheon.
Urbina, Martin, and Sara Kreitzer. 2004. "The Practical Utility and Ramifications of RICO: Thirty-Two Years after Its Implementation." *Criminal Justice Policy Review* 15(3): 294–323.

Varese, Federico. 2001. *The Russian Mafia*. Oxford: Oxford University Press.
Wagley, John R., 2006. "Transnational Organized Crime: Principal Threats and U.S. Responses." CRS Report for Congress, March 20. Washington, DC: Congressional Research Service.
Williams, Phil. 2002. "Organized Crime and Cyber-Crime: Implications for Business." Pittsburgh, PA: CERT Coordination Center, Carnegie Mellon University.
Woodiwiss, Michael, and David Bewley-Taylor. 2005. "The Global Fix: The Construction of a Global Enforcement Regime." Transnational Institute Briefing Series. Amsterdam: TNI.
Zhang, Sheldon. X. 2007. *Smuggling and Trafficking in Human Beings: All Roads Lead to America*. Stanford, CA: Stanford University Press.

CHAPTER 13

ENVIRONMENTAL CRIME

PETER CLEARY YEAGER AND
SALLY S. SIMPSON

As Mary Clifford (1998, p. 7) points out, the term *environmental crime* has been used "almost indiscriminately without any universally accepted definition." The phenomenon can include such diverse behaviors as someone tossing trash from a car window and a corporation dumping toxic waste into the air or waterways, harming a "protected" species such as the snail darter or spotted owl and failure to properly dispose of common household products such as latex paint. Such imprecision makes it difficult to study how extensive, pervasive, and costly these behaviors are to society and its victims, as well as the best mechanisms for the prevention and control of environmental crime.

For the purposes of our discussion, we combine Clifford's (1998, p. 26) two proposed definitions of environmental crime:

- "An act committed with the intent to harm or with a potential to cause harm to ecological and/or biological systems and for the purpose of securing business or personal advantage."
- "Any act that violates an environmental protection statute."

In this chapter we do not focus on all behaviors that fall under this definitional rubric. Although we recognize that individuals may be among the most significant contributors to current environmental problems (Vandenbergh 2001, p. 192) and that other organizations, both legitimate (for example, government agencies) and illicit (for example, organized crime), can be environmental lawbreakers, our interest lies in the acts of legitimate business organizations and their officers that violate environmental laws regardless of whether the laws are criminal, civil, or regulatory in nature ("corporate crime," as defined by Clinard and Yeager, 1980). In this vein, we focus on environmental offenses and policy within the United States, on which most of the research published in English has focused. However, more recently scholars have begun to study environmental offenses and policies in other nations, and we incorporate their findings into the discussion that follows, with particular emphasis on legal approaches in other countries.

In this essay we draw several conclusions:

- While pollution by major industrial point dischargers has decreased over time in the United States, a relatively small number of companies is disproportionately responsible for violations of environmental laws, and violation rates vary by industry.
- The limited research on environmental compliance and lawbreaking by companies, research that is concentrated in the United States, has produced mixed results on such questions as the effects of financial strain, firm size, and deterrence.
- Although nations around the world approach environmental regulation in many similar ways, particularly in favoring more cooperative approaches over strict adversarial approaches, there is substantial variation in the effects of nations' environmental laws on pollution control. This variation especially distinguishes Western capitalist societies from the formerly state-dominated and increasingly market-oriented economies of China and Russia.
- The emphasis on negotiation, discretion, and delegation to local levels in much environmental law enforcement constrains environmental protection on behalf of economic interests. It can also result in enforcement bias favoring larger, more powerful polluters. Potential consequences of such patterns include reductions in both deterrence and the legitimacy of law.
- Future research should seek to assess which combination of persuasion, inducement, and compulsion devices contribute most to industrial and state commitments to environmental protection.

In section I we describe types and patterns of environmental lawbreaking by business organizations after first describing some of the data and measurement issues that perplex and challenge researchers. Focusing next on theory, in section II we explore individual, organizational, and structural explanations for environmental crime. In section III we examine national and international policies for regulating the environmental behaviors of business. Here we examine constraints on policy that shape environmental outcomes. We conclude with consideration of the implications of these findings for both future research and public policy.

I. Environmental Conduct in Business

Like other kinds of corporate crime, it is difficult to measure the extent and pervasiveness of environmental lawbreaking. There are few analyses of self-reports of offending in this area and no environmental victimization surveys.[1] Consequently, estimates are drawn from official records collected by federal and state regulatory agencies (mainly the U.S. Environmental Protection Agency [EPA]), the Administrative Office of the U.S. Courts, the Executive Office for U.S. Attorneys, and the U.S. Sentencing Commission, among other sources (see, for example, Scalia 1999). For the most part, these sources count only offenses that have come to the attention of authorities through proactive (such as inspections) or reactive (public reports of fish kills, bad smells) processes. Generally, an alleged violation must have moved far enough in the justice process to have generated an investigation or a deliberative outcome (for example, case dismissal, guilty verdict, EPA warning letter) to show up in the statistics. Because the criteria for moving cases forward vary from agency to agency and from one system of justice to another, it is difficult to compare estimates or counts across data sources (Simpson, Harris, and Mattson 1993).

Official statistics also portray environmental crime from the perspective and processes of the state. The matter of perspective leads some environmentalists and industrialists alike to suggest that official data serve more of a political purpose than an environmental one. Thus critics suggest that official counts of crime are symbolic tools utilized to demonstrate that environmental offending is taken seriously by the state without affecting the pollution problem itself. As Adler (1998, p. 40) points out, "Evaluating environmental protection by the number of enforcement actions taken is a bit like rating a mutual fund on the number of stocks bought and sold in a given year. Such actions make for a good bureaucratic bean-counting exercise, but it is a poor proxy for actual results." Similarly official environmental crime rates are poor measures of corporate violations of environmental laws because enforcement processes and policies commonly handle such offenses with noncriminal sanctions and sometimes without taking any enforcement action. Moreover, individual corporations—typically larger companies—have often been able to influence the definition of their own compliance with environmental laws, thereby shaping the profile of offenses in systematic ways (Yeager 1991).

Sensationalized cases of environmental offending are also utilized to extrapolate offending patterns absent systematic data without much regard to the "worst-case scenario" nature of these types of events. For example, although pollution from the Exxon *Valdez* was monumental, the size and scope of the tragedy is out of scale compared with more commonplace oil spills. On its Web site (http://www.uscg.mil/hq/g-m/nmc/response/stats/summary.htm) the U.S. Coast Guard reports 3,897 recorded spills for 2004, but only four incidents fall into the highest spill categories (between 100,001 and 1 million gallons), whereas 3,677 are in the lowest spill category (between 1 and 100 gallons). Sensationalized offenses such as the *Valdez* incident are useful for publicizing environmental harms (the bulk of environmental damage is associated with the high spill categories), but the data do not tell us how much environmental offending actually occurs or how many offenses are "owned" by each business.

Measurement problems like these led, in part, to the creation in 1986 of the Toxic Release Inventory. The TRI is a mandatory reporting system created as part of the Emergency Planning and Community Right-to-Know Act, through which toxic releases and transfers are reported by facilities of a certain size (10 or more employees), in designated industrial sectors, by chemical type. The TRI is a dynamic reporting system: requirements change from year to year, affecting which facilities participate and which chemicals are reported. According to EPA officials and scholars (Cohen 2001), the TRI has given communities a means to hold companies accountable for the amount of toxins released locally. This kind of public awareness has sensitized businesses to better environmental accounting and management, ultimately prompting some firms to voluntarily reduce emissions beyond legal requirements. But, as Cohen points out, the exact mechanism that prompts firms to voluntarily reduce emissions is not well understood. More empirical work is needed to determine whether voluntary "overcompliance" is linked to market sensitivity, informal community pressure, or social norms, and whether the same set of factors also predict corporate noncompliance (Simpson, Gibbs, and Slocum 2008).

A. Types and Patterns of Environmental Behavior

Neither official data nor extrapolation offers a precise approximation of the actual amount of offending, and both introduce their own kind of systematic bias. Depending on which data sources are used, estimates of offending levels are highly variable and show different patterns. Given our focus on business organizations, it makes sense to concentrate on offending patterns and trends at the firm level. Yet EPA data are collected at the facility or plant level, and though it is possible to aggregate data to parent companies, it is not easy to do so. The EPA does not mandate the collection of this data element, nor is the information necessarily updated when plants are sold and ownership changes.

In the aggregate, official EPA data show a recent three-year reduction of pollutants by 3 billion pounds (although 2006 reductions were lower than those in 2004 and 2005), and defendants in civil cases were required to spend $20 billion for pollution controls. Both of these accomplishments set records. In addition the EPA concluded nearly 5,000 civil administrative and judicial cases in 2006 (an increase of 100 percent over the previous year), while criminal enforcement produced $43 million in fines and restitution and 154 years in jail for sentenced defendants (Nakayama 2007; U.S. Environmental Protection Agency 2007). Criminal prosecutions were down, however, suggesting a change in enforcement policies at the federal level away from criminal cases and toward the handling of offenses under administrative and civil law. Environmental prosecutions declined 36 percent between 2001 and 2006, from 919 to 584. Relatedly, EPA investigators opened 37 percent fewer cases in 2006 than in 2001; in 2007, the agency employed only 172 of the 200 criminal investigators required as a minimum by the 1990 Pollution Prosecution Act. Whereas EPA officials emphasized the reduced pollution loads and forced expenditures on improved pollution control systems, critics—including some former EPA personnel—argued that a changing political climate was weakening the deterrent effect of environmental law (Environmental Integrity Project 2003; Mintz 2004; Solomon and Eilperin 2007).

Obviously it is not possible to ascertain whether such changes in aggregate enforcement data over time also capture changes in offending trends generally, or for business organizations specifically. However, there is some evidence that point-source pollution by EPA-designated industrial "majors" has declined over the past two decades, leading some to conclude that small firms and individuals are responsible for the bulk of environmental pollution in the United States today (Vandenbergh 2001). This observation comes nearly 15 years after Hammit and Reuter (1988) concluded that small-quantity generators (i.e., responsible for less than 1 percent of the total hazardous waste in the United States) have a high rate of criminality when it comes to disposing of that waste.

Firm-level characteristics, such as organizational profitability and size, have figured into a number of studies that explore whether financial and structural characteristics are associated with environmental noncompliance and overcompliance. Although corporate environmental research is not as well developed as investigations into the etiology of conventional crime (or even other forms of corporate offending such as antitrust), results of these investigations are mixed (see Cohen, Fenn, and Konar 1997 for their review) and appear to vary according to offense, program or media type, unit of analysis (plant or facility versus company), and the industry under investigation.

B. Overcompliance

In their study of Standard and Poor's 500 companies ranked according to their level of environmental performance, Cohen, Fenn, and Konar (1997) find financial performance to be positively (but rarely significantly) correlated with environmental effectiveness. Attempting to unravel the causal relationship between being "green" and profitability, the authors offer preliminary evidence that "financial distress *may* be a precursor to poor environmental performance" (27; emphasis added). DeCanio and Watkins (1998), on the other hand, found strong relationships between firm characteristics and company investment in energy efficiency (i.e., predicting whether a firm will join an EPA voluntary "green lights" program that commits the company to adopt lighting upgrades). Larger companies (measured by the number of employees) and firms that were good financial performers (measured by a variety of indicators) were significantly more likely to join the Green Lights Program.

Other research on firm participation in voluntary pollution abatement programs has found a link between firm size and program participation, in that large firms with the greatest amount of pollution emissions were more apt to participate (Arora and Cason 1996). Khanna and Damon (1999) suggest that firms most likely to adopt innovative environmental management systems are those with older assets and larger on-site hazardous waste releases, but research by King (as cited in Hileman 2001) challenges the notion that program participants are better environmental citizens than nonparticipants, noting the deleterious "free rider" effect. Program participation may not necessarily indicate good citizenship and a commitment to lower environmental pollution. Laufer (2003, p. 257) warns about the potential for corporate "greenwashing," arguing that the "very firms that wash their reputations through public relations, complex front coalitions, sponsored 'think tanks,' and who publicly lead the fight against global warming, nuclear waste, and water pollution, remain some of the worst corporate offenders."

Consistent with some earlier corporate crime studies (e.g., Simpson 1986), DeCanio and Watkins (1998) found that industry measures of performance (for example, earnings per share growth rate performance) may be even stronger predictors of participation in Green Lights Programs than characteristics measured at the firm level. Participation in the program was also found to significantly vary across broad industry classifications. Relative to manufacturing companies (the excluded category), utilities were more likely to join Green Lights Programs, and service, finance, insurance, and real estate companies were less likely to do so. Arora and Carson (1996, p. 430) also note industry effects in their assessment of the EPA's 33/50 voluntary pollution reduction program. Although the industry effects were not as strong as the firm variables in their models (for example, size), participation was higher for companies operating in industries with high research and development and advertising expenditures.

In sum, overcompliance and extreme volunteerism by companies appear to be at least weakly associated with firm and industry characteristics. A critical question is whether these same factors (for example, size, financial performance, industry type) are associated with noncompliance.

C. Noncompliance

An extensive literature has developed over the past 25 years that links firm and industry characteristics to corporate offending. Very little of this literature concentrates exclusively (or at all) on environmental crime, and, absent evidence to the contrary, it is unwise to assume that all types of corporate offending are caused by the same etiological processes. As Simpson (1986) found in her study of antitrust offending—a broad offense type that includes many types of anticompetitive acts—firm and industry variables can operate differently. Thus we truncate our review to focus mainly on studies that are directly relevant to environmental offending, whose patterns also relate variously to potential explanatory factors.

Yeager (1991) found that company size was unrelated to firms' violations of pollution limits under the federal Clean Water Act, but he also found that large companies were in violation less often than small companies for failure to install pollution control equipment according to government-imposed schedules. In contrast, McKendall, Sanchez, and Sicilian's (1999) study of the largest 1,000 publicly owned manufacturing companies revealed a positive and significant effect for company size on environmental offending for both serious (agency and court orders or verdicts) and nonserious crimes (notices or warnings of violations), but company size had a diminished effect as it increased.

Size of polluting facilities may also shape violation rates. Although not examining violations as such, using TRI data for the chemical industry Grant, Jones, and Bergesen (2002, p. 402) discovered that large plants, especially those that were branches of a larger parent corporation, had significantly higher emissions rates when compared with small plants. As a particular kind of corporate form, subsidiaries may be more prone to pollute because of legal firewalls created between them and their corporate parents (Grant and Jones 2003). The researchers also noted that emission rates varied substantially by subindustry (for example, soaps and inorganic chemicals had lower emissions than paints and plastics).

In a study of air pollution violations in the pulp and paper industry Gray and Shadbegian (2005) find little evidence that firm characteristics affect compliance, but differences among plants or facilities do matter. For instance, facilities less likely to be in compliance are larger and older and include a pulping process. In his study of the same industry Nadeau (1997) found evidence that larger plants spent longer periods of time out of compliance with federal environmental regulations. Results also indicate that plants have similar kinds of records across regulatory requirements: "Plants with violations of other regulatory requirements, either in water pollution or OSHA regulation, are significantly less likely to comply with air pollution regulations. We do not see the same sort of effect for 'voluntary compliance' as represented by TRI emissions" (Gray and Shadbegian 2005, p.' 257). In their study of Clean Water Act violations Simpson, Garner, and Gibbs (2007) also found that plant and facility characteristics matter when aggregated to the firm level. Companies that owned more facilities had lower violation rates than those with fewer or only one plant or facility. Additionally they found a negative relationship between company size and offending.

Studies report a high degree of chronicity (or recidivism) and concentration of violations among some corporate offenders (Sutherland 1949; Clinard and Yeager 1980; Simpson 2000). Tracking offending records over time suggests that certain companies, like individuals, have a higher propensity for offending. In their study of 477 manufacturing companies Clinard and Yeager (1980, p. 116) report that "only 38 of the 300 manufacturing corporations cited for violations, or 13 percent (8 percent of all corporations studied), accounted for 52 percent of all violations charged in 1975–76, an average of 23.5 violations per firm." This degree of concentration held for environmental offenses as well as for violations of manufacturing, administrative, and labor rules (but not for violations of financial and trade laws). Looking specifically at point-source water pollution using the EPA's National Pollutant Discharge Elimination System, research by Simpson, Garner, and Gibbs (2007; compare Yeager 1991, p. 277) discovered a similar pattern. Most firms in their sample had very low violation rates over a six-year period,[2] with the average firm in violation about 2 percent of the time. Some firms, however, were in noncompliance as much as 75 percent of the time.

Firm-level violations also vary by industry. Clinard and Yeager (1980) observed that oil companies, in particular, had poor environmental records. Simpson, Garner, and Gibbs (2007) describe the uneven distribution of conventional and toxic pollution violations across the oil refining, pulp and paper, and steel industries. The steel industry, for example, accounted for the largest percentage of pollution violations even though it had fewer companies than any other industry analyzed. This was true even when pollutants were broken down into conventional (common pollutants such as organic waste, acid, bacteria, oil, and grease) and toxic pollutants. Due to differences between industries in production processes and technology, some conventional pollutants are a greater problem in some industries than in others (for example, biological oxygen demand is a greater problem for pulp and paper than for steel and oil). Additional evidence of industry effects can be found in the work of McKendall, Sanchez, and Sicilian (1999), who found negative associations between environmental offending levels and industry profitability and concentration. However, earlier work (McKendall and Wagner 1997) casts some doubt on these findings.

More consistently, the evidence does suggest that conventional and toxic pollution violations have decreased over time, perhaps because regulatory requirements, coupled with informal sanctions imposed by the public, have lowered pollution levels substantially. In the Simpson, Garner, and Gibbs (2007) study the total number of violations for the 63 companies in their sample (a number that fluctuates over the six years of their study) monotonically dropped from a high of nearly 1,000 violations to 600 between 1995 and 2000. Kagan, Gunningham, and Thornton's (2003) international study of environmental performance in the pulp and paper industry (tracking 14 manufacturing mills in the United States, Australia, New Zealand, and British Columbia) observes a gradual decline over time in environmentally harmful emissions. All of the mills reported experiencing pressure from their host communities to improve environmental performance. Importantly, the researchers found few substantial differences in pollution patterns over time across the different nations (and there was a fair amount of convergence in substantive pollution control standards across jurisdictions).

They did find, however, a significant relationship between corporate financial performance and environmental performance. "Mills owned by corporations with larger profit margins (ratio of income to sales) and larger annual sales income in the early 1990s generally had lower BOD, TSS, and AOX emissions late in the decade,[3] and also had better pollution control technology, although the relationships were not consistently significant for both measures of economic resources" (Kagan, Gunningham, and Thornton 2003, p. 67).

These findings, coupled with some empirical support that strain-inducing profit squeeze (at the firm or industry level and macro level) can increase corporate offending in the antitrust area (see Simpson 1986, 1987; Simpson and Koper 1997), have led some to suggest that constraints and pressures on companies from the economy and competition are related to fluctuations in environmental crime. This expectation was supported in the study of Clean Water Act violations by Simpson, Garner, and Gibbs (2007) and work by McKendall, Sanchez, and Sicilian (1999). Other studies have found modest (and mixed) statistical relations between indicators of economic strain and environmental offenses (Clinard et al. 1979; Clinard and Yeager 1980) or no relation at all (Yeager 1981). Nadeau (1997) found that pulp and paper plants facing improved demand for their products spent longer periods of time in noncompliance with environmental regulations. He suggested that these plants may have concluded that the opportunity costs of investing in pollution controls were too high when those funds could be instead invested in meeting growing demand for products.[4]

The gradual decline of pollutants over time also is documented in the U.S. EPA Sector Notebooks. The Notebooks provide researchers with holistic and comprehensive industry-specific environmental profiles that point to several possible explanations for the decline, including industrial process information, processes that influence the amount and type of pollutants discharged, and changes in legislation, regulations, and regulatory assistance, including EPA-sponsored pollution control programs. Also contained in the Notebooks are data on pollutant release, regulatory requirements (which vary by industry), and the compliance and enforcement history for the sector.

Although there is a paucity of quantitative studies in the environmental offenses area, several patterns and trends have emerged. First, it appears that industrial point-source pollution (and violations) among EPA-designated majors has decreased over time. Second, violations are concentrated: a small number of companies are responsible for a disproportionate amount of offenses. Third, company offending rates vary by industry. Fourth, there are more similarities than differences among Western nations (Australia, Canada, New Zealand, and the United States) in how regulation shapes corporate behavior. On the other hand, the relations between economic strain and firm size on environmental compliance remain to be further sorted out. Studies have found that larger firms are more likely to be among both the overcompliers and the offenders and have produced some mixed findings on the connection between financial health and compliance. In addition, whether the relationship between economic munificence and environmental record is causal or recursive is unknown.

II. Explanations for Environmental Offending

In this section we offer different explanations for environmental offending by firms. Because companies are aggregate entities, operating within complex political, economic, and social environments, and are populated with individuals, causal explanations range from theories about individuals to those that link corporate offending to the structure of economic systems. It is not possible to give a full accounting of all of these perspectives in this chapter, but we will cover a limited number for which there is some empirical support (albeit not necessarily from studies of environmental offending per se) and relevance for the emerging trends identified above.

A. Micro Level

Most explanations for corporate crime, including environmental offending, have focused on the small-scale features of the social environment. After all, organizations cannot act or behave on their own. Sutherland's (1949) theory of differential association, for instance, recognizes that there are multiple moralities in the social world of individuals. As such, it emphasizes the group transmission of definitions favorable to law violation (over definitions unfavorable), along with the conditions of interpersonal associations that enhance the social learning of crime (for example, intensity, priority, and duration). As Cressey (1986, p. 196) points out, "White-collar criminals, as well as street criminals, should be viewed as conformists rather than deviants because they have taken over behaviour patterns that are dominant in their social worlds."[5]

Benson (1985) shows how white-collar offenders develop and utilize symbolic accounts that allow them to deny their responsibility for crime (excuses) or the moral wrongfulness of their actions (justifications). To the extent that environmental offenders do not believe their actions are wrong (say, if such actions are common in their company or industry) and they are expected to do whatever is best for their company (loyalty), then the illegal act is neutralized and continued offending is likely. Geis's (1967) review of secondary sources from the heavy electrical equipment antitrust cases of 1961 revealed offenders who either believed they had done nothing wrong or, in the case of those who knew the behavior was illegal, lost sight of that fact because of a perceived obligation to job and organization. Simpson's (2002) research consistently shows that managers are willing to break the law (antitrust, environmental, accounting, bribery) if requested to do so by a supervisor, a finding confirmed in a recent study that focused exclusively on environmental offenses (Simpson, Gibbs, and Slocum 2008).

Yet it is unclear whether attitudes, behaviors, or both actually drive offending. In their test of differential association theory Zey-Ferrell, Weaver, and Farrell

(1979) find that the behavior of one's peers and one's own opportunity are better predictors of unethical conduct by marketers than what others think or one's own personal beliefs. Unfortunately their study is limited to unethical actions by managers in marketing (for example, padding an expense account, taking extra personal time, not reporting violations of company policy and rules) and does not include environmental offending. Flannery and May (2000), however, do study environmental decision making, and they find a modest relationship between managers' attitudes and ethical decision intentions. Importantly, they find that the magnitude or "moral intensity" of the consequences (for example, harmful effects for human or nonhuman victims) moderated the effect of attitudes on decision making. Environmental attitudes that tap into procedural, substantive, and conformity norms played virtually no role in noncompliance in the Simpson, Gibbs, and Slocum (2008, p. 32) study, once situational and manager characteristics were included in the analysis; thus environmental attitudes "might not be distinct from broader ethical and moral evaluations, some of which may emerge from one's position in the company, experiences on the job, or assessments of a firm's liabilities."

Rational choice theory (of which deterrence theory is a specialized case), on the other hand, assumes that offending decisions reflect rational processes—processes partially bounded by the amount, quality, and type of information individuals receive as well as their individual capacities to assess and process that information. Decisions to violate the law will take into account the benefits that result from the act as well as the potential costs associated with it (for both the decision maker and his or her company). Paternoster and Simpson (1993), for instance, argue that decisions by corporate managers to violate the law will take into account instrumental as well as normative considerations (morals, shame, and guilt).

The evidence surrounding corporate deterrence ("mere deterrence") is generally mixed. Several studies find limited, if any, support that the threat or application of legal sanctions inhibits offending (or reoffending) by firms (Simpson and Koper 1992) or the managers within them (Braithwaite and Makkai 1991; Simpson 2002). Studies specifically of environmental compliance have also produced mixed results. Cohen's (2000, p. 10246) review of deterrence studies of environmental law found that "both increased government monitoring and increased enforcement activities result in reduced pollution or increased compliance." On the other hand, Simpson, Garner, and Gibbs (2007) found no evidence of deterrence effects in their study of corporate compliance with the U.S. Clean Water Act.

Yet the relationship between sanctions and offending may be more complex. In their recent work Smith, Simpson, and Huang (2007) show that formal legal sanctions work indirectly on managers' offending propensities, through perceived morality and outcome expectations (costs and benefits). Similarly, Paternoster and Simpson (1996) demonstrate that sanction threats are superfluous for managers who believe corporate illegal acts are highly immoral, but operate in an expected manner for those lower on the morality scale. These findings, along with research by Braithwaite and Makkai (1991) that reveals a link between emotionality and the deterrent effect of sanction threats (low emotionality negates the threat), suggest that rational choice explanations that take into account individual differences and include situational, normative, and a broad range of instrumental considerations are promising. But, as Vaughan (1998) warns us, not all organizational decisions (including those that break laws) are explicitly rational and thus may not be amenable to a rational choice framework.

Like differential association, social control theory emphasizes the ways moral beliefs control deviant decision making. However, control theories view morality as a bond to conventional society. It is through our bonds to significant others (for example, parents, peers, teachers, colleagues) that we assess the negative consequences of illegal behavior. In the case of corporate offending, bonds can be conceptualized at the level of the company. Lasley (1988), for instance, suggests that bonds of attachment, involvement, commitment, and belief in a common value system are best measured within the context of an executive's most immediate source of control: the company.

Research reveals that informal costs (associated with stigma, attachment, and commitment) appear to have a substantial deterrent effect on offending and that managers care about informal sanction threats regardless of whether they are incurred by themselves or by the company (Paternoster and Simpson 1996; Simpson 2002). In his theory of reintegrative shaming, Braithwaite (1989) also emphasizes the important role of shame and shaming processes as a critical element of communitarian and interdependent societies.[6] Thus, social control theory offers a helpful way to think about constraints that promote conformity.

There is less support, however, for Gottfredson and Hirschi's (1990) newer version of control theory, which links offending propensity to differences in self-control (Reed and Yeager 1996; Simpson and Piquero 2002). Because there is relatively little empirical work in this area, it is premature to dismiss the approach entirely. There may be some important individual differences between managers who offend, given opportunity, and those who do not. Differences may not necessarily lie in self-control. We do know that emotionality affects offending propensity among nursing home executives in Australia and that desire for control—a psychological trait—predicts how managers in the United States evaluate and assess opportunities and crime choices (Piquero, Exum, and Simpson 2005). Managers with a high desire for control may not see limits to this desire, and this may affect how they understand risks.

On the whole, however, the micro-level perspectives do not provide a clear picture of the complexities of organizational life. As Boulding (cited in Fisse and Braithwaite 1983) reminds us, corporate managers come and go, but the firm, like an elephant, continues along its way fairly indifferent to its many riders. Why are some corporations good environmental citizens and others chronic offenders? Why do firms desist from crime? The organization and its environment provide the keys to understanding motivations for environmental offenses, the sources of and constraints from offending pressures, and how illegal opportunities emerge.

B. Organizational and Macro-Level Explanations

The corporation is a complex organizational entity, whose primary, if not exclusive, purpose is to be profitable and expand market share. Given these goals, perhaps the most popular explanation for corporate offending is strain. Strain can be induced internally (for example, by top executives who rely on quantitative evaluations of manager performance; see Clinard 1983) or by the external environment (a highly competitive market or new regulatory obligations that the firm must meet). Vaughan (1983, p. 59) suggests that "scarcity, combined with the differential standards for economic success, raises the possibility of blocked access to resources regardless of an organization's size, wealth, age, experience, or previous record." To put it differently, strain provides the motive for offending (the arousal of behavior), but offending will not occur absent opportunity and choice (McKendall and Wagner 1997).

As already discussed, some research has demonstrated a correlation between financial performance and environmental compliance at the firm and industry levels. Thus, under the right set of conditions, profit squeeze and loss of market share can place strain on managers to, say, cut back on environmental abatements as a cost-saving measure or not report emissions over permitted limits because of the potential for negative market consequences. It can also affect the amount of investment capital a firm can expend on environmental upgrades or the adoption of environmental management best practices. Intra-organizational strain may be exacerbated when a firm pursues a product-dominant strategy (concentrating on one product line), especially when the company is performing poorly in that market (see, for example, Simpson and Koper 1997).

Strain may also occur as a consequence of managerial philosophies, changes in top management (Daboub et al. 1995), and intra-organizational power struggles over resources and the strategic direction of a firm (Fligstein 1987). Offending may also be influenced by particular corporate strategies and structures (opportunities). Multidivisional forms (in contrast to functionally structured firms), for instance, are theorized to isolate subunits, decentralize decision making, and disperse oversight, thus increasing the risk of offending. Other structural characteristics that have been associated with corporate offending are company size (Clinard and Yeager 1980), political regime, and macro-economic pressures on companies such as a declining stock market, higher levels of unemployment, and decreases in GNP (Simpson 1987). Although these latter factors are tied to a strain argument, Vaughan (1983) suggests that because large firms tend to have more transactions, they have more crime opportunities, a point developed as well by Clinard and Yeager (1980) and Simpson (1986).

Many of these organizational influences and macro-level offending correlates figure prominently in Finney and Lesieur's (1982) contingency theory of corporate crime. This perspective assumes that corporate crimes emerge out of dynamic and contingent processes. There are a series of events, in a sequence, that lead decision makers to choose crime over other alternatives. But criminal behavior is consequential as well: crime can create deviant commitments, negative reactions by society, and organizational defenses. Thus the theory can explain why some companies are more deviant than others (different situational contingencies, internal controls, and responses to crime) and explain how some firms come to desist (adopting crime containment strategies postdiscovery). However, the theory has not been fully tested or applied specifically to environmental crime. In fact, few of these correlates of corporate offending have been specifically tied to environmental crime, and environmental offending may not have the same correlates as other kinds of corporate illegalities (Shover and Routhe 2005, p. 325). Therefore, more research is needed before we can theorize more fully about the organizational and macro (structural) sources of offending. However, the notion that offending is caused by a confluence of motive, opportunity, choice, and constraint (lack of control) is a consistent theme across micro- and macro-level theories, offering a promising conceptual scheme for cross-level integration (McKendall and Wagner 1997).

III. Environmental Law and Public Policy

Now institutionalized in many parts of the world, environmental law has achieved something of a taken-for-granted status in most economically developed societies. It can therefore come as a surprise to recall that law has been the instrument of choice for environmental protection for only four decades. Prior to the 1970s law was little involved in protecting the natural environment from industrial impacts on air, water, and land. Instead, in both market- and state-managed economies these vital resources were routinely consumed and despoiled without limit or cost to industrial producers.

In the brief span of time since, environmental law expanded rapidly over both ecological substance—from species protection to atmospheric conditions—and geographic terrain. Often under pressure from citizens and victims of industrial pollution, advanced nations began to pass and implement many such laws in the 1970s. There followed a number of international and regional compacts intended to control harmful environmental impacts that cross national boundaries and affect world populations, such as the trafficking of industrial wastes to developing nations and effects producing climate change.

As impressive as this diffusion of environmental regulation has been, equally impressive is the rapid evolution of diverse legal approaches to environmental pollution. These now range from the prescriptive regulations of the original U.S. air and water pollution control statutes, through cooperative regulatory approaches featuring more negotiation than legal threat, to market-like incentive and cooperative systems such as tradable pollution permits, emissions taxes, and corporate self-policing.[7]

In the U.S. context, all of these regulatory approaches are presently in use in the effort to reduce environmental harms from industrial pollution. Indeed, two or more of these approaches are commonly joined in a specific policy approach to pollution control. For example, since the enactment of the Clean Water Act in 1972, the federal Environmental Protection Agency has commonly used its discretion to negotiate compliance with many companies rather than strictly enforce the pollution control standards mandated by Congress (compare Yeager 1991). Similarly, accompanying market-based incentive systems is the threat of legal sanctions should companies exceed the pollution loads they have purchased the right to discharge.

These variations in legal approaches have implications both for environmental impacts (the policy issue) and for the understanding of patterns in environmental lawbreaking (the analytic or research issue). Among others, they mean that criminal law is but one of several legal tools used by nations to limit the environmental impacts of industry. In fact, it is the tool least often used to compel business compliance with environmental law.[8] Virtually everywhere, criminal cases constitute only a very small fraction of the enforcement and compliance actions taken by government agencies against pollution. Criminal prosecution is generally reserved for only the most egregious, wanton cases of willful environmental offenses. Somewhat counterintuitively, then, criminal cases do not routinely address the greatest threats to the natural environment, nor do they make the greatest impacts on environmental quality. Instead, governments typically address the violations that manifest these threats through shifting combinations of negotiation, incentives, and commands.

A. Environmental Laws around the World: A Brief Synopsis

Although governments began ruling against pollution at least as far back as the fourteenth century, and occasionally with draconian sanctions,[9] systematic and sustained environmental regulation was a product of the last decades of the twentieth century in countries experiencing the harmful ecological effects of industrial pollution. For example, although Japan passed early industrial water pollution laws in 1958, it was only in 1969 that the national government implemented effective regulation under the law. The government passed and strengthened environmental laws in the late 1960s and early 1970s and established its Ministry of Environment in 1971 (Yokoyama 2007). The Czech Republic (then Czechoslovakia) promulgated water pollution laws in 1973 and 1974 (Earnhart 2000). The United States created the federal Environmental Protection Agency in 1970, the same year that Congress passed the nation's first major pollution control law, the Clean Air Act. Soon to follow were the Clean Water Act (1972), the Safe Drinking Water Act (1974), the Toxic Substances Control Act (1976), the Resource Conservation and Recovery Act (1976), the Surface Mining Control and Reclamation Act (1977), and the Comprehensive Environmental Response, Compensation and Liability Act (1980), among other federal environmental laws (Yeager 1991, p. 181; Natural Resources Defense Council 2007).

China and Russia came later to sustained concern with environmental protection, each taking serious notice of accumulated ecological damage only as their governments initiated programs to spur economic growth by introducing degrees of privatization and markets into their previously tightly state-controlled economies. Although in the 1940s the USSR had passed some of the world's first laws to control toxic substances, later laws to control pollution in the 1960s and 1980s went largely unenforced as economic goals displaced environmental concerns. As part of its national restructuring (*perestroika*) a few years before its dissolution, the Soviet Union in 1988 established a new national environmental protection agency, the State Committee on Environmental Protection (Goskompriroda) to consolidate environmental regulation and to activate the country's moribund environmental laws. Although an early result was the closure or downsizing of more than 1,000 production plants in 1989 alone for violation of the nation's pollution laws, environmental protection efforts continued to struggle against the high value placed on economic growth in Russia. In the early years of the twenty-first century, President Vladimir Putin abolished the State Committee on Environmental Protection and transferred its responsibilities to the more economy-friendly Natural Resources Ministry, the municipal environmental police were eliminated, environmental impact studies were curbed, and an official report disclosed that three-fifths of Russians were affected by unsound environmental conditions (Robinson 1989; PBS 2002; Innset 2007).

Environmental policy has followed a similar trajectory in China but has left, if anything, a more troubled ecological legacy. At the outset of Deng Xiaoping's reform movement to open China's economy to market forces, the Chinese Constitution declared in 1978 that protection of the environment was a key to modernization of the nation. The next year the national government enacted the country's first major environmental protection law, and there followed many additional laws over the next two decades, including the Water Pollution Prevention and Control Law (1984), the Air Pollution Prevention and Control Law (1987), the Solid Waste Law (1995), and the Energy Conservation Law (1997). In 1998 China's State Environmental Protection Agency was given ministry status (Wang 2000; PBS 2002). But enforcement has largely been sacrificed to China's aggressive and successful pursuit of rapid economic growth. As a result, the country's environment today remains among the world's worst. Of the 20 cities on the World Bank's recent list of those with the worst air, 16 were Chinese. The European Union estimates that only 1 percent of China's 560 million urban dwellers breathes safe air. According to another estimate, nearly half a billion Chinese are without access to safe drinking water. The World Health Organization has estimated that polluted air and water cause some 750,000 deaths a year, while much of China's rivers and lakes have been found unfit for industrial and agricultural uses. In a speech before the National People's Congress in 2007

Prime Minister Wen Jiabao asserted that China was failing to reach its pollution control goals and that it must improve environmental protection; he also emphasized that the nation's top priority must be to maintain its strong economic growth (Yardley 2004, 2007; Kahn and Yardley 2007).

In addition to national laws and regulation, the transnational migration of pollution problems has resulted in a number of international and multilateral treaties, rules, directives, conventions, and protocols. For example, 170 nations have ratified the 1992 Basel Convention, which establishes legal obligations regarding the import and export of hazardous waste among the parties to the Convention. More recently, 174 nations have ratified the Kyoto Protocol of the United Nations Framework Convention on Climate Change. The Protocol took effect in 2005 and requires developed nations to reduce their greenhouse gas emissions below specified target levels between 2008 and 2012, with these commitments to be reviewed and enforced by UN-based organizations. Importantly, the United States has not ratified either the Basel Convention or the Kyoto Protocol.[10]

The European Union also produces legislation that binds its member states. For example, a new EU regulation on transnational shipments of waste became effective in July 2007. This law, which built on EU commitments under the Basel Convention, bans hazardous waste exports from EU nations to developing countries and specifies information and other requirements for the shipment of waste between countries. It also provides for enhanced enforcement measures, requiring member states to carry out inspections of shipments and to report on their legislation and penalties for illegal shipments.[11]

In June 2007 the EU put into effect new legislation governing the manufacture and use of chemicals and establishing the European Chemicals Agency to administer it. Known as the Registration, Evaluation, and Authorization of Chemicals law, the legislation requires chemical companies to provide government regulators with information on the health and environmental effects of chemicals they produce over specified volumes. The burden is on the companies to demonstrate that the chemicals they produce do not pose risks or that measures have been identified for safe handling of the material. This approach reverses the burden of proof found in the counterpart law in the United States, the 1976 Toxic Substances Control Act. Under this Act, the EPA is required to show that chemicals may pose risks to human health or the environment before the agency can require manufacturers to provide data on health and environmental effects (U.S. Government Accountability Office 2007*a*).

Stimulated by the 1992 United Nations Conference on Environment and Development in Rio de Janeiro, more than 200 multilateral environmental agreements have been entered into by many nations, ranging from agreements between small groups of countries to those comprising 180 and more members. These agreements cover a variety of transnational environmental concerns, from biodiversity and desertification to the marine environment and air pollution. For a variety of reasons, however, effective enforcement of these agreements often remains elusive (see below; Tomkins 2004–5; United Nations Environment Programme 2005, 2006).

B. The Means and Ends of Environmental Regulation

Law addresses industrial pollution to achieve a number of goals: protecting the natural environment, safeguarding the public health, and husbanding nature's resources for future uses are key. But these goals include as well the maintenance of the state's legitimacy and, increasingly, the provision of environmental justice. A number of constraints, especially in political economy, limit the achievement of all of these ends but do not frustrate them entirely or evenly over time and place. Always, however, such constraints shape the ability of law to reach its goals.

As we noted earlier, a variety of legal approaches to controlling industrial pollution have evolved, yet in both modern and modernizing nations around the world cooperative regulatory approaches have been dominant while adversarial and criminal modes of control have remained largely in the background. This appears to be as true of modern capitalist democracies such as the United States, in which the foundational environmental laws of the 1970s appeared in the adversarial language of "command-and-control" state regulation (Yeager 1991; Hunter and Waterman 1992), as it is of the world's principal communist state, China (Lo and Fryxell 2003). In both cases environmental laws made by national governments are delegated to regulatory personnel in the countries' regions, states, and locales, where officials commonly negotiate compliance with business interests rather than insist on the letter of the law. Researchers have also noted such cooperative approaches in Sweden (Marald 2001), Britain (Lo and Fryxell 2003, p. 86), and the Netherlands, where van de Bunt and Huisman (2007) describe recent policy moves toward self-regulation alongside more punitive mechanisms such as administrative fines.

A further move away from adversarial regulation has been the increasing use of market mechanisms to control industrial pollution. In one common approach the government sets permissible pollution levels and allows companies to buy and sell rights to pollute: companies that are not meeting the specified pollution limits can buy rights to exceed them by specified amounts from firms that are discharging pollutants at levels below the specified limits. Applied most often to problems of air pollution, these "tradable permit" policies have been implemented in the United States (Freeman and Kolstad 2007*a*), China (Lo and Fryxell 2003), the Netherlands (van de Bunt and Huisman 2007), and the European Union (European Commission 2007; Freeman and Kolstad 2007*b*).

Meanwhile the criminal sanction maintains two functions. First, it backstops the regulatory regimen to handle cases of business recalcitrance when the cooperative or market-based approaches fail, much the role Braithwaite (2002) has proposed in his arguments for "responsive regulation." Second, criminal penalties are used as a first-line response to some types of environmental offenses. These typically involve the illegal shipping or dumping of hazardous wastes and often involve organized crime activities, along with the witting or unwitting role of legitimate companies that dispose of such wastes, as in the United States (Szasz 1986). Crimes involving the mishandling of hazardous wastes are a focus of current U.S. Sentencing Guidelines for environmental crimes, including as they may relate to acts of terrorism.[12]

Such environmental crimes have also become a focus of international policing agencies such as Interpol, Europol (European Law Enforcement Organization), and Aquapol, a partnership comprising European water police forces and inland navigation inspectorates. Other areas of the criminal law focus in international policing include illegal trafficking in species of wild flora and fauna and illegal trafficking in radioactive or nuclear materials. One of Interpol's current concerns involves links between pollution crimes and terrorism. (On these points see, for example, Tomkins 2004–5; White 2004–5; Interpol 2006, n.d.)

In each of these types of criminal cases identifiable intent is commonly married to disreputable perpetrators, just the sort of combination that is congenial and familiar to criminal law and prosecutors. In contrast, the routine emissions associated with ongoing production processes in legitimate businesses are infrequently considered for criminal prosecution.

The more cooperative regulatory approaches taken for the latter type of environmental offenses may generate adequate compliance rates, as some scholars suggest (e.g., Braithwaite 2002). As we noted, pollution loads have declined in a number of areas. Moreover, recent comparative case study research in the United States and Europe found that neither economic incentive approaches nor prescriptive regulatory approaches to industrial pollution substantially exhibited systematic advantage over the other in achieving compliance; indeed, the authors note that almost all of the national policies they studied comprised a mix of both types of approach (Harrington and Morgenstern 2007).

But more cooperative approaches also carry the risk of co-optation, injustice, and reduced pollution control. Such risks are especially likely where environmental regulators face powerful industrial interests and their state sponsors who prioritize economic growth over environmental protection. In China, despite the centralized rule of the Communist Party, the environmental enforcement function is largely delegated to regional and local officials. This creates regional variation in official approaches to industrial compliance (Lo and Fryxell 2003). But it also places enforcement in the hands of officials who are responsible for maintaining high levels of industrial growth in their locales, and who are therefore typically unwilling to sacrifice that growth to substantial pollution control costs. Provincial officials have often ignored environmental rules, even to the extent of reopening mines and factories that had been closed by central authorities. These officials have also scuttled President Hu Jintao's initiative to create a "green gross domestic product" measure that would incorporate the losses due to environmental damages in calculating the nation's real economic growth. This effort was abandoned in 2007, when pollution-adjusted growth rates in some provinces were reduced to near zero, generating effective political resistance from the provinces. Also revealing the central government's ambivalence regarding environmental protection is the size of China's State Environmental Protection Agency: it has about 200 full-time employees, compared to approximately 18,000 at the U.S. Environmental Protection Agency (Wang 2000; Yardley 2004; Kahn and Yardley 2007).

Although U.S. environmental regulation does not manifest China's levels of overt resistance to and corruption of environmental law, it displays limitations that stem similarly from the state's dual roles as facilitator of economic growth and chief protector of the environment. Research suggests that this is the case with the federal laws regulating industry's water pollution and its handling of hazardous waste.[13]

Atlas's (2007) study of the federal EPA's delegation of enforcement of the nation's hazardous waste law to the states found that on average states levied fines for business violations that were "less than half of what the federal government would impose in similar circumstances" (p. 972). His findings suggest that the states may be more lenient because their governments do not wish to strictly enforce the laws against local businesses, whether to protect general economic well-being or (relatedly) to keep or attract businesses from moving to states with weaker penalties for infraction.[14] Indeed, not only have U.S. EPA policies explicitly allowed for such state reductions in imposed penalties, but the federal agency's own regional offices have been found to commonly impose fines less than those its policies call for (Atlas 2007, pp. 948, 972–73). Because much of the enforcement of the nation's environmental laws generally is delegated to the individual states, these results suggest that penalties may not have the deterrent effects originally intended in the federal laws. Glicksman and Earnhart's (2007) recent research on the deterrent effects of enforcement of the U.S. Clean Water Act in the chemical industry found evidence that federal fines were a greater deterrent than state fines, and that corporate environmental managers perceive fines as a deterrent.

Related deference to economic interests has been found in the language and implementation of the U.S. Clean Water Act (Yeager 1991). Hesitant to intrude on the capitalist prerogatives of private sector businesses, legislators inscribed in this law the government's dependence on industrial firms' knowledge and extant technologies for legal definitions of required pollution controls, rather than engaging in government research and development of cleaner technologies. Subsequent enforcement of the pollution control requirements employed a form of negotiated compliance that relies on persuading noncompliant companies with informal communications and warnings; the use of stricter, more formal, and adversarial sanctions was considerably less common. Thus compliance was often delayed. Pollution control was further limited when companies successfully appealed to the federal EPA for reduced pollution control requirements for their factories (Yeager 1991; compare Hunter and Waterman 1992). Van de Bunt and Huisman (2007, p. 27) cite a study of environmental regulation in the Netherlands that reports compliance delays owing to a similar enforcement approach based on persuasion, and in her research Du Rées (2001) finds that Swedish supervisory agencies' dual roles as advisors and enforcers with respect to polluting facilities constrain the effectiveness of environmental criminal law.

Environmental law enforcement also raises issues of equity. In his study of the U.S. Clean Water Act Yeager (1991) found that larger companies were sanctioned less often than smaller firms, in part because larger companies more successfully argued for reduced pollution controls on their plants. A later study of several U.S. environmental laws found that, controlling for the harm of the violation, small firms were twice as likely to face criminal sanctions as were large corporate violators, except in the case of the Clean Water Act (Firestone 2003). A number of earlier studies of environmental law enforcement suggested that large firms benefit from a credibility or reputational advantage over small firms in the minds of regulators, such that the former receive more favorable enforcement outcomes, holding violations constant. In the United States Shover, Clelland, and Lynxwiler (1986; see also Lynxwiler, Shover, and Clelland 1983) found that large companies were fined smaller sums of money than small ones for violations of the surface mining law because the former were better able to negotiate the nature of offenses with field inspectors, who also viewed the larger firms as more likely to appeal harsh fines. In Britain Hawkins (1983, 1984) similarly discovered that large firms were more successful in persuading water pollution control inspectors that they were socially responsible, as one result of which their pollution violations were more likely to be viewed as accidents than as willful offenses. More recently in the United States Stretesky (2006) found that larger companies more often used the federal EPA's self-policing policy to report their own violations than did smaller companies, perhaps conferring a reputational advantage to the former that lowers their regulatory costs relative to those of smaller firms.

Unequal enforcement outcomes are made more likely under conditions of limited enforcement resources, which require regulatory officials to make choices regarding targets and tactics. The research record reviewed here suggests that regulators commonly choose cautiously by proceeding cooperatively rather than aggressively, especially with powerful business polluters. And enforcement resources are always scarce relative to the environmental protection responsibilities set by law. These resources are also vulnerable to changing political winds. A study in the United States found that industries' investments in pollution control equipment is associated with the federal EPA's enforcement budget, and that that budget is positively related to Democratic Party strength in the Congress (Regens, Seldon, and Elliott 1997). Other evidence suggests that Republican administrations are more likely than Democratic ones to constrain environmental regulation by budgetary restrictions or other means at their disposal (Yeager 1991; Steinzor 2003; Mintz 2004).

Inequitable and inconsistent enforcement of laws undermines the legitimacy of law for regulated companies. In turn, weakened legitimacy spurs higher rates of violation, other factors held constant (Yeager 1995, 2007). The importance of a level playing field in enforcement is suggested in interview-based research on environmental compliance in two U.S. industries. In this study "respondents indicated that they would be far less inclined to voluntary compliance if others were perceived to be 'getting away with it'" (Gunningham, Thornton, and Kagan 2005, p. 310). Decentralized enforcement systems commonly create challenges to the goal of equity in enforcement. Recent federal investigations of U.S. EPA oversight of enforcement across regions and by individual states indicate ongoing difficulties in ensuring consistent and equitable enforcement, including those stemming from reduced budgeting for environmental protection (U.S. Government Accountability Office 2006, 2007*b*).

The integrity of environmental law enforcement is also threatened by the globalization of both pollution and production. When, to lower their production costs, the multinational corporations of developed states export their polluting operations to less developed nations with lax environmental controls, distributing the health and other environmental costs to poor populations while expropriating the profits to the companies' home states, normative commitments to environmental protection are everywhere challenged.[15] For example, in the face of both home and international complaints about the vast environmental damages associated with China's rapid industrial growth, Chinese leaders point to the numerous foreign multinational corporations and their customers for whom polluting Chinese factories are making products. They also say that China will not limit its economic growth by imposing mandatory limits on its carbon dioxide emissions, the principal greenhouse gas contributing to global climate change, because wealthy countries are the original sources of global warming (Kahn and Yardley 2007). The United States is the home base of many of the multinational corporations either contracting their manufacturing to Chinese firms or building factories there, and has yet to ratify the Kyoto Protocol, adding weight to Chinese resistance to such regulation. Such international dynamics also underscore the difficulties in enforcing multilateral environmental agreements, noted earlier.

IV. Conclusions

For forty years now, environmental law and regulation have made some substantial impacts on industrial pollution loads, especially in the United States and the more advanced nations of Europe. Research on compliance and enforcement of environmental laws has grown in tandem with these developments. But both the cause of environmental protection and research on its ways and means require greater efforts to secure sustainable environments and a greater measure of justice for future generations.

There are many areas of investigation that would benefit from future research. Much of the research to date has focused on specific industries, statutes, time frames, and nations (again, especially in the United States and Europe), so there is ample need for additional research that examines industrial compliance and enforcement activities in other sectoral combinations of laws and business and over time. This is particularly true in an area of public policy as dynamic as environmental law. Especially volatile and uncertain in the increasingly globalized world economy are the effects of national and international laws on the levels and distribution of harms from industrial pollution across ecosystems and populations, as reports from Russia and China indicate.

Among the more prominent influences on regulatory policy and industrial compliance with environmental laws are the evolution both of national ideologies and international agreements in the competitive world economy (for example, regarding competing priorities for economic growth vs. environmental protection) and of the corporate cultures of powerful multinational businesses regarding stewardship of the environment. These are closely linked phenomena; among other ways, they are connected by the legitimacy effects of law on compliance rates of businesses. Modern and modernizing nations alike generally proclaim the importance of environmental protection in their formal laws. Future research can help identify the combinations of persuasion, inducement, and compulsion that contribute most to a commitment to compliance with environmental laws on the part of regulated industries and national states over time and socioeconomic contexts.

Analysis of the roles played by national and international publics in the legislation-enforcement-compliance nexus is also important. Here we have in mind research on the political and economic conditions under which public sentiment for greater environmental protection coalesces and expresses itself effectively at various stages of legislation, regulatory implementation, and enforcement. Effective expression of citizens' desires for environmental protection can increase state action in enforcement, strengthen the basis for the legitimacy of environmental law (which, other things being equal, should improve compliance rates), and engender citizen enforcement of laws through direct public pressure on polluting facilities or, as in the United States, lawsuits against polluters and state agencies when the government fails to enforce environmental rules.[16]

Such research may not only discover the bases of effective environmental protection, but may also thereby contribute to both safer environments and a more just distribution worldwide of the benefits and costs of economic growth.

NOTES

1. Some self-report data from corporations do exist. For example, the U.S. Environmental Protection Agency collects periodic discharge monitoring reports from industrial facilities discharging pollutants into rivers and streams; these reports are required to include occasions in which the facilities violate their pollution control permits. See, for example, Yeager (1991).

2. Firm-level violation rates were calculated by dividing a firm's yearly count of violations by the number of DMRs (Discharge Monitoring Reports) per year it was required to submit to EPA.

3. Conventional pollutants: BOD is biological oxygen demand, TSS is total suspended solids, and AOX measures the level of absorbable organic halides in mills' effluent waters (see Kagan, Gunningham, and Thornton 2003, pp. 55–56).

4. It is likely that the variation in the findings of these studies is due, at least in significant part, to methodological differences and limitations (for example, limited samples and focus on specific industries).

5. Sutherland's (1949) differential association theory was developed to explain all types of offending, with its emphasis on individual-level processes. However, he also applied the theory to explain variations in crime between organizations.

6. Braithwaite (1989) also emphasizes how negative relationships between regulatory authorities and companies may produce a defiant effect, increasing the risk of recidivism (see Makkai and Braithwaite 1994).

7. In using the language of "prescriptive regulations" for the more traditional legal approach to pollution control, we seek to avoid the ideological bias that commonly afflicts the alternative label of "command-and-control" regulation. This bias is especially likely when such regulation is counterposed to the alternative market-based or economic incentives approaches to the extent that the former is associated with state command and the latter with choice in the context of free markets. For this language we are indebted to Freeman and Kolstad (2007*b*).

8. But see O'Hear (2004) on the increase in use of the criminal sanction for federal environmental offenses in the United States since the 1980s. On the other hand, 2007 data show a decline in federal criminal enforcement of environmental laws during the administration of George W. Bush (Solomon and Eilperin 2007; compare Environmental Integrity Project 2003; Mintz 2004).

9. According to Wenner (1976, p. 7), "As far back as 1307 in England a royal proclamation was issued prohibiting the burning of coal in furnaces because of the resultant acrid condition in the air above London. Admittedly most such statements of policy have gone unenforced, but at least one unfortunate found that the 1307 English edict was more than symbolic when he was executed for the offense the following year." See also Yeager (1991, pp. 51–83).

10. The United States did sign the Basel Convention in 1990, but has yet to pass the legislation necessary to complete its ratification. For information on the Basel Convention, see "Basel Convention" at http://www.basel.int/ (accessed December 3, 2007) and U.S. Environmental Protection Agency, "International Waste Activities: Basel Convention" at http://www.epa.gov/epaoswer/osw/internat/basel.htm (accessed November 21, 2007). For information on the UN Framework Convention on Climate

Change and the Kyoto Protocol, see, respectively, http://unfccc.int/essential_background/convention/items/2627txt.php and http://unfccc.int/kyoto_protocol/items/2830txt.php.

11. See "Environment: New EU Waste Shipment Legislation Comes into Force Today," Europa: Gateway to the European Union, July 12, 2007. http://europa.eu/rapid/pressReleasesAction.do?reference=IP/07/1078&..... (accessed November 21, 2007).

12. The first two sections in the U.S. Sentencing Commission *Guidelines Manual* describe the criminal penalty levels for "Knowing Endangerment Resulting from Mishandling Hazardous or Toxic Substances, Pesticides or Other Pollutants" (§ 2Q1.1) and for "Mishandling of Hazardous or Toxic Substances or Pesticides; Recordkeeping, Tampering, and Falsification; Unlawfully Transporting Hazardous Materials in Commerce" (§ 2Q1.2). The latter section also refers to increased penalties for such offenses if they relate to acts of terrorism; see also § 3A1.4. See U.S. Sentencing Commission (2007).

13. The Clean Water Act and the Resource Conservation and Recovery Act, respectively.

14. Compare Glicksman and Earnhart (2007, p. 338): "Some evidence indicates that state regulators may be more averse to following up inspections with rigorous enforcement for fear that a state with a reputation for strong environmental enforcement may become comparatively less attractive to new business than a state with a reputation for weak environmental enforcement."

15. This problem mirrors the issues of equity and fairness that are at the heart of scholarship on environmental justice in the United States, which focuses on class and race disparities in the distribution of environmental harms and in enforcement of environmental law (see, for example, Lynch, Stretesky, and Burns 2004; Mohai and Saha 2007).

16. On citizen suits, see, for example, Yeager (1991) and Zinn (2002).

REFERENCES

Adler, Jonathan H. 1998. "Bean Counting for a Better Earth: Environmental Enforcement at the EPA." *Regulation* (Spring): 40–48.

Arora, Seema, and Timothy N. Cason. 1996. "Why Do Firms Volunteer to Exceed Environmental Regulations: Understanding Participation in EPA's 33/50 Program." *Land Economics* 72: 413–32.

Atlas, Mark. 2007. "Enforcement Principles and Environmental Agencies: Principal-Agent Relationships in a Delegated Environmental Program." *Law and Society Review* 41: 939–80.

Benson, Michael L. 1985. "Denying the Guilty Mind: Accounting for Involvement in White Collar Crime." *Criminology* 23: 583–607.

Braithwaite, John. 1989. *Crime, Shame and Reintegration*. New York: Cambridge University Press.

———. 2002. *Restorative Justice and Responsive Regulation*. New York: Oxford University Press.

Braithwaite, John, and Toni Makkai. 1991. "Testing an Expected Utility Model of Corporate Deterrence." *Law and Society Review* 25: 7–40.

Clifford, Mary. 1998. *Environmental Crime: Enforcement, Policy, and Social Responsibility.* Gaithersburg, MD: Aspen.

Clinard, Marshall B. 1983. *Corporate Ethics and Crime: The Role of Middle Management.* Beverly Hills, CA: Sage.

Clinard, Marshall B., and Peter C. Yeager. 1980. *Corporate Crime.* New York: Free Press.

Clinard, Marshall B., Peter C. Yeager, Jeanne M. Brissette, David Petrashek, and Elizabeth Harries. 1979. *Illegal Corporate Behavior.* Washington, DC: U.S. Government Printing Office.

Cohen, Mark A. 2000. "Empirical Research on the Deterrent Effect of Environmental Monitoring and Enforcement." *Environmental Law Reporter* 30: 10245–52.

———. 2001. "Information as a Policy Instrument in Protecting the Environment: What Have We Learned?" *Environmental Law Reporter* 31: 10425–31.

Cohen, Mark A., Scott A. Fenn, and Shameek Konar. 1997. "Environmental and Financial Peformance: Are They Related?" Working Paper, Owen Graduate School of Management, Vanderbilt University.

Cressey, Donald R. 1986. "Why Managers Commit Fraud." *Australian and New Zealand Journal of Criminology* 19: 195–209.

Daboub, A. J., A. M. S. Rasheed, R. L. Priem, and D. A. Gray. 1995. "Top Management Team Characteristics and Corporate Illegality." *Academy of Management Review* 20: 138–70.

DeCanio, Stephen J., and William E. Watkins. 1998. "Investment in Energy Efficiency: Do the Characteristics of Firms Matter?" *Review of Economics and Statistics* 80(1): 95–107.

Du Rées, Helena. 2001. "Can Criminal Law Protect the Environment?" *Journal of Scandinavian Studies in Criminology and Crime Prevention* 2: 109–26.

Earnhart, Dietrich. 2000. "Environmental Crime and Punishment in the Czech Republic: Penalties against Firms and Employees." *Journal of Comparative Economics* 28: 379–99.

Environmental Integrity Project. 2003. "Paying Less to Pollute." http://www.environmentalintegrity.org/pubs/PayingLesstoPollute_final.pdf.

European Commission. 2007. "Combating Climate Change: The EU Leads the Way." http://ec.europa.eu/publications/booklets/move/70/en.pdf.

Finney, Henry C., and Henry R. Lesieur. 1982. "A Contingency Theory of Organizational Crime." In *Research in the Sociology of Organizations,* edited by Samuel B. Bacharach. Greenwich, CT: JAI.

Firestone, Jeremy. 2003. "Enforcement of Pollution Laws and Regulations: An Analysis of Forum Choice." *Harvard Environmental Law Review* 27: 105–76.

Fisse, Brett, and John Braithwaite. 1983. *The Impact of Publicity on Corporate Offenders.* Albany: State University of New York Press.

Flannery, Brenda L., and Douglas R. May. 2000. "Environmental Ethical Decision Making in the U.S. Metal-Finishing Industry." *Academy of Management Journal* 43: 642–62.

Fligstein, Neil. 1987. "The Intraorganizational Power Struggle: The Rise of Finance Presidents in Large Corporations, 1919–1979." *American Sociological Review* 52: 44–58.

Freeman, Jody, and Charles D. Kolstad, eds. 2007*a*. *Moving to Markets in Environmental Regulation: Lessons from Twenty Years of Experience.* New York: Oxford University Press.

Freeman, Jody, and Charles D. Kolstad. 2007*b*. "Prescriptive Environmental Regulations versus Market-Based Incentives." In *Moving to Markets in Environmental Regulation:*

Lessons from Twenty Years of Experience, edited by Jody Freeman and Charles D. Kolstad. New York: Oxford University Press.

Geis, Gilbert. 1967. "The Heavy Electrical Equipment Antitrust Cases of 1961." In *Criminal Behavior Systems*, edited by Marshall B. Clinard and Richard Quinney. New York: Holt, Rinehart and Winston.

Glicksman, Robert L., and Dietrich H. Earnhart. 2007. "The Comparative Effectiveness of Government Interventions on Environmental Performance in the Chemical Industry." *Stanford Environmental Law Journal* 26: 317–71.

Gottfredson, Michael, and Travis Hirschi. 1990. *A General Theory of Crime*. Palo Alto, CA: Stanford University Press.

Grant, Don, and Andrew W. Jones. 2003. "Are Subsidiaries More Prone to Pollute? New Evidence from the EPA's Toxics Release Inventory." *Social Science Quarterly* 84: 163–73.

Grant, Don, Andrew W. Jones, and Albert J. Bergesen. 2002. "Organizational Size and Pollution: The Case of the U.S. Chemical Industry." *American Sociological Review* 67: 389–407.

Gray, Wayne B., and Ronald J. Shadbegian. 2005. "When and Why do Plants Comply? Paper Mills in the 1980s." *Law and Policy* 27: 238–61.

Gunningham, Neil A., Dorothy Thornton, and Robert A. Kagan. 2005. "Motivating Management: Corporate Compliance in Environmental Protection." *Law and Policy* 27: 289–316.

Hammit, James K., and Peter Reuter. 1988. *Measuring and Deterring Illegal Disposal of Hazardous Waste*. Santa Monica, CA: RAND.

Harrington, Winston, and Richard D. Morgenstern. 2007. "International Experience with Competing Approaches to Environmental Policy: Results from Six Paired Cases." In *Moving to Markets in Environmental Regulation: Lessons from Twenty Years of Experience*, edited by Jody Freeman and Charles D. Kolstad. New York: Oxford University Press.

Hawkins, Keith. 1983. "Bargain and Bluff: Compliance Strategy and Deterrence in the Enforcement of Regulation." *Law and Policy Quarterly* 5: 35–73.

———. 1984. *Environment and Enforcement: Regulation and the Social Definition of Pollution*. New York: Oxford University Press.

Hileman, Bette. 2001. "Regulatory Over Compliance." *Government and Policy* 79(26): 27–28.

Hunter, Susan, and Richard W. Waterman. 1992. "Determining an Agency's Regulatory Style: How Does the EPA Water Office Enforce the Law?" *Western Political Quarterly* 45: 403–17.

Innset, Ola. 2007. "Already Wounded Environmental Laws in Russia Getting Brushed Under the Carpet." Translated by Jens Chr. Brugge. *Bellona*. http://www.bellona.org/articles/krivo_nos.

Interpol. 2006. "Interpol Pollution Crimes Working Group: Assessing the Links between Organised Crime and Pollution Crimes." http://www.interpol.int/Public/EnvironmentalCrime/Pollution/organizedCrime.pdf.

———. n.d. "International European Police Co-operation on the Water." http://www.interpol.int/Public/EnvironmentalCrime/Pollution/Aquapol.pdf.

Kagan, Robert A., Neil Gunningham, and Dorothy Thornton. 2003. "Explaining Corporate Environmental Performance: How Does Regulation Matter? *Law and Society Review* 37: 51–90.

Kahn, Joseph, and Jim Yardley. 2007. "As China Roars, Pollution Reaches Deadly Extremes." *New York Times* (August 26). http://www.nytimes.com/2007/08/26/world/asia/26china.html.

Khanna, Madhu, and Lisa Damon. 1999. "EPA's Voluntary 33/50 Program: Impact on Toxic Releases and Economic Performance of Firms." *Journal of Environmental Economics and Management* 37: 1–25.

Lasley, James R. 1988. "Toward a Control Theory of White-Collar Offending." *Journal of Quantitative Criminology* 4: 347–62.

Laufer, William S. 2003. "Social Accountability and Corporate Greenwashing." *Journal of Business Ethics* 43: 253–61.

Lo, Carlos W. H., and Gerald E. Fryxell. 2003. "Enforcement Styles among Environmental Protection Officials in China." *Journal of Public Policy* 23: 81–115.

Lynch, Michael J., Paul B. Stretesky, and Ronald G. Burns. 2004. "Slippery Business: Race, Class, and Legal Determinants of Penalties against Petroleum Refineries." *Journal of Black Studies* 34: 421–40.

Lynxwiler, John, Neal Shover, and Donald A. Clelland. 1983. "The Organization and Impact of Inspector Discretion in a Regulatory Bureaucracy." *Social Problems* 30: 425–36.

Makkai, Toni, and John Braithwaite. 1994. "The Dialectics of Corporate Deterrence." *Journal of Research in Crime and Delinquency* 31: 347–73.

Marald, Erland. 2001. "The BT Kemi Scandal and the Establishment of the Environmental Crime Concept." *Journal of Scandinavian Studies in Criminology and Crime Prevention* 2: 149–70.

McKendall, Marie A., Carole Sanchez, and Paul Sicilian. 1999. "Corporate Governance and Corporate Illegality: The Effects of Board Structure on Environmental Violations." *International Journal of Organizational Analysis* 7: 201–23.

McKendall, Marie A., and John A. Wagner III. 1997. "Motive, Opportunity, Choice, and Corporate Illegality." *Organizational Science* 8: 624–47.

Mintz, Joel A. 2004. "'Treading Water': A Preliminary Assessment of EPA Enforcement During the Bush II Administration." *Environmental Law Reporter* 34: 10933–53.

Mohai, Paul, and Robin Saha. 2007. "Racial Inequality in the Distribution of Hazardous Waste: A National-Level Reassessment." *Social Problems* 54: 343–70.

Nadeau, Louis W. 1997. "EPA Effectiveness at Reducing the Duration of Plant-Level Noncompliance." *Journal of Environmental Economics and Management* 34: 54–78.

Nakayama, Granta Y. 2007. "Getting Results at the EPA." *Washington Post* (October 3), p. A22. http://www.washingtonpost.com.

Natural Resources Defense Council. 2007. "Environmental Laws and Treaties." http://www.nrdc.org/reference/laws.asp.

O'Hear, Michael M. 2004. "Sentencing the Green-Collar Offender: Punishment, Culpability, and Environmental Crime." *Journal of Criminal Law and Criminology* 95: 133–276.

Paternoster, Raymond, and Sally Simpson. 1993. "A Rational Choice Theory of Corporate Crime." In *Routine Activity and Rational Choice*, vol. 5 of *Advances in Criminology Theory*, edited by Ronald V. Clarke and Marcus Felson. New Brunswick, NJ: Transaction Press.

Paternoster, Raymond, and Sally Simpson. 1996. "Sanction Threats and Appeals to Morality: Testing a Rational Choice Model of Corporate Crime." *Law and Society Review* 30: 549–83.

PBS. 2002. *Commanding Heights* (section on history of environmental law in Russia, China). http://www.pbs.org/wgbh/commandingheights/lo/countries/ru/ru_env.html.

Piquero, Nicole Leeper, M. Lyn Exum, and Sally S. Simpson. 2005. "Integrating the Desire-for-Control and Rational Choice in a Corporate Crime Context." *Justice Quarterly* 22: 252–80.

Reed, Gary E., and Peter Cleary Yeager. 1996. "Organizational Offending and Neoclassical Criminology: Challenging the Reach of a General Theory of Crime." *Criminology* 34: 357–82.

Regens, James L., Barry J. Seldon, and Euel Elliott. 1997. "Modeling Compliance to Environmental Regulation: Evidence from Manufacturing Industries." *Journal of Policy Modeling* 19: 683–96.

Robinson, Nicholas A. 1989. "Soviet Environmental Protection: The Challenge for Legal Studies." *Pace Environmental Law Review* 7: 117–50. http://digitalcommons.pace.edu/cgi/viewcontent.cgi?article=1382&context=la wfaculty.

Scalia, John. 1999. "Federal Enforcement of Environmental Laws, 1997." *Bureau of Justice Statistics Special Report* (November). Washington, DC: U.S. Department of Justice.

Shover, Neal, Donald A. Clelland, and John Lynxwiler. 1986. *Enforcement or Negotiation: Constructing a Regulatory Bureaucracy.* Albany: State University of New York Press.

Shover, Neal, and Aaron S. Routhe. 2005. "Environmental Crime." In *Crime and Justice: A Review of Research,* vol. 32, edited by Michael Tonry. Chicago: University of Chicago Press.

Simpson, Sally S. 1986. "The Decomposition of Antitrust: Testing a Multi-Level, Longitudinal Model of Profit-Squeeze." *American Sociological Review* 51: 859–75.

———. 1987. "Cycles of Illegality: Antitrust Violations in Corporate America." *Social Forces* 65: 943–63.

———. 2000. "Corporate Crime." In *Introduction to Sociology,* edited by George Ritzer. Hightstown, NJ: McGraw-Hill.

———. 2002. *Corporate Crime, Law, and Social Control.* New York: Cambridge University Press.

Simpson, Sally S., Joel Garner, and Carole Gibbs. 2007. *Why Do Corporations Obey Environmental Law? Assessing Punitive and Cooperative Strategies of Corporate Crime Control.* Final Technical Report, National Institute of Justice, Grant No. 2001-LJ-CX-0020. Washington, DC: U.S. Department of Justice.

Simpson, Sally S., Carole Gibbs, and Lee Ann Slocum. 2008. "Comparing Predictors of Corporate Anti- and Pro-Social Environmental Behavior." Working Paper, Department of Criminology and Criminal Justice, University of Maryland, College Park.

Simpson, Sally S., Anthony R. Harris, and Brian Mattson. 1993. "Measuring Corporate Crime." In *Understanding Corporate Criminality,* edited by Michael B. Blankenship. New York: Garland.

Simpson, Sally S., and Christopher Koper. 1992. "'Deterring' Corporate Crime." *Criminology* 30: 347–75.

Simpson, Sally S., and Christopher Koper. 1997. "The Changing of the Guard: Top Management Characteristics, Organizational Strain and Antitrust Offending." *Journal of Quantitative Criminology* 13: 373–404.

Simpson, Sally S., and Nicole Leeper Piquero. 2002. "Low Self-Control, Organizational Theory, and Corporate Crime." *Law and Society Review* 36: 509–48.

Smith, N. Craig, Sally S. Simpson, and Chun-Yao Huang. 2007. "Why Managers Fail to Do the Right Thing: An Empirical Study of Unethical and Illegal Conduct." *Business Ethics Quarterly* 17: 633–67.

Solomon, John, and Juliet Eilperin. 2007. "Bush's EPA Is Pursuing Fewer Polluters." *Washington Post* (September 30), p. A1. http://www.washingtonpost.com.

Steinzor, Rena. 2003. *Testimony before the Subcommittee on Fisheries, Wildlife, and Water of the U.S. Senate regarding Implementation of the Clean Water Act. U.S. Senate.* http://www.epw.senate.gov/108th/Steinzor_091603.htm.

Stretesky, Paul B. 2006. "Corporate Self-Policing and the Environment." *Criminology* 44: 671–708.

Sutherland, Edwin H. 1949. *White Collar Crime*. New York: Dryden.

Szasz, Andrew. 1986. "Corporations, Organized Crime, and the Disposal of Hazardous Waste: An Examination of the Making of a Criminogenic Regulatory Structure." *Criminology* 24: 1–27.

Tomkins, Kevin. 2004–5. "Police, Law Enforcement, and the Environment." *Current Issues in Criminal Justice* 16: 294–306.

United Nations Environment Programme. 2005. "Envisioning the Next Steps for MEA Compliance and Enforcement." http://www.unep.org/dec/support/mdg_meeting_col.htm.

———. 2006. "Developing Responses to Factors Inhibiting Implementation and Enforcement of Multilateral Environment Agreements." http://www.unep.org/dec/support/mdg_meeting_col.htm.

U.S. Environmental Protection Agency. 2007. "FY 2006 OECA Accomplishments Report." Office of Enforcement and Compliance Assurance. Washington, DC. http://www.epa.gov/compliance/resources/reports/accomplishments/oeca/fy06accomplishment.pdf.

U.S. Government Accountability Office. 2006. "Environmental Compliance and Enforcement: EPA's Effort to Improve and Make More Consistent Its Compliance and Enforcement Activities." *Testimony before the Committee on Environment and Public Works, U.S. Senate,* by John B. Stephenson, director, Natural Resources and Environment. GAO-06–840T. June. http://www.gao.gov/new.items/d06840t.pdf.

———. 2007*a*. "Chemical Regulation: Comparison of U.S. and Recently Enacted European Union Approaches to Protect against the Risks of Toxic Chemicals." GAO-07–825. August. http://www.gao.gov/new.items/d07825.pdf.

———. 2007*b*. "Environmental Protection: EPA-State Enforcement Partnership Has Improved, but EPA's Oversight Needs Further Enhancement." GAO-07–883. July. http://www.gao.gov/new.items/d07883.pdf.

U.S. Sentencing Commission. 2007. *Guidelines Manual,* §3E1.1. (November). http://www.ussc.gov/2007guid/GL2007.pdf.

van de Bunt, Henk, and Wim Huisman. 2007. "Organizational Crime in the Netherlands." In *Crime and Justice in the Netherlands,* edited by Michael Tonry and Catrien Bijleveld. Vol. 35 of *Crime and Justice: A Review of Research,* edited by Michael Tonry. Chicago: University of Chicago Press.

Vandenbergh, Michael. 2001. "The Social Meaning of Environmental Command and Control." *Virginia Environmental Law Journal* 20: 191–219.

Vaughan, Diane. 1983. *Controlling Unlawful Organizational Behavior.* Chicago: University of Chicago Press.

———. 1998. "Rational Choice, Situated Action, and Social Control." *Law and Society Review* 32: 23–61.

Wang, Alex. 2000. "The Downside of Growth: Law, Policy and China's Environmental Crisis." *Perspectives* 2 (October 31). http://www.oycy.org/Perspectives/8_103100/downside_of_growth.htm.

Wenner, L. M. 1976. *One Environment under Law: A Public Policy Dilemma*. Pacific Palisades, CA: Goodyear.

White, Rob. 2004–5. "Environmental Crime in Global Context: Exploring the Theoretical and Empirical Complexities." *Current Issues in Criminal Justice* 16: 271–85.

Yardley, Jim. 2004. "Rivers Run Black, and Chinese Die of Cancer." *New York Times* (September 12). http://www.nytimes.com/2004/09/12/international/asia/12china.html.

———. 2007. "Chinese Premier Focuses on Pollution and the Poor." *New York Times* (March 5). http://www.nytimes.com/2007/03/05/world/asia/05china.html.

Yeager, Peter C. 1981. "The Politics of Corporate Social Control: The Federal Response to Industrial Water Pollution." Ph.D. dissertation, University of Wisconsin, Madison.

———. 1991. *The Limits of the Law: The Public Regulation of Private Pollution*. New York: Cambridge University Press.

———. 1995. "Management, Morality and Law: Organizational Forms and Ethical Deliberations." In *Corporate Crime: Contemporary Debates,* edited by Frank Pearce and Laureen Snider. Toronto: University of Toronto Press.

———. 2007. "Understanding Corporate Lawbreaking: From Profit Seeking to Law Finding." In *International Handbook of White-Collar and Corporate Crime,* edited by Henry N. Pontell and Gilbert Geis. New York: Springer.

Yokoyama, Minoru. 2007. "Environmental Pollution by Corporations in Japan." In *International Handbook of White-Collar and Corporate Crime,* edited by Henry N. Pontell and Gilbert Geis. New York: Springer.

Zey-Ferrell, Mary, Mark Weaver, and O. C. Farrell 1979. "Predicting Unethical Behavior among Marketing Practitioners." *Human Relations* 32: 557–69.

Zinn, Matthew D. 2002. "Policing Environmental Regulatory Enforcement: Cooperation, Capture, and Citizen Suits." *Stanford Environmental Law Journal* 21: 81–174.

CHAPTER 14

MONEY LAUNDERING

MICHAEL LEVI AND PETER REUTER

THE conversion of criminal incomes to forms that allow the offender unfettered spending and investment has been an ongoing concern to both criminals and the state since at least the early days of the American Mafia. Meyer Lansky's claim to fame was partly his supposed skill in concealing the origins of funds used to buy real estate and legitimate businesses. The goal was to avoid tax evasion charges, which had famously brought down Al Capone, by making it difficult to trace the connection between wealth, its ownership and its criminal sources.[1] One reason for this systematic approach to crime control was the growth of organized crime, itself stimulated by Prohibition. Laws against handling stolen property traditionally referred only to the physical property obtained in the course of the crime. Only in the past generation has the disguise or concealment of funds obtained from crimes itself become a criminal activity, created by a new set of laws and regulations aimed at what is now called "money laundering."

Developed initially in the United States to combat use of international banks for tax evasion, money laundering controls became a significant component of the war on drugs in the 1990s and the more localized Italian struggle against the *brigate rossi* (Red Brigades) in the 1980s. More recently the regime has grown into an extensive and global set of controls aimed at a wide array of offenses, from cigarette smuggling to corruption of high-level officials and terrorist finance. The fundamental innovation is to shift to the financial system (very broadly defined) the responsibility for keeping criminal money out and reporting instances when they suspect that criminal money has successfully entered or is being inserted into legitimate institutions. The liability has both criminal and regulatory penalties to induce compliance by banks, insurance companies, pawnbrokers, and an expanding array of other businesses and professions, including, most controversially in some countries, lawyers. In both the United Kingdom and the United States the result has been a modest flow of cases against banks and their employees for violation of these laws, occasionally accompanied by fines in the tens of millions of dollars.

The Financial Action Task Force (FATF), a collection of 34 governments (as of 2007) of wealthy nations, has created the rules that are now on the books of almost every nation, rich and poor. A complex collaborative system, including the International Monetary Fund and the World Bank, monitor compliance with the rules.

Money laundering is difficult to study in part because it is conceptually elusive. Is it a separate activity, like the fencing of stolen goods, or is it better thought of as an element of certain criminal acts, such as conspiracy is? Sometimes it is indeed very like conspiracy, an inherent part of the act; for example, Andrew Fastow, the treasurer of Enron, pled guilty to money laundering as well as fraud, but they were two dimensions of the same act. Just as some thieves fence the goods they have stolen, some fraudsters, drugs traffickers, and robbers may put proceeds into bank accounts or businesses they run. In other instances laundering clearly is a distinct act, involving parties with no other connection to the predicate crime; for example, Lucy Edwards, a senior executive in charge of Eastern European operations at the Bank of New York, and her husband, the businessman Peter Berlin, earned large sums by laundering $7 billion dollars for some Russians who were either evading taxes or concealing the fruits of criminal enterprise (Block and Weaver 2004).

Our focus here is on money laundering itself rather than the controls, though we cannot avoid some discussion of the latter and their effects, since the offense is so shaped by the regime.[2] We describe the market for money laundering services. Who seeks to launder money? What crimes are they involved in, and in what countries? Who provides the services, and what sorts of services are provided to what sorts of people? The incompleteness of our answers to these descriptive questions is not a function of the brevity of the chapter but of the small amount of serious research and the difficulty that the phenomenon itself represents for research purposes. We also provide a brief assessment of the consequences of the control system.

Our conclusions are readily summarized:

- There is a great deal of uncertainty as to how much money is laundered and what share of criminal proceeds are laundered through the financial system rather than spent or stored for future use.
- The methods used for laundering are frequently unsophisticated.
- Professional money launderers certainly exist, but they may account for a small share of all laundering (at least by volume of offenders) and seem to occupy narrow niches.
- Although a huge amount of data is generated by the control system, little is utilized for investigation.

- The system of money laundering controls has weak conceptual foundations, and there is no evidence that it does much more than allow prosecutors to occasionally add additional criminal charges and obtain more severe penalties.

In the first section we define and describe the offense. Section II then presents examples that illustrate the variety of methods available and kinds of persons involved, along with some classifications. In section III we discuss the relationship of money laundering to corruption control, a major current motivation for the control system. In section IV we analyze the effects of anti–money laundering controls and offer a few comments on policy.

I. Defining Money Laundering in Law and Practice

Legally, money laundering refers only to concealing the proceeds of specific crimes (the *predicate* crime). The list of predicates varies cross countries but has gradually been extended in most nations to all crimes with a maximum sentence of at least one year of imprisonment (e.g., the European Union Third Directive of 2005). Beyond the bare bones description of the act in terms of its intent, the question of what constitutes the act is more difficult. A standard but much critiqued description of the laundering process (e.g., by van Duyne 2003; van Duyne and Levi 2005) identifies three components: placement, layering, and integration.

Placement is the process of putting illicit funds into the financial system. This may be the riskiest stage for the criminal as it is only here that there is a clear connection between the money and the crime itself. As a result of this enhanced risk, much of the enforcement has been targeted at this stage of the process (Lilley 2006). The U.S. State Department (2003) claims that the regulations in place in the United States have resulted in most placement being done abroad, though it offers no supporting evidence.

Layering is the process of moving the money through the financial system in order to further conceal the connection between the money and the crime. It is common—though no one except the offenders knows how common—to use a variety of identities, shell companies, and trusts in a number of countries to make the trail more difficult to follow. The FATF annual *Typology* reports provide a useful introduction into some of the ways the financial system can be exploited to make illegitimate funds both hard to trace and seemingly legitimate.

Integration is the final stage, in which the funds reenter the legitimate economy. The launderer might choose to invest the funds into real estate, luxury assets, or business ventures or might consume the resources with the claim, if challenged, that the funds were legitimately acquired.

Many parties can be involved in laundering, but the number can be as low as one. When Andrew Fastow used offshore banks to remove money from the principal accounts of the Enron Corporation, he committed both the predicate felony and the money laundering itself. There has been no claim that any one at the relevant banks *knowingly* assisted him. This insider involvement is not uncommon for large-scale financial frauds (see Levi, this volume); just as Cressey (1955) argued that all accountants could commit embezzlement, the perpetrator has exactly the skills required to also conceal the sources of his or her funds. At the other end of the sophistication spectrum, if drug dealers or thieves put the cash they have obtained from crime into a bank account in their own names, this is legally considered to be the offense of laundering in the United States and the United Kingdom (though not in countries where self-laundering is not criminalized). Thus one finds many newspaper reports stating that people have been charged both with drug trafficking and money laundering.

Frequently, however, there is a customer for and a supplier of money laundering services. Once this individual generates a volume of business too large to spend immediately, the predicate drug dealer will need someone with other skills to launder his or her revenues. Both will be guilty of money laundering, a useful fact to remember when interpreting statistics from the criminal justice system. It may be even more common that there are three parties: the money launderer could be an intermediary who recruits someone inside a financial institution to make the transaction or opens accounts to facilitate transactions in violation of due diligence Know Your Customer regulations that the institution is required by law to follow.

Although there are hundreds of articles and books that review responses to money laundering, and even specialist periodicals such as the *Journal of Money Laundering Control,* the empirical research literature on the phenomenon of money laundering is very slight indeed; key references are Beare and Schneider (2007), van Duyne and Levi (2005), Levi and Reuter (2006), Naylor (2004), Passas (2003), and Reuter and Truman (2004). In contrast to drug dealing, there are no ethnographic studies of money laundering; money launderers are better able to protect themselves from intrusion by researchers. There are occasional books written by reporters about particular cases, some of which are very useful; see, for example, Woolner (1994), who chronicles a money laundering investigation that reached the highest level of the Colombian cocaine trade. Criminal and civil complaints in the United States and elsewhere sometimes also provide useful details. None of these sources provide a basis for generalizing patterns of laundering over time and place.

More might be expected from official overviews; after all, given the political, bureaucratic, regulatory, and enforcement resources devoted to combating laundering, one might hope to see some systematic analysis of the modus operandi developed by launderers. Each year the FATF produces the oddly named *Typologies* report, which provides examples of different kinds of money laundering methods, often clustered around a particular theme, such as the use of professional intermediaries, trade-based value transfers, or wire transfers, or the laundering of funds from particular activities, such as Value-Added Tax frauds. These are intended to be highly schematic representations which are often hard to understand, but they do provide a useful additional set of descriptions. However, it would be a mistake to think that these are always based on a rigorous examination of a run of cases; rather, they may represent just whatever those consulted are aware of and choose to volunteer. Enforcement agencies typically are too busy dealing with cases and processing inputs such as reports from banks to review systematically what they might learn from the cases they deal with, though occasionally deeply sanitized reports are issued. Otherwise we are reliant on what appears in the press concerning specific high-level cases. The *Wall Street Journal* has provided detailed and insightful coverage of some major cases, such as the Beacon Hill case (involving J. P. Morgan-Chase) and the ABN-AMBRO scandal concerning payments in the Middle East (e.g., Simpson 2005). The growing literature on corruption in developing countries has also generated some writing on money laundering (Levi, Dakolias, and Greenberg 2007), though mostly about governance and law (e.g., Pieth, Low, and Cullen 2007) and scandals rather than economic analysis.[3]

It is rare for a description to be complete; instead, it will be focused on a particular transaction or individual and omit a lot of the contextual detail. An exception is the case of John Mathewson, whose activities are briefly described in the next section. He had strong incentives to provide everything to the U.S. authorities and did manage to give them his complete electronic records (U.S. Senate 2001).

II. Money Laundering Methods and Markets

There is both a demand and a supply component to money laundering. It takes little to create a legal basis for the offense of laundering: concealment or disposal of the proceeds of any crime. Anyone minded to store crime proceeds for a short or long period may be said to be seeking to launder money, and anyone actually supplying those facilities is a de facto launderer. Likewise, all ambitious offenders who try to hide their assets from the authorities, to make it harder to connect them to the crimes and thus confiscate their wealth, will seek to launder. All that is needed is a bank account or some similar relationship with a financial institution that allows the movement of funds from one location and owner to another location and owner. Any businesspeople willing (for profit or in exchange for vice opportunities or relief from debts) to run up additional revenues on their cash registers or to sell antiques, art, and jewelry (especially for cash) can help criminals conceal the proceeds of crime. This may put at risk their own businesses and assets, as well as their liberty.

However, many money laundering *cases* involve more elaborated and distinct roles than this. We offer here a few brief descriptions of figures involved in different ways as providers or intermediaries. Our tentative conclusion, still in the nature of a conjecture, is that most money launderers occupy quite narrow niches. Some, perhaps most, have only a very few customers; they will be cautious in taking on new business. This has important implications for the market for money laundering services.

John Mathewson was a U.S. businessman who in 1984 started a bank in the Cayman Islands that catered primarily to U.S. tax evaders, as indicated by the flurry of convictions that emerged after he turned state's evidence. His customers learned about his services through word of mouth or through advertisements at the airport on the British colony's main island, Grand Cayman. They usually came to his Guardian Bank and Trust Company offices with a letter of reference and enough cash to pay the $8,000 fee to set up and maintain the non-interest-bearing accounts. Mathewson had no prior criminal record; he had been a moderately successful small-town businessman.

A recent case involves allegations that a banker with a long record of involvement in other questionable activities (e.g., busting UN sanctions against supplying oil to South Africa, defrauding the Soviet government in oil transactions) operated a Caribbean bank that laundered money from what is called "carousel fraud."[4] The U.K. authorities have identified 2,500 persons involved in such fraud with accounts at that one bank, and over £50 million in tax evaded. No allegations have been made that the banker had any involvement in the fraud itself. He appears to have occupied a narrow, though lucrative niche.

A Russian national, Alexander Yegmenov, laundered funds for numerous Russian criminals by setting up literally thousands of shell companies in New York State, where the requirement to identify owners and directors is not (or certainly was not then) enforced (Komisar 1999). Yegmenov may himself have been involved in some of the offenses in Russia but seemed to spend much of his time on the U.S. laundering activities. No charges have been brought against the banks he used for these purposes. Other than this, along with many aspects of "organized crime" there are many allegations and ongoing investigations about real estate and other business moguls acting as launderers for the underworld, but evidence in the form of convictions is thin on the ground. (Another aspect of this, the involvement of lawyers and other professionals, is discussed later.) Moreover, as with other investment firms, launderers can lose as well as gain money from their investments, for example in real estate (van Duyne and Levi 2005).

A. How Much Money Laundering Is There?

A modern problem requires estimation of its scale, so that it can be compared to other problems and so that performance measures can be developed against which to judge the efforts of those who aim to combat it. Thus there have been modest efforts to develop estimates of money laundering at the national and global levels (see Reuter and Truman 2004, chapter 2, for a review).

It is not clear that it is either useful or feasible to estimate the figure. Numbers are frequently cited with minimal documentation, becoming "facts by repetition." For example, the IMF estimated a total of $590 billion to $1.5 trillion globally in 1996. In 2005 the United Nations cited the range of $500 billion to $1 trillion (http://www.unodc.org/unodc/en/money_laundering.html, accessed June 2, 2005). A sustained effort between 1996 and 2000 by the FATF to produce a fully documented estimate failed. There are, however, a few estimates of the potential demand for money laundering that are regularly treated as actual money laundering estimates. The estimates fall into two categories: macroeconomic and microeconomic. Neither yields estimates that can be considered anything more than indicative. The macroeconomic estimates are methodologically flawed: they generate implausibly high figures. For example, taken at face value they indicate that the German economy grew 50 percent faster than measured officially over the period 1991–2001 (Schneider and Enste 2000). The microeconomic estimates lack a credible empirical base. For example, fraud, the largest source of criminal revenues for the United States, is estimated from a survey that had only a 10 percent response rate and asked questions very imperfectly related to the relevant quantity (Association of Certified Fraud Examiners 2002 and follow ups to 2008).

Even taken at face value these numbers are only weakly related to money laundering. Much of this income is earned by people who use the cash to purchase legal goods directly without making use of any financial institution. Small-time thieves earning $25,000 annually are unlikely to make use of a bank or any other means of storing or transferring money. It is impossible to estimate or even guess what share of these revenues will require laundering.

The aim of laundering is to conceal the derivation of funds from crime and yet retain control over them. This involves trust of a particular person or persons—perhaps a member of one's family or ethnic or religious group—or trust of an institution, such as a bank or a money service business (MSB). The imagery of money laundering may involve cross-border transfers, but it is not clear how often this happens; logically it should depend on the risks and advantages of keeping funds within one's own jurisdiction. But sending money via institutions is not the only technique; the point is to transfer *value* by whatever means, including mispricing and misdescribing exported goods (Zdanowicz 2004) or matching those businesspeople or tourists who want dollars or euros with those who have those currencies as proceeds of crime (Passas 2003; FATF 2006). Such financial matchmaking can be undertaken by banks, but it can also be done by partly legitimate networks, usually within the same ethnic or nationality group. The global trade in money is assisted by the vast sums repatriated by millions of expatriate workers around the world, making it hard to distinguish legitimate- from illegitimate-source funds. The authorities have tried to regulate this market by requiring MSBs to register and to identify both the senders and the recipients of funds.

It is helpful to look at laundering techniques in terms of the problems that offenders have to confront. The laundering methods used may depend on the nature of the regime that is in place (see section III). The identification of "suspiciousness" by professionals and others with a legal responsibility to combat money laundering is often a judgment that the people or transactions are "out of place" for the sort of account they have and the people they purport to be. If the would-be predicate offenders start out with a business that is being used as a medium for what looks like legitimate activity, such as Enron before its collapse, then placement of funds may look unproblematic: corporate lawyers may be falling over themselves to offer well-paid services in the construction of corporate vehicles. They will not routinely suspect senior corporate staff of being major criminals, perhaps especially because they were appointed by them and would like to be paid by them in the future. Because many frauds would be unsuccessful if they did *not* look like legitimate activity, this gives violators a structural advantage over other types of offenders. We now turn to examine what is known about patterns of laundering, and because many studies are country-specific, we examine European evidence before turning to the laundering of the proceeds of corruption. (See also Beare and Schneider 2007 for a broad range of Canadian cases based on investigations by the Royal Canadian Mounted Police.)

B. Drugs and Money Laundering in Europe

Although European research on laundering is patchy, it is more extensive than in the United States and on a par with the Canadian work. The relative lack of research is surprising, given that the United States has been the policy leader in this field.

Van Duyne and Levi (2005) review what is known about money management by European offenders. The classification in table 14.1 aims to map the ways Dutch drug perpetrators attempt to hide from government the crime money itself, or the illegal ways of acquisition. The categories are not mutually exclusive because more than one way of handling proceeds of crime may be employed in the same case

Table 14.1. Methods of disguising and laundering crime proceeds

Forms of concealment/disguise	Frequency
Export of currency	31
Disguise of ownership	10
False justification	
Loan-back	3
Payroll	2
Speculation	1
Bookkeeping	7
"Untraceable"	4

Source: van Duyne and Levi 2005.

and with the same money. For example, a portion of the money may be exported, part of which is subsequently brought back by means of a loan-back construction, while the expensive car is paid for in cash, to be subsequently put in the name of a relative to retain effective ownership in the event of proceeds confiscation. Subsequent gangland killings in the Netherlands have targeted (previously blackmailed) wealthy real estate magnates such as Willem Endstra, who was alleged to be the banker for the underworld and whose murder in 2004 supposedly left some serious criminals uncertain of where "their" assets were (personal interviews). The issue of *how* offenders get proceeds into those property purchases is often more obscure, though some notaries have been suspected of being conduits (Lankhorst and Nelen 2005). Many British cases involve lawyers depositing substantial sums in cash in the law firm's client and even office accounts (Bell 2002; Middleton 2008). In one case, £193 million was passed through the client account of the law firm in which the accused, who was not himself a solicitor, worked. This enabled the fraudsters to say that these solicitors could confirm the authenticity of the companies concerned, and that the transactions were taking place on behalf of their legitimate clients (Middleton 2008).

Bearing in mind that these observations derive only from identified cases, and some may have derived from an era in which it was expected that money hidden abroad was safe from the clutches of the courts, it seems plausible to interpret the evidence as follows.

1. *Export of Crime Money*

As can be observed in table 14.1, in most cases the money was simply exported: the 31 observations, covering 17 cases, concerned €16.6 million that had been found in foreign bank accounts (over a time span of eight years). In four additional cases there was evidence of money export to foreign bank accounts, though either these accounts were already cleared before the police arrived or the files did not mention any figures. In the cases of Turkish and Moroccan drug entrepreneurs, this export appeared to be an obvious option, given their country of origin. Either through bureaux de change or by means of physically transporting the cash, the crime moneys were brought safely to their home countries.

2. *Disguise of Ownership*

The second most frequently observed form of safeguarding assets while still being able to use them is the simple *disguise of ownership* by putting them in someone else's name. Only in a few cases was this done with any sophistication, for example, when corporate structures (legal persons) were used. The usual defects were the closeness of the relationship between the nominal owner and the beneficiary and the difficulty of the nominal owners to prove having possessed the means to acquire the assets in the first place. Nominal owners were frequently acquaintances or relatives; some found themselves to be the involuntary owner of unknown property. For example, the mother of one middle-level Dutch cocaine trafficker, who lived only on a meager pension, was surprised to learn that she owned a villa. In other cases, criminals (ab)used relatives by putting (moveable) assets or bank accounts in their names.

Though preexisting legal persons were used to channel drug money, few of them were actually set up for the purpose of disguising ownership. The notable exceptions were a British crime entrepreneur, two Dutch cannabis traffickers, and a Turkish heroin wholesaler, all of whom invested in real estate using legal persons for the beneficial ownership. Another Dutch hash trafficker established an extensive network of legal persons to disguise the ownership of cash, bank accounts, and vehicles. These corporate constructions to *disguise* real ownership overlap with the laundering (*justification*) category discussed below: tampering with paperwork and with other evidence.

3. *False Justification*

From the point of view of "real" laundering, the successful *justification* (in the event of investigation) of ill-gotten moneys or assets is the core craft: providing documentary evidence that the increase in wealth, whether in terms of money, assets, or valuables, has a legitimate source. One of the methods most frequently used is *loan-back construction*. Given the frequent references in the literature to this method, it is surprising to learn that its sophistication is shallow. Van Duyne, Kouwenberg, and Romeijn (1990) described a professional provider of loan-back constructions who designed professional loan contracts, complete with related correspondence and a real money flow of interest and repayments to the lender corporation abroad in order to imitate perfectly real loan transactions (and deduct the interest paid from tax liabilities). The loan-back provider saw to it that his clients did pay the required monthly interest and repayment. Except for one case, such professional conduct could not be observed in this study. Loan contracts were sometimes missing, or the apparent "contracts" did not mention the repayment and interest terms, nor was there any record that the required demonstrable "flow back" of interest and installment payments were carried out.

In two cases the laundering of a monthly income by means of salary payment could be observed. In one case €75,000 was loaned to an independent but friendly small firm which subsequently handed out a modest monthly salary. This laundering was not intended to justify the millions of euros in proceeds, but to placate the Inland Revenue Service and create the illusion of a genuine income.

"Real" laundering, by setting up *phony bookkeeping* to make the money really "white," appeared to be a craft mainly used by drug entrepreneurs who lived in the Netherlands, mimicking the sort of business they were in. For example, a florist, using his horticulture as a cover for growing cannabis plants, had to obtain invoices to cover expenses as well as the income from the cannabis sales. In the cocaine traffic with Colombians, certificates of transportation of goods and accompanying phony paperwork with commodities (sugar) on the parallel market was carried out to justify the return flow of the money to Colombia. Such cover stories were easily busted by investigators.

4. *The Untraceability of Crime Profits*

This is a "default" category, consisting of supposed moneys that could not be found.

C. Worldwide Laundering?

A recurrent refrain in the money laundering literature and political speeches is the transnational dimension: money trails around the world through impenetrable accounts held in sunny, faraway resorts. Such far-flung hideaways do exist, but the question remains to what extent wholesale drug entrepreneurs are customers of these facilities. Dutch convicted drug wholesalers were certainly not customers: the exotic "financial secrecy havens" rarely figured as target countries for depositing drug money. The frequency distribution over the foreign countries clustered around *neighboring* countries: Belgium, Luxembourg, Germany, and (depending on nationality) Morocco and Turkey. Other jurisdictions were infrequent: bank accounts in Panama, Gibraltar, Liechtenstein, Jersey, the British Virgin Islands, and Dubai did occur, but in only six cases. It seems that the Dutch drug entrepreneurs favored Belgium and Luxembourg, the Turks and Moroccans their own countries. A Dutch-Thai couple held bank accounts in Thailand because of the nationality of one of the partners. This finding contradicts the usual image of "transnational" criminals spreading their ill-gotten profits worldwide over the "bad" financial secrecy havens. Instead, it seems that the choice of banking jurisdiction is largely determined by proximity to the drug entrepreneur's economic home.

Suendorf's (2001) German-language study of laundering in Germany contains 40 examples of money laundering in the broad juridical meaning of the word: that is, every subsequent handling of illegal profits aimed at disguising their origins. Two cases can be considered to fall into the category of thoroughly organized money management: organizations were established to move the crime moneys of heroin wholesalers to their respective home countries. One of them, the Bosporus case, identified an extensive and complex network of money-exchange bureaus directed by an Iranian entrepreneur, who served a Kurdish heroin wholesaler. The funds were collected in various cities in Germany, carried to branches of the Iranian or associated independent bureaus. Subsequently the cash was placed in German banks and transferred to bank accounts of allied money change offices in New York. From these accounts the moneys were diverted to Dubai and—if required—back to Germany or Turkey. To fool the German police, the bureau de change submitted occasional suspicious transaction reports (van Duyne and Levi 2005). In 11 of the 40 cases examined by Suendorf, there was an attempt to make an investment in the upperworld, though with variable success and degrees of professionalism. Three examples illustrate this:

- Three instances of insolvent real estate enterprises; one was a construction firm that obtained a suspicious Italian infusion of money but nevertheless went bankrupt (Suendorf, 2001, pp. 208–10). No relationship with drugs is mentioned.

- A greengrocer, whose son was involved in heroin traffic and who invested part of the proceeds in the father's firm, which expanded quickly (207).
- A designer bathroom store, whose licit Russian owner was pressured to accept a compatriot as a manager. Money laundering is suspected (208–9). Likewise, no drug relationship is mentioned.

Most of the other examples concerned only the channeling of funds into accounts rather than full integration of suspected moneys. Overall, the sophistication and professionalism displayed was modest.

Finally, a recent British interview-based study of drugs dealers suggests a pattern of expenditure and laundering (Matrix Research and Consultancy 2007, p. 39). Table 14.2 summarizes key findings.

Some dealers stressed that they "did not do anything flashy with their earnings," for example, "just spending the money on the kids ... and paying the mortgage." The information collected pointed to unsophisticated money laundering techniques with a tendency to use friends and family, for example by investing in their businesses or bank accounts. One interviewee reported establishing a fraudulent painting and decorating business and buying winning betting slips that he cashed at betting shops across the country. One freelance hauler involved in the drug trade reported that his boss would identify a firm in financial trouble but that still had regular consignments coming into the country. He offered them a deal so he could use their legitimate consignment as a front to enable drug importation.

The danger (not avoided by van Duyne and Levi 2005) of this sort of analysis is that although it throws some appropriately skeptical light on official claims and popular assumptions about money laundering sophistication, it rests on those cases successfully dealt with by the authorities to conviction. It therefore excludes those cases that are difficult to prosecute, including those persons involved as victims or offenders in gangland killings.

Table 14.2. Uses of profits by U.K. drug dealers

Use of profit	Often	Sometimes	Never	Nonresponse	Total
Profits spent on lifestyle	68	2	5	29	104
Profits reinvested in drug trafficking	48	1	7	48	104
Profits invested in property or other assets	25	12	29	38	104
Profits laundered through legitimate business	19	2	39	44	104
Profits spent on drug habit	17	11	10	66	104
Profits sent overseas	8	8	48	40	104

Source: Matrix Research and Consultancy 2007.

III. Corruption and Money Laundering

Money laundering controls are an important tool for dealing with corruption, particularly in developing countries (Levi, Dakolias, and Greenberg 2007). The recovery of illicitly acquired assets is one of the centerpieces of the UN Convention against Corruption of 2005. The Iraq Oil for Food Program was merely one example of the circumvention of sanctions (Independent Inquiry Committee 2005). The range of activities and the ways wealth transfers are effected illustrate some of the difficulties in using anti–money laundering (AML) measures to punish corruption. Whereas Grand Corruption is identified with notorious dictators and their cronies, many other forms of corruption are not insubstantial. Large bribes are paid to border or internal law enforcement officials and to judicial officers or those who control them not to proceed against criminals or their goods. The goods can be illegal (e.g., narcotics), counterfeit (software and other intellectual property, alcohol, medicines, cigarettes, tobacco), or legal but untaxed smuggled dutiable genuine goods. Corruption can arise in any area of procurement. But no formal bribes in the form of direct transfer of cash or bank transfer need take place, making the identification of the offense, proof of corruption (and laundering), and appropriate sanctions nearly impossible. Sometimes it is simply understood that if people want to do business in a particular town or country they have to buy or sell via businesses or professionals whom they know to be connected to elites, criminals, or both.

Value transfers need not take place via electronic funds transfer or other banking methods. They may involve false invoicing or more convoluted chains of agreements that rely on family relationships and minimize direct financial flows in the short term. For example, consider that X is a central government official with authority over logging permits in a district suitable for tourism and villa development, the market being residents of the provincial capital. He issues a permit to Y and asks him to bribe a provincial official Z, to give high priority to a road in a forthcoming regional infrastructure project that will connect capital and district. The father Q of X's son-in law R owns 3,000 acres in the district, which is ideal for real estate development. The land has little value without the road. Q, for his daughter's sake, agrees to sell land to his son-in law, who hangs onto it until land values rise. He then sells the land and helps to support his father X's retirement. It is not obvious how this typical roundabout kind of trade in favors requires money laundering or can be inhibited by AML controls.

Nonetheless, money laundering is an important correlate of corruption, embezzlement, and other serious crimes for gain.[5] This may mean the assets are expatriated illicitly or, when the procurements are large enough, placed by the companies paying the bribes, perhaps via "commission payments" to intermediaries. It is common for falsified documentation—the overpricing or even invention of services—to be used. Again, payments do not occur in either country but go offshore. Unlike proceeds of crimes such as drug trafficking that result in cash payments, many corrupt transactions are not easy to arrange through informal value transfer systems (Maimbo 2003; Maimbo and Passas 2004; Maimbo et al. 2005). They are more suited to formal systems, at least where the corrupted persons wish to place their assets overseas.

Two examples of major long-running corruption cases are described in boxes 14.1 and 14.2: "Kazakhgate" and "The Montesinos Case." That both involve Switzerland is almost accidental; although Switzerland historically was the destination of choice for many plundered assets—having the desirable combination of honest safe-keeping, political stability, and ethical neutrality toward the sources of funds—there is no longer any reason to suppose that it is the destination of choice for corrupt assets nowadays. Indeed, the activism of the Swiss authorities might be regarded as a deterrent, though large forfeitures remain quite rare.

IV. Anti–Money Laundering Measures and Their Effectiveness

AML measures were first developed at a national level in the United States and the United Kingdom in the mid-1980s (though bulk cash deposit Currency Transaction Reporting was introduced as early as 1970 in the United States). Since that time, by

Box 14.1. Kazakhgate

James Giffen had long-standing ties with the Kazakh leadership. Through a company called Mercator he became a special advisor to President Nazarbayev when he took office in 1991. The company received success fees for deals between the government and U.S. oil giants Chevron and Mobil between 1995 and 2000. Giffen allegedly diverted approximately $70 million that had been paid by oil companies into escrow accounts at Swiss banks for oil and gas rights in Kazakhstan to secret accounts under his control. Mobil paid a $5 million "advance" to Mercator for the first contract, the right to negotiate a share in the Khazakh company Tengiz. For the second, Mobil agreed to finance an assetless shell company called Vaeko Europe to purchase, transport, and process condensate (a liquid form of natural gas) from Kazakhstan for a refinery in Orenburg, across the Russian border. Millions of dollars of Kazakh customs revenues were lost, as the processed material appears to have been sent on to Europe rather than being reimported to Kazakhstan. In March 1996 $1.1 million was transferred from Vaeko's bank account into a secret Swiss account controlled by Giffen. Giffen subsequently wired $1 million to the account of former oil minister Balgimbaye's Orchard account. He allegedly used the money, inter alia, to purchase over $180,000 worth of diamond jewelry and a spa vacation for his family.

Box 14.2. The Montesinos Case

In September 2000 Vladimiro Lenin Montesinos Torres, former head of the Peruvian National Intelligence Service, was charged with a host of illegal activities, including drug trafficking, arms dealing, embezzlement of public funds, and violations of human rights. He fled Peru but was later arrested in Venezuela and extradited to Peru, where he was sentenced to a 15-year prison term on corruption charges. In September 2006 Montesinos was sentenced to a 20-year prison term for his direct involvement in an illegal arms deal aimed at providing 10,000 assault weapons to Colombian rebels.

Thanks to the proactive attitude of the Swiss judicial and police authorities, the illegal assets Montesinos had deposited in Swiss accounts were frozen and the Peruvian authorities notified. The Swiss started money laundering proceedings involving $113.6 million in several different accounts. The investigations revealed that the funds belonging to Montesinos originated from corruption-related crimes. Since 1990 Montesinos had received "commissions" on arms deliveries to Peru and had this bribe money paid to his bank accounts in Luxembourg, the United States, and Switzerland. Montesinos received bribes for at least 32 transactions, each worth 18 percent of the purchase price. He also collected $10.9 million in "commissions" on the purchase of three planes bought by the Peruvian Air Force from the state-owned Russian arms factory. In return, Montesinos used his position to ensure that certain arms dealers were given preference when these orders were issued. On the basis of these facts, a total of $80.7 million was transferred to the Peruvian National Bank. In addition, one of the arms dealers who enjoyed preferential treatment "voluntarily" repatriated from his Swiss bank accounts his $7 million commission from these transactions. General Nicolas de Bari Hermoza Rios also accepted bribes relating to arms deliveries to Peru and also agreed to return the money ($21 million). In August 2004 U.S. officials returned to Peru $20 million in funds embezzled by Montesinos that had been deposited in U.S. banks by two men working for him.

In a separate action, the Swiss Federal Banking Commission (SFBC) investigated the activities of five banks in connection with the Montesinos case. The SFBC found that after due diligence, despite significant amounts deposited and indication of activities in arms dealing, one bank did not investigate any further. It failed to recognize Montesinos's politically exposed person quality, even though publicly accessible information would have enabled it to do so with reasonable effort. Because of the general manager's position in the hierarchy of the bank's management, the SFBC held him responsible for the bank's organizational deficiencies. The general manager also was alleged to have personally approved the opening of accounts with Montesinos despite formal shortcomings in the opening procedure. Furthermore, he was held co-responsible for not recognizing Montesinos as a politically exposed person. The SFBC held that the general manager was not fit to hold his position and ordered that he be removed immediately; he left by September 15, 2001. The banking commission also ordered that a special audit of the bank be conducted by an outside auditor in 2002.

With the exception of UBS Ltd., none of the banks involved contacted Montesinos directly but based decisions on opening accounts solely on information provided by third parties. The commission said that was insufficient in the case of significant private banking relationships.

Source: Levi, Dakolias, and Greenberg 2007, pp. 402–4.

a combination of imitation, political peer pressure, and technical assistance, the world has witnessed an extraordinary growth in efforts to control crime for gain (and more recently, terrorism) via measures to identify, freeze, and confiscate the proceeds of crime nationally and transnationally.[6] This is an attempt to deal with the crime-facilitating consequences of the core policy to open up money flows via the liberalization of currency restrictions and marketization in developing countries, including former communist societies. Stripping the proceeds of crime from offenders, both by criminal and, increasingly, by civil process, is politically popular and has a positive demonstration effect in local communities. It is expected a priori to inhibit criminal careers of individuals and organized crime groups by restricting their ability to save and to integrate their funds, which remain at risk. Moreover, many on the political left who would ordinarily be civil libertarian see pro-transparency AML activities as mechanisms to reduce the kleptocracy and Grand Corruption that has damaged Central and Eastern European countries as well as much of Africa, Asia, and South America; hence the passage of the UN Convention against Corruption 2005, to match the previous UN Vienna Drugs Convention (1988) and the UN Transnational Organised Crime Convention (2002).

More and more entities and professions are being brought into the AML network. Banks must train their staff and report suspicions that are fairly standard throughout the EU under the 2001 and 2005 European Directives. In addition, accountants, art and car dealers, casinos, jewelers, lawyers, and notaries are required to identify clients and report them to the authorities if their transactions are in cash over €15,000 or are deemed "suspicious." Few such reports would have been made without the threat of criminal and regulatory sanctions. One useful way of conceptualizing the issue is as a global crime risk management exercise that seeks to conscript as unpaid deputy sheriffs those parts of the private sector and foreign governments that seem unwilling to volunteer for social responsibility (Favarel-Garrigues, Godefroy, and Lascoumes 2008). Many former communist European countries, having rejected all-knowing invasive states, find themselves pressured into establishing central databases for financial transfers and sharing data on these reports across the EU.

In 2006 in the United States over 1 million Suspicious Activity Reports (SARs) were filed; indeed, between 1996 and 2006 4.2 million SARs were filed there (FinCEN 2007). From a few informal tip-offs from bankers to police in 1986, the number of SARs filed in the United Kingdom rose to 20,000 in 2000 and then to 213,561 in 2006. Over the same period, Dutch reports more than doubled; this rise has occurred throughout the 47 countries of the Council of Europe (not just the EU) covering some 800 million citizens, reflecting the increased training and number of bodies covered by AML legislation, plus political pressures of the EU *acquis communautaire*, the detailed criteria with which countries must comply before they are admitted to the EU.

Nonetheless, the totals still vary enormously between countries. By contrast with the U.S. and U.K. figures, in 2006 Switzerland filed 619 reports (involving

815 million Swiss Francs; Money Laundering Reporting Office Switzerland 2007). What are the implications of this? At first sight, the data suggest that Swiss authorities are doing little about money laundering. However, a suspicious transaction report has much graver consequences in Switzerland. When an account is reported as suspicious there, it is *automatically* frozen for up to five days pending investigation of whether or not a formal criminal investigation should be opened, placing a premium on having few ill-founded suspicions. If 1 million Americans (there are fewer customers than there are SARs because some attract multiple filings) had their accounts frozen, there would be a significant outcry and increased investigative resource would be needed to process the reports within a few days! Takats (2006) has developed a model that suggests the government can be flooded and rendered less effective by an overly broad reporting system.

One way of looking at the impact of AML laws is to examine the famous 1983 Brinks' Mat gold bullion robbery at London Heathrow, which netted around $52 million in gold. This happened before any money laundering legislation in the United Kingdom. The gold was largely smelted down and used to make jewelry, leading to sudden very large increases in the business turnover of one suspect, funds from whose company were withdrawn in cash to the extent that the regional Bank of England branch ran out of £50 notes with which to supply the local bank branch. Yet no one made any report to the authorities, nor were they obliged to do so. In the absence of corruption or intimidation, that would not happen now. On the other hand, in a separate prosecution linked to the Brinks' Mat robbery, solicitor Michael Relton set up a Liechtenstein foundation into which £3.16 million was paid and at one stage had bought property for £5.4 million in London. Had AML laws been in force, Relton would have been vulnerable to prosecution for transferring the proceeds of criminal conduct; but because, unusually, the funds could be traced directly to the robbery, he was convicted anyway and was jailed for 12 years for handling stolen property.

What other kinds of effects of AML can we deduce? Levi and Reuter (2006) have reviewed the evidence of impact of AML and have concluded that there has been little crime suppression to date, nor—given the poor quality and vast range of estimates of proceeds from drugs, for example—is it plausible that we would be able to detect any effects and separate them from error. Given the small direct operational costs of recent European terrorist attacks—less than $10,000—it seems very unlikely that sufficient sums from legal or illegal sources can be denied, though the ready availability of funds for facilitating movement between countries, indoctrination, and preparation undoubtedly makes terrorism easier. As for the impact of AML on improving criminal justice performance, the few analytical studies carried out show that this has been very modest to date. The extent to which this is attributable to low resource investment and to poor communications between public and private sectors, especially cross-border, remains to be determined. No one knows what the total number of *persons* subjected to extra surveillance is in Europe (EU and beyond), but it is a significant feature in the policing landscape, even though scarce financial investigation resources mean that relatively little is done about many of the reports that are received.

In many respects the policy transfer process in AML and anti-corruption methods, assisted by foreign aid for particular developments and economic sanctions for noncooperation, has been a major success. Nevertheless, the goal of affecting the organization and levels of serious crimes has been displaced in practice by the more readily observable goal of enhancing and standardizing rules and systems; the critical evaluation of what countries actually do with their expensively acquired suspicious transaction report data remains in its infancy; and the punishment for poor AML performance, though apparently similar internationally, in practice has focused more sharply on smaller and weaker jurisdictions than on the Great Powers, raising questions about the equity of the process. The mechanisms that facilitate laundering are intricately linked to those that enable wealthy corporations and individuals to hide their assets from public knowledge and—a separate issue—to minimize the taxes that they are obliged to pay (Blum et al. 1998; Godefroy and Lascoumes 2007). However, it remains a fact that in wider Europe, out of the billions of euros obtained and then in part saved from crimes annually, far less than 1 billion is confiscated, and, for all their successes in individual cases, the shift to civil forfeiture independent of prosecution in the United Kingdom and in the Irish Republic has hitherto had only a modest impact on this, especially net of the costs of investigation, court action, and asset management (Public Accounts Committee 2007; Harvey 2008). What has happened to these unconfiscated billions over the decades? What social harm do they do, and where?

A. Effectiveness

How should the effectiveness of the AML regime be assessed? Money laundering itself is only the intermediate target; the true target is the volume of predicate crimes, perhaps weighted in terms of their harmfulness. Reduction in the volume of the money laundered is not a conceptually strong measure of the effectiveness of the regime; subtler outcome measures are needed. Levi and Reuter (2006) examine in detail the problem of finding such measures to reduce crimes other than terrorism and bribery or kleptocracy, since the bulk of AML activities have been devoted to such criminal activities as drugs, other illegal markets, and white-collar crimes.

In terms of crime control the AML regime may generate two other benefits. First, part of the social appeal of proceeds of crime confiscation is the public satisfaction that offenders are denied the fruits of crime. Second, seizure of funds generates revenue for the government, and the incarceration of those who conspire to make the profits of crime appear legitimate punishes senior offenders. The seizures attack the negative role models offered by offenders living high on the hog. Research in Europe finds ample illustrations of law enforcement officers stressing the pain that asset confiscation brings to offenders, both in absolute terms and compared with at least European levels of imprisonment (Levi and Osofsky 1995; Nelen 2004);[7] though plausible, this has not been independently verified on a large sample of offenders, nor is it clear how it affects the willingness of these or other offenders to commit crimes in the future. Given the stakes that financial and legal professionals have in maintaining their employment and licensure, they may be relatively deterrable (Lankhorst and Nelen 2005; Middleton and Levi 2005; Middleton 2008). That is, unless they are being blackmailed or threatened or unless they or their firms are at serious risk of going bust anyway, modest expected risks of apprehension and punishment may be enough to discourage many from participating. In some instances the only way to apprehend those principal offenders who separate themselves from the predicate offenses is to convict them of money laundering offenses associated with predicate crimes that have been committed by others. Such cases show that, with respect to a wide range of predicate crimes, the law applies to everyone.

However, it is also important to think about what the AML system does not affect. Because scrutiny of sources of criminal earnings for low earners is limited, it is probably only criminal incomes of more than perhaps $50,000 annually that create a need for concealing the source of the revenues. Thus unless the AML processes stop all bigger league criminals from importing drugs or committing frauds, most offending by volume will be unaffected. However, it seems unlikely that laundering is such a scarce skill that incarcerating a few hundred will have a major impact on availability. The rise of artificial tanning and nail parlors in the United Kingdom is an illustration of cash-hiding self-laundering potential, especially since tax agencies do not profit from and are not set up to investigate over-reporting of taxable income. Although professional money launderers certainly exist,[8] they are surprisingly infrequent in reported cases. Terrorist financing cases also seem to involve people who belong very much to the cause rather than being mere commercial launderers; the latter, after all, might be more likely to trade in their sources in exchange for liberal official treatment of their own past and future delinquencies.

This is important for both policy and research purposes. The rationale behind the current AML regime is based in part on the implicit assumption that the regime provides tools to apprehend and punish a set of actors who provided a critical service for the commission of certain kinds of crime and who had previously been beyond the reach of the law—an assumption that makes the market model a useful heuristic device for analyzing the effects of laws and programs. However, if money laundering is mostly done by predicate offenders or by nonspecialized confederates, then the regime accomplishes much less. For research purposes, the prominence of the amateur launderer—at least in cases of which we have public knowledge—implies that the market-model concept is a strained analogy, since most laundering is done by amateurs who are not regular players.

In short, AML performance measures are difficult to develop because they would have to link the AML actions to changes in the predicate crimes; this is hard enough in the case of drugs, on which evidence is best, though one might expect bank detections to be better for frauds. High-level dealers, the only ones who need money laundering services, account for no more than 25 percent of total drug revenues. Assume that in the current regime money launderers charge customers approximately 10 percent of the amount laundered. Now assume that an improved system raised the price for money laundering services by half, to 15 percent. The result would be an increase in the price of drugs of only 1.25 percent, far too small to be picked up by existing monitoring systems. This is not an argument that money laundering controls are not effective or cost-effective, but only that their success cannot be empirically assessed by examining prices and quantities in drug markets.

B. Improving Performance

AML regimes might have two other benefits in addition to controlling crime: improving the efficiency of the system and catching offenders who otherwise would escape. Cuéllar (2003) agrees that such regimes might have improved efficiency in drug control and in reducing a few related criminal activities, but argues that they have failed in the second area. The principal use to which the U.S. AML regime has been put has been to increase the penalties with which prosecutors can threaten predicate offenders. The regime has had little success in apprehending professional money launderers or high-level criminals. In Europe there has been some activity against professionals, such as lawyers and bankers—though more by regulatory than criminal sanctions—but the extent to which this has incapacitated crime networks, reduced the variety of their offending, or reduced the scale of their growth as criminal organizations remains unknown and largely unanalyzed (Levi and Maguire 2004; Nelen 2004; van Duyne and Levi 2005). There are limits to the extent to which the police (or, for that matter, bankers) can pursue the rationale behind suspected transactions without interviewing suspects. However, greater attention to beneficial ownership of assets should logically help with asset recovery compared with postarrest or even postcharge financial investigations that were commonplace before; in this sense, AML has an influence on law enforcement methodologies, from drugs to Grand Corruption. Thus in the U.K. regime since passage of the Proceeds of Crime Act 2002, developed further by the financial reporting orders (for up to 20 years following a court order) in the Serious Organised Crime and Police Act 2005 and increased powers in the Serious Crime Act 2007, investigators can place monitoring orders on suspected offenders' accounts that prospectively allows them to track fund movements and to require forfeiture of cash over £1,000 inland as well as at borders unless the suspect can convince the court that the funds were legitimately acquired. This introduces a conviction-to-grave process of financial self-reporting by offenders, in which provable lying introduces extra risks. In terrorism investigations, though few money laundering reports may have triggered preventive interventions against pending attacks, financial investigations are deemed useful for tracking movement and associates (see Biersteker and Eckert 2007).

It is generally agreed that there is scope for better use of the data generated by the AML system. Greater skilled commitment to financial investigation and adjudication is likely to improve criminal justice and disruption yields, whatever effect this may have on levels of offending of different kinds. There are many individual cases in which SARs have added to (or, more rarely, stimulated) investigations and proceeds of crime recoveries (Gold and Levi 1994; Fleming 2005; Lander 2006; Serious Organised Crime Agency 2007; see also Harvey 2008).

The paucity of cases against stand-alone launderers and investigations that have their origin in money laundering information supports the criticism that the AML regime has brought in few new offenders. There are no systematic data on the origins of cases against major criminals, such as principal drug dealers, so it is impossible to tell whether more of them are being captured through money laundering laws and investigations. Furthermore, where heads of state or their families are involved in Grand Corruption (including embezzlement and, sometimes, illicit trafficking and other major crimes) it is far from obvious to whom either domestic or foreign institutions should report without fear of retaliation, or who has sufficient motivation to take serious action. In this respect, the national Financial Intelligence Unit model, like most national crime investigation and prosecution models, breaks down when confronted with key elites, even where they have no formal immunity for acts performed in office.[9]

Finally, whatever the gains from money laundering controls, there are also a variety of costs that need to be considered. Reuter and Truman (2004) offer a very rough estimate of $7 billion for the costs of the U.S. AML regime in 2003. That figure includes costs to the government ($3 billion), the private sector ($3 billion), and the general public ($1 billion). It does not include two potentially important cost elements: the effect on the international competitive position of business sectors subject to AML rules and the costs of errors.[10] There has been a rise in demand for money laundering reporting officers—who must by law be appointed in every regulated institution, though they do not have to be exclusively devoted to that role—and escalating use of expensive software that tries to identify suspicious transactions on the basis of pattern analysis.

V. Concluding Remarks

Money laundering, though a traditional activity, is a very modern crime, created by the late twentieth-century state to enlist the financial sector in its pursuit of the proceeds of crime and deterrence of career criminality, particularly transnational crime. There can be no doubt that many billions of dollars are laundered, but whether that is 1 percent or 10 percent of GDP in developed economies is very much a matter of guesswork.

Money is laundered in many ways by offenders of very different kinds. It is one of the few activities that connect Al Qaeda, Colombian drug dealers, and Enron officers. There are many different techniques for laundering, involving both the most respectable and the most marginal of institutions. Given the commitment of state authority and individual privacy to the pursuit of money laundering, it would be worthwhile learning a great deal more about laundering itself.

A broad and intrusive set of controls has been erected to prevent money laundering. These controls have potentially large effects. For example, U.S banks have at times made it difficult for MSBs to wire remittances of immigrant workers back to their home countries, or even handle MSBs' accounts, because they fear that bank regulators will monitor them more closely for possible money laundering violations, and that they might be penalized themselves if the MSBs do launder proceeds of crime. The AML requirements of extensive documentation before opening an account can reduce the access of poor persons to the financial system. Showing that the system generates substantial crime or corruption control benefits ought to be high on the agenda of the relevant policy-making community.

NOTES

1. Mark Haller provided helpful clarifying comments on this matter.

2. A more extensive review of the regime is presented in Reuter and Truman (2004). For a good ethnographic study of the French private sector regime with some universal application, see Favarel-Garrigues, Godefroy, and Lascoumes (2008).

3. Many such scandals may be found in the publications and press releases of Transparency International.

4. The scheme takes advantage of the fact that value-added tax (VAT) is rebated if the item is exported to another country. Sales are made to dummy foreign corporations, and rebates are then fraudulently claimed, while companies owing the VAT to the national tax authorities typically go bust and cannot pay their bills. Often the difficulty is proving the connection between companies and managers, since they claim to be independent of each other. See FATF (2007) for a description of the scheme. This is a far from trivial phenomenon, costing several billion dollars worth of losses annually and forcing a restatement of the U.K. balance of payments (Levi, Dakolias, and Greenberg 2007). The fact that relatively little is known about what happens to the money therefore is interesting in itself.

5. Often such acts could be labeled corruption, embezzlement, *and* theft, as the terms are not mutually exclusive.

6. For a sound legal and institutional history of these changes, see Gilmore (2004). For a more sociological history, see Levi (2007).

7. These are supported by interviews with U.K. law enforcement personnel, 2002–5.

8. According to the Dutch investigative authorities, in Dutch organized crime investigations in 2004 a third of those under investigation were described as having laundering as their primary and another third as a secondary aspect of their criminal work. The significance of laundering to the final third was unknown (Council of Europe 2006). We are not in a position to test these ascriptions, but van Duyne and Levi (2005) note the relative lack of sophistication in those laundering schemes that make it through to final conviction after appeals.

9. This is not uniquely a problem for the countries of the South, especially Africa: scandals engulfed Prime Minister Berlusconi (Italy) and President Chirac (France) while in office, as well as, at a more modest level, former German chancellor Kohl. In the wealthier as well as some poorer countries many of these scandals involve campaign finance.

10. Z-Yen (2005) estimated annual AML costs for U.K. banks as £85–120 million, with total costs of £220–90 million ($440–580 million). See also Harvey (2008).

REFERENCES

Association of Certified Fraud Examiners. 2002. *2002 Report to the Nation on Occupational Fraud and Abuse*. Austin, TX: ACFE.

Beare, Margaret, and Stephen Schneider. 2007. *Money Laundering in Canada: Chasing Dirty and Dangerous Dollars*. Toronto: University of Toronto Press.

Biersteker, Thomas, and Sue Eckert, eds. 2007. *Countering the Financing of Global Terrorism*. London: Routledge.

Block, Alan, and Constance Weaver. 2004. *All Is Clouded by Desire*. Westport, CT: Greenwood.

Blum, Jack, Michael Levi, Tom Naylor, and Phil Williams. 1998. *Financial Havens, Banking Secrecy and Money-Laundering*. Issue 8, UNDCP Technical Series. UN document V.98–55024. New York: United Nations.

Council of Europe. 2006. *Organised Crime Situation Report 2005*. Strasbourg, France: Council of Europe. http://www.coe.int/t/dg1/legalcooperation/economiccrime/organisedcrime/Report2005E.pdf.

Cressey, Donald. 1955. *Other People's Money*. New York: Free Press.

Cuéllar, Mariano-Florentino. 2003. "The Tenuous Relationship between the Fight against Money Laundering and the Disruption of Criminal Finance." *Journal of Criminal Law and Criminology* 93: 312–466.

Favarel-Garrigues, Gilles, Thierry Godefroy, and Pierre Lascoumes. 2008. "Sentinels in the Banking Industry: Private Actors and the Fight against Money Laundering in France." *British Journal of Criminology* 48(1): 1–19.

Financial Action Task Force. Annual. *Report on Money Laundering Typologies*. Paris: Financial Action Task Force.

———. 2006. *Trade Based Money Laundering*. http://www.fatf-gafi.org/dataoecd/60/25/37038272.pdf.

———. 2007. *Laundering the Proceeds of VAT Carousel Fraud*. http://www.fatf-gafi.org/dataoecd/16/3/38335020.pdf.

FinCEN. 2007. *The SARs Activity Review 2007—by the Numbers*. http://www.fincen.gov/sars/btn_8/sar_btn_Issue8.pdf.
Fleming, Matthew. 2005. "U.K. Law Enforcement Agency Use and Management of Suspicious Activity Reports: Towards Determining the Value of the Regime." http://www.jdi.ucl.ac.uk/downloads/publications/research_reports/Fleming_LEA_Use_and_Mgmt_of_SARs_June2005.pdf.
Gilmore, William. 2004. *Dirty Money*. 3rd ed. Strasbourg, France: Council of Europe.
Godefroy, Thierry, and Pierre Lascoumes. 2007. *Capitalisme Clandestin*. Paris: Decouverte.
Gold, Michael, and Michael Levi. 1994. *Money-Laundering in the U.K.: An Appraisal of Suspicion-Based Reporting*. London: Police Foundation.
Harvey, Jackie. 2008. "Just How Effective Is Money Laundering Legislation?" *Security Journal* 21: 189–211.
Independent Inquiry Committee. 2005. "Manipulation of the Oil-for-Food Programme by the Iraqi Regime." http://www.iic-offp.org/documents/IIC %20Final%20Report%2027Oct2005.pdf.
Komisar, Lucy. 1999. "Russian Cons and New York Banks." *Village Voice*, December 1–7.
Lander, Sir Stephen. 2006. *Review of the Suspicious Activity Reports Regime*. http://www.soca.gov.uk/downloads/SOCA/theSARsReview_FINAL_Web.pdf.
Lankhorst, Francien, and Hans Nelen. 2005. "Professional Services and Organised Crime in the Netherlands." *Crime, Law and Social Change* 42(2–3): 163–88.
Levi, Michael. 2007. "Pecunia non olet? The Control of Money-Laundering Revisited." In *The Organised Crime Community*, edited by F. Bovenkerk and M. Levi. New York: Springer.
Levi, Michael, Maria Dakolias, and Ted Greenberg. 2007. "Money Laundering and Corruption." In *The Many Faces of Corruption: Tracking Vulnerabilities at the Sector Level*, edited by J. Edgardo Campos and S. Pradhan. Washington, DC: World Bank.
Levi, Michael and Mike Maguire. 2004. "Reducing and Preventing Organised Crime: An Evidence-based Critique." *Crime, Law and Social Change* 41(5): 397–469.
Levi, Michael, and Lisa Osofsky. 1995. *Investigating, Seizing and Confiscating the Proceeds of Crime*. Police Research Group Paper 61. London: Home Office.
Levi, Michael, and Peter Reuter. 2006 "Money Laundering: A Review of Current Controls and Their Consequences." In *Crime and Justice: An Annual Review of Research*, vol. 34, edited by Michael Tonry. Chicago: University of Chicago Press.
Levine, Steve. 2007. *Oil and Glory*. New York: Random House.
Lilley, Peter. 2006. *Dirty Dealing: The Untold Truth about Global Money Laundering and International Crime*. 3rd ed. London: Kogan Page.
Maimbo, Sam M. 2003. *The Money Exchange Dealers of Kabul: A Study of the Informal Funds Transfer Market in Afghanistan*. Washington, DC: World Bank.
Maimbo, Sam, R. Adams, R. Aggarwal, and Nikos Passas. 2005. *Migrant Labor Remittances in the South Asia Region*. Washington, DC: World Bank.
Maimbo, Sam M., and Nikos Passas. 2004. "The Regulation and Supervision of Informal Remittance Systems." *Small Enterprise Development* 15(1): 53–62.
Matrix Research and Consultancy. 2007. *The Illicit Drug Trade in the United Kingdom*. 2nd ed. London: Home Office. Online Report 20/07. http://www.homeoffice.gov.uk/rds/pdfs07/rdsolr2007.pdf.
Middleton, David. 2008. "Lawyers and Client Accounts: Sand through a Colander." *Journal of Money Laundering Control* 11(1): 34–46.

Middleton, David, and Michael Levi. 2005. "The Role of Solicitors in Facilitating 'Organized Crime': Situational Crime Opportunities and Their Regulation." *Crime, Law and Social Change* 42(2–3): 123–61.

Money Laundering Reporting Office Switzerland (MROS). 2007. *Report 2006: Annual Report by the Money Laundering Reporting Office*. Bern: Federal Office of Police, Swiss Federation.

Naylor, R. Tom. 2004. *Wages of Crime*. Ithaca, NY: Cornell University Press.

Nelen, Hans. 2004. "Hit Them Where It Hurts Most? The Proceeds-of-Crime Approach in the Netherlands." *Crime, Law and Social Change* 41: 517–34.

Passas, Nikos. 2003. *Informal Value Transfer Systems, Terrorism and Money Laundering*. http://www.ncjrs.gov/pdffiles1/nij/grants/208301.pdf.

Pieth, Mark, Lucinda Low, and Peter Cullen. 2007. *The OECD Convention on Bribery: A Commentary*. Cambridge: Cambridge University Press.

Public Accounts Committee. 2007. *Assets Recovery Agency: Report*. http://www.publications.parliament.uk/pa/cm200607/cmselect/cmpubacc/391/391.pdf.

Reuter, Peter, and Edwin M. Truman. 2004. *Chasing Dirty Money*. Washington, DC: Institute for International Economics.

Schneider, Friedrich, and Dominik Enste. 2000. "Shadow Economies: Size, Causes, and Consequences." *Journal of Economic Literature* 381: 77–114.

Serious Organised Crime Agency. 2007. *The Suspicious Activity Reports Regime Annual Report 2007*. http://www.soca.gov.uk/assessPublications/downloads/SARsAnnualReview221107.pdf.

Simpson, Glenn. 2005. "How Top Dutch Bank Plunged into a World of Shadowy Money." *Wall Street Journal* (December 30), p. 1.

Suendorf, Ulrike. 2001. *Geldwäsche: Eine Kriminologische Untersuchung*. Neuwied, Germany: Luchterhand.

Takats, Elod. 2006. "A Theory of 'Crying Wolf': The Economics of Money Laundering Enforcement." International Monetary Fund Working Papers. Washington, DC.

U.S. Senate, Minority Staff of the Permanent Subcommittee on Investigations. 2001. *Correspondent Banking: A Gateway for Money Laundering*. February 5. http://freedom.orlingrabbe.com/money_laundering/correspondent_banking.pdf.

U.S. State Department. 2003. *International Narcotics Control Strategy Report*. Washington, DC: Government Printing Office.

van Duyne, Petrus C. 2003. "Money Laundering Policy: Fears and Facts." In *Criminal Finance and Organizing Crime in Europe*, edited by Petrus C. van Duyne, Klaus von Lampe, and James L. Newell. Nijmegen, Netherlands: Wolf Legal.

van Duyne, Petrus, C., Rolf Kouwenberg, and Georg Romeijn. 1990. *Misdaadondernemingen Ondernemende misdadigers in Nederland*. Arnhem, Gouda Quint.

van Duyne, Petrus C., and Michael Levi. 2005. *Drugs and Money: Managing the Drug Trade and Crime-Money in Europe*. Abingdon, UK: Routledge.

Woolner, Ann. 1994. *Washed in Gold: The Story behind the Biggest Money Laundering Investigation in U.S. History*. New York: Simon and Schuster.

Zdanowicz, John. 2004. "Detecting Money Laundering and Terrorist Financing via Data Mining." *Communications of the ACM* 47(3): 53–55.

Z-Yen. 2005. *Anti–Money Laundering Requirements: Costs, Benefits and Perceptions*. London: Corporation of London. http://www.zyen.com/Knowledge/Research/AMLR_FULL.pdf.

CHAPTER 15

TAX EVASION

VALERIE BRAITHWAITE

Tax evasion is a crime that adversely affects a nation's economy and the tax morale of citizens by reducing the nation's capacity to provide government services or manage its debt and by placing a disproportionate burden on those who pay their share (Burman 2003; Bajada and Schneider 2005, pp. 3–5; Kirchler 2007, p. 24). Tax evasion has political as well as economic significance (Internal Revenue Service 2005*b*). Institutions of taxation are part of how nations define themselves (Schmölders 1970; Stiglitz 2002, p. 177), and taxes regulate activity (J. P. Smith 1993; Mumford 2002, pp. 6–7; Moran 2003). For instance, taxes on tobacco increase price disincentives for dangerous consumption (Geis, Cartwright, and Houston 2003). Taxation also makes a statement about how a society practices social justice, expressing a nation's values regarding resource redistribution from the rich to the poor (progressive taxation) or from the poor to the rich (regressive taxation; Stiglitz 2002, p. 177). Taxes can deepen the oppression of taxpaying communities, at times with catastrophic consequences (for example, wars of independence in the United States and India or revolution in France).

In stable democracies with well-established taxation institutions, state-citizen reciprocity underlies most people's understanding of taxpaying (Scholz and Lubell, 1998*a*, 1998*b;* Frey and Feld 2001; Rawlings, 2003; Feld and Frey, 2007). In some circumstances, however, paying tax may be regarded as little more than legally ordained extortion. Presumably for this reason, Moran (2003, p. 378) offers the following definition: "A tax occurs when a government requires contributions for its operations from individuals, firms, or groups within its jurisdiction without returning a clear quid pro quo." Feeling reciprocity is a subjective social phenomenon, and as Moran implicitly recognizes, cannot be imposed on an individual who pays tax.

Nevertheless, reciprocity and obligation occur in taxpaying insofar as a "psychological contract" is made between the taxpayer and the state (Frey and Feld

2001; Feld and Frey 2007). This extra layer to Moran's (2003) definition means that citizens and taxpayers generally buy into taxpaying as an obligation. In return, governments provide the community with infrastructure and services. When government fails to deliver expected and promised benefits to the satisfaction of taxpayers, discontent is expressed as a breach of trust (Scholz and Lubell 1998*a*, 1998*b*; Feld and Frey 2002; Rawlings 2003).

At sufficiently high levels tax evasion signals a threat to a society's economic security, political stability, and social capital. It is no surprise, then, that the regulation of taxpaying is well institutionalized in mature democracies. The institution depends on social mores and elaborate systems of tax law and procedure. In many democratic societies the law is complex, the administration cumbersome and bureaucratic. The remarkable feature of these tax systems is that they work as well as they do (Alm, McClelland, and Schulze 1992), but there is widespread belief that they are in trouble, with a growing gap between expected and collected taxes (Hasseldine and Li 1999; Avi-Jonah 2000; Tanzi 2000; Rossotti 2002; Burman 2003). In a globalized world where wealth is mobile and sovereign states are unable to successfully identify and isolate the wealth that is "theirs" to tax, tax evasion is not easy to track down (Tanzi 1996). Pinpointing evasion is made difficult by different tax laws in different countries (Moran 2003), complexities in tax law that generate uncertainty (Picciotto 2007), and an attitude to the law that makes it fair game for exploitation by those who abide by black letter interpretation while dismissing the spirit that the law embodies (McBarnet 1992).

In this chapter I briefly map the domain of tax evasion, draw on the best data available from the United States to illustrate the magnitude of the problem, review the scientific literature on the primary drivers of tax evasion, and consider some of the strategies that governments are using to try to rebuild the effectiveness and integrity of their tax systems to ensure future sustainability. The main conclusions are the following:

- Tax evasion needs to be understood holistically: perceptually, people are capable of linking different forms of taxation to each other and to the quality of governance.
- The nature and extent of tax evasion vary across contexts and time depending on opportunity to evade tax and the enforcement processes in place.
- Efficiency considerations in tax collection influence which groups will be taxed and the success of evasion strategies. The result is that when methods of taxation change the message of moral obligation needs to be renegotiated with the public, particularly in circumstances where commitment to overarching law-abidingness is absent.
- In the United States underreporting of taxable income explains a large part of tax evasion, but tax avoidance through deposits in offshore financial centers lies outside these estimates. Worldwide these deposits are thought to be in excess of $5 trillion.

- The wheel of social alignments is proposed as a way of integrating three spheres of tax research: the optimal design of the tax system, the deliberations that enable individuals to voluntarily accept taxpaying (benefits, moral obligation, and justice), and the role played by others beyond the tax authority and the taxpayer (accountants, tax advisors, financial planners, work colleagues, and family). Sometimes these influences are sympathetic to the tax system, other times not.
- Interlocking the three spheres of design, taxpayer perceptions, and influential networks to build a cooperative taxpaying culture requires increased engagement of tax authorities with the taxpaying public through high standards of procedural justice, meaningful dialogue, and responsiveness.

I. Domain

Taxes take different forms "depending on each nation's history, administrative capacity, and culture" (Moran 2003, p. 378). For example, income tax, corporate tax, land tax, capital gains tax, death tax, inheritance tax, sales tax, customs and excise tax, and value-added tax are all available to governments and generally are used in combination, albeit to different degrees in different places. Moran regards levels of economic development as critical to differentiating the tax mix of former British colonies: "Australia, Canada, the United Kingdom, and the United States raise most of their revenues from income, wage, and corporate taxes while the Anglophone African nations and India raise more of their tax revenues from customs duties" (Moran 2003, p. 381). Indeed, the United States, Canada, and Australia raise half of their tax revenue from income tax, while Britain raises a third in this way (Moran 2003).

This is undoubtedly the reason so much of the literature on tax evasion has focused on income tax (an exception is Slemrod 1999). The tax mix, however, matters. Understanding interdependencies and how people see the relative merits of different forms of taxpaying is at the heart of understanding tax evasion. Two examples illustrate, one in the area of development, the other in the area of corporate taxation.

Global pressures on developing countries to lower trade barriers is particularly detrimental to poorer nations that have a tax mix that is heavily weighted toward customs and excise duties (Moran 2003). As underresourced and inexperienced tax administrators are trying to collect customs and excise tax from global business enterprises, they are no doubt grappling with a mixed message about how worthwhile their activities are. It is of little wonder that such tax authorities struggle to establish effective tax systems that will withstand problems of corruption. The degree to which a society can harness a moral imperative to pay tax within its population is an important predictor of levels of tax evasion (Torgler 2003).

The role of the global economy in legitimizing particular forms of tax evasion and undermining efforts to communicate a moral imperative to pay tax calls for further study.

The question of corporate tax contributions is ideologically fraught, with some scholars arguing that entities should not be taxed on their profits if their shareholders and owners are paying personal income tax (Sørensen 1999; Moran 2003). Such a view, however, does not have the support of the general public (Steinmo 1993, p. 158; V. Braithwaite 2003*c;* V. Braithwaite and J. Braithwaite 2006). The economic and social harms caused by the collapse of a corporation such as Enron, which paid no taxes for four of its last five years (J. Braithwaite 2005), have sharpened concerns about corporate social responsibility, including taxpaying (V. Braithwaite et al. 2001; Happé 2007).

Although corporations and the public may be at odds about their "rightful" contributions to the tax system, the reality is that many companies pay no tax at all (J. Braithwaite 2005, p. 20), and most member nations of the Organisation for Economic Co-operation and Development have seen a drop in the proportion of revenue they collect through company tax due to global tax planning by large corporations (Steinmo 1993, p. 20). Profits are moved from countries with high tax rates to those offering more favorable tax conditions, in particular, tax havens. The result has been a race to the bottom as far as corporate and individual income tax rates are concerned (Avi-Jonah 2000; Genser 2001; Maranville 2004).

A policy imperative for governments is to guard against public perceptions of corporate free riding. Such perceptions cast doubt over a government's capacity to enforce the law and create justification for widespread community defiance (Mason and Calvin 1984; Rossotti 2002; V. Braithwaite et al. 2003). From a policy perspective, evasion in relation to corporate income tax is not disconnected from other types of tax evasion (Schneider and Enste 2002).

II. Magnitude

Estimating tax evasion and avoidance is difficult. Part of the problem is definitional, part is the reliability of data on the magnitude of the problem. Tax evasion can be defined as an illegal act of commission or omission that reduces or prevents tax liability that would otherwise be incurred (Webley et al. 1991, p. 2). Specifying what these acts are is impossible. As Tanzi and Shome (1994, p. 328) explain, tax evasion covers a "truly remarkable" array of activities, continually being invented by those looking for ways of not paying tax.

When attention turns from evasion to avoidance, problems of specification deepen. The distinction between avoidance and evasion has been expressed simply: "It is the difference between working within the law (though against its spirit) and working outside it (Woellner et al. 2005, p. 1615)" (cited in Evans 2005). When tax law is as complex as it is, opportunities arise for finding loopholes and ambiguities, so that "the arrangement of one's affairs, within the law, to reduce one's tax liability" becomes possible (James and Nobes 2000, p. 300) in circumstances where these actions are "contrary to the spirit of law" (p. 100). Recent legislative changes in some countries that have introduced general anti-avoidance rules (principles) have sought to bring avoidance under the control of the legal system (see Jones 1996; Freedman 2004; J. Braithwaite 2005). These general tax principles make it illegal to act in ways that are counter to the spirit of the law for no other purpose than to minimize tax (or when the dominant purpose is avoidance).

The Internal Revenue Service (IRS; 2005*a*, 2005*b*) has invested heavily in measuring the "tax gap" to provide an estimate of U.S. taxpayers' compliance with their federal tax obligations. The tax gap refers to the difference between the tax that taxpayers should pay and what they actually pay on a timely basis. The data for 2001 was collected from audits of 46,000 tax returns of individuals. Data for the corporate contribution to the tax gap was not updated from 1988.

Individual income tax constitutes about half of the tax gap (IRS 2005*b*). Other taxes that are included in the tax gap estimate are corporation tax, employment tax, and estate and excise tax. The IRS has broken down the tax gap into three forms of evasion: underreporting income, nonfiling of tax returns, and nonpayment of a tax debt. The largest component (80 percent) involves the underreporting of income (IRS 2005*a*). IRS (2005*a*) audits have shown that the majority of individuals underreporting were understating income, mainly from business activities, rather than overclaiming deductions to reduce their taxable income. The remaining forms of evasion each account for about 10 percent of the tax gap: failure to pay the reported taxes owed and failure to file a tax return (IRS 2005*a*).

Of note is what the tax gap does not cover. It does not include taxes from the illegal sector of the economy (IRS 2005*b*), which includes crimes of drug trafficking and smuggling of various kinds. Also excluded from the tax gap, because of its invisibility in many cases, is the "legitimate" work performed by illegal immigrants and those who are paid in cash outside the official economy.[1] The tax gap also does not include revenue lost through avoidance measures that the IRS feels ill-equipped to challenge or that are beyond reach; as an example, Tanzi (2000) cites the impenetrable veil around transactions in offshore financial centers, citing a 1998 UN report that estimates that deposits in these centers exceed $5 trillion.

The tax gap for the tax year 2001 in the United States is estimated as falling in the range of $312 billion to $353 billion (IRS 2005*a*, 2005*b*). IRS enforcement activity and late payments have reduced this gap by $55 billion, that is, by 16 to 18 percent. Obviously, figures on U.S. tax evasion cannot be generalized to other parts of the world, nor should it be assumed that the United States is leading the way in tackling tax evasion. The United States is unusual, however, in the rigorous and systematic way it has gone about collecting data. Therefore, the U.S. tax gap data are a useful benchmark for gauging the seriousness of tax evasion for countries around the world.

Although the dollar value of tax evasion is substantial, most studies confirm that the majority of people pay their tax. Hasseldine and Li (1999) summarize international survey work reporting that about a quarter of people who file a tax return will admit to deliberately underreporting income. Using data from the IRS Taxpayer Compliance Measurement Program audits, Andreoni, Erard, and Feinstein (1998) reported that 25 percent of all taxpayers underpaid their taxes by $1,500 or more. Tax evasion appears to be a relatively common crime, perhaps even the most common. Even so, a very sizable proportion obey the law without the need for intervention (IRS 2005*b*). Given the low risks of detection and punishment (Rossotti 2002), most people comply with tax law in an economically irrational way most of the time (Alm, McClelland, and Schulze 1992; Andreoni, Erard, and Feinstein 1998).

III. Changes in Tax Evasion

The 2001 analysis of the tax gap led the Internal Revenue Service (2005*a*) to conclude that there had been "modest deterioration in tax compliance among individual taxpayers since the last study was conducted in 1988." In 2002 Charles Rossotti, then commissioner of the Internal Revenue Service, reported to the IRS Oversight Board, "We are winning the battle, but losing the war. Over the last ten years, the size and complexity of the tax system increased enormously. Beyond the simple increase in number of taxpayers and revenue dollars, the majority of tax revenues now come from sources that are more subject to manipulation by those who wish to pay less than the law requires and much more difficult and time consuming for our agents to uncover" (pp. 1–2). Rossotti continued with an admission that the IRS had no overall strategy for dealing with corporate tax shelters, had not concentrated efforts on high-income individuals, and had not revised their auditing priorities to focus attention on offshore accounts, partnerships, and trusts through which vast sums of income flowed, resulting in a burgeoning market in "tax schemes and devices designed to improperly reduce taxes to taxpayers based on the simple premise they can get away with it" (p. 2).

IV. What Change Means in the Tax Context

The literature supports Rossotti's (2002) analysis that swings in levels of evasion at the national level reflect opportunity to evade, created by change in enforcement activity and by change in socioeconomic conditions that alter ease of collection. Aggressive tax planning, for instance, appears to be responsive to enforcement activity. John Braithwaite (2005) has proposed a cyclical theory of aggressive tax planning that recognizes the role that tax authorities play in signaling what is not acceptable. Braithwaite tracks the way the wealthy engage in tax planning with innovative game plans that are ahead of what tax authorities are looking for in their auditing activities. Schemes that have met with some success at elite levels are then repackaged for marketing to an unsuspecting public eager to jump on the next financial planning bandwagon and save tax. In the repackaging process, many of the niceties that protect against challenges from tax authorities are lost. It is therefore at the mass-marketing stage that tax authorities feel confident that they have the ammunition to challenge the schemes and close them down. By this time promoters have made their financial killing, and small investors are left to their own devices to fight their case against the tax authority. This sequence of elite marketing, mass marketing, and tax authority challenge means that aggressive tax planning occurs in cycles, with the greatest risk occurring at the end of the cycle, when smaller players regard such schemes as safe, smart investments and join the stampede. Until tax authorities become more adept at intervening in a timely fashion tax avoidance activities will fluctuate substantially across time.

Enforcement intervention is not the only factor shaping what the figures tell us about tax evasion over time. As economic conditions change, the costs of collecting a particular form of tax may exceed the revenue collected from that tax. To preserve the tax base without additional collection expense, governments change the tax mix. As the tax mix changes, opportunities for tax evasion will also change.

By tracking Australia's transition during the twentieth century from having a predominantly customs, excise, and land tax base to an income tax base that relies heavily on wage and salary earners, J. P. Smith (1993) has shown how adaptive tax systems are to changing economic and social conditions. These changes have been used by John Braithwaite (2005) to explain why Australia's progressive tax regime (like the regime in the United States) has become more regressive in the course of the century. At the turn of the twentieth century, the working classes were poorly paid, itinerant, often working in rural Australia. Collecting tax from such a group was far less cost effective than collecting tax from those with money, land, and inheritance or from highly paid workers in urban areas. As smaller family businesses corporatized and became part of larger companies and as workers found steady jobs with better salaries in urban areas, the opportunity to tax the working classes in a new and highly cost-effective way emerged. Increasing wages gradually drew workers into the income tax net originally designed for the rich, and tax was extracted by employers on behalf of the government at source through a withholding system.

Thus by the end of the twentieth century the tables had turned, not only in Australia, but also in the United States (see Browlee 2000 for the U.S. history). Wage and salary earners were a "captured" population: their income could be easily tracked through third parties (employers and financial institutions), and tax could be withheld by government. Those with wealth, on the other hand, were able to move their money to places where third-party reporting and withholding tax could be avoided. This is not to suggest that there are no options for the working class to avoid tax. Shadow economy activity leaves no audit trail and occurs commonly when goods and services can be sold or traded completely outside the official economy (Schneider and Enste 2002).

V. Special Features

The above analysis illustrates tax evasion as a white-collar crime, the substance of which is sometimes poorly specified and changes with economic and social conditions. One might be forgiven for thinking of tax evasion as a failure to comply with "arbitrary" legal rulings (Schmölders 1970). If there is a moral underpinning to tax evasion, it is not transparent in the specific rules (Picciotto 2007). The moral underpinning is more abstract; it is a belief in the rule of law and accepting responsibility for being a law-abiding citizen, or a commitment to the psychological contract between the taxpayer and the state (Frey and Feld 2001; Orviska and Hudson 2002). The relatively abstract nature of the moral underpinnings to taxation probably explains why tax authorities and tax systems so readily look to coercion as their ultimate enforcement weapon, not necessarily through punishment but through a tax design that gives the taxpayer little choice.

VI. The Wheel of Social Alignments

The dominant theoretical lens for understanding tax evasion has grown out of deterrence theory (Allingham and Sandmo 1972), with its presumption that people will evade tax when the benefits of evasion outweigh the costs. However, research findings have led to modification of this basic theoretical model. The odds of detection and penalties are so low that it is mostly rational to cheat, yet people tend to do the right thing and pay their taxes (Alm, McClelland, and Schulze 1992; Slemrod 1992; Alm, Sanchez, and de Juan 1995). Personal interpretations of risk and gain, knowledge of taxation, cognitive heuristics, social norms, shame, guilt, and identity are among the factors that have been shown to influence an individual's propensity to evade tax (see Webley et al. 1991; Kirchler 2007). Moreover, the process through which these influences operate can involve the individual in a conscious, deliberative assessment of gain and loss, or very little deliberation (V. Braithwaite

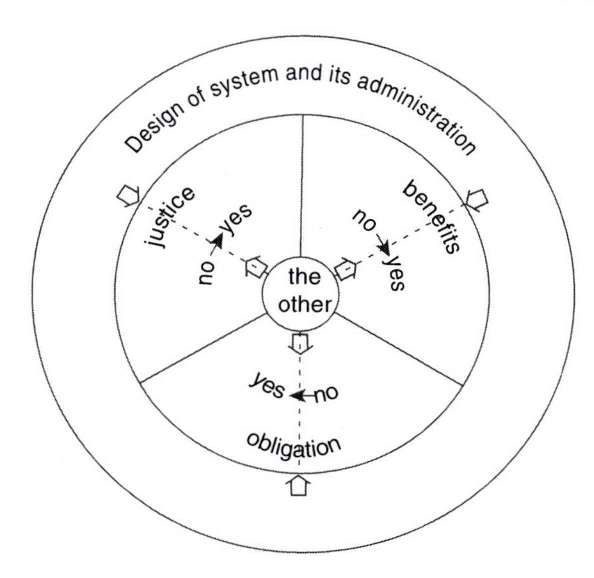

Figure 15.1. The wheel of social alignments.
Source: V. Braithwaite and Wenzel 2008.

and Wenzel 2008). Tax evasion can occur through modeling the behavior of significant others (V. Braithwaite and J. Braithwaite 2006) or through the use of general heuristics (Scholz and Pinney 1995; Scholz and Lubell 1998*a*, 1998*b*).

The varied and multiple pressures that increase or decrease tax evasion can be integrated for the purposes of policy analysis through the wheel of social alignments depicted in figure 15.1 (V. Braithwaite and Wenzel 2008). The wheel of social alignments displays the segments that tax authorities need to be constantly monitoring and improving in order to collect tax efficiently in keeping with the democratic will. The outer band of the wheel represents the tax system, its laws, codes, and administration. This is the institution of taxation that commonly constrains individuals, makes demands, and ensures that demands are met. Ideally it is also where lie responsiveness to taxpayers (K. W. Smith 1992; V. Braithwaite 2003*a*), respect for taxpayer rights (Bentley 2007), and tax system integrity (V. Braithwaite 2003*d*).

The middle band represents how individuals deliberate and make choices about taxation. Opportunities for conflict with the tax authority arise around benefits accrued from contributions, obligation or coercion to make contributions, and justice in collecting contributions. If a tax system is to be sustainable and honor democratic principles, these conflicts must be resolved by most people most of the time in ways that are sympathetic rather than antagonistic to taxpaying.

The inner core of the wheel in figure 15.1 represents "the other" who is sought out by the taxpayer as a role model who affirms the taxpayer's identity, particularly ethical identity (Harris 2007). The other may be a friend of the tax system or an enemy, or an alternative authority (for example, the financial planning industry).

The other provides taxpayers with direction when personal deliberation leaves them unsure and confused about the demands of the system (the outer band).

The width of the three bands in figure 15.1 varies with culture and context. When tax authorities wish to impose a system without scope for noncompliance (for example, a simple withholding system), the outer band will be wide, leaving the middle band of dialogue with little practical utility and rendering the inner core irrelevant. The situation may change, however, if the tax is unduly oppressive and comes to the attention of the population as harmful or unfair. The middle band and the inner core may then combine forces to weaken the outer rim of institutional constraint. The inner core and middle band are also likely to be wide, comparatively speaking, in a self-assessment system where individuals are required to make an investment in thinking about the tax they are paying.

When taxation is a subject that is deliberated and the state seeks to bring the tax system into line with the democratic will, the outer band, the middle band, and the inner core should all have a noticeable presence. Through dialogue, the bands have opportunity to interlock to form a unified whole that can move forward. The forward movement is propelled by the deliberation that takes place within the community about the tax system: Will it bring benefits now or in the future? Does it elicit a feeling of obligation? Does it resonate with a sense of social justice? If these questions are answered in the affirmative, the wheel moves forward and accumulates the momentum that sets up mutual trust and cooperation between taxpayers and their tax authority. If they are not answered in the affirmative, the wheel may roll backward and disintegrate, or it may oscillate in confusion from feelings of discontent while holding on to some faith in the system. If discontent is squashed and deliberation outlawed, the outer rim operates as a clamp, holding things in place, allowing no scope for movement or development. When processes are in place to respond to concerns and gain forward momentum, the tax regime is optimally effective, operating largely on cooperation and earning such cooperation by acting with integrity.

VII. Primary Drivers

In this section I briefly review the literature on why individuals evade tax and discuss all five segments and bands in figure 15.1. Benefits, coercion, obligation, and justice have been identified in the literature as components in the story of why people evade tax (Cullis and Lewis 1997; Tanzi 2001; also see more general reviews by K. W. Smith and Kinsey 1987; Slemrod 1992; Alm, Sanchez, and de Juan 1995; Andreoni, Erard, and Feinstein 1998; Hasseldine and Li 1999). Tax system design also has been linked with evasion, although in the tax design literature the emphasis has been on raising revenue in accord with normatively desirable principles

(Tanzi and Shome 1994; Brand 1996; Tanzi 2000, 2001). The role of the other in tax evasion has assumed greater importance more recently, adding a dynamic element to how communities come to defy the structural design of the system (Organisation for Economic Co-operation and Development 2001*a*).

A. Tax System Design and Administration

Drawing on Adam Smith's four canons of taxation—equity, certainty, convenience, and economy—tax experts such as Tanzi (2000, 2001), Tanzi and Shome (1994), and Brand (1996) converge in their views on what the gold standards of tax design are, and maintain that evasion and avoidance will be lower when good design principles are followed. Of widespread concern is complexity, the central argument being that unintentional evasion increases when there is confusion about what is required (Long and Swingen 1988; Tanzi and Shome 1994; Brand 1996). As well as being simple, tax systems should be cost-effective. Where taxpayer compliance costs are high, compliance is less rational or even impossible (Sandford 1995). K. W. Smith and Stalans (1991) have brought together complexity and psychological compliance costs, suggesting that a simplified tax system would create more comfort for taxpayers (that is, reduce emotional costs), and in this way serve as a positive incentive for compliance. The principles of efficiency and equity involve keeping taxes as low as possible and spreading the burden as widely as possible. In line with these standards is the previously observed need to be sensitive to the different tax mixes of different countries and to curb tax avoidance. Finally, the revenue agency must be designed in such a way that it can prove itself a credible enforcer. Brand (1996, p. 14) expresses this design principle as having "a presence across the spectrum," being everywhere in the public eye, educating, persuading, and sanctioning.

The above are normative principles of tax design that may serve a broader governance agenda, not simply an agenda of reducing tax evasion. In terms of keeping evasion in check, strong empirical support can be found for some design features, most consistently in limiting the opportunity that would-be tax evaders have for avoiding detection (Wärneryd and Walerud 1982; Witte and Woodbury 1985; Long and Swingen 1988; K. W. Smith 1992; Andreoni, Erard, and Feinstein 1998; Richardson and Sawyer 2001; Taylor and Wenzel 2001). For example, tax withholding systems clearly have worked (White, Harrison, and Harrell 1993; Hasseldine 1998; IRS 2005*a*, 2005*b*), not only reducing opportunity for evasion, but also saving on compliance costs, at least for taxpayers and tax authorities. Third-party reporting has also been shown to improve compliance, lending credibility to enforcement capacity in the process (IRS 2005*a*, 2005*b*). In the experimental tax literature the probability of audit and of penalties has been associated with less tax evasion (Andreoni, Erard, and Feinstein 1998; Slemrod and Yitzhaki 2002). The evidence for other principles as a means for reducing evasion is more ambiguous. Research on the empirical relationship between tax rates and compliance has produced mixed results (Andreoni, Erard, and Feinstein 1998; compare Clotfelter 1983 and Feinstein 1991), as has the research on complexity and compliance costs and evasion (Carroll 1992; Richardson and Sawyer 2001).

In all these areas the caveat is how fair and reasonable people regard the actions of tax authorities operating under these principles. Trading complexity for simplicity needs to be balanced against an understanding that complexity is often the cost of governments pleasing their constituents or being fair (Carroll 1992; Warskett, Winer, and Hettich 1998; Slemrod and Yitzhaki 2002). Forest and Sheffrin (2002) demonstrate empirically that unfairness overshadows complexity in the prediction of evasion.

Likewise, the effects of audits and penalties are complex. From the authority's perspective, these effects need to be sufficiently negative to signal that noncompliance is unacceptable, though not so negative as to undermine enforcement capability. If too heavy, penalties may be applied sparingly by authority, and when applied may lead to lengthy appeals that undercut the credibility of the revenue agency as an enforcer (Tanzi and Shome 1994). Instead of deterring, taxpayers can learn through the process of ineffective audit and successful challenge how to get away with evasion. Even withholding systems can bring risks. There is some evidence that when constraints are tightened in one area of taxation, defiance moves to another area where noncompliance is less easily detected (Yaniv 1992; Ahmed and V. Braithwaite 2005). Tax evasion is like a squishy ball: pressuring one part results in an extrusion elsewhere.

B. Benefits

Empirical evidence for whether perception of benefits from taxation protect against evasion and avoidance is at best partial and indirect, although theoretical work has led to an expectation that such a relationship should exist in the real world (Falkinger 1988). Andreoni, Erard, and Feinstein (1998) reviewed the research on satisfaction with government and concluded that taxpayers who felt that their tax dollars were not well spent may refuse to pay their full tax liability. Richardson and Sawyer (2001) were more circumspect, warning against generalizations because of variations in what is meant and measured when considering satisfaction with government, for example, whether the reference point is satisfaction with government expenditure for the common good or satisfaction with government spending for oneself.

Western democracies are experiencing high levels of disillusionment with government (Dean, Keenan, and Kenney 1980; La Free 1998; V. Braithwaite et al. 2001), and some studies have linked this general form of alienation with tax evasion (Webley et al. 1991; V. Braithwaite et al. 2003). Mason and Calvin (1984) have disputed the claim that individuals who are dissatisfied with government will engage in tax evasion, but they suggest that indirect effects may occur, involving a watering down of the legitimacy of government authority.

Ahmed and V. Braithwaite (2005) found that dissatisfaction with government on tertiary education loans generated dismissiveness of government authority, in turn predicting defiance.

C. From Coercion to Moral Obligation

Each individual is expected to accept his or her legal obligation to comply with the tax laws. If a cooperative response is not forthcoming, coercion makes its presence felt through the revenue authority's enforcement powers: legal sanctions, social stigma, and appeals to an individual's conscience (Grasmick and Bursik 1990).

Fear of sanctioning (particularly being caught) has emerged as a significant predictor of tax compliance in some studies (Mason and Calvin 1978; Grasmick and Bursik 1990; K. W. Smith 1992; V. Braithwaite et al. 2003), but not others (Hessing et al. 1992). Effectiveness of deterrence at the level of individuals varies depending on how those individuals engage with the tax system (Hessing et al. 1992; Scholz and Pinney 1995; Wenzel 2004*b*).

Of particular policy significance is the finding that personal ethical norms can drive tax compliance, with deterrence playing a role when obligation and social pressure fail (Wenzel 2004*b*). Adherence to personal ethical norms has been investigated in many guises in the tax literature. Moral obligation, ethical responsibility, and anticipated feelings of shame and guilt have emerged as significant factors in containing evasion (Schwartz and Orleans 1967; Grasmick and Scott 1982; Grasmick and Bursik 1990; Porcano and Price 1993) and are regarded as among the most consistent predictors in the literature (for reviews, see Andreoni, Erard, and Feinstein 1998; Richardson and Sawyer 2001).

Mason and Calvin (1984) have pointed out the interdependencies among obligations, sanctions, and legitimate and credible law. They have argued that when compliance norms are allowed to weaken in a society, particularly as a result of perceptions of unfairness, the shared sense of moral obligation and the accompanying guilt feelings also weaken. Coercive efforts to reverse this downward compliance spiral will not necessarily lift moral obligation. They may increase perceptions of unfairness and crowd out a moral commitment to pay tax (Frey 1997).

D. Justice

Although there is evidence that injustice is an important correlate of tax evasion at a general level (Spicer and Becker 1980; K. W. Smith 1992), there is little consistency in the literature on which aspects of injustice precipitate evasion in contemporary Western democracies (Andreoni, Erard, and Feinstein 1998; Richardson and Sawyer 2001; Wenzel 2003). Contextual variation and whether or not justice is salient in the minds of taxpayers have been proposed as likely explanations for this inconsistency of findings (Hite 1997; Scholz and Lubell 1998*b*).

Both vertical and horizontal equity have received attention in the tax literature because of their normative importance, if not their explanatory significance, in relation to evasion. Horizontal equity is a central tenet for the design of tax systems, ensuring that the same tax is paid by members of groups of comparable taxpaying capacity, both in terms of what is expected and what is actually collected (Dean, Keenan, and Kenney 1980). Vertical equity attracts attention because of its political dimension. In many Western countries, progressivity is widely endorsed as politically desirable. In principle, each should pay according to capacity; in practice, the rich pay more (Slemrod 2000; V. Braithwaite et. al. 2001; Edlund 2003). In Australia, as elsewhere (for the United States, see Slemrod 2000; for the United Kingdom, see Commission on Taxation and Citizenship 2000), perceptions of low vertical equity in the tax system invite a great deal of criticism (V. Braithwaite 2003*c;* Rawlings 2003).

Interestingly, experimental interventions have supported the importance of justice. In the United States Hite (1997) was successful in demonstrating improved compliance when a vertical equity message was given for the amount of tax the wealthy pay. Wenzel (2005) had similar success in Australia with a message that others were paying their fair share of tax.

E. "The Other"

"The other" in figure 15.1 comprises tax advisors, friends, family, work colleagues, celebrities, and newspaper columnists—in other words, those with whom we may identify (Sigala, Burgoyne, and Webley 1999; Wenzel 2002, 2004*a*, 2007). The influence of the other may be pro-tax or antitax. Most of us most of the time take our cue as to what we should do by watching how others observe rules, a form of behavioral modeling that McAdam and Nadler (2005) refer to as the coordinating function of law. For this reason, whenever people pay taxes the predominant role of the other is assumed to be positive. The negative role is nevertheless present as well, most notably when people believe others are free riding the system (Wenzel 2005).

The influence of the other in tax research is most commonly investigated in terms of the role of tax advisors, tax agents, or tax practitioners in "leading" taxpayers into and out of compliance, and of taxpayers demanding aggressive tactics from their agents, who then feel pressured into supplying riskier advice than they would otherwise give (see, e.g., Klepper and Nagin 1989; Klepper, Mazur, and Nagin 1991). Whereas most taxpayers want a tax advisor who is honest and will keep them out of trouble with the authorities, there is clearly a market in aggressive tax planning. High risk takers find tax advisors who specialize in aggressive advice and creative compliance, whereas cautious, no-fuss taxpayers find advisors who deliver a competent and honest service (Tan 1999; Karlinsky and Bankman 2002; Sakurai and V. Braithwaite 2003).

VIII. Procedural Justice and Dialogue for Effectiveness and Integrity of Tax Systems

In summary, the story of figure 15.1 is that a high integrity tax system is not only well-designed, but also is respectful of and responsive to the democratic will (V. Braithwaite 2003*d*). Three approaches to showing respect and responsiveness have empirical support in the scientific literature and have been used to guide policy decisions. The first approach is to treat taxpayers with procedural justice, manifested in taxpayers' charters or bills of rights (see Organisation for Economic Co-operation and Development 2001*b*). The second approach is to listen to the public on matters relating to raising and spending taxes, illustrated through direct democracy referenda (e.g., in Switzerland), government reform (e.g., U.S. Tax Reform Act of 1986; see Scholz, McGraw, and Steenbergen 1992; Kinsey and Grasmick 1993), government task forces (e.g., Cash Economy Task Force; see Australian Taxation Office 1998), and best practice guidelines for tax administrations (Organisation for Economic Co-operation and Development 2001*a*). The third approach is to engage in dialogue with taxpayers, described by J. Braithwaite (2005) in the Australian context and Happé (2007) in the Dutch.

Research showing the importance of procedural justice for compliance with the law has been pioneered by Tyler and his colleagues (see Tyler's 1990 seminal work). Procedural justice prioritizes dealing with people in a manner that is transparent, impartial, respectful, and inclusive of others' interests and concerns. The important message from this work for tax research is that authorities develop trust and build their legitimacy, not through giving people the outcomes they want, which is often impossible, but rather through observing their right to a fair hearing and respectful treatment. Kristina Murphy's (2003, 2004, 2005) work with Australians prosecuted for involvement in mass-marketed aggressive tax planning schemes has shown that concessions on penalties, though important, were less significant in fueling long-term anger and resistance than were perceptions of procedural injustice.

The importance of procedural justice is linked to another development: democratic deliberation and consultation (Dryzek 1990; V. Braithwaite 2003*d*). The democratic voice seems to have been lost (Commission on Taxation and Citizenship 2000), partly because of the complexity of tax systems (Picciotto 2007) and partly because of the common view that people don't want to pay tax (Alm 1999) and therefore cannot deliberate on the matter constructively. Loss of hope that authorities will listen and consider different interests has been at the heart of much of the recent loss of legitimacy of governments (La Free 1998; V. Braithwaite 2004). Cutting the public out of deliberation about the rights and wrongs of tax evasion and avoidance may also be a key factor in escalating what many depict as a

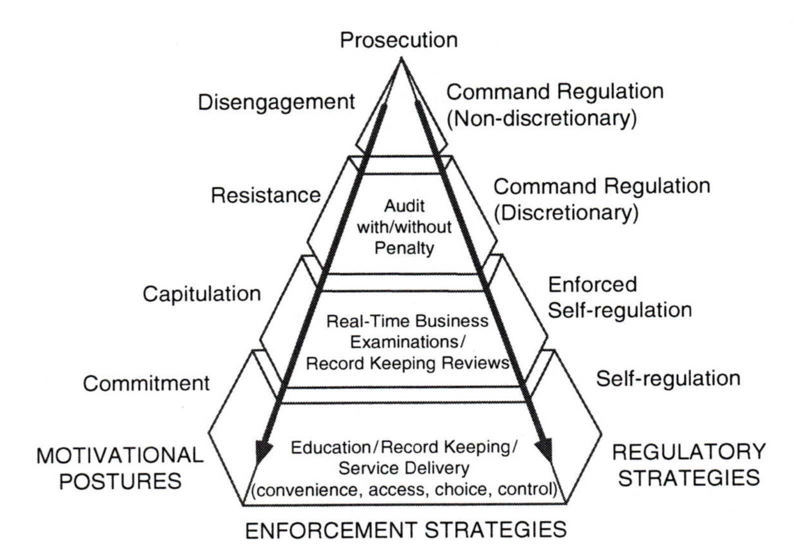

Figure 15.2. Example of regulatory practice with the Australian Taxation Office's compliance model.
Source: V. Braithwaite 2003*a*.

cat-and-mouse game of law invention that leads eventually to loss of respect for law (McBarnet 2003). The research of Kinsey and Grasmick (1993) and Scholz, McGraw, and Steenbergen (1992) on the U.S. Tax Reform Act of 1986 provides evidence of how changes to the tax system can create a far better climate of compliance when the changes are championed through deliberative fora. Bruno Frey and his colleagues have shown that among the Swiss cantons, tax jurisdictions where direct democracy is practiced have higher compliance and, more generally, that deliberative processes and inclusiveness lower prospects of tax evasion (Pommerehne, Hart, and Frey 1994; Feld and Kirchgässner 2000; Frey and Feld 2001; Feld and Frey 2002, 2005; Frey 2003; Torgler, 2003). As well as being responsive to administrative capabilities, tax design needs the endorsement of the people.

The theoretical account that frames these findings is that when tax authorities and taxpayers have a psychological contract that communicates mutual respect, loyalty, and commitment to the deliberative process, the individual takes on the persona of a citizen who is engaged in the democratic process and accepts responsibility for contributing to the collective good (Feld and Frey 2007). The theory of motivational posturing shows that taxpayers slip in and out of this cooperative stance and demonstrates why tax authorities must work at keeping cooperation at the forefront in tax deliberations (V. Braithwaite 2003*b;* V. Braithwaite, Murphy, and Reinhart 2007).

These ideas are seen at work in contexts where tax authorities are in dispute with taxpayers. Happé (2007) has described the process of negotiation with corporations in the Netherlands, and John Braithwaite (2005) has described resolution of transfer pricing agreements in Australia in similar terms. The Compliance Model in figure 15.2 developed by the Australian Taxation Office (V. Braithwaite 2003*a*) and now adapted to suit the needs of a number of other countries (Job, Stout, and Smith 2007) sets out a process whereby dialogue, persuasion, and mutual understanding proceed before the application of penalties. The application of the science of regulatory pyramids, as seen in the Compliance Model, recommends only as much intervention as is required to elicit compliance under the law. Commitment to respectful treatment and openness to cooperation exist at all times, but the pyramid threatens ever-increasing steps of regulatory intervention if evasion persists. A conversation can escalate into a warning, a warning into a wider conversation with stakeholders, conversations into sanctioning, and sanctioning into incapacitation at the pyramid's peak. The use of the Compliance Model requires well-trained staff, tax officers who are technically and interpersonally skilled in dealing with irregularities and escalating sanctions where necessary. This can be a challenge for large bureaucratic tax administrations (Hobson 2003; Job and Honaker 2003; Job, Stout, and Smith 2007; Waller 2007). Pyramidal strategies can deliver an extra thousand dollars in revenue from each dollar spent on the strategy (J. Braithwaite 2005, p. 95).

IX. Conclusion

Understanding and effectively managing tax evasion is a complex task, made more so when the objective is evidence-based policy making. Many different research perspectives have been offered for analyzing the problem, with the result that it is difficult for policy makers to tackle tax evasion in a systemic and holistic way. So how do we integrate what we know? Is there a framework for allowing these perspectives to coexist as policy is formulated? The wheel of social alignments (fig. 15.1) reminds us that although the system may be designed in accordance with normatively desirable principles and is expected to affect individuals in predictable ways, the effects may be other than expected. System designers have little control over meanings that individuals give to their experience and share with others, socially constructing narratives that affect levels of cooperation and compliance with authority. Moreover, taxpayers can turn words of defiance into actions of defiance more readily in the twenty-first century because they have greater control over how they manage their tax affairs with support from a burgeoning global financial industry.

Tax authorities can no longer afford to design their systems as they please and ignore public perceptions. Nor is the answer bringing the community onboard through "spin," which is a short-term approach to a serious problem. Tax authorities need to engage in a reflective process with the community about tax design, tax administration, tax benefits, moral obligation, coercion, justice, and alternative tax authorities. This discussion needs to be augmented by evidence acquired through field experiments and rigorous data analysis. Only then will tax authorities have the knowledge and moral authority required to manage the difficult problems of evasion and avoidance currently besetting tax systems.

NOTE

1. The audits conducted in the National Research Program (NRP) will detect a proportion of shadow economy activity but will not detect activity by individuals who are not connected in any way to the official economy. Estimates of the size of the cash economy vary with method, and differences between nations is great; estimates for the United States range from 6 to 14 percent of GNP (see Schneider and Enste 2002, pp. 29–42).

REFERENCES

Ahmed, Eliza, and Valerie Braithwaite. 2005. "A Need for Emotionally Intelligent Policy: Linking Tax Evasion with Higher Education Funding." *Legal and Criminological Psychology* 10(2): 1–19.

Allingham, Michael, and Agnar Sandmo. 1972. "Income Tax Evasion: A Theoretical Analysis." *Journal of Public Economics* 1: 323–38.

Alm, James. 1999. "Tax Evasion." In *The Encyclopedia of Taxation and Tax Policy,* edited by Joseph J. Cordes, Robert D. Ebel, and Jane G. Gravelle. Washington, DC: Urban Institute Press.

Alm, James, Gary McClelland, and William Schulze. 1992. "Why Do People Pay Taxes?" *Journal of Public Economics* 48: 21–38.

Alm, James, Isabel Sanchez, and Ana de Juan. 1995. "Economic and Noneconomic Factors in Tax Compliance." *Kyklos* 48(1): 3–18.

Andreoni, James, Brian Erard, and Jonathan Feinstein. 1998. "Tax Compliance." *Journal of Economic Literature* 36: 818–60.

Australian Taxation Office. 1998. *Improving Tax Compliance in the Cash Economy.* Canberra: Commonwealth of Australia.

Avi-Jonah, Reuven S. 2000. "Globalization, Tax Competition, and the Fiscal Crisis of the Welfare State." *Harvard Law Review* 113: 1575–676.

Bajada, Christopher, and Friedrich Schneider. 2005. Introduction to *Size, Causes and Consequences of the Underground Economy: An International Perspective,* edited by Christopher Bajada and Friedrich Schneider. Aldershot, UK: Ashgate.

Bentley, Duncan. 2007. *Taxpayers' Rights: Theory, Origin and Implementation.* Alphen aan den Rijn, Netherlands: Kluwer Law International.

Braithwaite, John. 2005. *Markets in Vice, Markets in Virtue.* Sydney: Federation Press.

Braithwaite, Valerie. 2003*a*. "A New Approach to Tax Compliance." In *Taxing Democracy: Understanding Tax Avoidance and Evasion,* edited by Valerie Braithwaite. Aldershot, UK: Ashgate.

———. 2003*b*. "Dancing with Tax Authorities: Motivational Postures and Non-Compliant Actions." In *Taxing Democracy: Understanding Tax Avoidance and Evasion,* edited by Valerie Braithwaite. Aldershot, UK: Ashgate.

———. 2003*c*. "Perceptions of Who's Not Paying Their Fair Share." *Australian Journal of Social Issues* 38(3): 335–62.

———. 2003*d*. "Tax System Integrity and Compliance: The Democratic Management of the Tax System." In *Taxing Democracy: Understanding Tax Avoidance and Evasion,* edited by Valerie Braithwaite. Aldershot, UK: Ashgate.

———. 2004. "The Hope Process and Social Inclusion." *Annals of the American Academy of Political and Social Science* 592: 128–51.

Braithwaite, Valerie, and John Braithwaite. 2006. "Democratic Sentiment and Cyclical Markets in Vice." *British Journal of Criminology* 46(6): 1110–27.

Braithwaite, Valerie, Kristina Murphy, and Monika Reinhart. 2007. "Threat, Motivational Postures and Responsive Regulation." *Law and Policy* 29(1): 137–58.

Braithwaite, Valerie, Monika Reinhart, Malcolm Mearns, and Rachelle Graham. 2001. *Preliminary Findings from the Community Hopes, Fears, and Actions Survey.* Working Paper No. 3. Canberra: Centre for Tax System Integrity, Australian National University.

Braithwaite, Valerie, Friedrich Schneider, Monika Reinhart, and Kristina Murphy. 2003. "Charting the Shoals of the Cash Economy." In *Taxing Democracy: Understanding Tax Avoidance and Evasion,* edited by Valerie Braithwaite. Aldershot, UK: Ashgate.

Braithwaite, Valerie, and Michael Wenzel. 2008. "Integrating Explanations of Tax Evasion and Avoidance." In *Cambridge Handbook of Psychology and Economic Behaviour,* edited by Alan Lewis. Cambridge: Cambridge University Press.

Brand, Phil. 1996. "Compliance: A 21st Century Approach." *National Tax Journal* 49(3): 413–19.

Browlee, W. Elliot. 2000. "Historical Perspective on U.S. Tax Policy toward the Rich." In *Does Atlas Shrug? The Economic Consequences of Taxing the Rich,* edited by Joel Slemrod. New York: Russell Sage Foundation.

Burman, Leonard E. 2003. "On Waste, Fraud and Abuse in Federal Mandatory Programs." Statement before the Committee on the Budget, U.S. House of Representatives, July 9. http://www.taxpolicycenter.org/publications/url.cfm?ID=900641

Carroll, John S. 1992. "How Taxpayers Think about Their Taxes: Frames and Values." In *Why People Pay Taxes,* edited by Joel Slemrod. Ann Arbor: University of Michigan Press.

Clotfelter, Charles. 1983. "Tax Evasion and Tax Rates: An Analysis of Individual Returns." *Review of Economics and Statistics* 65(3): 363–73.

Commission on Taxation and Citizenship. 2000. *Paying for Progress: A New Politics of Tax for Public Spending.* London: Fabian Society.

Cullis, John G., and Alan Lewis. 1997. "Why People Pay Taxes: From a Conventional Economic Model to a Model of Social Convention." *Journal of Economic Psychology* 18: 305–21.

Dean, Peter, Tony Keenan, and Fiona Kenney. 1980. "Taxpayers' Attitudes to Income Tax Evasion: An Empirical Study." *British Tax Review* 28: 28–44.

Dryzek, John S. 1990. *Discursive Democracy: Politics, Policy, and Political Science.* Cambridge: Cambridge University Press.

Edlund, Jonas. 2003. "Attitudes towards Taxation: Ignorant and Incoherent?" *Scandinavian Political Studies* 26(2): 145–67.

Evans, Chris. 2005. "Avoiding the Issue: Countering the Termites in the Australian Tax System." http://www.australianreview.net/digest/2005/09/evans.html.

Falkinger, Josef. 1988. "Tax Evasion and Equity: A Theoretical Analysis." *Public Finance* 43(3): 388–95.

Feinstein, Jonathan. 1991. "An Econometric Analysis of Income Tax Evasion and Its Detection." *RAND Journal of Economics* 22(1): 14–35.

Feld, Lars P., and Bruno S. Frey. 2002. *Trust Breeds Trust: How Taxpayers Are Treated.* Working Paper No. 32. Canberra: Centre for Tax System Integrity, Australian National University.

Feld, Lars P., and Bruno S. Frey. 2005. *Tax Compliance as the Result of a Psychological Contract: The Role of Incentives and Responsive Regulation.* Working Paper No. 76. Canberra: Centre for Tax System Integrity, Australian National University.

Feld, Lars P., and Bruno S. Frey. 2007. "Tax Compliance as the Result of a Psychological Tax Contract: The Role of Incentives and Responsive Regulation." *Law and Policy* 29(1): 102–20.

Feld, Lars, and Gebhard Kirchgässner. 2000. "Direct Democracy, Political Culture, and the Outcome of Economic Policy: A Report on the Swiss Experience." *European Journal of Political Economy* 16: 287–306.

Forest, Adam, and Steven Sheffrin. 2002. "Complexity and Compliance: An Empirical Investigation." *National Tax Journal* 55(1): 75–88.

Freedman, Judith. 2004. "Defining Taxpayer Responsibility: In Support of a General Anti-Avoidance Principle." *British Tax Review* 4: 332–57.

Frey, Bruno S. 1997. "A Constitution for Knaves Crowds Out Civic Virtues." *Economic Journal* 107(443): 1043–53.

———. 2003. "The Role of Deterrence and Tax Morale in Taxation in the European Union." Jelle Zijlstra Lecture, Netherlands Institute for Advanced Study in the Humanities and Social Sciences,Wassenaar. http://www.nias.knaw.nl/en/new_3/new_1/new_12/.

Frey, Bruno S., and Lars P. Feld. 2001. "The Tax Authority and the Taxpayer: An Exploratory Analysis." Paper presented at the Second International Conference on Taxation, Centre for Tax System Integrity, Australian National University, Canberra, December 10–11.

Geis, Gilbert, Sophie Cartwright, and Jodie Houston. 2003. "Public Wealth, Public Health, and Private Stealth: Australia's Black Market in Cigarettes." *Australian Journal of Social Issues* 38(3): 363–78.

Genser, Bernd 2001. *Corporate Income Taxation in the European Union: Current State and Perspectives.* Working Paper No. 17. Canberra: Centre for Tax System Integrity, Australian National University.

Grasmick, Harold G., and Robert J. Bursik Jr. 1990. "Conscience, Significant Others, and Rational Choice: Extending the Deterrence Model." *Law and Society Review* 24(3): 837–61.

Grasmick, Harold G., and Wilbur J. Scott. 1982. "Tax Evasion and Mechanisms of Social Control: A Comparison with Grand and Petty Theft." *Journal of Economic Psychology* 2: 213–30.

Happé, Richard. 2007. "Multinationals, Enforcement Covenants and Fair Share." *International Tax Review* 35(10): 537–47.

Harris, Nathan. 2007. *Shame, Ethical Identity and Conformity: Lessons from Research on the Psychology of Social Influence.* Regulatory Institutions Network Occasional Paper No 12. Canberra: Regulatory Institutions Network, Australian National University.

Hasseldine, John. 1998. "Prospect Theory and Tax Reporting Decisions: Implications for Tax Administrators." *Bulletin for International Fiscal Documentation* 47: 501–5.

Hasseldine, John, and Zhuhong Li. 1999. "More Tax Evasion Research Required in New Millennium." *Crime, Law and Social Change* 31: 91–104.

Hessing, Dick J., Henk Elffers, Henry S. J. Robben, and Paul Webley. 1992. "Does Deterrence Deter? Measuring the Effect of Deterrence on Tax Compliance in Field Studies and Experimental Studies." In *Why People Pay Taxes,* edited by Joel Slemrod. Ann Arbor: University of Michigan Press.

Hite, Peggy. 1997. "Identifying and Mitigating Taxpayer Non-Compliance." *Australian Tax Forum* 14: 155–76.

Hobson, Kersty. 2003. "Championing the Compliance Model: From Common Sense to Common Action?" In *Taxing Democracy: Understanding Tax Avoidance and Evasion,* edited by Valerie Braithwaite. Aldershot, UK: Ashgate.

Internal Revenue Service. 2005*a*. "New IRS Study Provides Preliminary Tax Gap Estimate." IR-2005–38. http://www.irs.gov/newsroom/article/0,,id=137247,00.html.

———. 2005*b*. "Understanding the Tax Gap." FS-2005–14. http://www.irs.gov/newsroom/article/0,,id=137246,00.html.

James, Simon, and Christopher Nobes. 2000. *The Economics of Taxation: Principles, Policy and Practice.* 7th ed. Harlow, UK: Prentice Hall.

Job, Jenny, and David Honaker. 2003. "Short-Term Experience with Responsive Regulation in the Australian Tax Office." In *Taxing Democracy: Understanding Tax Avoidance and Evasion,* edited by Valerie Braithwaite. Aldershot, UK: Ashgate.

Job, Jenny, Andrew Stout, and Rachel Smith. 2007. "Culture Change in Three Taxation Administrations: From Command-and-Control to Responsive Regulation." *Law and Policy* 29(1): 84–101.

Jones, John. 1996. "Tax Law: Rules or Principles?" *Fiscal Studies* 17(3): 63.

Karlinsky, Stuart, and Joseph Bankman. 2002. "Developing a Theory of Cash Businesses: Tax Evasion Behavior and the Role of Their Cash Preparers." Paper presented at the Fifth International Conference on Tax Administration, Australian Taxation Studies Program, University of New South Wales, Sydney, April 4–5.

Kinsey, Karyl A., and Harold G. Grasmick. 1993. "Did the Tax Reform Act of 1986 Improve Compliance? Three Studies of Pre- and Post-TRA Compliance Attitudes." *Law and Policy* 15(4): 239–325.

Kirchler, Erich. 2007. *The Economic Psychology of Tax Behaviour.* Cambridge: Cambridge University Press.

Klepper, Steven, Mark Mazur, and Daniel Nagin. 1991. "Expert Intermediaries and Legal Compliance: The Case of Tax Preparers." *Journal of Law and Economics* 34: 205–29.

Klepper, Steven, and Daniel Nagin. 1989. "Tax Compliance and Perceptions of the Risks of Detection and Criminal Prosecution." *Law and Society Review* 23(2): 209–40.

La Free, Gary. 1998. *Losing Legitimacy: Street Crime and the Decline of Social Institutions in America.* Boulder, CO: Westview.

Long, Susan B., and Judyth A. Swingen. 1988. "The Role of Legal Complexity in Shaping Taxpayer Compliance." In *Lawyers on Psychology and Psychologists on Law,* edited by Peter J. Van Koppen, Dick J. Hessing, and Grat Van Den Heuvel. Amsterdam: Swets and Zeitlinger.

Maranville, Deborah. 2004. "Unemployment Insurance Meets Globalization and the Modern Workforce." *Santa Clara Law Review* 44(4): 1129–58.

Mason, Robert, and Lyle D. Calvin. 1978. "A Study of Admitted Income Tax Evasion." *Law and Society* 1978: 73–89.
Mason, Robert, and Lyle D. Calvin. 1984. "Public Confidence and Admitted Tax Evasion." *National Tax Journal* 37: 489–96.
McAdam, Richard H., and Janice Nadler. 2005. "Testing the Focal Point Theory of Legal Compliance: The Effect of Third-Party Expression in an Experimental Hawk/Dove Game." *Journal of Empirical Legal Studies* 2: 87–123.
McBarnet, Doreen. 1992. "Legitimate Rackets: Tax Evasion, Tax Avoidance, and the Boundaries of the Law." *Journal of Human Justice* 3(2): 56–74.
———. 2003. "When Compliance Is Not the Solution but the Problem: From Changes in the Law to Changes in Attitude." In *Taxing Democracy: Understanding Tax Avoidance and Evasion,* edited by Valerie Braithwaite. Aldershot UK: Ashgate.
Moran, Beverly I. 2003. "Taxation." In *The Oxford Handbook of Legal Studies,* edited by Peter Cane and Mark Tushnet. New York: Oxford University Press.
Mumford, Ann. 2002. *Taxing Culture: Towards a Theory of Tax Collection Law.* Burlington, VT: Ashgate.
Murphy, Kristina. 2003. "Procedural Justice and Tax Compliance." *Australian Journal of Social Issues* 38(3): 379–407.
———. 2004. "The Role of Trust in Nurturing Compliance: A Study of Accused Tax Avoiders." *Law and Human Behavior* 28(2): 187–209.
———. 2005. "Regulating More Effectively: The Relationship between Procedural Justice, Legitimacy and Tax Non-Compliance." *Journal of Law and Society* 32: 562–89.
Organisation for Economic Co-operation and Development. 2001*a*. *Principles for Good Tax Administration—Practice Note GAP001.* Paris: Centre for Tax Policy and Administration.
———. 2001*b*. *Taxpayer Rights and Obligations—Practice Note GAP002.* Paris: Centre for Tax Policy and Administration.
Orviska, Martha, and John Hudson. 2002. "Tax Evasion, Civic Duty and the Law Abiding Citizen." *European Journal of Political Economy* 19(1): 83–102.
Picciotto, Sol. 2007. "Constructing Compliance: Game Playing, Tax Law and the Regulatory State." *Law and Policy* 29(1): 11–30.
Pommerehne, Werner W., Albert Hart, and Bruno S. Frey. 1994. "Tax Morale, Tax Evasion, and the Choice of Policy Instruments in Different Political Systems." *Public Finance* 49(Supplement): 52–69.
Porcano, Thomas M., and Charles E. Price. 1993. "The Effects of Social Stigmatization on Tax Evasion." *Advances in Taxation* 5: 197–217.
Rawlings, Greg. 2003. "Cultural Narratives of Taxation and Citizenship: Fairness, Groups and Globalisation." *Australian Journal of Social Issues* 38(3): 269–306.
Richardson, Maryann, and Adrian J. Sawyer. 2001. "A Taxonomy of the Tax Compliance Literature: Further Findings, Problems and Prospects." *Australian Taxation Forum* 16: 137–320.
Rossotti, Charles O. 2002. *Report to the IRS Oversight Board: Assessment of the IRS and the Tax System.* Washington, DC, September. http://www.nteuirswatch.org/documents/numbers/Rossotti%2002%20report%20to%20oversight%20board.pdf.
Sakurai, Yuka, and Valerie Braithwaite. 2003. "Taxpayers' Perceptions of Practitioners: Finding One Who Is Effective and Does the Right Thing?" *Journal of Business Ethics* 46(4): 375–87.

Sandford, Cedric, ed. 1995. *Tax Compliance Costs, Measurement and Policy*. Bath, UK: Fiscal Publications.
Schmölders, Gunter. 1970. "Survey Research in Public Finance—A Behavioural Approach to Fiscal Theory." *Public Finance* 25: 300–6.
Schneider, Friedrich, and Dominik H. Enste. 2002. *The Shadow Economy: An International Survey*. Cambridge: Cambridge University Press.
Scholz, John T., and Mark Lubell. 1998*a*. "Adaptive Political Attitudes: Duty, Trust, and Fear as Monitors of Tax Policy." *American Journal of Political Science* 42(3): 903–20.
Scholz, John T., and Mark Lubell. 1998*b*. "Trust and Taxpaying: Testing the Heuristic Approach to Collective Action." *American Journal of Political Science* 42(2): 398–417.
Scholz, John T., Kathleen M. Mcgraw, and Marco R. Steenbergen. 1992. "Will Taxpayers Ever Like Taxes? Responses to the U.S. Tax Reform Act of 1986." *Journal of Economic Psychology* 13(4): 625–56.
Scholz, John T., and Neil Pinney. 1995. "Duty, Fear, and Tax Compliance: The Heuristic Basis of Citizenship Behavior." *American Journal of Political Science* 39: 490–512.
Schwartz, Richard, and Sonya Orleans. 1967. "On Legal Sanctions." *University of Chicago Law Review* 34: 274–300.
Sigala, Maria, Carole Burgoyne, and Paul Webley. 1999. "Tax Communication and Social Influence: Evidence from a British Sample." *Journal of Community and Applied Social Psychology* 9: 237–41.
Slemrod, Joel. 1992, ed. *Why People Pay Taxes*. Ann Arbor: University of Michigan Press.
———, ed. 1999. *Tax Policy in the Real World*. Cambridge: Cambridge University Press.
———. 2000. "The Economics of Taxing the Rich." In *Does Atlas Shrug? The Economic Consequences of Taxing the Rich,* edited by Joel Slemrod. Cambridge, MA: Harvard University Press.
Slemrod, Joel, and Shlomo Yitzhaki. 2002. "Tax Avoidance, Evasion and Administration." In *Handbook of Public Economics,* vol. 3, edited by Alan J. Auerbach and Martin Feldstein. Amsterdam: Elsevier.
Smith, Julie P. 1993. *Taxing Popularity: The Story of Taxation in Australia*. Canberra: Federalism Research Centre, Australian National University.
Smith, Kent W. 1992. "Reciprocity and Fairness: Positive Incentives for Tax Compliance." In *Why People Pay Taxes: Tax Compliance and Enforcement,* edited by Joel Slemrod. Ann Arbor: University of Michigan Press.
Smith, Kent W., and Karyl A. Kinsey. 1987. "Understanding Taxpayer Behavior: A Conceptual Framework with Implications for Research." *Law and Society Review* 21(4): 639–63.
Smith, Kent W., and Loretta J. Stalans. 1991. "Encouraging Tax Compliance with Positive Incentives: A Conceptual Framework and Research Directions." *Law and Policy* 13(1): 35–53.
Sørensen, Peter B. 1999. "Changing Views of the Corporate Income Tax." In *Tax Policy in the Real World,* edited by Joel Slemrod. Cambridge: Cambridge University Press.
Spicer, Michael W., and Lee A. Becker. 1980. "Fiscal Inequality and Tax Evasion: An Experimental Approach." *National Tax Journal* 33: 171–75.
Steinmo, Sven. 1993. *Taxation and Democracy: Swedish, British and American Approaches to Financing the Modern State*. New Haven, CT: Yale University Press.
Stiglitz, Joseph. 2002. *Globalization and Its Discontents*. New York: Norton.
Tan, Lin M. 1999. "Taxpayers' Preference for Type of Advice from Tax Practitioner: A Preliminary Examination." *Journal of Economic Psychology* 20: 431–47.

Tanzi, Vito. 1996. "Globalization, Tax Competition and the Future of Tax Systems." International Monetary Fund Working Paper, WP/96/141, Washington, DC, December. http://ideas.repec.org/p/imf/imfwpa/96–141.html.

———. 2000. *Globalization, Technological Developments and the Work of Fiscal Termites*. International Monetary Fund Working Paper, WP/00/181, Washington, DC, November. http://www.imf.org/external/pubs/ft/wp/2000/wp00181.pdf.

———. 2001. "Creating Effective Tax Administrations: The Experience of Russia and Georgia." In *Reforming the State: Fiscal and Welfare Reform in Post-Socialist Countries,* edited by Janos Kornai, Stephan Haggard, and Robert R. Kaufman. Cambridge: Cambridge University Press.

Tanzi, Vito, and Parthasrathi Shome. 1994. "A Primer on Tax Evasion." *International Bureau of Fiscal Documentation* 48: 328–37.

Taylor, Natalie, and Michael Wenzel. 2001. *The Effects of Different Letter Styles on Reported Rental Income and Rental Deductions: An Experimental Approach*. Working Paper No. 11. Canberra: Centre for Tax System Integrity, Australian National University.

Torgler, Benno. 2003. *Tax Morale and Institutions*. CREMA Working Paper No. 2003–09. Basel, Switzerland.

Tyler, Tom R. 1990. *Why People Obey the Law*. New Haven, CT: Yale University Press.

Waller, Vivienne. 2007. "The Challenge of Institutional Integrity in Responsive Regulation: Field Inspections by the Australian Taxation Office." *Law and Policy* 29(1): 67–83.

Wärneryd, Karl-Erik, and Bengt Walerud. 1982. "Taxes and Economic Behaviour: Some Interview Data on Tax Evasion in Sweden." *Journal of Economic Psychology* 2: 187–211.

Warskett, George, Stanley L. Winer, and Walter Hettich. 1998. "The Complexity of Tax Structure in Competitive Political Systems." *International Tax and Public Finance* 5: 123–51.

Webley, Paul, Henry Robben, Henk Elffers, and Dick Hessing. 1991. *Tax Evasion: An Experimental Approach*. Cambridge: Cambridge University Press.

Wenzel, Michael. 2002. "The Impact of Outcome Orientation and Justice Concerns on Tax Compliance: The Role of Taxpayers' Identity." *Journal of Applied Psychology* 87(4): 629–45.

———. 2003. "Tax Compliance and the Psychology of Justice: Mapping the Field." In *Taxing Democracy: Understanding Tax Avoidance and Evasion,* edited by Valerie Braithwaite. Aldershot, UK: Ashgate.

———. 2004*a*. "Social Identification as a Determinant of Concerns about Individual-, Group-, and Inclusive-Level Justice." *Social Psychology Quarterly* 67: 70–87.

———. 2004*b*. "The Social Side of Sanctions: Personal and Social Norms as Moderators of Deterrence." *Law and Human Behavior* 28: 547–67.

———. 2005. "Misperceptions of Social Norms about Tax Compliance: from Theory to Intervention." *Journal of Economic Psychology* 26: 862–83.

———. 2007. "The Multiplicity of Taxpayer Identities and Their Implications for Tax Ethics." *Law and Policy* 29(1): 31–50.

White, Richard A., Paul D. Harrison, and Adrian Harrell. 1993. "The Impact of Income Tax Withholding on Taxpayer Compliance: Further Empirical Evidence." *Journal of the American Taxation Association* 15: 63–78.

Witte, Ann D., and Diane F. Woodbury. 1985. "The Effect of Tax Laws and Tax Administration on Tax Compliance: The Case of the U.S. Individual Income Tax." *National Tax Journal* 38: 1–13.

Woellner, Robin, Stephen Barkoczy, Shirley Murphy, and Chris Evans. 2005. *Australian Taxation Law*. 15th ed. Sydney: CCH.

Yaniv, Gideon. 1992. "Collaborated Employee-Employer Tax Evasion." *Public Finance* 47: 312–21.

PART IV

TRANSNATIONAL CRIME

CHAPTER 16

HUMAN SMUGGLING AND HUMAN TRAFFICKING

EDWARD R. KLEEMANS

In social and political debate there is much confusion about human smuggling and human trafficking. The terms are often used interchangeably, although they refer to two different phenomena that share common elements. Human *smuggling* primarily relates to illegal immigration and the violation of immigration laws. It often involves the mutual consent of smugglers and illegal immigrants. Although travel conditions may be harsh and prices may be high, smuggling rings provide a desired connection between poor or dangerous countries and affluent, safe countries such as the United States, Canada, the member states of the European Union, Australia, and Japan. Human smugglers may be viewed as good guys for saving political refugees or helping family or friends to build up a new life or as bad guys who unscrupulously abuse dependent, illegal immigrants by demanding high prices, providing bad or perilous travel arrangements, or exploiting clients who have to pay off high debts (debt bondage). This ambiguity explains why many legal definitions explicitly require smugglers to act to obtain, directly or indirectly, "a financial or other material benefit" (e.g., United Nations [UN] 2000*a*). This ambivalence also complicates the normative debate about combating human smuggling, not the least because making illegal immigration processes more difficult may also adversely affect travel conditions, prices, and the position of illegal immigrants.

Human *trafficking* focuses on exploitation by the use of force, fraud, coercion, or deceit. The UN Protocol to Prevent, Suppress and Punish Trafficking in Persons defines "trafficking in persons" as "the recruitment, transportation, transfer, harboring or receipt of persons, by means of the threat or use of force or other forms of coercion, of abduction, of fraud, of deception, of the abuse of power or of a position of vulnerability or of the giving or receiving of payments or benefits to achieve the consent of a person having control over another person, for the purpose of exploitation" (UN 2000*b*, Article 3a). Although this definition is quite wide, just like many other UN definitions, human trafficking most notably refers to forced prostitution or other forms of sexual exploitation, forced labor or services, slavery or practices similar to slavery, servitude, and the removal of internal organs. Forced prostitution and sexual exploitation, particularly of women and children, have a long history and are the main focus of the antitrafficking debate. Bad labor conditions and economic exploitation also have a long history, but opinions vary substantially about how harsh labor conditions and restrictions on free will should be to warrant calling them "modern slavery." This is one reason the UN definition explicitly makes the consent of the victim irrelevant. Nevertheless, which phenomena qualify as trafficking—and under which conditions—is open to debate.

Legal definitions in many countries follow this distinction between human smuggling and human trafficking. In practice the two different phenomena may be intertwined. Sexual exploitation may be preceded by (assisted) illegal immigration, whereas for some illegal immigrants human smuggling may end up in debt bondage and bad labor conditions. Nevertheless, human smuggling is mainly characterized by mutual consent; many clients may be better referred to as customers—often even family or friends—than as victims. In human trafficking, however, the relationship between traffickers and trafficked people is dominated by exploitation and the use of force, fraud, coercion, or deceit.

In this chapter I highlight the following main points:

- Human smuggling and human trafficking are different phenomena that require different policy responses.
- Human smuggling basically involves mutual consent between illegal immigrants, their families, and smugglers.
- Much illegal immigration makes use of entirely "regular" channels and is closely intertwined with political asylum and immigration policies.
- Opportunity-reducing initiatives may target mechanisms actually used by human smugglers and illegal immigrants, but may also have negative side effects, for example, on true political refugees, travel conditions, and prices. Law enforcement operations may target the part of the smuggling business that is dominated by criminal groups, large volumes, and bad travel conditions.
- Human trafficking is different from human smuggling, as the basic aspect of the former offense relates to exploitation and the violation of human rights. Particularly in human trafficking for sexual exploitation, types of victims and types of traffickers involved differ substantially from those

involved in human smuggling, and human rights violations of women, boys, and girls are far more severe.
- The position of prostitutes and the opportunities of pimps to exploit prostitutes largely depend on the ways governments try to deal with the contested nature of prostitution. In combating human trafficking, involuntary prostitution, helping victims, and prosecuting offenders are key issues.

In section I, I summarize data, figures, and patterns concerning human smuggling and human trafficking. In section II I focus on the processes of human smuggling, and in section III I elaborate on processes of human trafficking. Although other forms of exploitation, such as labor trafficking, also occur, this section focuses particularly on human trafficking for sexual exploitation. Section IV is devoted to policy measures and interventions. In section V I summarize my main conclusions and highlight research priorities for the coming decade.

I. Facts, Figures, and Patterns

Although much research has been published on human smuggling and human trafficking, it is hard to give an accurate estimate of their prevalence and incidence. For many reasons, national and international data are scarce, unreliable, and not comparable (e.g., Laczko 2005; Lehti and Aromaa 2006; Savona and Stefanizzi 2007; Zhang 2007). First, much research does not distinguish between human smuggling and human trafficking, mingling data relating to trafficking, smuggling, and irregular immigration. Second, governments, law enforcement agencies, and nongovernmental organizations (NGOs) maintain their own data sets and their own reasons for defining and presenting the trafficking problem in particular ways. Third, both human smuggling and human trafficking are phenomena that are seriously underreported. Illegal immigrants have few reasons to report illegal border crossing, and a substantial part of irregular immigration makes use of entirely "regular" channels and procedures, such as tourist visas, business invitations, counterfeit documents, asylum systems, and marriage fraud. The actions of immigrants and the assistance of family and friends provide ample opportunity, even without involvement of professional human smugglers. Several types of human trafficking also make use of the victim's initiation of the first leg of the journey: women are not abducted, but travel voluntarily to another country and end up in situations of exploitation only later on. Moreover, victims of trafficking do not report to the police for many reasons, including emotional attachment to the perpetrator, dependency, weak legal status, and fear of negative repercussions. As a result, existing data are most often either general estimates created on the basis of unclear methodologies or administrative data kept by the various involved authorities or organizations on the victims they assist (Laczko 2005).

Despite these problems much progress has been made (e.g., Salt 2000; Kyle and Koslowski 2001; Laczko and Gozdziak 2005; Savona and Stefanizzi 2007). Lehti and Aromaa (2006, pp. 183–215) give a detailed account of the various estimates of the number of people trafficked each year worldwide for sexual or economic exploitation, varying between 600,000 and more than 4 million. They conclude that the usual assumption that prostitution-related trafficking makes up 70 to 80 percent of all global trafficking in persons is probably false. It is likely that other forms of trafficking, particularly traffic for economic exploitation as domestic servants and as laborers in agriculture, construction, and sweatshop industries, are at least as common as trafficking for sexual exploitation. However, according to these authors, aggravated abuses of human rights are substantially more common in trafficking for sexual exploitation than in other types of trafficking.

Another interesting conclusion they offer is that most global trafficking for sexual exploitation is short distance. According to the available estimates, about 60 to 80 percent of the trade takes place *within* countries. The percentage of cross-border trafficking is only 25 to 30 percent of the total global volume, and the bulk is regional, taking place between neighboring countries. The major flows run from rural places to cities and from economically depressed regions to affluent ones. This finding is salient, as many policy makers tend to focus on cross-border trafficking and many criminal justice agencies and NGOs tend to underestimate the amount of local or regional trafficking.

Furthermore, most trafficking is not related to the major industrialized countries (only 10 to 20 percent). The bulk of trafficking takes place within and between third world and Eastern European countries. Western and Japanese sex tourism forms a substantial part of the clientele of local prostitution in several third world countries and in parts of Russia. Major growth in prostitution in Asia started in the 1960s and was stimulated by wars and large foreign armies in the area (e.g., in Vietnam). Later these sex industries were reconstructed to serve European, Australian, North American, and Japanese sex tourism, often with the consent and open support of local governments. Globalization and the increasing ease of travel have stimulated both sex tourism and the influx of foreign sex workers into Western prostitution markets. Another major event was the collapse of the Soviet empire and the sudden emergence of free travel between poor, Eastern European countries and rich, Western European countries, creating a fertile breeding ground for migrant prostitution inside Europe.

Although Lehti and Aromaa (2006) conclude that most global trafficking for sexual exploitation is short distance, they also elaborate on data regarding large-scale long-distance trafficking. Distance, history (e.g., former colonies), and particular economic and social relationships with particular countries influence which countries become sources of trafficking. The main source countries are Brazil, the Dominican Republic, Russia, Sri Lanka, China, Thailand, the Philippines, and

Nigeria. According to Lehti and Aromaa, all these countries have in common an exceptionally good infrastructure for such trafficking: either strong domestic organized crime or long-standing traditions of female economic emigration with established global migration networks and immigrant communities.

II. Processes of Human Smuggling

Politicians and NGOs alike frequently relate human smuggling and human trafficking to the involvement of organized crime. More generally, the discussion tends to gravitate toward images of cruel offenders and helpless victims. In Europe public debate was fueled by the awful Dover incident in 2000, when 58 Chinese immigrants suffocated in a lorry while trying to reach the United Kingdom; two survivors were able to recollect this tragedy in detail. In the United States a similar role is played by the June 1993 grounding of the *Golden Venture,* a Chinese smuggling ship, off New York City's harbor with a cargo of nearly 300 illegal immigrants. At least six and perhaps 10 of the passengers died while floundering in the bone-chilling surf (DeStefano 2007, p. 5). Cruel and reckless Snakeheads (Chinese human smugglers) are the common subject of daunting tales in many countries. A well-known example is Sister Ping, the "Snakehead Queen," who, according to U.S. law enforcement agencies, was a ruthless, underworld mafia-type boss in New York's Chinatown and a cutthroat underground banker. For more than a decade she eluded law enforcement agencies. Eventually, she was arrested, extradited, and sentenced in 2006 to 35 years' imprisonment on charges of conspiring to commit alien smuggling, hostage taking, money laundering, and laundering ransom money (Zhang 2007, pp. 79–86).

We can understand the political or emotional reasons why these events and persons appeal to media and politics. Yet such images severely misrepresent the problem and misdirect policy discussions. Human smuggling basically involves mutual consent between illegal immigrants and "smugglers," who are either family members, friends, or more distant professional smugglers. There are many reasons people want to migrate despite increasingly repressive Western migration regimes: imminent danger, discomfort, and poverty, combined with the prospect of a better life elsewhere. Next to these push factors, major pull factors are wage differences, dual labor markets in Western countries (stable, high-paying jobs combined with labor shortages for unstable, low-paying jobs), and the welfare state, particularly in Europe.

Portes (1995) has added to this mainly economic perspective the important role of migrant networks across the world, as migrants do not make isolated decisions. Social networks are important in providing information and assistance, which explains "chain migration" and collective decisions on migration by (extended) families to increase family revenues. If migration is viewed this way, we can understand why many actors—migrants, smugglers, family, and friends, but also employers, organizations, and some governments—may have a clear common interest in successful migration, through legal or illegal means. It also explains why much illegal migration occurs through entirely legal channels. With some creativity and manipulation, the options that are open for legal immigration can also be used for illegal immigration. Zhang (2007, pp. 22–56) reviews the ways several legal channels are used: entering as a legal immigrant (by using forged documents); marriage fraud; the use of tourist, student, or scholar visas; and business invitations. In Europe much attention has also been paid to the use of asylum procedures and counterfeit documents, providing access to the welfare state (e.g., Neske and Doomernik 2006).

Two preliminary conclusions abide. First, many more people may be involved in human smuggling than professional smugglers alone, whereas much smuggling can be done entirely without the involvement of professional smugglers. Second, smuggling occurs through many more channels than the most visible, which are overrepresented in the media (physical transportation of illegal immigrants by land, sea, and air).

International migration may be viewed as a global business with licit and illicit aspects (Salt and Stein 1997). It involves migrants and their social networks, trying to migrate and send money home, and professional as well as amateur smugglers who make a living out of their business. A range of actors are involved in the smuggling process, which may be divided into three stages: mobilization (country of origin), en route (transit countries), and insertion (country of destination).

An analysis of 10 police investigations into human smuggling shows that the prime suspects in these cases very often have social ties with both the countries of origin and the countries of destination (Kleemans and van de Bunt 2003; Kleemans 2007). Smugglers and clients often share the same ethnic background. Before they start smuggling, many smugglers have been smuggled themselves. Smuggling networks emerge in which the organizers of (sub)routes are the major players. The prime suspects are not distant masterminds but are often involved in the day-to-day activities. The cases also illuminate the crucial role of forged documents. The logistics of smuggling are made far less complicated through use of forged documents: smuggled immigrants, who have an equal interest in a successful journey, can simply travel alone, for instance by airplane. The cores of these smuggling rings can be relatively small, consisting of a few people in the country of origin, in a transit country (if necessary), and in the country of destination. Many prime suspects are also closely involved in forging documents.

Without forged documents the journey is much longer, more complicated, and more uncomfortable. Additional barriers, transfers, and stops are necessary, as well as reliance on local knowledge and local contacts to transfer and cater to people on the move. A longer chain also involves more complex coordination, communication, and payment schemes. Sometimes these chains are coordinated from start to finish, but in other instances clients are successively passed through the hands of groups that are only very loosely connected (see also Neske and Doomernik 2006; Zhang 2007). Some scholars emphasize the substantial agency on the part of smuggled immigrants (e.g., Herman 2006; van Liempt and Doomernik 2006).

There is a recurring debate in the literature about the amount of organization involved and the role of organized crime, particularly in smuggling Chinese (e.g., Chin 1999). Zhang and Chin (2002) tend to deny the involvement of organized crime or large criminal groups. Based on extensive ethnographic research, they claim that Chinese human smuggling is dominated by ordinary citizens, a point also stressed in research on the U.S.-Mexican border (Spener 2004). Familial networks and fortuitous social contacts have enabled these individuals to pool resources to smuggle human beings around the world. According to Zhang and Chin, Chinese human smuggling organizations consist of mostly peer group entrepreneurs and dyadic networks (see also Zhang and Gaylord 1996; Zhang 1997). However, much research based on law enforcement information takes a wider view of the variety of organizational structures involved (e.g. Aronowitz 2001; Schloenhardt 2001; Kleemans and van de Bunt 2003; Staring et al. 2005; Soudijn 2006). For instance, Soudijn carried out extensive research on the smuggling of Chinese immigrants, mainly through European countries into the United Kingdom, by analyzing 88 Dutch court files (1996–2003). Two conclusions diverge from what is typically found in ethnographic research. First, although many ethnic Chinese are involved, about a quarter of the suspects were not ethnic Chinese often acting as large-scale transporters. Field interviews would miss such an observation, as these tend to focus on Chinese smugglers and the Chinese community. Second, the Chinese smuggling scene does not consist of individuals who form temporary business alliances. Perhaps this description might be adequate when considering the whole smuggling route, as different legs of the journey are managed by different smuggling groups. The analyzed groups take on assignments from several organizations abroad, and different alliances are continued if smuggling operations run smoothly. Rather than by central coordination, smuggling is harmonized by looser organizations through social networks. Yet on a lower level, police and court files show much more cohesion, as the relationships among offenders are relatively stable. Social bonds are not flexible and fluid but durable and consistent if no problems arise. Furthermore, large-scale smuggling groups handle a continuous flow of migrants waiting to be smuggled, which results in a need to have reliable people at hand and to construct some division of labor (Soudijn 2006).

A view of human smugglers as ruthless offenders preying on helpless victims is sometimes correct—when criminal groups are involved, violence is used, travel conditions are harsh, and prices are exorbitant. Yet generally such a view neglects the driving force behind human smuggling: human smuggling basically involves mutual consent between illegal immigrants and smugglers. Smuggling rings, even when involving criminal groups, have a clear interest in keeping their clients satisfied, as satisfied customers and their families bring in new business. In migrant communities communication about smuggling is relatively open, and advertising by word of mouth is a common way to attract new clients. Furthermore, many migrant communities do not regard smuggling illegal immigrants as a serious offense. On the contrary, smugglers are not viewed as criminals but as service providers, offering the opportunity to find a better future elsewhere. Hence policy makers are well advised not to neglect the basic rationale behind human smuggling as a combined effort of immigrants, their social environment, and smugglers to circumvent immigration laws.

III. Processes of Human Trafficking

Human trafficking is very different, as the basic aspect of this offense relates to exploitation and the violation of human rights. Particularly in human trafficking for sexual exploitation, both the types of victims and the types of traffickers involved differ substantially from those involved in human smuggling. To put it briefly, victims are much more vulnerable and dependent, and offenders are much more violent and exploitive. The relationships between victims and offenders are much more complex, ranging from intimate or perverted relationships to very strict monitoring and outright violence and intimidation. This also blurs the difference between coercion and free will, which is a central element in public debates about prostitution as a "normal" profession. I do not elaborate on this public debate; suffice it to say that a too moralistic view of prostitution tends to neglect the reality that prostitution is a relatively profitable business for people who lack other opportunities and that many prostitutes are not forced directly into prostitution. However, viewing prostitution as a perfectly normal business tends to neglect some basic realities that are exploited by traffickers: prostitution is also very lucrative for those who profit from the work of prostitutes, and much prostitution is simply degrading and dangerous.

Victims of forced prostitution tend predominantly to be young, poor, and dislocated and have troubled backgrounds. In South and Southeast Asia and in some regions of Latin America the majority of victims of prostitution-related trafficking are believed to be minors. In Western industrialized countries the average age in forced prostitution is also younger than that of domestic prostitution and independent migrant prostitution. The bulk of victims originate from the most economically depressed and politically most unstable areas in the world and from the most disadvantaged social and ethnic groups in those areas (Lehti and Aromaa 2006, pp. 147–54). A disproportionately high percentage of victims come from broken or abusive family relations (see also Surtees 2008). Forced prostitution typically tends to thrive on dependency, deprivation, and dislocation.

Dislocation and a high turnover are also part of the prostitution business. Brothel owners and people renting rooms in window prostitution are in constant need of new girls to bring in extra money. Prostitutes and pimps also travel to different locations and countries in search of new clients and profitable opportunities. A study by van Dijk (2002, pp. 99–102, reviewed in Kleemans 2007) on human trafficking in the Netherlands in the period 1997–2000, involving 521 suspects, shows that victims are bought and sold more than once and the turnover rate is high. Many victims report that they have worked in various cities and in various countries. In the police investigations analyzed, some victims were active in street prostitution or escort services, but most worked in brothels or in window prostitution. Forty clubs were owned by trafficking suspects, 27 clubs cooperated (the owners usually turned a blind eye), and 21 clubs were used by traffickers (the owners being unaware). People renting rooms in window prostitution were never directly involved in trafficking. They rented rooms to pimps without checking on whether the prostitutes were illegal or exploited. Sometimes the girls were recruited abroad, but more often they were simply bought from other pimps or recruited domestically.

Complex recruiting processes, domestically and abroad, have been investigated in many studies. Three conclusions are particularly relevant. First, outright abduction or selling into prostitution is not common. Nevertheless, outside the industrialized world, abduction and selling by relatives are much more prevalent (Lehti and Aromaa 2006, pp. 154–62). Many victims are recruited by promises of employment opportunities, often in hotel service, catering, and entertainment or as domestic workers and nannies. What's more, many victims are aware that they will work in prostitution or are at risk of ending up in prostitution or sex-related jobs. Second, dislocation may capture the essence of trafficking much better than border crossing. Much trafficking occurs domestically or regionally, whereas many cross-border victims travel voluntarily and end up in situations of exploitation only later on. Third, recruitment and exploitation often involve personal relationships. Recruitment occurs through acquaintances, friends, or relatives or through (former) prostitutes and traffickers. In many cases, intimate relationships are involved: parents or relatives force children into prostitution, male sexual partners become parasites on the woman's prostitution activities, and traffickers seduce vulnerable girls and move them gradually into (forced) prostitution through a perverted relationship characterized by a combination of grooming, bullying, and violence. The involvement of close, intimate relationships in cases of exploitation explains why free will is a relative phenomenon in this context, why many victims feel reluctant to report to the authorities, and why victims often don't want to be liberated and, after being liberated, may soon return to prostitution.

Once victims are recruited, the principle means of exploitation are manipulation through perverted social relationships, close monitoring, intimidation, and outright violence. According to many studies, implied and actual violence is common and ever present (e.g., Lehti and Aromaa 2006, pp. 158–62; Surtees 2008). However, this violence may be integrated in complex, personal relationships and (economic) dependency situations. Furthermore, debt bonding is very common, as recruiting expenses or travel costs have to be paid to the traffickers. Traffickers tend to perpetuate this debt situation through inflated housing and living expenses and arbitrary fines for "misconduct." This exploitation strategy is often accompanied by close monitoring of the daily lives and earnings of the victims. If women are sold to another pimp, the story repeats itself. Finally, particularly in cross-border trafficking, exploiting the illegal residence status of victims is a common control method; this involves confiscating passports and other identity documents as well as abusing illegal immigrants' fear of local authorities and the prospect of expulsion.

Some situations are more conducive to exploitation than others. Prostitution involves subsectors such as window prostitution; prostitution in clubs, brothels, private houses, massage parlors, and couples clubs; home prostitution; escort prostitution; and streetwalking. Streetwalking and escort prostitution are the most dangerous forms of prostitution, as prostitutes have little control over the locations where activities take place (private homes, hotels, cars) and it is difficult to screen customers. Such dangers produce an implicit demand for protection, for example by pimps, and protection and monitoring clients may easily end up in monitoring and exploiting prostitutes as well. Other forms of prostitution, such as window prostitution, may also involve protection and extortion by male relatives or pimps. The conditions for independent, voluntary prostitution are most favorable in clubs and brothels, as more prostitutes are present at the same time, clients can be checked in advance, and control can be exercised over the locations where and the conditions under which sexual activities take place. Still, much depends on the intentions of the operators of these brothels and clubs (they may also play a part in forced prostitution) and government policies toward these clubs.

A still underexposed phenomenon in the literature is the role women play in forced prostitution. Though usually viewed as victims, women often play prominent roles as recruiters, transporters, or exploiters (Kleemans and van de Bunt 1999; Lehti and Aromaa 2006; Siegel and de Blank 2008). Former victims may be used as recruiters or may be offered more favorable working conditions if they recruit replacements; relatives of male traffickers or prostitutes may be involved in monitoring and exploiting prostitutes; and some women make a career of prostitution, for example victims of Nigerian trafficking who become *mamans,* controlling other victims. Although men play a prominent role in forced prostitution, the business of prostitution is also very much a women's business, which explains why women should be regarded not only as victims, but also as potential accomplices or traffickers themselves. A similar point can be made about the underexposed role of women in other criminal activities, such as (Chinese) human smuggling (e.g., Soudijn 2006; Zhang, Chin, and Miller 2007).

Finally, a much discussed element in forced prostitution is the involvement of criminal groups and organized crime. Forced prostitution is a profitable criminal activity that attracts several kinds of offenders, criminal groups, and criminal networks (for reviews, see Lehti and Aromaa 2006; Surtees 2008). Three main forms of criminal cooperation can be distinguished (see van Dijk 2002). Solo offenders have forced one or more girls into prostitution. Self-supporting criminal groups control the entire process, from recruitment to prostitution, and have no established contacts with other offenders or groups involved in human trafficking; the main suspects are often in charge of brothels or sex clubs, relying on personal contacts to recruit and transport victims. Criminal macro networks include solo offenders and criminal groups clustered by geographical proximity, family ties, friendships, commercial circuits, or similarity in criminal activities. In trafficking networks, clusters evolve around recruitment in particular countries, sometimes around transport, and around forced prostitution locations. There may be prostitution carousels and the selling and reselling of victims, producing never-ending debt and dependency situations.

Due to space limitations, I do not devote much attention to trafficking for labor exploitation, though it is part of the UN definition of human trafficking. The literature on labor trafficking shows that the processes involved are very different from the ones involved in forced prostitution, particularly in terms of the relationships between victims and offenders, the nature of victims and offenders involved, the amount of agency, the amount of force and deceit, and the exit options. The worst cases may be appalling in terms of human rights violations: victims may experience debt bondage, withholding of identity documents, threats and abuse, reduced or no pay, excessive working hours, dangerous conditions, poor accommodations, and discrimination (for a literature review, see Dowling, Moreton, and Wright 2007). Victims are found in a variety of employment sectors, including agriculture, construction, nursing, domestic work, and hospitality. These industries typically require large numbers of low-paid, flexible, seasonal workers, sometimes in difficult and dangerous conditions. Hence the key driver of such trafficking is the demand for cheap and malleable labor, and illegal immigration is one of the key sources. Yet, generally, opinions vary substantially about how harsh the labor conditions and restrictions on free will should be to warrant calling it "modern slavery" or "human trafficking."

IV. Policy Measures and Interventions

A traditional way to combat human smuggling and human trafficking is to increase border controls, build higher fences, and target physical smuggling processes. The deficiencies of this approach are clear. For one, most human trafficking for sexual exploitation turns out to be short distance, and cross-border trafficking frequently involves victims who travel voluntarily and end up in exploitive situations later on. In cases of human smuggling, this approach passes over a significant part of smuggling through entirely regular channels: entering as a legal immigrant (using forged documents), marriage fraud, business invitations, and the use of tourist, student, or scholar visas. Another important impediment of this approach concerns the considerable negative side effects, in terms of human lives, injuries, and perilous travel conditions, as is demonstrated by research on securing the U.S.-Mexican border (Frost 2007; Guerette 2007). The attacks of September 11, 2001, have turned U.S. border control into a national security issue, even though all 19 terrorists involved entered the country on valid student and tourist visas (Frost 2007). Guerette shows that since the year 2000 more than 300 migrant deaths are recorded along the U.S.-Mexican border each year, and it is believed that many more perish but remain unfound. Nevertheless, there is a strong focus on additional border security measures—more fences, more surveillance, and more advanced technology—as well as on proactive harm-reduction strategies such as educational campaigns informing would-be migrants of the dangers of crossing in remote areas, provision of live-saving equipment and training for line agents and search and rescue operations by Border Search Trauma and Rescue teams, and lateral repatriation programs to return apprehended migrants to less hazardous places along the border. Although there has been no overall reduction in the rate of migrant deaths since the U.S. Border Security Initiative was created, evidence collected by Guerette seems to indicate that these last two mechanisms may have prevented some migrant deaths.

The U.S.-Mexican border is just one of the corridors producing a cat-and-mouse game between border control authorities and illegal immigrants and smugglers. Other corridors involving committed illegal immigrants trying to reach affluent countries are the eastern, "green" borders of the European Union and the "blue" borders between the European Union and Africa and Asia (particularly Spain, Italy, and Greece) and between continental Europe and the United Kingdom (the channel).

Next to general living conditions and dual labor markets, an additional attractive factor of EU countries involves the welfare state and access through asylum systems. During the 1990s the rate of migrants applying for asylum in Europe rose to unprecedented numbers, partly because the asylum system was one of the few opportunities to enter Europe legally (Neske and Doomernik 2006). The sheer number of applicants and the difficulty of distinguishing between true political refugees and economic immigrants seriously undermined the efficiency and legitimacy of asylum adjudication processes. Careful, protracted, and individualized procedures were an easy prey for smugglers and immigrants who forged or destroyed documents and used fabricated stories about countries of origin and travel routes. As a result, many procedures, for true political refugees and economic immigrants alike, have become shorter, stricter, and less individualized (e.g., general "safe" areas and regions) and are accompanied by more meager facilities. Furthermore, visa regulations have been changed, preboarding checks have been strengthened, and carrier sanctions have been imposed, for instance making airline companies responsible for checks on irregular migration. Whether or not these opportunity-reducing initiatives are effective is open to debate, as are the negative side effects for true political refugees and for smugglers and their clients. What is known is that these initiatives do target mechanisms actually used by human smugglers and illegal immigrants.

Another policy line involves demand-reducing initiatives such as curbing access to the welfare state and making employers or companies responsible for contracting illegal laborers (e.g., sanctions, inspections). These initiatives may indeed reduce demand, yet at the same time they make life much harder for illegal immigrants and their families. Engbersen, van der Leun, and de Boom (2007) point to the unintended side effects of the very effective way Northern European welfare states are able to exclude illegal immigrants from the formal economy and public services: illegal immigrants have to participate in various informal economies or, when lacking access through social networks, engage in criminal activities.

Hence several policy proposals focus on decriminalizing illegal immigration through labor market initiatives such as temporary or permanent foreign worker programs or selective regularization. Whether or not labor market initiatives are a viable option depends very much on the local situation. Particularly in the European Union, complicating factors for such alternatives are the attractiveness of such programs for low-skilled workers (and their families), combined with an elaborate welfare state, and spillover effects to neighboring countries.

Selective regularization programs have been carried out in several countries (Levinson 2005). The main bottlenecks of this approach relate to the development of objective criteria for regularization and the attractiveness of these programs for new immigrants and illegal immigrants in neighboring countries. Various international examples have shown that regularization programs are seldom a one-off solution and that implementing such programs consistently is very difficult (for a review, see Cornelius, Martin, and Hollifeld 1994). Due to space limitations, I do not elaborate on different policies for controlling immigration. Yet the modus operandi of human smugglers and illegal immigrants demonstrates that illegal immigration and human smuggling are closely intertwined with political asylum and immigration policies (for a review, see Guild and Minderhoud 2006).

Just as human smuggling thrives on the "wicked" problem of irregular migration with no easy solutions, human trafficking for sexual exploitation thrives on the contested nature of prostitution and the different views on how authorities should deal with this ambiguous market. Over the years prostitution policies in many countries have oscillated between harm reduction (focused on public health issues such as sexually transmitted diseases, and more recently HIV/AIDS) and prohibition and criminalization versus regularization, favored by opposing interest groups.

In many countries prostitution is de facto tolerated to some extent, though different forms of prostitution and exploitation are regulated or combated in different ways (see Munro 2006). A recent study commissioned by the Norwegian government compared two widely opposing policy approaches, one in Sweden (criminalization) and the other in the Netherlands (regularization; Norwegian Ministry of Justice and the Police 2004). In Sweden the main policy assumption is that voluntary prostitution does not exist; prostitution is viewed as a form of violence, committed by men against women. The Swedes consider prostitution to be a serious social problem that inflicts damage on individuals and society. Hence in 1999 the purchase of sexual services became punishable by law (prostitutes themselves are not punishable). In this way, authorities hope to deter clients and generate new norms about the social unacceptability of the purchase of sexual services. Yet preliminary results show that the enforcement of the new act is quite difficult and generates negative side effects for prostitutes (Norwegian Ministry of Justice and the Police 2004).

A totally different approach is taken by the Dutch authorities. In October 2000, after years of leniency and de facto tolerance, the general ban on brothels was lifted. The essence of this regularization approach was that, under certain conditions, voluntary prostitution by prostitutes of legal age is no longer prohibited and that brothels are legal if they comply with certain licensing conditions. At the same time, policy makers intended to crack down forcefully on unacceptable forms of prostitution, such as prostitution of minors and illegal aliens and involuntary prostitution. An extensive evaluation shows that this regularization approach of location-bound prostitution (brothels, sex clubs, and window prostitution) produced some positive effects: business owners tend to comply with licensing conditions, and the number of prostitutes without legal documents has decreased (matched by an increase in prostitutes from Eastern European countries that fall under the European Economic Area).

Yet at the same time, the position of prostitutes has not improved much, and pimps are still a common phenomenon: the number of prostitutes with a pimp has not decreased (Daalder 2007). What's more, law enforcement investigations show that human trafficking still thrives behind the legal façade of regularization. The main reason for this ambiguous outcome is that the policy is focused too much on business owners, whereas we know from research that the exploitation of women is more often carried out by pimps. The legal change seems to have effectively deterred business owners from getting directly involved in human trafficking, yet it has failed to address the main problem of exploitation by pimps. Prostitutes with pimps mainly work behind the windows, in the escort business, and at home.

Involuntary prostitution—even in the regulated sector—is also very difficult for inspecting authorities to detect. The same applies to prostitution of minors because it is often difficult to determine the age of young prostitutes. These hidden phenomena can be detected, however, by intrusive law enforcement investigations. Next to capacity and priority problems, the main problems for mounting effective law enforcement operations are identifying abuse and the complex motives of the women involved. People involved in the business and clients have little interest in law enforcement attention. Nevertheless, an interesting finding from the evaluation is that some clients are willing to report on involuntary prostitution. The campaign "Appearances Are Deceptive," stimulating clients to call an anonymous tip line, was found to be a useful instrument (Daalder 2007). Also, for a variety of reasons many women do not report to the police. The closed world of victims, produced by displacement, the involvement of close intimate relationships, and daily monitoring by human traffickers all beg the question for policy makers of what victims have to expect from cooperating with the authorities. A recent study on victims of trafficking demonstrates that some victims decline assistance because they want to go home—without any fuss, stigma, or repercussion—or because they want to return to work, mainly for economic reasons. It also demonstrates that several supply-driven programs and facilities, often managed by NGOs, are not attuned to the basic needs of these victims (Brunovskis and Surtees 2007).

Furthermore, government agencies and government-sponsored agencies sometimes have different, conflicting views on how to approach abuse: Do we want to help or empower victims? Do we want victims to exit prostitution? Do we want victims to collaborate in mounting successful investigations? Caring for victims—often accompanied by anonymity—frequently conflicts with prosecuting offenders, regardless of whether they are close relatives or daily present bullies. What's more, during protracted investigations, a victim's cost-benefit balance may shift, producing conflicting or withdrawn statements or outright defection. Yet defection in the eyes of the authorities may be the same as loyalty or fear toward the perpetrators, or a decision to be the captain of one's soul again. Some policy measures explicitly address this cost-benefit balance, such as by allowing temporary residence to victims only on the condition of their cooperation in judicial investigations (e.g., Bureau Nationaal Rapporteur Mensenhandel 2007).

Finally, combating human trafficking also involves an important international dimension (e.g., United Nations Office for Drug Control and Crime [UNODC] 2006; U.S. Department of State 2007; U.S. Government Accountability Office [GAO] 2007). Many governments, particularly the U.S. government, and international organizations (e.g., UNODC, International Labor Organization, International Organization for Migration, UNICEF, and The Office of the United Nations High Commissioner for Refugees) are involved in antitrafficking programs and projects. These interventions generally aim to prevent human trafficking through public awareness, outreach, education, and advocacy campaigns; to protect and assist victims by providing shelters, health care, and psychological, legal, and vocational services; and to investigate and prosecute human trafficking by providing training and technical assistance for police, prosecutors, and judges. However, little is known about the effectiveness of these interventions, as they often lack some important elements that allow programs and projects to be monitored (GAO 2007).

V. Conclusion

Human smuggling and human trafficking, though sharing some common characteristics, are different phenomena. For policy reasons it is important to acknowledge that human smuggling basically involves mutual consent between illegal immigrants, their families, and smugglers. Many clients may be better referred to as customers—or even family or friends—than as victims. Opportunity-reducing initiatives may target mechanisms used by human smugglers and illegal immigrants. Yet illegal immigration and human smuggling are closely intertwined with political asylum and immigration policies. For this reason opportunity-reducing initiatives may also have negative side effects, for example on true political refugees, travel conditions, and prices. Law enforcement operations may target the part of the smuggling business that is dominated by criminal groups, large volumes, and bad travel conditions.

In contrast, the basic characteristics of human trafficking are exploitation and the violation of human rights. Particularly in human trafficking for sexual exploitation, types of victims and types of traffickers involved differ substantially from those involved in human smuggling, and human rights violations of women, boys, and girls are far more severe. Although other forms of exploitation, such a labor trafficking, also exist, this chapter has focused on human trafficking for sexual exploitation. The position of prostitutes and the opportunities of pimps to exploit prostitutes largely depend on the ways governments try to deal with the contested nature of prostitution. In combating human trafficking, key issues are identifying involuntary prostitution, helping victims, and prosecuting offenders. Much has yet to be learned about the effectiveness of several countertrafficking initiatives, as the moral outrage about human trafficking is not paralleled by an equal amount of sound empirical research and policy evaluation.

In the coming decade more research should be done on the complex relationships between victims and offenders to understand why some women don't report to the authorities or why they decline assistance. Because much of the research is focused on victims who are actually assisted, victim profiles may be biased. Much can be learned from other sources, such as field interviews and law enforcement investigations. Another important area for research is the victimization of minors, boys and girls, and of very young girls ending up in prostitution, and the roles played by their social environment. Lehti and Aromaa (2006) point out that there may be serious underreporting of human trafficking in minors. Furthermore, research should focus not only on victimization, but also on agency, particularly voluntary prostitution and conditions of (in)dependency, economic motivations, women making a career in prostitution, and women who become involved in trafficking as (co-)offenders.

Another important area for research is how different prostitution and enforcement policies affect the opportunities and restrictions of various parties: clients, owners, operators, pimps, and prostitutes. The same applies to different immigration policies and antismuggling initiatives. More research on the financial aspects of human smuggling and human trafficking might also reveal much about the profits of different actors and the social organization of these illegal activities. The contested nature of both prostitution and illegal immigration and widely opposing views on these matters seem to block sound empirical research on matters policy makers should know about.

REFERENCES

Aronowitz, A. 2001. "Smuggling and Trafficking in Human Beings: The Phenomenon, the Markets That Drive It and the Organisations That Promote It." *European Journal on Criminal Policy and Research* 9(2): 163–95.

Brunovskis, A., and R. Surtees. 2007. *Leaving the Past Behind? When Victims of Trafficking Decline Assistance.* Oslo: Fafo. http://www.fafo.no/pub/rapp/20040/20040.pdf.

Bureau Nationaal Rapporteur Mensenhandel. 2007. *Mensenhandel: Vijfde Rapportage van de Nationaal Rapporteur* (Trafficking in Human Beings: Fifth Report of the National Rapporteur). The Hague: Bureau Nationaal Rapporteur Mensenhandel.

Chin, K. L. 1999. *Smuggled Chinese: Clandestine Immigration to the United States.* Philadelphia: Temple University Press.

Cornelius, W. A., P. L. Martin, and J. F. Hollifeld. 1994. *Controlling Immigration: A Global Perspective.* Stanford, CA: Stanford University Press.

Daalder, A. L. 2007. *Prostitution in the Netherlands since the Lifting of the Brothel Ban.* The Hague: WODC.

DeStefano, A. M. 2007. *The War on Human Trafficking: U.S. Policy Assessed.* New Brunswick, NJ: Rutgers University Press.

Dowling, S., K. Moreton, and L. Wright. 2007. *Trafficking for the Purposes of Labour Exploitation: A Literature Review.* Home Office Online Report 10/07. London: Home Office.

Engbersen, G., J. van der Leun, and J. de Boom. 2007. "The Fragmentation of Migration and Crime in the Netherlands." In *Crime and Justice in the Netherlands,* edited by M. Tonry and C. Bijleveld. Vol. 35 of *Crime and Justice: A Review of Research,* edited by M. Tonry. Chicago: University of Chicago Press.

Frost, N. 2007. "Securing Borders and Saving Lives." *Criminology and Public Policy* 6(2): 241–44.

Guerette, R. 2007. "Immigration Policy, Border Security, and Migrant Deaths: An Impact Evaluation of Life-saving Efforts under the Border Safety Initiative." *Criminology and Public Policy* 6(2): 245–66.

Guild, E., and P. Minderhoud, eds. 2006. *Immigration and Criminal Law in the European Union: The Legal Measures and Social Consequences of Criminal Law in Member States on Trafficking and Smuggling in Human Beings.* Leiden: Martinus Nijhoff.

Herman, E. 2006. "Migration as a Family Business: The Role of Personal Networks in the Mobility Phase of Migration." *International Migration* 44(4): 191–221.

Kleemans, E. R. 2007. "Organized Crime, Transit Crime, and Racketeering." In *Crime and Justice in the Netherlands,* edited by M. Tonry and C. Bijleveld. Vol. 35 of *Crime and Justice: A Review of Research,* edited by M. Tonry. Chicago: University of Chicago Press.

Kleemans, E. R., and H. G. van de Bunt. 1999. "The Social Embeddedness of Organized Crime." *Transnational Organized Crime* 5(2): 19–36.

Kleemans, E. R., and H. G. van de Bunt. 2003. "The Social Organisation of Human Trafficking." In *Global Organized Crime: Trends and Developments,* edited by D. Siegel, H. van de Bunt, and D. Zaitch. Boston: Kluwer Academic.

Kyle, D., and R. Koslowski, eds. 2001. *Global Human Smuggling: Comparative Perspectives.* Baltimore: Johns Hopkins University Press.

Laczko, F. 2005. Introduction to "Data and Research on Human Trafficking: A Global Survey." Special issue of *International Migration* 43(1/2): 5–16.

Laczko, F., and E. Gozdziak, eds. 2005. "Data and Research on Human Trafficking: A Global Survey." Special issue of *International Migration* 43(1/2).

Lehti, M., and K. Aromaa. 2006. "Trafficking for Sexual Exploitation." In *Crime and Justice: A Review of Research,* vol. 34, edited by Michael Tonry. Chicago: University of Chicago Press.

Levinson, A. 2005. *The Regularization of Unauthorized Migrants: Literature Surveys and Country Case Studies.* Oxford: University of Oxford, Centre on Migration, Policy and Society.

Munro, V. E. 2006. "Stopping Traffic? A Comparative Study to Responses to the Trafficking in Women for Prostitution." *British Journal of Criminology* 46: 318–33.

Neske, M., and J. Doomernik, eds. 2006. "Comparing Notes: Perspectives on Human Smuggling in Austria, Germany, Italy, and the Netherlands—Cluster Introduction." *International Migration* 44(4): 39–58.

Norwegian Ministry of Justice and the Police. 2004. *Purchasing Sexual Services in Sweden and the Netherlands: Legal Regulations and Experiences: An Abbreviated English Version.* Report by a Working Group on the Legal Regulation of the Purchase of Sexual Services. Oslo, Norway.

Portes, A. 1995. "Economic Sociology and the Sociology of Immigration: A Conceptual Overview." In *The Economic Sociology of Immigration: Essays on Networks, Ethnicity, and Entrepreneurship,* edited by A. Portes. New York: Russell Sage.

Salt, J. 2000. "Trafficking and Human Smuggling: A European Perspective." *International Migration* 38(3): 31–56.

Salt, J., and J. Stein. 1997. "Migration as a Business: The Case of Trafficking." *International Migration* 35(4): 467–89.

Savona, E. U., and S. Stefanizzi. 2007. *Measuring Human Trafficking: Complexities and Pitfalls.* New York: Springer.

Schloenhardt, A. 2001. "Trafficking in Migrants: Illegal Immigration and Organised Crime in Australia and the Pacific Region." *International Journal of Sociology of Law* 29: 331–78.

Siegel, D., and S. de Blank. 2008. "Vrouwen die in Vrouwen Handelen: De rol van Vrouwen in Mensenhandelnetwerken" (Women Trading in Women: The Role of Women in Human Trafficking Networks). *Tijdschrift voor Criminologie* 50(1): 35–48.

Soudijn, M. 2006. *Chinese Human Smuggling in Transit.* The Hague: Boom Juridische Uitgevers.

Spener, D. 2004. "Mexican Migrant Smuggling: A Cross-Border Cottage Industry." *Journal of International Migration and Integration* 5(3): 295–321.

Staring, R., G. Engbersen, H. Moerland, N. de Lange, D. Verburg, E. Vermeulen, and A. Weltevrede. 2005. *De Sociale Organisatie van Mensensmokkel* (The Social Organization of Trafficking in Human Beings). Zeist, Netherlands: Uitgeverij Kerckebosch.

Surtees, R. 2008. "Traffickers and Trafficking in South and Eastern Europe: Considering the Other Side of Human Trafficking." *European Journal of Criminology* 5(1): 39–68.

United Nations. 2000*a*. *Protocol against the Smuggling of Migrants by Land, Sea and Air, Supplementing the United Nations Convention against Transnational Organized Crime.* http://www.uncjin.org/Documents/Conventions/dcatoc/final_documents_2/convention_smug_eng.pdf.

———. 2000*b*. *Protocol to Prevent, Suppress and Punish Trafficking in Persons, Especially Women and Children, Supplementing the United Nations Convention against*

Transnational Organized Crime. http://www.uncjin.org/Documents/Conventions/dcatoc/final_documents_2/convention_%20traff_eng.pdf.

United Nations Office for Drug Control and Crime. 2006. *Trafficking in Persons: Global Patterns*. Vienna: UNODC.

U.S. Department of State. 2007. *Trafficking in Persons Report*. Washington, DC: U.S. Department of State.

U.S. Government Accountability Office. 2007. *Human Trafficking: Monitoring and Evaluation of International Projects Are Limited, but Experts Suggest Improvements*. Washington, DC: U.S. Government Accountability Office.

van Dijk, E. 2002. *Mensenhandel in Nederland 1997–2000* (Trafficking in Human Beings in the Netherlands 1997–2000). Zoetermeer, Netherlands: KLPD.

van Liempt, I., and J. Doomernik. 2006. "Migrant's Agency in the Smuggling Process: The Perspective of Smuggled Migrants in the Netherlands." *International Migration* 44(4): 165–90.

Zhang, S. 1997. "Task Force Orientation and Dyadic Relations in Organized Chinese Alien Smuggling." *Journal of Contemporary Criminal Justice* 13(4): 320–30.

Zhang, S. 2007. *Smuggling and Trafficking in Human Beings: All Roads Lead to America*. Westport, CT: Praeger.

Zhang, S., and K. L. Chin. 2002. "Enter the Dragon: Inside Chinese Human Smuggling Organizations." *Criminology* 40(4): 737–67.

Zhang, S., K. L. Chin, and J. Miller. 2007. "Women's Participation in Chinese Transnational Human Smuggling: A Gendered Market Perspective." *Criminology* 45(3): 699–733.

Zhang, S., and M. S. Gaylord. 1996. "Bound for the Golden Mountain: The Social Organization of Chinese Alien Smuggling." *Crime, Law and Social Change* 25(1): 1–16.

CHAPTER 17

TERRORISM

LAURA DUGAN

WITH the consuming attention given to terrorism it is surprising how little of our knowledge is based on systematic empirical analysis. Schmid and Jongman (1988), in their encyclopedic review of political terrorism, found that most of the more than 6,000 published works on the topic is impressionistic, making broad generalizations based on episodic evidence. More recently, as part of the Campbell Collaboration's systematic review program, Lum, Kennedy, and Sherley (2006) conducted a thorough and systematic review of counterterrorism evaluations. From the more than 20,000 writings on terrorism between 1971 and 2004, only seven met their criteria of being moderately rigorous evaluation studies. For comparison, a similar review of criminal justice evaluations 10 years earlier found more than 500 rigorous and scientifically sound program impact evaluations (Sherman et al. 1997), raising a stark contrast between what we know about criminal justice and what we know about terrorism. The dearth of rigorous evaluations of counterterrorism efforts raises an obvious question: On what are policy makers basing their strategies to counter terrorism?

To be fair to researchers and policy makers, until recently comprehensive data on terrorism activity have been unavailable. Although several organizations now maintain databases on terrorist incidents,[1] these data sources face at least three serious limitations. First, most of the existing data sources use extremely narrow definitions of terrorism. For example, RAND (Memorial Institute for the Prevention of Terrorism 2007) includes only attacks in which the perpetrator is motivated by political objectives, thus excluding attacks motivated by religious or other social objectives. Furthermore, by restricting their targets to civilians, ambiguous terrorist attacks on noncombatant military are systematically omitted.

Second, terrorism databases are limited because many of them are collected by government entities, thus assuring that definitions and counting rules are influenced by political considerations. For example, the U.S. State Department (2008) maintains a list of foreign terrorist organizations (FTOs), which designates FTO status according to, among other things, an organization's threat to U.S. interests. Yet others might perceive some of the FTOs as revolutionaries fighting a just cause. For example, Hamas is listed as an FTO despite its status among the Palestinian people as a legitimate operation using justified tactics.

The third and most important limitation is that although instances of domestic terrorism greatly outnumber instances of international terrorism, domestic terrorism is excluded from all existing long-term publicly available databases.[2] The gravity of this omission can be felt when we consider two of the most noteworthy terrorist events of the 1990s. By excluding domestic terrorism, the March 1995 nerve gas attack on the Tokyo subway and the April 1995 bombing of the federal office building in Oklahoma City would remain unrecorded since both lack any known foreign involvement.

This chapter uses a newly available data source on terrorist attacks that overcomes all three limitations to provide an overview of terrorism worldwide and in the United States from 1970 to 2004. The data from 1970 to 1997 were originally collected by Pinkerton Global Intelligence Services (PGIS), a private agency that assesses global risk for its international clientele. As a private agency, PGIS was unaffected by political incentives to label some attacks as terrorist and others as justified. Instead, they adopted a broad-based definition used by the U.S. Army and included every attack that met those criteria, regardless of whether the U.S. Department of State would have considered the act terrorism. The political neutrality of the PGIS data protects them from obvious biases imposed on other, government-funded data sets.

The PGIS data were electronically coded and combined with data from other sources by researchers at the University of Maryland to form the Global Terrorism Database (GTD; see LaFree and Dugan 2007 for a thorough introduction). This database later became one of the key contributions leading to the establishment of the Department of Homeland Security's fifth Center of Excellence at the University of Maryland, the National Center for the Study of Terrorism and Response to Terrorism (START). As part of its mission, START (2007*a*) "aims to provide timely guidance on how to disrupt terrorist networks, reduce the incidence of terrorism, and enhance the resilience of U.S. society in the face of the terrorist threat." With the availability of GTD data and the expertise and commitment of scholars from diverse disciplines, including criminology and criminal justice, progress can be made toward providing a sound rigorous research base to estimate the policy effects on terrorism. Since the original PGIS data ended in 1997, the START Center has begun efforts to extend the GTD to the present (hereafter referred to as GTD2), relying on the expertise of a criteria committee to develop a codebook and inclusion criteria for each incident.[3] The GTD2 captures information on more than 120 variables and stores the original open source texts on which each case is based. Data collection is completed for the years 1998 through 2004.[4] Both versions of the

GTD are available for browsing (http://www.start.umd.edu/data/gtd/) and will be released to researchers on a regular basis, according to the Web site.[5]

The main conclusions I offer in this chapter concerning terrorism are the following:

- Comprehensive data on global terrorist attacks are now available for rigorous policy analysis.
- The distribution of attacks varies greatly over time and space.
- Terrorism in the United States from 1970 to 1997 was mostly perpetrated by antiabortion activists and by people who fail to claim the attack.
- Attempts to control terrorism have been mostly unsuccessful, with the exception of a few important cases that are context-specific.
- We need a comprehensive data set that includes the full range of policy responses to terrorism that will enable us to more thoroughly and more rigorously analyze the policy responses to terrorism.

I begin by summarizing efforts to measure terrorism in section I. In Section II I provide an overview of the distribution of global terrorist violence over time and space from 1997 to 2004 using the GTD data. The chapter then turns to terrorist activity in the United States in section III, describing perpetrators, targets, and weapons. In Section IV I describe two efforts that assessed the effectiveness of very different policy interventions in very different contexts using the GTD data, as well as other efforts that rely on other data sources. The chapter concludes in section V with a discussion of the policy implications of deterring terrorism.

I. Measuring Terrorism

I begin by discussing the complications of measuring terrorism arising from the vast disagreement on how to define it. I then introduce the Global Terrorism Database and compare it to existing sources of incident-based terrorism data.

A. Defining Terrorism

Before terrorism can be measured it must be defined. This point is much easier to state than to resolve. Each of the dozens of academic disciplines now studying terrorism has its own interpretation of what counts as a terrorist event. Even within disciplines scholars argue about the specific targets, motives, or other criteria that qualify an event as terrorism. Thus many of the most influential academic books on terrorism (e.g., Schmid and Jongman 1988; Hoffman 1998) devote their first chapters to definitions of terrorism. The reasons for the difficulty are apparent. As Fairchild and Dammer (2001, p. 281) and many others note, "One man's terrorist is another man's freedom fighter." One of the most common challenges to the empirical study of terrorism (Falkenrath 2001, p. 165) is that the various publicly available databases have used different definitions.

This discord extends beyond academia. Even agencies within the U.S. government employ different definitions that include components tailored to their unique missions. The original PGIS data, and consequently the GTD data, adopted the broadest definition of terrorism, based on the U.S. Army standard (LaFree et al. 2006, pp. 21–22): "the threatened or actual use of illegal force and violence to attain a political, economic, religious or social goal through fear, coercion or intimidation." Neither the State Department nor the FBI definition of terrorism includes threats of force. Yet as Hoffman (1998, p. 38) points out, "Terrorism is as much about the threat of violence as the violent act itself." Many, perhaps most hijackings involve only the threatened use of force (e.g., "I have a bomb and I will use it unless you follow my demands"). Similarly, kidnappers almost always employ force to seize victims, but then threaten to kill, maim, or otherwise harm victims unless demands are satisfied. The State Department definition is limited to "politically motivated violence." The FBI definition is somewhat broader, including social and political objectives as fundamental terrorist aims.

The GTD definition includes all of these, and adds economic and religious objectives. Thus, unlike other databases, the GTD includes attacks against noncombatant military if the motives appear to meet its broad criteria. Each case in the GTD preserves enough information to allow other researchers to filter out cases that may not meet their definition. For example, in another project where we are integrating the GTD cases into the RAND chronology, RAND staff examined all kidnapping cases and filtered out those that seemed to have exclusively economic motivations, despite being perpetrated by a known terrorist organization (Dugan et al. 2008). RAND also removed all attacks against military targets.

Analyses in this chapter use the complete GTD data set. By incorporating the broadest definition overall we may see trends influenced by the distribution of attacks that others might not perceive as terrorist.

B. The GTD and Other Sources of Terrorism Data

The GTD is based on data originally collected by PGIS. From 1970 to 1997 PGIS trained researchers to identify and record terrorism incidents from a wide variety of sources, including wire services, U.S. State Department reports, other U.S. and foreign government reporting, U.S. and foreign newspapers, PGIS offices around the world, such special interests as organized political opposition groups, and data furnished by PGIS clients and other individuals in official and private capacities (see LaFree and Dugan 2007 for a discussion of how sources may have changed over time). About two dozen persons were responsible for coding information over the years spanned by the data collection, but only two individuals were in charge of supervising data collection during the entire period.[6]

In LaFree and Dugan's (2007) introduction to the GTD, the original database, PGIS, is compared to seven other terrorism open source event databases. In all cases PGIS is more comprehensive, documenting more incidents than any other source. PGIS reports about seven times more events than the next three largest—ITERATE, the U.S. State Department, and Tweed (these are described below). Two important reasons PGIS stands out is that it was collected over a wider period, 1970 through 1997, with a broader scope, both international and domestic.

The ITERATE (International Terrorism: Attributes of Terrorist Events) database, originally collected by Edward Mickolus (1982), has probably been the most widely used archival source of terrorism data for empirical research (Enders and Sandler 2006).[7] ITERATE contains two different types of files: quantitatively coded data on international terrorist incidents and a qualitative descriptions of each incident. Yet, compared to PGIS's 67,179 attacks, ITERATE counts only 10,837 over a broader period of time (LaFree and Dugan 2007).

In addition to PGIS, three of the other data sources discussed by LaFree and Dugan (2007) are private risk assessment companies: Cobra, Triton, and Tweed.[8] Tweed prepares an annual register that details political, economic, and social events related to terrorist activities. Triton assembles a list of current global activities of specific terrorist groups. The Cobra Institute is developing a chronology of world terrorism events and detailed information about known terrorist groups. Tweed collects information only from domestic incidents; Triton began documenting terrorism only in the middle of 2000; and Cobra collects information only on international attacks.

The U.S. State Department began publishing an annual report on international terrorism in 1982 (reporting 1980 incidents) and in 1984 began calling the report *Patterns of Global Terrorism* (Pluchinsky 2006). The Patterns Report reviews international terrorist events by year, date, region, and terrorist group and includes background information on terrorist organizations, U.S. policy on terrorism, and progress on counterterrorism. Because the *Patterns of Global Terrorism* report lacked comprehensiveness, the U.S. Congress mandated that, starting in 2004, the terrorism statistics be compiled by the newly created National Counter-Terrorism Center. These new data are available to the public on a government Web site (http://wits.nctc.gov).

Finally, RAND has collected a detailed set of secondary data on international terrorist events from 1968 to 1997. In recent years RAND has also collaborated with the Oklahoma City National Memorial Institute for the Prevention of Terrorism to develop a detailed secondary database on both international and national terrorism since 1998 (http://tkb.org/Home.jsp).[9] The coincidence that the GTD database ends in 1997 and the RAND collaboration database begins in 1998 led the START Center and RAND to seek funding to combine the two data sets (LaFree and Dugan 2005). As part of this project, cases in GTD that fail to match the more restrictive RAND definition will be removed from the files.[10] The GTD-RAND data set was completed in early 2008 (Dugan et al. 2008).

Another ongoing data collection effort conducted by START is to update the GTD from 1998 to the present, more closely preserving the original definition. However, because the criteria, collection strategies, and quality control procedures changed from the original data collection (1970–97) to the recent data collection (1993, 1998–2004), the extent to which the inclusion criteria used for the original data collection match the criteria being used today is unknown. We are reassessing the original GTD using the coding rules currently employed to assure a consistent time series. Until this is complete, distinctions between the two time series will be preserved to avoid misinterpretations in the trends. In other descriptions the data sets will be combined.

All these databases vary in many important ways. Two important advantages that the GTD has over the others is that collection was supervised by the same two persons over a 27-year period and the definition is broad enough to be useful for a larger number of users. The following analysis describes global terrorism activity and local U.S. terrorism activity using GTD data. Because the database is constantly evolving, it is important to note that the data used for these analyses were last downloaded May 7, 2007.

II. The Distribution of Global Terrorism

Figure 17.1 compares trends in total attacks and fatal attacks worldwide from the GTD, 1970 to 2004.[11] The difference in the magnitude of the lines shows that attacks were fatal less than half of the time over this period. On average, about 40 percent of total attacks each year are fatal. Through 1976 terrorist attacks were relatively infrequent, with fewer than 1,000 incidents each year. But from 1978 to 1979 the frequency nearly doubled. The broad increases were characterized by smaller peaks in 1984 (3,486 total, 1,100 fatal) and 1989 (4,309 total, 1,840 fatal). Both total and fatal attacks reached the highest peak in 1992 (5,261 total and 2,205 fatal). Afterward, the number of terrorist attacks declined to just over 3,500 at the end of the original data collection in 1997—a 33 percent decline.

The vertical line in figure 17.1 separates the first and second GTD data collection efforts. We cannot directly compare trends before and after 1998 because the two databases have not yet been synthesized. However, we can say that based on the original data collection there was a major drop in total and fatal attacks starting in 1993 and continuing to the end of the original data collection in 1997. We can also conclude that total attacks increased from 1998 (913) to a peak in 2001 (1,414), then dropped to 1,123 in 2004 (resulting in a 23 percent rise from 1998). Fatal attacks over this period increased by 65 percent, from 431 to 711.

In addition to great variation in terrorism over time, there is also large variation in the distribution in terrorist attacks and fatalities across global regions. Figure 17.2 shows the distribution of terrorist attacks and fatalities

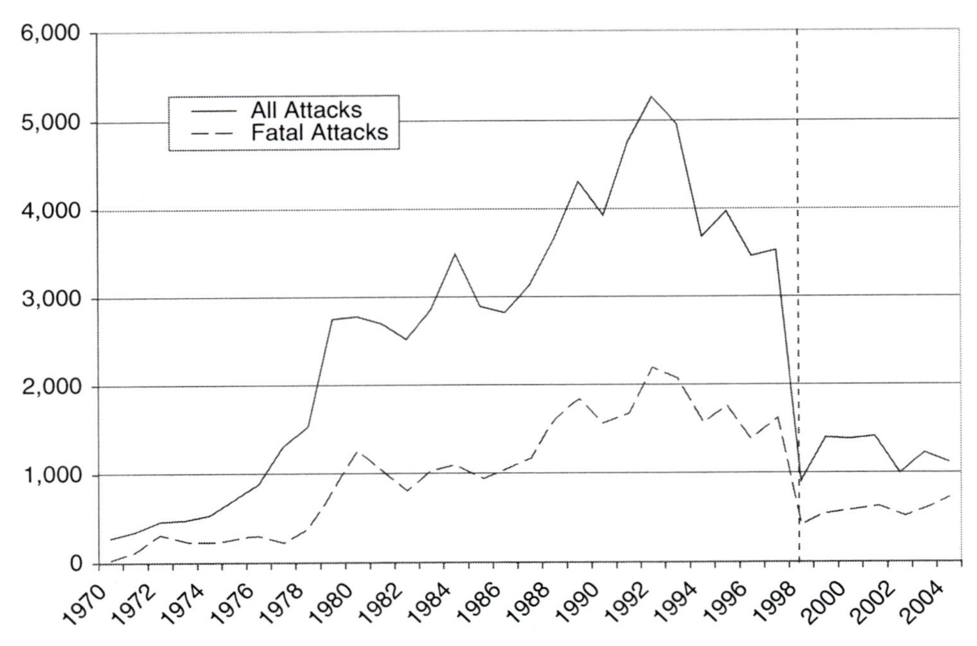

Figure 17.1. Global trends in terrorism, 1970–2004.
Source: Global Terrorism Database.

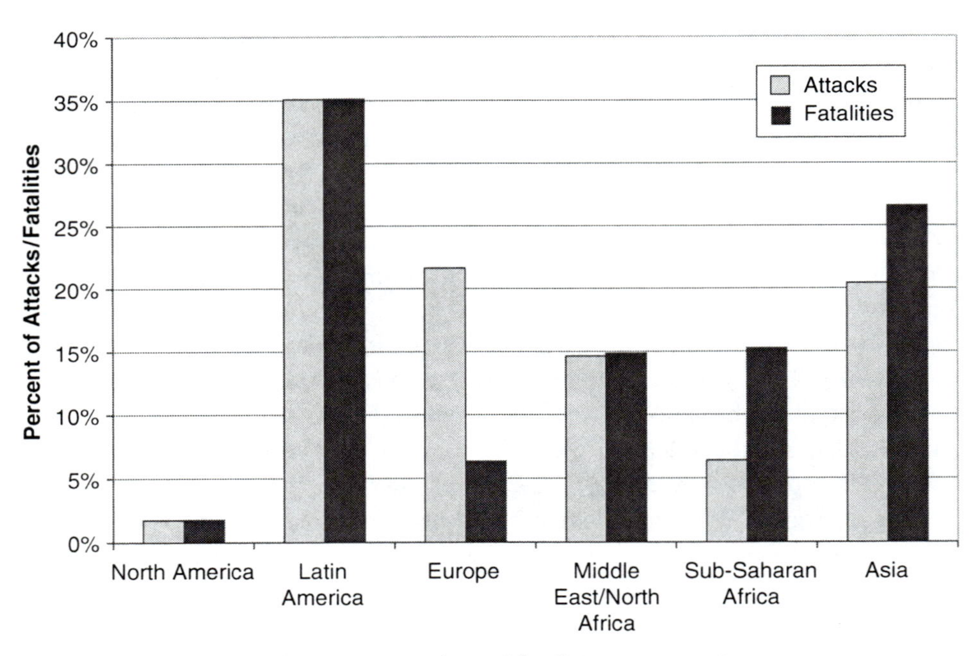

Figure 17.2. Global terrorist attacks and fatalities across regions, 1970–2004.
Source: Global Terrorism Database.

across the six major regions of the world, as delineated by PGIS (for a list of countries in each region, see the appendix). Most apparent is that terrorism and terrorism-related fatalities occur in Latin America nearly twice as often as in any other region, more than five times as often as in sub-Saharan Africa, and more than 20 times more often than North America.[12] Europe rates second in terms of total attacks with more than 21 percent of all global terrorism, followed closely by Asia at nearly 20 percent. The Middle East/North Africa region follows with just under 15 percent of the attacks, and sub-Saharan Africa and North America account for the smallest proportion of terrorism events (6.4 and 1.7 percent).

Figure 17.2 also shows that the distribution of fatalities across regions matches the distribution for total attacks only in three regions: North America, Latin America, and the Middle East. Asia and sub-Saharan Africa have a higher proportion of fatalities than attacks, averaging 3.1 and 5.7 fatalities per attack, respectively. Thus, although sub-Saharan Africa has relatively few attacks compared to the rest of the world (except for North America), when attacks occur, they are more likely to produce high fatalities. By contrast, Europe has a smaller proportion of fatalities compared to attacks, averaging less than one death (0.71) per incident. Latin America remains the leader in fatalities, but Asia has the second highest percentage of fatalities by region, accounting for nearly 27 percent of all terrorism-related fatalities. The reasons for the differences in lethality remain to be explained, although parts of the explanation may include media policies on reporting and differences in access to medical care.

Given the distribution shown in figure 17.2, it is not surprising that the three countries with the most terrorist attacks over this period are located in Latin America: Colombia, Peru, and El Salvador with 6,871, 6,134, and 5,556 total attacks, respectively.[13] The remainder of the 20 most active countries are as follows, listed from most active to least; India, Northern Ireland,[14] Spain, Turkey, Pakistan, Sri Lanka, Philippines, Chile, Guatemala, Israel, Nicaragua, Lebanon, Algeria, South Africa, Italy, United States, and France, with activity ranging from 3,979 attacks in India to 1,255 in France.

To understand better how terrorism has changed over time for select countries, figure 17.3 shows the trends of attacks for the most active country in each region, marking the different data collection strategies with a vertical line. Most apparent is their distinct patterns of activity over the same period. Colombia most closely resembles the overall trends found in figure 17.1, rising to a peak in 1992 with 528 attacks. However, after a sharp drop after that year, reaching a low of 129 attacks in 1995, Colombia rises to an even higher peak in 1997 with 653 attacks. Even in Colombia's least active year, terrorists in that country still attacked more frequently than in any single year in the United States. India, Turkey, and South Africa also peak later in the series, followed by declines. All three countries have very little activity early in the series, with the exception of Turkey, which has a burst of activity from 1976 to 1980. Activity first rises above 100 attacks per year

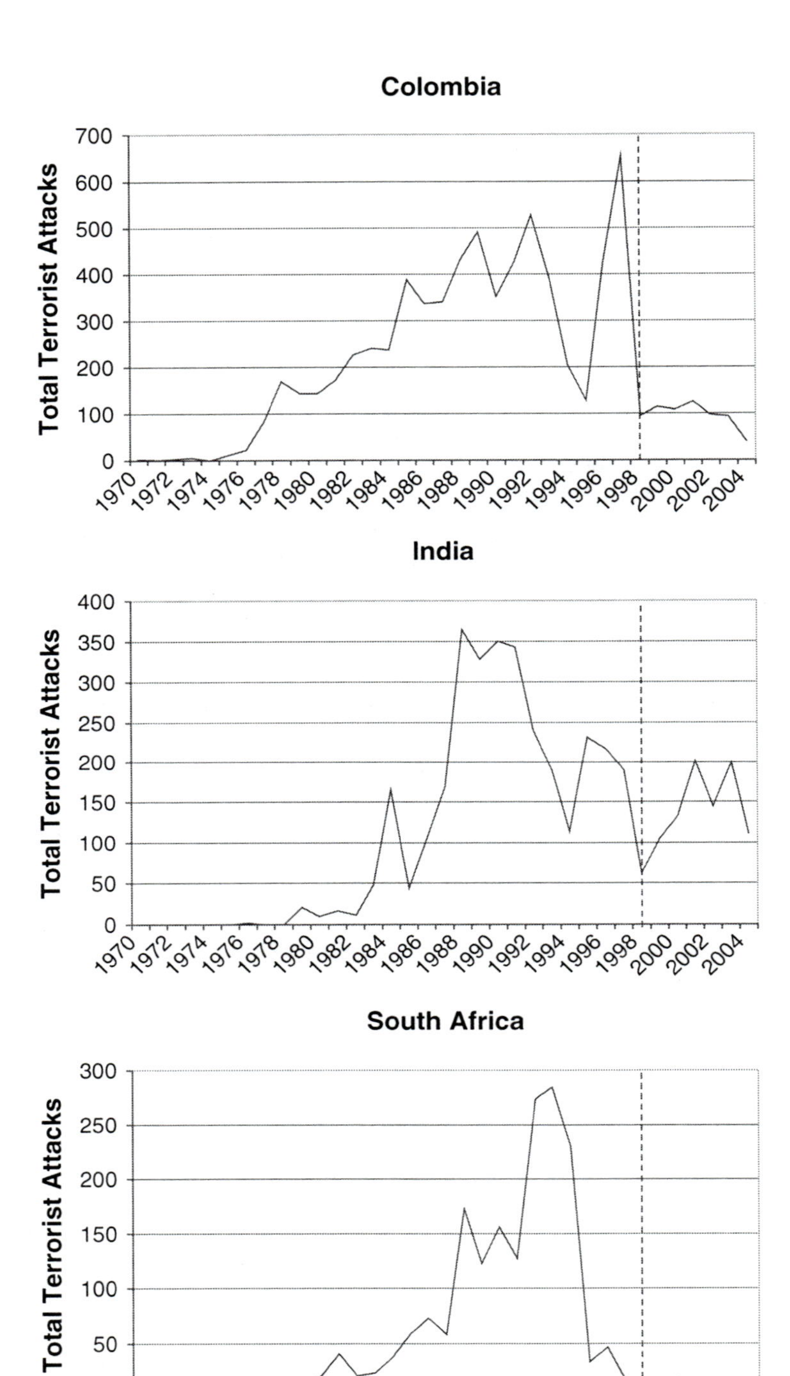

Figure 17.3. Country with most active terrorism in each region, 1970–2004.
Source: Global Terrorism Database.

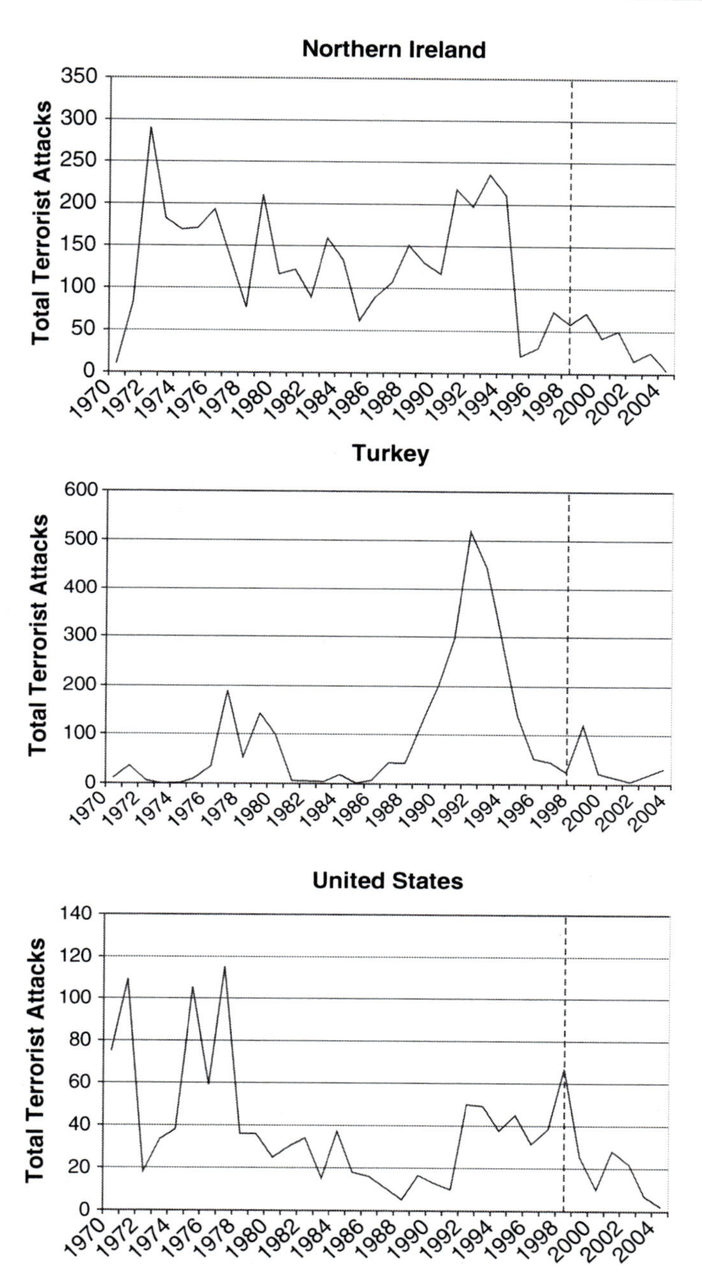

Figure 17.3. (continued)

in 1984 for India, 1989 for Turkey, and 1988 in South Africa, peaking in 1988 in India and 1992 in Turkey and South Africa. Northern Ireland and the United States follow a similar pattern, each peaking in the 1970s and then again in the 1990s after a relative drop during the 1980s.

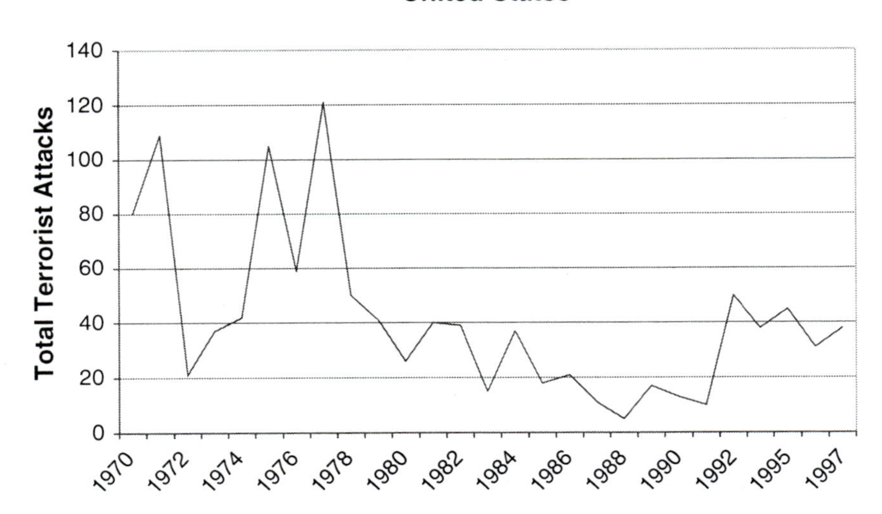

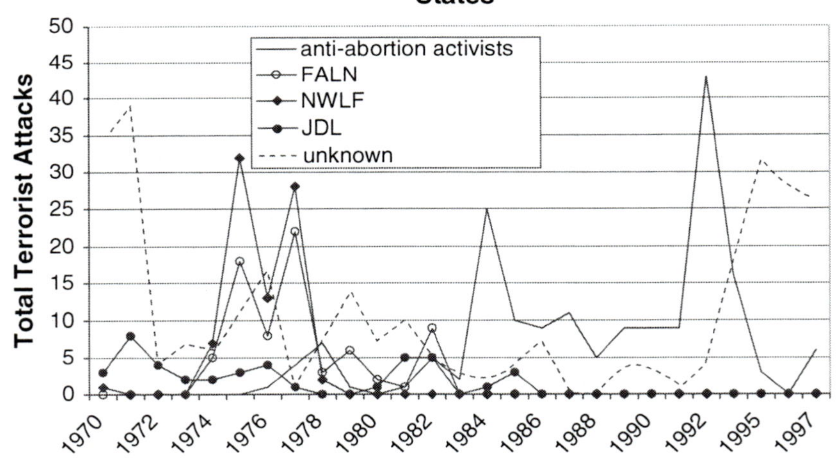

Figure 17.4. Most active terrorist groups in the United States, 1970–97.
Source: Global Terrorism Database.

III. Terrorism in the United States

Figure 17.4 repeats the trend of activity for the United States for the years 1970 to 1997 and then shows the patterns of activity for four of the most active perpetrators over this period; antiabortion activists, Fuerzas Armadas de Liberacion Nacional (FALN), New World Liberation Front (NWLF), and the Jewish Defense League

(JDL).[15] Also included in the graph is the pattern of unclaimed terrorist events over this period. Most apparent in this figure is that the first peak in U.S. attacks in 1971 seems to be driven by an unusually high number of unclaimed incidents (39). Without data prior to 1970 it is difficult to discern whether this is part of an ongoing trend or whether 1970 and 1971 had an unusual amount of unclaimed terrorism for that time. The drop in unclaimed attacks in 1972 does suggest an important break between 1970 and 1971 and the remainder of the 1970s and 1980s. Not until 1994 does the number of unclaimed events rises again, peaking in 1995 with 32 attacks. Between 1971 and 1994 the United States had on average 5.6 unclaimed terrorist attacks a year. This is a promisingly low number for investigators, given that there was an average of 37 terrorist attacks each year in the United States during those years. Thus investigators had leads on nearly 85 percent of all terrorist attacks during that period.

The second two peaks of U.S. terrorism activity, in 1975 and 1977, appear to be driven by the activities of the NWLF and FALN, two of the most active organizations of that time. The NWLF claimed to be a "moral" revolutionary group that was at war with the establishment, attacking corporations, media, utility companies, and other symbols of elitism (Wolf 1981). In 1976 they attempted to bomb Senator Dianne Feinstein's home when she was a member of the San Francisco Board of Supervisors, according to testimony in 1995 Senate hearings (Baggett 2007). In the list of the 10 most active perpetrators of terrorism from 1970 to 2004 shown in table 17.1, the NWLF was identified as the perpetrator in as many as 83 attacks (which killed only one person).

Table 17.1. Ten most active terrorist perpetrators in the United States, 1970–2004

Perpetrator	Years active	Attacks	Primary target
Unclaimed	———	345	Diverse
Antiabortion group	1976–2003	245	Abortion providers
New World Liberation Front	1970–78	83	Symbols of corporate capitalism
Fuerzas Armadas de Liberacion Nacional	1970–82	71	U.S. citizens and facilities
Jewish Defense League	1970–85	43	Anti-Semites
Weather Underground, Weathermen	1970–81	40	Publicity targets
Omega-7	1975–83	31	Castro supporters
Black Liberation Army	1970–84	27	Publicity targets
Independent Armed Revolutionary Commandos	1977	19	U.S. politicians
Armed Revolutionary Independence Movement	1970–71	16	Publicity targets

Source: Global Terrorism Database, http://www.start.umd.edu/data/gtd.

The FALN is ranked fourth on this list with 71 recorded attacks. The FALN was one of several Puerto Rican nationalist terrorist groups fighting to gain independence from the United States (Memorial Institute for the Prevention of Terrorism 2007). As shown at the top of figure 17.4, after the decline in leftist and Puerto Rican nationalist activity in the early 1980s there were no other large peaks of terrorism activity. Yet the bottom graph shows the rise in a newer and more active movement of violence, this time targeting abortion providers. The antiabortion movement was not organized by any one entity. Instead, individuals and local organizations formed a larger movement that was responsible for at least 245 attacks from 1976 to 2003, with the two most active years being 1984 (25 attacks) and 1992 (43 attacks). Finally, the fifth-ranking perpetrator in the United States during this period was the JDL with 43 recorded attacks that usually targeted people alleged to be anti-Semitic. During its tenure JDL averaged only about 2.5 attacks per year, with 1971 as its most active year at eight attacks.

The next five most active perpetrators of terrorism violence during this period were the Weather Underground, another leftist revolutionary organization that formed out of the anti–Vietnam War movement; Omega-7, an anti-Castro Cuban group; the Black Liberation Army, a militant splinter group of the Black Panther Party; Independent Armed Revolutionary Commandos, an organization that repeatedly failed to assassinate U.S. politicians; and the Armed Revolutionary Independence Movement, another Puerto Rican nationalist organization (Memorial Institute for the Prevention of Terrorism 2007).

Figure 17.5 presents the distribution of persons and entities targeted by terrorists in the United States. The right side of the pie clearly reflects the activities of the most active organizations. More than 70 percent of all attacks were aimed at the preferred targets of the antiabortion movement, leftist revolutionary groups, and Puerto Rican nationalists (abortion-related entities, businesses, government, diplomats, and police). Other targets include private citizens, police, nongovernmental organizations, airports and airlines, and utilities.

Figure 17.6 presents the distribution of primary weapons that were used in terrorist attacks in the United States. More than 80 percent of all attacks used explosives, fire, or firebombs. This in unsurprising because the primary weapon of choice for most of the organizations listed in table 17.1 was explosives. Common explosives include car bombs, dynamite, and incendiaries. Nine percent of attacks used firearms as their primary target. The group that most commonly used firearms was the Black Liberation Army, which used them in 22 of 27 attacks. More than 50 percent of all attacks that used firearms were assassinations or assassination attempts. Chemical agents were used in 8.5 percent of attacks. Of the chemical agents, the most common used was butyric acid (46 percent), followed by gasoline (3 percent). Other chemical agents include paraffin, cyanide, and mercury. The butyric acid was mostly used by antiabortion activists against clinics.

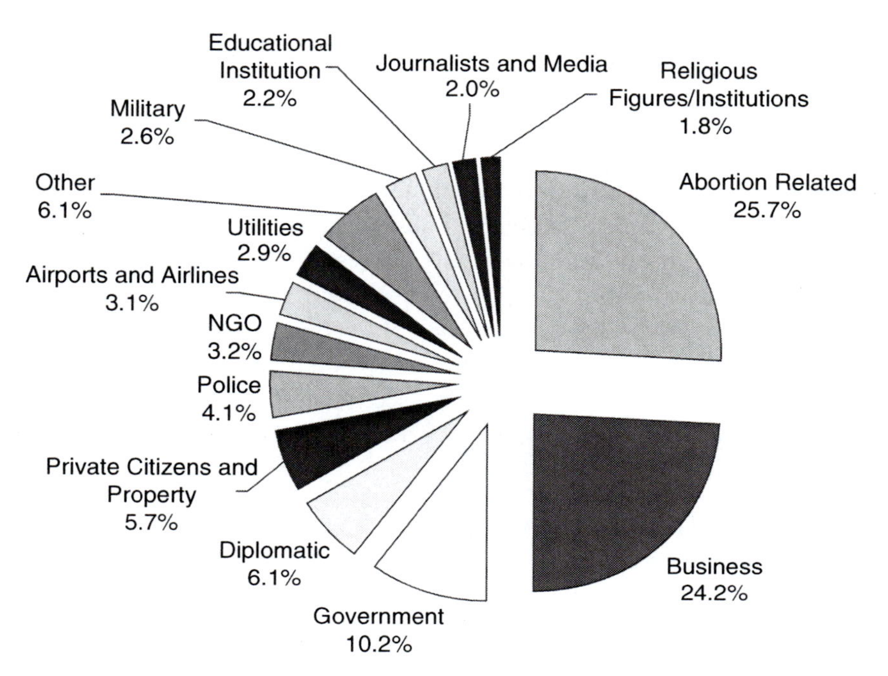

Figure 17.5. Primary terrorist target types in the United States, 1970–2004.
Source: Global Terrorism Database.

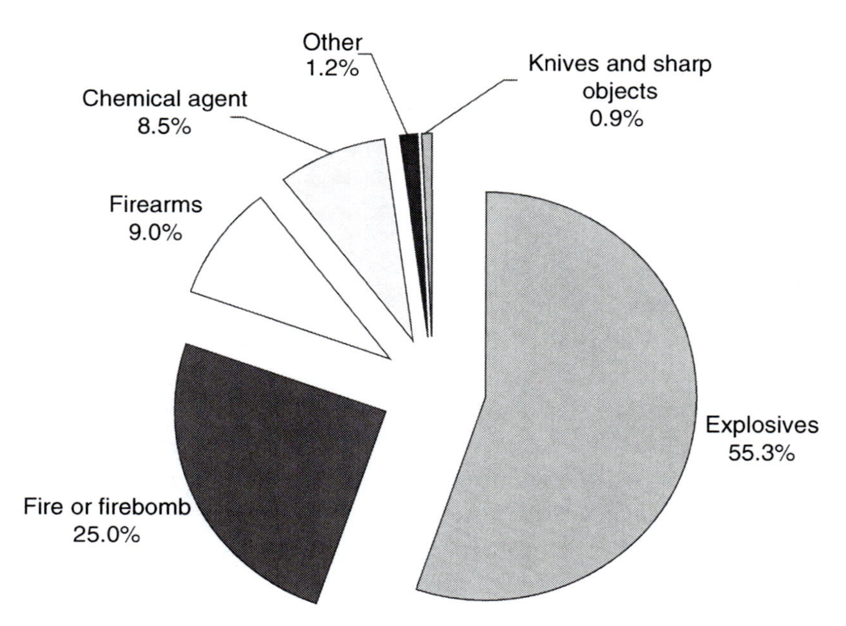

Figure 17.6. Primary terrorist weapon types in the United States, 1970–2004.
Source: Global Terrorism Database.

IV. "Effectiveness" of Control Strategies

In this section I describe two studies that used the GTD data to attempt to understand how well government action was able to deter terrorist activity. The first project, by LaFree, Dugan, and Korte (2007), assesses the effectiveness of six strategies implemented by the British government to control republican terrorist activity in Northern Ireland. The second project (Metelsky 2006) compares patterns of antiabortion terrorism in the United States before and after the passage of federal policy to end antiabortion violence.[16] This section ends with a summary of other efforts to estimate the impact of counterterrorism efforts.

A. Northern Ireland

Approximately 60 percent of Northern Ireland's 1.5 million people are Protestants, and most of the remaining population is Catholic. But the conflict in Northern Ireland is more complex than simple conflict between these two religions. The mixture of nationalist ideals and religious differences led to ongoing struggle within the country. The escalation of terrorist violence in the late 1960s can be traced back to at least 1920, when Britain divided Ireland into two administrative units in an attempt to ensure a loyalist (predominantly Protestant) majority in Northern Ireland that supported the union between Britain and Ireland (O'Leary and McGarry 1993; McGloin 2003; O'Leary 2005). In the late 1960s Irish republicans (predominantly Catholic) began a movement to protest perceived political and economic discrimination against Northern Ireland (O'Leary and McGarry 1993). The Irish Republican Army (IRA), a paramilitary group supporting the republican agenda, was committed to the goal of a united Ireland independent of Britain. According to Irish republicans, Britain was occupying their country by force and therefore an armed struggle was justifiable and necessary to rid Northern Ireland of its occupiers (Alonso 2001; McGloin 2003). Although the IRA is the most active and best known of the Irish republican groups that have employed terrorist methods, there are several less visible groups, notably the Irish National Liberation Army and the Irish People's Liberation Organization. We examine the combined activity of all republican organizations. The other active terrorist movement during this period was formed by groups of loyalist organizations that supported British control of Northern Ireland.

Northern Ireland provides a strategic test of the effects of counterterrorist measures on the risk of future terrorist attacks because Britain imposed a variety of discrete counterterrorist interventions over several decades. After an extensive literature review, we identified six highly visible British interventions that seemed mostly directed toward republican terrorism. Two were primarily based on criminal justice (internment and criminalization or Ulsterization) and four were

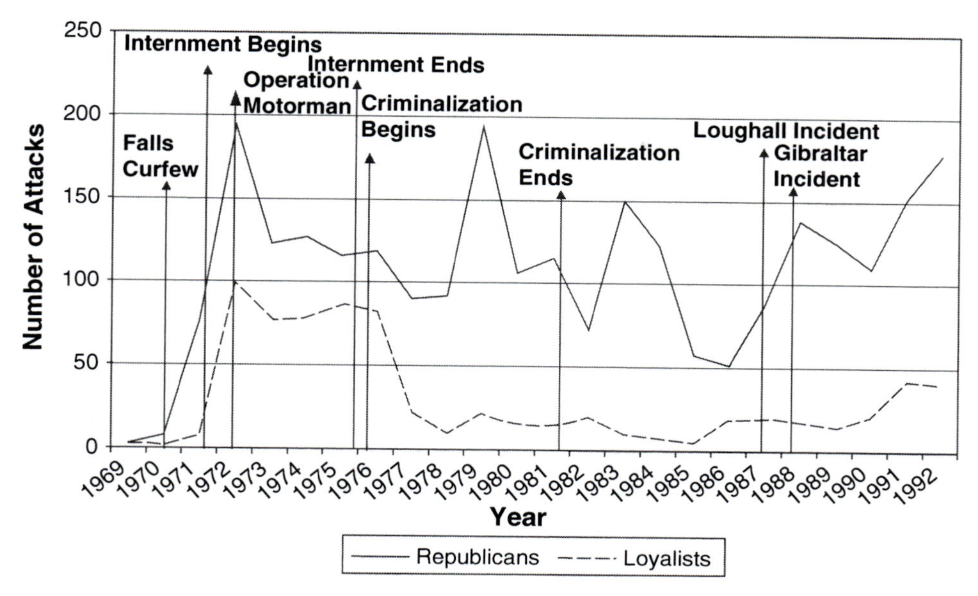

Figure 17.7. Terrorist attacks by republicans and loyalists, Northern Ireland, 1969–92.
Source: Global Terrorism Database.

primarily military (Falls Curfew, Operation Motorman, and the Loughall and Gibraltar incidents). During the internment period of about four months nearly 2,000 suspected terrorists (mostly Catholics or republicans) were detained by the authorities. Criminalization and Ulsterization were strategies aimed at treating terrorist suspects as criminals rather than political prisoners and thereby reducing the perceived legitimacy of their actions (McEvoy 2001, p. 21).

Falls Curfew was a 36-hour military curfew and search operation to locate IRA members and weapons stockpiles, which resulted in four deaths and severely damaged several homes. Operation Motorman was a massive British military deployment that was aimed at eliminating "no go" areas in Londonderry and Belfast, deploying more than 30,000 armed service personnel in the area. The Loughall incident was a planned ambush carried out by the British Special Air Service that resulted in the deaths of eight IRA members. Similarly, during the Gibraltar incident, the British Special Air Service shot and killed three IRA members as part of a planned military operation. Figure 17.7 shows the patterns of republican and loyalist terrorism over this period, with the above interventions marked by the vertical lines.

We estimated the effect of these interventions using a modified hazard model to accommodate repeated events over time. Three of the interventions—internment, criminalization, and the Gibraltar incident—led to an increased risk of terrorism, the opposite of what was intended. During the period of internment, the risk of more attacks was nearly 2.2 times greater than before and after internment. Results suggest that Falls Curfew and Operation Motorman had short-term and longer term effects opposite those desired. Immediately after Falls Curfew there was a drop in the risk of more attacks, but over time the hazard rose to well above precurfew levels. Operation Motorman appeared to result in an immediate rise in the hazard of republican attacks that eventually dropped to levels below the hazard levels prior to the operation. In sum, only Operation Motorman seemed to show any lasting evidence of deterrence against terrorist activity. Four of the other five interventions suggest more of a defiant effect, leading to increased terrorism activity.

B. Abortion Clinic Attacks in the United States

Research by Metelsky (2006) examines more closely the violent activity of the anti-abortion movement in the United States, depicted by the perpetrators of attacks in figure 17.4 and table 17.1. This movement turned violent after the U.S. Supreme Court recognized a constitutional right to abortion (*Roe v. Wade*, 410 U.S. 113 [1973]) and abortion clinics were opened throughout the country. According to Metelsky (2006, p. 6), since the first abortion clinic attack in 1976 there have been 212 bombings and arsons, 100 butyric acid attacks, and 7 murders associated with the movement. In 1994 the federal government passed the Freedom of Access to Abortion Clinic Entrances (FACE) Act as a response to the increased threat to the safety of abortion providers and the women who sought their services.

The federal FACE Act imposes civil and criminal penalties on persons using "force, threat of force, or physical obstruction to prevent a person from providing or receiving reproductive health services." Additionally, penalties can be applied to a person who "intentionally damage[s] or destroy[s] the property of a facility or attempts to do so because such a facility provides reproductive health services" (18 U.S.C. 248 1994). Persons convicted of a first offense face fines and imprisonment up to a year, and those with previous convictions face fines and imprisonment up to three years for each act.

Metelsky (2006) examined the trends of abortion-related violence before and after the passage of the 1994 FACE Act. The two years prior to the Act were the most violent, totaling 242 attacks in 1992 and 186 in 1993. In 1994 there were 89 attacks, followed by 57 in 1995. Overall the average number of attacks per year dropped from 114.2 during the 10 years prior to the FACE Act to 77.2 for the 10 following years. Although these trends are insufficient to determine causality, a closer examination of their tactical components provides a strong case to hypothesize the effectiveness of the Act.

The operational tactics of antiabortion activists explicitly changed after the passage of the 1994 FACE Act. The timing of these shifts suggests that the movement was responding to the potential penalties imposed by the Act. According to Metelsky (2006), the number of specific types of antiabortion attacks that were targeted by FACE dropped after its passage. These include murders, bombings, arsons, butyric acid attacks, invasions, and blockades. Conversely, acts that fall outside the purview of FACE, such as hate mail and picketing, increased substantially after its passage. Together these trends suggest a substantial shift in tactics from violent to nonviolent as a result of the legislation and set us up for a more thorough and rigorous evaluation of FACE.

C. Other Assessments on Controlling Terrorism

The studies discussed so far represent only two efforts to understand how policy may or may not deter terrorism. Yet these studies account for a large proportion of a relatively small group of quantitative evaluations (Lum, Kennedy, and Sherley 2006). The mixed results suggest that effectively deterring terrorism will require an evolving understanding of the complexity of the terrorist players and situational context. The following examples of policy evaluations sometimes report success and in most cases suggest increased hazardous consequences during state attempts to deter terrorist violence.

Enders and Sandler (1993) provide one of the few studies of the impact of counterterrorist strategies using empirical data (ITERATE) and statistical tests. They examine the deterrent effect of six counterterrorist strategies: (1) the installation of metal detectors in U.S. airports in January 1973; (2–4) the fortification of U.S. embassies in 1976, 1985, and 1986; (5) the enactment in October 1984 of tougher U.S. laws for terrorist-related acts; and (6) the U.S. decision to bomb Libya in 1986 for its alleged involvement in the terrorist bombing of a West Berlin discotheque. Although Enders and Sandler find a significant deterrent effect for both metal detectors and embassy fortifications, these effects are counterbalanced by a significant increase in other kinds of hostage-based attacks and assassinations.

Two nonstatistical studies that examine the consequences of the 1998 attempt by the United States to subdue terrorist activity in Afghanistan argue that the efforts made things worse rather than better. The military strikes apparently increased Osama bin Laden's popularity throughout the region and intensified public animosity toward the United States (Malvesti 2002). Collateral damage caused by the bombings prompted accusations that the United States placed little value on Afghan lives, thereby undermining the legitimacy of the U.S. strikes (Roberts 2002).

Similarly, in Eppright's (1997) evaluation of Israel's 1996 incursion into Lebanon, he concludes that there was a significant drop in Hezbollah's rocket attacks in Israel. However, Eppright also points out that because of Israel's actions in Lebanon, local and international support for Hezbollah dramatically increased (see also Greener-Barcham 2002).

More systematically, the overall assessment of the seven robust studies detected by Lum, Kennedy, and Sherley (2006) found mixed results. They summarized the set of 86 findings from the seven studies by classifying them into the following six categories: (1) installing metal detectors and security screening; (2) fortifying embassies and protecting diplomats; (3) increasing severity of punishment; (4) United Nations resolutions against terrorism; (5) Israeli military-led retaliation attacks on the PLO and Lebanon and U.S. retaliatory raids on Libya; and (6) changes in political governance. Some of the findings on metal detectors were drawn from Enders and Sandler (1993). Efforts to secure airlines may result in increases in other types of violence (see also Cauley and Im 1988). Furthermore, the combined findings from all seven studies provide no evidence that fortifying embassies or protecting diplomats has been effective at reducing attacks on these targets.

Landes (1978) found no evidence that increasing the severity of punishment for apprehended hijackers reduces hijacking. Later work by Dugan, LaFree, and Piquero (2005), however, demonstrated that when Cuba made it a crime to hijack airplanes, hijacking attempts to Cuba dropped substantially. However, this finding was specific only to those who hijack to get to Cuba. In most cases the hijackers were not terrorists. That analysis found no evidence that any of the policy initiatives in the 1970s were effective in reducing terrorist-related hijacking.

Similarly, United Nations resolutions were found to show no discernible statistical effectiveness on their own (Lum, Kennedy, and Sherley 2006). Also, consistent with the Northern Ireland example detailed earlier, the overall findings on the effects of military retaliation strongly suggest that these retaliations often lead to more terrorism, not less. Finally, the Lum, Kennedy, and Sherley review found that changes in political parties seemed to lead to an overall increase in terrorist attacks.

Fundamental to all of the research just described is the question of whether we can comfortably conclude that the findings were causal. Although many of the studies attempted to rule out rival causes, producing strong evidence suggesting a causal link, by relying on a quasi-experimental design we necessarily fall short of unequivocal causality. Yet practical and ethical considerations preclude researchers from adopting a pure experimental design to estimate the causal relationship between intervention and prevention strategies and terrorism activity. In other words, the contextual dynamics in the social and political environment of terrorism are so complex that rival causes will almost always influence terrorism activity despite any intervention or prevention attempts. However, we now have enough data on terrorism incidents over a relatively long period of time that can be combined with the wealth of qualitative information on the context of terrorism activity to help us begin to disentangle the effects from competing influences.

V. Policy Implications

The projects described above show very different responses to government efforts to deter terrorist violence. In the Northern Ireland case, terrorists may have become even more motivated to attack after British deterrent efforts. This is especially true when the British government detained nearly 2,000 suspected terrorists for four months. One IRA member has been quoted as saying, "The British security forces are the best recruitin' officer we have" (Geraghty 2000, p. 36). Yet when the U.S. government imposed harsher sanctions against those convicted of abortion-related violence, the level of violence appeared to decrease, suggesting that there is some value in government deterrence efforts. The British government did eventually adopt more successful strategies—bigovernmentalism, consociation, and federalizing institutions—that in recent years have brought hope for a permanent peace (O'Leary 2005). Still, the divergent reactions by terrorists in these and other studies strongly suggest that selecting an appropriate deterrence strategy is not a task that should be taken lightly. Casual generalizations from one context to another could cost more than wasted resources; it could lead to more loss of life.

Despite these mixed findings, one point seems clear. Most terrorist organizations are unlikely to be deterred by traditional sanctions, especially because they are often wholly willing to exchange their lives or their freedom to strike a blow against their enemies (Pedahzur 2005). Of the eight reasons that Cronin (2006) gives for a terrorist group's decline, only two are directly related to deterrence: the capture or killing of the leader and military force or repression.[17] Even here, she warns that the effectiveness of capturing the leader depends on specific organizational characteristics, such as its structure, the charisma of the leader, and the presence of a viable successor (Cronin 2006). Israel's 1992 deportation of top Hamas leaders backfired when the more radical midlevel leaders took over using more deadly tactics against the Israelis (Hoffman and Cragin 2002). This strategy can also backfire if the group raises its captured or killed leader to the status of martyr, motivating further attacks (U.S. Institute of Peace 1999; Cronin 2006).[18]

In some cases military intervention or repression has contributed to a group's decline, such as the Shining Path in Peru and the Kurdistan Workers' Party in Turkey (Cronin 2006). Again, these strategies must be used with caution because, as noted above, sometimes repression leads to increased violence, as with the Chechen rebels in Russia and the Irish Republican Army (Cronin 2006; LaFree, Dugan, and Korte 2007). Furthermore, long-term repressive measures may challenge civil liberties and human rights, which can undermine government legitimacy (Cronin 2006).

Clarke and Newman (2006) suggest that we adopt a situational approach to preventing terrorism, similar to that used to control more common crimes. By systematically analyzing the opportunities that terrorists exploit, these authors suggest that we can direct our efforts toward developing reasonable means to block those opportunities. Of course, their strategy is adaptive because terrorist organizations will exploit new avenues of attack. The strength of this approach is that it assumes that terrorists will always attempt to attack vulnerable targets. Thus we need not rely on efforts to eliminate terrorists or to change the long-term conditions that spawn terrorists before enhancing our safety from terrorist attacks.

A thorough understanding of the possible policy responses to terrorism requires cooperation across disciplines. By applying only the criminal justice perspective to deterring terrorism, we can develop only one set of policy alternatives and possible responses. By incorporating the motivations of the individual actors, the organizational structure, and the situational context we can better account for a broader and more realistic set of policy alternatives and possible outcomes. Those who study the psychology of the terrorist (McCauley 2001; Horgan, 2005) can work with those who understand the organizational complexities (Laqueur 1999; Crenshaw 2001; Cronin 2006) and those who are well practiced at studying the complexity of criminal behavior (LaFree and Dugan 2004) to inform policy makers. The START Center has been bringing together social scientists from many disciplines to better understand the formation and continuation of terrorism activity.[19]

By developing a global terrorism database of attacks we have clearly made some advances in our understanding of how to effectively control terrorism. However, we also need a global database on the responses to terrorism and the characteristics of terrorist organizations in order to conduct broader analyses that reach beyond the case study. Any data on responses to terrorism need to include a broad range of strategies from conciliatory policies—such as repentance policies, amnesty policies, territorial concessions, and other positive inducements—to violent or repressive counterterrorism tactics. We need to put as much effort into collecting terrorism-related data as we have in collecting criminal justice–related data if we are to effectively inform policy.

APPENDIX: COUNTRIES INCLUDED IN EACH REGION

Region	*Countries/Territories*
North America	Canada, the French territory of St. Pierre and Miquelon, and the United States
Latin America	Anguilla, Antigua and Barbuda, Argentina, Aruba, Bahamas, Barbados, Belize, Bermuda, Bolivia, Bonaire, Brazil, Cayman Islands, Chile, Colombia, Costa Rica, Cuba, Curacao, Dominica, Dominican Republic, Ecuador, El Salvador, Falkland Islands, French Guiana, Grenada, Guadeloupe, Guatemala, Guyana, Haiti, Honduras, Jamaica, Martinique, Mexico, Montserrat, Nicaragua, Panama, Paraguay, Peru, Puerto Rico, Saba, St. Barthelemy, St. Eustatius, St. Kitts and Nevis, St. Lucia, St. Maarten, St. Martin, St. Vincent and the Grenadines, Suriname, Trinidad and Tobago, Turks and Caicos, Uruguay, Venezuela, and the Virgin Islands (British and U.S.)

Europe	Albania, Andorra, Armenia, Austria, Azerbaijan, Belgium, Bosnia-Herzegovina, Bulgaria, Byelarus, Croatia, Czech Republic, Denmark, Estonia, Finland, France, Georgia, Germany, Gibraltar, Greece, Greenland, Hungary, Iceland, Ireland, Italy, Kazakhstan, Kyrgyzstan, Latvia, Liechtenstein, Lithuania, Luxembourg, Macedonia, Malta, Isle of Man, Moldova, Monaco, Netherlands, Norway, Poland, Portugal, Romania, Russia, San Marino, Serbia, Montenegro, Slovak Republic, Slovenia, Spain, Sweden, Switzerland, Tajikistan, Turkmenistan, Ukraine, United Kingdom, and Uzbekistan
Middle East and North Africa	Algeria, Bahrain, Cyprus, Egypt, Iran, Iraq, Israel, Jordan, Kuwait, Lebanon, Libya, Morocco, Oman, Palestine, Qatar, Saudi Arabia, Syria, Tunisia, Turkey, United Arab Emirates, and Yemen
Sub-Saharan Africa	Angola, Benin, Botswana, Burkina Faso, Burundi, Cameroon, Cape Verde, Central African Republic, Chad, Comoros, Congo, Djibouti, Equatorial Guinea, Eritrea, Ethiopia, Gabon, Gambia, Ghana, Guinea, Guinea-Bissau, Ivory Coast, Kenya, Lesotho, Liberia, Madagascar, Malawi, Mali, Mauritania, Mauritius, Mozambique, Namibia, Niger, Nigeria, Reunion, Rwanda, Sao Tome and Principe, Senegal, Seychelles, Sierra Leone, Somalia, South Africa, Sudan, Swaziland, Tanzania, Togo, Uganda, Zaire, Zambia, and Zimbabwe
Asia	Afghanistan, Australia, Bangladesh, Bhutan, Brunei, Cambodia, China, Cook Islands, Fiji, French Polynesia, Guam, Hong Kong, India, Indonesia, Japan, Kiribati, Laos, Macao, Malaysia, Maldives, Marshall Islands, Micronesia, Mongolia, Myanmar, Nauru, Nepal, New Caledonia, New Zealand, Niue, North Korea, Northern Mariana Islands, Pakistan, Palau, Papua New Guinea, Philippines, Samoa (U.S.), Singapore, Solomon Islands, South Korea, Sri Lanka, Taiwan, Thailand, Tonga, Tuvalu, Vanuatu, Vietnam, Wallis and Futuna, and Western Samoa

NOTES

1. These include the U.S. Department of State (2001); the Jaffee Center for Strategic Studies in Tel Aviv (see Falkenrath 2001); the RAND Corporation (see Jongman 1993); and the ITERATE database (see Mickolus 1982).

2. The term *domestic terrorism* refers to terrorism that is perpetrated within the boundaries of a given nation by nationals from that nation targeting nationals of that nation.

3. In an effort to maintain the broadest criteria that allow users to select cases relevant to their research, the committee required that all three of the following criteria must be met for an incident to be included (START 2007*b*, pp. 10–11): (1) the incident must be intentional, the result of a conscious calculation on the part of a perpetrator; (2) the incident must entail some level of violence (includes property violence); (3) there must be subnational perpetrators (this database does not look at state terrorism, or, to phrase it more accurately, it limits itself to acts of nonstate terrorism). Furthermore, at least two of the following criteria must be present: (1) the act must be aimed at attaining a political, economic, religious, or social goal; in terms of economic goals, the exclusive pursuit of profit does not satisfy this criterion; (2) there must be evidence of an intention to coerce, intimidate, or convey some other message to a larger audience (or audiences) than the immediate victims; (3) the action must be outside the context of legitimate warfare activities, that is, the act must be outside the parameters permitted by international humanitarian law (particularly the admonition against deliberately targeting civilians or noncombatants).

4. Since the original PGIS and the GTD2 were collected differently (prospective versus retrospective), using strategically different criteria, we are currently exploring ways to integrate the two data sets. Until then, we will clearly discern between the two original sources.

5. An earlier version of the GTD data is currently available through the Inter-University Consortium for Political and Social Research (ICPSR).

6. During the transfer of the data from PGIS to the University of Maryland it was discovered that the boxes containing data from 1993 were missing. Those data were never recovered, although we have made several attempts to replace them through open sources. According to the PGIS reports, 4,954 attacks occurred that year.

7. The ITERATE data are available for a fee from the Social Science Data Collection library at the University of California at San Diego. http://ssdc.ucsd.edu/ssdc/ite00001.html.

8. Cobra appears to have collected data only during 1998 and 1999 (Shanty and Picquet 2000). Currently they are operating under the name Terrorism Research Center and can be reached at http://www.terrorism.com/. The Triton data are collected by Hazard Management Solutions, Ltd., a private agency. The data are unavailable publicly, but report summaries are available through subscription (http://www.hazmansol.com/research-and-analysis/triton-report-subscription/). The Tweed data can be downloaded from the University of Bergen, Department of Comparative Politics Web site (http://www.uib.no/People/sspje/tweed.htm).

9. In spring of 2008, MIPT lost its funding and removed the RAND Terrorism Chronology from its Web site. This data is no longer available for browsing.

10. RAND defines terrorism as follows:

> Terrorism is violence, or the threat of violence, calculated to create an atmosphere of fear and alarm. These acts are designed to coerce others into actions they would not otherwise undertake, or refrain from actions they

desired to take. All terrorist acts are crimes. Many would also be violation[s] of the rules of war if a state of war existed. This violence or threat of violence is generally directed against civilian targets. The motives of all terrorists are political, and terrorist actions are generally carried out in a way that will achieve maximum publicity. Unlike other criminal acts, terrorists often claim credit for their acts. Finally, terrorist acts are intended to produce effects beyond the immediate physical damage of the cause, having long-term psychological repercussions on a particular target audience. The fear created by terrorists may be intended to cause people to exaggerate the strengths of the terrorist and the importance of the cause, to provoke governmental overreaction, to discourage dissent, or simply to intimidate and thereby enforce compliance with their demands. (Memorial Institute for the Prevention of Terrorism 2007)

11. Because we had access to PGIS's reports we were able to use the total count of 1993 attacks to interpolate subsets of the data for 1993. We used the following formula:

$$Attacks93(subset) = \frac{\frac{Attacks92(subset) \times Attacks93(total)}{Attacks92\ (total)} + \frac{Attacks94(subset) \times Attacks93(total)}{Attacks94\ (total)}}{2}$$

Because this graph captures all global attacks, all countries are included regardless of their current regime. For example, prior to 1990 attacks in Germany are recorded under either West Germany (FRG) or East Germany (GDR). After reunification, all attacks in Germany are recorded under Germany.

12. Mexico and Puerto Rico were counted as part of Latin America instead of North America.

13. After much consideration, I report the frequency of attacks rather than the rate of attacks because terrorist attacks are less population-sensitive than crimes, where there is often a one-to-one correspondence between the crime and the offender or the crime and the victim. Reporting the frequency is not ideal, but it is much cleaner than adding error by reporting it relative to the population. Terrorist organizations are drawn to attack in particular countries more for political or social reasons than for reasons of opportunity (which is usually a function of population).

14. I treat Northern Ireland as separate from the United Kingdom because its terrorism is highly specialized to that region.

15. The year 1993 was not included in the figure to avoid misleading interpolation of organizational activity, as they have relatively low frequencies.

16. Metelsky (2006) states that she uses data from the National Abortion Federation (2000, 2003, 2005). Since then, all of the violent cases have been integrated into the GTD.

17. Other reasons that terrorist groups might end include unsuccessful generational transition, achievement of the cause, transition to a legitimate political process, and transition out of terrorism to another form of violence (crime or insurgency; Cronin 2006).

18. Examples of this include the killing of Che Guevera by the Bolivian Army, and the case of Sheikh Omar, who is imprisoned for life in the United States (Cronin 2006).

19. For a list of publications, see http://www.start.umd.edu/publications/other_pubs.asp#journal_articles.

REFERENCES

Alonso, Rogelio. 2001. "The Modernization in Irish Republican Thinking toward the Utility of Violence." *Studies in Conflict and Terrorism* 24: 131–44.

Baggett, Jay. 2007. "Ellison's Support for Terrorism Not a Concern." WorldNetDaily.com, January 27.

Cauley, John, and Eric Iksoon Im. 1988. "Intervention Policy Analysis of Skyjackings and Other Terrorist Incidents." *American Economic Review* 78: 27–31.

Clarke, Ronald V., and Graeme R. Newman. 2006. *Outsmarting the Terrorists*. Westport, CT: Praeger Security International.

Crenshaw, Martha. 2001. "Theories of Terrorism: Instrumental and Organizational Approaches." In *Inside Terrorism Organizations*, edited by David C. Rapoport. London: Frank Cass.

Cronin, Audrey Kurth, 2006. "How al-Qaida Ends." *International Security* 31: 7–48.

Dugan, Laura, Gary LaFree, Kim Cragin, and Anna Kasupski, 2008. *Building and Analyzing a Comprehensive Open Source Data Base on Global Terrorist Events.* A Final Report to the National Institute of Justice. University of Maryland, College Park, MD.

Dugan, Laura, Gary LaFree, and Alex Piquero. 2005. "Testing a Rational Choice Model of Airline Hijackings." *Criminology* 43: 1031–66.

Enders, Walter, and Todd Sandler. 1993. "The Effectiveness of Antiterrorism Policies: A Vector-Autoregression-Intervention Analysis." *American Political Science Review* 87: 829–44.

Enders, Walter, and Todd Sandler. 2006. *The Political Economy of Terrorism*. Cambridge: Cambridge University Press.

Eppright, Charles T. 1997. "'Counter terrorism' and Conventional Military Force: The Relationship between Political Effect and Utility." *Studies in Conflict and Terrorism* 20: 333–44.

Fairchild, E., and H. R. Dammer. 2001. *Comparative Criminal Justice Systems*. Belmont, CA: Wadsworth/Thomson Learning.

Falkenrath, R. 2001. "Analytic Models and Policy Prescription: Understanding Recent Innovation in U.S. Counterterrorism." *Journal of Conflict and Terrorism* 24: 159–81.

Geraghty, Tony. 2000. *The Irish War*. Baltimore: Johns Hopkins University Press.

Greener-Barcham, Beth K. 2002. "Before September: A History of Counter-Terrorism in New Zealand." *Australian Journal of Political Science* 37: 509–24.

Hoffman, Bruce. 1998. *Recent Trends and Future Prospects of Terrorism in the United States*. Santa Monica, CA: RAND.

Hoffman, Bruce, and Kim Cragin. 2002. "Four Lessons from Five Countries." *RAND Review*, Summer 2002 http://www.rand.org/publications/randreview/issues/rr.08.02/fourlessons.html

Horgan, John. 2005 *The Psychology of Terrorism*. New York: Routledge.

Jongman, A. J. 1993. "Trends in International and Domestic Terrorism in Western Europe, 1968–88." In *Western Responses to Terrorism*, edited by Alex P. Schmid and Ronald D. Crelinsten. London: Frank Cass.

LaFree, Gary, and Laura Dugan. 2004. "How Does Studying Terrorism Compare to Studying Crime?" In *Terrorism and Counter-Terrorism: Criminological Perspectives*, edited by Mathieu DeFlem. New York: Elsevier.

LaFree, Gary, and Laura Dugan. 2005. *Building and Analyzing a Comprehensive Open Source Data Base on Global Terrorist Events, 1968 to 2005*. Grant proposal to National Institute of Justice, University of Maryland, College Park.

LaFree, Gary, and Laura Dugan. 2007. "Introducing the Global Terrorism Database." *Terrorism and Political Violence* 19: 181–204.

LaFree, Gary, Laura Dugan, Heather Fogg, and Jeffrey Scott. 2006. *Building a Global Terrorism Database*. A Final Report to the National Institute of Justice. University of Maryland, College Park.

LaFree, Gary, Laura Dugan, and Raven Korte. 2007. "Is Counter Terrorism Counterproductive? Northern Ireland 1969–1992." Unpublished manuscript. University of Maryland, College Park.

Landes, W. M. 1978. "An Economic Study of U.S. Aircraft Hijackings, 1961–1976." *Journal of Law and Economics* 21: 1–31.

Laqueur, Walter. 1999. *The New Terrorism*. New York: Oxford University Press.

Lum, Cynthia, Leslie W. Kennedy, and Alison J. Sherley. 2006. "Are Counter-Terrorism Strategies Effective? The Results of the Campbell Systematic Review on Counter-Terrorism Evaluation Research." *Journal of Experimental Criminology* 2: 489–516.

Malvesti, Michele L. 2002. "Bombing bin Laden: Assessing the Effectiveness of Air Strikes as a Counter-Terrorism Strategy." *Fletcher Forum of World Affairs* 26: 17–29.

McCauley, Clark. 2001. "What Do Terrorists Want?" *Psychological Science Agenda* 14: 5.

McEvoy, Kieran. 2001. *Paramilitary Imprisonment in Northern Ireland: Resistance, Management, and Release*. New York: Oxford University Press.

McGloin, Jean Marie. 2003. "Shifting Paradigms: Policing in Northern Ireland." *Policing: An International Journal of Police Strategies and Management* 26: 118–43.

Memorial Institute for the Prevention of Terrorism. 2007. "MIPT Terrorism Knowledge Base." http://tkb.org/Home.jsp.

Metelsky, Lauren. 2006. "From Violence to Protest: The Freedom of Access to Clinic Entrances Act and the Shifting Tactics of Anti-Abortion Activists." Unpublished manuscript. University of Maryland, College Park.

Mickolus, Edward F. 1982. *International Terrorism: Attributes of Terrorist Events, 1968–1977*. Ann Arbor, MI: Inter-University Consortium for Political and Social Research.

National Abortion Federation. 2000. "NAF Violence and Disruption Statistics: Incidents of Violence and Disruption against Abortion Providers in the U.S. and Canada." http://www.prochoice.org/pubs_research/publications/downloads/about_abortion/violence_statistics2000.pdf.

———. 2003. "NAF Violence and Disruption Statistics: Incidents of Violence and Disruption against Abortion Providers in the U.S. and Canada." E-mail communication.

———. 2005. "NAF Violence and Disruption Statistics: Incidents of Violence and Disruption against Abortion Providers in the U.S. and Canada." http://www.prochoice.org/pubs_research/publications/downloads/about_abortion/violence_statistics.pdf.

O'Leary, Brendan. 2005. "Looking Back at the IRA." *Field Day Review*, March–April, pp. 216–46.

O'Leary, Brendan, and John McGarry. 1993. *The Politics of Antagonism*. London: Athalone.

Pedahzur, Ami. 2005. *Suicide Terrorism*. Cambridge, UK: Polity.

Pluchinsky, Dennis. 2006. "The Evolution of the U.S. Government's Annual Report on Terrorism: A Personal Commentary." *Studies in Conflict and Terrorism* 29: 91–98.

Roberts, Adam. 2002. "Counter-Terrorism, Armed Force and the Laws of War." *Survival* 44: 7–32.

Schmid, Alex P., and A. J. Jongman. 1988. *Political Terrorism: A New Guide to Actors, Authors, Concepts, Databases, Theories and Literature*. Amsterdam: North-Holland.

Shanty, Frank, and Raymond Picquet. 2000. *International Terrorism: An Annual Event Data Report, 1998*. Collingdale, PA: DIANE.

Sherman, Lawrence W., Denise Gottfredson, Doris L. MacKenzie, John Eck, Peter Reuter, and Shawn Bushway. 1997. *Preventing Crime: What Works, What Doesn't, What's Promising: A Report to the United States Congress*. Washington, DC: National Institute of Justice.

START. 2007*a*. "The Department of Homeland Security's Center of Excellence, the National Center for the Study of Terrorism and Response to Terrorism." http://www.start.umd.edu/about/.

———. 2007*b*. "GTD2 (1998–2004) Global Terrorism Database Codebook Draft 1.0." http://209.232.239.37/gtd2/gtd2_codebook.pdf.

U.S. Department of State. 2001. "Introduction: Patterns of Global Terrorism, 2000." http://www.state.gov/s/ct/rls/crt/2000/.

U.S. Department of State. 2008. "Foreign Terrorist Organizations." Fact sheet. http://www.state.gov/s/ct/rls/fs/08/103392.htm.

U.S. Institute of Peace. 1999. *How Terrorism Ends*. Special Report No. 48. Washington, DC: U.S. Institute for Peace.

Wolf, John B. 1981. *Fear of Fear: A Survey of Terrorist Operations and Controls in Open Societies*. New York: Plenum.

CHAPTER 18

TRAFFICKING IN CULTURAL ARTIFACTS

A. J. G. TIJHUIS

TRANSACTIONS involving cultural artifacts make up one of the least studied forms of transnational crime. Cultural artifacts encompass both antiquities and works of art. Although there is no standard definition for these crimes, Conklin (1994, p. 2) provides a broad and practical one: criminally punishable acts that involve works of art.

Art crimes can be divided into a number of different types: the theft of works of art, the faking and forging of works of art, the looting of antiquities, and those involving the nexus between cultural artifacts and organized crime.

Academic interest in art crimes, though limited, has been approached from different angles, mostly by noncriminologists. Archaeologists have extensively described the looting and smuggling of antiquities (e.g., Brodie, Doole, and Renfrew 2001). In addition, a number of books by journalists have shed light on specific cases (Middlemas 1975; Watson 1998; Watson and Todeschini 2006).

Lawyers have dealt with the main legal instruments with regard to the illicit trade in cultural artifacts, such as the conventions established by L'Institut international pour l'unification du droit privé (International Institute for the Unification of Private Law; UNIDROIT) and UNESCO (Prott 1997; Rascher 2000). The UNIDROIT Convention of 1995 laid down regulations for the restitution and return of cultural objects between two contract states (http://www.unidroit.org/english/conventions/1995culturalproperty/main.htm). These regulations are basically self-executing; that is, legal claims arise directly without the regulations having to be implemented into national law. The contract states thus operate on a unified basis regarding civil and administrative law. The 1970 UNESCO Convention (http://portal.unesco.org/culture/en/ev.php-URL_ID=2633&URL_DO=DO_TOPIC&URL_SECTION=201.html) is an international treaty that formulates basic principles for the protection of cultural goods and contains minimum standards for legislative, administrative, and international treaty measures, which the member states must implement to prevent illicit trafficking of cultural goods.

A few criminologists have focused on some aspects of crimes related to cultural artifacts. Conklin's (1994) *Art Crime* is the best known introduction to the subject. A recent PhD project by Laurence Massy (2000), a Belgian criminologist and art historian, examined the motivations of art thieves and the link between art crime and other types of (organized) crime. A PhD study by the author focused on the interface between licit and illicit trade in art and antiquities (Tijhuis 2006). Several Australian criminologists, for example Aarons (2001) and Polk and Alder (2002), have focused on art crime. Aarons performed an exploratory study of the illegitimate art market in Australia. Polk and Alder studied the market for antiquities as a criminal market.

Data on stolen artifacts can be gathered to some extent from several databases that register stolen objects. The most important are the private Art Loss Register (ALR) and Trace and the police registers Leonardo, Treima, and Stolen Works of Art. The ALR (http://www.artloss.com) records stolen and missing objects and among other things, searches auction catalogues to recover them. The ALR keeps records of over 10,000 losses from insurers, owners, and law enforcement agencies, adding to its database each year. In total, the ALR currently lists about 180,000 objects. Trace (http://www.trace.com/about.aspx?t=1) registers stolen, seized, and recovered works of art. Besides Trace, which focuses on stolen art in general, Trace Looted Art (http://www.tracelootedart.com) was developed to help both victims of Nazi spoliation and members of the art market by building a comprehensive database of Holocaust-era looted art.

The police register with the largest database is Leonardo, the register of stolen art and antiquities maintained by the Italian military police. It has more than one million entries that are actively compared with catalogues from auctions held worldwide. A comparable database, though smaller in numbers, is Treima, used by the French art police. The international police organization Interpol also maintains a database of stolen art registered by it member states (http://www.interpol.int/Public/WorkOfArt/CDrom/default.asp); it consists of about 31,500 objects on CD-ROMs distributed by Interpol.

Besides maintaining databases, the national police agencies mentioned and others are actively engaged in solving national and transnational cases of art crimes. Besides the specialized Italian and French agencies, the FBI in the United States and the Federal Police in Germany are important in this field.

To counter the trade in stolen art and antiquities, several international treaties have been drafted for this purpose. Besides the UNESCO and UNIDROIT

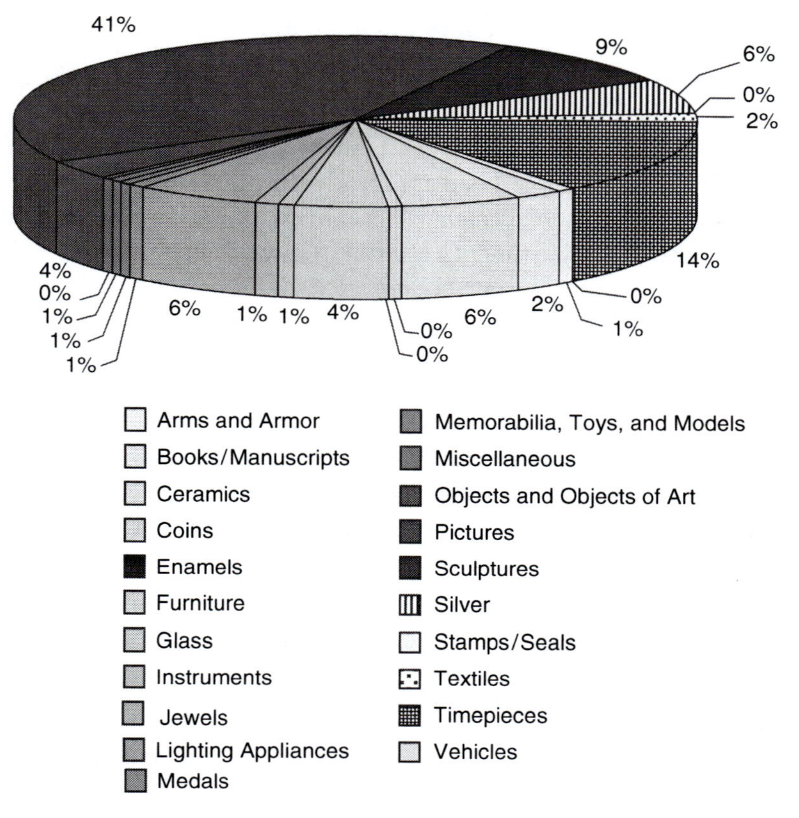

Figure 18.1. Categories of artworks recovered, 2007.
Source: Art Loss Register.

conventions, several others can be mentioned. In 1954 the Convention for the Protection of Cultural Property in the Event of Armed Conflict was adopted in The Hague (http://portal.unesco.org/culture/en/ev.php-URL_ID=8450&URL_DO=DO_TOPIC&URL_SECTION=201.html). The EU has adopted a directive on the restitution of illegally exported cultural objects between member states, as well as regulations concerning the importation of objects from Iraq. The United States has entered into a range of bilateral treaties with particular countries to protect certain types of objects (see http://exchanges.state.gov/culprop/overview.html); these countries are Bolivia, Cambodia, Colombia, Cyprus, El Salvador, Guatemala, Honduras, Italy, Mali, Nicaragua, and Peru.

This chapter focuses on art crimes that involve cross-border activities. In section I I discuss the different types of art crimes; their incidence is the topic of section II. Causal mechanisms and influences are discussed in section III. Law enforcement efforts and other policy approaches are described in section IV. Finally, in section V I discuss the policy implications and research priorities.

A number of general observations can be offered:

- No credible knowledge exists on the scale or on trends in art theft and looting.
- Police agencies specializing in art theft are few in number and typically small; Italy's is the largest and apparently the most effective.
- Databases on registered stolen objects are maintained by the French, Italian, and U.S. governments; the International Council of Museums; Interpol; and several private organizations.
- Numerous treaties and conventions on art theft and looting have been negotiated, but no evidence exists that their ratification has any effect on art crime prosecutions or recovery of objects.
- Looting of cultural sites is common throughout the world, especially in places experiencing conflict and extreme disorder.
- Art crime is a little studied subject; no serious work has been done on the structure, functions, and operations of markets in stolen and looted art.

I. Types of Crime

Transnational crime related to cultural artifacts can be divided into several types. This section discusses these types and look at the nexus with other types of (organized) crime.

A. Art Theft

Many articles on art crimes or art theft mention the theft in 1990 from the Isabella Stewart Gardner Museum in Boston, usually considered the largest art theft ever (see http://archives.cnn.com/2002/LAW/11/26/ctv.traces.museum.heist/index.html). Paintings by Rembrandt, Vermeer, Degas, and Manet were stolen. According to the FBI, the total value may be as high as $300 million (http://www.fbi.gov). Other often discussed thefts include the four separate robberies of the Alfred Beit Collection in Russborough House in Ireland, in which Old Masters were taken each time. The first robbery was committed by members of the IRA in 1974; thereafter, the collection was robbed by others in 1986, 2001, and 2002. Despite the spectacular nature of such large thefts, they make up a minor part of all art thefts. However, as these thefts are relatively often solved, a lot can be learned from them about perpetrators and their motives.

Most art is stolen from domestic dwellings and galleries, not from museums. The first category ranges from art stolen during a burglary to well-planned thefts from large private collections. The large majority of objects are not recovered, and it is difficult to say what happens to these objects.

A specific category of thefts involves religious art and objects. In many countries churches, temples, and other religious places are popular with thieves. Catholic churches are stripped of their precious objects by thieves who profit from the lack of security. Especially in Italy this type of theft is a huge problem, but other European countries, particularly France and Belgium, experience the same problem on a smaller scale (Massy 2000; Carabinieri 2004; Interpol 2007). In Russia and some other Eastern European countries religious icons have been stolen in substantial numbers. Icons only rarely are recovered, partly because of the difficulty of identifying individual icons and the sheer number of icons that have entered the market (Interpol 2007). In Asia the theft of Buddhas and other statues has been a major problem in several countries (Nagashima 2002). Nepal has been particularly hard hit by these thefts (Schick 1998).

Rare books and manuscripts are also often stolen. Although not as well-known as thefts of fine art from museums, this type of theft has victimized many libraries (Thompson 1968; Brown-Syed 1999; Abbott 2001).

B. Fakes and Forgeries

"Fakes are works of art made to resemble existing ones; forgeries are pieces that are passed off as original works by known artists. The mere production of a work that resembles an existing one is not a crime, but intentionally and deceptively passing it off as someone else's work is forgery, a type of fraud" (Conklin 1994, p. 48).

At first glance, the field of fakes and forgeries seems to be different from the trade in stolen and smuggled art and antiquities. It is well known that fakes and forgeries are part of the art trade and probably part of many museum and private collections. How many fakes and forgeries exist is a matter of debate and also depends on the definition used. According to Thomas Hoving (1996), the former director of the Metropolitan Museum in New York who devoted a book to the history of fakery and forgery, about 40 percent of all fine art objects in museum collections are fakes or forgeries. Although Hoving's estimate is not based on thorough academic research, several factors suggest that a significant part of museum and other collections consists of fakes and forgeries. One is the ease with which forgers can funnel their products into the legitimate art market; another is that fakes and forgeries are often discovered only decades after they are produced.

Many cases of fakes and forgeries have a transnational element. Two main categories can be distinguished: fakes of objects of fine art that are moved abroad to be sold and forgeries of antiquities that are moved from the source country to the market country to be sold. Often works of modern art, including works attributed to Picasso or Dalí, are faked or forged. However, Old Masters are also successfully faked or forged, as can be learned from the work of serial faker and forger Eric Hebborn (1997). His drawings penetrated some of the world's most prestigious museums for over forty years. In 1996 Hebborn published a book in which he outlined his methods; a week after it was published he was killed in Rome.

The second category consists of forgeries of antiquities. All kinds of antiquities, from Buddha statues to African masks and Roman statues, are faked. In daily practice this can have confusing consequences, for example in the case of fake Buddha statues. When these are sent abroad without export permits they will initially be considered smuggled and probably looted items. They may be seized and action may be taken against the supposed smuggler. Only after it has been established that the objects are fakes does it turn out that no crime has occurred (in most cases). One Mexican forger was so successful that he was arrested and accused of looting pre-Columbian sites; he was released only after he demonstrated his craft (Brodie and Watson 2000, p. 19).

C. Antiquities Looting and Smuggling

The looting of antiquities is often discussed together with art theft. Although they are related problems, it is important to note the differences between the two. Art theft concerns known objects, owned by someone, that are stolen. Looted antiquities are usually objects that were not known before as individual objects, for example because they were still buried in tombs or elsewhere. Many states claim unearthed antiquities within their territorial jurisdiction as their property, but most national laws will not enforce this claim against owners outside their jurisdiction. One reason for this is that it is often impossible to prove unequivocally that an object comes from the territory of a particular country.

However, a trial in 2002 might indicate some change on this point. Frederick Schultz, a New York antiquities dealer and former president of the National Association of Dealers in Ancient, Oriental and Primitive Art, was found guilty by a U.S. court of conspiring to receive and handle stolen Egyptian antiquities (Baker 2002; O'Keefe 2004). He bought antiquities that had been smuggled out of Egypt. The smuggling was organized by an antiquities restorer from the United Kingdom, Jonathan Tokeley-Parry, who worked with a local network in Egypt. They smuggled more than 2,000 items out of the country. Tokeley-Parry was caught and prosecuted in the United Kingdom. These convictions in the two largest art market countries, together with the accession of the United Kingdom to the UNESCO Convention, may signal an emerging change in the interpretation of the legal status of smuggled antiquities (O'Keefe 2004).

Besides Egypt there are numerous countries from which antiquities are looted and smuggled abroad, including Iraq, Jordan, and Syria. Both in the colonial era and recently, the Middle East has always played a part in the illicit supply of antiquities. International and civil wars have made things worse, as can be observed most recently in Iraq (Bogdanons 2005; Tijhuis 2007). Latin America also suffers from illicit excavations and smuggling; pre-Columbian objects are looted in Peru, Columbia, and Ecuador. Some countries have struggled with looting for ages and still have plundered sites (e.g., from the Spanish colonial period). In Belize legislation to protect its cultural heritage has been in place for over a hundred years. According to Belizean law, all antiquities belong to the state and cannot be exported; nevertheless, there is a lively trade in illicit material (Gilgan 2001, pp. 73–89). According to a PhD study by Matsuda (1998), as many as 30,000 to 50,000 people in Belize may hunt and gather artifacts; as many as 3 percent of this group loots full time.

Several countries in Africa are sources for illicit antiquities. Nok statues, terracotta, bronzes, and pottery are looted and smuggled from such countries as Mali, Niger, Ghana, and Burkina Faso. In several countries the trade in illicit antiquities is organized in open and diverse ways due to the inability and sometimes unwillingness of their governments to do anything to stop it. Networks of native traders connect the remotest villages with the main ports for shipment overseas. European traders directly buy their merchandise in regional centers and sometimes live in Africa for long periods or even permanently. This marks a difference from other regions where antiquities originate. In South America the trade tends to be more secretive and seems to involve more private collectors, besides dealers, looters, middlemen, and others (Alva 2001). In Southeast Asia the trade is more open and well developed in centers like Hong Kong and Bangkok. However, the structure of the trade before it ends up in these centers is less clear (Nagashima 2002; Soudijn and Tijhuis 2003).

Asia has several regions that provide input for both licit and illicit trade. The main regions are Southeast Asia, China, India, and the border areas of Pakistan, Afghanistan, and India. Some categories of objects are regularly intercepted at borders or claimed from foreign collections as stolen objects (Watson 1998; Nagashima 2002; Soudijn and Tijhuis 2003). These include Gandharan statues from the border regions of Pakistan and Afghanistan, Khmer objects from Cambodia and Thailand, and all kinds of objects from China.

Europe and the United States are primarily important as markets. However, several developed countries face the problems discussed above. Italy is the best known example; it loses significant amounts of antiquities, in addition to the works of art discussed earlier (Watson 1998; Watson and Todeschini 2006). The United Kingdom, although always discussed as a typical market country, has experienced a significant problem with illicit excavations with metal detectors (Gill and Chippindale 2002; Tubb 1995). According to some experts, this played an important role in the country's ratification of the 1970 UNESCO treaty and the relatively far-reaching legislation adopted to implement the treaty. In the United States the cultural heritage of Native Americans and others is often the object of theft, illicit excavations, and smuggling (Conklin 1994; Canouts and McManamon 2001).

A Case Study

Usually, the trade in stolen art and antiquities is hidden behind a veil of secrecy and the discretion of the art scene. However, a police raid on a warehouse at Geneva's Freeport, a trade zone exempt from Swiss customs, started a process that showed the functioning of the global illicit antiquities trade to the general public.

The warehouse contained 10,000 unprovenanced antiquities, valued at £25 million (Brodie and Watson 2000). The antiquities belonged to an Italian national, Giacomo Medici, an art dealer working from Switzerland. Medici had been active in the illicit trade for over three decades when he was arrested and later sentenced to a long prison sentence and payment of damages in the millions of euros. He had started as a smuggler himself before he progressed through the hierarchy of the illicit trade in Italy and became the coordinator of massive smuggling operations and sales through the auction house Sotheby's and directly to private and public customers (Brodie and Watson 2000; Watson and Todeschini 2006). The antiquities came from illicit excavations in Italy and were smuggled in bulk to Switzerland, where they were stored in warehouses in Geneva's Freeport. The raid on the warehouse was followed by years of intensive investigations by the Italian authorities. This led to the discovery of numerous sales from Medici to a range of top-end U.S. museums.

Most prominent was the Getty Museum in Los Angeles, which admitted to buying dozens of extremely precious objects from Medici. The New York Metropolitan Museum has allegedly dozens of looted objects in its collection and has been negotiating with the Italian government over restitution of objects. In Italy and Greece both a civil lawsuit and criminal charges were initiated against Marion True, a former curator of the Getty Museum. When an agreement was reached about the return of 40 objects to Italy the civil lawsuit was dropped. However, the criminal charges of conspiring to deal in looted art continued (Povoleda 2007). In Greece True was accused of acquiring an illegally excavated object for the Getty; however, this case was dismissed as the statue of limitations had run out ("Greece Drops Charges" 2007).

The revelations around Medici seem to confirm the often reiterated, but usually unproven, suspicions that the legitimate antiquities trade is inherently linked with the trade in looted and smuggled antiquities.

D. Cultural Artifacts and Organized Crime

A recurrent theme in the literature on art crime is a posited connection with drug trafficking and money laundering. Bernick (1998, p. 92) observed, "Law enforcement agents frequently have reported links between stolen art, money laundering and drug deals."

Experts point to three potential connections between the illicit art and antiquities trade, drug trafficking, and money laundering. First, precious stolen works of art are said to be used as collateral or means of payment in major drug deals. Second, stolen art or looted antiquities are trafficked together with drugs from source to market country. Third, stolen art is thought to be used to launder proceeds from drug trafficking or other criminal activities.

The first connection is often illustrated with a 1999 Spanish case. In January of that year the Spanish police broke up an international art smuggling ring and seized stolen masterpieces by Giacometti, Braque, Miro, Goya, and Picasso, as well as pre-Columbian sculptures, estimated to be worth $35 million. Most of the items had allegedly been stolen in 1997 from a chalet near Geneva. The perpetrators had planned to trade the objects for cocaine from drug traffickers (Brodie and Watson 2000). Not many other examples of art thefts linked to either drugs or other illegal trades can be found. It seems a real but relatively rare phenomenon that cannot explain a significant proportion of international art thefts.

A second connection is assumed to be present in the trade in illicit antiquities. It is claimed that drugs and antiquities are often shipped together. Brodie and Watson (2000) describe an example in which a smuggler's plane, arriving in Colorado from Mexico, carried 350 pounds of marijuana together with many pre-Columbian antiquities. In Guatemala and Belize secret airstrips in the rain forest have been discovered from which cocaine and Mayan objects were flown to Miami and other U.S. cities (Brodie and Watson 2000). Gilgan (2001) noted many links between marijuana growers and traders and antiquities looters. It seems that these are not mere examples, however, but the sum of almost all known cases, because other credible cases are almost impossible to find in the literature, media reports, or other sources.

The last link between the illicit art and antiquities trade and the drug trade has to do with money laundering. It is hypothesized that stolen art and antiquities are used to launder funds generated by drug trafficking. According to Brodie and Watson (2000, p. 18), Miami is a crossroad for illicit art and antiquities from Ireland, Peru, Guatemala, Mexico, and Greece. Drug profits pay for the art and antiquities that are sent for auction so as to obtain a good pedigree for the cash. However, empirical evidence is scarce. Despite the theoretical potential for money laundering with regular (nonstolen art), this mode of money laundering seems to be rare. In one case, two art dealers were charged with conspiring to launder $4.1 million in drug funds. They had tried to sell two paintings to someone who wanted to pay with drug money. The alleged buyer turned out to be an informant, and before concluding the deal the two art dealers were arrested ("Art Dealer" 2001; "Two New Yorkers" 2001). However, cases like this one do not prove the occurrence of money laundering schemes but only the willingness of some individuals to be helpful in such schemes.

The data on the various connections between the illicit art and antiquities trade and other illegal markets seem to consist primarily of a few incidents. Yet despite the difficulties in obtaining sufficient and reliable data in this field, one cannot conclude that the claimed connections lack any credible evidence. The U.K. Ministerial Advisory Committee on the Illicit Trade in Cultural Objects (2000, p. 13) noted with regard to this topic, "Evidence from law enforcement agencies also shows that the illicit trade in cultural property is in some instances (and in some parts of the world very frequently) linked with other illegal activities. While this evidence is inevitably anecdotal, we nevertheless find it persuasive." The anecdotal evidence, though perhaps persuasive, is too scant to serve as the basis

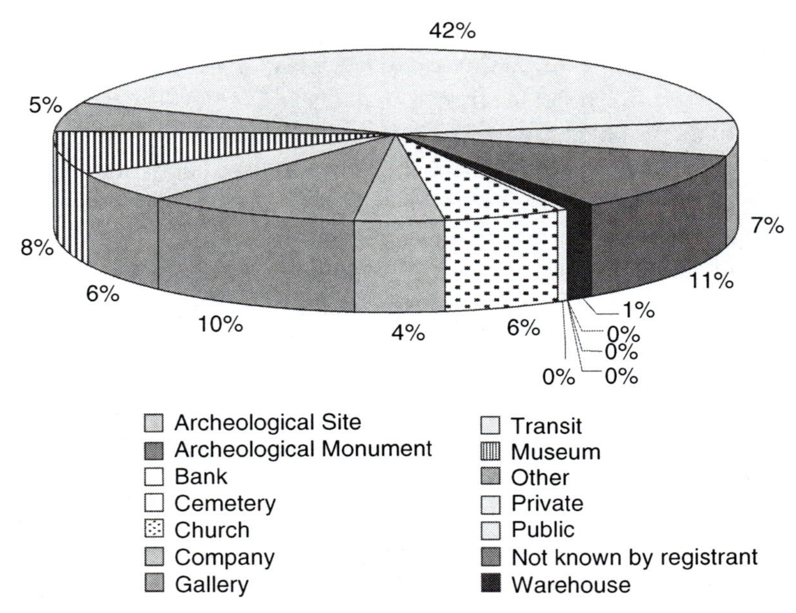

Figure 18.2. Theft of artworks by location, worldwide, 2007.
Source: Art Loss Register.

for well-informed conclusions. There are definitely cases in which the illicit trade is connected with other types of crime, but a systematic connection has neither an empirical nor a theoretical basis.

II. The Incidence of Crimes with Cultural Artifacts

The extent of the transnational trade in stolen art and antiquities and in fakes and forgeries is impossible to estimate with any degree of plausibility. Several factors play a role; most prominent is that art crime is not a clear-cut concept or category that has more or less the same meaning around the globe. To the contrary, large differences exist in how art crimes are defined; some countries have no legislation that outlaws the import or export of stolen art and antiquities, and, setting definitional problems aside, most countries do not (or barely) prosecute and record crimes related to art. As the crimes are not prosecuted or registered, no statistics are available for analysis.

There are some bits and pieces of information that provide some indication of the scale of the trade. First, data can be gathered from the private ALR. Figure 18.2 shows the different locations of thefts as percentages of the total number of registered thefts. Registered thefts are thefts of objects that were registered with one of the offices of the ALR. All numbers refer to 2007.[1] Stolen or missing items are identified primarily by searching auction catalogues (51 percent) and by ad hoc searches by the police (31 percent).

Brodie and Watson (2000), two researchers from Cambridge's Illicit Antiquities Research Centre, provide numbers from several sources that give some impression of the scale of the illicit trade. The complete overview can be read in their study (pp. 21–23). The authors do not provide the names of their sources, although some numbers can also be found in other publications (Rose 1998; Slayman 1998). The 1997 raid in the Geneva Freeport that yielded 10,000 antiquities from sites all over Italy is one example. In late 1998 a raid on a villa in Sicily revealed more than 30,000 Phoenician, Greek, and Roman antiquities worth more than £20 million. Between 1993 and 1995 the Turkish police were involved in 17,500 official police investigations into stolen antiquities.[2] Raids on an antiquities dealer carried out by the German police in Munich in 1997 recovered about 60 crates full of material ripped from the walls of churches in North Cyprus, including 139 icons, 61 frescoes, and four mosaics (Rose 1998). In Mali a survey of 125 square miles identified 834 archaeological sites and found that 45 percent had been looted, 17 percent badly. According to Brodie and Watson, the history of Mali is literally disappearing from beneath the feet of its inhabitants. In Pakistan a survey in the Charsadda district showed that nearly half of the Buddhist shrines, stupas, and monasteries had been badly damaged or destroyed by illegal excavations for salable antiquities (p. 22).

Isman (2001) described the activities of the art squad of the Italian police. The art squad is the largest in any country worldwide and has more than 150 members. From its start in 1969 through 2001, they recorded 630,000 thefts in a database that contains more than 1.1 million objects. Investigations led to the recovery of 180,000 works of art and 360,000 archaeological objects.

III. Causal Mechanisms and Influences

The transnational trade in stolen art and antiquities can be placed in the context of several causal mechanisms and influences. This discussion is not based on systematic criminological studies or sufficient pools of police data, as these are simply unavailable.

A. Causal Mechanisms

Although art has always been stolen, thefts from museums and private collections have become more frequent with the rapid rise in prices of fine art since the late 1950s. At a number of auctions toward the end of the 1950s and the beginning of the

1960s the idea of masterpieces as objects with spectacular and ever-increasing value was established as more or less an undisputed fact for the public at large (Lacey 1998; Koldehoff and Koldehoff 2004). Before the 1950s prices were moderate and seldom surpassed the $100,000 mark. However, in 1958 Cezanne's *Boy in a Red Waistcoat* raised $483,000, and in 1959 Ruben's *Adoration of the Magi* fetched $610,000. In November 1961 Rembrandt's *Aristotle Contemplating the Bust of Homer* sold for $2.3 million (McLeave 1981). Since the 1960s it has become more and more common for paintings to capture prices above the $1 million mark. In recent years both classical and modern art have sold for prices in the tens of millions of dollars. As prices rose, paintings and other objects may have seemed an easy way for criminals to earn a lot of money without too much risk. One could try to sell the objects or to persuade insurance companies or owners to pay for their safe return. In many cases the stolen objects were taken abroad.

Two important general mechanisms can be observed. First, the tremendous rise in value of art and antiquities has probably been the primary cause of the growth of art-related crimes.[3] Second, the trade in stolen art and antiquities is primarily demand-driven. Depending on the actors and objects involved, one can distinguish more specific mechanisms and influences.

Most thefts occur because offenders expect to make a profit by selling the stolen objects. This counts for antiquities looters and thieves of art from museums and private collections. These crimes can probably be understood most productively from a routine activity perspective (see, e.g., Conklin 1994, p. 119). A number of offenders are part of the so-called art scene; many thefts are committed by persons with a connection to the objects (Tijhuis 2006). They may be scholars, students, collectors, museum curators, or dealers. Furthermore, these persons are often serial thieves who operate for years and in many places. Their chances of getting caught are lower than those of regular thieves. They are especially active in a number of niche markets, such as rare prints, antique books, and civil war memorabilia.

As opposed to the for-profit thieves, offenders may be motivated by their desire to obtain objects for themselves. A small group of offenders falls into this category, but they are responsible for many thefts.

The trade in stolen art and antiquities usually starts with a thief or looter, but he or she is only one part of the trade. Thieves sell to middlemen or directly to art dealers and collectors who buy or sell stolen objects. As the available pools of works of art and antiquities are limited, they can try to obtain objects through their collaboration with thieves and fences that they cannot otherwise obtain. The trade in antiquities depends on objects that have been looted and smuggled. The case of Giacomo Medici and various U.S. museums discussed earlier provides an illustration.

B. Wars and Other Conflicts

The regular thefts of works of art and the illicit excavations of archaeological sites are in many countries associated with wars and political disturbances (Chamberlin

1983; Fuchs 1992). Such unrest has always led to significant looting, smuggling, and confiscation of art and antiquities. Because of the international character of the art trade this topic needs to be explored if we are to understand the links between this type of crime and political developments and actors. In the literature on the illicit art and antiquities trade, however, this topic is often underexamined and focused primarily on World War II. Warfare, revolutions, and civil wars, however, are a permanent fact of life and continually provide opportunities for looting and smuggling. Many works of art and antiquities that have been stolen or taken abroad without permit originate from such situations.

The occupation of many countries by Nazi Germany led to systematic theft and confiscation of cultural goods on an unprecedented scale. Thanks to renewed interest in this topic during the 1990s, many objects were returned to their original owners and knowledge about this topic increased substantially. The theft of artworks from Germany by the Soviet Union at the end of World War II has been described in recent years, although receiving far less attention than do Nazi atrocities (Akinsja and Kozlov 1995). During the 1950s the Soviet Union returned approximately one and a half million objects to East Germany. After the fall of the Berlin Wall a debate about works of art stolen during and after the war emerged again and led to new exchanges of stolen art (Greenfield 1996, pp. 220–35).

In the former German Democratic Republic a specialized government organization existed that engaged in smuggling operations to obtain foreign currency. Part of this involved the sale of works of art that were confiscated from East German citizens and museums during the 1970s and 1980s. Large quantities of works of art were sold abroad, although the authorities told victims that the items would go to museums in the GDR (Blutke 1990; Bischof 2003).

Long before World War II art and antiquities were looted by many other conquerors, notoriously including Napoleon during his military campaigns. Egypt, Venice, and Rome were among the places that were especially badly hit by the looting campaigns of the French (Chamberlin 1983). During the nineteenth century many antiquities were stolen from the colonies of European countries. The British are known for the plunder of antiquities from Ghana and Benin (Lloyd 1964; Chamberlin 1983).

After World War II a number of other territories were occupied and looted. Traditional wars receive less importance than do civil wars in which organized crime and transnational crime often play a significant role (Crefeld 1998). In recent decades numerous internal conflicts have had a major influence on the proliferation of looted art and antiquities. Many source countries have seen civil wars, anarchy, or revolutions during extended periods. Afghanistan, Lebanon, China, Cambodia, Vietnam, the Democratic Republic of Congo, Nigeria, Colombia, and Nicaragua are countries that have lost large parts of their cultural heritage to looting (Fuchs 1992; Brodie, Doole, and Renfrew 2001).

Due to the chaos caused by the U.S. occupation of Iraq and the lack of interest by the occupation forces to protect Iraq's unique cultural heritage, looting of antiquities rapidly developed to dramatic proportions in that country. The well-known case of the looting of the National Museum is just one example, and paradoxically seems to have had a relatively modest impact (Bogdanons 2005).

The loss of cultural heritage can have quite different causes. First, the chaos of civil war may create a perfect situation for looting of sites or institutions. Second, both authorities and their opponents may engage in looting and smuggling to finance their activities. Third, they may simply be corrupt and fill their own pockets with the revenues of illicit trade. Finally, the cultural heritage is sometimes "simply" destroyed for ideological reasons or as a result of hostilities. The destruction of the Buddhas at Bamijan in Afghanistan by the Taliban is a recent example.

Often the same countries will experience both regular looting and looting due to (civil) war or revolution. Cambodia illustrates this. During the era of the Khmer Rouge antiquities were looted and sold by members of the Khmer Rouge to generate funds while the same Khmer Rouge sometimes destroyed antiquities as well (Nagashima 2002). After the Khmer Rouge were ousted from power antiquities continued to be looted and smuggled across the border to Thailand. Another example is Afghanistan, where times of both war and "peace" were marked by large-scale looting and destruction.

A parallel can be drawn with other transnational crimes, such as the illicit arms trade, drug trafficking, and trafficking "blood" diamonds. These crimes are also strongly connected with unstable countries or regions. In some countries illicit arms sales were financed by the smuggling of blood diamonds, for example in Angola and Sierra Leone. The same holds for drug trafficking and the arms trade in Afghanistan and Colombia. The involvement of foreign intelligence organizations further complicates things in several countries.

IV. Law Enforcement Efforts and Other Approaches

Several law enforcement agencies are committed to fighting the trade in stolen art and antiquities. Compared with other agencies devoted to fighting other types of transnational crime, such as drug trafficking and human smuggling, these are small organizations and few in number. The most important are briefly discussed in this section, followed by a discussion of other approaches.

A. Law Enforcement Agencies

Since 1947 the international police organization Interpol has collected data on art thefts from its members around the world. In that year a notice was published for a stolen rare stamp; since then, Interpol has increasingly distributed notices on famous stolen works of art, as well as lists of all registered stolen objects. In 1995 Interpol started to collect the data on stolen objects on a CD ROM that could be consulted by police agencies and others (http://www.interpol.int/Public/WorkOfArt/Default.asp). In August 2006 Interpol switched to DVDs that offered better quality images. The aim is to help recover stolen objects and to make it harder to sell them. Yet this register contains only a fraction of all stolen objects. As a result, and due to the intervals between the issuance of updated CD ROMs and slow communication between police agencies, the use of this tool has been limited. However, Interpol is currently enabling member states to access its database directly. As of 2008 more than 65 countries were making use of this opportunity.[4]

The database of Interpol is fed by national police agencies. The most important agencies are those in the main art markets: the United States, the United Kingdom, France, Germany, and Italy. In the United States, the most important art market in the world, the FBI has a special Art Crime Team as well as a National Stolen Art File. The Art Crime Team consists of 12 special agents to investigate art crimes, supported by three specialist trial attorneys for prosecutions (http://www.fbi.gov/hq/cid/arttheft/arttheft.htm). The National Stolen Art File is a database of reported stolen art accessible by law enforcement agencies around the world. Many countries are party to multilateral treaties governing the criminalization and adjudication of cases of stolen art and antiquities. In contrast, the United States has signed only bilateral treaties, mostly with countries of South America. However, the bilateral treaties have produced more concrete results compared with measures such as the UNESCO Treaty, which have not had as many known successes in over 35 years of the treaty's existence.

An active and central bureau for art crimes exists in Paris: Office central de lutte contre le trafic des biens culturels (http://www.interieur.gouv.fr/sections/a_l_interieur/la_police_nationale/organisation/dcpj/trafic-biens-culturels). With a staff of about 35, this is one of the most effective art squads in Europe in terms of arrests and returns of stolen objects, although it is not the largest organization. In Italy an art unit of more than 150 persons exists as part of the Carabinieri, or military police (http://www.beniculturali.it/menu_servizio/TutelaCulturale.asp). Both France and Italy also operate advanced databases to search for stolen art. Items in these databases are constantly compared with objects in auction catalogues and other open sources.

In Germany police attention to art crimes varies between states; some are quite active, while others pay little perceptible attention to the topic. The National Police Service, Bundeskriminalamt (BKA), in Wiesbaden registers stolen objects although the BKA Web site (http://www.bka.de); the list extends only from 1997 through 2001. Since 2001 no new information has been added.

B. Other Approaches

Private initiatives play an important role in countering the trade in stolen art and antiquities. Private registers of stolen art help recover objects and hinder dealers in stolen objects. Lists of categories of antiquities that are considered outlawed try to limit demand for these objects and to deter dealers from selling them. The most important private register is the ALR. The register can be checked by anyone for a fee. Objects can also be checked in the register from Trace.

The so-called Red List of the International Council of Museums (ICOM) contains categories of items that are regarded as particularly vulnerable. The ICOM is committed to the conservation, continuation, and communication to society of the world's natural and cultural heritage, present and future, tangible and intangible. Created in 1946, the ICOM is a nongovernmental organization maintaining formal relations with UNESCO.

Dealing in items on the Red List is seen by many in the art world as a criminal act or at least as "not done," irrespective of the precise legal or illegal character of these dealings in a particular jurisdiction. Examples of items that have been on a Red List for some time are so-called Nok statues. Currently four Red Lists have been published, for Africa, South America, Iraq, and Afghanistan (http://icom.museum/redlist). The ICOM also has an ethical code for its members, a large group of museums all over the world (http://icom.museum/ethics.html). This ethical code demands compliance with the rules set by the UNESCO Convention. Neither the ethical code nor the Red List is legally binding for the members of the ICOM.

V. Policy Implications and Research Priorities

On the basis of the current body of knowledge about the trade in stolen art and antiquities several tentative recommendations can be offered for both public policies and research in this field.

A. Policy Implications

Discussions about public policies with regard to the trade in stolen art and antiquities tend to focus on ratification of multilateral treaties. However, no concrete evidence or anecdotal indications exist that ratification of these treaties by itself has a significant effect on the trade. The trade is primarily demand-driven and impossible to control with law enforcement means alone.

Legislation in market countries should raise the responsibility of all actors involved by increasing and extending due diligence standards. This should mean that one can claim to be a good faith purchaser of art or antiquities only when all available registers of stolen art or valid export licenses have been checked. Statutes of limitations for art crimes should be prolonged or abolished, depending on the types of objects.

More practical changes can also be recommended. First, law enforcement agencies in market countries should increase their efforts with respect to this type of crime. In several countries this means initiating activity on this topic, as specialized police units do not now exist. Furthermore, the registration of stolen art should be started in countries that lack any registration or increased in countries that have outdated or incomplete registries. The information in these registers should be exchanged between countries to assist in the recovery of stolen objects. It is relatively easy technically to connect databases of stolen art. Besides the national registers and the exchange between national registers the use of the Interpol register should be stimulated and the register itself made more efficient. Finally, and not least important, ways should be found to stimulate an awareness that the illicit art and antiquities trade matters—not because it is illegal, not because it is the most important transnational crime in numbers or monetary terms (it clearly is not), but because major components of human history and culture are being stolen and often are lost forever.

B. Research Priorities

Several research topics demand further empirical study. The destinations of most stolen works of art remain unknown. A minor percentage turns up at some point in auction houses or galleries, but the trajectory of most objects usually cannot be fully reconstructed. Future studies should be guided by several research questions: What kinds of perpetrators are responsible for art thefts? Where do all the stolen objects go? Are they sold to unsuspecting private persons or to complicit dealers? What is the role of insiders in the theft of and trade in works of art?

The trade in looted antiquities has been somewhat more transparent than the trade in stolen art. However, some topics demand further study. Perhaps most important is to determine the scale of the illicit trade, which is largely unknown with respect to many objects and destinations. Furthermore, the role of (civil) wars and similar phenomena should receive much more attention, as unrest is clearly an integral stimulus of illicit trade. Finally, with respect to legislative instruments, research should examine whether more effective legislation can be formulated or whether the existing legislation can be used and interpreted in a more productive way. Despite the great importance that is granted to well-known treaties, there is no convincing evidence that the ratification of these treaties by itself substantially decreases the illicit trade in the countries involved.

NOTES

1. The author would like to express his gratitude for the kind cooperation of the ALR, which provided these numbers.

2. Although this information is relatively old, Turkish authorities are regularly sending long lists of stolen items to foreign governments, which might illustrate their active approach to this problem. At the same time, several authors have pointed to the tremendous loss of cultural heritage in Cyprus due to the Turkish occupation of a part of the island.

3. *Value* is meant here in both real as well as imagined terms. Although prices for the most appreciated works of art have risen to astronomical levels, some economists have pointed out that the rise in prices in the overall market has hardly (or not) outperformed prices of other assets, if all factors are taken into account (such as insurance and maintenance costs, absence of interest or dividends).

4. The author expresses his gratitude to Interpol for providing information on Interpol initiatives.

REFERENCES

Aarons, Lisette. 2001. "Art Theft: An Explanatory Study of the Illegitimate Art Market in Australia." *Australian and New Zealand Society of Criminology* 34(1): 17–37.

Abbott, E. Carl. 2001. "People Who Steal Books." *Left Atrium* 165(12): 1646–47.

Akinsja, Konstantin, and Grogori Kozlov. 1995. *Stolen Treasure: The Hunt for the World's Lost Masterpieces*. London: Weidenfeld and Nicolson.

Alva, Walter. 2001. "Destruction of the Archaeological Heritage of Peru." In *Trade in Illicit Antiquities: The Destruction of the World's Cultural Heritage,* edited by Neil Doole, Jenny Brodie, and Colin Renfrew. Oxford, UK: Oxbow Books.

"Art Dealer Served Time for Fencing Stolen Art." 2001. *Museum Security Network Report,* June 3. http://www.museum-security.org/01/120.html#4.

Baker, Alexi S. 2002. "Selling the Past: United States vs Frederick Schultz." *Archaeology OnlineFeature*. April 22. http://www.archaeology.org/online/features/schultz/index .html.

Bernick, Lauren. 1998. "Art and Antiquities Theft." *Transnational Organized Crime* 4(2): 91–116.

Bischof, Ulf. 2003. *Die Kunst and Antiquitaten Gmbh in Bereich Kommerzielle Koordinierung—Schriften zum Kulturgutenschutz* (*The Art and Antiquities Inc. within Commercial Coordination – Publications on the Protection of Cultural Goods*). Berlin: De Gruyter Recht.

Blutke, Gunther. 1990. *Obskure Geschafte mit Kunst und Antiquitaten—Ein Kriminalreport* (*Shady Dealings with Art and Antiquities – A Crime Report*). Berlin: Links Verlag.

Bogdanons, Matthew. 2005. "The Casualties of War: The Truth about the Iraq Museum." *American Journal of Archaeology* 109(3): 477–525.

Brodie, Neil, and Peter Watson. 2000. *Stealing History—The Illicit Trade in Cultural Material*. Cambridge, UK: McDonald Institute for Archaeological Research.

Brodie, Neil, Jenny Doole, and Colin Renfrew, eds. 2001. *Trade in Illicit Antiquities: The Destruction of the World's Archaeological Heritage*. Cambridge, UK: McDonald Institute for Archaeological Research.

Brown-Syed, Christopher. 1999. "Some Observations on Systematic Book Theft." *Library and Archival Security* 15(1): 83–89.
Canouts, Veletta, and Francis P. McManamon. 2001. "Protecting the Past for the Future: Federal Archaeology in the United States" In *Trade in Illicit Antiquities: The Destruction of the World's Cultural Heritage* edited by Neil Brodie, Jenny Doole, and Colin Renfrew. Oxford, UK: Oxbow Books.
Carabinieri. 2004. *Agenda 2004 Attivita operative*. Rome: Ministry of Culture.
Chamberlin, Russell E. 1983. *Loot—The Heritage of Plunder*. London: Thames and Hudson.
Conklin, John. 1994. *Art Crime*. Westport, CT: Praeger.
Crefeld, Martin van. 1998. *The Transformation of War*. London: Simon and Schuster.
Fuchs, Elisa. 1992. *Göttinnen, Gräber und Geschäfte—Von der Plünderung fremder Kulturen (Goddesses, Graves and Deals – On the Plunder of Foreign Cultures)*. Bern, Switzerland: Erklärung von Bern.
Gilgan, Elizabeth. 2001. "Looting and the Market for Maya Objects: A Belizean Perspective." In *Trade in Illicit Antiquities: The Destruction of the World's Cultural Heritage*, edited by Neil Brodie, Jenny Doole, and Colin Renfrew. Oxford, UK: Oxbow Books.
Gill, David, and Christopher Chippindale. 2002. "The Trade in Looted Antiquities and the Return of Cultural Property: A British Parliamentary Inquiry." *International Journal of Cultural Property* 11(1): 50–64.
"Greece Drops Charges against Getty Curator over Looted Golden Wreath." 2007. CBC News online, November 27. http://www.cbc.ca/world/story/2007/11/27/true-greece-court.html?ref=rss.
Greenfield, Jeanette. 1996. *The Return of Cultural Treasures*. Cambridge: Cambridge University Press.
Hebborn, Eric. 1997. *The Art Forger's Handbook*. New York: Overlook.
Hoving, Thomas. 1996. *False Impressions: The Hunt for Big-Time Art Fakes*. New York: Simon and Schuster.
Interpol. 2007. *Stolen Works of Art DVD*. Lyon, France: Interpol.
Isman, Fabio. 2001. "For That Stolen Vermeer, Follow the Art Squad." *UNESCO Courier*, April, http://www.findarticles.com/p/articles/mi_m1310/is_2001_April/ai_74652534.
Koldehoff, Nora, and Stephan Koldehoff. 2004. *Aktenzeichen Kunst—Die Spektakularsten Kunstdiebstahle der Welt (The Art File – The Most Spectacular Art Thefts in the World)*. Cologne, Germany: DuMont.
Lacey, Robert. 1998. *Sotheby's Bidding for Class*. New York: Little, Brown.
Lloyd, Alan. 1964. *The Drums of Kumasi*. London: Panther.
Massy, Laurence. 2000. *Le Vol d'Oeuvres d'Art—Une Criminalité Méconnue (The Theft of Works of Art – A Misunderstood Crime)*. Brussels: Bruylant.
Matsuda, David J. 1998. *Subsistence Digging in and around Belize*. Ann Arbor, MI: Union Institute.
McLeave, Hugh. 1981. *Rogues in the Gallery—The Modern Plague of Art Thefts*. Boston: David R. Godine.
Middlemas, Keith. 1975. *The Double Market—Art Theft and Art Thieves*. Westmead, UK: Saxon House.
Ministerial Advisory Committee on the Illicit Trade in Cultural Objects. 2000. *Report of the Illicit Trade Advisory Panel*. London: Department for Culture Media and Sport.
Nagashima, Masayuki. 2002. *The Lost Heritage—The Reality of Artifact Smuggling in Southeast Asia*. Bangkok: Post Books.

O'Keefe, Patrick J. 2004. "Preparing for Litigation in the United States: The Schultz Case." Paper presented at the conference Illicit Traffic in Cultural Property in Southeast Asia, Bangkok, Thailand, March 24–26.
Polk, Kenneth, and Christine Alder. 2002. "Stopping This Awful Business: The Illicit Traffic in Antiquities Examined as a Criminal Market." *Art, Antiquity and Law* 11(1): 35–55.
Povoleda, E. 2007. "Progress Seen in Talks on Antiquities." *New York Times Online,* December 1. http://www.nytimes.com/2007/12/01/arts/design/01anti.html.
Prott, Lyndell. 1997. *Commentary on the Unidroit Convention.* Leicester, UK: Institute of Art and Law.
Rascher, Andrea. 2000. *Kulturgütertransfer und Globalisierung* (*Globalism and the Transfer of Cultural Goods*). Zurich, Switzerland: Schulthess Juristische Medien.
Rose, Mark. 1998. "From Cyprus to Munich." *Archaeology Online Features,* April 20. http://www.archaeology.org/online/features/cyprus.
Schick, Jurgen. 1998. *The Gods Are Leaving the Country.* Bangkok: White Orchid Books.
Slayman, Andrew. 1998 "Geneva Seizure." *Archaeology Online Features,* September 14. http://www.archaeology.org/online/features/geneva.
Soudijn, Melvin, and Edgar Tijhuis. 2003. "Some Perspectives on the Illicit Antiquities Trade in China." *Art, Antiquity and Law* 8(2): 149–65.
Thompson, Lawrence S. 1968. *Bibliokleptomania.* Berkeley, CA: Peacock.
Tijhuis, Edgar. 2006. *Transnational Crime and the Interface between Legal and Illegal Actors: The Case of the Illicit Art and Antiquities Trade.* Nijmegen, Netherlands: Wolf Legal Publishers.
———. 2007. "Task Force to Fight Illicit Trafficking in Cultural Property Stolen in Iraq." In *Organized Crime: From Trafficking to Terrorism,* edited by Frank Shanty and Patit Mishra. Santa Monica, CA: ABC CLIO.
Tubb, Kathryn W., ed. 1995. *Antiquities—Trade or Betrayed: Legal, Ethical and Conservation Issues.* London: Archetype.
"Two New Yorkers, Man from Connecticut Charged with Money Laundering." 2001. *Portsmouth Herald,* Massachusetts, June 1. http://www.seacoastonline.com/2001news/6_1_sb1.htm.
Watson, Peter. 1998. *Sotheby's Inside Story.* London: Bloomsbury.
Watson, Peter, and Cecilia Todeschini 2006. *The Medici Conspiracy: The Illicit Journey of Looted Antiquities from Italy's Tomb Raiders to the World's Greatest Museums.* New York: Public Affairs.

CHAPTER 19

CYBERCRIME

SAMUEL C. MCQUADE III

TECHNOLOGICALLY advanced societies offer many and fast-evolving behavioral opportunities and often experience new forms of social deviance and criminality. Crimes enabled by information technology (IT) involving networked computers and other interoperable electronic devices constitute a prevalent, harmful, rapidly growing, and misunderstood phenomenon.

The term *cybercrime* is widely though neither universally nor consistently used. As Wall (2001, p. 1) wrote, "The term cybercrime does not actually do much more than signify the occurrence of a harmful behavior that is somehow related to a computer... [and yet] ... like sticky paper on a shoe, it is a term that cannot be easily shaken off and dismissed as it has quickly become absorbed into popular parlance." *Cybercrime* is a general label for many evolving and emerging types of IT-enabled abuse and crime and builds on previous categorizations of high-tech offending (e.g., Lee 1991; Parker 1998; Denning 1999; Wall 2001). The term encompasses harmful behaviors occurring via cyberspace that transcend geopolitical jurisdictions and confound traditional law enforcement investigation tactics and methods.

Cybercrime includes existing and emerging forms of criminality carried out with electronic IT devices and information systems, including but not limited to the Internet. By *electronic IT devices* I mean servers, desktops, laptops, and mini-computers along with combinations of scanners, copiers, fax machines; telephones and cellular phones; personal digital assistants; pagers; gaming consoles; and other devices capable of connecting to computerized networks. Increasingly IT devices are smaller, interoperable, cost less, and have greater processing speed and memory than earlier versions. They are capable of more extensive multitasking by users (e.g., listening to music, watching movies, or playing electronic games while sending or receiving text messages and other data). Capabilities built into a single device often include Web browsing, audio recordings, digital pictures, and real-time video streams for easy uploading or downloading. All of this can occur in standalone modes or via wired or wireless telecommunications networks. Otherwise known as *information systems,* these computer-controlled networks consist of organizational intranets that connect devices to servers or the Internet (and therefore the World Wide Web).

In this chapter I begin by discussing cybercrime as an evolving technology-based crime construct. This is followed by examples and explanations of emerging IT-enabled abuse and crime and discussion of major types of cybercrime and categories of cyber offenders. The prevalence of cyber offending and victimization is reviewed on the basis of a limited number of available studies. I then discuss responses to cybercrime by numerous investigative, regulatory, and technical assistance entities. I conclude with suggestions for research and discuss possibilities for mounting and sustaining coordinated research, evaluation, and prevention initiatives.

A number of generalizations can be offered:

- Labels and constructs for IT-enabled crime date to Sutherland's (1940) differentiation of white-collar crime from ordinary street crime, yet criminological theory-building that takes account of the role of technology in the evolution of crime remains largely undeveloped.
- An emerging theory of technology-enabled crime, policing, and security (McQuade 2006) provides a new framework for understanding cybercrime.
- Understanding cybercrime requires some knowledge of technical vernaculars and nuanced awareness of behaviors facilitated by IT devices and information systems.
- Complex forms of "malware" (i.e., malicious software such as computer viruses, worms, Trojans, spyware, and adware) and remotely controlled "bot networks" are among the most perplexing and potentially harmful forms of cybercrime.
- Child pornography associated with "child morphing" digitization and human trafficking for sexual purposes are particularly insidious; large-scale research reveals, however, that a considerable amount of what passes for online sex crimes against youth involves teenagers exploring their sexuality and courting one another.
- Categorizations of cybercrimes and cyber offenders are seldom grounded in theory or empirical analysis, but are nonetheless useful and necessary for understanding distinct and potentially observable offending behaviors in specific periods.
- Studies of the nature and extent of cybercrime, and its social and economic effects, are few in number, often focus narrowly on particular types of offending or victimization, and are often weak in definitions and metrics.
- Many forms of cybercrime are increasing, becoming more technologically complex and difficult to manage, and causing seemingly immeasurable harm.

- Many organizations in the United States and other nations are actively attempting to prevent and control cybercrime. The effects of these efforts are seldom evaluated. Information about law enforcement successes typically comes from successful investigations and prosecutions of high-profile incidents.
- Large-scale cyber attacks affecting information infrastructures may constitute threats to national security. Prevention efforts require interagency and departmental coordination at the federal level and capacity building in government and industry partnerships.

I. An Evolving Crime Construct

Technology-enabled crime is nothing new. People have always used tools and techniques to cause harm and commit crimes. The term *cybercrime* was first coined by Sussman (1995) and Heuston (1995) amid a jumble of contemporary IT-related crime labels (e.g., electronic crime, digital crime, Internet crime, high-tech crime, and new age crime). This term naturally developed from earlier conceptualizations and constructs, including computer-related crime, computer crime, computer abuse, economic crime, corporate crime, organized crime, financial crime, and white-collar crime. Conceptual confusion about the meaning and significance of these constructs is attributable to inventions, innovations, and technological diffusion. Nearly 70 years after Sutherland's (1940) identification of "white-collar criminality" we continue to struggle to find meaningful labels for IT-enabled crime.

Technological invention and innovation make new forms of deviance, abuse, and crime inevitable. Some criminologists worry about the usefulness of operationalizing crime constructs, claiming that doing so is unrealistic and impractical. Other scholars disagree. Recognizing that evolving forms of criminality necessarily present new challenges, they accept the need for crime constructs for undertaking research needed to develop prevention and control strategies (National White Collar Crime Center and West Virginia University 1996). Labeling and defining criminological phenomena as they emerge and evolve, and before they can be systematically observed, categorized, and analyzed, presents challenges.

Classical School scholars were concerned with the problems of eighteenth-century legal systems and with punishments imposed without regard for human rights (Williams and McShane 1993), but did not consider how technology, even in those simpler times, enabled deviant, abusive, or criminal behaviors to occur and evolve. Nineteenth-century Positivist School scholars also ignored technology even while exploring "use of scientific methodology, assumption of pathology, classification of criminal types, prediction of criminality, and treatment of criminals" (Williams and McShane 1993, p. 5).

More recently, Sutherland's (1947) differential association theory identified simple-to-complex techniques as an aspect of criminal learning.[1] Cohen and Felson (1979) took account of technology in routine activities theory, and Brantingham and Brantingham (1998, 1999, 2004) identified key crime analysis factors and technologies to be used in environmental criminology. A unifying theory about criminal use of tools, techniques, and systems versus countervailing policing and security technology has only recently been proposed and remains substantially untested (see McQuade 1998, 2001, 2005, 2006, pp. 175–79).

The essence of technology-enabled crime, policing, and security theory is its integration of earlier writings about crime causation with technology principles relating to invention, innovation, adoption, adaptation, implementation, personnel training, supervised use of tools and systems, maintenance, evaluation, and diffusion. It builds on the work of many theorists, including Sutherland (1940), Cohen and Felson (1979), and Akers (1985). "It is based on elements of classical criminology (i.e., choice and deterrence theories), as well as components of various social process, social structure and conflict theories and takes into account aspects of trait theories, especially arousal, cognitive, and behavioral trait theories" (McQuade 2006, p. 176).

The theory proposes 10 essential hypotheses (McQuade 2006, pp. 176–79). First, technologies are combinations of tools, techniques, and systems ranging from simple to complex in their design, materials, construction, manufacturing processes, adoption, social implementation, technical and systems integration, and applications. Criminals, police, and security professionals employ a full range of available technologies for similar and countervailing purposes.

Second, forms of deviance, social abuse, and crime, that is *new crimes,* are committed through innovative uses of technology. Initially new crime is not well understood, and is therefore relatively complex, because investigative experts tend not to be able to explain to other investigative experts how criminals are using technologies.

Third, faced with relatively complex crime and attendant management problems, police, security professionals, and prosecutors innovate with countervailing technologies to overcome and try to stay ahead of technological gains made by criminals. With increased understanding and law enforcement interdiction, new crimes transform into better understood *adaptive crimes,* and laws criminalizing adaptive behaviors begin to be enacted.

Fourth, formulating and enacting new crime laws and regulations raise public awareness. Attitudinal and behavioral changes begin to emerge in ways that precipitate arrest and prevention of adaptive crimes.

Fifth, eventually laws are adopted and diffused as a form of legal or social technology that leads to increased investigation and prosecution. When this happens, formerly new and then adaptive crime transforms into *ordinary crime* that is much better understood, routinely recognized, and systematically targeted.

Sixth, enhanced enforcement, combined with technological advances, compel criminals to adopt new technologies. This begins anew the cycle of technological competition between criminals and the police.

Seventh, criminals who do not adopt new technologies are at greater risk of being caught unless and until their technological capabilities exceed those of law enforcement and security professionals. Similarly, law enforcement and security professionals must consistently develop, adopt, and diffuse new technologies or risk falling behind in their crime-fighting capabilities. Recurring criminal and police innovation cycles have a "ratcheting-up" effect akin to a military arms race.

Eighth, crime and policing become increasingly complex as a function of increasingly complex tools and techniques employed by criminals, police, and security professionals. The result is perpetually complex technology-enabled crime, policing, and security management.

Ninth, once developed, adopted, and understood, tools and techniques tend to remain in use because of their continuing functionality and constraints to technology development or adoption. The result is a full range of relatively simple (ordinary) to relatively complex (new) forms of crimes and countervailing investigation and prevention methods.

Tenth, criminals and police always wonder about their adversaries' activities, and each group may not fully understand the consequences of their own uses of technology. This can result in unintended positive and negative spin-off effects. Over time, technology becomes better understood, thus relatively less complex, and crimes become more manageable, except to the extent that criminal innovations disrupt relatively stable technological competitions between law-abiding and violating forces in society.

These propositions provide a framework for understanding all forms of criminality with respect to their technological underpinnings and societal contexts of prevention and control. The framework was developed (McQuade 1998) and later expanded and provisionally tested in doctoral research that triangulated findings using three methodologies: content analysis of purposive expert interview transcripts; historical reconstruction of the technology of money laundering in the United States as a proxy for several increasingly complex IT-enabled crimes; and archival research comparing federal money laundering prosecution records for evidence of increasing technological complexity in two time periods, 1986–92 and 1993–99 (McQuade 2001).

Crime and policing coevolve. Technological complexity generally facilitates high-tech criminality and impairs effective policing because of long-standing bureaucratic routines, law enforcement and security organization inertia, inefficiencies associated with centralized government technology procurement, technology-driven operating platforms, constrained organizational missions, relatively simplistic, limited, or non-use of IT in law enforcement organizations, technology-oriented leadership that fails to recognize and use the potential of emerging IT, and lagged perceptions in police cultures of new versus old technology needs and skills.

We should not be surprised that it takes a long time for scientific findings to take shape and take hold, especially because criminology is an eclectic field amalgamating insights from sociology, cultural anthropology, psychology, economics, public administration, and public policy. Still, more than 50 years have passed since the onset of computer abuse, a case of financial account "salami slicing" in a Minneapolis bank (Parker 1989).[2]

Criminologists have relied on a limited set of theories and concerned themselves primarily with understanding why crime occurs rather than why and how it occurs and evolves technologically and the implications of this knowledge for justice system administration. Technology tends to be taken as given, an inevitable function of technological development, the marketplace, and other societal developments (i.e., as background noise).

An increasing number of criminologists recognize what many criminal justice and security practitioners have long known: assessing emerging technological threats posed by criminals is necessary for protecting critical information infrastructures on which modernized nations depend (see, e.g., National Research Council 1991; McLoughlin 1996; President's Commission on Critical Infrastructure Protection 1997). Agencies of the U.S. government and other nations have taken up the cause.

II. IT-Enabled Abuse and Crime

Preventing or controlling IT-enabled abuse, crime, and victimization requires the understanding of some technical vernacular along with technological aspects of behaviors involving information systems and electronic devices. *Information systems* include wired and wireless telecommunications networks controlled by computerized switches. Examples are intranets that connect computer workstations of individual users to servers within facilities, and the Internet, on which the World Wide Web rests. Networks allow people using computers and other IT devices to create, change, manipulate, send, receive, save, archive, and destroy digitized information.[3]

Information systems and electronic devices are principally used to send, receive, manipulate, and save data. Sending and receiving capabilities enable a condition that IT professionals colloquially refer to as "talking to each other." Interoperable telecommunications, coupled with harmful behaviors of human beings, underpin cybercrime and distinguish it from many other forms of crime.

Commoditization implies that such devices are becoming readily available, less expensive, more versatile, easier to use, and more commonly used. IT devices are also becoming more functional. As commodities they have greater memory and processing speed and are able to support multitasking such as sending and receiving text messages, simultaneous Web browsing, listening to music, or watching movies, among other types of online or standalone activities. IT commoditization combined with a steady stream of inventions and innovations has produced worldwide Internet connectivity that has transformed manufacturing, commerce, transportation, education, and governance in ways that as recently as 1995 were unimaginable.

Computerization has introduced new forms of criminality and circumstantially changed many aspects of traditional crimes. For example, whereas certain varieties of spam (massively distributed e-mail) represent relatively new forms of legally proscribed behavior, street drug trafficking may now also involve various IT devices used to coordinate sales via encrypted text or voice messaging. Computer trespassing (i.e., unlawfully accessing an information system or exceeding authorized permissions on a network) has been transformed through the technological specter of "bot networks" (also known as "botnets" or simply "bots") that can facilitate simultaneous intelligence gathering, hacking, and launching of distributed denial-of-service attacks, among other crimes, via remotely seized and controlled computers (McQuade 2006, chapter 3).

A wide variety of forms of malware (i.e., malicious software) now exist. "Cryptoviruses" are designed to attack computers, encrypt data, and orchestrate threats, sometimes in the form of a ransom note demanding payment lest valuable data be destroyed, released to competitors, or used for blackmail (Symantec 2004). "Metamorphic worms" are sophisticated codes capable of shifting their design according to security measures encountered so that firms may not recognize their true destructive power until their information systems have been compromised. Viruses, Trojans, worms, and adware or spyware can infect digital cell phones and other types of mobile devices in ways that stick unsuspecting victims with huge phone bills, damaged operating systems or software applications, lost or damaged data, or worse (see, e.g., item 3 in Thompson 2004).

These and other IT-enabled crimes greatly expand the number of potential offenders and victims. This has unprecedented implications for protecting information systems worldwide and for international criminal justice system administration. Even new devices with increasingly high levels of information security installed by manufacturers may be vulnerable immediately or soon after they come to market. Apple's iPhone, released in June 2007, for example, was criticized three months later because its calculator software was found to be vulnerable to being hacked and granting root file authority to online perpetrators. Zetter (2007) reported that a hacker could potentially remotely hijack an iPhone to operate the unit's built-in camera, make and receive phone calls, intercept and send text messages, or trace the owner's location via WiFi network systems without the owner's knowledge.

IT devices not adequately safeguarded with security updates to their operating systems and software applications are highly vulnerable. Media accounts contain many examples of government agencies, financial institutions, universities, and federal research labs, such as Lawrence Livermore, that have not adequately protected sensitive data. Numerous cases have involved unauthorized releases of thousands of personal account records, leading the federal government and many state governments to enact legislation requiring victim notification in such events. IT devices, software application, operating systems, and malware design complexities are expanding potential effects (i.e., with respect to the variety and scale of denial, disruption, destruction, or theft of data and associated financial costs of restoring information systems integrity; CERT Coordination Center 2003). This qualitatively distinguishes cybercrimes from traditional crimes such as theft, assault, and burglary, even when such traditional crimes are incidentally facilitated with IT devices offline.

Many observers point out that cybercrimes are more ominous than traditional crimes because they allow offenders to carry out multiple attacks at any time, from anywhere, partly or completely anonymously, against information systems, and thus to target very large numbers of potential victims simultaneously in ways that may go undetected for extended periods. There are additional qualitative differences between cybercrimes and traditional crimes that, if not understood, compromise both research and intervention strategies (McQuade 2007*b*). First, cybercrime occurs because someone uses information systems and electronic IT devices to invade and possibly damage technology and digitized data of other people. Second, organizations are physical environments in which illicit uses of electronic devices, and activities for which they are used, are easily concealed and possibly detected only via electronic monitoring of information systems (i.e., online or network) activity. Third, cybercrimes can result in damage to hardware, software, and data. This can occur intentionally or inadvertently as the result of what a perpetrator does online, combined with insufficient security knowledge or countermeasures. Fourth, accessing, possessing, and then using data of varying value and confidence (i.e., privacy expectations) are central to committing cybercrimes. Data that do not already exist in digital form can be digitized with scanners and then transposed into or onto various media for illicit online or offline purposes. Fifth, different types of cybercrime can co-occur in single or multiple incidents and be committed by individuals or groups whose combined expertise facilitates commission of increasingly numerous and complex crimes. Sixth, cybercrimes can occur separately or in combination with traditional crimes depending on knowledge, skills, organizational means, and resources, including access to information systems. Seventh, cybercrimes invariably involve physical activities that underscore cyber transactions: someone, initially at least, must have an input device; only then can illicit online activities occur. Eighth, offenders can use multiple information systems and electronic devices located in single or multiple locations from which to launch cyber attacks physically or remotely; these can be staged to occur sequentially or simultaneously against targets anywhere in the connected world. Ninth, many victims know perpetrators in person or online beforehand. Having been targeted, contacted, and manipulated, victims are often tricked into divulging personal or organizational information, which is then used to commit crimes. Tenth, social engineering tactics are fundamental to intelligence gathering for nearly all forms of cybercrime. Phishing is a quasi-automated example used for online manipulation to acquire passwords or other valuable personal account data, intelligence gathering, and attacks against information systems.

III. Cybercrime and Cyber Criminals

The evolving nature of IT-enabled crime implies that victimization is not predicated on illicit behaviors being proscribed in criminal laws or even by organizational policies. Such behaviors may initially involve abuse of information systems, computers, and other IT devices in ways not yet criminal. IT devices are increasingly networked via intranets and other networks such as the Internet. Social norms, perceptions of abuse, criminal laws, justice system policies, and crime prevention and control strategies evolve in response to criminal innovations using technological systems, tools, and techniques. Different labels for overlapping and validated crime constructs remain important (e.g., white-collar crime, financial crime, organized crime). Observable and measurable variables needed for research into the nature and extent of IT-enabled crime exist and can be put into use even though things are constantly changing.

A fundamental problem in labeling and categorizing crime is that all typologies suffer from questionable cut points (i.e., what qualifies as this rather than something else?). Categories in high-tech crime have derived from theoretically scattered perspectives, have not been consistently operationalized, and have not generally been empirically validated. Examples of categorizations include hackers, crackers, phreakers, and pirates (Lee 1991); utopians, cyberpunks, cyber spies, and cyber terrorists (Young 1993); pranksters, hackers, malicious hackers, personal problem solvers, career criminals, extreme advocates, and a catchall group consisting of malcontents, addicts, and irrational or incompetent people (Parker 1998); and activists, hactivists, and cyber terrorists (Denning 1999).

These and similar typologies were well-intended efforts to characterize offending in particular periods on the basis of media accounts, limited interview and survey research, occasional content analysis of online traffic among suspected offender groups (e.g., from hacker forums), examination of police records, and a mixture of anecdotes and informed opinions. In 2004 a colleague and I (McQuade and Castellano 2004) surveyed 873 randomly selected college students attending Rochester Institute of Technology and identified five statistically significant and distinct forms of cyber offending among this population: *hackers* who disrupt or deny computer services, publicly disclose security flaws, and write or distribute harmful software; *harassers* who use computers to harass, threaten, and distribute passwords without permission; *pirates* who illegally download music, movies, or software; *academic cheats* who use computers or other IT devices to plagiarize or cheat on assignments or exams; and *data snoops* who guess passwords or illegally gain access to information systems solely to look at data or files. Although findings from this single study cannot be generalized, they demonstrate technological preferences and specialization in relatively high to low tech and in more modern to traditional types of criminal offending.

The field seems forever destined to pursue meaningful labels, categories, and typologies and the people who engage in such behaviors (see e.g., Chung et al. 2006; S. Gordon and Ford 2006). Nonetheless, developing categories of offending behavior is integral to and needed for research and warrants continual reconsideration when designing and undertaking cybercrime studies. It is important that categories be logically deduced and reasonably comprehensive, but not conceptually overlapping, and validated with respect to a certain population. Given what we know or suspect about cyber abuse and IT-enabled criminal offending by individuals, the 12 categories listed in box 19.1, "Categories of Cyber Offenders," emerge (McQuade 2006, p. 132).

Those categories are not mutually exclusive because any offender can conceivably engage in any of the described behaviors. The typology has not been empirically tested with any population, much less a general population, nor is it likely to be. Convenience samples (traditionally of college or secondary school students when it comes to IT-enabled crime studies) do not represent general populations and therefore cannot provide an accurate picture of cybercrime offending or victimization. Gaining access to subsets of criminals who use IT for illicit behaviors, much less acquiring truthful information from them, is difficult to impossible.

All users of computers or other IT devices have probably inadvertently or intentionally committed some form of online abuse or offending described in the box. In the Rochester Institute of Technology study (McQuade and Castellano 2004) a large proportion of students acknowledged sharing network passwords in violation of university policies, and a large majority acknowledged illegally downloading music, movies, or software. None of these behaviors was construed by students as being deviant, even though they are all abusive, potentially harmful, or criminal.

The category "cyber terrorists" is as yet only a theoretical possibility, although it is now well-established in military and intelligence circles that many nations, including the United States, engage in the doctrine of network-centric warfare that includes use of information systems to launch attacks against critical information infrastructures of enemy states. In April 2007 the Associated Press reported strong evidence that Russian government computer servers were used to launch attacks against the highly developed information infrastructure of Estonia, temporarily crippling government, media, and financial sector Web sites. In the aftermath, Estonian leader Toomas Hendrik Ives and U.S. President George W. Bush convened

Box 19.1. Categories of Cyber Offenders

Major categories of cyber offenders are as follows:

- *Negligent users* who use information systems while violating security policies or who do not practice sound information security practices and thereby expose their data or that residing on a network to harm.
- *Traditional criminals* who use computers or other electronic IT devices for communications or record keeping in support of their illegal activities.
- *Fraudsters and thieves,* including those who phish, spoof, spam, or otherwise deceive people online for financial gain.
- *Hackers, computer trespassers, and password crackers* who break computer account passwords or unlawfully enter information systems to commit online or offline crimes, or, in the tradition of the original hacker ethic (Levy 1984, p. 40), use computers to explore, learn about, and take control of systems illegally in order to commit pranks or find, exploit, or expose security vulnerabilities.
- *Malicious code writers and distributors* who create, copy, or release disruptive or destructive viruses, Trojans, worms, or adware or spyware programs.
- *Music, movie, and software pirates* who use IT to violate copyright laws by illegally copying, distributing, downloading, selling, or possessing software applications, data files, or code.
- *Harassers and extortionists* who use technologies to threaten, embarrass, annoy, or coerce. (Young offenders in this category are conventionally referred to as "cyber bullies.")
- *Stalkers, pedophiles, and other sex offenders* who use online or in-person methods to gain illegal sexual pleasure from or power over people. This includes offenders who use the Internet to facilitate sex tourism or human trafficking for sexual purposes.
- *Academic cheats* who use IT tools and techniques to plagiarize or cheat on assignments or exams, or who fake research methods or findings for profit or fame.
- *Organized criminals* who use computers or electronic devices in the course of their legal and illegal business enterprise.
- *Corporate, government, and freelance spies* who use simple to complex tools and methods of espionage, including spyware and key logger applications, to snoop for personal or professional purposes.
- *Cyber terrorists* who try to advance their social, religious, or political goals by instilling widespread fear or by damaging or disrupting critical information infrastructure.

Source: McQuade 2006, p. 132.

talks that discussed the possibility of developing a NATO research center to focus on such cyber attacks (McKinnon 2007).

One chapter on cybercrime cannot discuss detailed aspects of all forms of online offending. However, child pornography deserves special explanation and comment because it is so offensive and potentially exasperating for investigators, and because enormous legislative, enforcement, and media attention have been given to it. U.S. federal law forbids the creation, distribution, and possession of child pornography (i.e., photographic or video images of juveniles engaged in sexual activities or exposing their genitals). The same is true of most, but not all, other nations. Consequently online content legally created, distributed, or accessed online in one nation may be illegal elsewhere even though child pornography is abundant on the Internet despite international conventions to the contrary. The ubiquity of online child pornography hinges on the existence of clandestine rings of offenders who use encrypted Web or Internet newsletters that employ code words for types of victims illustrated (Jenkins 2001), as well as on ubiquitous searching for and consumption of legal pornography by millions of paying customers and other people who drive market demands for online adult entertainment.

Online child pornography involves underage persons being lured into pornographic productions or being sold or forced into cyber sex or lives of prostitution (CNN staff author 2001). Southeast Asian nations, Cambodia in particular, have been cited for being duplicitous regarding human trafficking (Hughes 2003). However, many nations, including the United States, fall short of taking necessary actions to control this abhorrent form of crime (U.S. Department of State 2007). "Kidnapping and international smuggling of young girls and boys for these purposes is now a transnational crime phenomenon often instigated in impoverished nations where victims face dire economic circumstances" (Chinov 2000). But to the extent that minors themselves engage in the creation and distribution of nude photographs and videos, such as when using cell phones or social computing forums to show off or court each other, they too are violating child pornography laws.

Pornography that features child and adolescent models can be especially challenging because law enforcement officers must make determinations about a victim's identity, whereabouts, and true age at the time of photographing or filming. U.S. investigators must also determine whether depicted content is of real persons or merely of holographic images made to look like underage persons posing in sexually explicit ways (McQuade 2006, pp. 97–98). Although not illegal in the United States, digital imaging technologies and computers combined with makeup, lighting, and camera angles make it easy to create real or contrived images of real girls and boys being older or younger than they actually are (a process known as child morphing). McQuade (2006) describes child morphing in some detail.

IV. Prevalence

The limited number of studies examining computer abuse and IT-enabled offending is stunning. Several things have contributed to this, including a primary focus by practitioners and researchers alike on violent and other traditional forms of crime. U.S. state and national crime reporting systems exclude or significantly limit data gathering on these types of IT-related crime and the technologies used in their commission. Financial and other organizations are often unwilling to report losses for fear of losing consumer or investor confidence. And only a small number of scholars are interested in computer crime issues. This is probably because criminology graduate training is rooted in established criminal justice issues and criminological theories, with some other social science perspectives, and includes very limited or no cross-training in science, technology, and society studies. Very limited funding and publishing outlets for high-tech crime behavioral research have also contributed to the dearth of empirical studies. Few scholars have been able to secure tenure on the basis of publishing solely on high-tech crime.

Scholars who investigated computer-related crime issues from 1970 to 2000 did so with little or no grant funding. A select few were commissioned by the National Institute of Justice (NIJ) for specific projects in the late 1980s (e.g., Conly 1989; Hollinger 1989; McEwen, Fester, and Nugent 1989; Parker 1989; Rosenblatt 1989). But only recently have NIJ and other agencies of the federal government begun to develop a comprehensive technology R&D and behavioral research agenda focused on IT-enabled deviancy, abuse and offending. Government-sponsored studies in other nations have been equally rare. Consequently more than half a century following the onset of computer abuse we know fairly little about the nature and extent of IT-enabled offending and victimization behaviors or effective criminal justice system countermeasures.

There have been a few exceptions. First, identity theft has been documented by investigations sponsored by the Federal Trade Commission (Synovate 2003), the National Institute of Justice (Newman and McNally 2005), and, most recently, the Bureau of Justice Statistics in the National Crime Victimization Survey (Baum 2006): "About 1.6 million households experienced theft of existing accounts other than a credit card (such as a banking account), and 1.1 million households discovered misuse of personal information (such as social security number)....Ten percent of the households with incomes of $75,000 or higher experienced identity theft; that was about twice the percentage of households earning less than $50,000. [And] across all types of identity theft, the average amount lost per household was $1,620" (Baum 2006, p. 1).

Second, cybercrime technology tools, methods, and technological countermeasures (G. R. Gordon et al. 2002; McQuade 2006, chapters 3, 9, 10) have been investigated, along with capability assessments and the capacity-building and intervention needs of local, state, and federal law enforcement and prosecution agencies (e.g., Stambaugh et al. 2000; Nasheri 2004; National Institute of Standards and Technology 2004; Burd 2006; McQuade 2007*b*).

Third, international perspectives about the global reach and effects of cybercrime along with descriptions of needed intervention strategies and efforts have become available, including, for example, the Council of Europe's International Convention on Cybercrime, which took effect in July 2004, and recent symposia intended to maintain and expand international cooperation (see, e.g., United Nations 1997, 2001; Commission of the European Communities 2002; Council of Europe 2007).

Fourth, various measures of cybercrime and information systems security effectiveness as indicated by unscientific reports are periodically released by practitioner organizations and well-respected academic institutions, such as those in the United States, including the Computer Security Institute in partnership with the San Francisco Regional Office of the FBI, the National White Collar Crime Center, and Carnegie Mellon University's Computer Emergency Response Team (CERT) Coordination Center.

As criminology and criminal justice programs of study generate interest in high-tech crime issues commensurate with course offerings in computer crime issues and digital immigrant experiences (Prensky 2001), research findings about the prevalence of other types of cybercrime are beginning to emerge, especially those involving youth as offenders and victims. These include several small studies and a few larger surveys of youth of varying ages using either random or convenience sampling to ascertain levels and correlates of pirating, online sex crimes and promiscuity, and cyber bullying (see, e.g., Finn 2004; Jones and Lenhart 2004; McQuade and Castellano 2004; Princeton Survey Research Associates International 2007).

Notable studies include the national Youth Internet Safety Surveys of 1999 and 2005. The first of these found that among 1,501 youths ages 10 to 17 randomly surveyed (Finkelhor, Wolak, and Mitchell 2000), 6 percent were harassed online within the past year; 2 percent were extremely upset or afraid due to a harassment episode; 25 percent were exposed to unwanted sexual material; 5 percent received unwanted solicitations for sex; 3 percent received a solicitation that included an attempt to contact the youth in person, over the phone or via postal mail; 97 percent of solicitations were made by people the victim had met online; 48 percent of overall solicitations for sex and 48 percent of unwanted solicitations were made by juveniles themselves (under 18 years old); 65 percent of solicitations occurred in chat rooms and 24 percent via instant messenger; and 49 percent of victims did not tell anyone about the incidents. Findings from the 2005 survey of 1,388 randomly selected respondents ages 6 to 17 were similar and included that one in three were victimized online and victims felt angry, sad or depressed and often did not tell their parents what was going on for fear of losing computer privileges (Wolak, Mitchell, and Finkelhor 2006).

The combined behaviors of online gaming, cellular phone text messaging, and social networking on forums such as UTube, MySpace, and Facebook have inspired additional research into the nature and extent of Internet activities by and among youth, along with risks they encounter while online (see, e.g., studies by Mitchell, Finkelhor, and Wolak 2001; Daniel 2002; Cyberspace Research Unit 2002; Berson and Berson 2005; Lenhart and Madden 2007). Research is also beginning to expose possibilities of so-called Internet or computer addiction (Shaffer, Hall, and Vander

Bilt 2000; Vaugeois 2006) and to correlate time spent online gaming with cyber bullying among other IT-enabled activities (McQuade 2007*a*).

The largest and most comprehensive survey research of youth IT offending and victimization has now been completed by the author and colleagues in the region of Rochester, New York. Preliminary findings based on a randomized selection of school classrooms and a survey of 40,079 students in kindergarten through 12th grade in 14 school districts confirm that children begin using the Internet at very young ages. Most students use their home computers, cell phones, and other mobile devices, as well as those of their friends, without close parental supervision, positive role modeling, or school instruction on how to be safe, secure, and ethical online. Specific findings (McQuade and Sampat 2008) reveal that within the prior year:

- Most kindergarten-age children use the Internet and are exposed to content that makes them feel uncomfortable, yet one in four do not report disturbing incidents or materials to grownups.
- Cyber bullying begins in second grade; at the same age, 8 percent of children report seeing or being told private things about the bodies of other people online.
- Illegal pirating of music, movies, and software via p2p networks begins in fourth grade, as does children's sharing of personal information about themselves with friends and strangers online.
- By middle school (grades 7–9) approximately 11 percent of students report defeating Internet filtering and blocking software installed on home computers by parents. They engage in many forms of cyber-enabled offending, spanning academic dishonesty to purchasing illegal and prescription drugs online. They are also victims of many types of online abuse and crime, not limited to those of a sexual nature, and many youth are victimized in more than one way every year.

Our research also reveals that these trends continue through high school and into college years; that cybercrime against young people involves much more than adult sex offenders targeting adolescents; and that most online abuse and crime involving youth goes unreported and undetected. Youth victimize each other online even as they are victimized by adults. They often know offenders beforehand (McQuade and Sampat 2008). Research indicates that as youth age and use the Internet to socially interact through instant messaging, electronic gaming, chat rooms, blogs, and Web forums, most of them will eventually experience and engage in some form of online abuse or crime. For millions of young Internet users online victimization and offending experiences are common, tolerated, and even expected (i.e., nondeviant and a normal aspect of being online). By traditional standards of civility, good and alarming if not actually harmful, aspects of what I have come to call "contemporary digital youth culture" are of increasing concern to parents, educators, criminal justice officials, and mental health professionals. The emerging picture is that online abuse and crimes begin early in life, are ubiquitous, and, though we have no reliable metrics or research mechanisms to estimate monetary effects, may cause billions of dollars in social and economic harm (McQuade 2006, pp. 203–9).

V. Prevention and Control Capabilities

Youth in most nations grow up largely without benefit of systematic education or training in information security, Internet safety, or cyber ethics. Most parents, teachers, and other adults in positions of responsibility for children are misinformed or complacent about online threats to child safety and about youth offending. Despite federally sponsored programs beginning in the mid-1990s, such as NetSmartz and i-Safe (along with dozens of other online instructional resources for primary and secondary education), most children are left to their own devices and online networking. Throughout 2008 the Internet Safety Technical Task Force established by the Berkman Center for Internet and Society at Harvard Law School explored online safety technologies that could be used or developed by many companies across multiple platforms. However, Congress, most state legislatures, the media, and policing agencies continue to emphasize enforcement and regulatory strategies concerning online sexual predators rather than education as a means to prevent cyber offending.

Prevention of cybercrime cannot be limited to youth. Nor is preventing cybercrime the purview or responsibility of any single nation, justice system, or agency. The many forms of cybercrime, its evolving nature and ubiquity, and IT critical information infrastructures dictate worldwide responses. IT administrators, information security professionals, and high-tech crime investigators and prosecutors have important roles to play. So do common and professional users of devices and information systems (President's Commission on Critical Infrastructure Protection 1997).

Numerous U.S. federal and state regulations and laws affecting cybercrime have been enacted since the late 1970s. Federal laws have four primary purposes (Science Applications International Corporation 1995): protecting individual privacy and access to government information, securing U.S. government information and information services, ensuring critical information infrastructure availability and reliability, and defining IT-enabled misuse, abuse, and crime. Many agencies have regulatory authority for overseeing IT security practices and standards via key legislation. The Sarbanes-Oxley Act of 2002 governs financial accounting and reporting practices of publicly held corporations. The Financial Services Modernization (Gramm-Leach-Bliley) Act of 1999 authorizes eight federal agencies to protect personal and financial privacy. The Health Insurance Portability and Accountability Act of 1996 requires medical service providers to assure the privacy and security of patient treatment data. Other agencies are entrusted with investigating cybercrimes or lending support for their prevention and control.

Following the September 11 terrorist attacks the USA Patriot Act strengthened the cybercrime investigation powers of federal agencies by enabling them to seek support from Internet service providers and telecommunications companies. This controversial law also authorized the creation of regional electronic crimes task forces that, under the direction of the U.S. Secret Service, facilitate information sharing among government, industry, and academia. The FBI maintains an organizational network known as InfraGard that fosters sharing of critical infrastructure protection information with state and local law enforcement agencies, private corporations, and academic institutions. The Financial Crimes Task Force, spearheaded by the Financial Crimes Enforcement Network of the U.S. Department of the Treasury, has achieved greater cooperation among financial organizations in reporting of money laundering and other online financial crimes.

Private security firms provide information security and cybercrime investigative services to financial institutions experiencing incidents that are not reported to public police. The extent to which public and private policing and security services overlap is not documented, nor are the number and relative capabilities of organizations engaged in this effort. The vast majority of public law enforcement agencies lack capabilities to engage in cybercrime investigations and have good reason not to do so. Political imperatives, limited resources, prevailing practices, and limited understanding often result in police and prosecutors paying more attention to crime problems in human and legal terms rather than with respect to technology. Consequently only the most egregious cybercrimes are investigated and prosecuted, usually by federal, state-level, or large metropolitan police agencies with specialized high-tech crime units. Such units are able to provide only limited technical support to smaller agencies.

Key national and international cybercrime investigative and technical assistance agencies include Carnegie Mellon's CERT Coordination Center; the FBI Cyber Division; the Financial Crime Division of the U.S. Secret Service; the High Technology Crime Investigators Association; the Information Systems Security Association; the International Criminal Police Organization (Interpol); the National Center for Missing and Exploited Children; the National White Collar Crime Center; the SysAdmin, Audit, Network, Security Institute; the U.S. Computer Emergency Readiness Team of the U.S. Department of Homeland Security; and the Computer Crime and Intellectual Property Section of the U.S. Department of Justice. Mission objectives of most of these organizations have been described by McQuade (2006, pp. 337–41).

VI. Policy and Research

Cybercrime is constantly evolving, transcends physical places and spaces, and has no geopolitical boundaries. Cybercrime includes new forms of online crime sometimes combined with traditional crimes. Scholars have contributed relatively small and incremental though important advances to understanding of the nature and extent of computer abuse, computer crime, computer-related crime, and particular forms of cybercrime. There is broad consensus that cybercrime threatens many institutional sectors and critical information infrastructure. Many countries are developing capabilities to prevent and control many forms of cybercrime. These efforts are scattered across public and private sectors in a complicated web of laws, policies, organizations, data systems, and programs, of which only a few have been described here. Fewer still have been evaluated.

Too often policy making responds to innovative use of technology by criminals rather than acting systematically to prevent increasingly complex crimes. Recent proposals to require sex offenders to register their e-mail and instant message accounts and Web sites, and to direct police to crack down on teenagers exchanging nude pictures of themselves, are in the main ill-conceived. The challenge for research is to discover causes and correlates of cybercrime offending and victimization, including the roles of technology. The challenge for policy making is to promote physical and cyber environments conducive to legal use of technologies by law enforcement, security officials, and the public while thwarting harmful deviance and crime.

More research needs to be undertaken in all areas of cybercrime offending and victimization. Agreement is needed as to what constitutes cybercrime and various types of cyber offending. The emerging theory of technology-enabled crime, policing, and security, earlier described, is a useful start. A full range of exploratory and confirming research is needed to develop and test hypotheses. Metrics, especially for assessing social and economic effects, need to be developed and validated. Special attention and research investments should be directed toward further understanding of the nature, extent, and causal factors of cybercrime experienced by youth and young adults who, on a worldwide basis, represent the future majority of online victims and offenders. The Committee on Law and Justice of the National Research Council should formally assess the strength of scientific research and findings on cybercrime issues. U.S. R&D institutions, including the National Science Foundation, the Department of Homeland Security, the Department of Justice, and agencies within the military and intelligence community, should consider whether large-scale cybercrimes constitute national security threats. Interventions by civilian law enforcement and private security apparatuses compared with those by the military and intelligence communities should be documented and assessed (see discussion of this by McQuade 2006, pp. 106–8, 247–65).

Current research sponsored by the National Science Foundation into trusted information systems is important to national economic security, but so are studies that seek to correlate deviant and unlawful behaviors with invention, innovation, and adoption of information systems and electronic IT devices. The United States can learn from the British Home Office's long-standing interest in advancing situational crime prevention by designing opportunities for crime out of technological products. This approach is contrary to that historically taken by the NIJ leadership in supporting new technology R&D primarily to aid in detecting contraband and apprehending offenders, advance interoperable communications technologies used by law enforcement agencies, and promote officer and public safety during field encounters with suspects or those already incarcerated. The NIJ has seldom integrated its technology R&D with its behavioral research and evaluation agenda. Moreover, the U.S. government is loath to pick technology winners among manufacturers, so industrial sectors involved in technology development for criminal justice systems improvement must often engage in their own R&D while relying on government primarily for standards setting.

Finally, the United States should ponder whether the time has come for a presidential commission on the prevention of cybercrime. Three times since the onset of computerization eminent bipartisan and scientific panels have considered the fundamental areas of crime prevention and criminal justice systems reform in contexts of emerging technology-enabled crime threats. The President's Commission on Law Enforcement and Administration of Justice (1967) addressed the challenge of crime in a free society, along with implications for science and technology improvements needed in policing, courts, and corrections. This commission did not explicitly recognize the ominous threat that computer abuse then presented.

The President's Commission on Organized Crime (1984) explored the national and international aspects of computer abuse. Development over the next 20 years fundamentally changed understanding of organized crime and set the stage for what is now unraveling in cyberspace. Computerization has greatly expanded the potential structuring, methods, and markets through which organized crime can profit. Gambling can now take place online and internationally, as can the sale of illegal pornography, sex-related services, tobacco, and alcoholic beverages. However, organized crime takes these and other classical means of profit to new sophisticated levels involving encrypted, coded, and wireless communications; Web-based data mining for intelligence gathering on potential targets; creation and distribution of malware that can be used for online extortion or in bot-enabled distributed denial-of-service attacks; spam and phishing schemes coupled with mass credit card fraud and identity theft; password cracking and computer hacking to facilitate all the above, along with corporate espionage in search of trade secrets; and theft of intellectual property, including pirating and international sales of music, movies, and software. Many combinations and variations of these methods and goals are now technologically possible and frequently involve offenders going to great lengths to disguise their identity (McQuade and Kozak, forthcoming).

The President's Commission on Critical Infrastructure Protection (1997) examined links between cyber and physical assets of national importance and made policy recommendations concerning prevention and control of cybercrimes. Since then information assurance has become the watchword among information security professionals, but today's law enforcement officers remain largely occupied with crime fighting in traditional ways, occasionally venturing into high-tech crime investigations as resources, expertise, and political will insist or allow. Ten years and several IT generations later, it may be time for a fresh and comprehensive look at where America stands on this most exasperating of crime issues.

NOTES

1. See also Akers (1985, 1998); Burgess and Akers (1966).

2. "Salami slicing" refers to siphoning off rounded sums in digital financial transactions for automated deposits. For example, if a transaction involved $393.5848, an illicit computer code could direct posting of only $393.58 to the correct account and divert the remaining $.0048 to a foreign bank account, preferably in a country with strict bank secrecy laws.

3. Examples of other worldwide computing platforms are Milnet, used to support open source communications of the U.S. Department of Defense, and Internet2, a computerized network and organizational consortium consisting of university, industry, and government entities seeking to develop and deploy advanced computer network technologies.

REFERENCES

Akers, Ronald. L. 1985. *Deviant Behavior: A Social Learning Approach*. 3rd ed. Belmont, CA: Wadsworth.

———. 1998. *Social Learning and Social Structure: A General Theory of Crime and Deviance*. Boston: Northeastern University Press.

Baum, Katrina. 2006. *Identity Theft, 2004: First Estimates from the National Crime Victimization Survey*. Washington, DC: U.S. Department of Justice.

Berson, Ilene R., and Michael J. Berson. 2005. "Challenging Online Behaviors of Youth: Findings from a Comparative Analysis of Young People in the United States and New Zealand." *Social Science Computer Review* 23(1): 29–38.

Brantingham, Patricia L., and Paul J. Brantingham. 1998. "Environmental Criminology: From Theory to Urban Planning Practice." *Studies on Crime and Crime Prevention* 7(1): 31–60.

Brantingham, Patricia L., and Paul J. Brantingham. 1999. "Theoretical Model of Crime Hot Spot Generation." *Studies on Crime and Crime Prevention* 8(1): 7–26.

Brantingham, Patricia L., and Paul J. Brantingham. 2004. "Computer Simulation as a Tool for Environmental Criminologists." *Security Journal* 17(1): 21–30.

Burd, Steffani A. 2006. *Impact of Information Security in Academic Institutions on Public Safety and Security: Assessing the Impact and Developing Solutions for Policy and Practice*. Washington, DC: U.S. Department of Justice.

Burgess, Robert. L., and Ronald L. Akers. 1966. "A Differential Association-Reinforcement Theory of Criminal Behavior." In *Crime and Law Enforcement in the Global Village*, edited by Joseph E. Jacoby. Prospect Heights, IL: Waveland.

CERT Coordination Center. 2003. *Overview of Attack Trends*. Pittsburgh: Carnegie Mellon University.

Chinov, Mike. 2000. "Aid Workers Decry Growing Child Sex Trade in Cambodia." *CNN. Com*. http://archives.cnn.com/2000/asianow/southeast/09/18/cambodia.pedophile/index.html.

Chung, Wingyan, Hsinchun Chen, Weiping Chang, and Shihchieh Chou. 2006. "Fighting Cybercrime: A Review and the Taiwan Experience." *Decision and Support Systems* 41: 669–82.

CNN staff author. 2001. "Sex Slavery: The Growing Trade." *CNN.Com*. http://archives.cnn.com/2001/world/europe/03/08/women.trafficking/.

Cohen, Lawrence E., and Marcus Felson. 1979. "Social Change and Crime: A Routine Activity Approach." In *Crime and Law Enforcement in the Global Village*, edited by Joseph E. Jacoby. Prospect Heights, IL: Waveland.

Commission of the European Communities. 2002. *Proposal for a Council Framework Decision on Attacks against Information Systems*. Brussels: Commission of the European Communities.

Conly, Catherine H. 1989. *Organizing for Computer Crime Investigation and Prosecution*. Washington, DC: National Institute of Justice.

Council of Europe. 2007. *Summary of Proceedings, Octopus Interface Conference on Cooperation against Cybercrime*. Convened in Strasbourg, France, June 11–12. http://www.coe.int/t/dc/files/themes/cybercrime/default_en.asp.

Cyberspace Research Unit. 2002. *Young People's Use of Chat Rooms: Implications for Policy Strategies and Programs of Education*. Preston, UK: University of Central Lancashire.

Daniel, Annie. J. 2002. *An Exploration of Middle and High School Students' Perceptions of Deviant Behavior When Using Computers and the Internet. Proceedings of the Association of Small Computer Users in Education*. Conference convened in Myrtle Beach, South Carolina, June 9–13.

Denning, Dorothy E. 1999. "Activism, Hactivism and Cyberterrorism: The Internet as a Tool for Influencing Foreign Policy." Paper presented at the Nautilus Institute workshop Internet and International Systems: Information Technology and American Foreign Policy Decisionmaking, San Francisco, CA, December 10. http://69.44.62.160/archives/info-policy/workshop/papers/denning.html.

Finkelhor, David, Janis Wolak, and Kimberly Mitchell. 2000. *Online Victimization: A Report of the Nation's Youth*. Washington, DC: National Center for Missing and Exploited Children.

Finn, Jerry. 2004. "A Survey of Online Harassment at a University Campus." *Journal of Interpersonal Violence* 19: 468–83.

Gordon, Sarah, and Richard Ford. 2006. "On the Definition and Classification of Cybercrime." *Journal in Computer Virology* 2: 13–20.

Gordon, Gary R., Chet D. Hosmer, Christine Siedsman, and Don Robovich. 2002. *Assessing Technology, Methods, and Information for Committing and Combating Cyber Crime*. Washington, DC: U.S. Department of Justice.

Heuston, George Z. 1995. "Investigating the Information Superhighway: Global Views, Local Perspectives." *Journal of Criminal Justice Education* 6(2): 311–21.

Hollinger, Richard C., 1989. "Statistics on Computer Crime: A Review of the Research Questions." Paper presented at the National Institute of Justice Computer Crime Conference, Washington, DC, September 14–15.

Hughes, Donna M. 2003. "Sexual Exploitation and the Internet in Cambodia." *Journal of Sexual Aggression* 6(1–2): 1–23.

Jenkins, Phillip. 2001. *Beyond Tolerance: Child Pornography on the Internet*. New York: New York University Press.

Jones, Steve, and Amanda Lenhart. 2004. "Music Downloading and Listening: Findings from the Pew Internet and American Life Project." *Popular Music and Society* 27(2): 185–89.

Lee, M. J. 1991. "Computer Viruses, Computer Hackers: Security Threats of the 1990's." National Criminal Justice Reference Service. http://www.ncjrs.gov/app/publications/abstract.aspx?id=136939.

Lenhart, Amanda, and Mary Madden. 2007. *Social Networking Websites and Teens: An Overview*. Philadelphia: Pew Charitable Trusts.

Levy, S. 1984. *Hackers: Heroes of the Computer Revolution*. New York: Doubleday.

McEwen, J. T., D. Fester, and H. Nugent. 1989. *Dedicated Computer Crime Units*. Washington, DC: National Institute of Justice.

McKinnon, John D. 2007. "Estonia Presses Bush for Cyber-Attack Research Center." http://blogs.wsj.com/washwire/2007/06/25/estonia-presses-bush-for-cyber-attack-research-center/.

McLoughlin, Glenn J. 1996. *The National Information Infrastructure: The Federal Role*. Washington, DC: Congressional Research Service.

McQuade, Samuel C. 1998. *Towards a Theory of Technology Enabled Crime*. Fairfax, VA: George Mason University.

———. 2001. "Cops versus Crooks: Technological Competition and Complexity in the Co-evolution of Information Technologies and Money Laundering." PhD dissertation, George Mason University.

———. 2005. "Technology-Enabled Crime, Policing and Security." *Journal of Technology Studies* 31(1): 32–42.

———. 2006. *Understanding and Managing Cybercrime*. Boston: Pearson Education.

———. 2007*a*. "Cyber Bullying: Preliminary Findings and Early-Age Profiles." Paper presented at the Monroe County Cyber Bullying Conference, Monroe Community College, Rochester, NY, October 1.

———. 2007*b*. "High-Tech Abuse and Crime on College and University Campuses: Evolving Forms of Victimization, Offending, and Their Interplay in Higher Education." In *Campus Crime: Legal, Social and Policy Perspectives,* 2nd ed., edited by Bonnie Fisher and John Sloan. Springfield, IL: Charles C. Thomas.

McQuade, Samuel C., and Tom Castellano. 2004. "Computer Aided Crime and Misbehavior among a Student Population: An Empirical Examination of Patterns, Correlates, and Possible Causes." Paper presented at the Annual Conference of the American Society of Criminology, Nashville, TN, November 17.

McQuade, Samuel C., and Michael Kozak. Forthcoming. "Organized Crime." In *Encyclopedia of Cybercrime*, edited by Samuel C. McQuade III. Westport, CT: Praeger/Greenwood.

McQuade, Samuel C., and Neel Sampat. 2008. *Survey of Internet and At-Risk Behaviors*. Scholarship at Rochester Institute of Technology. Rochester, NY: Rochester Institute of Technology Libraries.

Mitchell, Kimberly J., David Finkelhor, and Janis Wolak. 2001. "Risk Factors for and Impact of Online Sexual Solicitation of Youth." *Journal of the American Medical Association* 285(23): 3011–14.

Nasheri, Hedi. 2004. *Addressing Global Scope of Intellectual Property Law*. Washington, DC: U.S. Department of Justice.

National Institute of Standards and Technology. 2004. *Forensic Examination of Digital Evidence: A Guide for Law Enforcement*. Washington, DC: U.S. Department of Justice.

National Research Council. 1991. *Computers at Risk: Safe Computing in the Information Age*. Washington, DC: National Academy Press.

National White Collar Crime Center and West Virginia University. 1996. *Proceedings of the Academic Workshop*. Bureau of Justice Assistance Grant No. 96-WC-CX-001. Morgantown, WV.

Newman, Graeme R., and Megan M. McNally. 2005. *Identity Theft Literature Review*. Washington, DC: U.S. Department of Justice.

Parker, Donn B. 1989. *Computer Crime: Criminal Justice Resource Manual*. 2nd ed. Washington, DC: National Institute of Justice.

———. 1998. *Fighting Computer Crime: A New Framework for Protecting Information*. New York: Wiley.

Prensky, Marc. 2001. "Digital Natives, Digital Immigrants." *On the Horizon* 9(5): 1–6.

President's Commission on Critical Infrastructure Protection. 1997. *Critical Foundations: Protecting America's Infrastructures*. Washington, DC: U.S. Government Printing Office.

President's Commission on Law Enforcement and the Administration of Justice. 1967. *The Challenge of Crime in a Free Society*. Washington, DC: U.S. Government Printing Office.

President's Commission on Organized Crime. 1984. *The Cash Connection: Organized Crime, Financial Crime, and Money Laundering*. Washington, DC: U.S. Government Printing Office.

Princeton Survey Research Associates International. 2007. *Cyberbullying and Online Teens*. Philadelphia: Pew Foundation.

Rosenblatt, Kenneth S. 1989. "Improving Techniques for Investigating and Prosecuting Computer Crime: Out of the Classroom and into the Field." Paper presented at the National Institute of Justice Computer Crime Conference, Washington, DC, September 14–15.

Science Applications International Corporation. 1995. *Information Warfare: Legal Regulatory, Policy, and Organizational Considerations for Assurance*. Washington, DC: Joint Staff, the Pentagon.

Shaffer, Howard. J., Mathew N. Hall, and Joni Vander Bilt. 2000. "Computer Addiction: A Critical Consideration." *American Journal of Orthopsychiatry* 70(2): 162–68.

Stambaugh, Hollis, David Beaupre, David J. Icove, Richard Baker, Wayne Cassaday, and Wayne P. Williams. 2000. *State and Local Law Enforcement Needs to Combat Electronic Crime*. Washington, DC: U.S. Department of Justice.

Sussman, V. 1995. "Policing Cyberspace." *U.S. News and World Report* (January 23), pp. 54–61.

Sutherland, Edwin. H. 1940. "White-Collar Criminality." In *Crime and Law Enforcement in the Global Village*, edited by Joseph E. Jacoby. Prospect Heights, IL: Waveland.

———. 1947. "Differential Association." In *Crime and Law Enforcement in the Global Village*, edited by Joseph E. Jacoby. Prospect Heights, IL: Waveland.

Symantec. 2004. "W32 Crypto Security Response." http://securityresponse.symantec.com/avcenter/venc/data/w32.crypto.html.

Synovate. 2003. *FTC Identity Theft Survey Report*. Washington, DC: Federal Trade Commission.

Thompson, Clive. 2004. "The Virus Underground." *New York Times*. http://www.nytimes.com/2004/02/08/magazine/08worms.html.

United Nations. 1997. *Manual on the Prevention and Control of Computer-Related Crime*. New York: United Nations.

———. 2000. "Global Challenge of High-Tech Crime." Workshop on Crimes Related to the Computer Network, Tenth United Nations Congress on the Prevention of Crime and Treatment of Offenders. Convened in Vienna, April 10–17. Published by the United Nations Asia and Far East Institute for the Prevention of Crime and Treatment of Offenders, Tokyo, Japan.

U.S. Department of State. 2007. *Trafficking in Persons Report, 2007*. Washington, DC: Bureau of International Information Programs.

Vaugeois, Pierre. 2006. *Cyberaddiction: Fundamentals and Perspectives*. Montreal: Centre Quebecois De Lutte Aux Dependances.

Wall, David S. 2001. *Cybercrime and the Internet*. London: Routledge.

Williams, Frank. P., and Marilyn D. McShane. 1993. *Criminology Theory: Selected Classic Readings*. Cincinnati: Anderson.

Wolak, Janis, Kimberley J. Mitchell, and David Finkelhor. 2006. *Online Victimization of Youth: Five Years Later*. Alexandria, VA: NCMEC.

Young, Lawrence F. 1993. "Utopians, Cyberpunks, Players and Other Computer Criminals: Deterrence and the Law." In *Security and Control of Information Technology in Society*, edited by Richard Sizer, Louise Yngström, Henrik Kaspersen, Simone Fischer-Hübner. Proceedings of the IFIP TC9/WG9.6 working conference on Security and Control of Information Technology in Society. Onboard M/S *Illich* and at St. Petersburg, Russia, August 12–17.

Zetter, Kim. 2007. "iPhone's Security Rivals Windows 95 (No, That's Not Good)." http://www.wired.com/politics/security/news/2007/10/iphone_windows.

PART V

CRIMES AGAINST MORALITY

CHAPTER 20

DRUGS

ROBERT J. MACCOUN AND
KARIN D. MARTIN

Psychoactive drugs are an especially rich topic for criminological scholarship. The topic is inherently multidisciplinary, involving neuroscience, psychology, cultural anthropology, history, microeconomics, and moral philosophy. And drug policy instruments extend beyond the usual arsenal (special and general deterrence, incapacitation, rehabilitation, retribution, and persuasion) to include social work, medicine, psychotherapy, social support groups, drug maintenance clinics, and mass-media campaigns.

To cover such a vast topic in a limited space it is necessary to be selective, making some general observations and pointing the reader to good secondary sources. We focus primarily on the currently illicit psychoactives, giving little attention to alcohol or tobacco. We trust that every educated reader will be familiar with the arguments for analyzing licits and illicits together, and we assure skeptics that we will not neglect the core question of how prohibition shapes drug behavior and drug outcomes.

We also limit our scope to policies and outcomes in the United States. We do this with some reluctance because there is much more innovation in drug policy in Canada, Australia, and Western Europe than in the United States, including experimentation with safe injection rooms, methadone buses, retail cannabis outlets, and government-provided heroin (see MacCoun and Reuter 2001, 2002).

Most readers will have at least passing familiarity with traditional scholarly ways of framing the topic, such as drug use as a victimless crime, the failure of drug prohibition and the merits of legalization, the relative emphasis on supply-side versus demand-side programs, the "punitive paradigm" versus the "public health paradigm," and neurochemical reasons why drugs are a unique social problem. We do not contend that any of these framings are wrong or misguided, just that they have become overly simplistic clichés that can stultify our thinking. We use an analytical framework that we hope provides a fresher and more pragmatic perspective on the topic.

We also try to avoid some hydraulic assumptions often implicit in drug policy debates, for example the assumption that if one approach (e.g., drug prohibition) has lots of problems, another approach (e.g., legalization) will work better, or that if we cut back our funding of one program (e.g., interdiction), we will end up spending more on another (e.g., treatment). It is not necessarily the case that any of our drug policy instruments, optimally deployed, will dramatically change our drug problems. Drug policies might not even be the most effective government responses, relative to, say, universal health care or improved education (see MacCoun and Reuter 2001). And offering more of anything that works modestly well doesn't guarantee we'll do even better.

The central empirical claim of this chapter is that existing policies have discouragingly modest effects on our drug problems. Our central normative claim is that we can advance our understanding of drug policies and outcomes by moving beyond a nearly exclusive reliance on the number of drug users as a metric for success (prevalence reduction). There are often important gains we can make in reducing the quantities that users consume (quantity reduction) and the harm that their use causes (harm reduction).

The first section sets out an analytical framework for thinking about drug use and abuse and about drug policy. The second summarizes current knowledge about patterns of drug use and patterns of drug-related harm. The third is an overview of policy responses to drug abuse and trafficking: interdiction and source-country programs, arrest and imprisonment, treatment, and prevention. In the conclusion we discuss a range of programs and offer a number of proposals—centering on the need to investigate not only the prevalence of drug use but also quantities consumed and harms associated with both drug use and drug policy strategies—for increasing our understanding of current patterns of drug use and of effects of drug policy. We close by calling attention to some emerging issues that are likely to force us to move beyond the clichés of late twentieth-century drug rhetoric.

A number of conclusions emerge:

- Understanding of the effects of drug use and drug policies would be enriched if the prevailing focus on the prevalence of drug use and whether people do or do not use drugs (with the aim of prevalence reduction) was extended to encompass quantity reduction (reducing the average amount used) and harm reduction (reducing the average harm per dose to users and nonusers).
- There is no simple relationship between drug use and crime: use can promote commission of crimes; criminality can promote drug use; both can be promoted by environmental, situational, dispositional, and biological factors.

- Use of most illicit substances peaked in the late 1970s and early 1980s, but this conclusion is based on national self-report surveys that underrepresent hard-core users.
- For most substances, a minority of heavy users account for a majority of the quantity consumed; most harms occur to heavy users.
- Interdiction and source-country antidrug efforts are not very effective; they could probably be cut back significantly but could probably not be eliminated without detectable effects.
- Current law enforcement emphasis on arrest and imprisonment is hard to defend and weighs disproportionately heavily on African American men.
- Drug treatment is effective and cost-effective, but treatment's effects are often fleeting.
- Drug prevention efforts in schools and via mass media are not conspicuously effective; school programs, however, are inexpensive and so do not need to be very effective to be cost-effective.

I. Analytical Framework

Framing drug policy in the language of supply-side versus demand-side programs reflects the increasing diffusion of economic thinking from the business place to other domains of American life. The idea is that some interventions involve supply (source-country controls, interdiction, drug market enforcement) and others involve demand (treatment, prevention), and that there is a drug control budget pie that can be sliced along these lines. But there are some drawbacks to this framing. As Murphy (e.g., 1994) has documented, the notion that we can simply shift monies from one portion of a federal drug budget to another is naïve; there is no single allocating authority, and the "budget" is a mythical post hoc construction assembled from a variety of conflicting sources and entities. Also, supply and demand factors are clearly interdependent and endogenous. The alternative idea of a public health framing of drug policy is refreshing, but in practice it tends to devolve to the "demand reduction" frame.

Instead, we try to keep the focus on strategies rather than tactics, goals rather than programs. Our framework for doing so is sketched here and is developed in greater detail elsewhere (MacCoun, Reuter, and Schelling 1996; MacCoun 1998; MacCoun and Reuter 2001).

A. Consequentialist versus Deontological Positions

Our perspective will not appeal to everyone. In particular, our framework is irrelevant for people who hold that certain moral beliefs trump any consideration of consequences. There are two such deontological positions. One is the *libertarian* belief that ingesting psychoactive substances is our birthright. At the other extreme is *legal moralism*, the belief that drug intoxication is intrinsically immoral. Based on an extensive analysis of drug policy rhetoric (MacCoun and Reuter 2001, chapter 3), we conclude that few people are strict libertarians or pure legal moralists with respect to drugs. Most people who argue that either drug use or drug prohibition is immoral usually cite empirical arguments in support of their positions.

MacCoun and Reuter (2001, p. 66) offered a thought experiment that can help people identify where they stand with respect to consequentialism.

> Imagine a newly invented synthetic psychedelic: "Rhapsodol." Rhapsodol provides an intense (but not unduly frightening) altered state, full of intellectually and aesthetically intriguing mental imagery, and a profound sense of love for all living creatures. These sensations last for approximately 30 minutes, then vanish completely, producing absolutely no detectable changes in one's life outlook or mental or physical functioning. They can be experienced only by sitting or lying in a completely stationary position; any abrupt physical movements end the psychedelic state and return one to a normal state. Moreover, because of neurochemical processes of adaptation, the effects can be experienced only once a day. Would you consider Rhapsodol use immoral? Should it be legally prohibited?

Readers who say yes to these questions may be less consequentialist than deontological in their opposition to drugs.

B. Goals for Drug Policy

At this point we bid pure libertarians and legal moralists adieu. For the consequentialists, we suggest three broad goals: *prevalence reduction* (reducing the number of users), *quantity reduction* (reducing the amount consumed by each user), and *micro harm reduction* (reducing the average harm per dose, including harms to users and harms to nonusers).

Practices and concepts most readily identified with prevalence reduction include abstinence, prevention, deterrence, and incapacitation. Practices and concepts most readily identified with harm reduction include safe-use and safe-sex educational materials, needle exchanges, and the free distribution of condoms to students (e.g., Drucker et al. 1998; Marlatt 1998; Ball 2007). Traditional discussions of prevention, treatment, deterrence, and incapacitation focus almost exclusively on the first category, with the implicit assumption that the best way to eliminate harm is to eliminate prevalence, turning users into nonusers. This is logically correct but not very realistic. Prevalence reduction may be employed in the hope of reducing drug-related harms, but because it directly targets use, any influence on harm is indirect. Harm reduction directly targets harms; any influence on use is indirect.

From an analytic standpoint, all three strategies contribute to the broader goal of macro harm reduction (reducing the total harm to society). For tangible (rather than purely symbolic) harms, *macro harm* = *micro harm* × *prevalence* × *quantity*, summed across types of harm (see below). The strategies are potentially in tension, particularly if efforts to reduce prevalence increase harm (as argued by many drug policy reformers), if efforts to reduce quantity discourage abstinence (as argued by opponents of controlled drinking), or if efforts to reduce average harm encourage the prevalence or quantity (e.g., the argument that harm reduction sends the wrong message). Thus any drug policy intervention should be evaluated with respect to all three criteria—prevalence reduction, quantity reduction, and harm reduction—because all three contribute to the reduction of total drug harm. Note that our use of "harm reduction" is unusual here, in that we are not referring to specific harm reduction programs such as needle exchange, but rather to a goal that is served, well or poorly, by any intervention. For that reason we discuss harm reduction in the context of traditional (and more widespread) interventions, such as policing, prevention, and treatment.

C. The Causes and Bearers of Drug-Related Harm

Why is psychoactive drug use a crime? And is there a sensible answer that also explains why tobacco and alcohol are on one side of the legal threshold, while marijuana, cocaine, the opiates, and the psychedelics are on the other? One way of tackling this question is historical, and there are a number of outstanding histories of the roles played by race, class, and economic interests in the evolution of drug, tobacco, and alcohol control (e.g., Musto [1971] 1987). Another approach is philosophical: If we were starting a society from scratch, which substances, if any, would we prohibit? The traditional first cut at this question uses John Stuart Mill's ([1859] 1999, pp. 72–73) harm principle: "The only purpose for which power can be rightfully exercised over any member of a civilized community, against his will, is to prevent harm to others. His own good, either physical or moral, is not a sufficient warrant."

MacCoun, Reuter, and Schelling (1996) listed nearly 50 different categories of drug-related harm, falling into three clusters: health, social, and economic functioning; safety and public order; and criminal justice. Many are quantifiable, at least in principle (e.g., public health care costs, reduced property values near drug markets, police and court costs), but others are not (e.g., infringement on personal liberty, devaluation of arrest as a moral sanction). The authors attempted to categorize these harms with respect to two questions: Who is the primary bearer of the harm? What is the primary source of the harm?

None of the harms could be confidently categorized as the exclusive burden of the user; in every category of harm there was a compelling case that others (dealers, intimates, employers, the neighborhood, or society) also suffered the harms. Thus the notion that drug use is a victimless crime seems untenable. Still, as MacCoun and Reuter (2001, p. 61) note: "Not every incident of drug use harms others; in fact, the vast majority do not.... Rather, each incident of drug use is accompanied by a risk that others will be harmed; some users, substances, settings, and modalities of use are riskier than others, but in no case is the risk zero.... Of course, this is true to some degree of most licit human activities." These harms to others meet Mill's criterion, but that hardly nails down the case for prohibition. MacCoun, Reuter, and Schelling (1996) argued that for over half of the harm categories, the primary source of the harm was either the illegal status of the drug or the enforcement of that law, at least under the current prohibition regime. (For arguments and evidence on this point, see MacCoun and Reuter 2001 and the collected essays in Fish 1998).

The notion that prohibition and its enforcement are partially responsible for drug harms is perhaps best illustrated by examining the relationship between an offender's illicit drug use and his or her involvement in other crimes. A considerable literature on this relationship suggests the following conclusions (Goldstein, Brownstein, and Ryan 1992; Parker and Auerhahn 1998; White and Gorman 2000; MacCoun, Kilmer, and Reuter 2003): drug use can promote other crimes; criminality can promote drug use; and both can be promoted by environmental, situational, dispositional, and biological third variables. All three pathways have empirical support in at least some settings and populations. But these causal influences are probabilistic, not deterministic. Most drug users are not otherwise involved in serious crime. Finally, the drug-crime link varies across individuals, over time within an individual's development, across situations, and possibly over time periods (as a function of the dynamics of drug epidemics and, possibly, drug control policies).

D. How Are Consumption and Its Consequences Distributed?

Like many things in life that are bounded at zero, the frequency distribution of drug consumption has a positively skewed log-normal shape (e.g., Edwards et al. 1994; Everingham and Rydell 1994). If one plots the proportion of all users (vertical axis) as a function of quantity consumed (horizontal axis), most users pile up on the low (left) side of the quantity distribution, but the plot will have a long narrow right tail representing a small proportion of users who use very large quantities. As a result, the harmful consequences of substance use are not uniform, but are disproportionately concentrated among the heaviest users. Everingham and Rydell used these features to explain why cocaine-related harms remained high even as total prevalence was dropping; one sees a similar logic today in methamphetamine statistics. There is a sophisticated treatment of these distributional features and their implications for the targeting of alcohol interventions (Edwards et al. 1994), but far less discussion in the illicit drug literature (MacCoun 1993).

Another consideration is how drug use and drug harms are distributed across geographic, class, and ethnic lines. African Americans use illicit drugs at a rate similar to (or sometimes lower than) European Americans, but they bear a disproportionate share of the law enforcement risk and market-related violence. This is partly due to the fact that poorer neighborhoods lack the social capital needed to resist open-air drug markets. But it also reflects the deleterious effects of our mandatory minimum sentencing policies, discussed below.

Finally, drug problems are distributed over time. Musto ([1971] 1987) argues that drug epidemics are dampened by a generational learning process in which new cohorts observe the harmful results of a drug on older users. Building on this idea, Caulkins (2005) and his colleagues have developed sophisticated models of how interventions (treatment, enforcement) may provide less or more leverage at different points in a drug epidemic. They argue, for example, that supply reduction measures will be more effective in the early stages of an epidemic but relatively ineffective in a large, mature, established market. Conversely, prevention and treatment may have limited effectiveness early in an epidemic—prevention because its effects are so lagged, and treatment because it interferes with generational learning about drug harms. This work is necessarily fairly speculative at present; we lack enough long-term time-series data to permit serious testing of such hypotheses. But their analyses are valuable in encouraging another dimension of more strategic thinking.

II. Epidemiology

Scholars rely heavily on counts of arrest rates and victimization reports to track trends in most categories of illicit behavior. In contrast, the literature on illicit drug use relies much more heavily on surveys of self-reported drug use, and to a lesser extent drug-related medical events. This probably reflects the sheer prevalence of drug use in the population (relative to property and violent crimes), as well as the more diffuse linkage between the criminal act and any harms to innocent victims.

A. Drug Use

In 2005 about 46 percent of Americans ages 12 and older had used an illicit drug at least once in their lifetime; 14 percent had done so in the past year, and 8 percent in the past month. Because illicit drug use is so often a fleeting encounter in adolescence, drug policy analysts usually view past-month prevalence use as a more meaningful indicator than lifetime prevalence.

The 2007 Monitoring the Future annual school survey (Johnston et al. 2008) has the longest running consistently measured time series for substance use in the United States. Figure 20.1 shows trends in past-month prevalence for selected

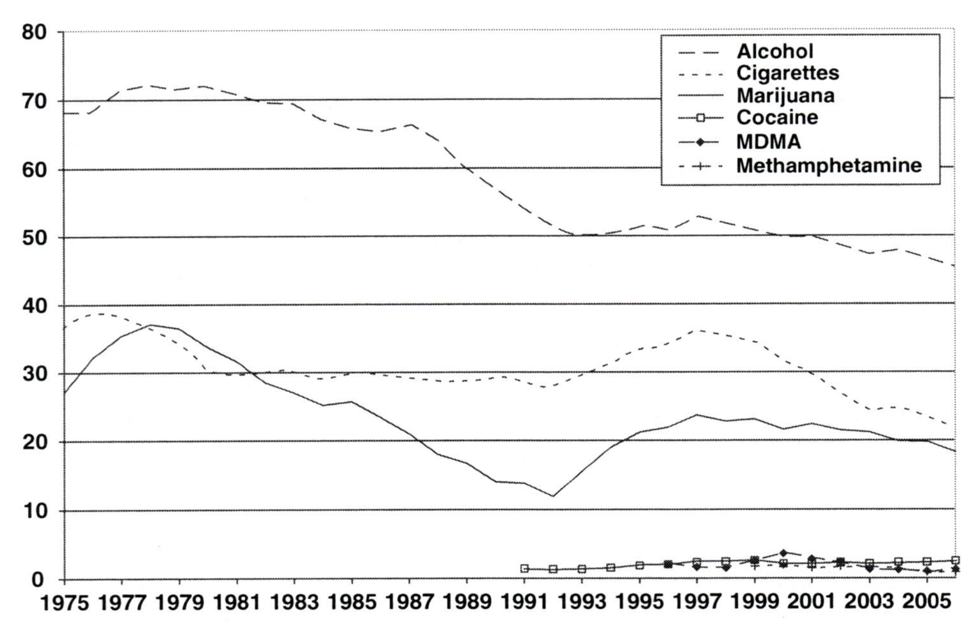

Figure 20.1. Trends in 30-day prevalence among 12th graders, 1975–2005.
Source: Johnston et al. 2007.

substances for 12th graders (Johnston et al. 2007). Several patterns are apparent. First, alcohol remains the most common psychoactive substance among high school seniors. Second, in the most recent year (2006), monthly alcohol and cigarette use each reached their lowest recorded levels. Third, past-month marijuana use reached its peak around 1979, hit a low in 1992, and has stabilized near 20 percent for the past decade. Finally, recent use of cocaine, MDMA, or methamphetamine is fairly rare among high school seniors. MDMA use seems to have peaked at 3.6 percent in the year 2000, cocaine use has remained fairly stable at around 2 percent, and methamphetamine has dropped from 1.9 percent in 2000 to 0.9 percent in 2006.

Table 20.1 shows past-month prevalence of various substances by age category, from the household-based 2006 National Survey on Drug Use and Health (Office of Applied Studies 2006). For each substance, young adults (ages 18–25) were the most frequent recent users, with one exception: heroin. New heroin initiation is rare; the U.S. heroin problem mostly involves an aging cohort of addicts who initiated use in their youth. The overall methamphetamine rates obscure the fact that prevalence remains considerably higher in the western United States (1.2 percent) than in the Midwest and South (0.5 percent) and the Northeast (0.1 percent), and is higher among whites and Latinos (0.3 percent) than among African Americans (0.1 percent). For a decade there have been claims that methamphetamine, originally a West Coast biker drug, is spreading east, but if so, the diffusion has been fairly slow, and there is no evidence that adolescent use is significantly increasing.

Table 20.1. Prevalence of use in the past month (%), by age

	Age group		
	12 to 17	18 to 25	26 and older
Alcohol	16.6	61.9	53.7
"Binge" alcohol use	10.3	42.2	21.4
Cigarettes	10.4	38.4	24.7
Marijuana	6.7	16.3	4.2
Nonmedical use of prescription psychotherapeutics	3.3	6.4	2.2
Cocaine	0.4	2.2	0.8
Hallucinogens	0.7	1.7	0.1
Methamphetamine	0.2	0.6	0.3
Heroin	0.1	0.1	0.2

Note: Entries are percentages of each age category in the 2006 U.S. household population.
Source: Office of Applied Studies 2006.

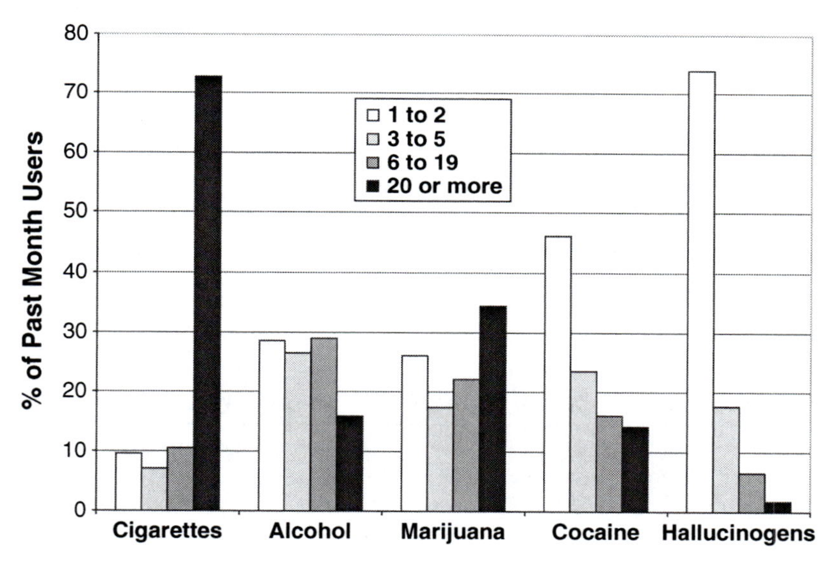

Figure 20.2. Number of days used in past month among past-month users, ages 12 and older, 2006.
Source: Office of Applied Studies 2007*a*.

The fact that someone has used a drug in the past month does not mean he or she uses the drug frequently. As seen in figure 20.2, cigarette smokers tend to be daily users, but most recent users of cocaine and the hallucinogens did so only once or twice in the past month. About a third of marijuana users use almost every day; surprisingly, only half as many alcohol users do so. (That difference is more rather than less pronounced if one examines only 18- to 25-year-olds.)

B. Drug-Related Harms

The prevalence of drug use provides a distorted picture of the actual health and safety harms posed by psychoactive drugs. There are several reasons for this. First, because drug use is only probabilistically related to drug harm, most harms to self and others are attributable to heavy users, and for most substances (except tobacco), a minority of users account for a majority of the quantity consumed. Second, school- and household-based surveys underrepresent hard-core users, who are more likely to be truants, school dropouts, homeless, or institutionalized. To track the harmful consequences of drug use analysts generally rely on three types of indicators: drug mentions in emergency room records, treatment statistics, and drug use among recent arrestees and prisoners. Table 20.2 shows recent data on the relative impact of the major illicit drugs on these harm indicators. As an additional index, we include the count of links produced in a search of Google News on November 3, 2007, for the terms *marijuana, cocaine, crack cocaine, methamphetamine, MDMA* or *(MDMA and Ecstasy)*, and *heroin*.

Another major category of drug-related harm is the transmission of HIV. Injection drug use accounts for about a third of all AIDS cases in the United States (Centers for Disease Control and Prevention 2002), and noninjection use is associated with an elevated risk of unsafe sexual practices. But there is no reliable way to attribute some fixed percentage of AIDS cases to cocaine use, to marijuana use, and so on.

In keeping with our general analytical framework, recall that *total harm is the product of prevalence × quantity × average harm*. Thus marijuana, by far the most prevalent illicit, accounts for a sizable share of all three harm indicators. But relative to their much lower prevalence, it is clear that heroin, cocaine, and methamphetamine are disproportionately harmful substances. A 2007 *Lancet* article by

Table 20.2. Relative contribution of major illicit drugs to various harm indicators

	Percent of drug-related emergency room visits	Primary drug (%) in admissions to treatment programs	Median percentage of arrestees testing positive	Past-month use among state prisoners (prior to offense)	Number of Google News mentions
All illicit drugs	56.4	–	70.3	56.5	–
Marijuana	16.7	15.8	44.1	39.2	21,463
Cocaine	30.9	3.9	30.1	25.0	20,459
Crack	–	10.0	–	–	3,453
Methamphetamine	7.5	8.2	4.7	10.8	3,771
MDMA (ecstasy)	0.7	0.9	–	5.9	2,853
Heroin/opiates	11.4	13.8	5.8	8.2	7,142

Sources: Column 1: Office of Applied Studies 2007*b;* column 2: Office of Applied Studies 2007*c;* column 3: National Institute of Justice 2003, tables 3–8; column 4: Pastore and Maguire 2008, table 6.21; column 5: Searches of news.google.com on November 3, 2007.

David Nutt and colleagues offers what is to date the most sophisticated attempt to rate psychoactive substances by their "intrinsic" health and behavioral harms. In decreasing order of harmfulness, the worst five drugs were heroin, cocaine, the barbiturates, street methadone, and alcohol. Tobacco was ninth, cannabis eleventh, LSD fourteenth, and MDMA eighteenth.

If one were starting a society from scratch, it is unclear where one might paint a bright line separating licit from illicit substances, but it is difficult to see why alcohol and tobacco would be more accessible than cannabis or MDMA. But of course, we are not starting a society from scratch. The data in table 20.2 are misleading if one wants to rank the intrinsic psychopharmacological harms of drugs—marijuana looming too large—but they are valid indicators if one wants to know the contributions of different substances to social harm under the current regime and with current patterns of use. These kinds of indicators tells us little about how harmful each substance might be in a regime of regulated legal access. Average harm per use might approximate the rating levels in Nutt et al. (2007), though heroin use would become a lot safer per dose. Total harm might differ, if for example legal LSD were to become massively popular. But this might be a short-term effect; societies seem to learn from experience and scale back on drugs that are obviously dysfunctional (Musto [1971] 1987).

III. Major Drug Policy Instruments

The FY2008 national drug control budget allocates 36 percent of drug funding for interdiction and source-country controls, 28 percent for domestic drug law enforcement, 23 percent for treatment, and 12 percent for prevention (Office of National Drug Control Policy 2007). We can offer only a whirlwind tour of the empirical literature on these interventions. Readers can find comprehensive (and hard-nosed) assessments in recent monographs by Boyum and Reuter (2005) and the National Academy of Sciences (Manski, Pepper, and Petrie 2001). The drug policy literature is enormous and yet remarkably thin, in that rigorous program evaluations are rare. There are some valuable cost-effectiveness analyses (most famously, Rydell and Everingham 1994), but these are limited by the available descriptive data and some daunting problems of causal inference (Manski, Pepper, and Petrie 2001), and many of the available evaluations were conducted by program developers, raising concerns about intellectual and financial conflicts of interest.

A. Interdiction and Source-Country Controls

In a classic analysis, Reuter, Crawford, and Cave (1988) explained why we should not expect big impacts of efforts to thwart drug production and trafficking. First, it is not possible to completely seal the borders against relatively small packages of chemicals that will be sold at very high prices; there are too many possible smuggling routes and tactics, and dealers are very adaptive. Second, the price structure of illicit markets is such that bulk drug products in source countries are dirt cheap compared to the high retail street prices in the United States. At the source, the economic value is low by U.S. standards but high by local standards; most of the markup in U.S. prices occurs in the last few links of the distribution chain, within U.S. borders. Caulkins and Reuter (1998) note that the wholesale price of cocaine or heroin in a source country is only about 1 percent of its U.S. retail street price. For example, $1,500 of cocaine in Colombia may be worth $15,000 at the U.S. border and $110,000 in the U.S. retail street market. Thus even very large seizures in other countries are unlikely to have big effects on local prices.

In recent years defense analysts have used time-series data to argue that interdiction and source-country campaigns actually do have a significant impact on street prices and U.S. demand. But these analyses have been debunked by a National Academy panel (Manski, Pepper, and Petrie 2001), arguing that the apparent correlations are spurious and amplified by selective focus on certain source-country interventions that happened to precede short-term price drops. It does not follow, however, that we could eliminate these programs entirely without a detectable effect. Most analysts believe that interdiction risks do raise prices; it is just that there are probably steeply declining marginal returns to such efforts. Presumably these programs serve other U.S. political, diplomatic, and economic goals beyond drug policy, laudable or otherwise. But we could probably cut back significantly on these efforts without seeing an increase in U.S. drug consumption.

B. Arrest and Imprisonment

It is estimated that we now have about a half a million drug offenders in state and federal prisons (Caulkins and Reuter 2006). The staggering increase in the federal prison population, and the role that drug offenses played in that increase, are shown in figure 20.3; state prisons show a similar pattern. Drug arrest rates (not shown) have remained stable in recent years, so much of the growth in the prison population has been fueled by declining parole rates.

What has this massive social experiment bought us? Early in the growth period, around 1992, one could argue that it was correlated with a considerable drop in drug use relative to the late 1970s (see fig. 20.1). But this period of optimism was short-lived. By 1996 about half of the gains were gone, and levels of use have remained fairly stable since then, even as the drug prison population continued to rise. In fact, illicit drug prices have plummeted during a period when massive law enforcement sought vigorously to make drugs more expensive (Caulkins and Reuter 2006). This is troubling because prices do matter; contrary to widespread belief, even addicts have been shown to be sensitive to drug prices (Caulkins and Reuter 1998). From the perspective of prevalence and quantity reduction, falling prices are a serious problem. But conceivably, falling prices may be beneficial from

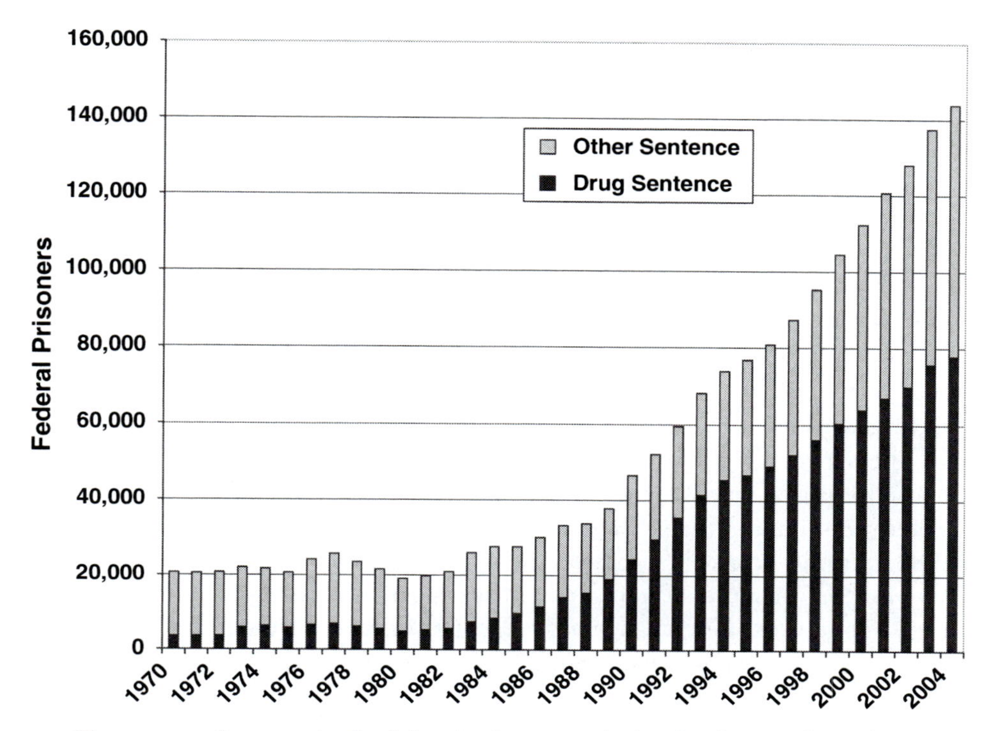

Figure 20.3. Increase in the federal prison population for drug and nondrug offenses, 1970–2004.
Source: Sourcebook of Criminal Justice Statistics Online, table 6.57; htt://www.albany.edu/sourcebook/wk1/0657.wk1 (accessed December 2007).

the perspective of harm reduction because addicts might be expected to conduct fewer income-generating crimes to feed their habit. This is another illustration of the need to confront hard trade-offs in thinking about drug policies.

The harshness of U.S. marijuana enforcement has long received considerable criticism, and indeed it is difficult to defend (MacCoun and Reuter 2001). But Caulkins and Sevigny (2005) warn against exaggerated concerns about unlucky marijuana smokers rotting away in a prison cell. Although 38 percent of state and federal incarcerations for drug offenses involved simple possession; "for only 2 percent of imprisoned drug-law violators was there no reason whatsoever to suspect possible involvement in distribution" (p. 411) and "depending on how strict a definition one preferred, one might argue that anywhere from 5,380 to 41,047 people were in prison in the United States solely for their drug use" (p. 417). On the other hand, many who avoid time in prison do spend time in jail—as much as a third of arrestees in a study of three counties in Maryland (Reuter, Hirschfield, and Davies 2001).

More troubling is the disproportionate imprisonment of African American men. In 2003 African Americans accounted for about half of all drug incarcerations (Pastore and Maguire 2008, tables 6.0001.2003 and 6.56). A major factor is the differential severity of mandatory minimum sentences for crack versus powder cocaine. Under these laws a dealer would have to sell 500 grams of powder cocaine but only 5 grams of crack cocaine to receive the same five-year sentence. Because crack is more likely to be sold in African American communities this has greatly widened the racial gap in sentencing. Even putting aside the questionable pharmacological and moral aspects of this differential policy, there is no evidence whatsoever for its effectiveness in controlling crime. Caulkins and colleagues (1997) show that conventional sentencing is significantly more cost-effective. The mandatory sentences for crack were trimmed somewhat in 2007, and the U.S. Supreme Court recently acted to restore some judicial discretion in these cases (*Kimbrough v. United States*, No. 06–6330, and *Gall v. United States*, No. 06–7949, both decided on December 10, 2007). Whether these changes will translate into a closing of the large racial differential remains to be seen.

The optimal level of drug law enforcement is surely well above zero, but just as surely it is well below current levels (MacCoun and Reuter 2001). Caulkins and Reuter (2006) argue that we could reduce the drug prisoner population by half without harmful consequences; they note that this would still leave us with system "a lot tougher than the Reagan administration ever was." Kleiman (2004) suggests tactics for getting more mileage out of less punishment through the use of small, quick sanctions, strategically deployed.

C. Treatment

In 2005 there were about 1.8 million people in substance abuse treatment in the United States, about 40 percent for alcohol, 17 percent for the opiates, 14 percent for cocaine, and 16 percent for marijuana (Office of Applied Studies 2007*c*).

There are certainly many thousands of people who need treatment and are not receiving it. Whether expanding the available treatment capacity would bring them in is an open question. We should be wary of assuming that a purely public health approach to drugs can work; the police and courts play a crucial role in bringing people into treatment—increasingly so with the expansion of drug courts and initiatives such as California's Proposition 36, the 2001 law that permits treatment in lieu of incarceration for those convicted for the first or second time for nonviolent drug possession (see Farabee et al. 2004). For most primary drugs of abuse, criminal justice referrals are a major basis for treatment: in 2005 57 percent of marijuana treatment, 49 percent of methamphetamine, and 27 percent of smoked cocaine. But 36 percent of clients in alcohol treatment were referred by the criminal justice system, so legal status may not be the crucial lever.

In a sophisticated cost-effectiveness analysis Rydell and Everingham (1994) estimate that the United States could reduce cocaine consumption by 1 percent by investing $34 million in additional treatment funds, which is considerably cheaper than achieving the same outcome with domestic drug law enforcement ($246 million), interdiction ($366 million), or source-country controls ($783 million). Treatment effects, however, are usually estimated using pre-post change scores that are vulnerable to two potential biases (Manski, Pepper, and Petrie 2001). First, the posttreatment reduction could reflect a simple regression to the mean in which an unusually extreme period of binge use would be followed by a return to the user's more typical levels, even in the absence of treatment. Second, treatment pre- and posttests are vulnerable to selection biases because clients who enter and remain in treatment until posttreatment measurement are a nonrandom and perhaps very unrepresentative sample of all users. Regression artifacts would inflate treatment estimates; selection biases could either inflate or deflate the estimates. We believe that the full weight of the evidence makes it clear that treatment is both effective and cost-effective, but until these problems are better addressed we cannot be sure that the benefits of expanded treatment would be as large as Rydell and Everingham implied.

Even its most passionate advocates recognize that treatment's benefits are often fleeting. About 75 percent of heroin clients and 50 percent of cocaine clients have had one or more prior treatment episodes (Office of Applied Studies 2007c). Forty to 60 percent of all clients will eventually relapse, though relapse rates are at least as high for hypertension and asthma treatment (McLellan et al. 2000). Importantly, Rydell and Everingham (1994) recognized that treatment can provide considerable health and public safety benefits *even if it reduces drug use only while the client is enrolled.* Held up to a standard of pure prevalence reduction (abstinence), treatment is unimpressive, but by the standards of quantity reduction and harm reduction, treatment looks pretty good. American providers, steeped in the Twelve Step tradition, often recoil at the phrase "harm reduction," but it is a service that they can and often do perform quite well.

Perhaps the most socially beneficial treatment modality is one that some are reluctant to view as treatment at all: methadone maintenance for heroin addicts. In 2006 there were 254,049 people receiving methadone, only about 20 to 25 percent of all opiate addicts in the United States (Office of Applied Studies 2006). The gap is partly due to spotty service provision outside major cities, but even in urban centers many addicts won't voluntarily seek out methadone, preferring heroin even with its attendant risks. Switzerland, the Netherlands, and Germany have amassed an impressive body of evidence that hard-core addicts significantly improve their health and reduce their criminality when they are able to obtain heroin directly from government clinics (van den Brink et al. 2003). Similar ideas were rejected in the United States several decades ago, but perhaps it is time for a second look (MacCoun and Reuter 2001).

D. Prevention

In the United States the dominant form of prevention takes place in the classroom, generally administered by teachers (Anderson, Aromaa, and Rosenbloom 2007). Ironically, prevention is the least well funded but most thoroughly tested drug intervention. Drug prevention has very modest effects on drug and alcohol use; for example, the mean effect size in the most recent comprehensive meta-analysis was about 1/20th of a standard deviation (Wilson, Gottfredson, and Najaka 2001). Considering that one-fifth of a standard deviation is usually considered the benchmark small effect size, this is not very encouraging. Making matters worse, the single most popular program, Drug Abuse Resistance Education (DARE), accounts for nearly a third of all school prevention programs (Anderson, Aromaa, and Rosenbloom 2007), but numerous studies show it has little or no detectable effect on drug use (Ennett et al. 1994). It is not clear whether its ineffectiveness stems from its curriculum or from its reliance on classroom visits by police officers.

But classroom-based prevention is quite inexpensive, so it doesn't have to be very effective to be cost-effective. Caulkins and colleagues (1999) estimate over $800 in social benefits from an average student's participation for a cost of only $150. Most of the benefits involve tobacco prevention, then cocaine, and only minimally marijuana. Classroom-based prevention materials can't be effective if the messages aren't salient in real-world settings where drug taking opportunities occur. But a well-funded campaign of magazine, radio, and television ads by the Office of National Drug Control Policy appears to have had no positive impact on levels of use (and possibly some negative impact; see U.S. Government Accountability Office 2006).

We should be wary of thinking we have evaluated the potential impact of mass media; it may just be that the messages we've been using aren't very helpful. Note that our prevention messages are almost exclusively aimed at prevalence reduction (i.e., primary prevention: "Don't use") rather than quantity reduction ("Use less") or harm reduction ("This kind of use is particularly dangerous"). A greater emphasis on secondary prevention and harm reduction might have real payoffs with respect to social costs, but we won't know unless we try (Rosenbaum 2007). Evidence from classroom sex education is instructive in this regard; programs that teach safe sex are reliably more effective at reducing risky behavior than are abstinence-based programs (Kirby, Laris, and Rolleri 2007; Trenholm et al. 2007).

IV. The Near Future

We can hazard some guesses about where U.S. drug policy might head in the future. The medical marijuana movement is likely to diminish in visibility as sprays such as Sativex reduce the role of marijuana buyers' clubs, yet adult support for marijuana legalization will continue to increase as the tumultuous generation gap of the 1960s becomes a distant memory. Methamphetamine will soon peak, if it hasn't already (in the United States, if not in Europe), leaving us to deal with a costly aging cohort of addicts, much like our earlier heroin epidemic. Vaccines against nicotine and cocaine addiction may soon hit the market, with both desirable and unintended consequences (MacCoun 2004).

But rather than developing the case supporting these speculations, we close with two trends that are already well under way, each of which has the potential to seriously subvert current cultural assumptions about drugs and drug control.

A. The Thizzle Scene

The conventional wisdom is that ecstasy (MDMA) is a "love drug" or empathogen, and that it is the drug of choice for European and Asian American college students and young professionals. But there are many reports of increased ecstasy use by minorities living in several cities (National Institute on Drug Abuse 2003). Many observers have noted its prevalence in the "hyphy" movement and the associated rap music (Hix 2006; Lee 2006; Swan 2006). There is evidence of an increase in the number of references to ecstasy use in hip-hop music starting in 1996 (Diamond, Bermudez, and Schensul 2006). The reported rise in ecstasy use in the hip-hop scene has ignited alarming claims that ecstasy is "the new crack" (e.g., Cloud 2001; Swan 2006); a CBS television report asked whether ecstasy was a "hug drug or thug drug" (CBS Broadcasting 2007).

In fact, researchers have only begun to examine the diffusion of ecstasy into inner-city neighborhoods (Yacoubian 2002; Urbach, Reynolds, and Yacoubian 2003; Boeri et al. 2005). There is laboratory evidence of heightened aggression in the week following MDMA ingestion (e.g., Hoshi et al. 2006), but in a 2001 study of arrestees, ecstasy use was not associated with race and was negatively associated with arrest for violent crimes (Hendrickson and Gerstein 2005). It is also unclear whether self-reported ecstasy use always involves MDMA, as opposed to closely related drugs such as methamphetamine (Avni 2007, but see Parrot 2004). Thus the emerging "thizzle" scene does raise intriguing questions about psychopharmacology, culture, and their intersection, but whether there is any meaningful causal connection between ecstasy, race, and crime is far from certain.

B. Cognitive Performance Enhancers

Earlier we offered a thought experiment about a hypothetical drug called Rhapsodol. We now ask the reader to consider a newly created synthetic stimulant, "Quikaine." Quikaine targets the neural system by increasing the speed of ion transfer between synaptic gaps. Thus it reduces reaction time and increases the speed with which physical tasks can be accomplished. It in no way alters the user's emotional state either during the time the drug is in the system or afterward. Neither does it affect intellectual functioning. Second, consider "Intellimine." Its sole impact on the human body is to improve cognitive capacity; it has no other emotional or physical impact and no lingering effect on mental functioning once the drug leaves the system. In addition, because variants of this drug have been used for decades to help with attention-deficit/hyperactivity disorder and Alzheimer's it has a long and empirically sound safety record. In fact, children and the elderly receive maximum benefit of the drug.

How should we regulate these drugs? Should they be legally available for purchase by adults? If not, are there more limited circumstances in which their use might be acceptable? For example, would Quikane's use be warranted by those charged with protecting others from danger, such as certain military operatives or police officers? What about for completing tasks faster and more safely, such as on an assembly line? How about for simply reducing the amount of time spent on household chores? Should we allow surgeons, crisis managers, and other high-stakes problem solvers to take Intellimine?

These drugs are hypothetical, but new synthetics already have some of their properties, and there is every reason to expect rapid advances in the development of performance enhancers in the near future (see Farah et al. 2004; Turner and Sahakian 2006). They will raise vexing questions about personhood, agency, freedom, and virtue. For centuries we have associated psychoactive substances with the pursuit of purely personal goals: fun, seduction, escape, transcendence, ecstasy. New drugs like Intellimine and Quikane will force us to come to grips with a radically new framing: drug use as a tool for enhanced economic competitiveness. Parents who now worry about how marijuana might jeopardize their children's Ivy League prospects may soon worry about whether abstinence lowers SAT scores. Employers who now screen urine for marijuana may come to view abstainers as slackers. It will be fascinating to see how we learn to reconcile these new pressures with our traditional attitudes toward drugs.

C. Priorities for Future Research

We close with a brief list of topics that are sorely in need of research attention. Rather than a long wish list, we confine our attention to priorities that are implied by our analytical framework, specifically the argument that quantity reduction and harm reduction deserve a footing more equal with prevalence reduction.

The first priority is to give far greater attention to the development of quantity and harm indicators in epidemiological research. Our national drug surveys devote far more attention to prevalence than to dosage, settings of use, or consequences of use, and the reliance on household and classroom populations overrepresents casual users and underrepresents the heaviest users (see Manski, Pepper, and Petrie 2001). We would like to see the Goldstein, Brownstein, and Ryan (1992) analysis of types of New York drug-related deaths replicated in many different cities on a periodic basis (MacCoun, Kilmer, and Reuter 2003).

The second priority is to incorporate more sophisticated quantity and harm measures into drug policy program evaluations. We rarely evaluate drug law enforcement, and when we do we typically seek changes in drug use without considering effects on patterns of drug use, much less the harms of drug use and the harms of aggressive policing. Treatment and prevention evaluators do attend to changes in quantity as well as prevalence, but they devote far less attention to changes in the harms. They are particularly resistant to assessing the possibility that participants who continue using might develop less harmful patterns of use.

Finally, we would endorse a greater willingness to directly test interventions designed to directly reduce drug-related harm. Only needle exchange has received much study in the United States, much of it conducted without any federal research support. More radical proposals, such as safe injection sites, "safer use" education, and government-regulated heroin maintenance, have been completely off the table despite receiving serious investigation in Europe. A more open inquiry could establish whether such policies are harmful or helpful, and it would do much to help restore the perceived legitimacy of the U.S. drug control establishment among elites and ordinary citizens alike.

REFERENCES

Anderson, Pamela, Susan Aromaa, and David Rosenbloom. 2007. "Prevention Education in America's Schools: Findings and Recommendations from a Survey of Educators." Boston: Join Together and Boston University School of Public Health.

Avni, Sheerly. 2007. "It's the Ecstasy, Stupid." http://www.truthdig.com/report/item/20070703_its_the_ecstasy_stupid/.

Ball, Andrew Lee. 2007. "HIV, Injecting Drug Use and Harm Reduction: A Public Health Response." *Addiction* 102: 684–92.

Boeri, Miriam, Miriam Williams, Claire E. Sterk, and Kirk W. Elifson. 2005 "Rolling beyond Raves: Ecstasy Use Outside the Rave Setting." *Journal of Drug Issues* 34(4): 831–60.

Boyum, David, and Peter Reuter. 2005. *An Analytic Assessment of U.S. Drug Policy.* Washington, DC: American Enterprise Institute.

Caulkins, Jonathan P. 2005. "Models Pertaining to How Drug Policy Should Vary over the Course of an Epidemic Cycle." In *Substance Use: Individual Behavior, Social Interactions, Markets, and Politics. Advances in Health Economics and Health Services Research,* vol. 16, edited by Bjorn Lindgren and Michael Grossman. Elsevier.

Caulkins, Jonathan, and Peter Reuter. 1998. "What Price Data Tell Us about Drug Markets." *Journal of Drug Issues* 28(3): 593–612.

Caulkins, Jonathan, and Peter Reuter. 2006. "Re-orienting Drug Policy." *Issues in Science and Technology Online.* http://www.issues.org/23.1/caulkins.html.

Caulkins, Jonathan P., C. Peter Rydell, Susan S. Everingham, James Chiesa, and Shawn Bushway. 1999. *An Ounce of Prevention, a Pound of Uncertainty: The Cost-Effectiveness of School-Based Drug Prevention Program.* Santa Monica, CA.: RAND.

Caulkins, Jonathan P., C. Peter Rydell, William L. Schwabe, and James Chiesa. 1997. *Mandatory Minimum Drug Sentences: Throwing Away the Key or the Taxpayers' Money?* Santa Monica, CA.: RAND.

Caulkins, Jonathan P., and Eric Sevigny. 2005. "How Many People Does the U.S. Imprison for Drug Use, and Who Are They?" *Contemporary Drug Problems* 32(3): 405–28.

CBS Broadcasting, Inc. 2007. "'Thizz' Use among Bay Area Teens a Growing Concern." http://cbs5.com/topstories/local_story_268000326.html.

Centers for Disease Control and Prevention. 2002. "Drug-Associated HIV Transmission Continues in the United States." http://www.cdc.gov/hiv/resources/factsheets/idu.htm.

Cloud, John 2001. "Ecstasy Crackdown." *Time* 157(14): 62–64.

Diamond, Sarah, Rey Bermudez, and Jean Schensul. 2006. "What's the Rap about Ecstasy?: Popular Music Lyrics and Drug Trends among American Youth." *Journal of Adolescent Research* 21: 269–98.

Drucker, Ernest, P. Lurie, A. Wodak, and P. Alcabes. 1998. "Measuring Harm Reduction: The Effects of Needle and Syringe Exchange Programs and Methadone Maintenance on the Ecology of HIV." *AIDS* 12: S217–30.

Edwards, G., P. Anderson, T. F. Babor, S. Casswell, R. Ferrence, N. Giesbrecht, C. Godfrey, H. D. Holder, P. Lemmens, K. Mäkelä, L. T. Midanik, T. Norström, E. Österberg, A. Romesljö, R. Room, J. Simpura, and O. Skog. 1994. *Alcohol Policy and the Public Good*. Oxford: Oxford University Press.

Ennett, S. R., N. S. Tobler, C. L. Ringwalt, and R. L. Flewelling. 1994. "How Effective Is Drug Abuse Resistance Education? A Meta-analysis of Project DARE Outcome Evaluations." *Journal of Public Health* 84(9): 1394–401.

Everingham, Susan S., and C. Peter Rydell. 1994. *Modeling the Demand for Cocaine*. Santa Monica, CA: RAND.

Farabee, David, Yih-Ing Hser, M. Douglas Anglin, and David Huang. 2004. "Recidivism among an Early Cohort of California's Proposition 36 Offenders." *Criminology and Public Policy* 3: 563–84.

Farah, Martha J., Judy Illes, Robert Cook-Deegan, Howard Gardner, Eric Kandel, Patricia King, Eric Parens, Barbara Sahakian, and Paul Root Wolpe. 2004. "Neurocognitive Enhancement: What Can We Do and What Should We Do?" Nature Reviews, *Neuroscience* 5: 421–26.

Fish, Jefferson M, ed. 1998. *How to Legalize Drugs*. Northvale, NJ: Jason Aronson.

Goldstein, Paul, Henry Brownstein, and Patrick Ryan. 1992. "Drug-Related Homicides in New York: 1984 and 1988." *Crime and Delinquency* 38(4): 459–76.

Hendrickson, James C., and Dean R. Gerstein. 2005. "Criminal Involvement among Young Male Ecstasy Users." *Substance Use and Misuse* 40: 1557–75.

Hix, Lisa. 2006. "Mistah F.A.B." *San Francisco Chronicle* (October 22).

Hoshi, Rosa, Hannah Pratt, Sachin Mehta, Alyson J. Bond, and H. Valerie Curran. 2006. "An Investigation into the Sub-Acute Effects of Ecstasy on Aggressive Interpretative Bias and Aggressive Mood—Are There Gender Differences?" *Journal of Psychopharmacology* 20(2): 291–301.

Johnston, Lloyd D., Patrick M. O'Malley, Jerald G. Bachman, and John E. Schulenberg. 2008. *Monitoring the Future National Survey Results on Drug Use, 1975–2007*. Vol. 1: *Secondary School Students*. NIH Publication No. 08–6418A. Bethesda, MD: National Institute on Drug Abuse.

Kirby, Douglas, B. A. Laris, and Lori Rolleri. 2007. "Sex and HIV Education Programs: Their Impact on Sexual Behaviors of Young People throughout the World." *Journal of Adolescent Health* 40(3): 206–17.

Kleiman, Mark A. R. 2004. "Toward (More Nearly) Optimal Sentencing for Drug Offenders." *Criminology and Public Policy* 3(3): 435–40.

Lee, Chris. 2006. "Up from the Underground: Hyphy, a Regional Strain of Rapid-fire Rap, Fuels a Scene of Both Community and Often-Unlawful Chaos. Is This Street Party Bound to Burn Out, or Is It Just Igniting?" *Los Angeles Times* (July 23).

MacCoun, Robert J. 1993. "Drugs and the Law: A Psychological Analysis of Drug Prohibition." *Psychological Bulletin* 113: 497–512.

———. 1998. "Toward a Psychology of Harm Reduction." *American Psychologist* 53: 1199–208.

———. 2004. "Anticipating Unintended Consequences of Vaccine-like Immunotherapies for Addictive Drug Use." In *New Treatments for Addiction: Behavioral, Ethical, Legal, and Social Questions,* edited by Henrick R. Harwood and Tracy G. Myers. National Research Council and the Institute of Medicine. Washington, DC: National Academy Press.

MacCoun, Robert J., Beau Kilmer, and Peter Reuter. 2003. "Research on Drug-Crime Linkages: The Next Generation." Commissioned paper. In *Toward a Drugs and Crime Research Agenda for the 21st Century.* Washington, DC: National Institute of Justice Special Report.

MacCoun, Robert J., and Peter Reuter. 2001. *Drug War Heresies: Learning from Other Vices, Times, and Places.* New York: Cambridge University Press.

MacCoun, Robert J. and Peter Reuter, eds. 2002. "The Varieties of Drug Control at the Dawn of the 21st Century." Introduction to the special issue of *Annals of the American Academy of Political and Social Science.* July: 7–19.

MacCoun, Robert J., Peter Reuter, and Thomas Schelling. 1996. "Assessing Alternative Drug Control Regimes." *Journal of Policy Analysis and Management* 15: 1–23.

Manski, Charles, John Pepper, and Carol Petrie. 2001. *Informing America's Policy on Illegal Drugs: What We Don't Know Keeps Hurting Us.* Washington, DC: National Academy of Sciences.

Marlatt, Gordon A. 1998. *Harm Reduction: Pragmatic Strategies for Managing High-Risk Behaviors.* New York: Guilford.

McLellan Thomas, David Lewis, Charles O'Brien, and Herbert Kleber. 2000. "Drug Dependence, a Chronic Medical Illness: Implications for Treatment, Insurance, and Outcomes Evaluation." *Journal of the American Medical Association* 284(13): 1689–95.

Mill, John Stuart. 1999. *On Liberty.* Peterborough, Canada: Broadview. (Originally published 1859.)

Murphy, Patrick. 1994. *Keeping Score: The Frailties of the Federal Drug Budget.* Santa Monica, CA: RAND.

Musto, David F. 1987. *The American Disease: Origins of Narcotic Control.* New York: Oxford University Press. (Originally published 1971.)

National Institute of Justice. 2003. *2000 Arrestee Drug Abuse Monitoring: Annual Report.* Washington, DC: National Institute of Justice. http://www.ncjrs.gov/nij/adam/ADAM2003.pdf.

National Institute on Drug Abuse. 2003. *Epidemiologic Trends in Drug Abuse,* Vol. 1: *Highlights and Executive Summary.* Community Epidemiology Work Group, National Institute on Drug Abuse. National Institutes of Health Publication No. 04–5364. Bethesda, MD: National Institutes of Health.

Nutt, David, Leslie A. King, William Saulsbury, and Colin Blakemore. 2007. "Development of a Rational Scale to Assess the Harm of Drugs of Potential Misuse." *Lancet* 369: 1047–53.

Office of Applied Studies. 2006. *State Profile—United States: National Survey of Substance Abuse Treatment Services.* http://wwwdasis.samhsa.gov/webt/state_data/US06.pdf.

———. 2007*a*. *Results from the 2006 National Survey on Drug Use and Health: National Findings.* DHHS Publication No. SMA 07–4293, NSDUH Series H-32. Rockville, MD: Substance Abuse and Mental Health Services Administration.

———. 2007*b*. *Drug Abuse Warning Network 2005: National Estimates of Drug-Related Emergency Department Visits.* DAWN Series D-29, DHHS Publication No. (SMA) 07–4256. Rockville, MD: Substance Abuse and Mental Health Services Administration.

———. 2007*c*. *Treatment Episode Data Set (TEDS): 1995–2005. National Admissions to Substance Abuse Treatment Services.* DASIS Series: S-37, DHHS Publication No. (SMA) 07–4234. Rockville, MD: Substance Abuse and Mental Health Services Administration.

Office of National Drug Control Policy. 2007. *National Drug Control Strategy FY2008 Budget Summary.* Washington, DC: Office of National Drug Control Policy.

Parker, Robert Nash, and Kathleen Auerhahn. 1998. "Alcohol, Drugs, and Violence." *Annual Review of Sociology* 24: 291–311.

Parrott A. C. 2004. "Is Ecstasy MDMA? A Review of the Proportion of Ecstasy Tablets Containing MDMA, Their Dosage Levels, and the Changing Perceptions of Purity." *Psychopharmacology* (Berlin) 173(3–4): 234–41.

Pastore, Ann L., and Kathleen Maguire, eds. 2008. *Sourcebook of Criminal Justice Statistics.* http://www.albany.edu/sourcebook/.

Reuter, Peter, Gordon Crawford, and Jonathan Cave. 1988. *Sealing the Borders: Effects of Increased Military Efforts in Drug Interdiction.* R-3594-USDP. Santa Monica, CA: RAND.

Reuter, Peter, Paul Hirschfield, and Curt Davies. 2001. "Assessing the Crackdown on Marijuana in Maryland." Unpublished manuscript. University of Maryland, College Park.

Rosenbaum, Marsha. 2007. *Safety First: A Reality-Based Approach to Teens, Drugs, and Drug Education.* San Francisco: Drug Policy Alliance.

Rydell, Peter, and Susan Everingham. 1994. *Controlling Cocaine: Supply versus Demand Programs.* Santa Monica, CA: Drug Policy Research Centre, RAND.

Swan, Rachel. 2006. "Feelin' Their Thizzle: How the Culture of Ecstasy Has Changed as the Drug Moved from Raves to Hip-hop." *East Bay Express* (March 15).

Trenholm, Christopher, Barbara Devaney, Ken Fortson, Lisa Quay, Justin Wheeler, and Melissa Clark. 2007. *Impacts of Four Title V, Section 510 Abstinence Education Programs.* Princeton, NJ: Mathematica Policy Research.

Turner, Danielle C., and Barbara J. Sahakian. 2006 "Neuroethics of Cognitive Enhancement." *Biosocieties* 1: 113–23.

Urbach, Blake, K. Michael Reynolds, and George Yacoubian. 2003. "Exploring the Relationship between Race and Ecstasy Involvement among a Sample of Arrestees." *Journal of Ethnicity in Substance Abuse* 1(4): 1–13.

U.S. Government Accountability Office. 2006. *ONDCP Media Campaign: Contractor's National Evaluation Did Not Find That the Youth Anti-Drug Media Campaign Was Effective in Reducing Youth Drug Use.* GAO-06–818. Washington, DC: U.S. Government Accountability Office.

van den Brink, Wim, Vincent M. Hendriks, Peter Blanken, Maarten W. J. Koeter, Barbara J. van Zwieten, and Jan M. van Ree. 2003. "Medical Prescription of Heroin to Treatment Resistant Heroin Addicts: Two Randomised Controlled Trials." *British Medical Journal* 327: 310.

White, Helene R., and D. M. Gorman. 2000. "Dynamics of the Drug-Crime Relationship." In *Criminal Justice 2000 The Nature of Crime: Continuity and Change*, edited by G. LaFree. Washington, DC: U.S. Department of Justice.

Wilson, David B., Denise Gottfredson, and Stacy S. Najaka. 2001. "School-Based Prevention of Problem Behaviors: A Meta-Analysis." *Journal of Quantitative Criminology* 17(3): 247–72.

Yacoubian, George S., Jr. 2002. "Assessing the Temporal Relationship between Race and Ecstasy Use among High School Seniors." *Journal of Drug Education* 32: 213–25.

CHAPTER 21

HATE CRIMES

VALERIE JENNESS

OVER the past three decades bias-motivated violence has been defined, promoted, and addressed as a criminal justice concern. What Lawrence (2006) calls "the Hate Crime Project" marks an important moment in the history of crime controls, the development of criminal and civil law, the allocation of civil rights, and expectations for law enforcement to do something about bias, prejudice, and hate-motivated conduct. The U.S. criminal justice system has begun to institutionalize data collection, systematize police responses to bias-motivated incidents, and set the stage for successful prosecutions.

The enforcement of hate crime law is taking place in many ways; hate crime law, policy, and practice are increasingly being institutionalized. Hate crime policy is not reducible to symbolic politics, as early analysts posited. A growing body of evidence controverts the notion that hate crime law goes unenforced, but, of course, that does not mean it is being fully enforced. Unfortunately the literature on enforcement of hate crime law, especially at the prosecutorial level, is not sufficiently well developed to support definitive conclusions or to answer a basic question about criminal justice policy in general and policing and prosecution more particularly: Is enforcement disparate?

Hate crime policies are proliferating at local, state, and federal levels in the United States and abroad. U.S. law enforcement officials increasingly are taking steps to enforce hate crime law. The result includes variations in reporting of hate crimes across jurisdictions and nascent efforts to prosecute predatory offenders.

My primary focus in this chapter is on criminal justice concerns related to hate crime. Section I presents a summary of early assessments of hate crime law and concerns about bias-motivated violence as "merely symbolic politics" with minimal enforcement effects. Section II contextualizes this assessment and includes a brief summary of federal and state hate crime law. Section III details the organization of hate crime enforcement and the outcomes of law enforcement practices, including data on the policing and prosecution of hate crime. In the last section I discuss how hate crime law and law enforcement practices that derive from it are unfolding beyond the United States.

A number of main points emerge:

- The term *hate crime* was coined in the United States in the second half of the twentieth century as the result of an anti–hate crime movement, which in turn was a product of the civil rights, women's, gay and lesbian, disabilities rights, and crime victims movements.
- By 2008 the U.S. federal government and almost every state had adopted a hate crime law.
- Police officers use discretion when defining what does and does not qualify as a hate crime; the social organization of policing and the compositions of communities affect how officers enforce hate crime law, and there are significant differences in response among types of police personnel, policing units, jurisdictions, and polities.
- Prosecutors are successfully prosecuting hate crime, albeit in small numbers compared with other types of crime.
- Hate crime—as a concept and a set of criminal justice policies and practices—has diffused across international borders, especially in English-speaking cultures.

I. Symbolic Politics

In *Hate Crimes: Criminal Law and Identity Politics,* Jacobs and Potter (1998, p. 65) argued, "Fundamentally, hate crime laws are symbolic statements requested by advocacy groups for material and symbolic reasons and provided by politicians for political reasons." They presented hate crime laws and related criminal justice policies as examples of legislators ceding policy making to interest groups. Hate crime laws, they argued, represent merely an exercise in symbolic politics. Likewise, Haider-Markel (1998, p. 69) posited that "hate crime policies and implementation efforts are largely attempts by politicians to satisfy organized interests in competitive political systems." Beale (2000) discussed the expressive function of federal hate crime law, especially its capacity to influence public perceptions of bias-motivated violence. More recently, Bell (2002, cited in Perry 2003, p. 431) demonstrated that "street level enforcers of hate crime have the power to effectively nullify hate crime statutes through non-enforcement, thereby reducing them to an empty symbolic gesture." These arguments suggest that hate crime laws are powerful symbols that result in few or no changes in practice.

These claims need to be put into context. From the introduction and politicization of the term *hate crime* (and its synonym *bias crime*) in the late 1970s to twenty-first century calls for increasing enforcement, social movements have constructed the problem of bias-motivated violence in particular ways (Jenness 1995*a*, 1995*b*, 1999; Jenness and Broad 1997; Maroney 1998), politicians at federal and state levels have enacted legislation that defines hate crime (Haider-Markel and Meier 1996; Jenness and Grattet 1996, 2004; Grattet, Jenness, and Curry 1998; Earl and Soule 2001; Soule and Earl 2001), judges have elaborated and enriched the meaning of hate crime as they grappled with constitutionality questions (S. Phillips and Grattet 2000; Gellman and Lawrence 2004), and law enforcement officials have varied in how they investigate, classify, and prosecute bias-motivated incidents (Martin 1995, 1996; Boyd, Berk, Hamner 1996; Haider-Markel 1998; Bell 2002; Grattet and Jenness 2005, 2008; Jenness and Grattet 2005; McPhail and Jenness 2006). Three decades after the passage of the first modern hate crime law, state attorneys general, governors, state commissions and task forces, social movement organizations, and citizens groups continue to call for enhanced efforts to enforce hate crime law.

II. Federal and State Laws

An assessment of hate crime–related criminal justice policy and law enforcement practices requires understanding the context in which *hate crime* emerged. As Maroney (1998) documented, the anti–hate crime movement in the United States arrived on the coattails of previously institutionalized social movements. Modern understandings of hate crime are a product of a confluence of several social movement discourses, most notably the black civil rights movement, the modern women's movement, the gay and lesbian movement, the disabilities rights movement, and the crime victims movement (see also Jenness and Broad 1997; Jenness and Grattet 2004).

Each of these social movements supported an institutionalized commitment to publicizing and combating violence directed at minorities because of their minority status. As liberal, progressive movements, the civil rights, women's, disabilities, and gay and lesbian movements "called attention to the personal costs of minority groups' political victimization," whereas the more conservative crime victims movement "called attention to the political context of personal victimization" (Maroney 1998, p. 579). Combined, they laid the foundation for a new movement to question, and make publicly debatable, issues of rights and harm as they relate to a variety of constituencies (Maroney 1998). This questioning took place in extralegal and legal realms at a time when the public was increasingly exposed to the interchangeable terms *bias crime* and *hate crime*.

Initially the movement promoted the concept of hate *crime* without the official backing of the state. Throughout the 1980s and 1990s rapid legal reform resulted in bias-motivated violence becoming criminalized in heretofore unknown ways, and the term *hate crime* came to signify a particular type of *criminal* conduct. Lawmakers began to respond to what they perceived to be an escalation of violence directed at minorities and political pressure by those promoting the interests of minorities by "making hate a crime" (Jenness and Grattet 2004). During the late twentieth century and continuing into the twenty-first century legislators criminalized discriminatory violence and laid the foundation for civil actions for bias-motivated violence. The federal government adopted hate crime legislation, as has almost every state.

A. Federal Law

In 1990 President George H. W. Bush signed the Hate Crimes Statistics Act (HCSA), which required the U.S. attorney general to collect statistical data on "crimes that manifest evidence of prejudice based on race, religion, sexual orientation, or ethnicity, including where appropriate the crimes of murder, non-negligent manslaughter; forcible rape; aggravated assault, simple assault, intimidation; arson; and destruction, damage or vandalism of property" (Pub. L. No. 101–275). The HCSA was amended by the Violent Crime Control and Law Enforcement Act of 1994; crimes motivated by a bias against persons with disabilities were also recognized as hate crime. The Federal Bureau of Investigation started collecting data on January 1, 2007. The HCSA requires the attorney general to gather data on bias-motivated crime and make these data available to the public.

The rationale for the HCSA, and its amendments, was to mandate collection of empirical data necessary to develop effective policies. HCSA supporters argued that involving the police in identifying and counting hate crimes would help law enforcement officials measure trends, design effective responses and prevention strategies, and develop sensitivity to the needs of hate crime victims. The HCSA does not establish new penalties for bias-motivated crimes or provide legal recourse for victims of bias-motivated crime.

In 1994 Congress passed the Hate Crimes Sentencing Enhancement Act (HCSEA) to increase penalties for crimes committed for bias-motivated reasons. The HCSEA identifies eight predicate crimes—murder; nonnegligent manslaughter; forcible rape; aggravated assault; simple assault; intimidation; arson; and destruction, damage, or vandalism of property—for which judges are allowed to enhance penalties under the federal sentencing guideline when "the finder of fact at trial determines beyond a reasonable doubt" that the crime committed was a hate crime (Pub. L. No. 103–322). *Hate crime* is defined by the HCSEA as criminal conduct in which "the defendant intentionally selected any victim or property as the object of the offense because of the actual or perceived race, color, religion, national origin, ethnicity, gender, disability, or sexual orientation of [the victim]" (Pub. L. No. 103–322). This law addresses only hate crimes that take place on federal lands and properties. It was invoked for the first time seven years after the passage of the HCSEA.[1]

The 1994 Violence Against Women Act (VAWA) specified that "all persons within the United States shall have the right to be free from crimes of violence motivated by gender" (Pub. L. No. 103–322). The VAWA originally allocated more than $1.6 billion over five years for education, rape crisis hotlines, training of justice personnel, victim services (especially shelters for victims of battery), and special units of police and prosecutors to deal with crimes against women; billions more have since been allocated. Title III provides a civil remedy for "gender crimes." It entitles victims to compensatory and punitive damages for a crime of violence if it is motivated, at least in part, by animus toward the victim's gender. This implicitly acknowledges that some, if not most, violence against women is not gender-neutral; establishes the possibility that violence motivated by gender animus is a proper subject for civil rights actions; and affixes the term *hate crime* to "a crime of violence committed because of gender or on the basis of gender, and due, at least in part, to animus based on the victim's gender" (Pub. L. No 103–322). Although this law was ruled unconstitutional on the grounds that it exceeded the constitutional reach of the Congress into the realm of the states (*United States v. Morrison,* 529 U.S. 598 [2000]), it received national attention and was predicated on and promoted the inclusion of gender in the concept of a hate crime (Angelari 1994).

B. State Laws

A plethora of state hate crime laws have been enacted. These take many forms, including statutes proscribing criminal penalties for civil rights violations, "ethnic intimidation" and "malicious harassment" statutes, and amendments to previously enacted statutes authorizing enhanced penalties. These laws diversely specify provisions for race, religion, color, ethnicity, ancestry, national origin, sexual orientation, gender, age, disability, creed, marital status, political affiliation, involvement in civil or human rights, and armed service personnel. Some states require authorities to collect data on hate- or bias-motivated crimes, mandate law enforcement training, prohibit the undertaking of paramilitary training, specify parental liability, and provide for victim compensation. Many states prohibit institutional vandalism and the desecration or defacement of religious objects, interference with or disturbance of religious worship, and cross burning.[2] Well over half of the penalty enhancement laws were based on a model developed and disseminated by the Anti-Defamation League (1997).

Hate crime laws differ in important ways but share common elements (Grattet, Jenness, and Curry 1998). They create or enhance penalties for criminal behavior motivated by bias. They include provisions that delineate axes of social differentiation, such as race, religion, national origin, sexual orientation, gender, and disability. They contain an "intent standard" or "motivational requirement" for conviction. The most robust hate crime law in the United States can be found in California: "No person, whether or not under color of law, shall by force or threat of force, willfully injure, intimidate, interfere with, oppress, or threaten any other person in the free exercise or enjoyment of any right or privilege secured to him or her by the Constitution or the laws of the United States because of the other person's race, color, religion, ancestry, national origin, disability, gender, or sexual orientation, or because he or she perceives that the other person has one or more of these characteristics" (California Penal Code 422.7).

As hate crime laws were proposed and adopted social scientists began to study them as a particular type of public policy making,[3] and legal scholars and the courts debated the constitutionality of hate crime law in ways that aligned with larger debates about the regulation of hate speech (Jones 1992; Lawrence 1993, 1999; Gould 2005) and the reach of federalism (Lee and Fernandez 1990; Lawrence 1999; Uhrich 1999; Chorba 2001). Some analysts argued that hate crime laws are "inherently unfair" (Goldberger 2004) and infringe on constitutionally guaranteed rights to free speech, equal protection, and due process. Nonetheless, by the turn of the twenty-first century the constitutionality of hate crime law was well-established. In their examination of 38 hate crime–related cases that came before appellate courts between 1984 and 1999, S. Phillips and Grattet (2000, p. 575) concluded, "The central constitutional issues regarding speech, due process and equal protection presented perplexing questions upon which reasonable people could, and did, disagree. Yet such questions have now been largely resolved [by the courts]." Hate crime laws are now a viable component of state-sanctioned formal social control and set the stage for newfound law enforcement mandates to police, prosecute, and punish bias-motivated violence.

III. Law Enforcement Responses to Hate Crime Law

Law enforcement officials have grappled with whether, when, and how to enforce hate crime laws. The mandate brings with it definitional ambiguities related to establishing the parameters of hate crime in general and motive in particular; political controversies surrounding hate crime and its relationship to political correctness in both law enforcement agencies and communities; and organizational dilemmas connected to agency structures, resource allocation decisions, and workplace culture (Cogan 2002; Franklin 2002). These dynamics have influenced how hate crime has been policed and prosecuted.

A. Policing

A growing number of studies shed light on how the organization and practice of policing shape whether, when, and how hate crime gets detected and reported.

According to Wexler and Marx (1986, p. 206), as late as the mid-1980s, a common municipal response to bias-motivated violence was "to look the other way in the hope that it will disappear. . . . Given the many other pressing demands on urban police, it is not surprising that law enforcement in this area (apart from the most extreme cases) has been minimal." They examined the Boston Police Department's efforts to respond to race- and ethnicity-based violence by implementing a departmentwide policy and creating a specialized unit that was effective in uncovering incidents that, under traditional reporting methods, appeared commonplace. They revealed that in 1978 the Boston police commissioner established written guidelines that "were to alter dramatically" how bias crimes would be handled in Boston (p. 210). New police practices related to bias-motivated crime resulted in intensive investigation after an incident, covert surveillance, victim decoys, and cover tests. These practices were well ahead of their time.

In the mid-1990s a series of studies documented the institutional, organizational, community, and individual factors that shape how policing of hate crime unfolds. Walker and Katz (1995) examined the creation of bias crime units as a significant new feature of U.S. law enforcement. Based on a study of 16 agencies that reported having a bias crime unit, this work revealed three important findings. First, there was considerable variation among departments that reported having a special bias crime unit, including the units being located in different subdivisions of the department bureaucracy and staffed by different types of officers. Second, personnel in these units used discretion to define their mission more broadly than other elements of law enforcement by addressing the more general problem of racial and ethnic conflict. Third, the most important factor related to the effective administration of a bias crime unit was the extent to which a department was committed to responding to the general problem of bias crime. The commonality across the specialized units was that they all had written procedures for handling bias crimes, even though the content of the procedures varied.

Outside of specialized units, the commitment to enforce hate crime laws is most visibly reflected in special policies and formal statements made by high-ranking law enforcement officials. As Jenness and Grattet's (2005; Grattet and Jenness 2005) recent empirical work reveals, there is a proliferation of hate crime policies among local law enforcement agencies in large states such as California,[4] even though many city and county law enforcement agencies have yet to adopt formal policies decades after hate crime laws were enacted. Many agency and community factors explain this variation in policy adoption, most notably the degree to which the law enforcement agency is susceptible to environmental influences and the degree to which the organizational culture aligns with the hate crime policy innovation (Jenness and Grattet 2005). Local policies vary immensely in how they define and operationalize hate crime, delineate an intent or motivation standard as well as status and conduct provisions, and codify guidelines for offi-

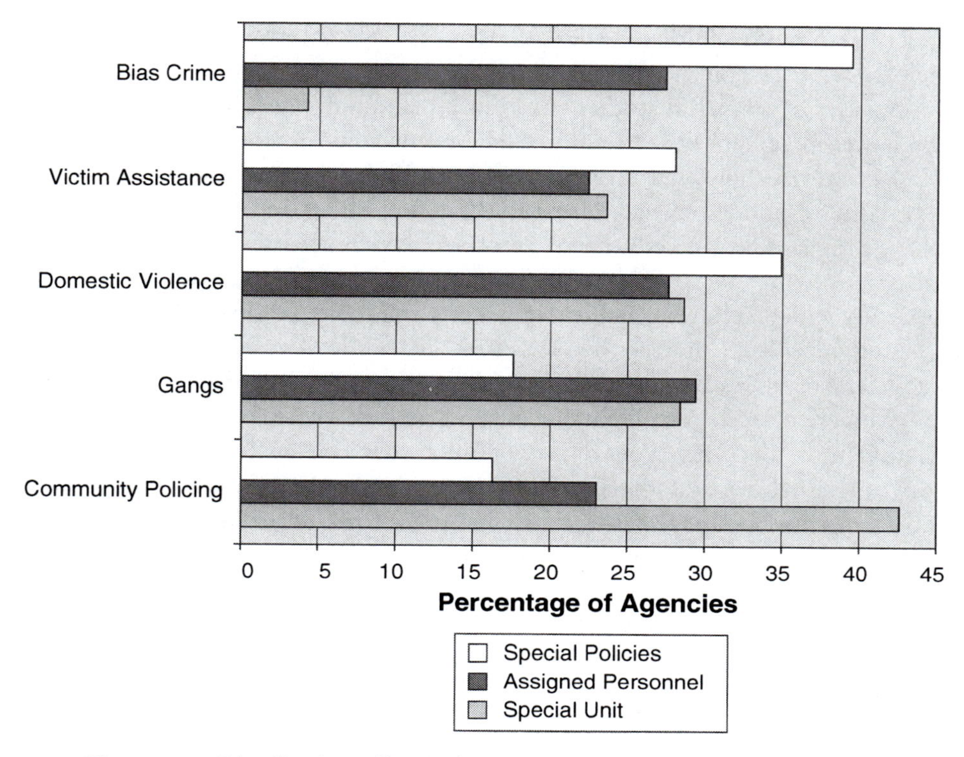

Figure 21.1. Distribution of law enforcement agency response to five major policing issues, 2000.
Source: Law Enforcement Management Administrative Statistics (U.S. Department of Justice 2000*b*).

cers to detect, report, classify, and investigate incidents that might qualify has hate crime (Grattet and Jenness 2005). Arguing that "the policies and the definitions of hate crime contained therein are an important venue through which local meaning-making related to hate crime occurs," Grattet and Jenness (2005, p. 911) demonstrate that what constitutes a hate crime from an enforcement (rather than a statutory) point of view is determined at the local level. This meaning making is informed by professional groups, social movements, federal and state sponsors, early prototypes of hate crime policy, community groups, and peer agencies and is a function of coercive, mimetic, normative, and actuarial processes (Grattet and Jenness 2005).

Data collected through the Law Enforcement Management Administrative Statistics survey of police departments conducted by the U.S. Bureau of Justice Statistics reveal that implementation of hate crime law enforcement is increasingly institutionalized. By the turn of the century enforcement of hate crime law was faring well compared with other policing pursuits, such as victim assistance, domestic violence, gangs, and community policing (fig. 21.1). Of course, the findings presented in figure 21.1 do not speak to how, in concrete terms, officers are enforcing hate crime law on the ground.

A series of empirical studies have illuminated how law enforcement agencies and law enforcement officers enforce hate crime law. For example, Martin (1995, 1996) examined how two jurisdictions, New York City and Baltimore County, Maryland, responded to hate crime in the 1990s. She found that these "agencies follow very similar procedures for identifying such offenses but employ different practices for investigating and verifying hate crimes" (Martin 1996, p. 459). In largely white, suburban Baltimore County the police embraced a community-oriented approach, whereas the New York City Police Department used a more traditional investigative approach. Martin's work emphasized the interpretive processes that demarcate whether incidents get classified as hate crime. She concludes, "Hate crimes, like other types of crimes, ultimately emerge through police definitions and situations and interpretations of laws and policies" (p. 471). Boyd, Berk, and Hamner's (1996, pp. 821–22) ethnography of the decision making of police detectives in a large urban police department concludes, "Far from finding it problematic to interpret and classify specific incidents, police detectives engage in certain routine practices in order to determine the hate-related status of an incident. Specifically, police rely on typifications and commonsense reasoning (Garfinkel 1967) regarding the constituent attributes of hate crimes and estimations of the proper role of the police as a basis for their interpretive decisions. These reasoning practices are inflected by the particular institutional arrangements of the division and the department in which the detectives operate." These typifications and reasoning practices are anchored in beliefs about the characteristics of "normal hate crimes" as well as efforts to determine what really happened that are geared toward arriving at assessments of bias motivation only when other motivations can be effectively eliminated.

In *Policing Hatred* Bell (2002) relies on ethnographic observations, interviews, police records, and media accounts to examine how a specialized detective unit, the Anti-Bias Task Force (ABTF) in "Center City," enforced hate crime law. Bell documents how the organizational history and structure of the ABTF, and the community in which it resided, determined the range of possibilities for policy development and hate crime enforcement. *Policing Hatred* explains how hate crime comes into being at the hands of those working the front lines of the criminal justice system.

Nolan and Akiyama's (1999, 2002) work on the enforcement of hate crime law suggests that differences in reporting can be attributed to variables that affect whether or not agencies report hate crime and variables that affect whether or not police officers record crime. These variables point to factors that affect law enforcement participation in hate crime reporting. Not surprisingly, one encourager is supportive organizational policies. Corroborating this view, Balboni and McDevitt's (2001, p. 15) research on factors that affect hate crime reporting among law enforcement personnel and across law enforcement agencies led them to conclude that "although individual officers may have differing opinions about the nature of the crime, if there is a policy about how to proceed with a hate crime investigation, officers will respect that policy." Grattet and Jenness (2008) used data from hundreds of California law enforcement agencies and hierarchical linear modeling to reveal that policies do, indeed, increase the rate of official hate crime reporting, regardless of other community and agency factors. Moreover, the degree to which law enforcement agencies are integrated into the communities in which they reside and to which they respond amplifies the effect policies have on official reporting.

B. Data Collection and Empirical Patterns: Police

Despite early analyses that anticipated obstacles to enforcement of the HCSA (Fernandez 1991; Uhrich 1999), law enforcement participation in the national data collection effort has steadily increased (table 21.1). By 2001, all 50 states were participating in this data collection effort, representing almost 12,000 law enforcement agencies covering over 80 percent of the population. However, over 80 percent of the reporting agencies routinely report zero hate crimes (Nolan, Akiyama, and Berhanu 2002; see also King 2007). In one of the most systematic

Table 21.1. Law enforcement participation in national hate crime data collection

Year	States and District of Columbia	Number of law enforcement agencies	% Population covered by participating agencies	Number of hate crimes reported	% of zero reporting agencies
1992	42	6,181	51	7,466	82
1993	47	6,865	58	7,587	81
1994	44	7,356	58	5,932	84
1995	46	9,584	75	7,947	84
1996	50	11,354	84	8,759	84
1997	49	11,211	83	8,049	85
1998	47	10,730	80	7,755	83
1999	49	12,122	85	7,876	85
2000	49	11,690	84	8,063	84
2001	50	11,987	85	9,730	82
2002	50	12,073	86	7,462	85
2003	50	11,909	83	7,489	84
2004	50	12,711	87	7,649	84
2005	50	12,417	83	7,163	84
2006	51*	12,620	85	7,722	83

* This number includes 49 states, the District of Columbia, and outlying areas (Guam).
Source: U.S. Department of Justice, various years.

analyses of the production of hate crime statistics, King (2007) demonstrates that compliance with the HCSA is less likely in places with larger black populations, and that this finding is contingent on region; that is, a positive correlation in the Northeast contrasts with an inverse association in the South. King also demonstrates that organizational facets of law enforcement affect compliance with the HCSA, with a commitment to community policing positively affecting compliance.

The implementation of the HCSA has resulted in production of a national inventory of officially reported incidents, offenses, and victims of hate crime in the United States.[5] The annual number of reported hate crime incidents ranged from 5,932 in 1994 to 9,730 in 2001. Race bias has consistently generated the most incidents, followed by religion, sexual orientation, ethnicity or nationality, and disability. In 2006 2,105 law enforcement agencies reported 7,722 hate crime incidents involving 9,080 offenses, 9,652 victims, and 7,330 offenders. In 2006 victims of hate crime were most often selected because of their race (52 percent); 66 percent of those were chosen because of antiblack sentiment, and 21 percent were selected because of antiwhite bias. Fewer than one-fifth (18 percent) of all hate crime victims were chosen because of religious affiliation, with the majority being targeted because of anti-Jewish sentiment. A little over 10 percent of victims targeted for religion were targeted due to their Muslim beliefs, and 5 percent were targeted because they are Catholic. Fifteen percent of victims were chosen because of their sexual orientation, with the majority being targeted because of anti–male homosexuality sentiment (62 percent). About 13 percent of those targeted were chosen because of their ethnicity or national origin; 63 percent of these were targeted because of their Hispanic heritage. One percent of all hate crime victims were targeted because of a bias against disability.

The majority of known offenders are white (59 percent); 21 percent are black. Of the 9,652 victims of hate crime in 2006, a little more than half (57 percent) were victims of crimes against persons, most commonly intimidation (46 percent) and thereafter simple assault (32 percent) and aggravated assault (22 percent). Fewer than half (43 percent) were victims of property crimes, most commonly destruction and damage or vandalism (80 percent), followed by larceny-theft (7 percent), robbery (5 percent), and burglary (4 percent). Fewer than 1 percent, 38 victims, were victims of crimes against society.

To put these patterns into perspective, it is useful to consider findings from the *National Crime Victim Survey* (*NCVS*) and the FBI's National Incident-Based Reporting System (NIBRS). A 2005 Bureau of Justice Statistics report revealed similar findings from multiple data sources (U.S. Department of Justice 2005). The *NCVS* and the Uniform Crime Reports demonstrate similar motivations for hate crimes. Motivations perceived by *NCVS* victims of crime not reported to the police are similar to ones reported to the police. Basic categories of offenses motivated by hate are similar for the *NCVS* and the Uniform Crime Reports.

However, there are also some differences. Some basic characteristics of hate crime victims differ in the *NCVS* and the NIBRS, with higher percentages of *NCVS* hate crime victims being women compared with the NIBRS hate crime victims (49 percent and 35 percent, respectively), a higher percentage of white victims in the *NCVS* data than the NIBRS data (84 percent and 67 percent, respectively), and a higher percentage of older victims in the *NCVS* data compared with the NIBRS data (64 percent and 45 percent, respectively, were over 30). Some basic characteristics of hate crime offenders also differ between the *NCVS* and the NIBRS, with a smaller percentage of offenses being committed by one person in the *NCVS* compared with the NIBRS (61 percent and 68 percent, respectively). Offenders reported by the *NCVS* were more likely to be strangers than offenders in the NIBRS (55 percent and 36 percent, respectively). The *NCVS* offenders were more likely than the NIBRS offenders to have a firearm, sharp implement, or blunt object (30 percent and 19 percent, respectively). Victims have reported an average of 191,000 hate crime incidents annually to the *NCVS* since 2000; however, only 44 percent of hate crimes are reported to the police. Victims who report hate crimes want to punish the offender and prevent further crimes; 40 percent of the victims who did not report hate crime to the police said they preferred to handle it another way.

Rubenstein (2004, p. 1220) reminds consumers of these data, "It is worth noting in this context that hate crimes constitute a very small percentage of all crimes, about .07 percent, or seven of every 10,000 crimes, nationwide." By adjusting for population size, Rubenstein demonstrates that these official data reveal that the gay population is the most at risk for hate crime victimization when compared to Jewish and black populations. Table 21.2 presents the annual rate of hate-related victimization per 1,000 persons, as computed by the Bureau of Justice Statistics; it does not include an estimate for sexual orientation.

C. Prosecution

The literature on prosecution of hate crime is considerably less developed. Maroney (1998, p. 607) reported, "No empirical research has been done to support or refute the premise of selective prosecution." Only recently has research on hate crime prosecutions begun to surface (King 2006; King, Messner, and Ballar 2006; McPhail and Jenness 2006; N. D. Phillips 2006). Lawrence (2006, p. 7) concedes that empirical data on hate crime law at the judicial decision-making level are "hard to come by" and that "broad legal or sociological generalizations will fill the gap. The better approach, of course, would be for these data to be collected and studied."

Some prosecutors have rejected hate crime laws as useless and unenforceable (Jacobs and Potter 1998; see also Lawrence 2006), whereas others have strongly embraced them (McPhail and Jenness 2006). For the former group, hate crime implies greater evidentiary burdens, more effort to explain hate crime laws to juries,

Table 21.2. Characteristics of victims of hate crime

Characteristics of victims	Annual rate of hate-related victimizations per 1,000 persons	
	All	Violent
Gender		
Male	1.0	0.9
Female	0.8	0.6
Race		
White	0.9	0.8
Black	0.7	0.5
Other*	1.4	1.1
Hispanic origin		
Hispanic	0.9	0.8
Non-Hispanic	0.9	0.8
Age		
17 or younger	1.6	1.6
18–20	1.6	1.6
21–29	1.1	1.0
30–39	0.9	0.6
40–49	1.0	0.7
50 or older	0.5	0.3
Marital status		
Never married	1.5	1.4
Married	0.5	0.4
Separated/divorced	2.6	1.2
Widowed	0.1	0.2**
Educational attainment		
Less than high school diploma	1.1	1.0
High school diploma	0.9	0.6
More than high school diploma	0.8	0.7
Household income		
Less than $25,000	1.3	1.0
$25,000–$49,000	1.0	0.9
$50,000 or more	0.7	0.7
Not reported	0.6	0.5
Location		
Urban	1.3	1.0
Suburban	0.8	0.7
Rural	0.7	0.6

Note: For property crimes, characteristics are those of the person reporting the incident to the *NCVS*.

* Includes American Indians and Asians. Persons of more than one race are excluded.

** Estimate is based on 10 or fewer sample cases.

Sources: U.S. Department of Justice, Bureau of Justice Statistics, 2005; *National Crime Victimization Survey, July 2000 through December 2003;* Harlow 2005.

and more time and energy to prepare cases. For prosecutors who are understaffed and have heavy caseloads, such laws may represent an extra set of burdens in an occupation often evaluated in terms of conviction rates. A prosecutor in Texas explained:

> If I believed personally that the case was racially motivated, but I thought that doing that [charging a hate crime] would detract from the actual commission of the crime and might jeopardize the guilty plea, then I would just try the case as a regular offense. The law allows us, in the code of criminal procedure, to offer anything in the punishment that the judge deems relevant for punishment. So, I would probably just save that for punishment, and call witnesses to prove that and then argue to the jury that that needs to move up the range of punishment. This is the safer course. (cited in McPhail and Jenness 2006, p. 97)

Other prosecutors view hate crime law as an extra tool for the management of crime and intergroup conflict in their community. Another Texas prosecutor explained, "I certainly would relish the opportunity to go after somebody who committed a crime and victimized somebody just because of their sexual orientation, or just because of race. I would love that and do it with glee. I would use every tool at my disposal to do it because I genuinely think that it is a worse person, a more dangerous person, who hurts somebody because of who they are rather than because of drugs, alcohol, or greed" (cited in McPhail and Jenness 2006, p. 107).

The federal and state governments increasingly have encouraged prosecution of hate crime by producing and disseminating resources in the form of periodicals. As early as 1992 the Department of Justice published *Hate Crime Statistics: A Resource Book* (U.S. Department of Justice 1992). In 1995 the Office for Victims of Crime created a National Bias Crimes Training curriculum designed to provide assistance for law enforcement officials and victim assistance professionals (U.S. Department of Justice 1995). In 1998 the National Institute of Justice created and distributed the guide *Prosecutorial Response to Hate and Bias-Motivated Crime* (American Prosecutors Research Institute 1998). In 2000 the Bureau of Justice Assistance published a booklet on *Addressing Hate Crimes: Six Initiatives That Are Enhancing Efforts of Criminal Justice Practitioners* (U.S. Department of Justice 2000*a*).

At the state level, prosecutors have produced and disseminated manuals that provide guidelines for prosecuting hate crime. In California the attorney general developed the Hate Crime Rapid Response Team Protocol for the Development of Department of Justice Resources. Some municipalities have sought to obtain compelling evidence for hate crime convictions. The city of Sacramento secured a $100,000 grant from the Bureau of Justice Assistance to deploy a sophisticated vehicle that permits close yet covert surveillance of hate crime suspects (U.S. Department of Justice 1997).

D. Data Collection and Empirical Patterns: Prosecution

Information on hate crime prosecution at the federal and state level is limited to official data from the U.S. Department of Justice, state attorneys general, and the *National Prosecutors Survey* conducted by the Bureau of Justice Statistics (U.S.

Department of Justice). There are no published studies of the degree to which hate crime is being prosecuted in the United States and the factors that predict prosecutors' decisions to pursue hate crime charges.

The Civil Rights Division of the U.S. Department of Justice is charged with enforcing and prosecuting federal hate crimes laws. Federal hate crime prosecutions are few in number, in part because of the narrow scope of the federal law and because of federal reluctance to preempt or disrupt local prosecutions. According to the Department of Justice, from fiscal years 1998 to 2001, the average number of prosecutions was 28.5.[6] In recent years the Department of Justice has prosecuted a number of high-profile hate crime cases. In fiscal year 2007 the Department of Justice convicted 189 defendants of civil rights violations, the largest number in the history of the department (http://www.usdoj.gov/opa/pr/2007/November/07_crt_921.html). Although it is difficult to determine what proportion of the Department of Justice's civil rights cases qualify as hate crime convictions proper, from fiscal year 2001 to fiscal year 2007 the department charged 62 defendants in 41 cross-burning cases (http://www.usdoj.gov/opa/pr/2007/November/07_crt_921.html).

In 2007 the Department of Justice reported the following examples of prosecuted cases.

- Conspiracy to threaten, assault, and murder African Americans. In *United States v. Saldana* four members of a violent Latino street gang in Los Angeles were convicted of participating in a conspiracy aimed at threatening, assaulting, and murdering African Americans in a neighborhood claimed by the defendants' gang. Three of the defendants were also convicted of a federal hate crime violation stemming from the murder of an African American who was killed because he was black and because he was using a public street claimed by the gang. All four defendants received life sentences.
- Racial cross burnings outside homes. In *United States v. Shroyer* and *United States v. Youngblood* individuals in Indianapolis and Detroit, respectively, were successfully prosecuted for burning crosses outside the homes of biracial families with the intent to interfere with victims' housing rights.
- Racial intimidation of a biracial family. In *United States v. Frederick and Kuzlik* two men were convicted in Cleveland, Ohio, for their roles in pouring mercury, a highly toxic substance, on the front porch and driveway of a biracial couple and their young child. This racially motivated act was done with the intent to force the victims out of their home.
- Assaults by members of a national white supremacist organization. In *United States v. Walker* three members of the National Alliance, a notorious white supremacist organization, were convicted for assaulting a Mexican American bartender at his place of employment in Salt Lake City, Utah. These same defendants allegedly assaulted an individual of Native American heritage outside another bar in Salt Lake City.

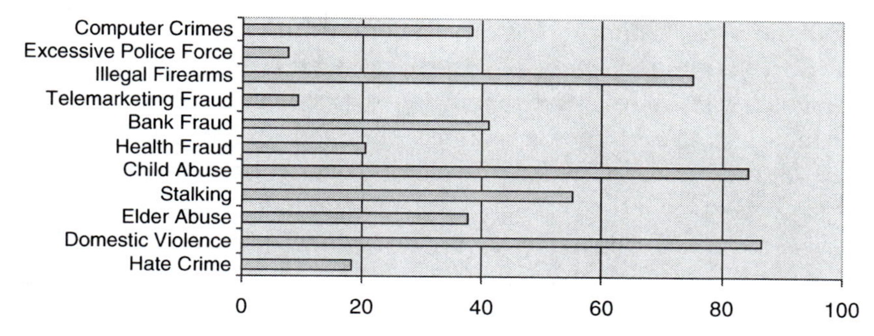

Figure 21.2. Percentage of prosecutors' offices in state court systems that have prosecuted select crimes, 2001.
Source: National Prosecutors Survey (U.S. Department of Justice).

- Race-based murder of an African American. In *United States v. Eye and Sandstrom,* a pending death penalty case in Kansas City, Missouri, the defendants have been charged with shooting and killing an African American man as he walked down the street. The government alleges that the defendants shot the victim because of his race and because he was walking on a public street.
- Cold case against a former Klansman for kidnapping and conspiracy in connection with the murder of two African Americans. *United States v. Seale* stemmed from the 1964 murders of 19-year-old Charles Moore and Henry Dee in Franklin County, Mississippi. In June 2007 a former Klansman, James Seale, 71, was convicted of kidnapping and conspiracy in connection with the murders of Moore and Dee. The defendant received two life sentences.

The Department of Justice continues to work with the National Association for the Advancement of Colored People, the National Urban League, and the Southern Poverty Law Center to identify additional unresolved civil rights era murders (http://www.usdoj.gov/opa/pr/2007/November/07_crt_921.html).

In 1992 the *National Prosecutors Survey* (U.S. Department of Justice), a biennial survey of chief prosecutors in state court systems that is designed to obtain detailed information on prosecutors' offices, asked, "During the past 12 months, did your office prosecute any of the following kinds of felony cases?" For the first time, hate crime was listed as an option. Of 271 respondents, 19.6 percent indicated yes, and 42.4 percent and 38 percent indicated no and "not applicable." In the 2001 *Survey,* of 2,341 respondents, the proportion that indicated yes remained about the same (18.2 percent), with 72.2 percent indicating no and 9.6 percent "missing data." Hate crime does not fare well when it comes to comparisons with the other felony offenses (fig. 21.2); prosecution of hate crime comes in toward the bottom of the list, above telemarketing fraud and excessive police force.

Of all the states, California has carried out the most impressive state data collection effort. In 1995 the California attorney general began to publish an annual report on hate crime in the state that includes a section on prosecution, summarized in table 21.3. The attorney general received a total of 1,306 hate crime reports. Of these, 363 cases were referred to prosecutors. From the 334 cases filed by district and city attorneys for prosecution, 272 were filed as hate crimes and 62 were filed as non-bias-motivated crimes. For the 249 cases with a disposition available for the report, 140 were hate crime convictions, 78 were for other convictions, and 31 were not convicted. Three-fourths (75 percent) of the hate crimes referred for prosecution were filed as a hate crime, and half (51 percent) of the hate crime cases filed resulted in hate crime convictions.

IV. Whither the Future?

As a concept and a set of criminal justice policies and practices, hate crime has crossed international borders. Other Western countries, especially English-speaking ones, have acted to criminalize bias-motivated conduct (Bleich 2007; Bleich and Hart 2008). England and Wales, for example, have enacted a series of laws designed to curb racial-ethnic violence, including in 1994 a clause in the penal code that allows for stiffer sentences if a crime is committed against a person as a result of the person's race, color, national or ethnic origin, religious beliefs, or similar circumstance (Ross 2006). Australia has outlawed at federal, state, and territory levels words and images that incite hatred toward particular groups of people and conduct that constitutes "vilification" or "racial hatred" (Hennessy and Smith 1994; Cunneen, Fraser, and Tomsen 1997). New Zealand's Human Rights Act of 1993 identifies "inciting racial disharmony" as an offense; an offense is committed when words are publicly said or written "with intent to excite hostility or ill-will against, or bring into contempt or ridicule, any group of persons in New Zealand on the ground of the color, race, or ethnic origins of that group" (Ross 2006, p. 31). Germany has forbidden "public incitement" and "instigation of racial hatred," including the distribution of Nazi propaganda or literature liable to corrupt the youth. Unlike the United States, however, other countries have adopted fairly limited conceptions of hate crime, focusing primarily on racial, ethnic, and religious violence. Many other countries, mostly in the non-Western world, have not adopted the term to reference racial, ethnic, religious, or any other forms of intergroup conflict.

How hate crime policies and law enforcement practices evolve and produce discernable consequences is a lengthy process that began with the invention of the term. It includes the social construction of the meaning of *hate crimes* in various institutional contexts and ends with the invocation of state authority to enhance punishment for those who manifest bigotry in criminal behavior. The study of

Table 21.3. California hate crime prosecutions, 1995–2006

	Year											
Processing activity	1995	1996	1997	1998	1999	2000	2001	2002	2003	2004	2005	2006
Reported hate crimes	1,754	2,054	1,831	1,750	1,962	1,957	2,261	1,659	1,491	1,409	1,397	1,306
Hate crimes referred for prosecution	–	366	–	–	1,039	–	–	539	462	407	448	363
Criminal case filings	187	182	313	244	372	360	360	425	374	371	396	334
Hate crime case filings	–	142	–	–	–	–	314	351	304	277	330	272
Non-bias-motivated crime filings	–	40	–	–	–	–	46	74	70	278	66	62
Hate crime case filings with a disposition	–	–	–	–	270	303	240	301	223	94	274	249
Not convicted	–	–	–	–	41	28	33	48	26	36	36	31
Hate crime convictions	–	87	223	131	174	213	136	164	128	139	197	140
Other convictions	–	75	57	43	55	62	71	89	69	103	101	78
Total Convictions	107	162	280	174	229	275	207	253	197	242	298	218

Source: California Department of Justice 2007.

hate crime proper is less about specific types of human conduct and more about a modern social and legal invention shaped by the modern politics of victimization, the varying contexts in which hate crime law has been adopted, and the ways law enforcement has—and has not—enforced the laws. To quote Cogan (2002, p. 173), hate crime signifies "a crime category worthy of policy attention," one that represents a profound shift in how criminal justice systems respond to crime connected to historic and contemporary inequalities.

The American literature focuses primarily on police and prosecution, demonstrating how hate crime law is being enforced in different contexts. It demonstrates that officers use discretion when defining what does and does not qualify as a hate crime. The social organization of policing and the structural composition of the communities in which hate crime law is enforced affect what officers do. There are significant differences in how the policing of hate crime unfolds across types of police personnel, policing units, jurisdictions, and polities. As a result, the enforcement of hate crime law often has been delayed and, when it happens, is quite variable (Franklin 2002).

Variability in enforcement aside, the modern hate crime project is alive and well and producing discernable enforcement effects. It is not reducible to symbolic politics in the United States. Rather, the systematic enforcement of hate crime law is an increasingly institutionalized part of the criminal justice system. The results include more robust detection, more systematic data collection, and more uniform enforcement. The history and future of hate crime parallel the trajectories of other kinds of crime that have recently received increased attention. The policing and prosecution of domestic violence is an obvious comparison case. Decades ago domestic violence law was controversial and to many law enforcement officials appeared ambiguous and unenforceable. Now it is an integral part of the fabric of U.S. criminal justice. The story of hate crime and criminal justice will, no doubt, be told as a story of increasing institutionalization. It is easy to anticipate that it will be increasingly institutionalized in other nations' criminal justice systems too.

NOTES

1. In 2001 Attorney General John Ashcroft announced the indictment of Darrell David Rice on homicide charges for stalking and murdering two lesbians camping in the Shenandoah National Park (U.S. Department of Justice 2001). In 2004 the charges were withdrawn "without prejudice."

2. For a routinely updated inventory of state-level hate crime law, see the Anti-Defamation League's map of state law (http://www.adl.org/learn/hate_crimes_laws/map.html (accessed April 15, 2008).

3. For example, see Haider-Markel and Meier (1996), Jenness and Grattet (1996, 2004), Grattet, Jenness, and Curry (1998), Earle and Soule (2001), Soule and Earl (2001), and Savelsberg and King (2005).

4. For more along these lines, see Wilson and Ruback's (2003) work on law enforcement in Pennsylvania.

5. Data summarized in this and the following paragraphs were provided by the Criminal Justice Information Services Division of the FBI.

6. Fiscal year 2001 prosecutions related to a September 11 backlash consider only the first few weeks following the attacks. According to an interview on July 23, 2003, with a staff member of the Criminal Section of the Civil Rights Division, only one September 11–related hate crime prosecution is included in the FY2001 data. U.S. Department of Justice, "Fiscal Year 2000 Performance Report and Fiscal Year 2002 Performance Plan: Appendix A," April 1, 2001, http://www.usdoj.gov:80/ag/annualreports/pr2000/AppAFY2000disc.htm (accessed July 22, 2003) and Human Rights Watch telephone interview with a staff member of the Criminal Section of the Civil Rights Division, Washington, DC, July 23, 2003. See also http://www.hrw.org/reports/2002/usahate/usa1102-02.htm#P173_21889 (accessed April 15, 2008).

REFERENCES

American Prosecutors Research Institute. 1998. "Prosecutorial Response to Hate and Bias-Motivated Crime." Report submitted to the National Institute of Justice, U.S. Department of Justice, Washington, DC.

Angelari, Marguerite. 1994. "Hate Crime Statutes: A Promising Tool for Fighting Violence against Women." *American University Journal of Gender and the Law* 2: 63–106.

Anti-Defamation League. 1997. *Hate Crimes Laws: A Comprehensive Guide*. New York: Anti-Defamation League.

Balboni, Jennifer, and Jack McDevitt. 2001. "Hate Crime Reporting: Understanding Police Officer Perceptions, Departmental Protocol, and the Role of the Victim: Is There Such a Thing as a Hate Crime?" *Justice Research and Policy* 3: 1–27.

Beale, Sara. 2000. "Federalizing Hate Crimes: Symbolic Politics, Expressive Law, or Tool for Criminal Enforcement?" *Boston University Law Review* 80: 1227.

Bell, Jeannine. 2002. *Policing Hatred: Law Enforcement, Civil Rights, and Hate Crime*. New York: New York University Press.

Bleich, Erik. 2007. "Hate Crime Policy in Western Europe: Responding to Racist Violence in Britain, Germany, and France." *American Behavioral Scientist* 51: 149–65.

Bleich, Erik, and Ryan K. Hart. 2008. "Quantifying Hate: The Evolution of German Approaches to Measuring 'Hate Crime.'" *German Politics* 17: 63–80.

Boyd, Elizabeth, Richard Berk, and Karl Hamner. 1996. "Motivated by Hatred or Prejudice: Categorization of Hate-Motivated Crimes in Two Police Divisions." *Law and Society Review* 30: 819–50.

California Department of Justice. 2007. *Hate Crime in California, 1995–2006*. Sacramento: Division of California Justice Information Services, Bureau of Criminal Information and Analysis, Criminal Justice Statistics Center.

Chorba, Christopher. 2001. "The Danger of Federalizing Hate Crimes: Congressional Misconceptions and the Unintended Consequences of the Hate Crimes Statistics Act." *Virginia Law Review* 87: 319–79.

Cogan, Jeanine C. 2002. "Hate Crime as Crime Category Worthy of Policy Attention." *American Behavioral Scientist* 46: 173–85.
Cunneen, Chris, David Fraser, and Stephen Tomsen, eds. 1997. *Faces of Hate: Hate Crime in Australia*. Leichardt, Australia: Federation Press.
Earl, Jennifer S., and Sarah A. Soule. 2001."The Differential Protection of Minority Groups: The Inclusion of Sexual Orientation, Gender, and Disability in State Hate Crime Law." *Research in Political Sociology: The Politics of Social Inequality* 9: 35–58.
Fernandez, Joseph. 1991. "Bringing Hate Crimes into Focus: The Hate Crimes Statistics Act of 1990, Pub. L. No 101–275." *Harvard Civil Rights–Civil Liberties Law Review* 26: 261–92.
Franklin, Karen. 2002. "Good Intentions: The Enforcement of Hate Crime Penalty Enhancement Statutes." *American Behavioral Scientist* 46: 154–72.
Garfinkel, Harold. 1967. *Studies in Ethnomethodology*. Englewood Cliffs, NJ: Prentice Hall.
Gellman, Susan B., and Frederick Lawrence. 2004. "Agreeing to Agree: A Proponent and Opponent of Hate Crime Laws Reach Common Ground." *Harvard Journal on Legislation* 41: 420–48.
Goldberger, David. 2004. "The Inherent Unfairness of Hate Crime Statutes." *Journal on Legislation* 41: 449–64.
Gould, Jon B. 2005. *Speak No Evil: The Triumph of Hate Speech Regulation*. Chicago: University of Chicago Press.
Grattet, Ryken, and Valerie Jenness. 2005. "The Reconstitution of Law in Local Settings: Agency, Discretion, Ambiguity, and a Surplus of Law in the Policing of Hate Crime." *Law and Society Review* 39: 893–942.
Grattet, Ryken, and Valerie Jenness. 2008. "Transforming Symbolic Law into Organizational Action: Hate Crime Policy and Law Enforcement Practice." *Social Forces* 87: 501–28.
Grattet, Ryken, Valerie Jenness, and Theodore Curry. 1998. "The Homogenization and Differentiation of Hate Crime Law in the United States, 1978–1995: Innovation and Diffusion in the Criminalization of Bigotry." *American Sociological Review* 63: 286–307.
Haider-Markel, Donald P. 1998. "The Politics of Social Regulatory Policy: State and Federal Hate Crime Policy and Implementation Effort." *Political Research Quarterly* 51: 69–88.
Haider-Markel, Donald P., and Kenneth J. Meier. 1996. "The Politics of Gay and Lesbian Rights: Expanding the Scope of the Conflict." *Journal of Politics* 58: 332–49.
Harlow, Caroline Wolf. 2005. *Hate Crime Reported by Victims and Police*. Washington, DC: Bureau of Justice Statistics, U.S. Department of Justice.
Hennessy, Nancy, and Paula Smith. 1994. "Have We Got It Right? NSW Racial Vilification Laws Five Years On." *Australian Journal of Human Rights* 1: 249–64.
Jacobs, James, and Kimberly Potter. 1998. *Hate Crimes: Criminal Law and Identity Politics*. New York: Oxford University Press.
Jenness, Valerie. 1995*a*. "Hate Crimes in the United States: The Transformation of Injured Persons into Victims and the Extension of Victim Status to Multiple Constituencies." In *Images and Issues: Typifying Contemporary Social Problems*, edited by Joel Best. New York: Aldine de Gruyter.
———. 1995*b*. "Social Movement Growth, Domain Expansion, and Framing Processes: The Gay/Lesbian Movement and Violence against Gays and Lesbians as a Social Problem." *Social Problems* 42: 145–70.
———. 1999. "Managing Differences and Making Legislation: Social Movements and the Racialization, Sexualization, and Gendering of Federal Hate Crime Law in the U.S., 1985–1998." *Social Problems* 46: 548–71.

Jenness, Valerie, and Kendal Broad. 1997. *Hate Crimes: New Social Movements and the Politics of Violence*. Hawthorne, NY: Aldine de Gruyter.
Jenness, Valerie, and Ryken Grattet. 1996. "The Criminalization of Hate: A Comparison of Structural and Policy Influences on the Passage of 'Bias-Crime' Legislation in the United States." *Sociological Perspectives* 39: 129–54.
Jenness, Valerie, and Ryken Grattet. 2004. *Making Hate a Crime: From Social Movement to Law Enforcement*. New York: Russell Sage.
Jenness, Valerie, and Ryken Grattet. 2005. "The Law-in-Between: The Effects of Organizational Perviousness on the Policing of Hate Crime." *Social Problems* 52: 337–59.
Jones, Charles H. 1992. "Proscribing Hate: Distinctions between Criminal Harm and Protected Expression." *William Mitchell Law Review* 18: 935–59.
King, Ryan. 2006. "Dormancy and Implementation in Criminal Law: The Case of Hate Crime Prosecution." Paper presented at the annual meeting of the American Society of Criminology, Toronto, Canada, April.
———. 2007. "The Context of Minority Group Threat: Race, Institutions, and Complying with Hate Crime Law." *Law and Society Review* 41: 189–224.
King, Ryan, Steven Messner, and Robert D. Ballar. 2006. "Resisting Hate Crime Law and the Legacy of Lynching." Paper presented at the annual meeting of the Southern Sociological Society, New Orleans, Louisiana.
Lawrence, Frederick M. 1993. "Resolving the Hate Crimes/Hate Speech Paradox: Punishing Bias Crimes and Protecting Racist Speech." *Notre Dame Law Review* 68: 673–721.
———. 1999. *Punishing Hate: Bias Crimes under American Law*. Cambridge, MA: Harvard University Press.
———. 2006. "The Hate Crime Project and Its Limitations: Evaluating the Societal Gains and Risk in Bias Crime Law Enforcement." Public and Legal Theory Working Paper No. 216, Legal Studies Research Paper No. 216. George Washington University Law School.
Lee, Virginia, and Joseph M. Fernandez. 1990. "Legislative Responses to Hate-Motivated Violence: The Massachusetts Experience and Beyond." *Harvard Civil Rights–Civil Liberties Law Review* 25: 287–340.
Maroney, Terry A. 1998. "The Struggle against Hate Crime: Movement at a Crossroads." *New York University Law Review* 73: 564–620.
Martin, Susan. 1995. "A Cross-Burning Is Not Just an Arson: Police Social Construction of Hate in Baltimore Country." *Criminology* 33: 303–26.
———. 1996. "Investigating Hate Crimes: Case Characteristics and Law Enforcement Responses." *Justice Quarterly* 13: 455–80.
McPhail, Beverly, and Valerie Jenness. 2006. "To Charge or Not to Charge—That Is the Question: The Pursuit of Strategic Advantage in Prosecutorial Decision-Making Surrounding Hate Crime." *Journal of Hate Studies* 4: 89–119.
Nolan, James J., and Yoshio Akiyama. 1999. "An Analysis of Factors That Affect Law Enforcement Participation in Hate Crime Reporting." *Journal of Contemporary Criminal Justice* 15: 111–27.
Nolan, James. J., and Yoshio Akiyama. 2002. "Assessing the Climate for Hate Crime Reporting in Law Enforcement Organizations: A Force-Field Analysis." *Justice Professional* 15: 87–103.
Nolan, James, Yoshio Akiyama, and Samuel Berhanu. 2002. "The Hate Crimes Statistics Act of 1990: Developing a Method for Measuring the Occurrence of Hate Violence." *American Behavioral Scientist* 46: 136–53.
Perry, Barbara, ed. 2003. *Hate and Bias Crime: A Reader*. New York: Routledge.

Phillips, Nickie D. 2006. "Prosecution of Bias-Motivated Crimes in New Jersey County, 2001–2004." PhD dissertation, City University of New York, Graduate Center, Department of Criminal Justice.
Phillips, Scott, and Ryken Grattet. 2000. "Judicial Rhetoric, Meaning-Making, and the Institutionalization of Hate Crime Law." *Law and Society Review* 34: 567–606.
Ross, Jennifer Marie. 2006. "Bias Crime Investigation: Does a Label Make a Difference?" Master's thesis, Victoria University of Wellington, Department of Sociology.
Rubenstein, William. 2004. "The Real Story of the U.S. Hate Crime Statistics: An Empirical Analysis." *Tulane Law Review* 78: 1213–46.
Savelsberg, Joachim, and Ryan King. 2005. "Institutionalizing Collective Memories of Hate: Law and Law Enforcement in Germany and the United States." *American Journal of Sociology* 111: 579–616.
Soule, Sarah A., and Jennifer S. Earl. 2001. "The Enactment of State Level Hate Crime Law in the United States: Intrastate and Interstate Factors." *Sociological Perspectives* 44: 281–305.
Uhrich, Craig L. 1999. "Hate Crime Legislation: A Policy Analysis." *Houston Law Review* 36: 1467–529.
U.S. Department of Justice. 1992. *Hate Crimes Statistics: A Resource Book*. Washington, DC: Federal Bureau of Investigation.
———. 1995. *National Bias Crime Training for Law Enforcement and Victim Assistance Professionals*. Washington, DC: Office of Justice Programs, Office for Victims of Crime.
———.1994–95. *Survey of Prosecutorial Responses to Bias-Motivated in Crime in the United States, 1994–1995*. Washington, DC: Office of Justice Programs. National Institute of Justice.
———. 1997. *Stopping Hate Crime: A Case History from the Sacramento Police Department*. Washington, DC: Office of Justice Programs, Bureau of Justice Statistics.
———. 2000*a*. *Addressing Hate Crimes: Six Initiatives That Are Enhancing the Efforts of Criminal Justice Practitioners*. Washington, DC: Office of Justice Programs, Bureau of Justice Assistance.
———. 2000*b*. *Law Enforcement Management Administrative Statistics*. Washington, DC: Bureau of Justice Statistics.
———. 2001. News Conference with USA John Brownlee: Indictment of Darrell David Rice. DOJ Conference Center, Washington, DC, April 10.
———. 2005. *National Crime Victimization Survey, July 2000 through December 2003*. Washington, DC: Bureau of Justice Statistics.
———. 2005. *Hate Crime Reported by Victims and Police*. Washington, DC: Office of Justice Programs, Bureau of Justice Statistics.
———.[multiple years]. *National Prosecutors Survey*. Washington, DC: Bureau of Justice Statistics.
Walker, Samuel, and Charles M. Katz. 1995. "Less Than Meets the Eye: Police Department Bias-Crime Units." *American Journal of Police* 14: 29–48.
Wexler, Chuck, and Gary T. Marx. 1986. "When Law and Order Works: Boston's Innovative Approach to the Problem of Racial Violence." *Crime and Delinquency* 32: 205–23.
Wilson, Mindy S., and R. Barry Ruback. 2003. "Hate Crime in Pennsylvania, 1984–99: Case Characteristics and Police Responses." *Justice Quarterly* 20: 373–96.

CHAPTER 22

PROSTITUTION

JODY MILLER

THERE is perhaps no criminalized activity as hotly—and broadly—contested as prostitution. The *terms* of these debates help illustrate. At the basest level, the host of derogatory words used to describe women who sell sex is unmatched. These are tied to patriarchal religious understandings of prostitutes as sinners who are the ultimate abandoners of women's proper place as virgins or wives and mothers, and even as morally depraved corruptors of innocent men (Adler 1992). Academics use their own set of politicized words. Individuals who exchange sexual acts for economic remuneration are variously referred to as prostitutes, sex workers, and prostituted women. They are simultaneously understood as criminal offenders, legitimate workers, gendered victims, vectors of disease, and the ultimate subversives. Which interpretation is accurate depends on who you ask.

Throughout most of the United States legislators and criminal justice practitioners weigh in on the debate through the criminalization of prostitution and (more or less rigorous) enforcement of laws against it. To most criminal justice officials prostitution is a public order offense that contributes to social disorder in communities, including "disorderly public conduct, potential harm to children, harassment of and violence against women," drugs, crime, and the proliferation of dangerous and unsightly paraphernalia (Brents and Hausbeck 2005, p. 274). From a public health perspective prostitution is a serious health problem, particularly in the realm of sexually transmitted diseases and HIV/AIDS. The association of prostitution with disease has deep historical roots (Walkowitz 1982) and is rigorously disputed by sex workers' rights advocates, who argue that the presumed association of prostitution with disease is perpetuated by the tendency to view sex work as a homogeneous activity in which the most coercive or exploitive contexts are generalized as prototypical (Jenness 1993; Kempadoo and Doezema 1998; Saunders 2005).

Prostitution is hotly contested among feminists. Sex radicals bring a libertarian approach, arguing against government interference in consensual sexual activities (Rubin 1984). Liberal feminist philosophy (if not liberal feminists), parallel with some sex workers' rights organizations, frames the issue as a legitimate occupation, emphasizing choice, consent, and civil rights (Jenness 1993). Marxist and socialist feminists recognize prostitution as a gendered economic strategy emerging from women's (and especially women of color's) labor exploitation under advanced capitalism (see Maher 1997), while some radical feminists define prostitution as the ultimate form of violence against women and the quintessential symbol of patriarchy (Barry 1995). Similar to the situation during intense pornography debates that began in the early 1980s (McElroy 1997; MacKinnon and Dworkin 1998), these radical feminists find seemingly incompatible partners in the religious right. Though with vastly different philosophical underpinnings, both groups share the desire to eradicate prostitution (see Chapkis 2003). In contrast, poststructuralist feminists define prostitution as the ultimate subversive act because of "its open challenge both to the identification of sex acts with acts of desire and to the opposition between erotic/affective activity and economic life" (Zatz 1997, p. 277).

Unfortunately, what we know—and what we don't know—about prostitution is very much driven by the ideological debates that frame our understandings of the issue. This is an important caveat to keep in mind when interpreting the available statistics and research on the topic and in considering policy and practice. As Saunders (2005, p. 344) notes, "Much of the material published...and resultant public policy has more to do with other social anxieties than with the human beings who engage in commercial sex." With this caution in mind, here is how this chapter is organized. Section I provides an overview of definitional issues concerning prostitution and their linkages to legal philosophies about how best to address commercial sex. In section II I describe what we know of patterns, trends, and varieties of prostitution. Section III reviews research evidence on the causes and correlates of prostitution, as well as direct and collateral consequences. I consider the range of policy responses to prostitution, including currently popular criminal justice and other intervention strategies in section IV. I conclude with suggestions of fruitful directions for research and policy.

As I review what we know about prostitution and prostitution-related policies, several important themes will be clear:

- Commercial sex comprises a vastly diverse set of phenomena. Both research and policy have been inadequately attentive to this diversity, leading to major gaps in the knowledge we have available and the approaches developed to address prostitution.
- Politicization of the issue—from a wide-ranging set of stakeholders—contributes to these inadequacies. In the United States this has resulted in the dominance of punitive and medicalized models of intervention that fail to address the social, economic, and spatial complexities of prostitution.

- The only national data on prostitution patterns come from the Uniform Crime Reports and the National Incident-Based Reporting System arrests. These data, relating mostly to street prostitution, show that women arrested for prostitution are disproportionately African American, Asian, and Hispanic.
- The onset of prostitution occurs most commonly in adulthood, except among juvenile runaways and homeless people.
- Limited information is available on participation in different types of prostitution; most estimates are that 10 to 30 percent of prostitutes, disproportionately minority, are street workers.
- There appears to be a strong connection between drug use and prostitution, although the causal nexus is unclear. The position and personal safety of street prostitutes were significantly diminished by the proliferation of crack cocaine markets.
- Physical and sexual abuse of street prostitutes is epidemic.
- The American prohibitionist approach to prostitution has failed and leads to a wide array of disadvantages for prostitutes. Most other Western countries have developed more effective policies that produce fewer harmful consequences.

I. Definitions of Prostitution

Definitions and meanings of prostitution are widely contested. It is generally agreed that prostitution involves the exchange of sexual activities for economic remuneration with individuals with whom no special relationship otherwise exists (Scott et al. 2005). However, several facets of this definition are notable. First, it concentrates on the *sellers* rather than the *purchasers* of commercial sex, and consequently this orientation has guided much research and policy until quite recently. Often this has also meant an exclusive focus on *women* engaged in prostitution. In the United States, for example, until as recently as the 1970s numerous states' prostitution laws specified that criminalized prostitutes were "female" (Monroe 2005), and the purchase of commercial sex was not criminalized in all states until the 1960s (Weitzer 1999). Even when definitions are gender-neutral, the archetypal prostitute remains a woman (Pettersson and Tiby 2003).

In addition, there are variations in definitions of what constitutes economic remuneration. Under the prohibitionist model in the United States prostitution involves *monetary* exchange. Many scholars agree, however, that economic remuneration can also include "the provision of one or more of the necessities of living (i.e., food, clothing, and protection) and/or other items of monetary value" (Scott et al. 2005, p. 322; see also Pettersson and Tiby 2003, pp. 161–63). Particularly in recent decades, researchers have also included sex-for-drug exchanges as an important form of prostitution and a prominent feature of public health risks associated with commercialized sex (Romero-Daza, Weeks, and Singer 2003; Cusick and Hickman 2005).

Such inclusions are problematic for prostitutes' rights advocates, as they incorporate a variety of problematic sexual exchanges that distract from recognition of prostitution as service work and thus lead "to a strengthening of the stigma that is attached to prostitution" (van der Poel 1995, p. 41). Indeed, the result is a dominant paradigm in which prostitution consists of "sexual acts which socially marginalized women with health difficulties initiate/conduct on the street with men who give them money in return... [thus] defining prostitution as comprising individuals from a markedly vulnerable social situation" (Pettersson and Tiby 2003, pp. 168–69).

The contested nature of prostitution definitions is brought into sharpest relief when considered in light of the dominant legal philosophies concerning whether and how to intervene on prostitution. Four legal paradigms have been identified to address prostitution: prohibition, abolition, decriminalization, and legalization or regulation (Coomaraswamy 1997). In the prohibitionist model prostitution as such is a crime. Technically, all parties involved are criminalized, including the sex worker, client, and others who profit (e.g., pimps, brokers, traffickers, managers). However, it is primarily sex workers who are arrested and prosecuted (Norton-Hawk 2001; Monroe 2005). Except in rural counties in Nevada (Brents and Hausbeck 2005), the United States adopts a prohibitionist stance toward prostitution.[1]

Under the prohibitionist paradigm, prostitution is criminalized as a morals offense for its perceived disruption of public order and its presumed criminogenic effects. Weitzer (1999, p. 85) summarizes:

> The public visibility of the [prostitution] enterprise increases the likelihood that it will have some adverse effect on the surrounding community.... Standard complaints center on conduct such as streetwalkers' brazen flagging down of customers' cars, arguing and fighting with people on the street, visible drug use, performing sex acts in public, and littering with used condoms and syringes (both unsightly trash and a public health hazard). Children are frequently mentioned in the litany of grievances: they witness transactions and sex acts being consummated; they sometimes discover discarded condoms and syringes; and they are occasionally approached by prostitutes or customers.

There are, however, a variety of critiques of the prohibitionist model and its characterization of prostitution. Regardless of the competing philosophical stance, there is widespread agreement that prohibition is the most oppressive intervention paradigm for individuals who sell sex, as it increases stigma, heightens risks for victimization and exploitation, and often functions to strip prostitutes of legal protection under the law (Scibelli 1987).

For those who promote an abolitionist model the prohibitionist stance is tantamount to punishing the victims of violent exploitation. From the abolitionist perspective *prostituted women* are, by definition, victims in commercial sexual exchanges. Thus their participation in prostitution is decriminalized, whereas third-party involvement, and in some cases the participation of purchasers, is a criminal offense.[2] The ultimate goal under abolitionist models is the eradication of commercial sexual exchanges. This is the approach outlined in U.S. antitrafficking legislation passed in 2000, but with stringent criteria for determining who the "truly innocent victims" are (see Chapkis 2003).[3] No country has adopted a purely abolitionist approach. Although the act of prostitution itself is not criminalized, such acts as street solicitation, loitering, and "kerb-crawling" remain criminal offenses (for example, see Scibelli 1987 regarding France and Thailand; Hatty 1989 regarding Australia; Lowman 1990 regarding Canada). In the United Kingdom, for example, antisocial behavior orders can be used to declare prostitution a public disorder; violation of such an order is then a criminal offense (Armitage 2002). Regardless, like the prohibitionist model, the abolitionist approach does not recognize women's right to choose prostitution as a legitimate occupation. This is another arena of contested meanings and definitions.

The argument that prostitution should be recognized as *sex work* emanates from two philosophical positions: a liberal or libertarian model that views prostitution as a legitimate occupational choice within the service economy but says little about gender, race, and class stratification (see Jenness 1993; van der Poel 1995), and a critical structural-economic perspective that suggests "women become involved in prostitution because of economic and structural barriers that prevent them from earning sufficient capital in both the licit and illicit economies" (Maxwell and Maxwell 2000, p. 791). Decriminalization is the paradigm advocated by those who define prostitution as work. Key issues include the need to challenge the sexual double standard of morality as a means of de-stigmatizing prostitution, as well as combating discriminatory labor practices and exploitive working conditions (Truong 1990, pp. 48–50).

Those who bring a liberal or libertarian orientation to prostitution tend not to critique the sex industry or its place in broadly inequitable economic and social systems. Those who bring a more critical approach view decriminalization as a short-term solution to improve sex workers' lives without losing sight of the larger patriarchal and otherwise unequal contexts in which it takes place. For instance, many feminists suggest that prostitution both results from and contributes to the sexual objectification of women and sexual double standards. They maintain "a crucial moral distinction between prostitutes as sex workers and prostitution as a practice and institution" (Overall 1992, p. 708), but diverge from abolitionist radical feminists because they "defend prostitutes' entitlement to do their work but [do not] defend prostitution itself as a practice under patriarchy" (p. 723). Others argue that the ultimate goal is to overcome economic, employment, and migration inequalities based on gender, race, class, and nation. Whether prostitution might look different under more equitable social and economic arrangements, and whether women would choose sex work were a wider range of income-generating options available, would be open questions unfettered from current practices within unjust systems. Thus Zatz (1997, p. 291) argues, "It is not sex work per se that promotes oppressive values of capitalist patriarchy but rather the particular cultural and legal production of a marginalized, degraded prostitution that ensures its oppressive characteristics while acting to limit the subversive potential that might attend a decriminalized, culturally legitimate form of sex work."

Finally, legalization or regulation is the predominant legal approach for addressing prostitution in a number of Western and non-Western countries and in rural counties of Nevada.[4] Under this model there is state tolerance of prostitution through government regulatory schemes. Regulation includes direct government interventions such as the licensing and registration of brothel houses and neoregulatory systems such as mandatory health exams for sex workers (Scibelli 1987; Brents and Hausbeck 2005). This approach might best be understood from a conservative or functionalist interpretation of (male) sexuality and the role of prostitution: "Since male sexual needs cannot be satisfied within the framework of non-commercial arrangements, prostitution is regarded as a complement to marriage. The control of prostitution itself is viewed as both undesirable and doomed to failure, whilst various forms of social disruption that may arise in connection with prostitution ought to be dealt with" (Pettersson and Tiby 2003, pp. 157–58). Understanding legalization from this perspective provides insight into why it is only those who *sell* sex that are subject to regulation, including regular medical intervention, and why women's mobility is often severely restricted once they are registered sex workers, with regulations governing when and with whom they can be in public space (Brents and Hausbeck 2005).[5] For these reasons sex workers' right advocates are opposed to the legalization, in contrast to decriminalization, of prostitution.

II. Patterns and Trends in Prostitution

Given these vastly divergent orientations toward prostitution, what do we know about its patterns and trends? National and other systematic data are extremely limited. Because prostitution involves behaviors that are both stigmatized and almost uniformly illegal in the United States "the size and boundaries of the population are unknown, making it extremely difficult to get a representative sample" (Shaver 2005, p. 296). Most research uses samples identified through criminal justice or social service agencies or uses snowball sampling techniques. Each of these approaches results in selective or oversampling of "the most visible participants (such as street workers)," including those in crisis, whereas others, such as those who work in indoor venues of various kinds, are either not included or are undersampled (Shaver 2005, p. 296; Weitzer 2005). Kanouse and colleagues (1999) describe an innovative strategy they used to draw a probability sample of female street prostitutes in Los Angeles County, but note that they were unable to do so for indoor venues.[6] The result is a relatively homogeneous set of data on prostitution—in its most "multi-problematic" context (van der Poel 1995, p. 41)—with limited attention to the heterogeneity of prostitution or the diverse array of participants involved. This focus also results in a view of prostitution as a stigmatized identity category rather than a revenue-generating activity (Shaver 2005, p. 297).

Because prostitution is almost uniformly criminalized in the United States crime data are the primary source of systematic information. Consider the key sources we use for documenting crime patterns and trends. First, the Uniform Crime Reports have a primary concern with index offenses, those violent and property crimes deemed to be most serious in nature and impact. Because prostitution is a nonindex offense, data in the UCR are available only for arrests. There are a number of limitations to these data. First, the reporting category "prostitution and commercialized vice" includes an array of aggregated prostitution-related offenses. This category is defined by the FBI for reporting purposes as "the unlawful promotion of or participation in sexual activities for profit... includ[ing] prostitution; keeping a bawdy house, disorderly house, or house of ill fame; pandering, procuring, transporting, or detaining women for immoral purposes, etc.; [and] attempts to commit any of the above" (*Uniform Crime Reporting Handbook* 2004, p. 142). Thus it is not possible to identify what proportion of arrests are for solicitation to sell versus purchase sex, nor what proportion falls into the other commercialized sex offenses listed.

For example, in 2006 women were 64.2 percent of arrests in this offense category. Given evidence of the selective targeting of women engaged in (especially street-level) sex work, presumably the vast majority of these arrests involved women who were sellers of commercial sex. Though prostitution is often seen as *the* quintessential female offense, in 2006 only 1.5 percent of female arrests were for prostitution (Uniform Crime Reports 2006). Among the 35.8 percent of prostitution arrests in 2006 involving males (constituting 0.3 percent of male arrests), it is not known what proportion was arrested as a result of attempts to purchase commercial sex, as compared to selling sex or participating in the range of other offenses included in this UCR category.

Weitzer (1999) suggests that one-third of male arrests are for attempting to purchase commercial sex but does not provide evidence on how this estimate was calculated. Based on National Incident-Based Reporting System (NIBRS) data, Finkelhor and Ormrod (2004) report that between 1997 and 2000, 53 percent of adults arrested for prostitution were male and 47 percent were female. This includes only individuals arrested for engaging in prostitution as sellers, not purchasers. It is unclear why these data diverge so dramatically from UCR data, except that the NIBRS data are not yet nationally representative. Nonetheless, given disparate patterns of enforcement of prostitution laws across gender and variations in the extent to which jurisdictions target purchasers, these remain important questions.

Because selling sex is perceived as characteristically female, we know considerably less about patterns and trends involving men and transgendered individuals in the United States (but see Weitzer 2005 for an overview).

There are other significant problems with reliance on the Uniform Crime Reports to gauge patterns and trends in prostitution. First, there is extensive evidence that law enforcement interventions almost exclusively target individuals involved in street-level prostitution rather than indoor varieties (Weitzer 1999). This form of prostitution is most visible and is also considered most disruptive of public order, neighborhood safety, and community values. In addition, "gender bias persists in both arrest rates and penalties" for prostitution (p. 95). This is reflected, in part, in failures in many jurisdictions to arrest or otherwise penalize those who purchase sex. There are dramatic variations across jurisdictions and over time in the priority police agencies give to prostitution, and so-called "revolving door" policies in some jurisdictions often mean that the same individuals are arrested multiple times for the same offense (Weitzer 1999). In other cases, individuals suspected of prostitution may be arrested for other offenses (O'Leary and Howard 2001). These issues make reliance on UCR data problematic for understanding prostitution patterns and trends.

In view of these problems with official data, what other sources of information are available? Here we find further limitations. For example, because prostitution is considered a victimless or public order crime, data are not available from the *National Crime Victimization Survey*. This is the primary alternative to the UCR as a source of systematic national crime data. Self-report surveys, although not national in scope, are another major source of information on offending. However, such surveys are almost exclusively administered with adolescents, and systematic self-report surveys are often administered in school settings. This is problematic for several reasons. Unlike most other types of criminalized behaviors, the onset of prostitution appears to occur most often in early adulthood rather than adolescence (Maxwell and Maxwell 2000; but see Raphael and Shapiro 2002). This means youths are a unique subset of those involved in prostitution. Moreover, evidence consistently shows that youths at greatest risk for participation in prostitution are runaways and homeless (Nadon, Koverola, and Schludermann 1998; McClanahan et al. 1999; Raphael and Shapiro 2002; Weber et al. 2004), making it unlikely that they will be included in most self-report surveys.[7]

Finally, there is limited systematic information about both prosecution and sentencing patterns and trends for prostitution. For example, national data sources such as the Bureau of Justice Statistics' National Judicial Reporting System collect data only on felonies. Although anecdotal evidence suggests that prostitutes face a revolving door of criminal justice arrest, prosecution, and incarceration (Weitzer 1999; DeLisi 2002), researchers have not systematically examined the extent of disproportionate criminal justice intervention either for prostitution as compared to other arrestees or for various subcategories of those arrested for prostitution. Such data and research are much needed.

A. National Patterns and Trends in Arrest Data

For all of its flaws, the Uniform Crime Report is the best source of systematic information about prostitution, or at least patterns of arrest for prostitution-related offenses.[8] For this reason, UCR patterns and trends are worth consideration. Table 22.1 shows notable patterns of arrest trends by gender and age. Perhaps reflecting a shift in policy in some jurisdictions toward targeting men who purchase commercial sex, the late 1980s and early 1990s show an increase in arrests for men. This was followed, however, by a dramatic decrease in the late 1990s, which continued for adolescent males through 2006. In contrast, women's arrest trends were more inconsistent, with net declines from 1993 to 2006, but a small increase from 2002 to 2006. Arrests for adolescent girls show the most divergence from the overall trends: from the mid-1990s onward their rates of arrest have increased dramatically.

These patterns must be put in the context of the significant difference in the number of adult versus adolescent arrests. Across gender, adolescent arrests are, on average, 2 percent or less of total arrests for prostitution. This is in striking contrast to other common offense types. In 2006, for example, adolescent girls accounted for 16.2 percent of female violent index offense arrests, 27.1 percent of female property index offense arrests, and 8.7 percent of female drug abuse violation arrests (Uniform Crime Reports 2006). Although the adolescent proportion of prostitution arrestees increased from 1.3 percent in 1997 to 2.3 percent in 2006, these proportions are considerably lower than for other offenses.[9] Older women are a larger proportion of prostitution arrestees, as compared to other arrest categories.

It is not clear to what extent these arrest trends reflect patterns in women's rates of participation in prostitution across age. For example, based on their analysis of NIBRS data, Finkelhor and Ormrod (2004, p. 5) report that arrests are "less likely to be made in prostitution incidents involving juvenile offenders than in incidents involving adult offenders (74 percent and 90 percent of incidents, respectively)." In addition, arrest patterns by age may reflect variations in participation in prostitution across venues. Street-level prostitution bears the brunt of law enforcement

Table 22.1. Prostitution arrest trends by gender and age, 1988–2006

	% Change, 1988–97	% Change, 1993–97	% Change, 1997–2006	% Change, 2002–6
Male arrests	+16.9	+8.8	−31.5	−0.6
Male arrests, under 18	−14.3	+2.8	−31.2	−20.3
Female arrests	+5.0	−1.3	−14.8	+7.2
Female arrests, under 18	−35.1	+17.9	+48.2	+37.3
Total arrests	+9.4	+2.4	−21.6	+4.4

Source: Uniform Crime Reports 1997, 2006.

intervention (Weitzer 1999). Older women may be pushed into street-level work from other settings as a result of the association of youth with sexual desirability, and this may account for their disproportionate share of arrests. However, NIBRS data suggest that prostitution incidents involving juveniles are "considerably more likely to occur at homes and residences" (Finkelhor and Ormrod 2004, p. 5). Given that prostitution in such venues is less likely to come to police attention, official data may disproportionately underestimate juvenile prostitution.

Moreover, some arrests may reflect revolving-door practices in criminal justice interventions in prostitution (Weitzer 1999). DeLisi's (2002) analysis of arrest data for "female career criminals" includes, as illustration, the profile of a woman arrested 70 times for prostitution-related charges over a 12-year period. Notably, he also found that women classified as habitual offenders appeared to be late onset: their first arrests tended to occur in adulthood, and they had significant involvement in both prostitution and drug offenses. These are important relationships I return to below. It is safe to infer that age-related patterns for women in prostitution do appear distinct as compared with other criminalized behaviors. Unfortunately there is not sufficient evidence to draw conclusions about the precise nature of these distinctions.

Prostitution arrests are also patterned by race.[10] As shown in table 22.2, both African Americans and Asians are disproportionately arrested for prostitution, as compared with their shares of arrests for other offenses. For African Americans, this is especially pronounced among adolescents, while for Asians it is a pattern found only among adults. The only offenses for which African Americans were a larger share of arrestees in 2006 were murder, robbery, weapons offenses, and gambling. For Asians, this was the case only for running away, an adolescent behavior not associated with patterns of adult prostitution arrests.

There are likely several explanations for these patterns. For African Americans, patterns are tied to racial segregation and urban disadvantage. Rates of arrest for prostitution are highest in large cities and lowest in nonmetropolitan or rural

Table 22.2. Percentage distribution of arrests by race, 2006

	Arrests—all offenses	Prostitution arrests	Drug arrests
All arrests			
White	69.7	56.7	63.6
African American	28.0	39.6	35.1
American Indian	1.3	1.0	0.6
Asian	1.1	2.7	0.7
Arrests, under 18			
White	67.1	44.2	68.3
African American	30.3	53.9	30.1
American Indian	1.1	0.8	0.8
Asian	1.4	1.1	0.9

Source: Uniform Crime Reports 2006.

counties (Uniform Crime Reports 2006).[11] The association between prostitution and gendered or raced economic inequalities (Monroe 2005) and entrenched patterns of racial segregation associated with urban disadvantage and the coupling of urban drug economies with street and drug-house prostitution appear to contribute to these arrest patterns. Not surprisingly, African Americans' share of prostitution arrests is highest in cities, where they were 40.1 percent of arrestees in 2006, and lowest in nonmetropolitan and rural counties, where they were 16.3 percent of arrestees in 2006 (see table 22.3).[12] The disproportionate involvement of minority women in urban areas is even more pronounced in non–criminal justice samples. Raphael and Shapiro's (2002) rigorous snowball sampling in Chicago resulted in a large sample that was 55 percent African American, 13.1 percent Latina, 16.3 percent white, 12.2 percent biracial, 2.3 percent Asian, and 1.4 percent American Indian. Similarly, Kanouse et al.'s (1999) probability sample of female street prostitutes in Los Angeles County included more than 80 percent who were minority, primarily African American or Hispanic.

The particularly high proportion of African Americans under age 18 arrested for prostitution-related offenses may reflect additional patterns.[13] There is limited evidence that age of entry into prostitution is lower for minority as compared with white women (Kramer and Berg 2003). Finkelhor and Ormrod (2004) report that incidents of prostitution reported to the police that involved adolescent girls were more likely than other types to be referred to social services. There is evidence to suggest that African Americans, including adolescent girls, are more likely to be arrested and are less likely to be seen by criminal justice officials as in need of treatment (Visher 1983; Bridges and Steen 1998; Miller 1999). Though it remains an

Table 22.3. Percentage of prostitution arrests by race and population group

	Metro/suburban city	County	Nonmetro/rural county
2006			
White	56.4	61.9	73.1
African American	40.1	30.2	16.3
Asian	2.4	7.6	9.7
2002			
White	56.8	71.8	72.0
African American	40.6	23.4	21.0
Asian	2.0	4.0	3.5
1997			
White	57.3	71.8	83.3
African American	41.0	25.4	8.3
Asian	1.2	2.1	8.3

Source: Uniform Crime Reports 1997, 2002, 2006.

important empirical question, the disproportionate number of arrests of African American adolescents for prostitution may reflect these patterns.

The disproportionate rates of prostitution arrests among Asians raises additional questions. This appears to be a relatively new pattern. Although Asian adults were 1.0 percent of total arrests and 2.7 percent of prostitution arrests in 2006 (Uniform Crime Reports 2006), they were 1.2 percent of total and prostitution arrests in 1997, and 1.1 percent and 2.0 percent, respectively in 2002. More striking is that these patterns disproportionately reflect arrests made outside of cities, particularly in nonmetropolitan or rural counties and increasingly in metropolitan or suburban counties (see table 22.3). In contrast, total arrests for Asians occur disproportionately in cities.[14] These patterns warrant further investigation.

B. Venues, Juveniles, and Male Prostitutes and Customers

Law enforcement practices—and thus official data—tend to concentrate on those forms of prostitution that are most visible and most often perceived as disruptive of the public order. The sex industry is characterized not only by different sectors, but by status and economic hierarchies across them. Generally speaking, women working on the streets are among the lowest paid and most socially stigmatized, with the recent exception of women engaged in sex-for-crack exchanges or who work in drug houses. Women working through escort services or as "call girls" are at the high end. Not surprisingly, poor women and women of color are disproportionately represented on the streets and lower levels of prostitution, both as a result of race and gender economic inequalities and because of the "low value assigned to their sexuality" within racist constructs of desire (Austin 1998, p. 272; see also Kempadoo and Doezema 1998; Monroe 2005). Maher (1997) found this racialized hierarchy even among street-level sex workers. White women in the drug market she investigated were able to attract more and higher paying clientele than their Latina and, especially, African American counterparts.

However, limited data are available on what proportion of prostitution takes place on the streets as opposed to in various kinds of indoor venues, particularly in the United States, where all forms are prohibited. Two decades ago sex worker's rights advocate Priscilla Alexander (1988) estimated that just 10 to 20 percent of prostitutes worked on the streets. Though she did not provide evidence for how this calculation was made, it has since become a widely quoted figure. The challenge of creating probability estimates that allow for accurate approximations of prostitution across venues remains just that: a complex challenge for future research (Kanouse et al. 1999).

Most of the comparative research that has been done on indoor versus outdoor prostitution venues has taken place in countries with legal paradigms vastly different from that in the United States (but see Shaver 2005). Thus it is simply not clear whether the patterns and disparate experiences of workers found in Britain, Canada, Australia, and New Zealand—where abolitionist or legalization frameworks dominate—can be translated to the U.S. context (Weitzer 1999).

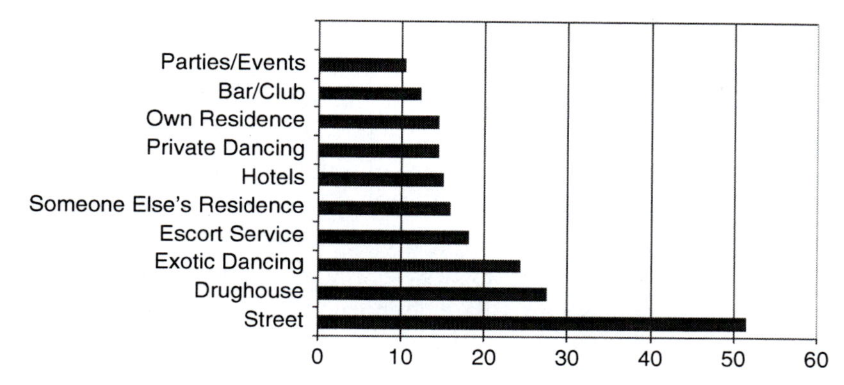

Figure 22.1. Women's participation in Chicago prostitution venues.
Source: Raphael and Shapiro 2002.

Research on legalized brothels in Nevada, for example, demonstrates that the policies adopted and workers' experiences in these settings are very much shaped by regulatory requirements, alliances with law enforcement, and profit incentives tied to legalization (Brents and Hausbeck 2005). There is no reason to believe that *illicit* indoor venues would share these characteristics.

Perhaps the most rigorous attempt to identify the variety in types of indoor prostitution venues was undertaken recently by the Center for Impact Research in Chicago. Through analyses of arrest statistics, extensive interviews with social service providers, investigation of Internet and print source materials advertising prostitution, and online communication with male purchasers, these researchers attempted to estimate the proportion of street versus off-street prostitution activities in the Chicago Metropolitan Area. Excluding sex-for-drug exchanges, they estimated that street prostitution constituted around 20 to 30 percent of prostitution activities, with escort services and prostitution in the context of exotic dance venues making up the bulk of off-street activities (O'Leary and Howard 2001).

Using snowball sampling techniques across "various segments of the prostitution industry," this research team interviewed 222 women involved in prostitution in Chicago (Raphael and Shapiro 2002, p. 10). These women identified 26 different venues in which they had engaged in prostitution. Figure 22.1 displays the rates for those most commonly identified. Although street-level and drug-house prostitution were most common, prostitution took place in a wide variety of additional venues, even among a sample that most likely represents the lower echelons of prostitution. Among low-frequency locales not included in figure 22.1 were Internet sites, peep shows, brothels, truck stops, massage parlors, and institutional settings (Raphael and Shapiro 2002, p. 11).

Though it is generally assumed that there is little or no mobility within the sex industry, these researchers found that social movement across venues was quite commonplace. Thus, because most research on prostitution in the United States has focused on women's experiences in the lower echelons of the sex industry—the streets, and more recently crack houses and other drug environments (Maher 1997; Romero-Daza, Weeks, and Singer 2003; Cusick and Hickman 2005)—important questions remain about the extent and nature of prostitution across venues.

Age is another important consideration. With the exception of runaways and homeless youth the onset of prostitution appears to occur primarily in young adulthood (Maxwell and Maxwell 2000). This gives credence to an understanding of prostitution as an income-generating strategy whose patterns diverge substantially from other criminalized behaviors (see Maher 1997). Nonetheless, research on juvenile prostitution is particularly important because of juveniles' greater vulnerabilities compared to adults. Recent analyses of NIBRS have provided new comparative information about patterns of prostitution among juveniles versus adults, but again, with the caveat that these data are generated based on incidents reported to the police (Finkelhor and Ormrod 2004).

Finkelhor and Ormrod's (2004) analysis reveals that juvenile males were more likely than females to come to the attention of the police for prostitution offenses (61 versus 39 percent). In addition, though most prostitution incidents involving juveniles occurred outdoors, juvenile incidents were more likely than adult incidents to occur indoors.[15] They were also more likely to come to the attention of the police in "multiple offender groups (59 percent of incidents)," whereas adult patterns were "composed overwhelmingly of single offender incidents (89 percent)" (p. 5). Juvenile prostitution was also disproportionately concentrated in large cities (27 percent of incidents, versus 10 percent for adults), despite the underrepresentation of such sites in the NIBRS data set.

Finkelhor and Ormrod (2004) also found distinct patterns across gender in juvenile prostitution, including somewhat younger female participants and extensive gender segregation. Most incidents involved exclusively juvenile males (117 incidents) or females (80 incidents). However, in mixed-age incidents (e.g., those with both juvenile and adult participants) "male juvenile offenders were primarily associated with male adult offenders... [and] female juvenile offenders were [also] most often (81 percent, or 29 of 36 incidents) associated with male adult offenders, suggesting the presence of pimps" (p. 7). Moreover, such mixed-age incidents with girls were more likely to take place in a residence or motel and "had the highest likelihood of containing an additional offense beyond prostitution (typically a drug-related or sex offense)" (p. 7). These findings suggest that juvenile prostitution is multifaceted and diverse, with distinct gendered dimensions.

There is limited systematic attention to adult male prostitution, at least in the United States. Weitzer (1999, pp. 220–21) provides the following synthesis of research about male prostitution from U.S., Western, and other cross-national research. Males tend to

- [be] involved in prostitution in a more sporadic and transitory way, drifting in and out of prostitution and leaving prostitution earlier...[16]
- [be] less dependent on prostitution as a source of income or for survival

- [be] more mobile across types of prostitution—moving between bars, massage parlors, and escort agencies or independent call boy operations...
- [be] more compelled to define their sexual orientation: while some self-identify as gay, others insist that they are heterosexual despite engaging in homosexual acts—a behavior-identity disparity that typically does not pertain to female prostitutes...
- [be] less likely to have been abused as children...
- [be] less likely to have been coerced into prostitution, less likely to have pimps, and subjected to much less violence from customers...
- [be] in greater control over their working conditions, because few have pimps and because males are able to exercise greater physical power over customers...
- derive more gratification from their sexual contacts with customers: males experience orgasm with clients much more often than females... and many male workers view prostitution as just another form of recreational sex, with the added benefit of material compensation...
- [be] less susceptible to arrest or harassment by the police, due to the fact that they dress less conspicuously than female prostitutes and are thus less obviously involved in prostitution, spend less time on the street, and because of police homophobia, which tends to discourage contacts with male workers.

The past decade has also witnessed increased research on men who purchase commercial sex, simultaneous with the development of law enforcement and criminal justice innovations that target them for intervention (Brooks-Gordon and Gelsthorpe 2003; van Brunschot 2003; Kennedy et al., 2004; Monto and McRee 2005; Lowman and Atchison 2006). As with sampling sex workers, sampling the purchasers of commercial sex is challenging. According to findings from the National Opinion Research Center's National Health and Social Life Survey, in the early 1990s approximately 16 percent of American men had purchased sex, but fewer than 1 percent had done so during the prior year (Michael et al. 1994 cited in Monto and McRee 2005).

More detailed studies of customers have tended to rely on samples of arrestees or those referred to diversion programs such as "john schools." These are nonrepresentative samples not only because of the critiques offered earlier of official data, but also because there is evidence to suggest that those customers who come to the attention of the police are disproportionately inexperienced rather than regular clientele (see Lowman and Atchison 2006 for a discussion). Comparing such men to nationally representative samples of men, Monto and McRee (2005, p. 505) found, "Customers were less likely to be married, less likely to be happily married if married, and more likely to report being unhappy in general.... Customers also expressed greater sexual liberalism and reported thinking about sex, masturbating, and participating in other aspects of the sex industry more frequently than men in general." On the whole, these differences were small in magnitude but were stronger for those men who reported being repeat users of commercial sex.

In addition, despite documented high rates of violence against street-level sex workers, research on male arrestees and undetected sex buyers suggests that "a relatively small proportion of sex buyers account for most of the violence" (Lowman and Atchison 2006, p. 292). Such findings, however, should be viewed as tentative. A great deal of research on violence against women demonstrates that men bring different interpretive meanings to such violence, often minimizing the seriousness of incidents women experience as violent (Scully 1990; King 2003). Such patterns may be heightened in the context of street prostitution due to the stigma attached and the unique configuration of rape myths surrounding it (Miller and Schwartz 1995).

III. Causes, Correlates, and Consequences

Research on causes, correlates, and consequences of prostitution tends to have significant methodological limitations tied to sampling challenges and the tendency to have access to and investigate only individuals at the lowest echelons of the industry. Many studies rely on convenience samples, including individuals in jail or treatment. Despite these limitations, there has been extensive research done on these issues, with fairly consistent patterns uncovered.

Many scholars, activists, and sex workers agree that women's primary motivation for involvement in the sex industry is economic (Monroe 2005). In markets characterized by intense gender, race, and class hierarchies prostitution provides a sometimes viable economic alternative among the limited options available. Both in the United States and abroad, despite the risks associated with sex work, no other occupation available to women who would otherwise be unskilled in the labor market provides a comparable income. It is also important to note that "in one person's lifetime, sex work is commonly just one of the multiple activities employed for generating income, and very few stay in prostitution for their entire adulthood" (Kempadoo and Doezema 1998, p. 4; see also Maher 1997; Austin 1998, p. 272).[17] Nonetheless, *prostitute* often becomes a master status for women involved in sex work, contributing to problems such as law enforcement discrimination, stigmatization, and violence.

Criminological and public health research—because it concentrates disproportionately on women involved in street-level prostitution and sex-for-drug exchanges—seeks to identify factors that put women and girls at risk for participation in prostitution. Because these investigations focus almost exclusively on women in lower echelons of prostitution, including street sex workers, drug users, and arrestees, they should not be viewed as generalizable among women across industry sectors. Perhaps the most heavily debated questions are whether childhood sexual abuse is causally related to prostitution, and what sequential relationship drug use or addiction plays in women's participation in prostitution.[18]

Studies of women engaged in street prostitution reveal high rates of experience with childhood violence, neglect, and abuse (Raphael and Shapiro 2002; Kramer and Berg 2003). Comparative studies have also revealed higher rates of childhood abuse, including sexual abuse, among prostitutes as compared with "heavy drinking and drug using women" (Vaddiparti et al. 2006, p. 451; see also Maxwell and Maxwell 2000) and other female jail detainees (McClanahan et al. 1999).[19] Widom and Kuhns's (1996) prospective cohort study provides strong evidence that childhood sexual abuse and neglect are associated with later participation in prostitution for women. Moreover, several recent studies suggest that sexual victimization, revictimization, and multiple victimizations in *adulthood* increase women's risk for participation in prostitution (West, Williams, and Siegel 2000; Campbell et al. 2003; Miner, Klotz Flitter, and Robinson 2006).

Some evidence suggests two distinct pathways into prostitution, with adolescent-onset prostitution tied more closely to running away than to childhood abuse (McClanahan et al. 1999). Several recent investigations, including a prospective study of female street youths' entry into prostitution (Weber et al. 2004) and a comparative study of adolescent female prostitutes and nonprostitutes drawn from the same neighborhoods, agencies, and detention facilities (Nadon, Koverola, and Schludermann 1998), did not find evidence that childhood abuse was a unique predictor of adolescent prostitution.

Instead, Weber et al. (2004) report that age of onset of homelessness, frequent drug use, use of hard drugs, and having a female sex partner distinguished those adolescent homeless girls who entered prostitution from those who did not. Nadon, Koverola, and Schludermann (1998, p. 216) report that "adolescent prostitutes were classified as runaways more frequently and used a wider variety of drugs, whereas nonprostitute youth had experienced more childhood physical abuse." Though girls involved in prostitution had higher rates of childhood sexual abuse (68 percent, versus 57 percent for girls not engaged in prostitution), these differences were not statistically significant. In contrast, Dunlap, Golub, and Johnson (2003, p. 73) suggest that the ecological context of the inner city results in high rates of compelled sex among girls. For some, these experiences lead to "sex-for-things" exchanges, and perhaps subsequently to prostitution.

Research on the drug-prostitution nexus reveals a strong relationship between drug use and street prostitution, though this is not a given (Shaver 2005, p. 309; see also Maxwell and Maxwell 2000). Some studies suggest that drug use precedes prostitution and may be a causal factor in the initiation of prostitution (Weber et al. 2004). This may be particularly likely with crack cocaine use (Maxwell and Maxwell 2000). Other studies have not found evidence that drug abuse consistently precedes prostitution (Maher 1997; McClanahan et al. 1999), and still others have found that childhood victimization has "a significant and direct association with both adult cocaine dependence and sex trading" (Vaddiparti et al. 2006, p. 451). Perhaps more sophisticated sampling and measurement strategies will further clarify these relationships.

Regardless of the causal sequence or sequences, there is widespread agreement that prostitution and drug abuse are often tightly coupled and mutually reinforcing on the streets (Miller 1995; Maher 1997; Cusick and Hickman 2005). Young, Boyd, and Hubbell (2000, p. 789) summarize: "Women may enter prostitution in order to fund their drug use; however, prostitutes likely increase their drug use in order to deal with distress caused by activities associated with their occupation." In addition there is evidence that such women's exposure to violence on the streets, including vicarious violence, increases their drug consumption, which then increases their frequency of participation in prostitution (Romero-Daza, Weeks, and Singer 2003).

It is not surprising, then, that street prostitution is widely believed to be the most dangerous setting in which sex work occurs in the United States.[20] Women engaged in street prostitution face widespread physical and sexual violence. Silbert and Pines (1982) conducted one of the earliest and largest studies of violence against street prostitutes in the United States, interviewing 200 women and girls in the San Francisco Bay Area. They report that 70 percent of their sample had been raped by clients, 65 percent beaten by clients, 66 percent were physically abused by pimps, and 73 percent "had experienced rapes totally unrelated to their work as prostitutes" (p. 128).

Such elevated rates of victimization have since been reported with consistency, with much of this violence described as routine (Miller 1993; Raphael and Shapiro 2002) and tied to the drug trade (Falck et al. 2001; Maher 1997). Some evidence suggests that rates of violence by intimates, whether partners or pimps, are higher than women's experiences of violence at the hands of customers (Dalla, Xia, and Kennedy 2003) and that women face victimization by a range of others on the streets, including drug dealers, users, the police, and others (Miller 1995; Maher 1997). Despite the consistency of these findings, we know more about the extent of such violence than its specific contextual dynamics (Lowman and Atchison 2006).[21]

The exception may be in the area of the prostitution–crack cocaine nexus. A wealth of evidence suggests that shifts resulting from the introduction of crack cocaine into the U.S. urban street scene have had detrimental effects on women engaged in sex work in these settings. Maher's (1997) longitudinal ethnography, for example, documented a rigid gender division of labor in the crack economy, shaped as well along racial lines, in which women found sex work one of the only available income-generating options. Changes brought about by the introduction of crack disadvantaged street sex workers further, resulting in lower payments, increased competition between women, and intensification of their degradation and mistreatment. Sexual exchanges in crack houses, particularly sex-for-crack exchanges, are believed to be among the most exploitive for drug-addicted women (see Bourgois and Dunlap 1993; Inciardi, Lockwood, and Pottieger 1993).

The intensity of violence against women working on the streets has been tied to both the organization and criminalization of prostitution, and stigmatization of street sex workers in particular. Particularly in locations characterized by rigorous law enforcement, prostitutes make decisions about their work with a primary goal of police avoidance. So, for example, they report getting into cars with clients hurriedly to minimize the possibility of being seen, completing transactions in isolated spots like dark alleys or side streets, and having clients drop them off in these areas in order to decrease visibility (Miller 1993). Such adaptation strategies increase their risk for victimization. Additional contributions to violence are ideologies that stigmatize street sex workers in particular, "marking violence against them as insignificant, deserved and/or justified" (Miller 1995, p. 437; see also Hatty 1989; Miller and Schwartz 1995; Austin 1998). Combined, these vulnerabilities also help explain why street sex workers are a primary target for serial killers (Lowman and Fraser 1995). As Scott et al. (2005, p. 533) summarize, "There appears to be little acknowledgement that sex workers might be endangered by public attitudes that present sex work in terms of... misogynistic behavior and legislation" (see also Sanders 2004).

Research suggests a number of additional problems encountered by street prostitutes. Most notable is discriminatory law enforcement, both with regard to the arrest of street sex workers and the handling of their victimization by criminal justice officials. Fairstein (1993) reports that in many communities in the United States complaints brought by sex workers are automatically dismissed. Even when such extreme measures are not adopted, issues of credibility and jury responsiveness appear to favor nonprosecution (Frohmann 1991). Street prostitutes routinely report not going to the police when they are victimized—for fear of criminal sanctions, because they have outstanding warrants for prostitution-related charges, or simply because they believe the criminal justice system will not take their victimization seriously (Miller 1993; Penfold et al. 2004).

There is also some evidence of police misconduct in the treatment of sex workers. Most of this work, however, is based on small or convenience samples or is limited to specific jurisdictions where policing is heavy. For example, several researchers have documented street prostitutes' experiences of sexual coercion at the hands of the police (Carmen and Moody 1985; Miller 1993), though the extent of the problem has not been well documented. Likewise, there is evidence of indiscriminate arrests in the application of loitering laws, making it more difficult for street prostitutes to escape criminal labeling (Carmen and Moody 1985; Scibelli 1987). More systematic research of such police misconduct is clearly warranted.

IV. Prostitution and Public Policy

The prohibitionist strategy adopted in the United States to address prostitution is widely understood as the most oppressive intervention paradigm for prostitutes

(Norton-Hawk 2001) and as ineffectual in systematically decreasing or eliminating commercial sex (Benson and Matthews 1995; Weitzer 1999; van Brunschot 2003). Although there are numerous calls for decriminalization, legalization, abolition, and even de facto decriminalization of some facets of prostitution, the current political reality in the United States makes a shift away from prohibition very unlikely.[22] There have been innovative policy initiatives in recent decades, though generally these have not considered prostitution outside the narrow confines of the lowest echelons of the industry and the most socially marginalized sex workers. Moreover, they remain wedded to criminal justice, public health, and social service frameworks without consideration of the structural inequities of gender, race, and class associated with prostitution in these contexts (Maher 1997; Monroe 2005).

A. Targeting Clients

Research documents that sex workers bear the brunt of law enforcement against prostitution, even where the law criminalizes all parties involved (Lowman 1990). When clients *are* arrested the penalties they face are not as harsh as those facing prostitutes (Scibelli 1987). This is also the case with most of the recent innovations created to target prostitution purchasers. For example, a number of cities in the United States and Canada have used sting operations to arrest customers and then send them to diversion programs commonly known as john schools (van Brunschot 2003; Kennedy et al. 2004).[23] A primary goal of such programs is deterrence, primarily through a brief educational process.[24]

These programs typically include six educational components, each of which implies particular understandings about prostitution: the law, the illegality of prostitution, sentencing, and risks for victimization; health risks, including sexually transmitted diseases and their long-term harms (often accompanied by explicit photographic evidence); lectures by health professionals, psychologists, or "sex addicts" about the nature of sexual addiction and associated harms; testimonials by prostitution "survivors," describing, for example, experiences of violence, drug addiction, childhood victimization, attitudes toward clients, and challenges exiting prostitution; evidence of harms caused to businesses and communities as a consequence of prostitution; and information about pimps and their role in entrapping and exploiting women (van Brunschot 2003).

Thus the orientation toward prostitution present in john schools is on deviance, disorder, disease, and prostitution as violence against women, drawing on a "medico-legal discourse" that perpetuates various facets of stigmatization (van Brunschot 2003, p. 224) but does not attend to structural inequalities. As Brooks-Gordon and Gelsthorpe (2003, p. 445) point out, "The school curriculum ignores gender and power issues, and the economic marginalization of women sex workers... 'abstract[ing] prostitution from its systemic and structural roots and treat[ing] it merely as a question of individual morality.'"

Moreover, while a punitive stance toward clients could be interpreted as an improvement over the traditional gender biases associated with the exclusive focus on sex sellers, there are numerous critiques vis-à-vis these issues. For example, john schools and other interventions against clients are criticized by prostitutes' rights advocates for interfering with sex workers' income-generating strategies and also heightening risks (Brooks-Gordon and Gelsthorpe 2003). Such diversion programs continue the unbalanced treatment of purchasers versus sellers, particularly when program participation is treated as an alternative to arrest (van Brunschot 2003). In comparison, sex workers often develop lengthy criminal records and in many jurisdictions even do fairly extensive jail time. Finally, the few studies that have attempted to evaluate whether john schools are successful in deterring recidivism have shown mixed results (Kennedy et al. 2004). Preliminary results suggest that being caught and arrested, rather than participation in the educational program, may be responsible for whatever deterrent effects are present.

B. Zoning Out Prostitution

A second, more traditional approach toward prostitution that continues to evolve is the use of law enforcement crackdowns and other measures to "zone out" prostitution and associated crime. Carter, Carter, and Dannenberg (2003), for example, report favorably on systematic steps taken in one area of Sarasota, Florida, to eradicate prostitution. Using principles from Crime Prevention through Environmental Design (CPTED), a partnership between local police and city planners and architects combined frequent, high-visibility police patrols targeting prostitution with new zoning policies to revitalize the area and incorporate CPTED principles. The project was unique because of its successful partnerships and comprehensive approach. Not surprisingly, however, although prostitution appeared to decline in this particular area, it occurred simultaneously with citywide increases, suggesting a displacement effect.

Such approaches tend to be viewed uncritically in the United States; researchers in the United Kingdom have taken a more critical stance in their analyses of similar processes in British cities.[25] Several studies have investigated initiatives in which citizen action groups organized—on their own or in partnership with the police—to displace street prostitution from their communities (Hubbard 1998; Sanders 2004). Their findings suggest that such efforts function to further marginalize sex workers and place them at greater risk for victimization and other negative outcomes. Sanders (2004, p. 1713) summarizes: "First, the way in which police and protesters control the sites of street prostitution has significant implications for the way in which the street [sex] market is organized and for the safety of individual women. Secondly, solutions sought through community safety policing result in the geographical displacement of prostitution.... Thirdly, local policies that focus on the 'disorder' in relation to the presence of prostitution inevitably criminalize individuals rather than tackling the issues associated with making the sex market safer for those who sell and buy commercial sex."

In contrast, such concerns rarely emerge in U.S. policy discussions about prostitution. It is thus not surprising that significant policy debates about the creation of managed zones for street prostitution are taking place in the United Kingdom. One recent investigation in Liverpool found support for such an approach among businesses, residents, the public, and sex workers themselves (Bellis et al. 2007). In contrast to the zero tolerance policies common in the United States, the goals of such efforts are to establish a space for street sex workers to more safely "operate according to regulations and... access health services" (p. 603). In a twist on the Sarasota model of crime prevention through environmental design, here the concern is in finding ways to effectively design out violence *against* sex workers. Moreover, the ultimate goal is to incorporate respect for individuals engaged in commercialized sex through policies that recognize and promote their citizenship and human rights (Sanders and Campbell 2007).

C. Harm Reduction

The closest corollaries to this approach in the United States are harm reduction approaches emerging from public health models of prostitution via the provision of social services, including mandatory treatment programs (Wahab 2005). Harm reduction initially emerged as a response to injection drug use and its association with HIV/AIDS and is based on principles of pragmatism, value neutrality, and concentration on achievable goals. Rather than abstinence and zero tolerance policies, the specific goals of such an approach are to reduce the net harms associated with drug use and prostitution. As Cusick (2006, p. 3) summarizes, "Harms associated with sex work include: the vulnerabilities that may lead to sex work; harms that are introduced by sex work; and mutually reinforcing harms such as problematic drug use. These harms are overwhelmingly concentrated in street sex markets and where sex workers' pre-existing vulnerabilities can be most exploited. They include predation and victimisation, violence and child abuse, trafficking and slavery, stigma, sanctions and penalties, STIs [sexually transmitted infections], exposure to mutually reinforcing harms and public nuisance."

In the U.S. context facets of this approach have been implemented in some cities through community-based outreach programs that focus on street sex workers' "psychosocial treatment needs" (Arnold, Stewart, and McNeece 2000, p. 117); efforts to improve access to victims' services for women (including prostitutes) who have "multiple barriers to services" (Zweig, Schlichter, and Burt 2002, p. 162); and through drug courts and diversion programs that mandate drug treatment, testing, and other interventions in lieu of jail time but often give less direct attention to prostitution-related service needs (Wahab 2005).

Outside the United States harm reduction approaches appear to incorporate more progressive strategies with greater frequency. These include explicit efforts to involve collaborative participation with current and former sex workers in the design and implementation of programming (Rabinovitch and Strega 2004;

Saunders 2005, p. 354) and the use of "Ugly Mugs" or "bad trick sheets" that allow sex workers to share information about dangerous men with one another and partner with law enforcement personnel to identify and arrest such offenders (Penfold et al. 2004).[26]

V. Conclusion

U.S. prostitution policy would do well to learn from the lessons and strategies available in international settings. The narrow scope of punitive, zero tolerance approaches combined with a medicalized model of social intervention fails to capture the social, economic, and spatial complexities of the commercial sex industry. Consequently our intervention strategies ultimately appear to enhance stigmatization, heighten the extent of violence within prostitution, and contribute to rather than ameliorate associated harms. Although no country has successfully tackled the complex issue of prostitution, the United States stands alone among Western nations in its exceptionally narrow orientation toward commercial sex.

Regardless of how prostitution is understood, it is clear that prohibition is a legal strategy that has not worked. There is strong evidence that this approach fails to recognize and address the human rights of those individuals, mostly women, engaged in commercial sex across strata and settings. In addition, it is a failed strategy given its explicit goals. One arena in which research can further contribute to our understanding of these issues is more systematic investigations of prosecution and sentencing trends for prostitution, as compared with other offenses. There is evidence of the failure of revolving-door policies but little other evidence of how criminal justice interventions affect those arrested, prosecuted, and incarcerated for prostitution. Given evidence of the disproportionate arrest of women and girls of color, research on racial inequalities in the operation of criminal justice is vital.

We also need more systematic research about the diversity of commercial sex markets, workers, victims, and clients. The highly politicized nature of debates about prostitution often results from generalizing the picture of prostitution in one context to all contexts. The complexity and variations of prostitution suggest the need for a comparably diverse and complex array of intervention strategies. A better understanding of the varieties of commercialized sex—and the settings in which it takes place—would better allow for the development of appropriately tailored policies.

Finally, it is clear from the research reviewed in this chapter that prostitution does not exist in a vacuum and is thoroughly grounded in racial, class, and gender inequalities that are both social and economic in nature. At the most basic and systemic levels policies developed to ameliorate these inequalities are needed.

More equitable social and economic arrangements would, at the very least, provide women (as well as men and children) a wider range of income-generating options and better and more systematic interventions into the root causes of prostitution for those at the lowest echelons and in the highest risk settings and would allow much-needed space for the recognition and promotion of the human rights of those engaged in commercial sex.

NOTES

1. So do, among others, China, Iceland, Japan, Malta, Nepal, the Philippines, Romania, Slovenia, Sri Lanka, Tanzania, Uganda, and Vietnam (Wijers and Lap-Chew 1997).

2. Most countries in Western Europe adopt a predominantly abolitionist approach, including Belgium, Denmark, Finland, France, Ireland, Italy, Norway, Portugal, Spain, Sweden, and the United Kingdom. Elsewhere, abolition is pursued in Bangladesh, Bulgaria, Cameroon, Canada, Czechoslovakia, Colombia, the Dominican Republic, Hong Kong, India, Lithuania, Nigeria, Poland, Thailand, and Ukraine (Wijers and Lap-Chew 1997).

3. Given space constraints and definitional complexities, trafficking is beyond the scope of my discussion here (see Lehti and Aromaa 2006). For analyses of definitions, methods, patterns and trends, and policy, see Kempadoo and Doezema 1998; Chapkis 2003; Saunders 2005.

4. Other countries include Australia, Austria, Germany, Greece, the Netherlands, and Switzerland, as well as Ecuador, Peru, and Turkey (Wijers and Lap-Chew 1997).

5. In Nevada, for example, sex workers are closely monitored even during nonworking hours. For example, in many brothels women are not permitted to leave the premises when they are under contract, even when they are not working a shift. "Most brothels identify specific days when women can go to the store or run errands; some do not even allow that. Others just require that women log in their specific locations... at all times" when they are off-site (Brents and Hausbeck 2005, p. 284).

6. Notably, their research suggests that jail-based samples are likely a better site for interviewing street prostitutes than drug programs or health clinics. While 68 percent of their probability sample had been arrested, only 29 percent and 46 percent, respectively, had entered drug rehab or visited STD clinics (Kanouse et al. 1999).

7. In fact, a recent NIBRS study notes only 28 reported incidents of prostitution in schools for the five-year period 2000 to 2004. Compare this to 15,298 incidents of aggravated assault, 1,662 incidents of forcible rape, 37 incidents of murder or nonnegligent manslaughter, 47,108 drug violations, and 14,371 weapons offenses (Noonan and Vavra 2007). Self-report studies do not simply collect information on school-based violations, but these patterns do suggest that youths involved in prostitution may not be attending school.

8. The NIBRS shows some promise for providing enhanced information about *reported* incidents of prostitution and commercialized vice, regardless of whether they lead to arrest. In addition, unlike the Uniform Crime Reports, incidents that involve

"engaging in sexual relations for profit" are differentiated from those that involve "assisting or promoting prostitution" (see Finkelhor and Ormrod 2004). As noted, NIBRS data are not yet systematically available, however, and incidents must have come to the attention of authorities for inclusion.

9. In 2006 just 26.9 percent of prostitution arrests involved individuals under the age of 25, compared with a total average for all crimes of 44.5 percent. The only other offenses for which a *smaller* proportion of arrests occur under the age of 25 were fraud (26.0 percent) and offenses against the family and children (22.0 percent; Uniform Crime Reports 2006).

10. Unfortunately the Uniform Crime Reports do not record data on ethnicity, thus it is not possible to determine patterns of prostitution arrest for those of Hispanic origin.

11. Moreover, prostitution as a proportion of total female arrests is lower outside cities. In 2006 prostitution arrests were 1.9 percent of female arrests in cities, 0.4 percent in metropolitan counties, and 0.1 percent in nonmetropolitan counties (Uniform Crime Reports 2006).

12. Although their proportion of arrestees remained stable in cities over the past decade, it that appears African Americans' proportion of arrests has increased in rural counties. In 1997 they were 8.3 percent of rural arrestees, compared to 21.0 percent in 2002 and 16.3 percent in 2006.

13. The only offenses for which African American youths were a larger share of arrestees in 2006 were murder, robbery, and gambling (Uniform Crime Reports 2006).

14. In 2006, for instance, Asians were 1.2 percent of total arrests in cities versus 0.6 percent in metropolitan counties and 0.9 percent in nonmetropolitan counties (Uniform Crime Reports 2006).

15. For example, 14 percent of juvenile incidents occurred in a home or residence, compared to 4 percent of adult incidents. While 68 percent of incidents involving juveniles occurred outside, this was the case for 84 percent of incidents involving only adults (Finkelhor and Ormrod 2004).

16. Ellipses refer to citations in the original. See Weitzer (1999).

17. Given these patterns, an important but as yet unanswered question is the lifetime prevalence of women's involvement in prostitution.

18. Very little research, in contrast, has examined desistance from prostitution (see Dalla 2006).

19. Several studies have found that the relationship between childhood abuse and prostitution is stronger for white than for African American women (Kramer and Berg 2003), though the evidence is far from conclusive.

20. Recent analyses undertaken by Raphael and Shapiro (2004) suggest that violence in some indoor venues is more widespread than is commonly assumed. Research showing minimal violence in indoor venues tends to concentrate on settings where strict regulation is present. Thus generalized conclusions about the relative safety of indoor venues may fail to take into account how setting effects are structured by the extent or absence of outside intervention. As Brents and Hausbeck (2005, p. 271) explain, "Legalization brings a level of public scrutiny, official regulation, and bureaucratization to brothels such that violence is far less likely to be a systemic problem as it is when prostitution is illegal but flourishing."

21. Arnold, Stewart, and McNeece (2001) also call for more contextual research on violence *by* street prostitutes, which we know even less about (but see Maher 1997).

22. Even the 2000 Trafficking Victims Protection Act, ostensibly an abolitionist policy toward trafficking into the United States, maintains a punitive undercurrent (Chapkis 2003).

23. Many would suggest that sting operations amount to entrapment. In fact, Lowman and Atchison's (2006, p. 288) survey research with customers suggests that "for a certain segment of the sex buyer population, their initial demand was, at least partly, supply driven"; that is, the opportunity presented itself. They suggest that the abolitionist approach recently adopted by Sweden, in which purchasing sex specifically is criminalized, is tantamount to institutionalized entrapment. Such concerns should be balanced, however, against ample evidence that entrapment strategies are routinely used against sex sellers as well (Scibelli 1987).

24. Several other deterrence methods have also been implemented, including publicizing the names of client arrestees in newspapers or on the Internet as a shaming mechanism (see Persons 1996), and even confiscating vehicles and sending notification letters to arrestees' homes (van Brunschot 2003, FN6).

25. For an overview of policy changes in Britain over the past decade, particularly the shift to "a more multi-faceted, multi-agency approach," see Matthews (2005, p. 893).

26. Ugly Mugs and bad trick sheets are locally produced fliers or reports in which sex workers provide descriptive accounts of men who have victimized them. Sanders and Campbell (2007) point out that such programs still place the onus of responsibility for safety on sex workers rather than on perpetrators or organizational features of street-level sex work. Nonetheless, such strategies appear more progressive than the systematic inattention to violence against street prostitutes in the United States.

REFERENCES

Adler, Jeffrey S. 1992. "Streetwalkers, Degraded Outcasts, and Good-for-Nothing Huzzies: Women and the Dangerous Class in Antebellum St. Louis." *Journal of Social History* 25: 737–55.

Alexander, Priscilla. 1988. "Prostitution: A Difficult Issue for Feminists." In *Sex Work: Writings by Women in the Sex Industry,* edited by Frederique Delacoste and Priscilla Alexander. London: Virago.

Armitage, Rachel. 2002. *Tackling Anti-Social Behaviour: What Really Works.* London: Nacro.

Arnold, Elizabeth Mayfield, J. Chris Stewart, and C. Aaron McNeece. 2000. "The Psychosocial Treatment Needs of Street-Walking Prostitutes: Perspectives from a Case Management Program." *Journal of Offender Rehabilitation* 30: 117–32.

Arnold, Elizabeth Mayfield, J. Chris Stewart, and C. Aaron McNeece. 2001. "Perpetrators as Victims: Understanding Violence by Female Street-walking Prostitutes." *Violence and Victims* 16: 145–59.

Austin, Regina. 1998. "'The Black Community,' Its Lawbreakers, and a Politics of Identification." *Southern California Law Review* 65: 1769–817.

Barry, Kathleen. 1995. *The Prostitution of Sexuality.* New York: New York University Press.

Bellis, Mark A., Fay L. D. Watson, Sara Hughes, Penny A. Cook, Jennifer Downing, Peter Clark, and Rod Thomson. 2007. "Comparative Views of the Public, Sex Workers,

Businesses and Residents on Establishing Managed Zones for Prostitution: Analysis of a Consultation in Liverpool." *Health and Place* 13: 603–16.
Benson, Catherine, and Roger Matthews. 1995. "Street Prostitution: Ten Facts in Search of Policy." *International Journal of the Sociology of Law* 23: 395–415.
Bourgois, Philippe, and Eloise Dunlap. 1993. "Exorcising Sex-for-Crack: An Ethnographic Perspective from Harlem." In *Crack Pipe as Pimp: An Ethnographic Investigation of Sex-for-Crack Exchanges*, edited by Mitchell S. Ratner. New York: Lexington Books.
Brents, Barbara G., and Kathryn Hausbeck. 2005. "Violence and Legalized Brothel Prostitution in Nevada: Examining Safety, Risk, and Prostitution Policy." *Journal of Interpersonal Violence* 20: 270–95.
Bridges, George S., and Sara Steen. 1998. "Racial Disparities in Official Assessments of Juvenile Offenders: Attributional Stereotypes as Mediating Mechanisms." *American Sociological Review* 63: 554–70.
Brooks-Gordon, Belinda, and Loraine Gelsthorpe. 2003. "Prostitutes' Clients, Ken Livingstone and the New Trojan Horse." *Howard Journal* 42: 437–51.
Campbell, Rebecca, Courtney E. Ahrens, Tracy Sefl, and Marcia L. Clark. 2003. "The Relationship between Adult Sexual Assault and Prostitution: An Exploratory Analysis." *Violence and Victims* 18: 299–317.
Carmen, Arlene, and Howard Moody. 1985. *Working Women: The Subterranean World of Street Prostitution*. New York: Harper and Row.
Carter, Sherry Plaster, Stanley L. Carter, and Andrew L. Dannenberg. 2003. "Zoning Out Crime and Improving Community Health in Sarasota, Florida: 'Crime Prevention through Environmental Design.'" *American Journal of Public Health* 93: 1442–45.
Chapkis, Wendy. 2003. "Trafficking, Migration, and the Law: Protecting Innocents, Punishing Immigrants." *Gender and Society* 17: 923–37.
Coomaraswamy, Radhika. 1997. *Report of the Special Rapporteur on Violence against Women: Its Causes and Consequences*. 53rd session of the United Nations Economic and Social Council, February 12.
Cusick, Linda. 2006. "Widening the Harm Reduction Agenda: From Drug Use to Sex Work." *International Journal of Drug Policy* 17: 3–11.
Cusick, Linda, and Matthew Hickman. 2005. "'Trapping' in Drug Use and Sex Work Careers." *Drugs, Education, Prevention, and Policy* 12: 369–79.
Dalla, Rochelle L. 2006. "'You Can't Hustle All Your Life': An Exploratory Investigation of the Exit Process among Street-Level Prostituted Women." *Psychology of Women Quarterly* 30: 276–90.
Dalla, Rochelle L., Yan Xia, and Heather Kennedy. 2003. "'You Just Give Them What They Want and Pray They Don't Kill You': Street-Level Sex Workers' Reports of Victimization, Personal Resources, and Coping Strategies." *Violence against Women* 9: 1367–94.
DeLisi, Matt. 2002. "Not Just a Boy's Club: An Empirical Assessment of Female Career Criminals." *Women and Criminal Justice* 13: 27–45.
Dunlap, Eloise, Andrew Golub, and Bruce D. Johnson. 2003. "Girls' Sexual Development in the Inner City: From Compelled Childhood Sexual Contact to Sex-for-Things Exchanges." *Journal of Child Sexual Abuse* 12: 73–96.
Fairstein, Linda A. 1993. *Sexual Violence: Our War against Rape*. New York: William Morrow.
Falck, Russel S., Jichuan Wang, Robert G. Carlson, and Harvey A. Siegal. 2001. "The Epidemiology of Physical Attack and Rape among Crack-Using Women." *Violence and Victims* 16: 79–89.

Finkelhor, David, and Richard Ormrod. 2004. *Prostitution of Juveniles: Patterns from NIBRS*. OJJDP Juvenile Justice Bulletin, Office of Justice Programs. Washington, DC: U.S. Department of Justice.

Frohmann, Lisa. 1991. "Discrediting Victims' Allegations of Sexual Assault: Prosecutorial Accounts of Case Rejections." *Social Problems* 38: 213–26.

Hatty, Suzanne. 1989. "Violence against Prostitute Women: Social and Legal Dilemmas." *Australian Journal of Social Issues* 24: 235–48.

Hubbard, Phil. 1998. "Community Action and the Displacement of Street Prostitution: Evidence from British Cities." *Geoforum* 29: 269–86.

Inciardi, James A, Donna Lockwood, and Ann E. Pottieger. 1993. *Women and Crack Cocaine*. New York: Macmillan.

Jenness, Valerie. 1993. *Making It Work: The Prostitutes' Rights Movement in Perspective*. New York: Aldine de Gruyter.

Kanouse, David E., Sandra H. Berry, Naihua Duan, Janet Lever, Sally Carson, Judith F. Perlman, and Barbara Levitan. 1999. "Drawing a Probability Sample of Female Street Prostitutes in Los Angeles County." *Journal of Sex Research* 36: 45–51.

Kempadoo, Kamala, and Jo Doezema. 1998. *Global Sex Workers: Rights, Resistance, and Redefinition*. New York: Routledge.

Kennedy, M. Alexis, Carolin Klein, Boris B. Gorzalka, and John C. Yuille. 2004. "Attitude Change Following a Diversion Program for Men Who Solicit Sex." *Journal of Offender Rehabilitation* 40: 41–60.

King, Neal. 2003. "Knowing Women: Straight Men and Sexual Certainty." *Gender and Society* 17: 861–77.

Kramer, Lisa A., and Ellen C. Berg. 2003. "A Survival Analysis of Timing of Entry into Prostitution: The Differential Impact of Race, Educational Level, and Childhood/ Adolescent Risk Factors." *Sociological Inquiry* 73: 511–28.

Lehti, Martti, and Kauko Aromaa. 2006. "Trafficking for Sexual Exploitation." In *Crime and Justice: A Review of Research*, vol. 34, edited by Michael Tonry. Chicago: University of Chicago Press.

Lowman, John. 1990. "Notions of Formal Equality before the Law: The Experiences of Street Prostitutes and Their Customers." *Journal of Human Justice* 1: 55–76.

Lowman, John, and Chris Atchison. 2006. "Men Who Buy Sex: A Survey in the Greater Vancouver Regional District." *Canadian Review of Sociology and Anthropology* 43: 281–96.

Lowman, John, and Laura Fraser. 1995. *Technical Report: Violence against Persons Who Prostitute: The Experience in British Columbia*. Vancouver, Canada: Department of Justice.

MacKinnon, Catharine A., and Andrea Dworkin, eds. 1998. *In Harm's Way: The Pornography Civil Rights Hearings*. Cambridge, MA: Harvard University Press.

Maher, Lisa. 1997. *Sexed Work: Gender, Race, and Resistance in a Brooklyn Drug Market*. New York: Oxford University Press.

Matthews, Roger. 2005. "Policing Prostitution: Ten Years On." *British Journal of Criminology* 45: 877–95.

Maxwell, Sheila Royo, and Christopher D. Maxwell. 2000. "Examining the 'Criminal Careers' of Prostitutes within the Nexus of Drug Use, Drug Selling, and Other Illicit Activities." *Criminology* 38: 787–809.

McClanahan, Susan F., Gary M. McClelland, Karen M. Abram, and Linda A. Teplin. 1999. "Pathways into Prostitution among Female Jail Detainees and Their Implications for Mental Health Services." *Psychiatric Services* 50: 1606–13.

McElroy, Wendy. 1997. *XXX: A Woman's Right to Pornography.* New York: St. Martin's.

Miller, Jody A. 1993. "'Your Life Is on the Line Every Night You're on the Streets': Victimization and Resistance among Street Prostitutes." *Humanity and Society* 17(4): 422–46.

———. 1995. "Gender and Power on the Streets: Street Prostitution in the Era of Crack Cocaine." *Journal of Contemporary Ethnography* 23: 427–52.

———. 1999. "An Examination of Disposition Decision-Making for Delinquent Girls." In *The Intersection of Race, Gender and Class in Criminology,* edited by Martin D. Schwartz and Dragan Milovanovic. New York: Garland.

Miller, Jody, and Martin D. Schwartz. 1995. "Rape Myths and Violence against Street Prostitutes." *Deviant Behavior* 16: 1–23.

Miner, Michael H., Jill M. Klotz Flitter, and Beatrice E. Robinson. 2006. "Association of Sexual Revictimization with Sexuality and Psychological Function." *Journal of Interpersonal Violence* 21: 503–24.

Monroe, Jacquelyn. 2005. "Women in Street Prostitution: The Result of Poverty and the Brunt of Inequity." *Journal of Poverty* 9: 69–88.

Monto, Martin A., and Nick McRee. 2005. "A Comparison of Male Customers of Female Street Prostitutes with National Samples of Men." *International Journal of Offender Therapy and Comparative Criminology* 49: 505–29.

Nadon, Susan M., Catherine Koverola, and Eduard H. Schludermann. 1998. "Antecedents to Prostitution: Childhood Victimization." *Journal of Interpersonal Violence* 13: 206–21.

Noonan, James H., and Malissa C. Vavra. 2007. *Crime in Schools and Colleges: A Study of Offenders and Arrestees Reported via National Incident-Based Reporting System.* Washington, DC: Federal Bureau of Investigation.

Norton-Hawk, Maureen. 2001. "The Counterproductivity of Incarcerating Female Street Prostitutes." *Deviant Behavior* 22: 403–17.

O'Leary, Claudine, and Olivia Howard. 2001. *The Prostitution of Women and Girls in Metropolitan Chicago: A Preliminary Prevalence Report.* Chicago: Center for Impact Research.

Overall, Christine. 1992. "What's Wrong with Prostitution? Evaluating Sex Work." *Signs* 17: 705–24.

Penfold, Clarissa, Gillian Hunter, Rosie Campbell, and Leela Barham. 2004. "Tackling Client Violence in Female Street Prostitution: Inter-Agency Working between Outreach Agencies and the Police." *Policing and Society* 14: 365–79.

Persons, C. 1996. "Sex in the Sunlight: The Effectiveness, Efficiency, Constitutionality, and Advisability of Publishing Names and Pictures of Prostitutes' Patrons." *Vanderbilt Law Review* 49: 1525–75.

Pettersson, Tove, and Eva Tiby. 2003. "The Production and Reproduction of Prostitution." *Journal of Scandinavian Studies in Criminology and Crime Prevention* 3: 154–72.

Rabinovitch, Jannit, and Susan Strega. 2004. "The PEERS Story: Effective Services Sidestep the Controversies." *Violence against Women* 10: 140–59.

Raphael, Jody, and Deborah L. Shapiro. 2002. *Sisters Speak Out: The Lives and Needs of Prostituted Women in Chicago—A Research Study.* Chicago: Center for Impact Research.

Raphael, Jody, and Deborah L. Shapiro. 2004. "Violence in Indoor and Outdoor Prostitution Venues." *Violence against Women* 10: 126–39.

Romero-Daza, Nancy, Margaret Weeks, and Merrill Singer. 2003. "'Nobody Gives a Damn If I Live or Die': Violence, Drugs, and Street-Level Prostitution in Inner-City Hartford, Connecticut." *Medical Anthropology* 22: 233–59.
Rubin, Gayle. 1984. "Thinking Sex: Notes for a Radical Theory of the Politics of Sexuality." In *Pleasure and Danger: Exploring Female Sexuality,* edited by Carole Vance. London: Routledge and Kegan Paul.
Sanders, Teela. 2004. "The Risks of Street Prostitution: Punters, Police and Protesters." *Urban Studies* 41: 1703–17.
Sanders, Teela, and Rosie Campbell. 2007. "Designing Out Vulnerability, Building In Respect: Violence, Safety and Sex Work Policy." *British Journal of Sociology* 58: 1–19.
Saunders, Penelope. 2005. "Traffic Violations: Determining the Meaning of Violence in Sexual Trafficking versus Sex Work." *Journal of Interpersonal Violence* 20: 343–60.
Scibelli, Pasqua. 1987. "Empowering Prostitutes: A Proposal for International Legal Reform." *Harvard Women's Law Journal* 10: 117–57.
Scott, John, Victor Minichiello, Rodrigo Mariño, Glenn P. Harvey, Maggie Jamieson, and Jan Browne. 2005. "Understanding the New Context of the Male Sex Work Industry." *Journal of Interpersonal Violence* 20: 320–42.
Scully, Diana. 1990. *Understanding Sexual Violence.* Boston: Unwin Hyman.
Shaver, Frances M. 2005. "Sex Work Research: Methodological and Ethical Challenges." *Journal of Interpersonal Violence* 20: 296–319.
Silbert, Mimi H., and Ayala M. Pines. 1982. "Victimization of Street Prostitutes." *Victimology* 7: 122–33.
Truong, Thanh-Dam. 1990. *Sex, Money and Morality: Prostitution and Tourism in Southeast Asia.* London: Zed Books.
Uniform Crime Reporting Handbook. 2004. Washington, DC: Federal Bureau of Investigation.
Uniform Crime Reports. 1997. Washington, DC: Federal Bureau of Investigation.
———. 2002. Washington, DC: Federal Bureau of Investigation.
———. 2006. Washington, DC: Federal Bureau of Investigation.
Vaddiparti, Krishna, Jane Bogetto, Catina Callahan, Arbi B. Abdallah, Edward L. Spitznagel, and Linda B. Cottler. 2006. "The Effects of Childhood Trauma on Sex Trading in Substance Using Women." *Archives of Sexual Behavior* 35: 451–59.
van Brunschot, Eric Gibbs. 2003. "Community Policing and 'John Schools.'" *Canadian Review of Sociology and Anthropology* 40: 215–32.
van der Poel, Sari. 1995. "Solidarity as Boomerang: The Fiasco of the Prostitutes' Rights Movement in the Netherlands." *Crime, Law and Social Change* 23: 41–65.
Visher, Christy A. 1983. "Gender, Police Arrest Decisions, and Notions of Chivalry." *Criminology* 21: 5–28.
Wahab, Stéphanie. 2005. "Navigating Mixed-Theory Programs: Lessons Learned from a Prostitution-Diversion Project." *Affilia* 20: 203–21.
Walkowitz, Judith. 1982. *Prostitution and Victorian Society: Women, Class, and the State.* New York: Cambridge University Press.
Weber, Amy E., Jean-François Boivin, Lucie Blais, Nancy Haley, and Élise Roy. 2004. "Predictors of Initiation into Prostitution among Female Street Youths." *Journal of Urban Health* 81: 584–95.
Weitzer, Ronald. 1999. "Prostitution Control in America: Rethinking Public Policy." *Crime, Law and Social Change* 32: 83–102.

———. 2005. "New Directions in Research on Prostitution." *Crime, Law and Social Change* 43: 211–35.

West, Carolyn M., Linda M. Williams, and Jane A. Siegel. 2000. "Adult Sexual Revictimization among Black Women Sexually Abused in Childhood: A Prospective Examination of Serious Consequences of Abuse." *Child Maltreatment* 5: 49–57.

Widom, Cathy Spatz, and Joseph B. Kuhns. 1996. "Childhood Victimization and Subsequent Risk for Promiscuity, Prostitution, and Teenage Pregnancy: A Prospective Study." *American Journal of Public Health* 86: 1607–12.

Wijers, Marjan, and Lin Lap-Chew. 1997. *Trafficking in Women, Forced Labour and Slavery-Like Practices in Marriage, Domestic Labour and Prostitution*. Amsterdam: Foundation against Trafficking in Women.

Young, Amy M., Carol Boyd, and Amy Hubbell. 2000. "Prostitution, Drug Use, and Coping with Psychological Distress." *Journal of Drug Issues* 30: 789–800.

Zatz, Noah. 1997. "Sex Work/Sex Act: Law, Labor and Desire in Constructions of Prostitution." *Signs* 22: 277–308.

Zweig, Janine M., Kathryn A. Schlichter, and Martha R. Burt. 2002. "Assisting Women Victims of Violence Who Experience Multiple Barriers to Services." *Violence against Women* 8: 162–80.

CHAPTER 23

ANTISOCIAL BEHAVIOR

MICHAEL TONRY AND
HARRIET BILDSTEN

ANTISOCIAL behavior often exists mainly in the eyes of beholders, as a 2008 *New York Times* story about the acquittal of one John Clifford of harassment and misdemeanor assault demonstrates. Said Mr. Clifford, a retired policeman, "I stand up for my right to be let alone," in explaining why he behaved in ways many would consider rude toward people whose loud talking and cell phoning regularly disturbed his daily commute on the Long Island Railroad (Hartocollis 2008).

That particular conflict of interests occurs daily. Whether you sympathize with Mr. Clifford or his antagonists probably depends on whether, when riding a train, you are more often a quiet reader or a cell phone talker. And whether you consider talking loudly in public spaces a small problem or a large one or no problem at all depends a lot on your personality and personal experience.

A larger ambiguity bedevils recent efforts in the United States to "maintain order" in urban areas and in England and Wales to address antisocial behavior. Antisocial behavior and disorder can encompass many inconsiderate, irksome, discomfiting, irritating, threatening, and damaging behaviors, ranging from littering to verbal harassment to drug selling to violent crimes.

The American development, often associated with "Broken Windows," an *Atlantic Monthly* article by James Q. Wilson and George L. Kelling (1982), is linked with law enforcement initiatives variously described as order maintenance, misdemeanor, zero tolerance, and quality-of-life policing. The English development, a totemic symbol for Tony Blair's Labour government, led to the creation and aggressive promotion of antisocial behavior orders (ASBOs). Issuance of an ASBO is a civil law matter, but its breach is a criminal offense. At their inception ASBOs were often aimed at "noisy neighbors," "neighbors from hell," "yobs," "hoodies," and unruly youngsters, people whose behavior, though often not criminal, can make other people's lives miserable. Sometimes they were aimed at criminal behaviors that for one reason or another were difficult to prosecute.

The broken windows hypothesis and its policy progeny and ASBOs implicate different categories of troubling behavior, each of which raises distinct normative and policy issues. The first is antisocial behavior exemplified by noisy neighbors who play music too loudly, too late, and too often; though violating no criminal law, this type of behavior is comparable to cell phone conflicts. People living in close quarters and rubbing together in crowded public spaces invade one another's personal space and get in one another's faces. College students may want to party late at night and celebrate the music of the moment, loudly, while weary middle-aged householders want uninterrupted sleep and complain mightily when they do not get it. Such things often make us unhappy and frustrated.

The second category of implicated behavior consists of things that may be legal, or may be minor crimes or ordinance violations, but are worrying because of their possible effects and not so much because of the behavior itself. J. Q. Wilson and Kelling's (1989, p. 3) examples are often quoted: "If the first broken window in a building is not repaired, then people who like breaking windows will assume that no one cares, and more windows will be broken.... Likewise, when disorderly behavior—say, rude remarks by loitering youths—is left unchallenged, the signal given is that no one cares. The disorder escalates, possibly to serious crime." Breaking windows may be a criminal offense, unless the windows are your own, but rude remarks seldom are. The speculation is that antisocial behavior can start or contribute to a spiral of neighborhood decline that leads people to become demoralized and alienated, which in turn leads to more serious forms of antisocial behavior. A related concern is that deteriorated or disordered neighborhoods may make people fearful. The overall logic is that antisocial behavior should be taken seriously lest neighborhoods slide down slippery slopes to deterioration, crime, and fear.

There are other means-to-an-end reasons to focus on antisocial behavior or disorder that is legal or constitutes only minor criminality. Police may want to encourage people, such as beggars, drunks, or prostitutes, whom they or other citizens see as troublesome to move along or stay away from particular areas. Or, as in order-maintenance policing in New York, police may stop people engaged in antisocial behavior as a pretext, on the logic that people who misbehave in minor ways often also misbehave in major ones; the stop provides a basis for temporary detention and for checking for outstanding arrest warrants or parole or probation absconding. In England officials emphasize that many speeding and parking scofflaws turn out to have serious criminal records and grounds for immediate arrest, and in New York City police officials make similar claims about squeegee men and unlicensed sidewalk merchants.

The third category of implicated behaviors consists of crimes that police and prosecutors find difficult to prosecute or do not think worth prosecuting. In addition, police and prosecutors often do not consider minor crimes—littering; being chronically, ear-shatteringly noisy in ways that arguably violate criminal laws against public nuisances—sufficiently important to invest much time or money in handling them. In encouraging use of ASBOs, Labour officials often spoke of behaviors that were criminal but about which witnesses felt intimidated from testifying.

Former British prime minister Tony Blair in 2005 made it clear that ASBOs were designed to circumvent the criminal law. To the Labour Party Conference in September 2005 he made his displeasure with the criminal justice system clear: "We are trying to fight twenty-first century crime—antisocial behaviour, drug dealing, binge-drinking, organized crime—with nineteenth century methods, as if we lived in the time of Dickens" (quoted in Morgan 2006, p. 110). There is a small irony here, which may explain why ASBOs often forbid behavior that is not criminal: Blair refers to antisocial behavior and binge-drinking as crimes; the latter, though perhaps unwise, is not criminal and the former need not be. After describing various measures taken to strengthen ASBOs, Blair explained, "All of these measures... have one thing in common: they bypass the traditional way the criminal justice system used to work.... The rules of the game have changed" (quoted in Morgan 2006, p. 97).

There are three fundamental problems with the policies discussed in this article. The first is that they violate fundamental norms about civil liberties and human rights: police should not stop citizens on pretexts, and governments should not adopt policies intended as end runs around the criminal law's procedural protections. The second is that the premises on which they rest do not appear to be valid: in England there is little evidence that ASBOs have achieved their ostensible goals, and in the United States the relevant research shows that the broken windows hypothesis cannot be confirmed. The third is that they assume a degree of state intrusion into private lives to which few people would voluntarily submit. In our crowded, urbanized, diverse twenty-first-century world, people get on one another's nerves and find themselves, like Mr. Clifford and his cell-phoning co-commuters, in circumstances in which their interests and behaviors collide. When the colliding behaviors are not criminal, or are crimes so minor that the police seldom or never choose to intervene, private citizens and their families and communities and local social service agencies should work such things out for themselves.

This chapter discusses ASBOs in England and Wales and recent U.S. policies based on the broken windows hypothesis. In sections I and II we discuss those developments and related research. The important questions about ASBOs are whether the prevalence of antisocial behavior has been reduced and whether people have become less concerned about it, and at what costs. With broken windows, the important questions are whether the slippery slope hypothesis is correct, whether police initiatives based on them substantially contributed to the crime rate declines of the past two decades, and whether the collateral costs of new policing policies are justified. In section III we discuss a series of normative and policy issues.

Here are our conclusions:

- ASBOs have not demonstrably reduced either the prevalence of antisocial behavior in England and Wales or peoples' concerns about it.
- ASBOS appear to have increased public dissatisfaction with neighborhood conditions by raising unrealistic expectations and to have reduced public confidence in government and support for traditional conceptions of civil liberty and procedural fairness.
- ASBOs have enabled local officials to circumvent traditional criminal law procedures and evidentiary rules and in some cases effectively to recriminalize behaviors that Parliament decriminalized (prostitution and begging are examples).
- Evidence concerning the broken windows hypothesis is mixed, with serious scholars reaching different conclusions; the weight of the evidence does not support the hypothesis.
- The clear weight of the evidence concerning the crime-preventive effects of policing initiatives related to the broken windows hypothesis—zero tolerance, misdemeanor, and order-maintenance policing—is that they have not contributed substantially to declines in crime rates.
- Initiatives supportive of the broken windows hypothesis, especially in New York City, increased alienation of minority citizens, diminished public perceptions of police legitimacy, and worsened police relationships with minority communities.

I. Antisocial Behavior in England and Wales

ASBOs were authorized by the Crime and Disorder Act 1998. The term *antisocial behavior* is broadly defined in that Act to include any action that "caused or was likely to cause harassment, alarm, or distress" to someone outside the actor's household. ASBOs constituted a radical attempt to circumvent protections the criminal law accords defendants. They allow police, local authorities, and others to initiate *civil* legal proceedings against individuals alleged to have engaged in acts someone considers antisocial. The prohibited behavior, however, need not be criminal; it can be as innocuous as "entering the city of Manchester." Because ASBO cases are tried in civil courts, they are subject to "more probable than not" standards of proof rather than the criminal law's "proof beyond a reasonable doubt" and are not subject to procedural and evidentiary rules that restrict admission of evidence in criminal courts. Sometimes they are issued ex parte, without a trial being held or the defendant being notified. Violations of ASBOs, however, constitute criminal offenses that can be prosecuted and punished in criminal courts with prison sentences up to five years, with the issue being not whether, for example, entering Manchester is itself criminal, but whether by entering Manchester the terms of the ASBO have been violated.

Not surprisingly in light of the unfairness of ASBOs, many police forces, local governments, and social service agencies were reluctant to seek ASBOs in the early years. In their first 30 months of operation, between April 1999 and September 2001, only 466 were issued in the entire country, and those disproportionately were in a small number of places (Campbell 2002).

Determined to increase use of ASBOs, the government aggressively promoted their use, broadened their scope in the Police Reform Act 2002, established an Antisocial Behaviour Unit in the Home Office in 2003, and announced that the Audit Commission would in future assess local governments' performance in attacking antisocial behavior. As a next step the government promoted a "Respect Agenda" and developed a large number of other policies—citations for minor misbehavior, ASBOs aimed at young children, systems of fines and court orders for underperforming parents—aimed at regulating private behavior considered unsuitable.

ASBOs have proliferated. In more recent years, as table 23.1 shows, they have been used extensively and targeted a wide range of behaviors; 1,336 were issued in 2003, 3,440 in 2004, 4,090 in 2005, and 2,822 in 2006. Presumably because of a combination of the government's strong support for ASBOs and the low burden of proof required, magistrates have turned down only 1 percent of applications for their issuance (Russell and McCormick 2005). Nearly half result in decisions that

Table 23.1. Antisocial behavior orders issued through December 2006

Period	Number issued	Number breached to date	Percent breached
4/1/99–5/31/00	104		
6/1/00–12/31/00	137		
2001	350		
2002	426		
2003	1,336		
2004	3,440		
2005	4,090		
Total to 2005	9,853	4,568*	47 percent*
2006	2,822		
Total to 2006	12,675		

* Based on 9,749 total ASBOs.

Source: Home Office Crime Reduction Web site (4/1/99–2005), http://www.crimereduction.homeoffice.gov.uk/asbos/asbos2.htm (accessed 2006).

their terms have been breached; through the end of 2003, 55 percent of breaches resulted in prison sentences (Burney 2005, table 5.1).

Many thousands of ASBOs have been issued, some of astonishing breadth. They have been used bizarrely (forbidding a woman to answer her doorbell in her underwear, an 88-year-old man to be sarcastic, a 13-year-old to ride his new dirt bike, an autistic child to stare over the fence from his family's yard, a child with Tourette's syndrome to shout at passers-by, a prostitute to possess condoms in the environs of a public health clinic that distributed them free, a suicidal woman to approach bridges) and have forbidden surprising activities (feeding seagulls, letting dogs bark, taxi drivers honking for passengers, pigs escaping from their sties). They have also been used illiberally (forbidding entry into any retail store in Devon or Cornwall, a family to enter a town where its home is located, young people under 16 to enter London's West End in the evening unaccompanied by an adult). Finally, they have been used unjustly (sentencing shoplifters to longer terms for violating ASBOs than they would have received had they been convicted of shoplifting, prostitutes to prison for engaging in noncriminal acts of prostitution, beggars to prison even though prison sentences are not authorized for criminal convictions for begging).[1]

British citizens were more troubled by antisocial behavior in 2007 than they were in 1992 or 1996, before the ASBO had been conceived of, or than they were in 1998, when the legislation creating it was enacted. The British Crime Survey (BCS), a representative annual survey of crime victimization and other topics, provides striking evidence of the perverse effects of overemphasis on antisocial behavior. Table 23.2 presents data from 12 waves of the BCS, beginning in 1992. It shows percentages of respondents who said particular types of disorder were "very" or "fairly" big problems at two-year intervals between 1992 and 1998 and annually since 2000. For most of the behaviors, the percentages have risen substantially since 1998, in most cases by 20 percent or more.

Elizabeth Burney (2005, p. 80) suggests that ASBOs have contributed to the growth of a "culture of complaint": "Service providers are increasingly expected to deal with problems that, before, might either have been ignored or dealt with between those involved." Home Office data bear that observation out. Table 23.3 presents data from the 2003–4 British Crime Survey on respondents' designations of antisocial behavior problems as "big" or "fairly big." Three patterns leap out. First, most of the behaviors listed are not crimes; they are everyday irritants of life everywhere, such as speeding and illegally parked cars, litter, irresponsible dog owners, and graffiti. Only drug dealing and vandalism typically involve criminal behavior. Second, levels of discontent are astonishingly high. Speeding was seen as a serious problem by 43 percent of respondents and illegal parking by 31 percent. Just under a third were troubled by litter, graffiti, and young people hanging about. Third, two of the items, loitering teenagers and rowdy people, are in effect complaints about other people's use of public space.

A very large majority of people receiving ASBOs have been children (Morgan and Newburn 2007, pp. 1038–39). Burney (2006, p. 206) observes that "ASBOs have

Table 23.2. Percentage of respondents saying antisocial behaviors are very or fairly big problems in their area, British Crime Survey, 1992–2007

Category	1992	1994	1996	1998	2000	2001–2	2002–3	2003–4	2004–5	2005–6	2006–7	2007
Noisy neighbors	8	8	8	8	9	10	10	9	9	10	11	10
Drunks, rowdies	N/A	N/A	N/A	N/A	N/A	22	23	19	22	24	26	25
Drug use/dealing	14	22	21	25	33	31	32	25	26	27	28	26
Teens hanging out	20	26	24	27	32	32	33	27	31	32	33	32
Rubbish, litter	30	26	26	28	30	32	33	29	30	30	31	31
Vandalism	26	29	24	26	32	34	35	28	28	29	28	28

Sources: for 1992–94: Simmons and colleagues 2002, table 9.13; for 1996 to 2006–7: Nicholas, Kershaw, and Walker 2007; for 2007: Home Office 2008.

Table 23.3. "Biggest" antisocial behavior problems reported by respondents, 2003–4 British Crime Survey

Category	Response, given in terms of percentage of respondents		
	Very big problem	Fairly big problem	Both combined
Speeding	12	31	43
Illegally parked cars	9	22	31
Rubbish, litter	9	20	29
Fireworks	10	19	29
Vandalism, graffiti	8	20	28
Loitering teens	9	19	28
Drug use, dealing	9	16	25
Loose dogs and mess	6	18	24
Drunk, rowdy people	5	14	19
Abandoned cars	4	11	15

Source: Wood 2004, figure 3.2.

become primarily used against children and young people and are seen as a way of dealing with unruly teenagers." Through the end of 2003, 52 percent of those receiving ASBOs were ages 10 to 17, and a significant number of the rest presumably were under 20 (Burney 2005, p. 96). It has long been known that the teenage years are a period of experimentation and include the peak years for criminality (let alone lesser acting out; Farrington 1986). A Home Office Survey on Young People and Crime showed that 25 percent of 10- to 25-year-olds admitted to committing a crime in the preceding 12 months (30 percent of males) and that just under 25 percent admitted to committing at least one of four forms of antisocial behavior in public (being rude or noisy so that people complained, behaving in a way that a neighbor complained, writing graffiti, or being racially abusive; D. Wilson, Sharp, and Patterson 2006). Among boys ages 14 to 19, well over a third admitted to antisocial behavior so defined. Those rates would have been much higher if all the behaviors listed in table 23.3 were surveyed.

ASBOs, and the intense publicity campaigns associated with them (Burney 2005; Morgan 2006), appear to have stoked the fires of adult resentment of teenagers' acting-out behaviors that are commonplace (Bottoms 2006). Table 23.4 shows data from the 2003–04 British Crime Survey on respondents' emotional responses to "young people hanging around." Fifty-four percent expressed annoyance and 24 percent expressed anger.

Whether the ASBO campaign has reduced the prevalence of antisocial behavior is unknown (Morgan 2006, p. 106). There are no data sources that allow measurement of temporal variation in the amorphous set of behaviors that have fallen within the scope of ASBOs. The BCS measures people's concern about antisocial behavior, not its incidence. If the BCS results are thought of as a proxy measure, the conclusion would have to be that antisocial behavior increased after

Table 23.4. Emotional responses to "young people hanging around" reported by respondents, 2003–4 British Crime Survey

Emotional response	Percentage of respondents*
Annoyance	54
Anger	26
Frustration	23
Worry	22

* Responses exceed 100 percent; multiple responses allowed.
Source: Wood 2004, table A 8.2.

1998. If the results are taken at face value as a measure of people's concern about particular forms of antisocial behavior, concerns have increased since 1998.

There are thus reasons to hypothesize that English government policies on antisocial behavior increased the public's discontent with the day-to-day circumstances of their lives and communities, fostered a culture of complaint, and exacerbated intergenerational resentment. This may be one reason why residents of the England and Wales are more likely than residents of any other developed country to invest in burglar alarms and other household security hardware, and why its residents have among the harshest preferences for sentencing offenders (van Dijk, van Kesteren, and Smit 2007).

ASBOs can be seen in three ways. First, in their own terms, at least, they are a new tool for reducing the incidence of antisocial behavior. Second, however, and probably as important, their creation is an adoption of an expressive policy intended to declare the unacceptability of antisocial behavior and, as government reports regularly avow (Home Office 2003), to increase public confidence. Third, they can be seen as a cynical ploy to gain electoral support by appealing to public anxieties, apprehensions, and resentments sometimes called "penal populism." Rod Morgan (2006, p. 111), formerly head of the Youth Justice Board of England and Wales, attributes the ASBO and other illiberal policies of England's Labour government to a tendency to seek "short-term electoral gain rather than effectiveness in changing behaviour or creating a safer world" (see also Downes and Morgan 2007, pp. 214–16, 221–22).

II. Broken Windows and Order Maintenance

James Q. Wilson and George L. Kelling's 1982 *Atlantic Monthly* article made "broken windows" a term of art. They were influenced by conclusions of a Police Foundation (1981) evaluation of a project in Newark, New Jersey, testing the effects of increased use of police foot patrol. Crime rates did not fall, but area residents felt safer and believed crime had declined.

J. Q. Wilson and Kelling (1982) argued that foot patrol had justified itself by enhancing residents' quality of life. They speculated that order-maintenance policing, focusing on signs of disorder and sources of insecurity and not just on violent crimes and reported incidents, would make communities safer: "At the community level, disorder and crime are usually inextricably linked, in a kind of developmental sequence. Social psychologists and police officers tend to agree that if a window in a building is broken and is left unrepaired, all the rest of the windows will soon be broken. This is as true in a nice neighborhood as in run-down ones.... One unbroken window is a signal that no-one cares" (p. 31).

The broken windows hypothesis gained some support among academics (e.g., Skogan 1992) and provoked a considerable amount of research that attempted to test it (e.g., Skogan 1992; Harcourt 1998; Kelling and Sousa 2001; Taylor 2001; Harcourt and Ludwig 2006). It also provoked substantial interest among policy makers, most famously in New York City, where it led to the policing innovations that established Mayor Rudolph Giuliani's credentials as a successful crime fighter and made the phrase *zero tolerance* part of the American (and subsequently world) criminal justice vocabulary. Empirical research, however, has largely refuted the hypothesis and shown that policing initiatives of the 1990s deserve little of the credit for New York City's substantial decline in crime rates.

A. Influence

New York City's Quality-of-Life Initiative, begun in 1994 by Mayor Rudolph Giuliani and Police Commissioner William Bratton, was the most extensive and publicized effort to date in the United States to implement order-maintenance policing (Harcourt 2002; Corman and Mocan 2005). The strategy emphasized aggressive enforcement of misdemeanor laws against quality-of-life offenses, including loitering and turnstile jumping (Harcourt 2002). Bratton observed that he supported Wilson and Kelling's ideas because in his policing experience he "had already lived it" (Bratton and Knobler 1998, p. 139).

Between 1994 and 1998 New York City's quality-of-life initiative resulted in between 40,000 and 85,000 additional adult misdemeanor arrests per year, greatly increased and more aggressive use of police stop-and-frisk powers, and sentencing of greatly increased numbers of people to prison and jail (Harcourt 2002, p. 101). Bratton credited the quality-of-life initiative with the arrests of many serious criminals, as minor offenders arrested under the program frequently had outstanding warrants for other and sometimes violent crimes (Treaster 1994).[2]

Several cities enacted ordinances giving police increased order-maintenance powers. The most famous of these did not withstand court challenges. For example, an antiloitering ordinance in New York, enforced by police as part of an order-maintenance initiative, was declared unconstitutional (*Loper v. New York City*

Police Department, 802 F. Supp. 1029 [S.D.N.Y. 1992]). The decision not only invalidated the ordinance but also criticized the broken windows theory and its potential effectiveness in dealing with community disorder. The U.S. Supreme Court rejected a comparable ordinance aimed at young people loitering on street corners in *City of Chicago v. Morales,* 527 U.S. 41 (1999). Justice Stevens, writing for the court, observed that myriad factors influence crime levels and that concern about disorder cannot justify overly broad criminal statutes.

Other cities enacted similar ordinances. Boston Mayor Thomas M. Menino announced that Boston police would crack down on misdemeanor offenses, including loud parties, public drinking, and littering, because community disorder is a precursor to violent crime (Brook 2006, pp. 2–3): "Today we are addressing what may sometimes appear to be smaller issues, but for those of us familiar with the 'broken windows' theory and reality, we know that these kinds of community disorder issues are the precursors to the violent crimes that may follow" (quoted in Brook 2006, p. 1).

In response to claims that the broken windows theory lacked empirical support, Boston police commissioner Kathleen O'Toole said, "We're not going to abandon our broken windows strategy. It's worked for us all along, and it will continue to work for us" (quoted in Brook 2006).

B. Effects

The broken windows hypothesis raises two major empirical questions: Does disorder necessarily lead to community deterioration and increased crime rates? What were the effects of police initiatives based on broken windows ideas; in particular, did they contribute substantially to crime rate reductions in the 1990s?

After a quarter-century's research, the broken windows hypothesis has not been validated, and one of its creators has backtracked. James Q. Wilson acknowledged the lack of empirical evidence in support of the hypothesis, explaining that it was based on an "assumption that a deteriorating quality of life caused the crime rate to go up" (quoted in Cohen 2000, p. B7). In a later interview Wilson said, "I still to this day do not know if improving order will or will not reduce crime. People have not understood that this was a speculation" (quoted in Hurley 2004, p. 1).

The basic ideas underlying the broken windows hypothesis are not implausible, which may be why it attracted such interest. For this reason, and because a couple of articles by leading academics seemed to confirm the basic ideas—neighborhood decline is associated with rising crime rates, proactive policing makes a difference—the theory seemed to be substantiated (Skogan 1986; Sampson and Cohen 1988). More recent work, however, has shown that evidence of the relationship between neighborhood decline and crime is much more complex than the broken windows theory allows for. Neighborhood decline is not related per se to crime rates (Sampson and Raudenbush 1999; Taylor 2001); underlying economic declines or preexisting levels of crime and disorder may explain both. Moreover, there are good reasons to doubt that order-maintenance policing deserves substantial credit for recent crime rate declines in New York City. Other cities not committed to order-maintenance policing experienced similar declines during the same period (Tonry 2004*b*). Close-grained analysis of New York's experience suggests that police tactics were but one of many things that affected crime rates (Harcourt and Ludwig 2006).

Wesley Skogan's 1986 article "Fear of Crime and Neighborhood Change" offered a grim view of the future of American cities and race relations as a result of the "cycle of fear and decline" (p. 222). In a later article, Skogan echoed Wilson and Kelling's thesis, citing disinvestment in neighborhood maintenance, demolition, demagoguery, and deindustrialization as "factors triggering neighborhood decline" (Skogan 1992).

Ralph Taylor (2001, p. 8) specified three ways in which "urban life" can be eroded: "through increasing neighborhood crime, through decreasing neighborhood quality, and by affecting residents' views about their neighborhood and their neighborhood safety." In a long-term study of crime in Baltimore neighborhoods Taylor used his findings to critique the broken windows hypothesis. He looked at changes over time in crime and in neighborhood fabric, comparing measures of incivilities, both perceived and assessed, and crime rates from 1981–82 to 1990–92. His aim was to determine whether incivilities contributed independently to crime rate changes or to basic neighborhood makeup (p. 179).

Taylor (2001, p. 193) noted that "deterioration spawns more deterioration when the deterioration betokens a neighborhood already in an underclass position relative to other neighborhoods." He suggested, however, that grime alone does not cause crime, and that the real source of neighborhood disorder and crime was economic decline.

Although Taylor's critique allows for the possibility that community policing targeting neighborhood deterioration may have some positive impacts, others have argued that the broken windows thesis is illogical and unprovable. Bernard Harcourt's (2002) *Illusion of Order: The False Promise of Broken Windows Policing* offers the most scathing critique. Harcourt criticized the hypothesis for failing to address the root causes of disorder and crime and for an almost complete lack of empirical support. He based his conclusions in large part on reanalyses of data in studies by Wesley Skogan (1992) and Robert Sampson and Jacqueline Cohen (1998).

Robert Sampson and Stephen Raudenbush, analyzing data from a long-term study of crime and neighborhood conditions in Chicago, similarly concluded that "the current fascination in policy circles on cleaning up disorder through law enforcement techniques appears simplistic and largely misplaced, at least in terms of directly fighting crime.... Attacking public order through tough police tactics may thus be a politically popular but perhaps analytically weak strategy to reduce crime"(Sampson and Raudenbush 1999, p. 638; see also Sampson and Raudenbush 2004).

Harcourt (2002) pointed out that correlations between disorder and crime are not proof of causation. He suggested a number of alternative explanations for falling crime rates in New York City and across the country in cities that implemented policing strategies akin to those in the quality-of-life initiative. He pointed to the 2,000 new police officers hired in 1992 under the Safe Streets, Safe City program and the 4,000 more added by Mayor Giuliani (pp. 98–100). The police force nearly doubled in size between 1992 and 1998; by 1998 New York City had the largest police force in the country and the highest number of officers per civilian in the country. Harcourt also noted internal police changes, including organizational overhauls, improved communication systems, and heavy reliance on geographical information systems in allocation of police personnel. Finally, Harcourt argued that changing drug use and trafficking, including a shift from crack cocaine to heroin beginning in the late 1980s, contributed to declining crime rates (p. 99). One of us has demonstrated that New York City's crime rate decline began three years before order-maintenance policing was initiated, and that New York City's declines in homicide and robbery rates in the 1990s were not significantly different from those in the other nine largest U.S. cities, several of which pointedly chose not to emulate New York City police policies (Tonry 2004*b*).

Harcourt and Jens Ludwig, in the most careful analysis of data on crime rate trends in New York City, reexamined data for 1989–98. They concluded:

> The pattern of crime changes across New York precincts during the 1990s that [is sometimes attributed] to broken windows policing is more consistent with what statisticians call mean reversion: those precincts that received the most intensive broken windows policing during the 1990s are the ones that experienced the largest increases in crime during the city's crack epidemic of the mid-to-late 1980s. Consistent with findings elsewhere from city-level data, jurisdictions with the greatest increases in crime during the 1980s tend to experience the largest subsequent declines as well. We call this Newton's Law of Crime: what goes up must come down (and what goes up the most tends to come down the most). (Harcourt and Ludwig 2006, p. 276)

Harcourt and Ludwig (2006) also examined new data from a five-city project and reexamined data in two studies (Kelling and Sousa 2001; Corman and Mocan 2005) that concluded that police innovations were largely responsible for the drop in New York City crime rates. They concluded, "Taken together, the evidence from New York City and from the five-city social experiment provides no support for a simple first-order disorder-crime relationship as hypothesized by Wilson and Kelling, nor for the proposition that broken windows policing is the optimal use of scarce law enforcement resources" (p. 271).

The findings just summarized substantially, if not entirely, undermine the broken windows hypothesis. Yet they have not persuaded convinced proponents. Bratton and Kelling (2006, p. 2) protested, "What particularly galls police about these critiques is that ivory-tower academics—many of whom have never sat in a patrol car, walked or bicycled a beat, lived in or visited regularly troubled violent neighborhoods, or collected any relevant data of their own 'on the ground'—cloak themselves in the mantle of an empirical 'scientist' and produce 'findings' indicating that broken windows has been disproved.... Police don't have time for these virtual-reality theories; they do their work in the real world." Whether the broken windows hypothesis has been decisively refuted depends on who is assigned the burden of proof. If proponents are assigned that burden, the hypothesis cannot be said to have been validated, as James Q. Wilson's recharacterization of it as a "speculation" appears to concede. The critics have much more evidence on their side. Reasonable people can differ over whether their evidence entirely refutes the hypothesis or merely seriously undermines it.

III. What Is Wrong with ASBOs and Order-Maintenance Policies?

ASBOs have demonstrably reduced neither the incidence of the behaviors they target nor public discontent with neighborhood conditions. There is a good chance that they increased public dissatisfaction and raised levels of public intolerance. Depending on your taste, the broken windows hypothesis has been refuted or seriously undermined. The weight of the evidence supports the conclusion that order-maintenance policing was not a substantial cause of declines in New York City crime rates in the 1990s.

This learning has been bought at heavy cost. By focusing on behaviors that are either not criminal or constitute only minor, seldom prosecuted forms of criminality, ASBOs and broken windows ideas have increased public intolerance. By insisting that traditional ideas about civil liberties, procedural protections, and human rights are expendable in the name of public order, they risk undermining normative beliefs and human rights policies long seen as fundamental in Western societies. They also risk exacerbating social cleavages between the comfortable haves and the unruly and awkward have-nots.

A. Intolerance

Both ASBOs and the broken windows theory risk increasing public intolerance. What sociologists sometimes call "the amplification of deviance" has taken place: things once seen as irritating or distasteful, but tolerable, are redefined as deviant and intolerable. The three forms of antisocial behavior respondents in the British Crime Survey most often complained about—speeding, parking illegally, and rubbish—are routine frictions of everyday life in crowded cities everywhere, and perceptions of their venality depend on perspective. Speeding is a nuisance to a resident of a crowded neighborhood but is a venial lapse to a driver who is late for an appointment. Ditto illegal parking. Not quite ditto rubbish; most people probably feel at least a twinge of a sense of wrongdoing tossing refuse on the street, but as sins go it is a minor and a ubiquitous one.

One of the two biggest problems according to the BCS is "teenagers hanging around" (Wood 2004, p. 12); speeding is the other. Speeding traffic is a fact of modern life for which speed cameras, speed bumps, speeding tickets, and traffic police are in most places seen as appropriate responses. Teenagers hanging around is a fact not of modern but of human life: kids do things in groups, and because home is a less appealing venue than most anywhere else, kids go somewhere else. That sometimes they are numerous, noisy, and untidy is not peculiarly characteristic of or endemic to England. The redefinition of speeding, illegal parking, and loitering teenagers as serious antisocial behavior in many British citizens' minds is not an accomplishment to celebrate.

The House of Commons Home Affairs Committee in 2005 expressed disappointment that "social service departments and other key players such as local education authorities, the Children and Adolescent Mental Health Service, Youth Services, and some children's NGOs are often not fully committed to local ASB strategies" (Home Office 2005, p. 7). The Committee, responding to criticisms about the trivial nature of many ASBOs, indignantly insisted that "activities such as playing football in the street are not necessarily harmless" (p. 6). That statement is bizarre. It is hard to imagine children playing in the street being portrayed as harmful, much less seriously harmful, anywhere but in England during the ASBO regime.

Loper v. New York City Police Department (802 F. Supp. 1029 [S.D.N.Y. 1992]), the decision striking down a New York City antiloitering ordinance that police used to target beggars, stressed the negative effects of fostering intolerance: "The peaceful beggar poses no threat to society. The beggar has arguably only committed the offense of being needy. The message one or one hundred beggars sends society can be disturbing. If some portion of society is offended, the answer is not in criminalizing these people,... but addressing the root cause of their existence. The root cause is not served by removing them from sight, however; society is then just able to pretend they do not exist a little longer" (at 1046).

B. Fundamental Norms

An important feature of both the U.S. broken windows and the U.K. ASBO stories is that policies that were initially seen as radical intrusions into individual liberty and as profoundly antiliberal in time became accepted as normal, and then led to adoption of broader policies that at the outset would have been almost unimaginable: pretextual arrests of people for minor misbehavior, running end runs around civil liberties and criminal procedure protections, imprisoning people for decriminalized behaviors such as prostitution and begging in England, criminalizing children playing soccer in the streets.

Prime Minister Blair in 2005 expressed his impatience with traditional criminal justice values and stressed his aim to focus on the interests of victims and potential victims: "The whole of our system starts from the proposition that its duty is to protect the innocent from being wrongly convicted.... But surely our *primary* duty should be to allow law-abiding people to live in safety" (quoted in Morgan 2006, pp. 110–11; emphasis added). In earlier years, in relation to crime, the Labour government made its impatience with the criminal justice system clear: "We must ensure that the criminal justice system is rebalanced in favour of victims" (National Victims Conference 2004, p. 10).

The public, policy makers, and policy critics became accustomed to policies that were once unthinkable and in a sense forgot about issues of principle that only a few years earlier had seemed terribly important. Sensibilities, prevailing ways of looking at and thinking about things, changed, and profoundly antiliberal policies became not only imaginable but difficult even to imagine as objectionable. There are many similar American examples. In the 1960s and before, few people thought it appropriate to try children in adult courts. Since then many laws have been passed, some reducing the juvenile court maximum age to 15, some allowing all serious crimes to be tried in adult courts whatever the defendant's age, and others that routinely treat children as if they are adults (Feld 2001).

There are many examples of such collective forgetting. In the United States preventive detention, confining criminal suspects before trial to prevent their committing new crimes, was highly controversial in the 1960s and 1970s. Passage of the first laws explicitly authorizing the practice was much delayed and highly contested. Suspects, after all, are legally presumed to be innocent. Confining someone before trial on any basis other than the reasonable suspicion that he or she may not appear violates the presumption. Nevertheless, the first laws were passed in the 1970s, and it is difficult now to find anyone who thinks there is anything controversial about them (Tonry 2004*b*).

By repeatedly insisting that the criminal justice system is not working satisfactorily governments undermine faith in the legal system. By insisting that traditional procedural rights and protections are unimportant and can be cut back without sacrifice of anything important, governments undermine public understanding and support for fundamental ideas about liberty, fairness, and justice.

Responding to the U.K. government's manipulations of language, John Humphrys of BBC Radio Four's *Today* show explained:

> Politicians from all parties tell us endlessly that the criminal justice system needs "rebalancing" in favour of the victim. That's a pretty safe proposition to defend. Surely we must all be on the side of victims. So if the system needs rebalancing in their favour let's get on with it....
>
> But this is a manipulation of the word's meaning. Those famous scales in the hands of Blind Justice are not meant to symbolize balancing the interests of the victim against the interests of the accused. They are there to weigh the evidence of the prosecution against that of the defence. That's it. (2004, p. 307)

C. Social Cohesion

Poverty, disadvantage, and diminished life chances are in no country randomly distributed. People who live lives of comparative disadvantage are much likelier than their more fortunate brethren to be poor, ill-educated, unemployed, mentally ill, drug dependent, and involved in "antisocial behavior" and crime. In the United States young blacks and Hispanics, especially males, are disproportionately poor and disadvantaged. In England young Afro-Caribbeans and young whites of working-class backgrounds, again mostly males, inhabit those social positions. Policies against crime and disorder that increase intolerance of the disadvantaged and diminish respect for their rights and liberties further marginalize the marginalized and lengthen the odds against their ever achieving normal, productive, satisfying patterns of life.

David Garland's magisterial *The Culture of Control* (2001) made "expressive policies" a widely recognized term of art. He observed that rising crime rates, coupled with widespread belief among officials in the 1970s and 1980s that they could do little that would significantly affect crime rates and patterns, led policy makers to search for ways they could acknowledge citizens' fears and anxieties and at least appear to be doing something about crime. Expressive policies were the answer. Whether or not they were likely to work, their adoption expressed solidarity with citizens and, if politicians were lucky, established tough-on-crime credentials for use in reelection campaigns. Zero-tolerance policing, mandatory minimum sentences, three-strikes laws, and the "War on Drugs" are the best known American examples, and ASBOs and "rebalancing the system in favour of the victim" in myriad ways are the best-known English examples (Tonry 2004*a*).

One characteristic of this strategy, Garland noted, is that it is often accompanied by a "criminology of the other," a tendency to target expressive policies on behaviors that are disproportionately committed not by members of the political majority but by more marginalized members of society. This is surely a reason why U.S. drug policies focus on drug dealing in the streets rather than in the suites, and on cocaine, methamphetamine, and marijuana rather than on the much more objectively dangerous drugs alcohol and nicotine.

Both ASBOs and the broken windows theory are primarily expressive policies. They are meant to allow governments to be seen to be taking citizen concerns seriously. But like other expressive policies, they primarily ensnare members of socially and economically disadvantaged groups, and especially of socially and economically disadvantaged minority groups.

Concerning New York City's zero-tolerance policing policies, Amnesty International (1996) reported that the annual number of citizens' lawsuits about police misconduct more than doubled between 1987 and 1994. Between 1993 and 1994 complaints to the police citizen complaints board increased by 37.43 percent.

Fifty percent of all complaints were filed by blacks and 26 percent by Hispanics; only 21 percent were filed by white New Yorkers. Bernard Harcourt (1998, pp. 379–80) summarizes evidence from a number of sources indicating that New York's policing policies produced substantially increased numbers of allegations of police brutality, especially against members of minority groups.

Concerning Boston's zero-tolerance policing policies, an editorial in the *Boston Herald* observed that antiloitering laws are most often enforced against unpopular groups and that they undermine the positive effects of good policing: "For many in law enforcement, the newly proposed anti-loitering laws feel like a reversion to the bad old days. They have the potential of pitting the police against the people. They weaken the trust that has been built up between the cops and Latino and other communities. And, they don't do anything to address the underlying causes of why kids join gangs in the first place" (Keane 2003).

D. The Future of ASBOs and the Broken Windows Theory

Antisocial behavior orders and police policies based on the broken windows hypothesis have done more harm than good. Neither set of initiatives has produced the gains their proponents promised. Both have produced unintended negative consequences that far outweigh any benefits that can reasonably be claimed for them. Countries facing the twenty-first-century challenges of globalization, increased population diversity, and anxieties associated with "late modernity" need to find ways to bring their fractured populations together rather than to split them, to narrow gaps between the haves and the have-nots rather than to spread them, and to strengthen the relations between majority and minority populations rather than to weaken them. Many of the putative goals of policies discussed in this chapter—improving the quality of urban life, lessening the frictions that divide people, and enhancing mutual respect—are worthy goals of government, but they need to be pursued in positive ways through a wide range of social, community, and public health programs rather than through the overreach of the criminal law.

NOTES

1. We have not cited the newspaper sources on which we draw. Web search engines can find the relevant stories and many others describing similar cases.

2. Harcourt (1998, p. 341) provides references to similar claims that arrests for minor offenses, including subway fare nonpayment, led to arrests for more serious crimes, such as the claim that "one out of seven fare evaders had prior warrants out for their arrest. One out of 21 was carrying a handgun."

REFERENCES

Amnesty International. 1996. *Police Brutality and Excess Use of Force in the New York City Police Department.* New York: Amnesty International.

Bottoms, Anthony E. 2006. "Incivilities, Offence, and Social Order in Residential Communities." In *Incivilities: Regulating Offensive Behaviour,* edited by Andrew von Hirsch and A. P. Simester. Oxford, UK: Hart.

Bratton, William, and George Kelling. 2006. "There Are No Cracks in the Broken Windows." *National Review* (February 28), p. 2.

Bratton, William J., and Peter Knobler. 1998. *Turnaround: How America's Top Cop Reversed the Crime Epidemic.* New York: Random House.

Brook, Daniel. 2006. "The Cracks in 'Broken Windows.'" *Boston Globe* (February 19). http://www.boston.com/news/globe/ideas/articles/2006/02/19/the_cracks_in_broken_windows/.

Burney, Elizabeth. 2005. *Making People Behave: Anti-social Behaviour, Politics, and Policy.* Cullompton, UK: Willan.

———. 2006. "No Spitting: Regulation of Offensive Behaviour in England and Wales." In *Incivilities: Regulating Offensive Behaviour,* edited by Andrew von Hirsch and A. P. Simester. Oxford, UK: Hart.

Campbell, Siobhan. 2002. *A Review of Antisocial Behaviour Orders.* Home Office Research Study 236. London: Home Office Research, Development, and Statistics Directorate.

Cohen, Patricia. 2000. "Oops, Sorry: Seems That My Pie Chart Is Half-Baked." *New York Times* (April 8), p. B7.

Corman, Hope, and Naci Mocan. 2005. "Carrots, Sticks and Broken Windows." *Journal of Law and Economics* 48(1): 235–66.

Downes, David, and Rod Morgan. 2007. "No Turning Back: The Politics of Law and Order into the Millennium." In *The Oxford Handbook of Criminology,* 4th ed., edited by Mike Maguire, Rod Morgan, and Robert Reiner. Oxford: Oxford University Press.

Farrington, David P. 1986. "Age and Crime." In *Crime and Justice: A Review of Research,* vol. 7, edited by Michael Tonry and Norval Morris. Chicago: University of Chicago Press.

Feld, Barry. 2001. *Bad Kids.* New York: Oxford University Press.

Garland, David. 2001. *The Culture of Control.* Oxford: Oxford University Press.

Harcourt, Bernard E. 1998. "Reflecting on the Subject: A Critique of the Social Influence Conception of Deterrence, the Broken Windows Theory, and Order-Maintenance Policing New York Style." *Michigan Law Review* 97: 291–389.

———. 2002. *Illusion of Order: The False Promise of Broken Windows Policing.* Cambridge, MA: Harvard University Press.

Harcourt, Bernard E., and Jens Ludwig. 2006. "Broken Windows: New Evidence from New York City and a Five-City Social Experiment." *University of Chicago Law Review* 73: 271–320.

Hartocollis, Anemona. 2008. "Noisy Train, a Fed-Up Rider and a Day in Court." *New York Times* (April 9). http://www.nytimes.com/2008/04/09/nyregion/09train.html.

Home Office. 2003. *Respect and Responsibility—Taking a Stand against Antisocial Behaviour.* Cm 5778. London: Her Majesty's Stationery Office.

———. 2005. *Antisocial Behaviour: The Government Reply to the Fifth Report from the Home Affairs Committee, Session 2004–05, HC 80.* Cm 6588. London: Her Majesty's Stationery Office.

———. 2008. *Crime in England and Wales—Quarterly Update to December 2007 (04/08)*. Home Office Statistical Bulletin. London: Home Office.

Humphrys, John. 2004. *Lost for Words: The Mangling and Manipulation of the English Language*. London: Hodder and Stoughton.

Hurley, Dan. 2004. *On Crime as Science (a Neighbor at a Time)*. http://crab.rutgers.edu/ goertzel/CollectiveEfficacyEarls.html.

Keane, Thomas M., Jr. 2003. "Anti-loitering Laws Aren't Gang-Busters." *Boston Herald* (March 26). http://www.provost-citywide.org/gang-busters-herald032603.htm.

Kelling, George L., and William H. Sousa Jr. 2001. *Do Police Matter? An Analysis of the Impact of New York City's Police Reforms*. New York: Manhattan Institute.

Morgan, Rod. 2006. "With Respect to Order, the Rules of the Game Have Changed: New Labour's Dominance of the 'Law and Order' Agenda." In *The Politics of Crime Control: Essays in Honour of David Downes,* edited by Tim Newburn and Paul Rock. Oxford: Oxford University Press.

Morgan, Rod, and Tim Newburn. 2007. "Youth Justice." In *The Oxford Handbook of Criminology,* 4th ed., edited by Mike Maguire, Rod Morgan, and Robert Reiner. Oxford: Oxford University Press.

National Victims Conference. 2004. *Conference Report: Supporting Victims—Making It Happen*. London: Home Office.

Nicholas, Sian, Chris Kershaw, and Alison Walker, eds. 2007. *Crime in England and Wales 2006/07*. Home Office Statistical Bulletin. London: Home Office.

Police Foundation. 1981. "The Newark Foot Patrol Experiment." Washington, DC: Police Foundation. Summary available at: http://www.policefoundation.org/docs/newark.html.

Russell, Ben, and Helen McCormick. 2005. "Doubling of Asbos Raises Concern over Misuse." *Independent* (June 30). http://findarticles.com/p/articles/mi_qn4158/is_20050630/ai_n14690856.

Sampson, Robert, and Jacqueline Cohen. 1988. "Deterrent Effect of the Police on Crime: A Replication and Theoretical Extension." *Law and Society Review* 22(1): 163–90.

Sampson, Robert J., and Stephen W. Raudenbush. 1999. "Systematic Social Observation of Public Spaces: A New Look at Disorder in Urban Neighborhoods." *American Journal of Sociology* 105(3): 603–51.

Sampson, Robert J., and Stephen W. Raudenbush. 2004. "Seeing Disorder: Neighborhood Stigma and the Social Construction of 'Broken Windows.'" *Social Psychology Quarterly* 67: 4.

Simmons, John, and colleagues. 2002. *Crime in England and Wales 2001/2002*. London: Home Office.

Skogan, Wesley. 1986. "Fear of Crime and Neighborhood Change." In *Communities and Crime,* edited by Albert J. Reiss Jr. and Michael Tonry. Vol. 8 of *Crime and Justice: A Review of Research,* edited by Michael Tonry and Norval Morris. Chicago: University of Chicago Press.

———. 1992. *Disorder and Decline: Crime and the Spiral of Decay in American Neighborhoods*. Berkeley: University of California Press.

Taylor, Ralph B. 2001. *Breaking Away from Broken Windows: Baltimore Neighborhoods and the Nationwide Fight against Crime, Grime, Fear, and Decline*. Boulder, CO: Westview.

Tonry, Michael. 2004*a*. *Punishment and Politics: Evidence and Emulation in the Making of English Crime Control Policy*. Cullompton, UK: Willan.

———. 2004*b*. *Thinking about Crime*. New York: Oxford University Press.
Treaster, Joseph B. 1994. "Crime Rate Drops Again in New York, Hastening a Trend." *New York Times* (June 22). http://query.nytimes.com/gst/fullpage.html?res=9907E3D6103BF931A35755C0A962958260.
van Dijk, Jan, John van Kesteren, and Paul Smit. 2007. *Criminal Victimization in International Perspective*. The Hague: Netherlands Ministry of Justice and Boom Juridische uitgevers.
Wilson, Debbie, Clare Sharp, and Alison Patterson. 2006. *Young People and Crime: Findings from the 2005 Offending, Crime, and Justice Survey*. Home Office Statistical Bulletin. London: Home Office.
Wilson, James Q., and George L. Kelling. 1982. "Broken Windows." *Atlantic Monthly* March: 29–38.
Wilson, James Q., and George L. Kelling. 1989. "Making Neighborhoods Safe: Sometimes 'Fixing Broken Windows' Does More to Reduce Crime Than Conventional 'Incident-Oriented' Policing." *Atlantic Monthly* February: 46–52.
Wood, Martin. 2004. *Perceptions and Experience of Antisocial Behaviour: Findings from the 2003/2004 British Crime Survey*. Home Office Online Report 49/04. London: Home Office Research, Development, and Statistics Directorate.

CHAPTER 24

GAMBLING

JOHN DOMBRINK

WHEN Massachusetts governor Deval Patrick announced in September 2007 a plan that supported bringing as many as three casinos to that state, he was met with support from certain quarters of the state government and opposition from other well-placed leaders and organizations. In detailing the plan, Patrick explained, "I believe authorizing three resort casinos will have significant economic benefits to Massachusetts. Done the right way, destination resort casinos can play a useful part, along with other initiatives in life sciences, renewable energy and education reform, in providing our Commonwealth with sustainable, long-term economic growth" (Commonwealth of Massachusetts 2007, p. 1). Though a relatively new governor, Patrick had chosen to address fiscal problems through the offset of gambling revenue, a path that many state governments have taken in various forms over the past 40 years, mostly for revenue enhancement or for economic development possibilities, or a combination of the two.

Certain vocal critics in Massachusetts have eyed gambling skeptically. They have tried to counter the exhortations of those who, in considering the state's geography, support gambling expansion as an opportunity to bring home some of the gambling dollars that go over the borders, to New Hampshire (as in the early lottery days) and to Connecticut (in the current casino lure of the Mohegan Sun and Foxwoods Indian casinos). Some critics immediately questioned the economic development and revenue potential of the 2007 Patrick plan (Maguire 2007*b*). Others warned of the possible deleterious effects on vulnerable populations, such as youth (Maguire 2007*a*). The Massachusetts legislature rejected the governor's proposal (Peter 2008).

In Illinois, where gambling expansion has been discussed recently as a method of offsetting budget demands, one report notes, "More casinos may be part of a deal to stave off service cuts and fare increases at the Chicago Transit Authority and suburban transit agencies" (Mendell 2007, p. 1). Meanwhile, in Kentucky the 2007 election of a new governor presaged more serious discussion about gambling in that decidedly conservative or "red" state (as political analysts have come to describe American states as "red" if they lean conservative or vote Republican, or "blue" if they lean liberal or vote Democratic) (Hegarty 2007). Across the various regions and political leanings of the United States, gambling has been normalized and legalized steadily over the past 40 years.

In the many considerations of gambling policy by state and federal entities during this time several factors have combined to produce a contemporary American approach in which gambling is widespread, participated in by many, increasingly seen as a common from of entertainment (often in combination with its retail, dining, and entertainment components), sought out by states and localities for its economic development boost, and relied on as a steady stream of state tax revenue separate from property and sales taxes.

Gambling, an activity that most cultures contain and many encourage, has been in many ways the least likely of the classic "victimless crimes" (such as prostitution, illegal drug use, pornography, abortion, and homosexuality) for the state to choose to limit through the strict use of the criminal sanction. That it moved from a largely tolerated but legally underground activity to an increasingly legalized activity in the United States after 1960, with an 800 percent increase in revenues from 1980 to 2005, speaks to the widespread nature of its embrace by various states.

In the first days of campaigns to legalize gambling in the 1960s moralistic opposition was often presented by various religious and civic groups (although it should be noted that Americans vary greatly by religiosity in their assessment of and participation in gambling activities). As gambling legalization spread, or underwent "normalization," these concerns proved to be less often successful, although gambling legalization did proceed more slowly than elsewhere in more Baptist-influenced southern states until recent years (Nelson and Mason 2007). Organized criminal influence, a major issue in the mid-twentieth-century days of Nevada gambling, has also receded as an issue of opposition, although it did affect the trajectory of casino legalization from the late 1970s forward (Dombrink and Thompson 1990).

More often, policy contests over gambling in the postmoralistic frame have turned to issues of problem gamblers, economic development, and ancillary crime. In this chapter I present the central argument of those critiques and conclude that, singly or together, they have not seriously impeded gambling expansion. However, these critiques may influence future skepticism or opposition, especially given the advent of increasingly facile communications technology.

A number of generalizations about gambling, its growth, and its societal and legal treatment can be drawn from the existing literature:

- Gambling in American society has been historically tolerated. Citizens consider it to have a low level of seriousness compared to other crimes and morally contested behaviors.
- The past 40 years have witnessed an explosive growth of legal gambling and revenues from legal gambling. Some forms, such as lotteries, have been dependent on state sponsorship. Others follow a private enterprise approach, with the state vitally involved and the recipient of tax revenues.
- Over these decades and through these processes gambling has become increasingly normalized in American society: accepted in public consideration, participated in by a large portion of the population, and relied on by the state.
- Nonetheless, gambling continues to be criticized in some quarters, especially because its expansion makes it more easily accessible to people who have difficulty controlling their gambling behavior. Because of this, gambling has not fully expanded in all possible forms in the states that allow it.
- Primarily due to the role of the state in allowing and promoting gambling, gambling's progress in all these dimensions has been uncoupled from the other victimless crimes.

In the first section of this chapter I discuss the scope and scale of legal gambling in the United States and examine various issues during this history, contextualizing U.S. treatment of this "normal vice," with continued toleration of gambling and its flourish in illegal forms. Section II details current forms of legal gambling and its symbolism. In section III I discuss critiques of legal gambling together with analyses of their salience and success in current discussions and legalization efforts. Section IV presents a number of unresolved issues in the legalization of gambling, including the capacity of communications technology to change the forms of gambling (and increase the worries of those critics). In section V I discuss why gambling has been uncoupled from legal treatment of other so-called victimless crimes.

I. America's Third Wave of Legal Gambling

Gambling has been described as America's pastime. The growth of legal gambling in the past 40 years suggests that such a statement may not be far from the truth. In 2005 legal gambling revenues totaled more than $84 billion (American Gaming Association 2007). Even though casinos have not spread Las Vegas–style gambling across the country, as was once predicted, almost $32 billion of this total (38 percent) was accounted for by the 460 commercial casinos in 11 states. Another nearly $23 billion (or 27 percent) came from Indian casinos, the parallel offerings of some 400 gaming establishments operated by about 230 tribes. Another 27 percent (almost $23 billion) came from state-run lotteries.

Revenues from legal gambling grew nearly 1,600 percent between 1976 and 1998. As one analyst notes, in comparison to legal gambling's $70 billion of revenue in 2000, "the sum total spent on tickets to all movies, plays, concerts, and live performances, plus all sports events, is only about $22 billion per year. Americans are now spending three times as much on gambling as on all other kinds of entertainment combined" (Christiansen Capital Advisors 2001). One author estimates that Americans now spend on slots five times the amount they spend on movie tickets (Cooper 2004).

Gambling has existed in the form of tolerated card games and bets on horseracing throughout American history. From colonial days gambling in various forms has often been legalized and used to support projects of the common good, such as education and public works. Parts of Harvard University were built with lottery proceeds, as were bridges and other public work projects (Ezell 1960; Cornell Law Project 1977). It was more tolerated in some eras than in others, but it persisted in subterranean locales even in the most restrictive times. Americans' tolerance waned following a mid-nineteenth-century scandal with the Louisiana Lottery, the early precursor of the national lottery, and legal forms of gambling receded (as did other forms of vice). Another resurgence was then quieted by the early twentieth-century movement that also led to the Volstead Act and the prohibition of alcoholic beverages. The State of Nevada passed a law in 1931 to reestablish legal gambling. Before the advent of the Las Vegas destination resort casinos, however, a law passed at the same time authorizing short-residence divorces brought more money into the state than did gambling legalization (Skolnick 1978).

In the 1950s gambling was still illegal in the United States, but law enforcement and prosecution were unsuccessful in limiting illegal gambling, as they had been in the prior two decades. During this period juries were reluctant to convict gambling defendants or to give them significant sentences when they did convict them (Mangione and Fowler 1979). This is consistent with Geis's (1979) observation that gambling generated a very low level of perceived seriousness by Americans. New Hampshire legalized the lottery in 1964, and other states soon followed. Las Vegas grew from a small desert town with legal gambling before World War II to a major world venue for legal casino gambling, built in part with the capital provided by organized crime groups.

The involvement of prominent organized crime groups in dominant forms of both illegal and legal gambling in the twentieth century has been well documented. Many scholars and journalists argue that the wealth of bootleggers of the 1920s and their nascent multiactivity crime groups expanded into gambling in the 1930s, making the most of the cash reserves they had amassed during Prohibition, at the same time that American society was experiencing the economic ravages of the Great Depression. The lore of gangster involvement in the genesis of the modern Las Vegas is mostly correct (Skolnick 1978; Denton and Morris 2002). Major crime organizations participated as hidden owners in a large number of Las Vegas casinos in the 1950s and 1960s. The arrival of corporate gaming through regulations passed in the late 1960s eventually allowed the Hiltons and Ramadas of the world entrée into Nevada gaming, to be eclipsed in turn by large gaming-centered, publicly traded corporations like MGM, Caesar's World, Mirage, Resorts, and Harrah's. The last vestiges of organized crime involvement were exposed in the late 1970s with the cases brought against corporations funded in part by the Teamsters Central States Pension Fund and connected to Chicago and Kansas City organized crime groups (Pileggi 1995).

In addition to legalized casino gambling in Nevada, the rise of what Nelson Rose (1980) has called the "third wave" of gambling legalization began in the 1960s, spurred by the New Hampshire lottery in 1964. By the 1970s, when other states had authorized lotteries, many states were experiencing what one economist termed the "fiscal crisis of the state" (O'Connor 1973). Gambling expanded as legalization efforts for lotteries continued, and legal casinos were authorized in New Jersey after a successful statewide vote there in 1976. The Commission on the Review of the National Policy toward Gambling (1976), an important national forum for consideration of various forms of regulation, found support in polls for legal forms of gambling. By the time Atlantic City opened casinos in 1978 as the second major venue for legal casino gambling in the United States, organized crime ownership and control was fading, being supplanted by publicly traded gaming corporations ("Special Report" 1978).

State-owned lotteries boomed during the 1980s. At the same time, a number of Indian reservations were experimenting with forms of gambling, leading to the U.S. Supreme Court ruling that upheld Indians' right to open casinos on tribal lands (*California v. Cabazon Band of Mission Indians*, 480 U.S. 202 [1987]) and the passage of the federal Indian Gaming Regulatory Act, which implemented the regulated proliferation of gambling on Indian lands. By 1982, gross legal gaming revenues in the United States were $10 billion. Of this, about 20 percent was derived from lotteries, 40 percent from casinos (not including Indian gaming), and the remainder from horse racing, dog racing, charitable games, legal bookmaking, and Indian gaming (Johnson 1991).

These multiple paths to legalization have produced legal gambling in the United States in many forms. One gaming executive sees a more integrated and diversified future for certain aspects of gambling: "Gaming has become almost ubiquitous around the United States, and I believe over time you will see a natural, common sense convergence between what is available in a casino with a wide range of other forms of entertainment. And hopefully what will come with that will be a normalization of gaming in the political environment, as well as the regulatory environment" (Loveman 2002, p. 38).

The U.S. model of legalized gambling typifies an approach taken by several countries that are similarly situated economically and politically. Although the United States is the largest contributor to the world's legal gambling revenue, with approximately 60 percent of the total, the involvement of large and small European countries is growing, and increasingly through online gambling. Many European countries have regulated online gambling, and some, such as Germany in 2008, have adopted the U.S. model and banned Internet gambling. Germany anticipates action from the European Union on its break from its sister countries. France may also reconsider its ban on Internet gambling to forge an EU consensus.

The British model has often been held up as the alternative (Skolnick 1978). Stringent requirements, such as membership in a gambling club and a waiting period of 24 hours—ostensibly to ward off impulsivity—make the model very different from the U.S. version. Popular and moralistic resistance have prevented some British entrepreneurs and politicians from grafting permission for Las Vegas–style large casinos onto the existing model of gaming regulation (Collins 2006).

Recent activity is making a gambling center of Macau, a small island that is currently a special district of China after four centuries as a Portuguese colony (Fallows 2007). Macau has long had a small casino presence, which exploded after U.S. companies arrived, in some cases partnering with the Hong Kong gambling magnate who had operated casinos there for four decades. With a nearly 50 percent rise in revenues in 2007, Macau is estimated to overtake the state of Nevada in gaming revenues in 2008, having already surpassed the Las Vegas Strip in 2007 (Greenlees 2008). Such growth helps make Asia the fastest growing gambling region in the world. Gambling experts predict that the Asian share of the world's legal gambling market will rise over 50 percent from its 2006 level to pass the European market by 2011 (PricewaterhouseCoopers 2007).

II. Current Scope and Forms

In a 2004 Gallup poll two-thirds of Americans reported that they had gambled in the prior year (Jones 2004), and U.S. states looking for revenues have increasingly fixed on legal gambling as a revenue source. A recent analysis by an organization that studies state governments captures this surge well: "Every state except Hawaii and Utah has some form of gaming. Bettors last year could try their luck at commercial casinos in 11 states, American Indian casinos in 28 and lotteries in all but eight. Some states, like Iowa and Louisiana, have scored a 'full house' with three kinds of casino gambling and the pair of lottery and track betting" (Prah 2007).

Researchers estimate that a third of American workers participate in Super Bowl office betting and that two-thirds of workers have bet in any betting pool. Poker, whether in-person, online, or on television, has emerged as a popular event, with the World Series of Poker an annual highlight. Poker has reasserted itself, along with the increasingly "machined" and technology-centric rise in slot machines, as a staple of legal gambling revenues since 1980. Whatever its contribution to the national gambling revenue pot, it also occupies a place of some symbolic importance because it epitomizes a game that is dependent on skill more than chance. News reports of middle school poker nights can be found alongside worries over problem gambling by college students.

Meanwhile, the spread of gambling, having reached 48 states, has clearly not been restricted to those "blue" or politically liberal states that have been noticeably reformist in decriminalizing other forms of formerly prohibited personal behavior. Indeed, as Nelson and Mason (2007) have shown, even the South, a major locus of the "values voters" on whom President Bush had come to rely as a socially conservative base for the Republican Party, has been receptive to the growth of gambling. As Ugel (2007, p. xvi) notes, "Casinos are no longer fantasy worlds, a faraway Vegas or Atlantic City. Now, they're just down the street or the next town over."

The ubiquity of gambling has generated concern and outcry from the opponents of legal gambling and gambling expansion, who fear that such easy access will have detrimental effects on people who are economically or psychologically less well positioned to ignore its lures. However, a 1999 Gallup Organization poll showed that only 26 percent of Americans saw gambling as immoral, and Skolnick (2001) has recently referred to gambling as the "normal vice" because of the widespread participation by most sectors of the American population. Harvard professor Howard Shaffer, director of Harvard Medical School's Division on Addiction, added, "This is the first time that a generation has grown up amid legalized gambling, in a social setting that not only permits but endorses the gambler" (quoted in Lambert 2002, p. 35). Frank Fahrenkopf (2005, p.14), president of the American Gaming Association (AGA), reported that a recent AGA survey of elected officials and community leaders in communities with gambling found " a stunning affirmation—by the most active and engaged people in the community—of our industry's value." Fahrenkopf was pleased to cite support by 79 percent of the respondents that "casinos have had a positive impact on the community," and a similar number who consider casinos as "good corporate citizens" (p.14). He later added, "According to the annual poll of adult Americans conducted for the *State of the States* survey... 82 percent... consider casino gaming to be an activity that's acceptable for themselves or others" (Fahrenkopf 2007, p. 20). He cited similar support on the issue of contribution to the common good: "Almost seven out of 10 interviewees see legalized casino gambling as a good way for state and local governments to generate revenue without draining taxes. There also is widespread agreement that casinos bring economic benefits to other industries and businesses" (p. 20). It appears that gambling has been normalized.

A. Varieties of Gambling

Las Vegas continued to evolve with the coming of the huge, theme-oriented hotel casinos in the 1990s. Hotel room capacity grew from 67,000 in 1989 to 105,000 in 1997 (Thompson 1998), and then to 127,000 in 2005. The occupancy rate for Las Vegas has remained high since then, at about 90 percent, undercutting the suspicion that the city had hit the end of its expansion. But by 2005 55 percent of Las Vegas Strip revenues came from nongaming venues, a 50 percent decrease in gaming's financial importance. One convention official noted, "The Sin City stigma is largely gone. . . . Las Vegas is almost a nation unto itself. . . . Everybody wants to go to Vegas—they want to go to a show, shop, eat, be entertained. It seems to have a formula that is working and not really showing any signs of slowing down" ("Las Vegas" 2006). Ferrari and Ives (2005, p. 6) write:

> Was Las Vegas . . . becoming a Mecca for the twenty-first-century American zeitgeist? . . . This nation has always had a paradoxical, if not downright hypocritical, relationship with Las Vegas. It is a city that America has loved to hate but cannot do without. It is the antithesis of the conventional, the established, and the traditional, and despite our false pretenses, we are drawn to it for precisely these reasons. We are a Puritan nation obsessed with sex, a self-proclaimed meritocracy that idolizes wealth, a hardworking, churchgoing law-abiding people that can't wait to party all night long. Las Vegas is the necessary dark side of our nature, the skeletons in our collective closet, the orgiastic expression of our own irrepressible id. It is our favorite dirty little secret. . . . A place that was once shunned as Sin City and considered beyond the pale of respectable society has now become the epicenter of mainstream leisure.

To them Las Vegas has become more like America, and, at the same time, America has become more like Las Vegas.

1. *Racinos*

One recent important development has been the expansion of slot machines to horse tracks, expanding the variety of gambling offered there. This innovation has allowed several states and locales to revive a moribund pari-mutuel wagering presence at the tracks, which had been faring less well than casinos and lotteries as a popular form of gambling, especially among younger people, for several decades now. Track betting hovers at a 5 percent share of legal gambling dollars. According to the American Gaming Association (2008), there were 36 racetrack casinos in 11 states in 2006, generating $1.44 billion in state tax revenues. Notably, these "racinos" had a tax rate of about 40 percent, far higher than typical state tax rates on casino operations (but in the neighborhood of lottery taxation).

Several jurisdictions, including New York and some Florida counties, have expanded their gambling presence with hybrid forms of gambling. Like lotteries, many racinos were promoted on the basis of their tax contributions for the common good. In New York Governor George Pataki claimed that the estimated $2 billion in funds from the racinos would allow the state of New York to satisfy a court order that the state provide a "sound basic education" for students without a steep tax increase.

2. *Poker Boom*

Every local Barnes and Noble and Borders bookstore has a sizable section of gambling books. Many explain the various games to be found in Las Vegas casinos, on riverboats, and at Indian casinos. Some books are pitched to specialty areas such as online gambling, for example *Complete Idiot's Guide to Online Gambling* (Balestra 2000) and *Winning at Internet Poker for Dummies* (Harlan and Derossi 2005). The boom in gambling at all levels in American society has produced cottage industries to assist the novice gambler.

Interspersed with these how-to manuals are memoirs of the gambling life by men and women of various ages. In *Moneymaker*, Chris Moneymaker (2005), an unlikely man with a fortuitous name, details the thrill of evolving from being a weekend college player to being an everyman who won the World Series of Poker. The appropriate subtitle of his book is *How an Amateur Poker Player Turned $40 into $2.5 Million at the World Series of Poker.*

If you venture into the once moribund poker areas of major Las Vegas casinos you will find that they have changed since the 1980s. Instead of a sparse gathering of players from various backgrounds you will find an infusion of young men, for poker has become an attractive game for younger Americans. The American Gaming Association notes in a 2006 report that one-third of Americans aged 21 to 39 reported playing poker in the prior year; they are clearly the most active age group (American Gaming Association 2006, p. 31).

The editor of *Global Gaming Business*, a gaming industry trade publication, writes in the inaugural issue of *PokerBiz*, his company's nod to the burgeoning poker business, "Five years ago, we would not have even considered an entire magazine dedicated to the business of running poker rooms. After all, poker was a 'dying' game, dwindling down to its core players and failing to match the pace of the overall growth of the gaming industry. But then two remarkable things happened: the debut of online poker, and the huge technological advances in televised poker. Each of these developments brought the excitement and allure of poker to the masses" (Gros 2005, p. 4). Poker commentator Phil Gordon addresses this phenomenon: "It's the only game that normal, everyday people can visualize themselves doing at the highest level. They know they will never be able to hit a Randy Johnson fastball or catch a Joe Montana pass, but they can imagine themselves sitting across from Phil Ivey and going all in. A plumber with marital difficulties can find himself suddenly rich and famous" (quoted in O'Brien 2006, p. 7).

3. *The New Slot Machines*

Then there is the 30-year rise of the slot machine and what it signifies. In 1976 slot machines accounted for maybe 25 percent of gaming revenues in America's legal casinos. In 2006 Nevada casinos reported three times more revenue from slot machines than from table games (State of Nevada 2007). Forty years ago, when Frank Sinatra and the Rat Pack roamed the bars and lounges of Las Vegas, slot machines were considered the gendered province of wives and girlfriends who were not serious gamblers. The illegal gambling spheres, where those who gambled learned their games—a combination of skill and chance—were very male domains. Unlike poker, winning at the slots is pure chance.

The biggest change in gambling in the 30 years since the report of the Commission on the Review of the National Policy toward Gambling (1976) has been the rise of slot machines. Slot machines are no longer the mechanical reel models that defined the "one-armed bandit" of decades past. Computerized displays and payout mechanisms are now dominant. A casino can now see payout percentages in slot machines from a central computer site and adjust them accordingly, something unthinkable 20 years ago.

As recently as 1980 slot machines came in only a few types. Then electronic games appeared and soon eclipsed the mechanical devices that had once been the mainstay. The introduction of progressive slot machines attracted players looking for the big jackpot. By 2005 devices such as the handheld "scratch-off" device were being touted at gaming expositions. Now a gambler can play on an "I Love Lucy" machine, in which players earn bonuses by trying to grab chocolates faster than Lucy did in her classic scene working on an assembly line. The "Star Wars" slot machine seems designed to attract those who have grown up on the six movies in the series and on the range of video games associated with it.

Opponents of gambling, such as the National Coalition against Gambling Expansion, focus on the allure of slot machines as a source of problem gambling, on the belief that such machines are particularly addictive (Batt 2007). At the 2003 International Gambling Conference in Vancouver the gambling expert William N. Thompson (2003) warned against the social costs of legal gambling: "If Bill Bennett, who had published several books and was a success in life, could be tripped up by poker machines, what about the average Joe?" One researcher concludes from her ethnographic study, "It really is no secret. The aim of these technologies is to make people play longer, faster and more intensively" (Batt 2007).

B. Politics, the Law, and Indian Gaming

Indian gaming represents a sector that is approaching the non-Indian casino industry in size. Indian gaming revenues grew from $5.4 billion nationally in 1995 to $19.4 billion in 2004 and $23 billion in 2005. In 2005 Indian gaming grew by 16 percent, ahead of other commercial gaming forms, including the newly expanding racinos. In 2006 some 400 gaming establishments, operated by about 230 tribes, earned over $25 billion in gaming revenue (National Indian Gaming Commission 2007); a third of the revenues came from California casinos.

Beginning with the federal Indian Gaming Regulatory Act in 1988, following the U.S. Supreme Court decision in *Cabazon*, a regulatory structure has been in place for tribes that operate gambling in the states that permit it. These multiyear "compacts," negotiated with the state through the office of the governor, vary dramatically between states and often within states. Some tribes have agreed to give as much as 25 percent of their revenues to their resident state, which has generally afforded them a gambling monopoly.

As one Indian official recently wrote, "In little more than 30 years, Indian gaming has provided more than 200 tribes the opportunity for self-determination and economic self-sufficiency. Indian gaming has replaced poverty with jobs bringing Indians back to Indian country. It's replaced disease with hospitals, doctors and medicine for our sick and elderly. We've replaced crime and dropouts with new schools and scholarships. And we've replaced despair with hope for a new generation of Indian people. With the help of gaming, tribal governments are beginning to rebuild communities that were all but forgotten" (Stevens 2004, p. 108).

These developments were at first embedded in an Indian appeal for self-reliance and economic development amid great poverty. Increasingly, however, Indian gaming has become a symbol of wealth and power, and although states are not rescinding their Indian gaming licenses, they may now be seeing the tribes as more mainstream commercial interests.

A 2004 *Los Angeles Times* poll found conflicting feelings among the residents of California regarding the burgeoning Indian casinos: the majority of respondents supported the Indian tribes in their efforts to develop casinos, but hoped for more in the way of tax revenues (Morain 2004, p. A1). How quickly the image of the deserving poor Indians has changed. The anthropologist Eve Darian-Smith describes the image in the popular media: "Native Americans are all now obscenely wealthy and fly regularly to Paris to drink champagne and live the good life. I argue that this public perception is fostering a new wave of animosity by the dominant society toward Native Americans, which is in turn shaping political and legal discourse surrounding regulation of Indian casinos" (Darian-Smith 2005, p. 1). The humorist Harry Shearer (2006) captures some of these themes in a recent satiric novel, in which embattled civic leaders reinvent themselves as an Indian tribe to compete for the gambling dollar.

There have been significant developments in the legalization and taxation of gambling in California and the 27 other states that have implemented gambling by Indian tribes over the years since *Cabazon*. Much of this growth has come from Indian casinos, whose scope is defined by state compacts, which are in current renegotiation. At the same time, other states have evolved policies that directly affect competitors to Indian gaming, for instance making horse racing venues more viable through the racino model.

This growth has begun to generate questions about the backgrounds of casino operators; the promise of economic development; the competition with other forms of industry and leisure; the reliance of the state on gambling as a revenue source; the effect of proximity on low-income populations; and the nature and growth of problem gambling, especially on vulnerable populations.

III. Discordant Voices: Problem Gambling and Other Impediments to Normalization and Expansion

Critics of gambling expansion focus on what some have called the ABCs of legal gambling: addiction, bankruptcy, and crime. Commenting in 2007 on one state's rejection of racinos, an analyst for the social conservative group Focus on the Family Action concluded, "You can dress up gambling, spend millions on public appeal and buy favor with state officials, but you cannot hide the stench of gambling addiction, crime, bankruptcy and destroyed lives" (Mesko 2007).

Whereas opposition to gambling used to be centered on moralistic attitudes, it has increasingly turned on issues of effects on vulnerable populations, such as the low-income population, those with a psychological propensity to gamble (or to be unable to control their gambling), and young people. Clotfelter and Cook (1989) demonstrate that legal lotteries generate revenues mostly from those at the lower end of the socioeconomic structure. Of course, this makes sense; unlike blackjack, lotteries hold out the promise of enormous gain for a small investment. Other critics, including many psychologists who are concerned with the prevalence of problem gambling behavior among vulnerable populations—notably youth—continue to challenge gambling's easy normalization. The psychologists Carmen Messerlian and Jeffrey Derevensky (2005, p. 1), authors of numerous studies, conclude, "With the continuous expansion of the gambling industry worldwide, more gambling opportunities and types of gambling exist today than in the past. With this increased exposure, more adolescents, already prone to risk-taking, have been tempted by the lure of excitement, entertainment, and potential financial gain associated with gambling."

There is also concern over what some critics believe are overblown economic development promises and state tax revenue related to gambling: "A state has economic problems, often due to a recession, and introduces gambling. Gambling revenues climb, then taper off, flatten out, and decline. At that point the state introduces some other form of gambling.... The trend is always toward more 'hard-core' forms of gambling.... Where will the states turn next? Now they are concerned about competition from offshore Internet casinos. The states may try to get in on Internet gambling" (Lambert 2002, pp. 4–5). Some critics argue that lottery contributions, though consistent, don't necessarily expand the education budget overall. A *New York Times* analysis in 2007 found that state lotteries provide 1 to 5 percent of a state's education funds (Stodghill and Nixon 2007). Other critics wonder why states are willing to help certain industries, such as racetracks, as a way to improve state revenues, favoring some forms of economic development over others. During 2007–8 considerations of expanded gambling in Maryland, a *Washington Post* editorial asked, "Why are horses more deserving of state handout than crabs and oysters?" ("Why Are Horses" 2008), comparing the racetracks with watermen who fish the local waters.

Other lines of opposition to legal gambling focus on the influence of new technology (especially as it could exacerbate problem gambling) and the effect on infrastructure.

The seeds of this ambivalence about legal gambling survive despite its significant growth and the steady trend toward normalization of gambling in Americans' attitudes and practices. The National Gambling Impact Study Commission (1999, pp. 19–20) issued their report with the following conclusions: "The two principal studies sponsored by this Commission found that the prevalence of problem and pathological gambling in America is troubling. [The National Research Center] estimates that, in a given year, approximately 1.8 million adults in the United States are pathological gamblers. [The National Opinion Research Center] found that approximately 2.5 million adults are pathological gamblers. Another three million of the adult population are problem gamblers. Over 15 million Americans were identified as at-risk gamblers."

A debate over how to frame gambling issues focuses on whether the percentage of Americans displaying problem gambling characteristics is a relative or an absolute concern. If the prevalence rate of problem drinking is estimated at 15 percent of those who drink, then the legal gambling industry would have to be buoyed by the National Gambling Impact Study Commission's acceptance of estimates of problem gambling far lower than that.

American Gaming Association President Fahrenkopf was pointed in his pleasure with the National Gambling Impact Study Commission's report: "When you get to the bottom line, the Commission report confirmed that the vast majority of Americans either gamble recreationally and experience no measurable side effects related to their gambling, or they choose not to gamble at all. The Commission puts to rest claims of organized crime involvement, of increased crime related to casinos, of exaggerated numbers of pathological gamblers, of economic benefits being outweighed by absurdly high social costs and a host of other outrageous charges we've had to deal with for years" (American Gaming Association 1999).

Dr. James Dobson, a leading social conservative and a member of the National Gambling Impact Study Commission, had a very different response to the Commission's work. He was upset that the Commission reported a far lower lifetime incidence rate for problem gambling compared with other problems such as alcoholism:

> Clearly, gambling is a destroyer that ruins lives and wrecks families. A mountain of evidence presented to our Commission demonstrates a direct link between problem and pathological gambling and divorce, child abuse, domestic violence, bankruptcy, crime and suicide. More than 15.4 million adults and adolescents meet the technical criteria of those disorders. That is an enormous number—greater than the largest city in this country. When other activities, such as smoking, have been shown to be harmful, the hue and cry

> for regulations to warn and protect the public has been loud and long. Today, the silence of most of our leaders about the risks of gambling is deafening. It is well past time for a Paul Revere to sound the alarm. Gambling is hazardous to your—to our—health! (Dobson 1999, p. 13)

In general, though, social conservatives are not finding much traction with their opposition to gambling. It has not become a leading issue in their organizational growth strategies, fund raising, or profiles.

As long ago as 1974, when New Jersey considered its first statewide initiative to legalize casinos, research showed that only a limited number of voters would respond to a religious or moralistic challenge to gambling on its face. Since then, opponents may have couched their opposition in part in moral terms, but as gambling has become increasingly normalized, more explicit moralistic opposition usually doesn't find large, receptive audiences. Nonetheless, at both the national level (the 1976 Commission on the Review of the National Policy toward Gambling, the 1999 National Gambling Impact Study Commission) and at state levels the appropriate role of the state has frequently been debated.

There may be limits to legal gambling. A Pew Research Center report in May 2006 found a "modest backlash" on attitudes toward the legalization of gambling, suggesting that Americans feel that we have enough gambling now. Fully 70 percent of respondents said that legalized gambling encourages people to gamble more than they can afford, suggesting a vein of ambivalence in even this very normalized activity. The highest level of support for legalizing gambling as a policy option was for lotteries, with 71 percent being in favor of that. Still, the Pew report concludes, "The negative turn in attitudes toward gambling appears to be driven by concerns that people are gambling too much rather than by any revival of the once common view that gambling is immoral" (Pew Research Center 2006, p. 2).

IV. Unresolved Questions

Despite the enormous growth in gambling, we don't have runaway gambling. If we did, we could expect to see some of the following: more Las Vegas–style casinos in many American states, legal sports gambling in many states, and Internet gambling legalized, advertised, supported by, or encouraged by the government.

The National Gambling Impact Study Commission (1999) estimated that Americans spend $380 billion in illegal gambling annually. The composition of such "dark numbers" is speculative (see Reuter 1984 on "mythical numbers' in a parallel sphere), yet if we take the expected revenue for the gambling operator from such bets (approximately 5 percent) and add on the portion of revenues that don't have to be paid in taxes (though there may be additional costs incurred to remain undetected), we end up with a figure of $19 billion. If that figure were indeed accurate—a big stretch—illegal gambling would comprise about 20 percent of the gambling that is done in the United States. It has been estimated that online sports betting generated over $4 billion in revenues in 2005. If the in-person amount of sports wagering was triple that, we would come close to the above estimate.

There are fears even among those who are content with the existing forms of gambling that expansion into any one of these three forms would be harmful, for different reasons. Sports gambling could conceivably increase the presence of organized crime and generate higher levels of problem gambling.

Gambling has been affected by the cyber revolution that has brought e-mail, Web pages, handheld devices, and superfast connectivity to nearly anyone in the developed world who wants it. The first Web sites devoted to gambling appeared in the mid-1990s. Within a few years, they proliferated. In 2007 it was estimated that there were 3,000 sites worldwide (Annenberg Public Policy Center of the University of Pennsylvania 2007).

The United States has chosen to cordon off this potential avenue for expansion of legal gambling, enacting the 2006 Unlawful Internet Gambling Enforcement Act (UIGEA) to prohibit banks from collecting debts incurred on such sites and to prohibit the establishment of sites on U.S. soil. This legal development put the United States in conflict with a number of European countries that have acted to authorize Internet gambling. The United States also ran afoul of the World Trade Organization, which considered claims by the Caribbean nation of Antigua that the United States, despite trade treaty understanding, was unfairly criminalizing an activity that Antigua was permitting and hosting. The United States has been recalcitrant in bringing state laws into conformity, while supporting its federal UIGEA (Rose 2006; Pontell, Geis, and Brown 2007).

Massachusetts Congressman Barney Frank, a liberal Democrat, oversaw hearings connected with a bill he was sponsoring to undo the UIGEA. Frank argued, "The existing legislation is an inappropriate interference on the personal freedom of Americans and this interference should be undone" (U.S. Congress 2007, p. 1). Several officials from various companies that work with the validation and control of online commerce testified at Frank's committee hearings that suitable controls could be enacted under a legalization scheme (Kitchen 2007; Prideaux 2007; Schmidt 2007).

Still, the various forms of handheld device gambling, access to gambling from home, and any easy connection of computers, gambling, and bank accounts or credit cards have not happened. If they do, U.S. states and the federal government may reassess the existing support for legal gambling.

V. The Normalization of Gambling

Legalized gambling is a once prohibited vice that has evolved and won acceptance in most quarters of American society. As Wolfe (2007) and others have observed, gambling has avoided becoming a key issue in the culture wars, unlike abortion and gay rights. How has gambling been normalized while these other, once victimless crimes have taken a different path, a rockier road, a series of dead ends and thwarted reform?

One reason gambling doesn't generate a backlash is that it doesn't involve a critique of the establishment or offer up a new paradigm of gender relations (as abortion does) or sex itself (as gay rights does). It also doesn't offer ties to the other major social movements of the day in the same way that marijuana decriminalization was tied to the Vietnam War. Gambling has separated itself from the other formerly prohibited victimless crimes by uncoupling itself from other vices (Dombrink and Hillyard 2007).

First, gambling hasn't challenged existing paradigms. Unlike entrenched bureaucratic issues such as the drug war, changing gambling policies didn't run directly against entrenched government entities. In earlier eras, police and prosecutors embraced de facto decriminalization. The economist Bill Eadington (2006) observes, "Gaming organizations have become mainstream in terms of objectives, management practices and corporate strategies."

Also of importance is the lack of successful opposition. Legal gambling proposals and initiatives haven't mobilized waves of committed, single-issue opponents. Even fervent gambling opponents eventually realized there were limits to their appeal to morality as a means of defeating gambling expansion proposals (Beato 2006).

A third consideration was the lack of a successful antigambling frame. In some locales and times organized crime was used against the expansion of legal gambling. Over time, the corporatization of the gaming industry (and the state operation of lotteries) has diluted this issue (though it would be raised very quickly under any discussion of a sports gambling legalization proposal). In other cases, the most salient issue for skeptics is compulsive or problem gambling. This continues to confront the legal casino industry, but the industry has integrated and advertised its own measures to address the problem. Analysts divide the responses to problem gambling by jurisdictions and operator as a choice or combination between providing informed choice, implementing consumer control, instituting restrictions (such as hours of operation), and placing a cap on the number and size of gaming venues. Many researchers and policy makers agree that the level of problem gambling is low compared to alcohol abuse, for instance.

A fourth issue has been crucial: the positive role of the state and the importance of tax revenues and economic development.

For all these reasons, and despite the opinion that we now have enough legal gambling in the United States, legal gambling is not partial birth abortion, not same-sex marriage, not the tobacco industry.

In 2007 stores pervasively sell lottery tickets, the newspaper *USA Today* runs the winning lottery numbers of 35 states ("Lotteries" 2008), and local newspapers discuss the betting line on various sports games for that weekend (e.g., "Behind the

Lines" 2007). Educators and law enforcement officials support legal gambling for its earmarked revenue, and developers and politicians tout its economic development potential. The United States may still be embroiled in a culture war about other issues, but the normalized issue of gambling is no longer considered in the same frame as those still much contested activities.

REFERENCES

American Gaming Association. 1999. "AGA on National Gambling Impact Study Commission." Press releases. http://americangaming.org.

———. 2006. "State of the States: The AGA Survey of Casino Entertainment." http://americangaming.org.

———. 2007. "Industry Information." http://americangaming.org.

———. 2008. "Industry Information: Tax Payments—Racetrack Casinos." http://americangaming.org.

Annenberg Public Policy Center of the University of Pennsylvania. 2007. "Card Playing Down among College-Age Youth; Internet Gambling Also Declines." Philadelphia: Annenberg Public Policy Center of the University of Pennsylvania, October 18.

Balestra, Mark. 2000. *Complete Idiot's Guide to Online Gambling.* New York: Alpha Books/Penguin.

Batt, Tony. 2007. "Gambling Issues: Rise of Slot Machines Decried." October 15. http://casinocitytimes.com.

Beato, Greg. 2006. "Sin Cities on a Hill: How Legalized Gambling Moved from the Strip to Main Street." *Reason.* May. http://www.reasononline.com.

"Behind the Lines: Underdog Irish Keep Their Label." 2007. *Los Angeles Times* (November 9), p. D12.

Christiansen Capital Advisors, LLC. 2001. "The Gross Annual Wager of the United States, 2000: Waiting to Exhale." http://www.cca-i.com.

Clotfelter, Charles, and Philip Cook. 1989. *Selling Hope: State Lotteries in America.* Cambridge, MA: Harvard University Press.

Collins, Peter. 2006. "The UK Gambling Act (2005): Lessons for Legislators." Address to the 13th International Conference on Gambling and Risk Taking, Lake Tahoe, May 23.

Commission on the Review of the National Policy toward Gambling. 1976. *Gambling in America.* Final Report. Washington, DC: U.S. Government Printing Office.

Commonwealth of Massachusetts. 2007. "Governor Patrick Unveils Plan for Casino Gambling in Massachusetts." Executive Department, Commonwealth of Massachusetts, September 18.

Cooper, Marc. 2004. *The Last Honest Place in America: Paradise and Perdition in the New Las Vegas.* New York: Nation Books.

Cornell Law Project. 1977. *The Development of the Law of Gambling; 1776–1976.* Washington, DC: National Institute of Law Enforcement and Criminal Justice.

Darian-Smith, Eve. 2005. "Paris, Diamonds, and Champagne: Casinos on Reservations and the New 'Rich Indian' Identity." Paper presented at the meeting of the Law and Society Association, Las Vegas, June. Abstract available at http://www.allacademic.com/meta/p17357_index.html.

Denton, Sally, and Roger Morris. 2002. *The Money and the Power: The Making of Las Vegas and Its Hold on America*. New York: Random House.
Dobson, James. 1999. "Summary Statement by Commissioner James C. Dobson, Ph.D." National Gambling Impact Study Commission Final Report, Appendix 1, Commissioner Members' Statements. http://govinfo.library.unt.edu/ngisc/reports/fullrpt.html.
Dombrink, John, and Daniel Hillyard. 2007. *Sin No More: From Abortion to Stem Cells. Understanding Crime, Law and Morality in America*. New York: New York University Press.
Dombrink, John, and William N. Thompson. 1990. *The Last Resort: Success and Failure in Campaigns for Casinos*. Reno: University of Nevada Press.
Eadington, William R. 2006. "Ten Challenges: Issues That Are Shaping the Future of Gambling and Commercial Gaming." Address to the 13th International Conference on Gambling and Risk Taking, Lake Tahoe, May 23.
Ezell, John Samuel. 1960. *Fortune's Merry Wheel: The Lottery in America*. Cambridge, MA: Harvard University Press.
Fahrenkopf, Frank. 2005. "A Fine State of Affairs." *Global Gaming Business* 4(4): 14.
———. 2007. "Milestones Reached." *Global Gaming Business* (May), p. 20.
Fallows, James. 2007. "Macau's Big Gamble." *The Atlantic*, September. http://www.theatlantic.com/doc/200709/macau.
Ferrari, Michelle, with Stephen Ives. 2005. *Las Vegas: An Unconventional History*. New York: Bulfinch.
Gallup Organization. 1999. "Gambling in America—1999: A Comparison of Adults and Teenagers." June 22. http://www.gallup.com.
Geis, Gilbert. 1979. *Not the Law's Business: An Examination of Homosexuality, Abortion, Prostitution, Narcotics, and Gambling in the United States*. New York: Schocken Books.
Greenlees, Donald. 2008. "Americans in the Action as Macao Casinos Soar." *New York Times* (January 18).
Gros, Roger. 2005. "Editor's Letter: A Pause for Poker." *PokerBiz* Spring: 4.
Harlan, Mark, and Chris Derossi. 2005. *Winning at Internet Poker for Dummies*. New York: For Dummies/Wiley.
Hegarty, Matt. 2007. "New Ky. Governor Supports Referendum." *Daily Racing Form* (November 7). http://www.espn.com.
Johnson, Dirk. 1991. "Gambling's Spread: Gold Rush or Fool's Gold?" *New York Times* (October 6).
Jones, Jeffrey. 2004. *Gambling a Common Activity for Americans*. Gallup Organization, March 24. http://www.gallup.com/poll.
Kitchen, Gerald. 2007. Testimony of Chief Executive, SecureTrading Group Limited, Before the House Committee on Financial Services, United States Congress, Legislative Hearing on H. R. 2046, Internet Gambling Regulation and Enforcement Act of 2007, June 8. http://www.house.gov/apps/list/hearing/financialsvcs_dem/htkitchen060807.pdf.
Lambert, Craig. 2002. "Trafficking in Chance." *Harvard Magazine* (July–August) 104(6): 32–41.
"Las Vegas: Sin City Still King of Colossal Conventions." 2006. *Reno Gazette-Journal* (May 1). http://www.rgj.com.
"Lotteries across the USA." 2008. *USA Today* (February 1), p. 15C.

Loveman, Gary. 2002. "Casino Communications: Q & A." *Global Gaming Business* (October 1), p. 38.
Maguire, Ken. 2007*a*. "Patrick's Casino Revenue Doubtful, Report Says." *Newsday* (October 25). http://www.newsday.com.
———. 2007*b*. "Some Warn Mass. Casino Plan Brings Risk for College Students." *Boston Globe* (October 14). http://www.boston.com.
Mangione, Thomas W., and Floyd J. Fowler Jr. 1979. "Enforcing the Gambling Laws." *Journal of Social Issues* 35(3): 115–28.
Mendell, David. 2007. "Gambling Expansion Now a Madigan Option: Sales-Tax Hike Still Pushed for Transit Funding." *Chicago Tribune* (October 30), p. 1. http://www.chicagotribune.com.
Mesko, Jennifer. 2007. "N.J. Voters Turn Down Massive Stem-Cell Research Plan." November 7. citizenlink.com.
Messerlian, Carmen, and Jeffrey L. Derevensky. 2005. "Youth Gambling: A Public Health Perspective." *Journal of Gambling Issues* 14 (September): 97–116.
Moneymaker, Chris. 2005. *Moneymaker: How an Amateur Poker Player Turned $40 into $2.5 Million at the World Series of Poker.* New York: HarperEntertainment.
Morain, Dan. 2004. "California on Path to Become Nation's Gambling Capital." *Los Angeles Times* (August 25), p. A1.
National Gambling Impact Study Commission. 1999. *National Gambling Impact Study Commission Final Report.* http://govinfo.library.unt.edu/ngisc/reports/fullrpt.html.
National Indian Gaming Commission. 2007. *Gaming Revenue Reports.* http://www.nigc.gov.
Nelson, Michael, and John Lyman Mason. 2007. *How the South Joined the Gambling Nation: The Politics of State Policy Innovation.* Baton Rouge: Louisiana State University Press.
O'Brien, Timothy. 2006. "Is Poker Losing Its First Flush?" *New York Times* (April 16), sec. 3, p. 1.
O'Connor, James. 1973. *The Fiscal Crisis of the State.* New York: St. Martin's.
Peter, Tom A. 2008. "Political Clash Sinks Massachusetts Casino-Gambling Plan." *Christian Science Monitor* (March 22). http://www.csmonitor.com/2008/0321/p25s09-uspo.html.
Pew Research Center. 2006. "Gambling: As the Take Rises, So Does Public Concern." May 23. http://pewresearch.org/assets/social/pdf/Gambling.pdf.
Pileggi, Nicholas. 1995. Casino: *Love and Honor in Las Vegas.* New York: Simon and Schuster.
Pontell, Henry, Gilbert Geis, and G. Christopher Brown. 2007. "Offshore Internet Gambling and the World Trade Organization: Is It Criminal Behavior or a Commodity?" *International Journal of Cyber Criminology* 1(1): 119–36.
Prah, Pamela M. 2007. "States Scramble for Gambling Jackpot." September 12. Stateline.org.
PricewaterhouseCoopers. 2007. "Global Entertainment and Media Outlook: 2007–2011." http://www.pwc.com.
Prideaux, Jon. 2007. Testimony of Independent Payments Consultant before the House Committee on Financial Services, United States Congress, Legislative Hearing on H. R. 2046, Internet Gambling Regulation and Enforcement Act of 2007, June 8. http://www.house.gov/apps/list/hearing/financialsvcs_dem/htprideaux060807.pdf.
Reuter, Peter. 1984. "The (Continued) Vitality of Mythical Numbers." *Public Interest* 14 (Spring): 135–47.

Rose, I. Nelson. 1980. "The Legalization and Control of Casino Gambling." *Fordham Law Review* 8: 245–300.

———. 2006. "Should Antigua Sue China?" August 26. http://www.gambling and the law.com.

Schmidt, Jeff. 2007. Testimony of Authis CEO before the House Committee on Financial Services, United States Congress, legislative hearing on H. R. 2046, Internet Gambling Regulation and Enforcement Act of 2007, June 8. http://www.house.gov/apps/list/hearing/financialsvcs_dem/htschmidt060807.pdf.

Shearer, Harry. 2006. *Not Enough Indians.* Boston: Justin, Charles.

Skolnick, Jerome H. 1978. *House of Cards: Legalization and Control of Casino Gambling.* Boston: Little, Brown.

———. 2001. "Normal Vice: The Evolution of Gambling." Paper prepared for the American Society of Criminology, New York University School of Law.

"Special Report: Gambling: The Newest Growth Industry." 1978. *Business Week* (June 26), pp. 110–29.

State of Nevada. 2007. *State Gaming Control Board, State of Nevada, Gaming Revenue Report.* January 2006–December 2006. http://gaming.nv.gov/documents/pdf/1g_06dec.pdf.

Stevens, Ernest, Jr. 2004. "The Rising Tide: Indian Gaming Is Bringing Opportunity to All Americans." *Global Gaming Business* (October), pp. 108–9.

Stodghill, Ron, and Ron Nixon. 2007. "For Schools, Lottery Payoffs Fall Short of Promises." *New York Times* (October 7).

Thompson, William N. 1998. "Uncertain Futures with Proven Entertainment Formulas: Las Vegas Approaches the Millennium." Unpublished paper, University of Nevada, Las Vegas, September 2.

———. 2003. "The Social Costs of Gambling: Old Questions and New Answers from a Las Vegas Survey." Presentation on panel, "Social Costs of Gambling." 12th International Conference on Gambling and Risk Taking, Vancouver, British Columbia, May 26–30.

Ugel, Edward. 2007. *Money for Nothing: One Man's Journey through the Dark Side of Lottery Millions.* New York: Collins.

U.S. Congress, House Committee on Financial Services. 2007. "Frank Introduces Internet Gambling Regulation and Enforcement Act of 2007." Press release. April 26.

Walker, Douglas M. 2008. "Challenges That Confront Researchers on Estimating the Social Costs of Gambling." *American Gaming Association,* January 3. http://americangaming.org.

"Why Are Horses More Deserving of State Handout Than Crabs and Oysters?" 2008. *Washington Post* (January 6). http://www.washingtonpost.com.

Wolfe, Alan. 2007. "What We Don't Know about Gambling, but Should." *Chronicle of Higher Education* (October 12), p. B8.

Index

CPSIA information can be obtained at www.ICGtesting.com
264269BV00004B/137-180/P

9 780199 844654